VOLUME TWO

*W*estern Civilization
Ideas, Politics & Society

FIFTH EDITION

MARVIN PERRY
Baruch College, City University of New York

MYRNA CHASE
Baruch College, City University of New York

JAMES R. JACOB
John Jay College of Criminal Justice, City University of New York

MARGARET C. JACOB
New School for Social Research

THEODORE H. VON LAUE
Clark University

George W. Bock, *Editorial Associate*

Houghton Mifflin Company   BOSTON   TORONTO
Geneva, Illinois   Palo Alto   Princeton, New Jersey

Senior Sponsoring Editor   *Sean W. Wakely*
Senior Associate Editor   *Jeffrey Greene*
Project Editor   *Helen Bronk*
Production/Design Coordinator   *Jennifer Waddell*
Senior Manufacturing Coordinator   *Marie Barnes*
Marketing Manager   *Pamela Shaffer*

Printed in the U.S.A.

Library of Congress Card Catalog Number: 95-77001

ISBN: 0-395-75044-X

Examination Copy: 0-395-766117

123456789-QM-99 98 97 96 95

CREDITS

Cover: Designer: Linda Wade, Linda Wade Productions
Image: *London Visitors,* oil painting by James Tissot,
1874. The Toledo Museum of Arts, Toledo, Ohio.

Text Credits
Pages 801–802: Reprinted with permission of Simon &
Schuster, Inc. from *The Poems of W.B. Yeats: A New Edi-
tion,* edited by Richard J. Finneran. Copyright 1924 by
Macmillan Publishing Company, renewed 1952 by Bertha
Georgie Yeats.

Contents in Brief

Contents

Maps

Chronologies

Preface

Western civilization is a grand but tragic drama. The West has forged the instruments of reason that make possible a rational comprehension of physical nature and human culture, conceived the idea of political liberty, and recognized the intrinsic worth of the individual. But the modern West, though it has unravelled nature's mysteries, has been less successful at finding rational solutions to social ills and conflicts between nations. Science, the great achievement of the Western intellect, while improving conditions of life, has also produced weapons of mass destruction. Though the West has pioneered in the protection of human rights, it has also produced totalitarian regimes that have trampled on individual freedom and human dignity. And although the West has demonstrated a commitment to human equality, it has also practiced brutal racism.

Despite the value that Westerners have given to reason and freedom, they have shown a frightening capacity for irrational behavior and a fascination for violence and irrational ideologies, and they have willingly sacrificed liberty for security or national grandeur. The world wars and totalitarian movements of the twentieth century have demonstrated that Western civilization, despite its extraordinary achievements, is fragile and perishable.

Western Civilization: Ideas, Politics, and Society examines the Western tradition—those unique patterns of thought and systems of values that constitute the Western heritage. While focusing on key ideas and broad themes, the text also provides a balanced treatment of economic, political, and social history for students in Western civilization courses.

The text is written with the conviction that history is not a meaningless tale. Without a knowledge of history, men and women cannot fully know themselves, for all human beings have been shaped by institutions and values inherited from the past. Without an awareness of the historical evolution of reason and freedom, the dominant ideals of Western civilization, commitment to these ideals will diminish. Without a knowledge of history, the West cannot fully comprehend or adequately cope with the problems that burden its civilization and the world.

In attempting to make sense out of the past, the authors have been careful to avoid superficial generalizations that oversimplify historical events and forces and arrange history into too neat a structure. But we have striven to interpret and to synthesize in order to provide students with a frame of reference with which to comprehend the principal events and eras in Western history.

CHANGES IN THE FIFTH EDITION

For the fifth edition every chapter has been reworked to some extent. The hundreds of carefully selected modifications and additions significantly enhance the text. Some changes deepen the book's conceptual character; others provide useful and illustrative historical details. The concluding essays in several chapters have been enlarged and improved. Chapters treating intellectual history have been expanded and additional quotations from original sources have been inserted. To help students focus on a chapter's key ideas, we have reduced the number of review questions and rewritten others. A new feature has been introduced in the fifth edition: each chapter now contains a profile, set off in a box, of a significant historical figure. Among the personalities featured are Jeremiah, Demosthenes, Cleopatra, Saint Boniface, Saladin, Babeuf, Toussaint-

L'Ouverture, Kierkegaard, Herzl, Isadora Duncan, and Charlie Chaplin.

Specific changes include a revised concluding essay, "The Religious Orientation of the Ancient Near East," in Chapter 1, "The Ancient Near East." A concluding essay, "The Legacy of the Ancient Jews," has been added to Chapter 2, "The Hebrews." In Chapter 3, "The Greek City-State," we illuminated more fully Homer's genius and expanded the treatment of women and slavery in Greek society. Chapter 4, "Greek Thought," contains improved discussions of Herodotus, Thucydides, and Euripides. The discussion of Alexandria and its cultural life was expanded in Chapter 5, "The Hellenistic Age." In Chapter 6, "The Roman Republic," we have added material on social stratification and on Cicero. New material on the status of women, on Stoicism, and on the Late Roman Empire has been incorporated into Chapter 7, "The Roman Empire." In Chapter 8, "Early Christianity," we have added new material on Jesus, Paul, the mystery religions, and Augustine, and sharpened the discussion in the concluding essay, "Christianity and Classical Humanism: Alternative World-Views." The most significant change in Chapter 9, "The Heirs of Rome," is the restructuring of the concluding section, "Medieval Society." Some additional information on town life, the Crusades, and Jewish-Christian relations has been incorporated into Chapter 10, "The High Middle Ages." We have somewhat altered the concluding essay, "The Middle Ages and the Modern World: Continuity and Discontinuity," in Chapter 12, "The Late Middle Ages." In Chapter 14, "The Reformation: Shattering of Christendom," new material on women has been added as well as revisions to the section, "Religious Reform or Social Revolution?," that assess the impact of Luther. A separate section on slavery has been added to Chapter 15, "European Expansion." More emphasis on the role of elites has been added to Chapter 16, "The Rise of Sovereignty: Transition to the Modern State," as well as new material on the rise of the Dutch Republic and reaction by French manufacturers to restrictions on economic activity. Chapter 18, "The Age of Enlightenment: Reason and Reform," has been revised considerably.

There is a new introduction based on recent research and new material on women.

In recent years, historians have rethought the question: was the French Revolution a bourgeois revolution? In Chapter 19, "The French Revolution," we have expanded the discussion of this issue. The relationship between romanticism and nationalism has been more clearly delineated in Chapter 22, "Thought and Culture in the Early Nineteenth Century." A new section, "Feminism, Extending the Principle of Equality," has been added to Chapter 24, "Thought and Culture in the Mid-Nineteenth Century." Chapter 26, "The Industrial West," condenses the political narrative and clarifies the connection of social and economic changes to politics. In Chapter 27, "Western Imperialism," the coverage of imperialism has been reorganized and abridged for better understanding. Chapter 28, "Modern Consciousness," now discusses Le Bon's theory of group psychology. All previous editions devoted two chapters to World War I; for this edition, we have consolidated the material into one chapter. While some sections were abridged, the concluding essay, "The War and European Consciousness," has been expanded and deepened. The treatment of the Holocaust has been somewhat enlarged in Chapter 33, "World War II."

The final part, "The Contemporary World," has been restructured and rewritten. Chapter 34, "Europe After World War II," interprets the years 1945–1985 from a post-Cold War perspective. The superpower rivalry provides the framework for the chapter, which emphasizes developments in Europe and the Soviet bloc. It also includes a section on decolonization around the world. Chapter 35, "The Troubled Present," covers the Gorbachev era, Eastern Europe in 1989, the collapse of the Soviet Union, the end of the Cold War, and realignments of power since 1991. It concludes with reflections on the world today—causes for optimism, causes for concern, and coping with the future.

More than half of the illustrations are new for this edition. The four-color art inserts and expanded art essays provide a comprehensive treatment of the evolution of Western art styles and are closely linked to the text.

DISTINCTIVE FEATURES

The text contains several pedagogical features. Chapter outlines and introductions provide comprehensive overviews of key themes and give a sense of direction and coherence to the flow of history. Many chapters contain concluding essays that treat the larger meaning of the material. Facts have been carefully selected to illustrate key relationships and concepts and to avoid overwhelming students with unrelated and disconnected data. Appropriate quotations, many not commonly found in texts, have been integrated into the discussion. Each chapter contains notes, an annotated bibliography, and review questions that refer students to principal points and elicit thought.

Western Civilization: Ideas, Politics, and Society is available in both one- and two-volume editions, and in a third edition, *From the 1400s*. *From the 1400s* (23 chapters) has been prepared for those instructors whose courses begin with the Renaissance or the Reformation.

Volume I of the two-volume edition treats the period from the first civilizations in the Near East through the Age of Enlightenment in the eighteenth century (18 chapters). Volume II covers the period from the growth of national-states in the seventeenth century to the contemporary age (20 chapters). Because some instructors start the second half of their course with the period prior to the French Revolution, Volume II incorporate the last three chapters of Volume I: "The Rise of Sovereignty," "The Scientific Revolution," and "The Age of Enlightenment." Volume II also contains a comprehensive introduction that surveys the ancient world, the Middle Ages, and the opening centuries of the modern era; the introduction is designed particularly for students who did not take the first half of the course. *From the 1400s* also contains an introduction that covers the ancient world and the Middle Ages.

ANCILLARIES

These learning and teaching ancillaries also contribute to the text's usefulness.

Two-volume Study Guide

Computerized Study Guide

Instructor's Resource Manual

Test Items

Computerized Test Items

Map Transparencies

Western Civilization Videodisc (or Videotape) and Guide

The *Study Guide,* available in two volumes, has been prepared and revised by Professor Lyle E. Linville of Prince George's Community College. For each text chapter, the *Study Guide* contains an introduction, learning objectives, words to know, identifications, a map study exercise, chronological/relational exercises, multiple-choice and essay questions, and a "transition," which reflects back on the chapter and looks forward to the next chapter's topic. For the map study questions, two copies of one or two different outline maps are provided and the student is asked to locate geographical features on one set of the maps. The second set is available for use by instructors in giving quizzes. In the chronological/relational exercises, students are asked to put a list of items in their chronological order; then in an exercise that brings to bear a deeper understanding of the material, students are asked to write a paragraph indicating the relationship of the items to one another, along with their historical significance. The *Study Guide*'s two volumes are designed so that Volume I covers all the chapters in Volume I of the text and Volume II covers all the chapters of Volume II and those of *From the 1400s*. So Volume II of the *Study Guide* can be used with either Volume II of the text or *From the 1400s*. The multiple-choice sections of the *Study Guide* are also available in a computerized version for IBM® computers. This interactive tutorial instruction program allows the student to answer the questions, then explains why the answer is right or wrong, and refers the student to the pages in the text where the question is discussed.

The *Instructor's Resource Manual* has been revised by Professor Diane Moczar of Northern Virginia Community College. The *Manual* contains learning objectives, chapter outlines, suggested lecture topics, topics for classroom discussion, ideas for student projects, and a film and multimedia bibliography. Professor Moczar has added new teaching suggestions throughout the *Manual* and has updated the bibliography. The accompanying *Test Items,* by Professor Dorothy Vogel of Indiana University of Pennsylvania, offers new and revised multiple-choice questions, identification terms, map questions, and essay questions for the fifth edition. The test questions are also available on computer disk for IBM® and Macintosh computers, both of which include editing capabilities. In addition, a complete set of map transparencies is available on adoption.

To add an exciting multimedia component to lectures and learning laboratories, we have created *The History of Western Civilization Videodisc/Videotape/Slide* program. The program allows the instructor to create customized multimedia classroom presentations using this rich collection of visual images. The program is divided into five chronological periods (ancient, medieval, early modern, modern, and twentieth century) and contains over 165 still images, 30 animated maps, and motion footage accompanied by period music. A companion *Videodisc/Videotape* instructor's guide provides descriptions, printed bar codes, bar code stickers to create customized lectures, and numeric codes. The program is available at no cost to adopters of the book. Please contact your local Houghton Mifflin representative for more information about this innovative and exciting multimedia program.

The text represents the efforts of several authors. Marvin Perry, general editor of the project, wrote Chapters 1–12, 19, 20, 22–25, 28, 29, and 31–33, and the section on the American Revolution in Chapter 18. James R. Jacob is the author of Chapters 13 and 15. Margaret C. Jacob provided Chapters 14 and 16–18. Myrna Chase wrote Chapters 21, 26–27, and contributed to the section on reform in Britain in Chapter 23. Theodore H. Von Laue is the author of Chapters 30 and 34–35. Marvin Perry and George W. Bock edited the manuscript for clarity and continuity.

ACKNOWLEDGMENTS

The authors would like to thank the following instructors for their critical reading of sections of the manuscript:

Gerald Anderson, *North Dakota State University*

Douglas C. Baxter, *Ohio University*

Dennis Frisch, *Santa Monica College*

Elizabeth Furdell, *University of North Florida*

Judith M. Ishkanian, *Santa Barbara City College*

Wendell Mauter, *Quincy University*

Wyatt Moulds, *Jones County College*

Timothy Myers, *Butler County Community College*

Walter Renn, *Middle Tennessee State University*

George Strong, *College of William & Mary*

D. A. Jeremy Telman, *University of Charleston*

Many of their suggestions were incorporated into the final version. We are also grateful to the staff of Houghton Mifflin Company who lent their considerable talents to the project. In particular we would like to thank Jeff Greene, developmental editor, and Helen Bronk, project editor, for their careful attention to detail; Irmina Plaszkiewicz-Pulc, whose copyediting skills are reflected in the manuscript; Marcia Mogelonsky for writing and choosing the images for the art essays; and Carole Frohlich, for supervising the choice of pictures in the text. This edition rests substantially on the editorial talents of Freda Alexander, who worked closely with us on previous editions of the text. I wish to thank Angela Von Laue for carefully reading the galleys of several chapters in Volume II. I am especially grateful to my friend George Bock who assisted in the planning of the text from its inception and who read the manuscript with an eye for major concepts and essential relationships. Once more, I thank my wife Phyllis G. Perry for her encouragement.

M.P.

Introduction

The Foundations of Western Civilization

Western Civilization is a blending of two traditions that emerged in the ancient world: the Judeo-Christian and the Greco-Roman. Before these traditions took shape, the drama of civilization was well advanced, having begun some five thousand years ago in Mesopotamia and Egypt.

Religion was the central force in these first civilizations in the Near East. Religion explained the operations of nature, justified traditional rules of morality, and helped people to deal with their fear of death. Law was considered sacred, a commandment of the gods. Religion united people in the common enterprises needed for survival, such as the construction of irrigation works. Religion also promoted creative achievements in art, literature, and science. In addition, the power of rulers, who were regarded as gods or as agents of the gods, derived from the religious outlook. The many achievements of the Egyptians and the Mesopotamians were inherited and assimilated by both the Greeks and the Hebrews, the spiritual ancestors of Western civilization. But Greeks and Hebrews also rejected and transformed elements of the older Near Eastern traditions and conceived a new view of God, nature, and the individual.

The Hebrews

By asserting that God was one, soverign, transcendent, and good, the Hebrews effected a religious revolution that separated them forever from the world-views of the Mesopotamians and Egyptians. This new conception of God led to a new awareness of the individual. In confronting God, the Hebrews developed an awareness of *self,* or I. The individual became conscious of his or her moral autonomy and personal worth. The Hebrews believed that God had bestowed on his people the capacity for moral freedom—they could choose between good and evil. Fundamental to Hebrew belief was the insistance that God had created human beings to be free moral agents. God did not want people to grovel before him, but to fulfill their moral potential by freely making the choice to follow, or not to follow, God's law. Thus, the Hebrews conceived the idea of moral freedom—that each individual is responsible for his or her own actions. Inherited by Christianity, this idea of moral autonomy is central to the Western tradition.

The Hebrew conception of ethical monotheism, with its stress on human dignity, is one source of the Western tradition. The other source derives from the ancient Greeks; they originated scientific and philosophic thought and conceived both the idea and the practice of political freedom.

The Greeks

In the Near East, religion dominated political activity, and following the mandates of the gods was a ruler's first responsibility. What made Greek political life different from that of earlier civilizations—and gives it enduring significance—was the Greeks' gradual realization that community problems were caused by human beings and required human solutions. The Greeks came to understand law as an achievement of the rational mind, rather than as an edict imposed by the gods. In the process, they also originated the idea of political freedom and created democratic institutions.

Greece comprised small, independent city-states. In the fifth century B.C., the city-state (*polis*) was in its maturity. A self-governing community, it expressed the will of free citizens, not the desires of gods, hereditary kings, or priests. The democratic orientation of the city-states was best exemplified by Athens, which was also the leading cultural center of Greece. In the Assembly, which was open to all adult male citizens, Athenians debated and voted on key issues of state.

Besides the idea of political freedom, the Greeks conceived a new way of viewing nature and human society. The first speculative philosophers emerged during the sixth century B.C. in Greek cities located in Ionia, in Asia Minor. Curious about the basic composition of nature and dissatisfied with earlier legends about creation, the Ionians sought physical, rather than mytho-religious, explanations for natural occurrences.

During this search, these philosophers arrived at a new concept of nature and a new method of inquiry. They maintained that nature was not manipulated by arbitrary and willful gods and that it was not governed by blind chance. The Ionians said that underlying the seeming chaos of nature were principles of order, that is, general rules that could be ascertained by human minds. The discovery marks the beginning of scientific thought. It made possible theoretical thinking and the systematization of knowledge. This is distinct from the mere observation and collection of data. Greek mathematicians, for example, organized practical experience with land measurements into the logical and coherent science of geometry. The Greeks also used the data collected by Babylonian priests, who observed the heavens because they believed that the stars revealed their gods' wishes. The Greeks' purpose was not religious—they sought to discover the geometrical laws underlying the motion of heavenly bodies. At the same time, Greek physicians drew a distinction between medicine and magic and began to examine human illness in an empirical and rational way. By the fifth century, the Greek mind had applied reason to the physical world and to all human activities. This emphasis on reason marks a turning point for human civilization.

In their effort to understand the external world, early Greek thinkers had created the tools of reason. Greek thinkers now began a rational investigation of the human being and the human community. The key figure in this development was Socrates.

Socrates' central concern was the perfection of individual human character and the achievement of moral excellence. Excellence of character was achieved, said Socrates, when individuals regulated their lives according to objective standards arrived at through rational reflection, that is, when reason became the formative, guiding, and ruling agency of the soul. Socrates wanted to subject all human beliefs and behavior to the clear light of reason and in this way to remove ethics from the realm of authority, tradition, dogma, superstition, and myth. He believed that reason was the only proper guide to the most crucial problem of human existence—the question of good and evil.

Plato, Socrates' most important disciple, used his master's teachings to create a comprehensive system of philosophy, which embraced the world of nature and the social world. Socrates had taught that there were universal standards of right and justice and that these were arrived at through thought. Building on the insights of his teacher, Plato insisted on the existence of a higher world of reality, independent of the world of things experienced every day. This higher reality, he said, is the realm of Ideas or Forms—unchanging, eternal, absolute, and universal standards of beauty, goodness, justice, and so forth. Truth resides in this world of Forms and not in the world revealed through the human senses.

Aristotle, Plato's student, was the leading expert of this time in every field of knowledge, with the possible exception of mathematics. Aristotle objected to Plato's devaluing of the material world. Possessing a scientist's curiosity to understand the facts of nature, Aristotle appreciated the world of phenomena, of concrete things, and respected knowledge obtained through the senses. Like Plato, Aristotle believed that understanding universal principles is the ultimate aim of knowledge. But unlike Plato, Aristotle held that to obtain such knowledge the individual must study the world of facts and objects revealed through sight, hearing, and touch. Aristotle adapted Plato's stress on universal principles to the requirements of natural science.

By discovering theoretical reason, by defining political freedom, and by affirming the worth and potential of human personality, the Greeks broke with the past and founded the rational and humanist tradition of the West. "Had Greek civilization never existed," said poet W. H. Auden, "we would never have become fully conscious, which is to say that we would never have become, for better or worse, fully human."

THE HELLENISTIC AGE

By 338 B.C., Philip of Macedonia (a kingdom to the north of Greece) had extended his dominion over the Greek city-states. After the assassination of Philip in 336 B.C., his twenty-year-old son Alexander succeeded to the throne. Fiery, proud, and ambitious, Alexander sought to conquer the vast Persian Empire. Winning every battle, Alexander's army carved out an empire that stretched from Greece to India. In 323 B.C., Alexander, not yet thirty-three years of age, died of a fever. His generals engaged in a long and bitter struggle to succeed him. As none of the general or their heirs could predominate, Alexander's empire was fractured into separate states.

The period from the early city-states that emerged in 800 B.C. until the death of Alexander the Great in 323 B.C. is called the *Hellenic Age*. The next stage in the evolution of Greek civilization (*Hellenism*) is called the *Hellenistic Age*. It ended in 30 B.C., when Egypt, the last major Hellenistic state, fell to Rome.

Although the Hellenistic Age had absorbed the heritage of classical (Hellenic) Greece, its style of civilization changed. During the first phase of Hellenism, the polis had given the individual identity, and it was believed that only within the polis could a Greek live a good and civilized life. During the Hellenistic Age, this situation changed. Kingdoms eclipsed the city-states in power and importance. Although cities retained a large measure of autonomy in domestic affairs, they had lost their freedom of action in foreign affairs. No longer were they the self-sufficient and independent communities of the Hellenic period.

Hellenistic society was characterized by a mingling of peoples and an interchange of cultues. As a result of Alexander's conquests, tens of thousands of Greek soldiers, merchants, and administrators settled in eastern lands. Greek traditions spread to the Near East, and Mesopotamian, Hebrew, and Persian traditions—particularly religious beliefs—moved westward. Cities were founded in the east patterned after the city-states of Greece. The ruling class in each Hellenistic city was united by a common Hellenism which overcame national, linguistic, and racial distinctions.

During the Hellenistic Age, Greek scientific achievement reached its height. Hellenistic scientists attempted a rational analysis of nature, engaged in research, organized knowledge in logical fashion, devised procedures for mathematical proof, separated medicine from magic, grasped the theory of experiment, and applied scientific principles to mechanical devices. Hellenistic science, says historian Benjamin Farrington, stood "on the threshold of the modern world. When modern science began in the sixteenth century, it took up where the Greeks left off."

Hellenistic philosophers preserved the rational tradition of Greek philosophy. Like their Hellenic predecessors, they regarded the cosmos as governed by universal principles intelligible to the rational mind. The most important philosophy in the Hellenistic world was Stoicism. By teaching that the world constituted a single society, Stoicism gave theoretical expression to the cosmopolitanism and universalism of the age. Stoicism, with its concept of a world-state, offered an answer to the problems of the loss of community and the alienation caused by the decline of the city-state. By stressing inner strength in dealing with life's misfortunes, Stoicism offered an avenue to individual happiness in a world fraught with uncertainty.

At the core of Stoicism was the belief that the universe contained a principle of order: the *logos* (reason). This ruling principle permeated all things; it accounted for the orderliness of nature. Because people were part of the universe, said the Stoics, they also shared in the logos, which operated throughout the cosmos. Since reason was common to all, human beings were essentially brothers and fundamentally equal.

Stoicism had an enduring impact on the Western mind. To some Roman political theorists, their Empire fulfilled the Stoic ideal of a world community in which people of different nationalities held citizenship and were governed by a worldwide law that accorded with the law of reason and by a natural law that operated throughout the universe. Stoic beliefs—that all human beings are members of one family; that each person is significant; that distinctions of rank are of no account; and that human law should not conflict with natural law—were incorporated into Roman jurisprudence, Christian thought, and modern liberalism. There is continuity between Stoic thought and the principle of inalienable rights stated in the American Declaration of Independence.

ROME

Rome, conquerer of the Mediterranean world and transmitter of Hellenism, inherited the universalist tendencies of the Hellenistic Age and embodied them in its law and institutions. Roman history falls into two periods: the Republic, which began in 509 B.C. with the overthrow of the Etruscan monarchy; and the Empire, which started in 27 B.C. when Octavian became, in effect, the first Roman emperor.

The Roman Republic

The history of the Roman Republic was marked by three principle developments: the struggle between patricians and plebeians, the conquest of Italy and the Mediterranean world, and the civil wars. At the beginning of the fifth century B.C., Rome was dominated by *patricians* (the landowning aristocrats). The *plebeians* (commoners) had many grievances; these included enslavement for debt, discrimination in the courts, prevention of intermarriage with patricians, lack of political representation, and the absence of a written code of law.

Resentful of their inferior status, the plebeians organized and waged a struggle for political, legal, and social equality. They were resisted every step of the way by the patricians, who wanted to preserve their dominance. The plebeians had one decisive weapon: their threat to secede from Rome, that is, not to pay taxes, work, or serve in the army. Realizing that Rome, which was constantly involved in warfare on the Italian peninsula, cold not endure without plebeian help, the pragmatic patricians begrudgingly made concessions. Thus, the plebeians slowly gained legal equality.

Although many plebeian grievances were resolved and the plebeians gained the right to sit in the Senate, the principal organ of govenrment, Rome was still ruled by an upper class. Power was concentrated in a ruling oligarchy, consisting of patricians and influential plebeians who had joined forces with the old nobility.

By 146 B.C., Rome had become the dominant power in the Mediterranean world. Roman expansion occurred in three main stages: the uniting of the Italian peninsula, which gave Rome the manpower that transformed it from a city-state into a great power; the struggle with Carthage, from which Rome emerged as ruler of the western Mediterranean; and the subjugation of the Hellenistic states of the eastern Mediterranean, which brought Romans into close contact with Greek civilization.

A crucial consequence of expansion was Roman contact with the legal experience of other peoples. Roman jurists, demonstrating the Roman virtues of pragmatism and common sense, selectively incorporated elements of the legal codes and traditions of these nations into Roman law. Thus, Roman jurists gradually and empirically fashioned the *jus gentium*, the law of nations or peoples.

Roman jurists then identified the jus gentium with the natural law (*jus naturale*) of the Stoics. The jurists said that law should accord with rational principles inherent in nature-universal norms capable of being discerned by rational people. The law of nations—Roman civil law (the law of the Roman state), combined with principles drawn from Greek and other sources—eventually replaced much of the local law in the Empire. This evolution of a universal code of law that gave expression to the Stoic principles of common rationality and humanity was the great achievement of Roman rule.

Another consequence of expansion was increased contact with Greek culture. Gradually, the Romans acquired knowledge from Greece about scientific thought, philosophy, medicine and geography. Adopting the humanist outlook of the Greeks, the Romans came to value human intelligence and eloquent and graceful prose and oratory. Rome creatively assimilated the Greek achievement and transmitted it to others, thereby extending the orbit of Hellenism.

During Rome's march to empire, all its classes had demonstrated spirit in fighting foreign wars. With Carthage and Macedonia no longer threats in Rome, this cooperation deteriorated. Rome became torn apart by internal dissension during the first century B.C.

Julius Caesar, a popular military commander, gained control of the government. Caesar believed that only strong and enlightened leaderhsip could permanently end the civil warfare destroying Rome. Rome's ruling class feared that Caesar would destroy the Republic and turn Rome into a monarchy. Regarding themselves as defenders of republican liberties and senatorial leadership, aristocratic conspirators assassinated Caesar in 44 B.C. The murder of Caesar plunged Rome into renewed civil war. Finally, in 31 B.C., Octavian, Caesar's adopted son, defeated his rivals and emerged as master of Rome. Four years later, Octavian, now called Augustus, became in effect the first Roman emperor.

The Roman Empire

The rule of Augustus signified the end of the Roman Republic and the beginning of the Roman Empire—the termination of aristocratic politics and the emergence of one-man rule. Under Augustus, the power of the ruler was disguised; in ensuing generations, however, emperors would wield absolute power openly.

Augustus was by no means a self-seeking tyrant, but a creative statesman. His reforms rescued a dying Roman world and inaugurated Rome's greatest age. For the next two hundred years the Mediterranean world enjoyed the blessings of the *Pax Romana,* the Roman peace.

The ancient world had never experienced such a long period of peace, order, efficient administration, and prosperity. The Romans called the Pax Romana a "Time of Happiness." It was the fulfillment of Rome's mission—the creation of a world-state that provided peace, security, ordered civilization, and the rule of law. The cities of the Roman empire served as centers of Greco-Roman civilization, which spread to the furthest reaches of the Mediterranean. Roman citizenship, gradually granted, was finally extended to virtually all free men by an edict in A.D. 212.

In the third century, the ordered civilization of the Pax Romana ended. The Roman Empire was plunged into military anarchy, as generals, supported by their soldiers, fought for the throne. Germanic tribesmen broke through the deteriorating border defenses to raid, loot, and destroy. Economic problems caused cities, the centers of civilization, to decay. Increasingly, people turned away from the humanist values of the Greco-Roman civilization and embraced Near Eastern religions which offered a sense of belonging, a promise of immortality, and relief from earthly misery.

The emperors Diocletian (285–305) and Constantine (306–337) tried to contain the forces of disintegration by tightening the reins of government and squeezing more taxes out of the citizens. In the process they divided the Empire into eastern and western halves, and transformed Rome into a bureaucratic, regimented, and militarized state.

Diocletian and Constantine had given Rome a reprieve, but in the last part of the fourth century, the problem of guarding the frontier grew more acute. At the end of 406, the border finally collapsed; numerous German tribes overran the Empire's western provinces. In 410 and again in 455, Rome was sacked by Germanic invaders. German soldiers in the pay of Rome gained control of the government and dictated the choice of emperor. In 476, German officers overthrew the Roman Emperor Romulus and placed a fellow German on the throne. The act is traditionally regarded as the end of the Roman Empire in the West.

EARLY CHRISTIANITY

When the Roman Empire was in decline, a new religion, Christianity, was sweeping across the

Mediterranean world. Christianity was based on the life, death, and teachings of Jesus, a Palestinian Jew who was executed by the Roman authorities. Jesus was heir to the ethical montheism of the Hebrew prophets. He also taught the imminent coming of the reign of God and the need for people to repent their sins—to transform themselves morally in order to enter God's kingdom. People must love God and their fellow human beings.

In the time immediately following the crucifixion of Jesus, his followers were almost exclusively Jews, who could more appropriately be called Jewish-Christians. To the first members of the Christian movement, Jesus was both a prophet, who proclaimed God's power and purpose, and the Messiah, whose coming heralded a new age. To Paul, another Jewish-Christian, Jesus was the redeemer who held out the promise of salvation to the entire world and the savior-god who took on human flesh annd atoned for the sins of humanity by suffering death upon the cross. Saint Paul carried this message to Jews and especially to non-Jews (Gentiles).

The Christian message of a divine Savior, a concerned Father, and brotherly love inspired men and women who were dissatisfied with the world of the here-and-now, who felt no attachment to city or Empire, who derived no inspiration from philosophy, and who suffered from a profound sense of loneliness. Christianity offered the individual what the city and the Roman world-state could not: a personal relationship with God, a promise of eternal life, a membership in a community of the faithful (the church) who cared for each other.

Unable to crush Christianity by persecution, Roman emperors decided to gain the support of the growing number of Christians within the Empire. By A.D. 392, Theodosius I had made Christianity the state religion of the Empire and declared the worship of pagan gods illegal.

The Judeo-Christian and Greco-Roman traditions are the two principle components of Western civilization. Both traditions valued the individual. For classical humanism, individual worth derived from the human capacity to reason—to shape character and life according to rational standards. Christianity also places great stress on the individual. It teaches that God cares for each person and wants people to behave righteously, and that he made them morally autonomous.

Despite their common emphasis on the individual, the Judeo-Christian and Greco-Roman traditions essentially have different world-views. With the victory of Christianity, the ultimate goal of life shifted from achieving excellence in this world through the full and creative development of human talent toward attaining salvation in a heavenly city. For Christians, a person's wordly accomplishments counted very little if he or she did not accept God and his revelation. Greek classicism held that there was no authority higher than reason; Christianity taught that without God as the starting point, knowledge is formless, purposeless, and error-prone.

But Christian thinkers did not seek to eradicate the rational tradition of Greece. Rather, they sought to fit Greek philosophy into a Christian framework. In doing so, Christians performed a task of immense historical significance—the preservation of Greek philosophy.

THE MIDDLE AGES

The triumph of Christianity and the establishment of Germanic kingdoms on once-Roman lands constituted a new phase in Western history: the end of the ancient world and the beginning of the Middle Ages. In the ancient world, the locus of Greco-Roman civilization was the Mediterranean Sea. The heartland of medieval civilization shifted to the north, to regions of Europe that Greco-Roman civilization had barely penetrated.

The Early Middle Ages

During the Early Middle Ages (500–1050), a common civilization evolved, with Christianity at the center, Rome as the spiritual capital, and Latin as the language of intellectual life. The opening centuries of the Middle Ages were marked by a decline in trade, town life, central authority, and learning. The Germans were culturally unprepared to breathe new life into classical civilization. A new civilization with its own distinctive style was taking root, however. It consisted of Greco-Roman survivals, the native traditions of the Germans, and the Christian outlook.

Christianity was the integrating principle of the Middle Ages, and the church its dominant institution. People came to see themselves as participants in a great drama of salvation. There was only one truth—God's revelation to humanity. There was only one avenue to heaven—the church. To the medieval mind, society without the church was as inconceivable as life without the Christian view of God. By teaching a higher morality, the church tamed the warrior habits of the Germanic peoples. By copying and preserving ancient texts, monks kept alive elements of the high civilization of Greece and Rome.

One German people, the Franks, built a viable kingdom, with major centers in France and the Rhine Valley of Germany. Under Charlemagne, who ruled from 768 to 814, the Frankish empire reached its height. On Christmas day in the year 800, Pope Leo crowned Charlemagne as "Emperor of the Romans." The title signified that the tradition of a world empire still survived, despite the demise of the Roman Empire three hundred years earlier. Because the pope crowned Charlemagne, this act meant that the emperor had a spiritual responsibility to spread and defend the faith.

The crowning of a German ruler as emperor of the Romans by the head of the church represented the merging of German, Christian, and Roman elements—the essential characteristic of medieval civilization. This blending of traditions was also evident on a cultural plane, for Charlemagne, a German warrior-king, showed respect for classical learning and Christianity, both non-Germanic traditions. During his reign, a distinct European civilization took root, but it was centuries away from fruition.

Charlemagne's successors could not hold the empire together, and it disintegrated. As central authority waned, large landowners began to exercise authority over their own regions. Furthering this movement toward localism and decentralization were simultaneous invasions by Muslims, Vikings from Scandinavia, and Magyars, originally from Western Asia. They devasted villages, destroyed ports, and killed many people. Trade was at a standstill, coins no longer circulated, and untended farms became wastelands. The European community collapsed, the political authority of kings disappeared, and cultural life and learning withered.

During these times, large landowners, or lords, wielded power formerly held by kings over their subjects, an arrangement called *feudalism.* Arising during a period of collapsing central authority, invasion, scanty public revenues, and declining commerce and town life, feudalism attempted to provide some order and security. A principle feature of feudalism was the practice of *vassalage,* in which a man in a solemn ceremony pledged loyalty to a lord. The lord received military service from his vassal, and the vassal obtained land, called a *fief,* from his lord.

Feudalism was built on an economic foundation known as manorialism. A village community (manor), consisting of serfs bound to the land, became the essential agricultural arrangement in medieval society. In return for protection and the right to cultivate fields, serfs owed obligations to their lords, and their personal freedom was restricted in a variety of ways.

Manorialism and feudalism presupposed an unchanging social order with a rigid system of estates, or orders—clergy who prayed, lords who fought, and peasants who toiled. The revival of an urban economy and the re-emergence of the king's authority in the High Middle Ages (about 1050–1270) would undermine feudal and manorial relationships.

The High Middle Ages

By the end of the eleventh century, Europe showed many signs of recovery and vitality. The invasions of Magyars and Vikings had ended, and kings and powerful lords imposed greater order in their territories. Improvements in technology and the clearing of new lands increased agricultural production. More food, the fortunate absence of plagues, and the limited nature of feudal warfare contributed to a population increase.

Expanding agricultural production, the end of Viking attacks, greater political stability, and a larger population revived commerce. In the twelfth and thirteenth centuries, local, regional, and long-distance trade gained such a momentum that some historians describe the period as a commercial revolution that surpassed commerce in the Roman Empire during the Pax Romana.

In the eleventh century, towns re-emerged throughout Europe, and in the next century became active centers of commerce and intellectual life. Socially, economically, and culturally, towns were a new and revolutionary force. Towns contributed to the decline of manorialism because they provided new opportunities for commoners, apart from food production.

A new class (the middle class) of merchants and artisans appeared; unlike the lords and serfs, the members of this class were not connected with the land. Townspeople possessed a value system different from that of lords, serfs, or clerics. Whereas the clergy prepared people for heaven, the feudal lords fought and hunted, and the serfs toiled in small villages, townspeople engaged in business and had money and freedom. Townspeople were freeing themselves from the prejudices of both feudal aristocrats, who considered trade and manual work degrading, and the clergy, who cursed the pursuit of riches as an obstacle to salvation. Townspeople were critical, dynamic, and progressive—a force for change.

Other signs of growing vitality in Latin Christendom (western and central Europe) were the greater order and security provided by the emergence of states. While feudalism fostered a Europe that was split into many local regions, each ruled by a lord, the church envisioned a vast Christian commonwealth, *Republica Christiana,* guided by the pope. During the High Middle Ages, the ideal of a universal Christian community seemed close to fruition. Never again would Europe possess such spiritual unity.

But forces were propelling Europe in a different direction. Aided by educated and trained officials who enforced royal law, tried people in royal courts, and collected royal taxes, kings enlarged their territories and slowly fashioned strong central governments. Gradually, subjects began to transfer their prime loyalty from the church and their lords to the person of the king. In the process, the foundations of European states were laid. Not all areas followed the same pattern. England and France achieved a large measure of unity during the Middle Ages; Ger-

many and Italy remained divided into numerous independent territories.

Along with economic recovery and political stability, the High Middle Ages experienced a growing spiritual vitality. This vigor was marked by several developments. The common people showed greater devotion to the church. Within the church, reform movements attacked clerical abuses, and the papacy grew more powerful. Holy wars against the Muslims drew the Christian community closer together. During this period, the church with great determination tried to make society follow divine standards, that is, to shape all institutions according to a comprehensive Christian outlook.

European economic and religious vitality was paralleled by a flowering of philosophy, literature, and the visual arts. Creative intellects achieved on a cultural level what the papacy accomplished on an institutional level—the integration of society around a Christian viewpoint. The High Middle Ages saw the restoration of some learning of the ancient world, the rise of universities, the emergence of an original form of architecture (the Gothic), and the creation of an imposing system of thought (scholasticism).

Medieval theologian-philosophers, called *scholastics* fashioned Christian teachings into an all-embracing philosophy, which represented the spiritual essence of medieval civilization. They achieved what Christian thinkers in the Roman Empire had initiated and what learned men of the Early Middle Ages were groping for: a synthesis of Greek philosophy and Christian revelation.

The Late Middle Ages

By the fourteenth century, Latin Christendom had experienced more than 250 years of growth, but during the Late Middle Ages, roughly the fourteenth and early fifteenth centuries, medieval civilization declined. The fourteenth century, an age of adversity, was marked by crop failures, famine, population decline, plagues, stagnating production, unemployment, inflation, devastating warfare, abandoned villages, and violent rebellions by the poor and weak of towns and countryside, who were ruthlessly suppressed by the upper classes. This century witnessed flights into mysticism, outbreaks of mass hysteria, and massacres of Jews; it was an age of pessimism and general insecurity. The papacy declined in power, heresy proliferated, and the synthesis of faith and reason erected by the Christian thinkers during the High Middle Ages began to disintegrate. All these developments were signs that the stable and coherent civilization of the thirteenth century was drawing to a close.

The Middle Ages and the Modern World

But the decline of medieval civilization in the fourteenth century brought no new dark age to Europe. Its economic and political institutions and technological skills had grown too strong. Instead, the waning of the Middle Ages opened up possibilities for another stage in Western civilization—the modern age.

The modern world is linked to the Middle Ages in innumerable ways. European cities, the middle class, the state system, English common law, universities—all had their origins in the Middle Ages. During the Middle Ages, importance advances were made in business practices, such as double-entry bookkeeping and the growth of credit and banking facilities. By translating and commenting on the writings of Greek philosophers and scientists, medieval scholars preserved a priceless intellectual heritage without which the modern mind could never had evolved. During the Middle Ages, Europeans began to lead the rest of the world in the development of technology.

Medieval philosophers, believing that God's law was superior to the decrees of states, provided a theoretical basis for opposing tyrannical kings who violated Christian principles. The idea that both the ruler and the ruled are bound by a higher law would become a principle element of modern liberal thought. The Christian stress on the sacred worth of the individual and on the higher law of God has never ceased to influence Western civilization. The Christian commandment to "love thy neighbor" has permeated modern reform movements.

Feudalism contributed to the history of liberty. The idea evolved that law should not be imposed by an absolute monarch but requires the collaboration of kings and subjects; that a king, too, should be bound by the law; and that lords should have the right to resist a monarch who violates agreements. Related to this development was the emergence of reperesentative institutions, notably the English parliament. The king was expected to consult its members on matters concerning the realm's affairs.

Despite these concrete elements of continuity, the characteristic outlook of the Middle Ages was much different from that of the modern world. Religion was the integrating feature of the Middle Ages, whereas science and secularism determine the modern outlook. Medieval thought began with the existence of God and the truth of his revelation as interpreted by the church, which set the standards and defined the purposes for human endeavor.

The medieval mind rejected the fundamental principle of Greek philosophy and modern thought—the autonomy of reason. Without the guidance of revealed truth, reason was seen as feeble. Unlike either ancient or modern thinkers, medieval scholars believed ultimately that reason alone could not provide a unified view of nature or society. To understand nature, law, morality, or the state, it was necessary to know its relationship to a supernatural order, a higher world.

In the modern view, both nature and the human intellect are self-sufficient. Nature is a mathematical system that operates without miracles or any other form of divine intervention. To comprehend nature and society, the mind needs no divine assistance; it accepts no authority above reason. The modern mind finds it unacceptable to reject conclusions of science on the basis of clerical authority and revelation or to base politics, law, and economics on religion; it rejects the medieval division of the universe into a heavenly realm of perfection and a lower earthly realm. Scientific and secular attitudes have driven Christianity and faith from their central position to the periphery of human concerns.

EARLY MODERN EUROPE

From the Italian Renaissance of the fifteenth century through the Age of Enlightenment of the eighteenth century, the outlook and institutions of the Middle Ages disintegrated and distinctly modern forms emerged. This radical change in European civilization could be seen on every level of society. On the economic level, commerce and industry expanded greatly, and capitalism largely replaced medieval forms of economic organization. In politics, central government grew stronger at the expense of feudalism. On the religious level, the unity of Christendom became fragmented by the rise of Protestantism. On the social level, middle-class townspeople, increasing in number and wealth, started playing a more important role in economic and cultural life. In consequence, the clergy lost its monopoly over learning, and the otherwordly orientation of the Middle Ages gave way to a secular outlook in literature and the arts. Theology, the queen of the sciences in the Middle Ages, surrendered its crown to mathematics and the study of nature.

The Renaissance

Many new tendencies manifested themselves dramatically during the Renaissance, a period beginning about 1350 and lasting for two centuries. The word *renaissance* means rebirth, and it is used to refer to the attempt by artists and thinkers to recover and apply the learning and standards of ancient Greece and Rome. The Renaissance was an age of transition during which the medieval outlook was rejected, classical cultural forms were revived, and modern attitudes emerged. The Renaissance was not a complete and sudden break with the Middle Ages; many medieval ways and attitudes persisted. Nevertheless, the thesis that the Renaissance represents the birth of modernity has much in its favor.

New economic, political, and social conditions presented new challenges, for which the old order of priests and feudal lords provided no answers. So the men and women of the Renaissance reached back beyond the feudal order—which they said belonged to the "Dark Ages"—to classical antiquity, where all seemed light, refinement, and civilization. They consciously modeled themselves on the standards set by ancient Greece and Rome. They ransacked monastic libraries for manuscript records of ancient wisdom and stud-

ied ancient ruins as examples of architectural and artistic perfection. They identified much more with the urban and urbane culture of antiquity than they did with the more recent, and to their minds, barbarous past.

The Renaissance started in the independent city-states of northern Italy in the fourteenth century; during the fifteenth and sixteenth centuries, its ideas spread to other lands in Europe. In the developed urban centers of Italy, commercial elites enjoyed the leisure and freedom that came with the wealth procured by trade. The wealthy Italian city-states acted as magnets. They attracted men of talent in every field—the military, government, business, the arts, and education—because of the rewards available to those who succeeded. Renaissance society was marked by a growing *secular outlook*. To be sure, the people were neither nonbelievers nor atheists. Increasingly, however, religion had to compete with worldly concerns. Members of the urban upper class did not allow religion to interfere with their quest for the full life. This worldliness found concrete expression in Renaissance art and literature.

Individualism was another hallmark of Renaissance society. The competitive marketplace in which they operated taught the urban elite to assert their own personalities, to demonstrate their unique talents, and to fulfill their ambitions. Often employed by this elite, Renaissance artists in turn sought to capture individual character and achievement in their works. At the same time, explorers ventured into uncharted seas, conquerors carved out empires in the New World, and merchant-capitalists amassed fortunes.

The most characteristic intellectual movement of the Renaissance was *humanism,* an educational program based on the study of ancient Greek and Roman literature. Renaissance humanists valued ancient literature for its clear and graceful style and for its insights into human nature. In contrast to medieval scholastic philosophers who used Greek philosophy to prove the truth of Christian doctrines, Italian humanists read classical literature to nourish their new interest in the worldly life.

A new curriculum was devised, aimed primarily at instructing not the clergy—as was the case in the Middle Ages—but the sons (rarely the daughters) of nobles and merchants. The new curriculum emphasized training in those skills of writing, speaking, politics and ethics that were most in demand at the Renaissance courts and that one had to master for a career in the expanding civil service. This educational ideal took such hold on the imagination of the European elite that it served until the twentieth century as the standard of what it meant to be educated.

The Renaissance wedded its vision of antiquity to its contemporary concerns. In the process, an entirely new culture was created, as different from the ancient world as it was from the Middle Ages. Thus, in art, the human form and rules of perspective were recovered from antiquity but were employed to represent a Christian idealism and a cult of the individual that were not antique. In politics, the ancient history of Greece and Rome was studied for clues to solve the problems of the Renaissance city-state, such as internal turmoil, mercenary armies, rivalries between city-states, and the menace of powerful foreign monarchies like France and Spain. Out of this intense political life came a rich experimentation in forms of government. Perhaps the most important were the efforts of the Florentines and Venetians, who tried for centuries to preserve the conditions of republican government and laid the theoretical foundations for modern republicanism.

The principal effect of this ferment was the gradual destruction of the medieval view that the world was static and the individual's place within it—whether as priest, warrior, or peasant—fixed. Instead, Renaissance culture emphasized the talents and creativity of an educated elite and the right of princes, as well as artists and merchants, to shape their own destiny. Embedded in this idea lay the germ of a completely new notion which was neither medieval nor ancient, but distinctly modern: the idea of secular progress.

The Reformation

Like the Renaissance, the Reformation, which began with Martin Luther's attack on the church, marked a break with the Middle Ages. Whereas the Renaissance turned away from medieval art and literary forms, the Reformation broke with the medieval religious outlook and ended the religious unity of the Middle Ages.

Continuing entrepreneural activity and the intellectual curiosity fostered by Renaissance learning produced a more sophisticated and independent urban elite. By the early sixteenth century, that elite became increasingly alienated from the traditional moral authority exercised by the church. Of course, the church had always had its dissenters, such as the medieval opponents of papal authority who favored placing ecclesiastical power into the hands of the church councils, or the late-fourteenth-century followers of John Wycliffe, who attacked church corruption and repudiated certain church doctrines. Not until the early sixteenth century, however, did church critics gather enough strength to challenge successfully the rule of the papacy and the moral authority of Catholic doctrines.

The Reformation began in German cities and spread throughout western Europe. Only in countries like Spain and Italy, where ecclesiastical authority was firmly entrenched, did the church repel the Protestant advance. Protestant reformers used the newly invented printing press to appeal to that urban elite and also to the traditional nobility, who had long coveted church lands and tax revenues. During the brief period from Luther's initial confrontation with a papal representative and seller of indulgences in 1517 until the death of of Henry VIII in England in 1547, nearly a quarter of the western European population had embraced one version or another of Protestantism.

Two doctrines formed the basis of this new version of Christianity: salvation comes to the believer as a result of divine mercy and not from the church's practices and rituals, and the essence of Christianity lies in the Bible. Religion is, therefore, accessible to any literate person, and in matters of salvation, all believers act as priests over their own spiritual fate. The motives of the thousands of Europeans who embraced a Protestant creed were many: anger at the corrupt lifestyle of some clergy, a restlessness with traditional authority coupled with the desire to search Scripture for themselves, the wish to bring about a social transformation that would indeed allow the poor to inherit the earth, and perhaps the need for a religion that glorified wordly activity rather than the cloister and its clergy.

Just as new clergy revitalized Europe intellectual life during the Renaissance and led Europeans to discard the medieval preoccupation with theology, a new religious outlook, personal faith, marked the Reformation. Personal faith, not adherence to the doctrines of the church, became central to the religious life of European Protestants. Like the Renaissance humanists, some Protestant leaders were trained in ancient learning, but they gave humanism a religious meaning. They wanted to restore the spirit of early Christianity, in which faith seemed purer, believers more sincere, and the clergy uncorrupted by luxury and power.

The Reformation shattered the religious unity of Europe, the chief characteristic of the Middle Ages, and weakened the church, the principal institution of medieval society. The church's moral authority was rejected by millions of Europeans, and its political power was curtailed.

By strengthening the power of kings at the expense of religious bodies, the Reformation furthered the growth of the modern state. Protestant rulers repudiated the pope's claim to temporal power and extended their authority over Protestant churches in their lands. In Catholic lands, the church, in reaction to Protestantism, tended to support rather than challenge monarchs. Protestantism did not create the modern secular state; it did, however, help to free the state from subordination to religious authority, an essential feature of modern political life.

The Reformation also promoted individualism. Protestants sought a direct and personal relationship with God and interpreted the Bible for themselves. They developed an inner confidence and assertiveness. This individualism may also have been expressed in a work ethic that was compatible with capitalist forms of economic activity.

The Commercial Revolution

One of the most decisive changes occurring between 1450 and 1750 was the Commercial Revolution. This transformation saw the breakdown of the largely self-sufficient agrarian economy, based on the manor, which characterized the Middle Ages. In its place came increased production and commercial activity. Perhaps the most dramatic change was that for the first time in human history the problem of providing an adequate food supply was solved in a few places (England, Holland, and British North America) by the late seventeenth century.

The Commercial Revolution was the product of two processes: overseas expansion and the price revolution. Western European monarchies carved out empires in other parts of the world—the Portuguese in Africa, India, and the East Indies in the fifteenth and early sixteenth centuries; the Spanish in Latin America in the sixteenth century; the French, the Dutch, and the English in North America, the East and West Indies, and India in the seventeenth and eighteenth centuries. Wherever they went, Europeans overcame armed opposition through their superior fire power in the form of the cannon, the musket, and especially the armed sailing ship. For four hundred years, one small part of the globe, western Europe, dominated and exploited much of the rest of the planet. Only in this century were the western European powers forced to relinquish their empires.

Overseas colonies played a vital role in the Commercial Revolution. They furnished raw materials, gold, and silver to stroke European economies; they also furnished protected markets for products made in Europe. Finally, colonies produced materials at low cost because of slave labor, which was widely used on plantations until the nineteenth century. Out of the colonies came immense profits to invest in further economic development.

The rapid and unprecedented rise in prices (inflation) throughout the sixteenth century was known as the *price revolution*. This inflation can be traced to two causes: an unexplained and perhaps inexplicable increase in population beginning in the second half of the fifteenth century and the influx of silver into western Europe from the mines of Mexico and Peru. There were more and more mouths to feed in the fifteenth and sixteenth centuries. Agricultural production expanded to meet this new demand but never expanded rapidly enough. So, prices, especially for primary products like wool and grain, shot up. The flooding of western Europe with silver from New World mines probably was also inflationary in an economy of scarcity. The money supply in the form of silver coin increased faster than the supply of goods, so prices rose faster.

The effect of the price revolution can hardly be overestimated. For the first time since the thirteenth century, demand was steadily rising. Investment in increased production was bound to yield increased profits, an enormous incentive to invest and reinvest.

In early modern Europe, the largest commercial endeavor by far was agriculture. Thus, the greatest investment was in land, and the most important changes produced by that investment took place on the land. Driven by the desire for profit, landlords saw that it would be necessary to reorganize their farms in order to increase production for an expanding market. The old manorial agriculture, based on the three-field system, was geared to the needs of the manor, not those of the market. The characteristic manorial pattern of farming in strips and of having communal access to common land was inefficient. So enterprising landlords denied their peasants the use of the commons and drove them from the manor. Having eliminated peasant holdings, the landlords tore down hedges and filled in ditches, dividing the strips, in this way consolidating the fields into single units, which they often let—if they themselves did not have the areas cultivated—at high rents to the most efficient producers.

This process of consolidation was known as *enclosure,* and its consequences were momentous. More and more land was turned over to commercial agriculture and returned increasing yields and profits. The peasants who had lost their customary use of the land either became agricultural laborers working for very low wages or left to find work in the towns or in the colonies overseas. Rural poverty and violence increased because of the displacement of the peasants.

This ruthless transformation of agriculture was matched by a comparable process in trade and industry. As commercial activity increased, the medieval guilds, essentially restrictive of production and exchange, became obsolete. The initiative passed to rich merchants whose operations were not local like the guilds, but regional, national, and sometimes even international in scale. They exploited cottage industry by monopolizing raw materials.

Raw wool, for example was put out by merchants to be processed by peasants in country villages (outside of towns, where guild restrictions did not apply). This procedure saved money on overhead by using the peasants' own cottages and on labor by paying low piece rates to peasants, who were only too glad to find work. The merchants then sold the finished product where it would fetch the best price. In industry as in farming, the effect was the same: increasing profits, investment, economic expansion, and a widening gap between rich and poor.

The Commercial Revolution represented a crucial stage in the development of modern capitalism. It ushered in a world economy and led to an earth dominated by Europeans, a situation that would endure until the twentieth century. We shall now examine other movements that helped shape the modern world: the growth of national states, the Scientific Revolution, and the Enlightenment.

NOTES

1. W. H. Auden, ed., *The Portable Greek Reader* (New York: Viking, 1952), p. 38.

2. Benjamin Farrington, *Greek Science* (Baltimore: Penguin Books, 1961), p. 301.

Geography of Europe

The map on the following pages shows the continent of Europe and the countries around the Mediterranean Sea, together with the physical features of the land such as major rivers and other bodies of water, mountains and changes of elevation, and the names of countries and their capitals. A knowledge of the geography of this area will help give a sense of the relationship between geography and history, of how the characteristics of the terrain and the availability of rivers and other bodies of water affected the movement of people and the relationship between people and environment throughout history.

Europe is the smallest continent in the world with the exception of Australia. The other continents are Africa, Asia, North America, South America, and Antarctica. The continent of Europe, which can be viewed as the western extension of the Asian landmass, is distinctive in its configuration. Peninsulas make up a significant portion of the continent's land area. This feature gives Europe an unusually long coastline, equal in distance to one and a half times around the equator (37,877 miles). Europe's western boundary is the Atlantic Ocean, while the Ural Mountains, Ural River, and Caspian Sea—in Russia and Kazakhstan—form its eastern boundary. Europe extends southward to the Caucasus Mountains, the Black Sea, and the Mediterranean Sea. The continent extends to the Arctic Ocean in the north. Off the mainland but considered by geographers to be part of Europe are thousands of islands, most notably the British Isles to the northwest.

North Americans are often surprised to discover the small size of the European continent. The geographic area of France, for example, is less than that of Texas; England is similar in size to Alabama. The distance from London to Paris is about the same as from New York to Boston; the distance from Berlin to Moscow is comparable to that of Chicago to Denver. And the entire continent of Europe is about the size of Canada.

MAJOR PENINSULAS AND ISLANDS   There are five major European peninsulas: the Iberian (Portugal and Spain); the Apennine (Italy); the Balkan (Albania, Bulgaria, Greece, and parts of the former Yugoslavian republics and Turkey); the Scandinavian (Norway and Sweden); and Jutland (Denmark). Ireland and the United Kingdom of England, Wales, and Scotland make up the British Isles. Major islands of the Mediterranean Sea include the Balearic Islands, Corsica, Sardinia, Sicily, Crete, and Cyprus.

SEAS, LAKES, AND RIVERS   Europe's irregular coastline encloses large areas of the surrounding waters into bays, gulfs, and seas. In the Mediterranean Sea are located, from west to east, the Tyrrhenian Sea (between Italy and Sicily, and Sardinia and Corsica), the Adriatic Sea (between Italy and the former Yugoslavian republics), the Ionian Sea (between Italy and Greece), and the Aegean Sea (between Greece and Turkey).

The Baltic Sea, in the north, is bordered by Finland, Estonia, Latvia, Lithuania, Poland, Germany, and Sweden, and connected by narrow channels to the North Sea, which lies between Great Britain and the countries of the northwestern mainland. The English Channel separates England and France, and the Bay of Biscay borders the west coast of France and the north coast of Spain. The Black Sea, on the southern border of Russia and Ukraine, is connected by water passages to the Aegean Sea. The Caspian Sea, which lies partly in Russia and

Kazakhstan, and partly in Asia, is the world's largest saltwater lake and is the lowest point in Europe at 92 feet below sea level.

Europe's many rivers have served as transportation routes for thousands of years. Several of the major rivers, including the longest, flow across the Russian plain. The Volga, Europe's longest river (2,194 miles), rises west of Moscow and empties into the Caspian Sea. It is also linked by canals and other river systems to the Arctic Ocean and the Baltic Sea. The Dnieper flows south through the agricultural heartland of Ukraine into the Black Sea.

Europe's second longest river, the Danube (1,777 miles), is the principal waterway in the southeastern part of the continent. It originates in Germany and flows through Austria, Slovakia, Hungary, the former Yugoslavian republics, Bulgaria, and Romania into the Black Sea. The Rhine winds northward from the Alps through western Germany and the Netherlands into the North Sea, which is also the destination of the Elbe River in eastern Germany. In France, the Rhône flows south into the Mediterranean, and the Seine and Loire flow west to the English Channel and the Bay of Biscay. Other important waterways are the Po in northern Italy, the Vistula in Poland, and the Thames in England.

The proximity of most areas of the European landmass to the coastline or to major river systems is important to understanding the historical development of European civilization. Trading routes and major cities developed along these waterways, and rivers have served as natural boundaries.

LAND REGIONS   Europe, despite its small size, presents a wide range of landforms from rugged mountains to sweeping plains. These landforms can be separated into four major regions: the Northwest Mountains, the Great European Plain, the Central Uplands, and the Alpine Mountain System. The mountains of the Northwest Region cover most of the region, running through northwestern France, Ireland, northern Great Britain, Norway, Sweden, northern Finland, and the northwest corner of Russia.

The Great European Plain covers almost all of the European part of the former Soviet Union, extending from the Arctic Ocean to the Caucasus Mountains. It stretches westward across Poland, Germany, Belgium, the western portion of France and southeastern England.

The Central Uplands is a belt of high plateaus, hills and low mountains. It reaches from the central plateau of Portugal, across Spain, the central highlands of France, to the hills and mountains of southern Germany, the Czech Republic and Slovakia.

The Alpine Mountain System is made up of several mountain chains. Included in this system are the Pyrenees between Spain and France, the Alps in southeastern France, northern Italy, Switzerland, and western Austria, and the Apennine range in Italy. Also included are the mountain ranges of the Balkan peninsula, the Carpathian Mountains in Slovakia and Romania, and the Caucasus Mountains between the Black and Caspian Seas. These mountain ranges have been formidable barriers and boundaries throughout history, affecting the movement of people and the relationship of people to each other and to the land.

When studying the map of Europe, it is important to notice the proximity of western areas of Asia, especially those at the eastern end of the Mediterranean Sea, to areas of North Africa. The cultures of these areas have not only interacted with those of Europe, but they have also played a significant role in shaping the history of Western civilization.

CHAPTER 16

The Rise of Sovereignty: Transition to the Modern State

*F*rom the thirteenth to the seventeenth century, a new and unique form of political organization emerged in the West: the dynastic, or national, state, which harnessed the power of its nobility and the material resources of its territory. Neither capitalism nor technology could have enabled the West to dominate other lands and peoples had it not been for the power of the European states. They channeled and organized violence into the service of national power by directing the energies of the ruling elite into national service and international competition. A degree of domestic stability ensued, and the states encouraged commerce and industry, which could in turn be taxed. Although they nurtured the aristocracy, many states also required that both lord and peasant serve in national armies for the purpose of foreign conquest, as well as for defense.

In most emerging states, monarchs and their courts were the key players in the process of state formation. Generally, they developed forms of government that historians describe by the term *absolutism.* For centuries, kings seemed invincible. Nevertheless, one other form of government emerged in early modern Europe: *republican,* or *constitutional,* states. By 1800, the future lay with this other, more participatory system, which gave greater power to landed or mercantile elites than to kings and their courts.

Although kings in some medieval lands had begun to forge national states, medieval political forms differed considerably from those that developed in the early modern period. During the Middle Ages, feudal lords gave homage to their kings but continued to rule over their local territories, resisting the centralizing efforts of monarchs. Local and even national representative assemblies, which met frequently to give advice to kings, at times acted as a brake on the king's

Henry VIII (*Reproduced by kind permission of Worshipful Company of Barbers*).

CHRONOLOGY 16.1 The Rise of Sovereignty

1469	Ferdinand and Isabella begin their rule of Castile and Aragon
1485	Henry VII begins the reign of the Tudor dynasty in England
1517	The Protestant Reformation starts in Germany
1519	Charles V of Spain becomes Hapsburg emperor of the Holy Roman Empire
1556–1598	Philip II of Spain persecutes Jews and Muslims
1559	Treaty of Cateau-Cambrésis between France and Spain
1560s–1609	Netherlands revolts against Spanish rule
1562–1589	Religious wars in France
1572	Saint Bartholomew's Day Massacre: Queen Catherine of France thought to have ordered thousands of Protestants executed
1579	*Vindiciae contra Tyrannos*, published by Huguenots, justifies regicide
1588	English fleet defeats the Spanish Armada
1590s	A reaction in Russia against Ivan IV, the Terrible
1593	Henry IV of France renounces his Protestantism to restore peace in France
1598	French Protestants granted religious toleration by the Edict of Nantes
1640–1660	English Revolution
1648	Treaty of Westphalia ends Thirty Years' War
1649	Charles I, Stuart king of England, is executed by an act of Parliament
1649–1660	England is coruled by Parliament and the army under Oliver Cromwell
1660	Charles II returns from exile and becomes king of England
1683	Turks attack Vienna and are defeated
1685	Louis XIV of France revokes the Edict of Nantes
1688–1689	Revolution in England: end of absolutism
1699	Treaty of Karlowitz marks Austrians' victory over Turks and affirms Austria's right to rule Hungary, Transylvania, and parts of Croatia
1701	Louis XIV tries to bring Spain under French control
1702–1714	War of the Spanish Succession establishes a balance of power between England and France
1740	Frederick the Great of Prussia invades Silesia, starting war with Austria
1789	French Revolution begins

power. The clergy supported the monarch but governed their congregations or monasteries as separate spiritual realms. The papacy challenged the authority of those monarchs who, it believed, did not fulfill their duty to rule in accordance with Christian teachings as interpreted by the church. In early modern times, powerful monarchs subdued these competing systems of political authority and established strong central governments.

MONARCHS AND ELITES AS STATE BUILDERS

At first the pivotal figures in the development of states were the kings. European elites, whether landed or urban, grudgingly gave allegiance to these ambitious, and at times ruthless, authority figures. In general, a single monarch seemed the only alternative to the even more brutal pattern of war and disorder, so basic to the governing habits of the feudal aristocracy. In the process of increasing their own power, the kings of Europe not only subordinated the aristocracy to their needs and interests, but also gained firm control over the Christian churches in their territories. Gradually, religious zeal was made compatible with and largely supportive of the state's goals, rather than papal dictates or even universal Christian aspirations. The demise of medieval representative assemblies—with the notable exception of the English Parliament—is a dramatic illustration of how monarchs subjected to their will all other political authorities, whether local, regional, or national.

Monarchs needed and employed a variety of tools for extending their power. All encouraged the use of vernacular languages—English, French, Spanish, and so on—because of common identity, as well as contrast with the church's monopoly over the international language of the time, Latin. But more important than words were arms. The foundations of monarchical power were the standing army and a system of tax collection that permitted war to be waged. The two were inseparable. The goal of the monarch was to have independent power, and only economic independence would make that possible. In gen-

eral, only war justified taxes. "Was [absolute monarchy] in reality ever anything but a constant search for new funds to pay for an over-ambitious foreign policy?" asks British historian William Doyle.[1] The rise and fall of the great European powers of the early modern period, first Spain, then France and England, can be traced directly in the fortunes of their armies on the battlefield and the fullness of the king's treasury. Only the rise of the Dutch Republic broke with the pattern of king-army-taxes as the key to the creation of a centralized state. The Dutch case was the very antithesis of absolutism because the rich, urban, Protestant elite loaned the state money at interest and in the process created the first system of national bonds and a citizen-financed national debt. As a result, a nation was created, but one without a strong central (as opposed to local) government. Local elites held most of the power.

In most monarchical states, however, anything that stood in the way of royal power had to be subdued, remolded, or destroyed. Where early modern monarchs succeeded in subduing, reconstituting, or destroying local aristocratic and ecclesiastical power systems, strong dynastic states emerged. Where the monarchs failed, as they did in the Holy Roman Empire and Italy, no viable states evolved until well into the nineteenth century. Those failures derived from the independent authority of local princes of city-states, and in the case of Italy, from the decentralizing influence of papal authority. In the Holy Roman Empire, feudal princes found allies in the newly formed Protestant communities, and in such a situation, religion worked as a decentralizing force. Successful early modern kings had to bring the churches under their authority and subordinate religion to the needs of the state. They did so not by separating church and state (as was later done in the United States), but rather by linking their subjects' religious identity with national identity. For example, in England, by the late seventeenth century, to be a true Protestant was to be a true English subject, while in Spain the same equation operated for the Catholic (as opposed to the Muslim or the Jew, who came to be regarded as non-Spanish).

In the thirteenth century, most Europeans still identified themselves with their localities: their villages, manors, or towns. They gave political allegiance to their local lord or bishop. They knew little, and probably cared less, about the activities of the king and his court, except when the monarch called on them for taxes or military service. By the late seventeenth century, in contrast, aristocrats in many European countries defined the extent of their political power in terms of their relationship to king and court. By then, the lives of very ordinary people were being affected by national systems of tax collection, by the doctrines and practices of national churches, and by conscription.

Increasingly, prosperous town dwellers, the bourgeoisie, realized also that their prosperity hinged, in part, on court-supported foreign and domestic policies. If the king assisted their commercial ventures, the bourgeoisie gave their support to the growth of a strong central state. In only two states, England and the Netherlands, did landed and mercantile elites manage to redistribute political power so that by the late seventeenth century it could be shared by monarchy and parliament or, in the Netherlands, monopolized by a social oligarchy.

The effects of European state building were visible in the world by the late seventeenth century. Commercial rivalry between states and colonial expansion, two major activities of the period, were directly related to the ability of elites to protect their interests under the mantle of the state, and to the state's willingness to encourage world trade in order to enrich its own treasury. Monarchs and the states they helped to create ushered in the modern world just as surely as did commercial expansion, capitalism, and science.

THE RISE AND FALL OF HAPSBURG SPAIN

The Spanish political experience of the sixteenth century stands as a model of the interconnectedness of king, army, and taxation. It was also one of the most spectacular examples in Western history of the rise and equally dramatic fall of a great power. In the course of their rise, the Spanish kings built a dynastic state that burst through its frontiers and encompassed Portugal, part of Italy, the Netherlands, and enormous areas of the

New World. Spain became an intercontinental empire—the first in the West since Roman times.

Hispania as a concept and geographical area existed in Roman times, and citizens of Portugal, Castile, Aragon, Catalonia, and Andalusia, to name only the larger and more important areas of the Iberian Peninsula, recognized a certain common identity—no more, no less. Until 1469, however, Spain did not exist as a political entity. In that year, Ferdinand, heir to the throne of Aragon, married his more powerful and prosperous cousin, Isabella, heiress of Castile. Yet even after the unification of Castile and the crown of Aragon (Catalonia, Aragon, and Valencia), relations among the fiercely independent provinces of Spain were often tense. Only through dynastic marriage of their offspring to a German-speaking family of central Europe, the Hapsburgs, did the Spanish monarchs emerge on the international scene.

Ferdinand and Isabella: Unity and Purity of "Blood" and Religion

During their rule (1479–1516), which took many years to establish firmly, Ferdinand and Isabella laid the foundation for the Spanish empire and Spanish domination of European affairs throughout the sixteenth century. Together, they sought to build the army and the state by waging a campaign to reconquer Spanish territory still held by the Muslims. At the same time, they strove to bring the church into alliance with the state and forge a Spanish identity based upon "blood" ancestry as well as religion.

In order to develop a strong monarchy, the Spanish rulers had to bring the church's interests in line with their own. Ferdinand and Isabella's alliance with the church and their war against the Muslims in the southern portion of the peninsula were interrelated. A crusade against the Muslims presupposed an energetic church and a deep and militant Catholicism, with the rulers committed to the aims of the church, and the church to the aims of the rulers. While other Europeans, partly under the impact of the Renaissance, questioned the church's leadership and attacked its corruption, the Catholic Kings (as Ferdinand and Isabella were called) reformed the church, making it responsive to their needs and also invulnerable

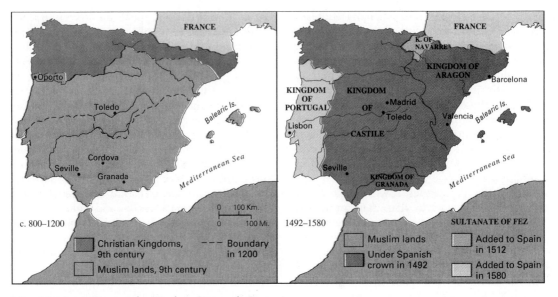

Map 16.1 Spain During the Ninth to Sixteenth Centuries

to criticism. Popular piety and royal policy led in 1492 to a victory over Granada, the last Muslim-ruled territory of Spain.

The five-hundred-year struggle for Christian hegemony in the Iberian Peninsula left the Spanish fiercely religious and strongly suspicious of foreigners. Despite centuries of intermarriage with non-Christians, by the early sixteenth century, purity of blood and orthodoxy of faith became necessary for, and synonymous with, Spanish identity. The Spanish state and church were actively engaged in persecuting Muslims and Jews, who for centuries had contributed substantially to Spanish cultural and economic life.

In 1492, in a move to enforce religious uniformity, the crown expelled from Spain Jews unwilling to accept baptism. Some 150,000 (some estimates are considerably higher) were driven out. The thousands of Jews who underwent conversion were watched by a church tribunal, the Inquisition, for signs of backsliding. The clerical inquisitors employed sophisticated means of interrogation and torture to ferret out newly converted Christians and their descendants suspected of practicing Judaism. Death by fire, sometimes in elaborate public ceremonies, was the ultimate penalty. Muslims also bore the pain of persecution: forced conversions; investigations, torture, and executions conducted by the Inquisition; and

finally, mass expulsion in 1609–1614. The Inquisition represented the dark side of Spanish genius for conquest and administration, and its shadow stretched down through the centuries well into the twentieth.

The wars against the Muslims gave the Spanish invaluable military experience and rendered their army one of the finest in Europe. The wars also created a pattern in the growth of the Spanish empire: its victories always lay in the south—in Italy, in Latin America, and against the Turks—while its defeats and setbacks occurred in the north—in the Netherlands, in opposition to the Lutheran Reformation in the Holy Roman Empire, and in war against England.

With a superior army, with the great magnates pacified, and with the church and the Inquisition under monarchial control, the Catholic Kings expanded their interests and embarked on an imperialist foreign policy in Europe and abroad, which had extraordinary consequences. Ultimately, it made Spain dominant in the New World.

Ferdinand and Isabella gambled on Columbus's voyage, and they won. Then, beginning in 1519 in Mexico, the conquistador Cortés defeated the Aztec nation with six hundred foot soldiers and sixteen horses. This feat was partly due to the superiority of Spanish technology, but it was also made possible by the condition of the Aztec nation, which was struggling to maintain a hold over its own people and over scores of other Mexican tribes that it had, in some cases, brutally subdued. The Spanish forces were led by members of the minor aristocracy, *hidalgos*. Their role was distinctive and yet typical of the role played by the minor aristocracy in the building of other European nation states. For them, as younger sons of impoverished aristocrats, war was a means to riches and land. They would serve the crown at home and abroad as soldiers and often as bureaucrats, and their loyalty to the king was matched only by their fierce ambition. The bureaucracy and army of the early modern states were very important avenues for obtaining or retaining elite status.

The Reign of Charles V: Hapsburg, King of Spain, and Holy Roman Emperor

Through a series of shrewd marriage agreements for their children, Ferdinand and Isabella strengthened their international alliances. As a result, their grandson, Charles, who ruled from 1516 to 1556, inherited Spain, the Netherlands, Austria, Sardinia, Sicily, the kingdom of Naples, and Franche-Comté. In 1519, the same year as the conquest of Mexico, he was also elected Holy Roman emperor (partly through bribery). Thus, he became the most powerful monarch in Europe. But in the course of his reign, he saw problems emerge that would eventually lead to Spain's decline and would weaken the Hapsburg dynasty to which, through marriage, he had been heir.

Charles's inheritance was simply too vast to be governed effectively. However, that was only dimly perceived at the time. The Lutheran Reformation proved to be the first successful challenge to Hapsburg power. It was the first phase of a religious and political struggle between Catholic Spain and Protestant Europe: a struggle that would dominate the last half of the sixteenth century and ultimately reduce Spanish influence.

The achievements of Charles V's reign rested on the twin instruments of army and bureaucracy. The Hapsburg Empire in the New World was vast, and, on the whole, effectively administered and policed. Out of this sprawling empire, with its exploited native populations, came the greatest flow of gold and silver ever witnessed by Europeans. Constant warfare in Europe, in Italy and against the Turks coupled with the immensity of the Spanish administrative network, required a steady intake of capital. But this easy access to income appears to have been detrimental in the long run to the Spanish economy (see Chapter 15). There was no incentive for the development of domestic industry, bourgeois entrepreneurship, or international commerce. Moreover, constant war engendered and perpetuated a social order geared to the aggrandizement of a military class rather than to the development of a commercial class. Although war expanded Spain's power in the sixteenth century, it also sowed the seeds for the financial crises of the 1590s and beyond, and for the eventual decline of Spain as a world power.

Philip II

In the reign of Philip II (1556–1598), the strengths and weaknesses of the Spanish state became fully evident. That period is pivotal in early modern Spanish history. Philip II inherited the throne from his father, Charles V, who abdicated in 1555 and left his son with a large empire in both the Old World and the New. Although this empire had been administered effectively enough, it was facing the specters of bankruptcy and heresy. Heresy, more than any other problem, compelled the attention of this obsessively devout monarch, whose zeal for Catholicism ruled his private conduct and infused his foreign policy. Philip bided his time with foreign infidels and heretics and waited for the moment when the crown would possess the revenue needed to launch an offensive against the Turks and international Protestantism.

To Philip II, being truly Spanish meant being Christian in faith and blood; the racist tendencies, already evident in the later fifteenth century, gained full expression during his reign. Increasingly, the country came to be ruled by an exclusive class of old Christians, who claimed to be untainted because for centuries they had refused to marry Muslims or Jews. Traditional in their thinking, the old Christians controlled the

ALLEGORY OF THE ABDICATION OF CHARLES V BY FRANS FRANCKEN II, 1556.
Emperor Charles V, who ruled half of Europe and most of the Americas, abdicated in 1555, giving his German imperial crown to his brother Ferdinand, archduke of Austria, and the kingdoms of Spain and the Netherlands to his son Philip II. The Hapsburg dynasty ruled Spain until the eighteenth century and Austria and Hungary until the early twentieth century. (*Rijksmuseum, Amsterdam*)

church, religious orders and the Inquisition—all to preserve an imperial system in need of reform.

Melancholic and standoffish by temperament, Philip II worked arduously and declined most of life's enjoyments. He pored over his ministers' reports, editing and commenting, yet in the end he was strangely indecisive. Some problems remained unsolved for years, as frustrated advisers begged in vain for the king to take action.

In the 1560s, Philip sent the largest land army ever assembled in Europe into the Netherlands with the intention of crushing Protestant-inspired opposition to Spanish authority. The ensuing revolt of the Netherlands lasted until 1609 (see page 366), and in losing the Netherlands, Spain lost its industrial heartland. In 1576, the Spanish army, in a desperate attempt to defeat the rebels, flooded and sacked Antwerp, the leading commercial and banking city in northern Europe. Antwerp's trade gradually moved to Amsterdam, a Protestant stronghold, which replaced its southern rival as an international capital and the center of the new Dutch national state.

By the 1580s, Philip's foreign policy was overextended in every direction, and his religious zeal shaped all of his decisions. He intervened in the French religious wars on the Catholic side, although his intervention gave little to Spain in the way of power or influence. Philip's disastrous attempt to invade England was also born of religious zeal.

Philip regarded an assault on England, the main Protestant power, as a holy crusade against the "heretic and bastard" Queen Elizabeth; he particularly resented English assistance to Protestant Dutch rebels. Sailing from Lisbon in May 1588, the Spanish Armada, twenty-two-thousand men strong, met with humiliating defeat. Its ships were too cumbersome to negotiate the treacherous English Channel, where the English ships easily outmaneuvered them and broke their formation by sending fire ships crashing into them. Moreover, strong winds, typical for this time of year, drove the Armada out of striking position.

This defeat had a psychological effect on the Spanish. They openly pondered what they had done to incur divine displeasure. Protestant Europe, on the other hand, hailed the victory as a sign of its election, and the "Protestant wind" stirred by divine intervention entered the mythology of English nationalism. In the rise and fall of nations, self-assurance has played a crucial, if inexplicable, role. The cultural renaissance associated with the England of Shakespeare owed its vigor and confidence in part to its pride at being Protestant and independent of Spanish influence.

The End of the Spanish Hapsburgs

After the defeat of the Armada, Spain gradually and reluctantly abandoned its imperial ambitions in northern Europe. The administrative structure built by Charles V and Philip II did remain strong throughout the seventeenth century; nevertheless, by the first quarter of the century, enormous weaknesses had surfaced in Spanish economic and social life. In 1596, Philip II was bankrupt, his vast wealth overextended by the cost of foreign wars. Bankruptcy reappeared at various times in the seventeenth century, while the agricultural economy, at the heart of any early modern nation, stagnated. The Spanish in their golden age had never devoted enough attention to increasing domestic production.

Despite these setbacks, Spain was still capable of taking a very aggressive posture during the Thirty Years' War (1618–1648). The Austrian branch of the Hapsburg family joined forces with their Spanish cousins, and neither the Swedes and Germans nor the Dutch could stop them. Only

French participation in the Thirty Years' War on the Protestant side tipped the balance decisively against the Hapsburgs. Spanish aggression brought no victories, and with the Peace of Westphalia (1648), Spain officially recognized the independence of the Netherlands and cut its ties with the Austrian branch of the family.

By 1660, the imperial age of the Spanish Hapsburgs had come to an end. The rule of the Protestant princes had been secured in the Holy Roman Empire; the largely Protestant Dutch Republic flourished; Portugal and its colony of Brazil were independent of Spain; and dominance over European affairs had passed to France. The quality of material life in Spain deteriorated rapidly, and the ever-present gap between the rich and the poor widened even more drastically. The traditional aristocracy and the church retained their land and power but failed conspicuously to produce effective leadership. With decline came rigidity of institutions and values. Spain remained authoritarian far longer than other European countries. Democratic revolutions did not occur in a country dominated by the landed elite and the church. The commercial elite that became increasingly important in England, the Netherlands, and France failed to develop in monarchical and agricultural Spain.

The Spanish experience illustrates two aspects of the history of the European state. First, the state as empire could survive and prosper only if the domestic economic base continued to expand. Living off the colonies ultimately meant economic stagnation and the absence of technological innovation at home. Second, the states where a vital and aggressive mercantile class developed generally prospered in the early modern period. In such states, the elite no longer consisted exclusively of those with landed wealth; rather, it comprised those who invested, or even participated, in the market and manufacturing. However, in Spain, the old aristocracy and the church continued to dominate and control society and its mores. They not only despised manual labor and profit taking through trade, but also showed little interest in science and technology.

Although the major states had been created by kings and shrewd dynastic marriages, after 1700 they were increasingly nurtured by an expansion of the elite to include merchants. Eventually, some of the merchants began to look and act like aristocrats. France became such an early modern absolutist state.

As the educated and commercial elites in the early modern states widened, courts and kings began to seem less and less necessary. The English constitutional model of government, complete with a representative assembly, started to look more attractive to reformers. Meanwhile, absolutist monarchies like France continued to function, but only with a vast and expensive bureaucracy that tried to stimulate commerce and industry.

THE GROWTH
OF FRENCH POWER

Two states in the early modern period succeeded most effectively in consolidating the power of their central governments: France and England. Each became a model of a very different form of statehood. The English model evolved into a constitutional monarchy, in which the king's power was limited by Parliament and the rights of the English people were protected by law and tradition. The French model emphasized at every turn the glory of the king and, by implication, the sovereignty of the state and its right to stand above the interests of its subjects. France's monarchy became absolute, although the evolution of the French state was a very gradual process; it was not completed until the late seventeenth century.

When Hugh Capet became king of France in 987, he was, in relation to France's other great feudal lords, merely first among equals. From this small power base, more symbolic than real, Hugh Capet's successors extended their territory and dominion at the expense of the feudal lords' power. To administer their territories, the Capetians established an efficient bureaucracy, composed of townsmen and trustworthy lesser nobles, who, unlike the great feudal lords, owed their wealth and status directly to the king. These royal officials, an essential element of monarchical power, collected the king's feudal dues and administered justice. At the same time, French kings emphasized that they had been selected by God to rule, a theory known as the divine right of kings. This theory gave monarchy a sanctity

that various French kings relied on to enforce their commands to rebellious feudal lords and defend themselves against papal claims of dominance over the French church.

Yet medieval French kings never sought absolute power. Not until the seventeenth century was the power base of the French monarchy consolidated to the extent that kings and their courts could attempt to rule without formal consultations with their subjects. In the Middle Ages, the French monarchs recognized the rights of, and consulted with, local representative assemblies, which represented the three estates, or orders, in society. These assemblies (whether regional or national) consisted of deputies drawn from the various elites: the clergy, the nobility, and significantly, the leadership of cities and towns in a given region. The Estates met as circumstances—such as wars, taxes, or local disputes—warranted, and the nationally representative assembly, the Estates General, was always summoned by the king. Medieval French kings consulted these assemblies mainly to give legitimacy to their demands and credibility to their administration. They also recognized that the courts—especially the highest court, the Parlement of Paris—had the right to administer the king's justice with a minimum of royal interference. Medieval kings did not see themselves as originators of law; they were its guarantors and administrators.

War came to serve the interests of a monarchy bent on consolidating its power and authority. As a result of the Hundred Years' War (1337–1453), the English were eventually driven from France and their claims to the French throne dashed. In the process of war, the French monarchy grew richer. The necessities of war enabled the French kings to levy new taxes, often enacted without the consent of the Estates General, and to maintain a large standing army under royal command. The Hundred Years' War also inspired allegiance to the king as the visible symbol of France. The war heightened the French sense of national identity; the English were a common enemy, discernibly different in manners, language, dress, and appearance.

With revenue and an army at their disposal, the French kings subsequently embarked on territorial aggrandizement. Charles VIII (1483–1498) invaded Italy in 1494. As Machiavelli, a shrewd assessor of the implications of power, observed,

Italy's weakness resulted from its lack of unity, whereas the power of this new cohesive state of France derived in large measure from the strength of its prince and his huge and mostly native-born army. Although the French gained little territory from the Italian campaign, they did effectively challenge Spanish power in Italy and intimidate an already weakened papacy.

Religion and the French State

In every emergent state, tension existed between the monarch and the papacy. At issue was control over the church within that territory—over its personnel, its wealth, and, of course, its pulpits, from which an illiterate majority learned what their leaders wanted them to know, not only in matters of religious belief, but also about questions of obedience to civil authority. The monarch's power to make church appointments could ensure a complacent church. A church that was willing to preach about the king's divine right and was compliant on matters of taxes was especially important in France because, legally, the church had to pay no taxes and had only to give donations to the crown. Centuries of tough bargaining with the papacy paid off when, in 1516, Francis I (1515–1547) concluded the Condordat of Bologna, by which Pope Leo X permitted the French king to nominate, and therefore effectively to appoint, men of his choice to all the highest offices in the French church.

The Concordat of Bologna laid the foundation for what became known as the *Gallican church*—a term signifying the immense power and authority of the Catholic church in France—which was sanctioned and overseen by the French kings. By the early sixteenth century, religious homogeneity had strengthened the central government at the expense of papal authority and the traditional privileges enjoyed by local aristocracy. This ecclesiastical and religious settlement lay at the heart of monarchical authority. Consequently, the Protestant Reformation threatened the very survival of France as a unified state. Throughout the early modern period, the French kings had assumed that their realms must be governed by one king, one faith, and one set of laws. Any alternative to that unity offered local power elites, whether aristocratic or clerical, the opportunity

to channel religious dissent into their service at the expense of royal authority. Once linked, religious and political opposition to any central government could be extremely dangerous.

During the decades that followed, partly through the efforts of the Huguenot (Protestant) underground and partly because the French king and his ministers vacillated in their attempts at persecution, the Protestant minority grew in strength and dedication. By challenging the authority of the Catholic church, Protestants were also inadvertently challenging royal authority, for the French church and the French monarchy supported each other. Protestantism became the basis for a political movement of an increasingly revolutionary nature.

From 1562 to 1598, France experienced waves of religious wars, which cost the king control over vast areas of the kingdom. In 1579, extreme Huguenot theorists published the *Vindiciae contra Tyrannos*. This theoretical statement, combined with a call to action, was the first of its kind in early modern times. It justified rebellion against, and even the execution of, an unjust king. European monarchs might claim power and divinely sanctioned authority, but by the late sixteenth century, their subjects had available the moral justification to oppose their monarch's will, by force, if necessary, and this justification rested on Scripture and religious conviction. Significantly, this same treatise was translated into English in 1648, a year before Parliament publicly executed Charles I, king of England.

The French kings floundered in the face of this kind of political and religious opposition. The era of royal supremacy ushered in by Francis I came to an abrupt end during the reign of his successor, Henry II (1547–1559). Wed to Catherine de' Medici, a member of the powerful Italian banking family, Henry occupied himself not with the concerns of government, but with the pleasures of the hunt. The sons who succeeded Henry—Francis II (1559–1560), Charles IX (1560–1574), and Henry III (1574–1589)—were uniformly weak. In this power vacuum, their mother, Catherine, emerged as virtual ruler—a queen despised for her foreign and nonaristocratic lineage, for the fact that she was a woman, and for her propensity for dangerous intrigue. One of the most hated figures of her day, Catherine de' Medici defies dispassionate assessment. She probably ordered the execution of Protestants by royal troops in Paris—the beginning of the infamous Saint Bartholomew's Day Massacre (1572). The massacre, with the blood bath that followed, became both a symbol and a legend in subsequent European history: a symbol of the excesses of religious zeal and a legend of Protestant martyrdom, which gave renewed energy to the cause of international Protestantism.

The civil wars begun in 1562 were renewed in the massacre's aftermath. They dragged on until the death of the last Valois king in 1589. The Valois failure to produce a male heir to the throne placed Henry, duke of Bourbon and a Protestant, in line to succeed to the French throne. Realizing that the overwhelmingly Catholic population would not accept a Protestant king, Henry (apparently without much regret) renounced his adopted religion and embraced the church. His private religious beliefs may never be known, but outward conformity to the religion of the Catholic majority was the only means to effect peace and reestablish political stability. Under the reign of Henry IV (1589–1610), the French throne acquired its central position in national politics. Henry granted to his Protestant subjects and former followers a degree of religious toleration through the Edict of Nantes (1598), but they were never welcomed in significant numbers into the royal bureaucracy. Throughout the seventeenth century, every French king attempted to undermine the Protestants' regional power bases and ultimately to destroy their religious liberties.

Louis XIV: The Consolidation of French Monarchical Power

The defeat of Protestantism as a national force set the stage for the final consolidation of the French state in the seventeenth century under the great Bourbon kings, Louis XIII and Louis XIV. Louis XIII (1610–1643) realized that his rule depended on an efficient and trustworthy bureaucracy, a renewable treasury, and constant vigilance against the localized claims to power by the great aristocracy and Protestant cities and towns. Cardinal Richelieu, who served as the young Louis XIII's chief minister from 1624 to 1642, became the great architect of French absolutism.

Richelieu's morality rested on one sacred principle, embodied in a phrase he invented: *raison d'état,* reason of state. Richelieu sought to serve the state by bringing under the king's control the disruptive and antimonarchical elements within French society. He increased the power of the central bureaucracy, attacked the power of independent, and often Protestant, towns and cities, and harassed the Huguenots. Above all, he humbled the great nobles by limiting their effectiveness as councilors to the king and prohibiting their traditional privileges, such as using a duel rather than court action to settle grievances. Reason of state also guided Richelieu's foreign policy. It required that France turn against Catholic Spain and join the Protestant, and hence anti-Spanish, side in the war that was raging at the time in the Holy Roman Empire. France's entry into the Thirty Years' War (1618–1648) resulted in a decisive victory for French power on the Continent.

Richelieu died in 1642, and Louis XIII the following year. Cardinal Mazarin, who took charge during the minority of Louis XIV (he was five years old when Louis XIII died), continued Richelieu's policies. Mazarin's heavy-handed actions produced a rebellious reaction, the *Fronde:* a series of street riots that eventually cost the government control over Paris and lasted from 1648 to 1653. Centered in Paris and supported by the great aristocracy, the courts, and the city's poorer classes, the Fronde threatened to develop into a full-scale uprising. It might have done so, but for one crucial factor: its leadership was divided. Court judges (lesser nobles who had often just risen from the ranks of the bourgeoisie) deeply distrusted the great aristocrats and refused in the end to make common cause with them. And both groups feared disorders among the urban masses.

When Louis XIV finally assumed responsibility for governing in 1661, he vowed that the events he had witnessed as a child in Paris, when the Fronde had brought street rioters to the palace windows, would never be repeated. In his reign, Louis XIV crafted the absolutist state, and he became the source of all power, which was in turn administered by his bureaucracy. The local elites or officials were expected to look to the central government for everything, from taxes to noble titles and exclusive privileges for perfume manufacturing or coal extraction. Provincial bureaucrats reported to ministers based in Paris.

THE ROYAL PALACE AT VERSAILLES: PAINTED BY PIERRE PATEL, 1668. Taking his father's royal hunting lodge as a base in 1661, the French king Louis XIV began construction of a magnificent palace at Versailles. This became the center of French royal government and kingly splendor and set the style for monarchical governments throughout Europe. (*Versailles/Cliche des Musées Nationaux*)

Indeed, even road engineers were sent out from Paris. The army was made larger and more professional, gaining, in addition, an architecture and engineering corps. The state also established a military school and sponsored academies for science, literature, and language. Intellectuals received court patronage and pensions but were expected to say what officials liked to hear.

Under Louis XIV, thus, the state became the major player in everything, from dredging the rivers to awarding manufacturing monopolies.

No absolute monarch in western Europe had ever before held so much personal authority or commanded such a vast and effective military and administrative machine. Louis XIV's reign represents the culmination of the process of increasing monarchical authority that had been under way for centuries. Intelligent, cunning, and possessing a unique understanding of the requirements of his office, Louis XIV became the envy of his age.

Perhaps the most brilliant of Louis XIV's many policies was his treatment of the aristocracy. He simply dispensed with their services as influential advisers. He treated the aristocrats to elaborate rituals, feasts, processions, displays, and banquets, but amid all these celebrations their political power dwindled. The wiser members of the aristocracy stayed home and managed their estates; others made their way at court as minor functionaries and basked in the glory of the Sun King. A lengthy visit to Versailles—a necessity for any aristocrat who wanted his views and needs attended to—could bankrupt the less well-to-do.

Louis XIV's domestic policies centered on his incessant search for new revenues. His palace at Versailles cost a fortune. So too did his wars, which Louis XIV waged to excess. To raise capital, he used the services of Jean Baptiste Colbert, a brilliant administrator, who improved methods of tax collecting, promoted new industries, and encouraged international trade. Such ambitious national policies were possible because Louis XIV had inherited an efficient system of administration, introduced by Richelieu. Instead of relying on the local aristocracy to collect royal taxes and to administer royal policies, Richelieu had appointed the king's own men as *intendants,* or functionaries dispatched with wide powers into the provinces. At first, their mission had been temporary and their success minimal, but gradually they became a permanent feature of royal administration. During the reign of Louis XIV, the country was divided into thirty-two districts, controlled by intendants. Operating with a total bureaucracy of about a thousand officials and no longer bothering even to consult the parlements or the Estates, Louis XIV ruled absolutely.

Why did such a system of absolute authority work? Did the peasants not revolt? Why did the old aristocracy not rise in rebellion? For the aristocrats, the loss of political authority was not accompanied by a comparable loss in wealth and social position; indeed, quite the contrary was true. During the seventeenth century, the French nobility—2 percent of the population—controlled approximately 20 to 30 percent of the total national income. The church, too, fared well under Louis, receiving good tax arrangements, provided it preached about the king's divinely given rights. Although there were peasant upheavals throughout the century, the sheer size of the royal army and police—more than 300,000 by the end of Louis's

reign—made successful revolt nearly impossible. When in the early 1700s, a popular religious rebellion led by Protestant visionaries broke out in the south, royal troops crushed it. Thus, absolutism rested on the complicity of the old aristocracy, the self-aggrandizement of government officials, the church's doctrines, the revenues squeezed out of the peasantry, and the power of a huge military machine.

Yet Louis XIV's system was fatally flawed. Without any effective check on his power and on his dreams of international conquest, no limit was imposed on the state's capacity to make war or on the ensuing national debt. Louis XIV coveted the section of the Holy Roman Empire that led to the Rhine; he also sought to curb Dutch commercial prosperity and had designs on the Spanish Netherlands. By the 1680s, his domestic and foreign policies turned violently aggressive. In 1685, he revoked the Edict of Nantes, forcing many of the country's remaining Protestants to flee. In 1689, he embarked on a military campaign to gain territory from the Holy Roman Empire. And in 1701, he tried to bring Spain under the control of the Bourbon dynasty. Louis XIV, however, underestimated the strength of his northern rivals, England and the Netherlands. Their combined power, in alliance with the Holy Roman Empire and the Austrians, defeated Louis XIV's ambitions.

The War of the Spanish Succession was essentially a land war, fought on the battlefields of northern Europe. Out of it, the Austrians acquired the southern Netherlands (Belgium) and thus a buffer against the possibility of a French overrun of the Low Countries. Most dramatically, however, the war created a balance of power in Europe, with Britain emerging as a major force in European affairs, the counterweight against the French colossus. The relative peace of the eighteenth century has often been attributed to the creation of this real, but fragile, balance among the major European powers.

Louis XIV's participation in these long wars emptied the royal treasury. By the late seventeenth century, taxes had risen intolerably, and they were levied mostly on those least able to pay: the peasants. In the 1690s, the combination of taxes, bad harvests, and plague led to wide-

MAP 16.2 Europe, 1648 ▶

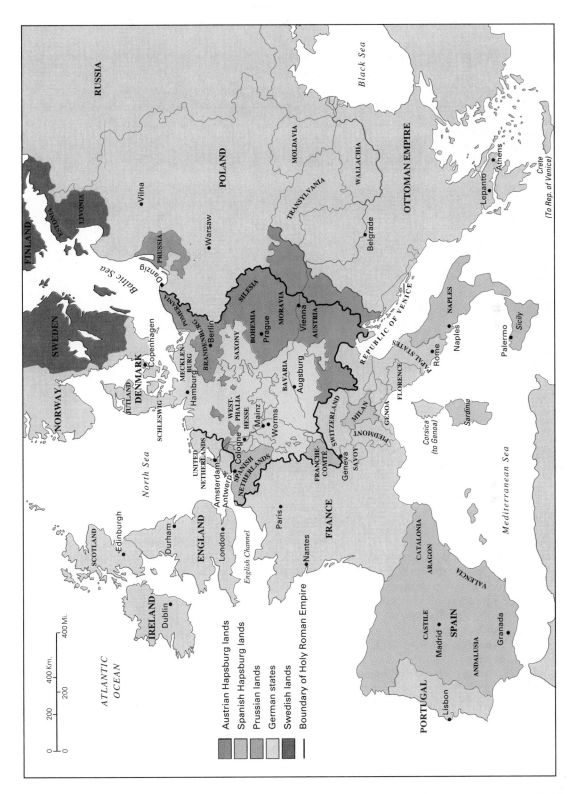

ATLANTIC
OCEAN

IRELAND
Dublin

SCOTLAND
Edinburgh

ENGLAND
Durham
London

English Channel

North Sea

UNITED
NETHERLANDS
Amsterdam
Antwerp
SPANISH
NETHERLANDS
Cologne
Mainz
WEST-
PHALIA
HESSE
Worms

FRANCE
Paris
Nantes

NORWAY

SWEDEN

DENMARK
Copenhagen
JUTLAND
SCHLESWIG
MECKLEN-
BURG
Hamburg

Baltic Sea

FINLAND

RUSSIA

ESTONIA
LIVONIA
Vilna

PRUSSIA
Danzig
POMERANIA
BRANDENBURG
Berlin
SAXONY
Warsaw

POLAND

SILESIA
BOHEMIA
Prague
MORAVIA
Vienna
AUSTRIA

MOLDAVIA

TRANSYLVANIA

WALLACHIA

Belgrade

OTTOMAN EMPIRE

Black Sea

BAVARIA
Augsburg

SWITZERLAND
Geneva
SAVOY
FRANCHE-
COMTÉ
PIEDMONT
MILAN

GENOA

REPUBLIC OF VENICE

PAPAL STATES
Rome
Florence
FLORENCE

NAPLES
Naples

Corsica
(to Genoa)

Sardinia

Palermo
Sicily

Mediterranean Sea

Lepanto
Athens

Crete
(To Rep. of Venice)

PORTUGAL
Lisbon

SPAIN
Madrid
CASTILE
CATALONIA
ARAGON
VALENCIA
ANDALUSIA
Granada

0   200   400 Mi.
0   200   400 Km.

Austrian Hapsburg lands
Spanish Hapsburg lands
Prussian lands
German states
Swedish lands
Boundary of Holy Roman Empire

KING LOUIS XIV AND MINISTER COLBERT VISIT THE GOBELINS FACTORY, GO-
BELINS TAPESTRY, C. 1699. The Gobelins tapestry factory was one of the first
examples of state-run enterprise in the West. Its fine fabrics became world
famous, but its success never led to other similar successes in state-sponsored
industries. Louis XIV's dream of an industrial France only became a reality in
the nineteenth century, after the French Revolution and the destrucrtion of royal
absolutism. (*Alinari/Art Resource, NY*)

spread poverty, misery, and starvation in large
areas of France. Thus, for the great majority of
French people, absolutism meant a decline in living standards and a significant increase in mortality rates. Absolutism also meant increased sur-
veillance of the population. Royal authorities
censored books, spied on heretics, Protestants,
and freethinkers, and even tortured and executed
opponents of state policy.

By 1715, France was a tightly governed society whose treasury was bankrupt. Protestants
had been driven into exile or forced to convert.
Strict censorship laws closely governed publishing, causing a brisk trade in clandestine books
and manuscripts. Direct taxes burdened the poor
and were legally evaded by the aristocracy. Critics of state policy within the church had been ef-

fectively silenced. And over the long run, foreign
wars had brought no significant gains.

In the France of Louis XIV, the dynastic state
had reached maturity and had begun to display
some of its classic characteristics: centralized bureaucracy; royal patronage to enforce allegiance;
a system of taxation universally but inequitably
applied; and suppression of political opposition,
either through the use of patronage or, if necessary, through force. Another important feature
was the state's cultivation of the arts and sciences
as a means of increasing national power and
prestige. Together, these policies enabled France
and its monarchs to achieve political stability, enforce a uniform system of law, and channel the
country's wealth and resources into the service of
the state as a whole.

Yet at his death in 1715, Louis XIV left his successors a system of bureaucracy and taxation that was vastly in need of overhaul. Because this system was still locked into the traditional social privileges of the church and nobility, reforming it was virtually impossible. Although the pattern of war, excessive taxation of the lower classes, and spending beyond revenues had damaged French finances, the bureaucracy of the absolutist state continued to function, extending its influence over every area of trade and manufacturing, transportation, and agriculture. To this day, perfectly preserved pieces of silk and cotton cloth made in the French provinces sit in the Parisian archives of the government. In the eighteenth century, they had been sent there for inspection. Only when the king's ministers had approved the samples could the cloth from which they had been cut be sold in the open market, with the king's seal. By the 1780s, manufacturers clamored for freer markets, fewer, or at least faster, inspections, and more freedom to experiment. They smuggled and cheated the inspectors while looking across the Channel at England with envy at the power, wealth, and freedom of its industry and its merchants. The discontent of French manufacturers contributed to the causes of the 1789 French Revolution.

THE GROWTH OF LIMITED MONARCHY AND CONSTITUTIONALISM IN ENGLAND

England achieved national unity earlier than any other major European state. Its fortunate geography freed it from the border disputes that plagued emerging states on the Continent. By an accident of fate, its administrative structure also developed in such a way as to encourage centralization. In 1066, William, duke of Normandy and vassal to the French king, had invaded and conquered England, acquiring at a stroke the entire kingdom. In contrast, the French kings took centuries to bring the territory of France under their domain.

As conquerors, the Norman kings pursued a policy of intermarriage and consultation. They consulted with their powerful subjects—archbishops, bishops, earls, and barons. By the middle of the thirteenth century, these consultations, or *parlays,* came to be called *parliaments.* Increasingly, the practice grew of inviting to these parliaments representatives from the counties—knights and burgesses. Gradually, these lesser-than-noble but often wealthy and prominent representatives came to regard Parliament as a means of self-expression for redressing their grievances. In turn, the later medieval kings saw Parliament as a means of exercising control and raising taxes. By 1297, the Lords (the upper house) and Commons (as the lower house was called) had obtained the king's agreement that no direct taxes could be levied without their consent. By the fourteenth century, Parliament had become a permanent institution of government. Its power was entirely subservient to the crown, but its right to question royal decisions had been established.

The English Parliament and Constitution

The medieval English Parliament possessed two characteristics that distinguished it from its many Continental counterparts, such as the various French Estates. The English Parliament was national, not provincial; more important, its representatives were elected across caste lines, with voting rights dependent on property, not on noble birth or status. These representatives voted as individuals, rather than collectively as clergy, nobles, or commoners, that is, as Estates (see pages 234–235). In the Middle Ages, Parliament and the monarchy were interdependent; they were seen not as rivals, but as complementary forms of centralized government. That very interdependence, however, would ultimately lead to conflict.

The constitution, too, emerged during the Middle Ages in England. It comprised unwritten and written precedents, laws, and royal acts that came to embody the basic principles of government. (In contrast to the French model, England developed into a *constitutional* monarchy.) This theoretical foundation—until then not written as a single constitution—grew out of legal practices and customs described under the generic title *common law*. Whereas feudal law, applied only to a local region, common law extended throughout the realm and served as a unifying force.

The Tudor Achievement

Emphasis on the medieval evolution of parliament and the constitution should not obscure the fact that England in the fifteenth century could be a lawless place, where local nobility ran their estates and made war on their neighbors largely unchecked by central government. One such war, the War of the Roses (1455–1485) pitted two noble families against each other in a struggle for domination. Out of it, the Tudors emerged triumphant, in the person of Henry VII (1485–1509), and he proceeded to spend much of his reign consolidating and extending his authority. In the process, he revitalized and remade the institutions of central government. Henry VII's goal was to check the unruly nobility. Toward this end, he brought commoners into the government. These commoners, unlike the great magnates, could be channeled into royal service because they craved what the king offered: financial rewards and elevated social status. Although they did not fully displace the aristocracy, commoners were brought into Henry VII's inner circle, into the Privy Council, into the courts, and eventually into all the highest offices of the government. The strength and efficiency of Tudor government were shown during the Reformation, when Henry VIII (1509–1547) made himself head of the English church. He was able to take this giant step toward increasing royal power because his father had restored order and stability.

The Protestant Reformation in England was a revolution in royal, as well as ecclesiastical, government. It attacked and defeated a main obstacle to monarchical authority: the power of the papacy. At the same time, the Reformation greatly enhanced the power of Parliament. Henry used Parliament to make the Reformation because he knew that he needed the support of the lords, the country gentry, and the merchants. No change in religious practice could be instituted by the monarchy alone. Parliament's participation in the Reformation gave it a greater role and sense of importance than it had ever possessed in the past. Nonetheless, the final outcome of this ad-

QUEEN ELIZABETH I (1558–1603) BY NICHOLAS HILLIARD. In this portrait, painted after England's victory in 1588 over the Spanish Armada, the queen's prestige is enhanced by the magnificent lace, pearls, and the rich jewels of her costume and crown. (*By kind permission of the Marquess of Tavistock, and the Trustees of the Bedford Estates*)

ministrative revolution enhanced monarchical power. By the end of his reign, Henry VIII easily possessed as much power as his French rival, Francis I. Indeed, until the early seventeenth century, the history of monarchical power in England, with its absolutist tendencies, was remarkably similar to the Continental pattern.

At Henry's death, the Tudor bureaucracy and centralized government were strained to the utmost, yet survived. The government weathered the reign of Henry's sickly son, Edward VI (1547–1553), and the extreme Protestantism of some of his advisers, and it survived the brief and deeply troubled reign of Henry's first daughter, Mary (1553–1558), who tried to return England to Catholicism. At Mary's death, England had come dangerously close to the religious instability and sectarian tension that undermined the French kings during the final decades of the sixteenth century.

Henry's second daughter, Elizabeth I, became queen in 1558 and reigned until her death in 1603. The Elizabethan period was characterized by a heightened sense of national identity. The English Reformation enhanced that sense, as did the increasing fear of foreign invasion by Spain. The fear was real enough and only lessened with the defeat of the Spanish Armada in 1588. For the English the victory was like that of David over Goliath, and its value was both symbolic and real. For the Spanish the defeat was also deeply affecting; only they asked how had they gone wrong. By contrast in the seventeenth century, the English would look back on Elizabeth's reign as a golden age. It was the calm before the storm, a time when a new commercial class was formed, which, in the seventeenth century, would demand a greater say in government operations.

The social and economic changes of the Elizabethan age can be seen, in microcosm, by looking at the Durham region in northern England. From 1580 to 1640, a new coal-mining industry developed there through the efforts of entrepreneurs—gentlemen with minor lands whose industry and skill enabled them to exploit their mineral resources. The wool trade also prospered in Durham. By 1600, social and political tensions had developed. The wool merchants and the entrepreneurial gentry were demanding a greater say in governing the region. They were opposed by the traditional leaders of Durham society: the bishops and the dozen or so aristocratic families with major lands and access to the court in London.

This split can be described as one between court and country. *Court* refers to the traditional aristocratic magnates, the hierarchy of the church, and royal officialdom. *Country* denotes a loose coalition of merchants and rising agricultural and industrial entrepreneurs from the prosperous gentry class, whose economic worth far exceeded their political power. The pattern found in Durham was repeated in other parts of England, generally where industry and commerce grew and prospered. The gentry gained social status and wealth. In the seventeenth century, these social and economic tensions would help foment revolution.

By the early seventeenth century in England, the descendants of the old feudal aristocracy differed markedly from their Continental counterparts. Their isolation from the great wars of the Reformation had produced an aristocracy less military and more commercial in orientation.

Furthermore, the lesser ranks of the landowning aristocracy, gentlemen without titles (the gentry), had prospered significantly in Tudor times. In commercial matters, they were often no shrewder than the great landed magnates, but they had in Parliament, as well as their counties, an effective and institutionalized means of expressing their political interests. The great nobles, on the other hand, had largely abandoned the sword as the primary expression of their political authority without putting anything comparable in its place. Gradually, political initiative was slipping away from the great lords into the hands of a gentry that was commercially and agriculturally innovative, as well as fiercely protective of its local base of political power.

Religion played a vital role in this realignment of political interests and forces. Many of the old aristocracy clung to the Anglicanism of the Henrican Reformation, with bishops and liturgy intact, and some even clung to Catholicism. The newly risen gentry found in the Protestant Reformation a form of religious worship more suited to their independent and entrepreneurial spirit. They felt that it was their right to appoint their own preachers and that the church should reflect local tastes and beliefs rather than a series of doctrines and ceremonies inherited from a discredited Catholicism. In late Tudor times, gentry and merchant interests fused with Puritanism—the English variety of Calvinism—to produce a political–religious vision with ominous potential.

The English Revolution, 1640–1660 and 1688–1689

The forces threatening established authority were dealt with ineffectively by the first two Stuart kings: James I (1603–1625) and Charles I (1625–1649). Like their Continental counterparts, both believed in royal absolutism. Essentially, these Stuart kings tried to do in England what later Louis XIV was to do in France: establish crown and court administrators as the sole governing bodies within the state. What the Stuarts lacked, however, was an adequate social and institutional base for absolutism, not least of all a standing army. They did not possess the vast independent wealth of the French kings.

Through the established church, the Stuarts

preached the doctrine of the divine right of kings. James I, an effective and shrewd administrator, conducted foreign policy without consulting Parliament. In a speech before Parliament, he stated that "it is sedition in subjects to dispute what a king may do in the height of his power . . . I will not be content that my power be disputed upon."[2]

James I made the standard moves toward creating an absolute monarchy: he centralized and consolidated the power of the government, and he tried to win over the aristocracy by giving them new offices and titles. This was an expensive policy, for which James I did not have a sufficient economic base. His successor, Charles I, took the same approach. After he suspended Parliament in 1629, Charles attempted to rule through his advisers. He had two major goals: to rid the nation of Puritans and to root out the "country" opposition. Charles also tried to collect taxes without the Parliament's consent. These policies ended in disaster; by 1640, the Puritans and the "country" opposition had grown closer together.

The English Revolution began in 1640 because Charles I needed money to defend the realm against a recent Scottish invasion. Being staunch Calvinists, the Scots had rebelled against Charles's religious policies. Moreover, their clan leaders saw rebellion as a way to get back at the Stuart kings, who long had been a thorn in their side, first when they had been in Edinburgh and now from their base in London. Charles had no alternative but to call Parliament, which could then dictate the terms: no concessions, then no taxes to fight the Scots, who were also demanding money for every day they occupied the northern territory. Parliament countered the king's requests with demands for rights: consultations with Parliament in matters of taxation, trial by jury, habeas corpus, and a truly Protestant church responsive to the beliefs and interests of its laity. Charles refused these demands, viewing them as an assault on royal authority. In 1642, civil war began. It was directed by Parliament, financed by taxes and the merchants, and fought by the New Model Army led by Oliver Cromwell (1599–1658), a Puritan squire who gradually realized his potential for leadership.

The English Revolution needs to be seen as a

crisis that lasted two generations: it began in 1640, turned into civil war in 1642, and culminated in regicide in 1649. After the restoration of monarchy in 1660, the crisis flared up again in 1679–81, and was finally resolved in 1688–89. It affected England, Scotland, Ireland, and Wales differently, but in all cases led to the consolidation of English power over these territories.

In the 1640s, the civil war generated a new type of military organization, one that looked toward the modern army. The New Model Army was financed by Parliament's rich supporters and led by gentlemen farmers. Its ranks were filled by religious zealots, along with the usual cross-section of poor artisans and day laborers. This citizen army defeated the king, his aristocratic followers, and the Anglican church's hierarchy.

In January 1649, Charles I was publicly executed by order of Parliament. During the interregnum (time between kings) of the next eleven years, one Parliament after another joined with the army to govern the country as a republic. In the distribution of power between the army and the Parliament, Cromwell proved to be a key element. He had the support of the army's officers and some of its rank and file, and he had been a member of Parliament for many years. However, he gained control over the army only after its rank and file was purged of radical groups. Some of these radicals wanted to level society, that is, to redistribute property by ending monopolies and to give the vote to all male citizens. In the context of the 1650s, Cromwell was a moderate republican who also believed in limited religious toleration for Protestants, yet history has painted him, somewhat unjustly, as a military dictator.

The English Revolution, understood as a constitutional crisis and civil war, was begun by urban merchants, as well as landed gentry, who were imbued with the strict Protestantism of the Continental Reformation. In the 1650s, however, the success of their revolution was jeopardized by growing discontent from the poor, who made up the rank and file of the army and who demanded that their economic and social grievances be rectified. Moreover, vast areas of the country were being administered inefficiently, and this increased popular discontent. The radicals of the English Revolution—men like Gerrard Winstanley, the first theoretician of social democracy in modern times, and John Lilburne, the Leveller—demanded redistribution of property, even communal property; voting rights for the majority of the male population; and abolition of religious and intellectual elites, whose power and ideology supported the interests of the ruling classes. The radicals rejected Anglicanism, moderate Puritanism, and even, in a few cases, the lifestyle of the middle class; they opted instead for radical politics and lifestyles. They spurned marriage, and the Quakers even allowed women to preach. The radicals terrified devoted Puritans like Cromwell. By 1660, two years after Cromwell's death, the country was adrift, without effective leadership.

Parliament, having secured the economic interests of its constituency (gentry, merchants, and some small landowners), chose to restore court and crown and invited the exiled son of the executed king to return to the kingship. Having learned the lesson his father had spurned, Charles II (1660–1685) never instituted royal absolutism, although he did try to minimize Parliament's role in the government. His court was a far more open institution than his father's had been, for Charles II feared a similar death.

But Charles's brother James II (1685–1688) was a foolishly fearless Catholic and admirer of French absolutism. Having gathered at his court a coterie of Catholic advisers (among them Jesuits) and supporters of royal prerogative, James attempted to bend Parliament and local government to the royal will. James's Catholicism was the crucial element in his failure. The Anglican church would not back him, and political forces similar to those that had gathered against his father, Charles I, in 1640 descended on him. The ruling elites, however, had learned their lesson back in the 1650s: civil war would produce social discontent among the masses. The upper classes wanted to avoid open warfare and preserve the monarchy as a constitutional authority, but not as an absolute one. Puritanism, with its sectarian fervor and its dangerous association with republicanism, was allowed to play no part in this second and last phase of the English Revolution.

In early 1688, Anglicans, some aristocrats, and opponents of royal prerogative (members of the Whig party along with a few Tories) formed a conspiracy against James II. Their purpose was to invite his son-in-law, William of Orange, stadholder (head) of the Netherlands and husband of James's Protestant daughter Mary, to invade England and rescue its government from James's control. It was hoped that the final outcome of this invasion would be determined by William and his conspirators, in conjunction with a freely elected Parliament. This dangerous plan succeeded for three main reasons: William and the Dutch desperately needed English support against the threat of a French invasion; James had lost the loyalty of key men in the army, powerful gentlemen in the counties, and the Anglican church; and the political elite was committed and united in its intentions. Defeated in Ireland, James II fled to France, and William and Mary were declared king and queen by act of Parliament.

This bloodless revolution—sometimes called the Glorious Revolution—created a new political and constitutional reality. Parliament gained the rights to assemble regularly and to vote on all matters of taxation; the rights of habeas corpus and trial by jury (for men of property and social status) were also secured. These rights were in turn legitimated in a constitutionally binding document, the Bill of Rights (1689). All Protestants, regardless of their sectarian bias, were granted toleration. The Revolution Settlement of 1688–89 resolved the profound constitutional and social tensions of the seventeenth century and laid the foundations of English government that lasted until now. The year 1688 created a new public and political order that would become the envy of enlightened reformers. The revolution, says historian J. H. Plumb, established "the authority of certain men of property, particularly those of high social standing, either aristocrats or linked with aristocracy, whose tap root was in land but whose side roots reached out to commerce, industry and finance."[3] Throughout the eighteenth century, England was ruled by kings and Parliaments that represented the interests of an oligarchy, whose cohesiveness and prosperity ensured social and political stability.

The English Revolution, in both its 1640–1660 and its 1688 phases established English parliamentary government and the rule of law; it also provided a degree of freedom for the propertied. In retrospect, we can see that absolutism

OLIVER CROMWELL SUPERVISES OVER AN END TO THE OLD ORDER, CARTOON, 1649. The Royal Oak symbolizing the authority held by Charles I was chopped down with his execution in 1649. Note that the Magna Carta and the Bible are seen as two of the literary stones that felled the monarchy. Not the least were the many ordinary choppers who, in the army and in countless battles, fought to bring Charles down. (*Courtesy of the Trustees of the British Museum*)

according to the French model probably never had a chance in England. There were simply too many gentlemen there who possessed enough land to be independent of the crown, and yet not so much that they could control whole sections of the kingdom. In addition, monarchs had no effective standing army. But to contemporaries, the issues seemed different: the English opponents of absolutism spoke of their rights as granted by their ancient constitution and the feudal law, of the need to make the English church truly Protestant, and, among the radicals, of the right of lesser men to establish their property. These opponents possessed an institution—Parliament—through which they could express their grievances. Eventually, they also acquired an army, which waged war to protect property and commercial rights. In 1689 the propertied classes invented limited monarchy and a constitutional

system based on laws made by Parliament and sanctioned by the king. Very gradually, the monarchical element in that system would yield to the power and authority of parliamentary ministers and state officials.

The Revolution of 1688–89 was England's last revolution. In the nineteenth and twentieth centuries, parliamentary institutions would be gradually and peacefully reformed to express a more democratic social reality. The events of 1688–89 have rightly been described as "the year one," for they fashioned a system of government that operated effectively in Britain and could also be adopted elsewhere with modification. The British system became a model for other forms of representative government, adopted in France and in the former British colonies, beginning with the United States. It was the model that offered a viable alternative to absolutism.

THE NETHERLANDS: A BOURGEOIS REPUBLIC

One other area in Europe developed a system of representative government that also survived for centuries. The Netherlands (or the Low Countries, that is, the seven Dutch provinces and Belgium), had been part of Hapsburg territory since the fifteenth century. When Charles V ascended the Spanish throne in 1516, the Netherlands became an economic linchpin of the Spanish empire. Spain exported wool and bullion to the Low Countries in return for manufactured textiles, hardware, grain, and naval stores. Flanders, with Antwerp as its capital, was the manufacturing and banking center of the Spanish empire.

The Spanish monarchy exploited its colonies in both the Old World and the New to finance wars against the Turks and the Italian city-states, and, by the 1540s, its crusade against Protestant Germany. Especially in the northern Low Countries, this tax burden joined with administrative inefficiency, unemployment, and religious repression to create the conditions that sparked the first successful bourgeois revolution in history.

During the reign of Charles V's successor, Philip II, a tightly organized Calvinist minority, with its popular base in the cities and its military strategy founded on sea raids, at first harassed and then aggressively challenged Spanish power. In the 1560s, the Spanish responded by trying to export the Inquisition into the Netherlands and by sending an enormous standing army there under the duke of Alva. It was a classic example of overkill; thousands of once-loyal Flemish and Dutch subjects turned against the Spanish crown. The people either converted secretly to Calvinism or aided the revolutionaries. Led by William the Silent (1533–1584), head of the Orange Dynasty, the seven northern provinces (Holland, Zeeland, Utrecht, Gelderland, Overijssel, Friesland, and Groningen) joined in the Union of Utrecht (1579) to protect themselves against Spanish aggression. Their determined resistance, coupled with the serious economic weaknesses of the overextended Spanish empire, eventually produced unexpected success for the northern colonies.

By 1609, the seven northern provinces were effectively free of Spanish control and loosely tied together under a republican form of government. Seventeenth-century Netherlands (that is, the Dutch Republic) became a prosperous bourgeois state. Rich from the fruits of manufacture and trade in everything from tulip bulbs to ships—and, not least, slaves—the Dutch merchants ruled their cities and provinces with a fierce pride. By the early seventeenth century, this new nation of only 1.5 million practiced the most innovative commercial and financial techniques in Europe.

In this fascinating instance, capitalism and Protestantism fused to do the work of princes; the Dutch state emerged without absolute monarchy, and indeed in opposition to it. From that experience, the ruling Dutch oligarchy retained a deep distrust of hereditary monarchy. The exact position of the House of Orange remained a vexing constitutional question until well into the eighteenth century. The oligarchs and their party, the Patriots, favored a republic without a single head, ruled by them through the Estates General. The Calvinist clergy, old aristocrats, and a vast section of the populace—all for very different reasons—wanted the head of the House of Orange to govern as stadholder of the provinces—in effect, as a limited monarch in a republican state. These unresolved political tensions prevented the Netherlands from developing a form of republican government that might have rivaled the stability of the British system of limited monarchy. The Dutch achievement came in other areas.

Calvinism had provided the ideology of revolution and national identity. Capital, in turn, created a unique cultural milieu in the Dutch urban centers of Amsterdam, Rotterdam, Utrecht, and The Hague. Wide toleration without a centralized system of censorship made the Dutch book trade, which often disseminated works by refugees from the Spanish Inquisition and later by French Protestants, the most vital in Europe right up to the French Revolution. And the sights and sounds of an active and prosperous population, coupled with a politically engaged and rich bourgeoisie, fed the imagination, as well as the purses, of various artistic schools. Rembrandt van Rijn, Jan Steen, Frans Hals, Jan Vermeer, and Jan van del Velde are at the top of a long list of great Dutch artists—many of them also refugees. They left timeless images portraying the people of the only republican national state to endure throughout the seventeenth century.

Collection Viollet

JOHN DE WITT

John de Witt (1625–1672) was one of the foremost European statesmen of the seventeenth century and grand pensionary of Holland. His international fame was all the more remarkable when we realize that he was one of the few representatives of a state who did not also speak on behalf of a monarch. The Dutch had won their independence from Spain, and they had embraced the republican form of government. As a committed republican, de Witt guided the United Provinces in wars against Cromwell's England during a time of extraordinary Dutch prosperity. De Witt and his wife

THE HOLY ROMAN EMPIRE: THE FAILURE TO UNIFY GERMANY

In contrast to the English, French, Spanish, and Dutch experiences in the early modern period, the Germans failed to achieve national unity. This failure led to frustration and eventually to antagonism toward the other powerful and unified European states. The German failure to unify is tied to the history of the Holy Roman Empire. That union of various distinct central European territories was created in the tenth century, when Otto I, in a deliberate attempt to revive Charlemagne's empire, was crowned emperor of the Romans. Later, the title was changed to Holy Roman emperor, with the kingdom consisting of mostly German-speaking principalities.

Most medieval emperors busied themselves not with administering their territories, but with attempting to gain control over the rich Italian peninsula and dealing with the challenges presented by powerful popes. In the meantime, the German nobility extended and consolidated their rule over their peasants and over various towns and cities. Their aristocratic power remained a constant obstacle to German unity. Only by incorporating the nobility into the fabric of the state's power, court, and army and by sanctioning their oppressive control of the peasants would German rulers manage to create a unified German state.

In the medieval and early modern periods, the Holy Roman emperors were dependent on their most powerful noble lords—including archbishops and bishops—because the office of emperor was an elective one and not the result of hereditary succession. German noble princes—some of whom were electors, such as the archbishops of Cologne and Mainz, the Hohenzollern elector of Brandenburg, and the duke of Saxony, were fiercely independent. All belonged to the empire, yet all regarded themselves as autonomous powers. These decentralizing tendencies were highly developed

were also avid devotees of reading and culture, and they belonged to a circle that discussed the latest ideas. This learned man also deeply distrusted the House of Orange, the closest institution to a monarchy that the Dutch possessed. There were, however, strong pressures in the Republic, often coming from the clergy and the common people who resented the wealthy regents, to restore the head of the House of Orange to the position of stadholder. In a riot that turned vicious, de Witt was murdered by a prostadholder mob that attacked him in The Hague. Today the spot of his murder is commemorated by a plaque.

by the thirteenth century, and the emperors gradually realized that the outer frontiers of their empire were slipping away. The French had conducted a successful military incursion into northern Italy and on the western frontier of the empire. Hungary had fallen to the Turks, and the Swiss were hard to govern (besides, given their terrain, they were impossible to beat into submission). At the same time, the Hapsburgs maneuvered themselves into a position from which they could monopolize the imperial elections.

The Holy Roman Empire in the reigns of the Hapsburg emperors Maximilian I (1493–1519) and Charles V (1519–1556) might have achieved a degree of cohesion comparable with that in France and Spain. Certainly, the impetus of war—against France and against the Turks—required the creation of a large standing army and the taxation to maintain it. Both additions could have worked to the benefit of a centralized, imperial power. But the Protestant Reformation, which began in 1517, meshed with the already well-developed tendencies toward local independence. As a result, it destroyed the last hope of Hapsburg domination and German unity. The German nobility were all too ready to use the Reformation as a vindication of their local power, and indeed Luther made just such an appeal to their interests.

At precisely the moment, in the 1520s, when Charles V had to act with great determination to stop the spread of Lutheranism, he was at war with France over its claims to Italian territory. Charles had no sooner won his Italian territories, in particular the rich city-state of Milan, when he had to make war against the Turks, who in 1529 besieged Vienna. Not until the 1540s was Charles V in a position to attack the Lutheran princes. By then, they had had considerable time to solidify their position and had united for mutual protection in the Schmalkaldic League.

War raged in Germany between the Protestant princes and the imperial army led by Charles V. In 1551, Catholic France entered the war on the Protestant side, and Charles V had to flee for his life. Defeated, Charles abdicated and retired to a Spanish monastery. The Treaty of Augsburg (1555) gave every German prince the right to determine the religion of his subjects. The princes had won their territories, and a unified German state was never constructed by the Hapsburgs.

When Emperor Charles V abdicated in 1556, he divided his kingdom between his son Philip and his brother Ferdinand. Philip inherited Spain and its colonies, as well as the Netherlands, and Ferdinand acquired the Austrian territories. Two branches of the Hapsburg family were thus created, and well into the late seventeenth century, they defined their interests in common and often waged war accordingly. The enormous international power of the Hapsburgs was checked only by their uncertain authority over the Holy Roman Empire. Throughout the sixteenth century, the Austrian Hapsburgs barely managed to control these sprawling and deeply divided German territories. Protestantism, as protected by the Treaty of Augsburg, and the particularism and provinciality of the German nobility continued to prevent the creation of a German state.

The Austrian Hapsburg emperors, however, never missed an opportunity to further the cause of the Counter Reformation and to court the favor of local interests opposed to the nobility. No Hapsburg was ever more fervid in that regard than the Jesuit-trained Archduke Ferdinand II, who ascended the throne in Vienna in 1619. He immediately embarked on a policy of Catholic revival and used Spanish officials as his administrators. His policies provoked a war within the empire that engulfed the whole of Europe.

The Thirty Years' War (1618–1648) began when the Bohemians, whose anti-Catholic tendencies can be traced back to the Hussite reformation, attempted to put a Protestant king on their throne. The Austrian and Spanish Hapsburgs reacted by sending an army into the kingdom of Bohemia, and suddenly the whole empire was forced to take sides along religious lines. The Bohemian nobility, after centuries of enforcing serfdom, failed to rally the rural masses behind them, and victory went to the emperor. Bohemia and Germany suffered an almost unimaginable devastation; the ravaging Hapsburg army sacked and burned three-fourths of each kingdom's towns and practically exterminated its aristocracy.

Until the 1630s, its looked as if the Hapsburgs would be able to use the war to enhance their power and promote centralization. But the intervention of Lutheran Sweden, led by Gustavus Adolphus and encouraged by France, wrecked Hapsburg ambitions. The ensuing military conflict devastated vast areas of northern and central Europe. The civilian population suffered untold hardships: soldiers raped women and pillaged the land, and thousands of refugees took to the roads and forests. Partly because the French finally intervened directly, the Spanish Hapsburgs emerged from the Thirty Years' War with no benefits. At the Treaty of Westphalia (1648), their Austrian cousins reaffirmed their right to govern the eastern states of the kingdom, with Vienna as their capital. Austria took shape as a dynastic state, while the German territories in the empire remained fragmented by the independent interests of their largely recalcitrant feudal nobility. In consequence, the war shaped the course of German history into the nineteenth century.

THE EMERGENCE OF AUSTRIA AND PRUSSIA

Austria

As a result of the settlement at Westphalia, the Austrian Hapsburgs gained firm control over most of Hungary and Bohemia, where they in-

stalled a virtually new and foreign nobility. At the same time, they strengthened their grip on Vienna. In one of the few spectacular successes achieved by the Counter Reformation, the ruling elites in all three territories were forcibly, or in many cases willingly, converted back to Catholicism. At long last, religious predominance could be used as a force—long delayed in eastern Europe because of the Protestant Reformation—for the creation of the Austrian dynastic state.

One severe obstacle to territorial hegemony remained: the military threat posed by the Turks, who sought to control much of Hungary. During the reign of Austrian Emperor Leopold I (1658–1705), warfare against the Ottoman Empire—a recurrent theme in Hapsburg history beginning with Charles V—once again erupted, and in 1683 the Turks again besieged Vienna. However, the Ottoman Empire no longer possessed its former strength and cohesiveness. A Catholic and unified Austrian army, composed of a variety of peoples from that kingdom and assisted by the Poles, managed to defeat the Turks and recapture the whole of Hungary and Transylvania and part of Croatia. Austria's right to govern these lands was firmly accepted by the Turks at the Treaty of Karlowitz (1699).

The Austrian Hapsburgs and their victorious army had now entered the larger arena of European power politics. In 1700, at the death of the last Spanish Hapsburg, Leopold I sought to place his second son, Archduke Charles, on the Spanish throne. But this brought Leopold into a violent clash with Louis XIV. Once again, Bourbon and Hapsburg rivalry, a dominant theme in early modern history, provoked a major European war.

In the War of the Spanish Succession, the Austrians, with their army led by the brilliant Prince Eugene of Savoy, joined forces with the English and the Dutch. This war brought rewards in western Europe to the Austrian Hapsburgs, who acquired the Spanish Netherlands (Belgium today), as well as Milan and small holdings in Italy. But the Hapsburgs did not succeed in capturing the Spanish throne.

Up to the early eighteenth century, the Austrian Hapsburgs had struggled to achieve territorial hegemony and to subdue the dissident religious groups (Protestant and Turkish Muslim), which in very different ways threatened to under-

FREDERICK THE GREAT RETURNING TO SANS-SOUCI AFTER MANEUVERS IN POTSDAM. Frederick II won Prussia military fame in Europe by leading his army in successful battles during the War of Austrian Succession and the Seven Years' War. These victories were due in part to Frederick's program of rigid training for his troops. (*Giraudon/Art Resource, NY*)

mine their authority. Warfare and the maintenance of a standing army had taken precedence over administrative reform and commercial growth. Yet military victory created the conditions within which centralization could occur.

The Austrian achievement of the eighteenth century, which made Austria a major force in European affairs, derived in large measure from the administrative reforms and cultural revival initiated by Charles VI (assisted militarily by Eugene of Savoy) and continued by his successors, Maria Theresa and Joseph II. These eighteenth-century monarchs embraced a style of government sometimes described as *enlightened* (see page 450–452). Through education and liberal policies, they sought to catch up with the more established and older dynastic states of Europe.

Prussia

By the seventeenth century in northern Europe, the cohesive state governed by an absolute monarch (or by oligarchs as in the Netherlands) had replaced feudalism as a system of government. Serfdom had largely disappeared in western Europe by the late sixteenth century, although it remained in parts of central and eastern Europe. No longer free to play at war or to control the lives of their peasants, progressive aristocrats improved their agricultural systems or sought offices and military commands in the service of the absolutist state. Thus, on the whole, western European aristocrats did not fare too badly under absolutism, but in the course of the early modern period, the state decisively checked their independent power.

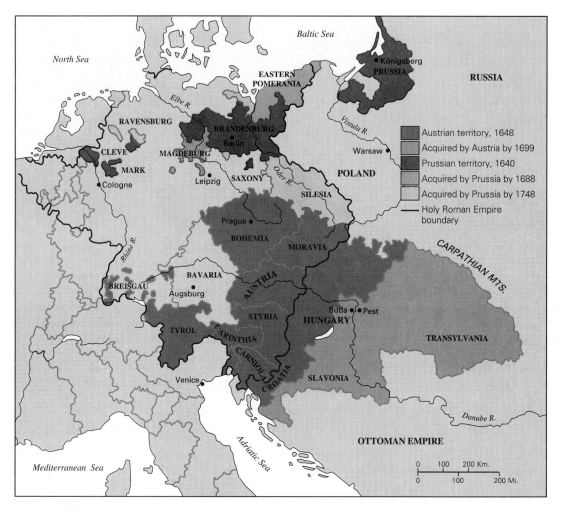

MAP 16.3 The Growth of Austria and Brandenburg-Prussia, c. 1650–1750

Prussia was different. Prussia was a state, within the Holy Roman Empire, that had emerged very late in northern Europe (in the late seventeenth century). Like Austria, Prussia displayed certain unique characteristics. Although it did develop an absolute monarchy like France, its powerful aristocracy acquiesced to monarchical power only in exchange for guarantees of their feudal power over the peasantry. In 1653, the Prussian nobility granted the elector power to collect taxes for the maintenance of a powerful army, but only after he issued decrees rendering serfdom permanent.

The ruling dynasty of Prussia, the Hohenzollerns, had a most inauspicious beginning in the later Middle Ages. These rulers were little more than dukes in the Holy Roman Empire until 1415, when Emperor Sigismund made one of them an imperial elector with the right to choose imperial successors. For centuries, the Hohenzollerns had made weak claims to territory in northern Germany. They finally achieved control over Prussia and certain other smaller principalities by claiming the inheritance of one wife (1608) and by single-minded, ruthless aggression.

The most aggressive of these Hohenzollerns was the elector Frederick William (1640–1688), who played a key role in forging the new Prussian state. Frederick William had inherited the territories of the beleaguered Hohenzollern dynasty, whose main holding, Brandenburg in Prussia, was very poor in natural resources. Indeed, Prussia had barely survived the devastation wrought by the Thirty Years' War, especially the Swedish army's occupation of the electorate.

A distaste for foreign intervention in Prussia, and for the accompanying humiliation and excessive taxes, prompted the Junker class (the landed Prussian nobility) to support national unity and strong central government. But they would brook no threat to their economic control of their lands and peasants. By 1672, the Prussian army, led by Junker officers, was strong enough to enter the Franco-Dutch war on the Dutch side. The war brought no territorial gains, but it allowed the elector to raise taxes. Once again, the pattern of foreign war, taxes, and military conscription led to an increase in the power of the central government. But in Prussia, in contrast to western lands, the bureaucracy was entirely military. No clerics or rich bourgeois shared power with this Junker class. The pattern initiated by the Great Elector (Frederick William) would be continued in the reigns of his successors: Frederick I (d. 1713), Frederick William I, and Frederick the Great.

The alliance between the aristocracy and the monarchy was especially strengthened in the reign of Frederick William I (1713–1740). In the older dynastic states, absolute monarchs in every case tried to dispense with representative institutions once the monarchy's power could stand on its own. So, too, did Frederick William finally undercut the Prussian provincial assemblies, the *Landtage,* which still had some power over taxation and army recruitment. Gradually, he rendered the Landtage superfluous. But he was able to do so only by incorporating the landowning Junker class into the machinery of government—especially into the army—and by keeping the tax-paying peasants in the status of serfs.

Since representative institutions in twentieth-century Germany have struggled, often unsuccessfully, for survival, it is interesting to note that in early eighteenth century Prussia such institutions did exercise considerable influence. Like the Austrian monarchy the Prussians embarked on a program of reforms, consolidation, and improvements, sometimes described as enlightened.

RUSSIA

Although remote from developments in western Europe, Russia in the early modern period took on some characteristics remarkably similar to those of western European states. It relied on absolute monarchy reinforced by a feudal aristocracy. As in Europe, the power of the aristocracy to wreak havoc had to be checked and its energies channeled into the state's service. But the Russian pattern of absolutism broke with the Western model and resembled that adopted in Prussia, where serfdom increased as the power of centralized monarchy grew. The award of peasants was the bribe by which the monarchy secured the aristocrat's cooperation in the state's growth.

Russian absolutism experienced a false start under Ivan IV, the Terrible (1547–1584). Late in the sixteenth century, Ivan sought to impose a tsarist autocracy. He waged a futile war against Sweden and created an internal police force that was entrusted with the administration of central Russia. His failure in war and an irrational policy of repression (fueled in part by his mental instability) doomed his premature attempt to impose absolutism. Much of Ivan's state building was undone with his death, which launched the Time of Troubles: a period of foreign invasion and civil warfare that endured for years.

Order was restored in the country only in 1613, when the Romanov dynasty gained the support of the aristocracy. The accession of Michael Romanov as tsar marks the emergence of a unified Russian state. Of that dynasty, by far the most important ruler was Peter the Great (1682–1725). He ruthlessly suppressed the independent aristocrats, while inventing new titles and ranks for those loyal to the court. The army was reformed in accordance with the standards of western lands. The peasants were made the personal property of their lords. From 1700 to 1707, taxes on the peasants multiplied five times over. Predictably, the money went toward the creation of a professional army along European lines and toward making war. The preparation led this time to victory over the Swedes. Finally, Peter brought the Russian Orthodox church under the control of the state by establishing a new office, called the Holy Synod; its head was a government official.

Peter managed to wed the aristocracy to the absolutist state, and the union was so successful that strong Russian monarchs in the eighteenth century, like Catherine the Great, could embrace enlightened reforms without jeopardizing the stability of their regimes. Once again, repression and violence in the form of taxation, serfdom, and war led to the creation of a dynastic state—one that proved least susceptible to reform and was eventually dismantled in 1917 by the Russian Revolution.

THE STATE AND MODERN POLITICAL DEVELOPMENT

By the early seventeenth century, Europeans had developed the concept of a *state:* a distinctive political entity to which its subjects owed duties and obligations. That concept became the foundation of the modern science of politics. The one essential ingredient of the Western concept of the state, as it emerged in the early modern period, was the notion of *sovereignty:* the view that within its borders the state was supreme, and other institutions and organizations—by implication even the church—were allowed to exist only if they recognized the state's authority. The art of government thus entailed molding the ambitions and strength of the powerful into service to the state. The state, its power growing through war and taxation, became the basic unit of political authority in the West.

Interestingly, the concept of human liberty, now so basic to Western thought, was not articulated first in the sovereign states of Europe. Rather, the idea was largely an Italian creation, discussed with great vehemence by the Italian theorists of the later Middle Ages and the Renaissance. These humanists lived and wrote in the independent city-states, and they often aimed their treatises against the encroachments of the Holy Roman emperor—in short, against princes and their search for absolute power. In the sixteenth and seventeenth centuries, the idea of liberty was rarely discussed and was generally found only in the writings of Calvinist opponents of absolutism. Not until the mid-seventeenth century in England did a body of political thought emerge that argued that human liberty can be ensured within the confines of a powerful national state: one governed by mere mortals and not by divinely sanctioned and absolute kings. In general,

despite the English and Dutch developments, absolutism in its varied forms (Spanish, French, Prussian) dominated the political development of early modern Europe.

Although first articulated in the Italian republics and then enacted briefly in England and more durably in the Netherlands, the republican ideal did not gain acceptance as a viable alternative to absolutism until the European Enlightenment of the eighteenth century. At the heart of that ideal lay the notion that the power of the state serves the interests of those who support and create it. In the democratic and republican revolutions of the late eighteenth century, western Europeans and Americans repudiated monarchical systems of government in response to the republican ideal. By then, princes and the aristocratic and military elites had outlived their usefulness in many parts of Europe. The states they had created, mostly to further their own interests, had become larger than their creators. Eventually, the national states of western Europe, as well as of the Americas, proved able to survive and prosper without kings or aristocrats, though they retained the administrative and military mechanisms so skillfully and relentlessly developed by early modern kings and their court officials.

By the eighteenth century, the power of the state had become the focal point of Western political life. Peace depended on the art of balancing the powers of the various European states so that no single state could expect to win domination, or *hegemony,* over all the others. Whenever a European state believed that it could dominate, war resulted. In early modern times, first the Spanish under Charles V and Philip II and then the French under Louis XIV sought, and for a brief time achieved, hegemony over European politics. Ultimately, however, these great states faltered because of the internal pressures that war making created. Nonetheless, the belief persisted, until 1945, that one state could dominate Western affairs. In the twentieth century, that belief produced not simply war but world war. By then, the power of Western states had overtaken vast areas of the world, and the ability to impose a balance of power became a matter of world survival.

MAP 16.4 The Expansion of Russia, 1300–1725 ▶

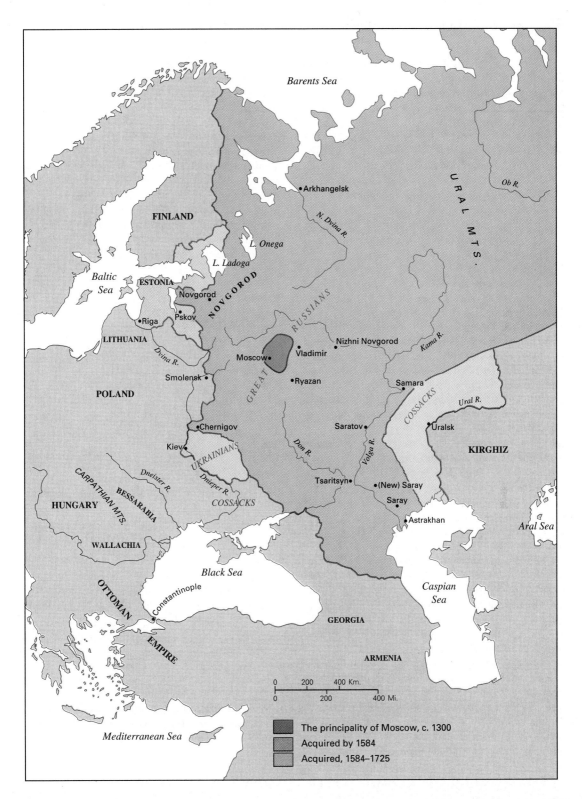

Barents Sea

U R A L   M T S .

Ob R.

• Arkhangelsk

N. Dvina R.

FINLAND

L. Onega

L. Ladoga

Baltic
Sea

ESTONIA

• Novgorod

N O V G O R O D

R U S S I A N S

• Riga

• Pskov

LITHUANIA

Dvina R.

Nizhni Novgorod •

Kama R.

Moscow •   Vladimir •

• Smolensk

G R E A T

• Ryazan

• Samara

C O S S A C K S

Ural R.

POLAND

Saratov •

• Uralsk

• Chernigov

Don R.

Volga R.

KIRGHIZ

Kiev •

U K R A I N I A N S

Dnieper R.

Tsaritsyn •

• (New) Saray

CARPATHIAN MTS.

Dneister R.

BESSARABIA

COSSACKS

• Saray

HUNGARY

• Astrakhan

Aral Sea

WALLACHIA

Black Sea

Caspian
Sea

O T T O M A N

Constantinople •

GEORGIA

E M P I R E

ARMENIA

| | 0 | 200 | 400 Km. |
| 0 | 200 | 400 Mi. |

Mediterranean Sea

The principality of Moscow, c. 1300

Acquired by 1584

Acquired, 1584–1725

◆ ◆ ◆

NOTES

1. William Doyle, *The Ancien Regime* (Atlantic Highlands, N.J.: Humanities Press, 1988), p. 19.

2. Quoted from *True Law of Free Monarchies,* excerpted in Marvin Perry et al., *Sources of the Western Tradition* (Boston: Houghton Mifflin, 1991), p. 23.

3. J. H. Plumb, *The Growth of Political Stability in England: 1675–1725* (London: Macmillan, 1967), p. 69.

SUGGESTED READING

Anderson, Perry, *Lineages of the Absolutist State* (1974). An excellent survey, sociological and Marxist in orientation.

Braudel, F., *The Mediterranean and the Mediterranean World in the Age of Philip II* (1973). One of the most important and beautifully written books ever done on early modern social and political development.

Brenner, Robert, *Merchants and Revolution. Commercial Change, Political Conflict, and London's Overseas Traders, 1550–1653* (1993). Lays to rest the notion that the English civil wars were just a contest between a stubborn king and his subjects who were religious fanatics.

Burke, Peter, *The Fabrication of Louis XIV* (1992). A good antidote for those who think that Madison Avenue invented advertising and image building.

Doyle, William, *The Ancien Régime* (1988). An excellent, short survey, which also reviews how historians have understood absolutism.

Elliott, J. H., *Imperial Spain, 1469–1716* (1963). Now a classic and the best account available of early modern Spain.

Jacob, Margaret C., and W. W. Mijnhardt, eds., *The Dutch Republic in the Eighteenth Century. Decline, Enlightenment, and Revolution* (1992). Essays survey Dutch history but also look at the republic in decline. A timely book for those worried about the decline of republics.

Kennedy, Paul, *The Rise and Fall of the Great Powers: Economic Change and Military Conflict 1550 to 2000* (1987). A courageous book that seeks to assess early modern militarism in relation to our own more recent American history.

Koenigsberger, H. G., *Early Modern Europe, 1500–1789* (1987). An excellent survey by a master historian.

Smith, Lacey Baldwin, *This Realm of England, 1399–1688,* rev. ed. (1983). A good, readable survey.

Sonnino, Paul, ed., *The Reign of Louis XIV* (1990). A brief, clear introduction.

REVIEW QUESTIONS

1. What role did elites play in the formation of the European states?

2. In what ways did early modern kings increase their power, and what relationship did they have to the commercial bourgeoisie in their countries?

3. What is meant by *raison d'état* and by the divine right of kings?

4. What role did religion and national churches play in creating the state?

5. Discuss the strengths and weaknesses of the Spanish state.

6. Why did England move in the direction of parliamentary government, while most countries on the Continent embraced absolutism? Indicate the main factors.

7. What made the Dutch state so different from its neighbors? Describe the differences. Are we justified in calling it "bourgeois"?

8. What made the Prussian, Russian, and Austrian experiences of statehood roughly comparable?

9. Discuss the differences between the treatment of the peasants in eastern and western Europe.

10. Government has sometimes been described as being, in the final analysis, organized violence. Is that an appropriate description of early modern European governments?

Art of the Seventeenth and Eighteenth Centuries

1. Caravaggio. *The Entombment.* Pinacoteca di Brera, Milan, Italy (Scala/Art Resource)

The influence of political, economic, and social change is seen in the visual arts of the seventeenth and eighteenth centuries. Perhaps most significant to the artists who made their living by providing paintings with religious themes for churches as well as for private patrons were the religious conflicts that were causing schisms throughout European society. All of a sudden, artistic interpretation of biblical themes was itself open to interpretation and scrutiny. Conflicts between Catholics and Protestants over doctrine and dogma were felt by artists who had to decide how best to please patrons who may have had newly developed or changed religious sympathies.

These two centuries also saw a great increase and redistribution of wealth in Europe, as explorers from that small continent began to explore new worlds and reap the benefit of increased trade. Politically, the seventeenth and eighteenth centuries are marked by a new sovereignty, when many of the countries we know from the modern map of Europe began to assert themselves as major powers.

2. Giovanne Benedetto Castiglione. *Melancholia*. Mid-Seventeenth Century. (Philadelphia Museum of Art. Pennsylvania Academy Fine Arts Collection)

While there are a number of terms used to describe these centuries politically, economically, and socially, they are given the collective term *baroque* in art historical parlance. Baroque literally means irregularly shaped, whimsical, grotesque, or odd. The origin of the word is French, but the origin of the Baroque style of art is agreed to be Rome.

As the art historian H. W. Janson explains, it is difficult to explain Baroque art within the context of the social and political changes that were sweeping Europe. While some historians see Baroque art as illustrative of the Counter Reformation, Janson points out that the style was equally appealing to Catholics and Protestants. Nor is Baroque art the art only of the absolute rulers of France or other newly established monarchies, for it was also a style of the bourgeois.

Unlike the art of the Renaissance, Baroque art is not intertwined with the philosophy or science of the seventeenth and eighteenth centuries. The artist stood apart from the mathematician and the poet, creating a style that was uniquely visual, lavish, and rich.

One of the most famous painters of the Italian Baroque was Caravaggio (1571–1610). Named for the city that was his birthplace, Caravaggio was, in fact, not a particularly successful artist in his own country. Although his canvases influenced a host of artists from other countries, most notably Rembrandt, his work, which portrayed biblical scenes with striking realism, was too vivid and not sufficiently reverent for his own countrymen.

Caravaggio's use of light and shadow is illustrated in *The Entombment* (1604) (Figure 1). The background of this work is almost flat and black; as we move into the foreground, the amount of focused light increases. The figure of Christ is almost completely illuminated. Compare the light beamed on him to the shadowy figure who supports his upper body to understand the extent to which Caravaggio manipulates light and its source.

Also noteworthy in this canvas is the depiction of the figures, who are clothed and coifed in a more contemporary than biblical style. This juxtaposition of scenes from the Bible with the flavor of everyday life in the seventeenth century may reveal more about the connection between the artist and his own surroundings. Caravaggio superimposed the contemporary on a scene from the Bible because religion had become more intertwined with worldly events.

The Baroque style of highly finished, realistic works is very familiar to us. But we must also recall that Baroque artists were skilled draftsmen. As an example, there is Giovanne Benedetto Castiglione's *Melancholia* (mid seventeenth century) (Figure 2), a brush drawing in oil with added red chalk. Works on paper do not always survive as well as those on board or canvas; they are more ephemeral and fragile. The drawings we do have attest to the artistic skill of seventeenth century artists, who use line and shadow as well as their Renaissance predecessors.

Melancholia is an almost abstract drawing, which may well address the conflicts that must have abounded during these centuries of great change. What is depicted is an allegory that illustrates the human dilemma between the worlds of art, religion, science, and learning. Symbols from each of these worlds—scientific tools, musical instruments, a globe, and the like—surround the figure of Genius, who sits in a contemplative fashion.

While the artists of the Baroque period were not usually the well-rounded humanists one associates with the Renaissance, nonetheless, it was not unusual for some of them to be able to work in two, as well as three dimensional art forms. Some, like Gian Lorenzo Bernini (1598–1680) distinguished themselves as sculptors as well as architects.

3. Gian Lorenzo Bernini. *The Ecstasy of Saint Teresa.* S. Maria della Vittoria, Rome (Scala/Art Resource)

Bernini was responsible for the sculptural program of St. Peter's Basilica in the Vatican. He also completed sculptures in other Roman churches, including the Cornaro Chapel in the church of Santa Maria della Vittoria. His *The Ecstasy of Saint Theresa* (1644–1647) (Figure 3) is a remarkable work not only in itself but also in its setting. The heart of Saint Teresa of Avila was said to have been pierced by an angel's golden arrow; the pain was exquisite, for not only was it the pain of death but also the pleasure of everlasting life in the arms of God. Bernini managed to capture the exact moment of Saint Teresa's ecstasy in a skillfully theatrical setting, using not only sculpture but the architectural elements of the chapel as well.

The saint and the angel are carved of white marble and seem to be floating on a cloud.

4. Nicolas Poussin. *The Rape of the Sabine Women* (Metropolitan Museum of Art, NY)

Golden rays that descend from a point above the figures and out of the view of spectators are bathed in light, courtesy of a window hidden behind the frame that surrounds the two figures. Bernini decorated the entire chapel to follow the theme of Saint Teresa; ceiling frescoes show clouds of angels celebrating the event.

While Bernini was gaining fame in Italy, a French painter—one who spent almost all of his career in Rome—was winning an international reputation. Nicolas Poussin (1593/4–1665) relied strongly on the art of the Classical, and especially the Hellenistic periods for his inspiration. His *The Rape of the Sabine Women* (c. 1636–37) (Figure 4), a lavish and richly painted canvas, captures the action like a carefully posed photograph. If Bernini was theatri-

cal in his portrayal of Saint Teresa, one could say that Poussin is cinematographic, with a canvas that could double as a movie still from a Cecil B. De Mille epic.

The story depicted in *The Rape of the Sabine Women* is derived from Classical mythology; the poses of the figures hearken back to the Hellenistic. Compare the positioning of the arms of the women on the left of the canvas to the tortured stance of the Laocoon. A close look at other groups in the Poussin canvas are also reminiscent of that sculpture. As another bow to the ancient past, Poussin paints buildings in the background that are faithful to Roman prototypes. His reliance on archaeology and mythology in this work are typical of much of his output. An artist with strong theoretical views, Poussin stressed form and composition over color and light. Many followed his theories, but he remained their master.

While paintings that depicted vast mythological, historical, or religious themes dominated the majority of the major art markets during the Baroque era, patrons in Holland sought paintings that related more to their own experience. For that reason, the genre of the still life—paintings of flowers, fruit, dishes, food, and other familiar objects—reached its zenith in that country.

Jan Davidsz de Heem, one of the most skilled of the Dutch still-life masters, was able to take a collection of objects and turn it into an object of art. His *Still Life* (Figure 5) showcases his meticulous, almost photo-realistic style. While some still lives are considered by modern art historians to be nothing more than ornamental displays of technical skill, there was a reason for them. The popularity of still lives, and of landscapes, probably has to do with the human desire for reassurance that "things are as they should be," that the status quo is being maintained, regardless of the religious or political turmoil that may inform other aspects of life. No matter what was going on politically, no matter what religious dispute was being negotiated, people could find a degree of comfort when surrounded by familiar objects or scenes.

While Heem distinguished himself as a still life painter, another Dutch master, Rembrandt van Rijn (1606–1669) gained fame for his historical and religious canvases. Rembrandt was influenced in his early years by Caravaggio, especially by the Italian's use of light. Unlike Caravaggio, however, he sought subject matter in the Old, rather than the New Testament. But that was not his only strength. His reputation as a portrait painter gained him fame and fortune in Amsterdam. He was also popular as a painter of many other subjects, including scenes from the Classical past.

Rembrandt's *Aristotle with a Bust of Homer* (1653) (Figure 6) shows some of the artist's hallmarks. The deep background of the work is almost black and without texture or light, just

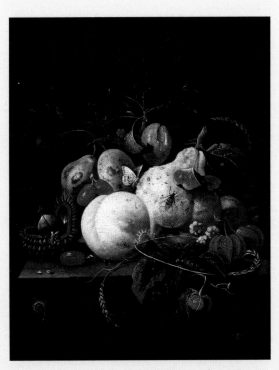

5. Jan Davidsz de Heem. *Still Life*. (Cameraphoto/Art Resource, NY)

as in Caravaggio's *The Entombment*. As one looks more to the foreground, figures and objects appear with more and more clarity and definition. The light moves from shadowy hues to a rich golden tone that bathes the face of the philosopher and the sculptured bust of the poet. With this manipulation of light and shadow, Rembrandt pays homage to Caravaggio.

Also like Caravaggio, Rembrandt clothes his Classical figure in contemporary dress. The Aristotle of Rembrandt's canvas is a Baroque being, not an ancient Greek. While contemporaries like Poussin revert to Classical prototypes, Rembrandt chooses instead to superimpose something of his era on the past.

The later part of the eighteenth century and the first decades of the nineteenth century mark the Rococo and Neoclassical periods in art history. Especially popular in France, the Rococo and Neoclassical movements owe much to political and social forces that governed other

6. Rembrandt. *Aristotle with a Bust of Homer.* 1653. (Metropolitan Museum of Art, NY)

aspects of life as well. The term "Rococo" describes a style that is frothy and frivolous, lacking in substance and importance. In 1698, King Louis XIV ordered the redecoration of his palace at Versailles with works that were light-hearted and youthful, instead of stodgy and serious. His dabbling with artistic matters led to quarrels and aesthetic disagreements in the artistic community. It also gave license for a new artistic style to take root.

A typical example of the Rococo may be seen in the work of François Boucher's (1703–70) *The Toilet of Venus* (1751) (Figure 7). Although some art historians describe his work as slick, artificial and frequently erotic—or precisely because of that description—Boucher became the darling of the French court. In his *The Toilet of Venus,* the goddess is full figured and lush, surrounded by all the sensual accouterments expected for a goddess of love and erotic pleasure. Boucher understood his audience well. His Venus would have been comfortable in a period dress, supervising the decor of her boudoir at the Palace of Versailles. The

7. Francois Boucher. *The Toilet of Venus.* (Metropolitan Museum of Art, NY)

overwhelming sensuality of the painting matched the sentiments of its limited audience.

While Boucher exemplified the light and airy sentiment of the Rococo, Jacques Louis David (1748–1825) typified the Neo-Classical. The Neo-Classical style represents a return to reason, a return to the rationality of the Classical past.

Justice, honor for one's country, and the need to portray inspirational themes were the philosophies that guided the Neo-Classical artists. Their training ground was in Italy, primarily because it was the source of Classical prototypes from which the artists could learn. David learned his lessons well. His *The Death of Socrates* (1787) (Figure 8) captures the essence of that event in a manner that combines the best of Poussin and Caravaggio.

The subject matter is important because it illuminates the Neo-Classical concept of virtue,

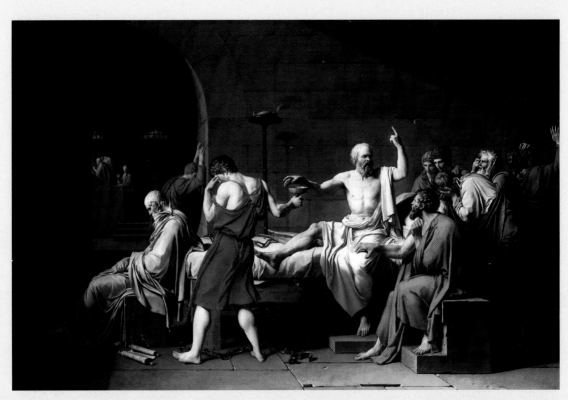

8. Jacques Louis David. *The Death of Socrates.* 1787. (Metropolitan Museum of Art, NY)

represented by Socrates' suicide. It also alludes to the philosopher's role as a person of reason. The style borrows from Poussin's ability to capture a scene with photographic stillness, rendering the figures in an almost sculptural way. But David has also appropriated the lighting techniques of Caravaggio and Rembrandt, skillfully juxtaposing light and shadow. While the Neo-Classicists paid homage to their distant past in subject matter, they also showed their reverence for the heritage of their less-remote ancestors.

CHAPTER 17

The Scientific Revolution:
The Mechanical Universe

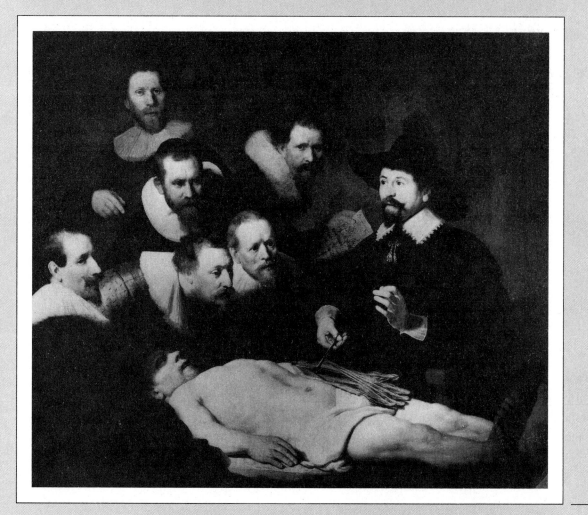

eginning in the fifteenth century, the cohesive medieval view of the world began to disintegrate. By the late seventeenth century, educated Europeans no longer believed in it. Thus, the collapse of medieval institutions such as feudalism and serfdom had an intellectual parallel. The Renaissance and the Reformation helped in disintegrating the medieval outlook, but no movement was as important in shaping the modern world-view as the Scientific Revolution of the seventeenth century. It made physical nature a valid object for systematic inquiry and mathematical calculation. For the new science to arise, a philosophical break with the medieval conception of nature had to occur. The medieval approach to nature sought to explain nature's appearances. To the naked eye, the earth seems to be in the center of our universe. Medieval philosophy explained how and why the earth was in the center; how and why heavy bodies fell toward it and light ones rose away from it. But the philosophical revolution of the seventeenth century demolished such explanations. At the heart of the Scientific Revolution was the assumption that appearances could lie, that truth lay in conceptualizing the universe as an abstract entity: as matter in motion, as geometrical shapes, and as weight and number.

The Scientific Revolution brought a new mechanical conception of nature, which enabled westerners to discover and explain the laws of nature mathematically. They came to see nature as composed solely of matter, whose motion, occurring in space and measurable by time, is governed by laws of force. This philosophically elegant construction rendered the physical world knowable, and even possibly manageable.

The Scientific Revolution also entailed the dis-

The Anatomy Lesson of Doctor Tulp, by Rembrandt, 1632. (*UPI/Bettmann*)

covery of a new, scientific methodology. Because of the successful experiments performed by scientists and natural philosophers such as Galileo Galilei, William Harvey, Robert Boyle, and Isaac Newton, Western science acquired its still-characteristic methodology of observation and experimentation. By the late seventeenth century, no one could entertain a serious interest in any aspect of the physical order without actually doing experiments or without observing, in a rigorous and systematic way, the behavior of physical phenomena. The scientific method, which entailed observation or experimentation that could be repeated, was now seen as an avenue to truth. The mechanical concept of nature, coupled with a rigorous methodology, gave modern scientists the means to unlock and explain nature's secrets.

Mathematics increasingly became the laguage of the new science. For centuries, Europeans had used algebra and geometry to explain certain physical phenomena. With the Scientific Revolution came a new mathematics, calculus; but even more important, philosophers became increasingly convinced that all nature—physical objects, as well as invisible forces—could be expressed mathematically. By the late seventeenth century, even geometry had become so complex that a gifted philosopher like John Locke (1632–1704), a friend and contemporary of Isaac Newton, could not understand the sophisticated mathematics used by Newton in the *Principia*. A new scientific culture had been born. During the eighteenth-century Enlightenment (see Chapter 18), it provided the model for progress in both the natural and human sciences.

MEDIEVAL COSMOLOGY

The unique character of the modern scientific outlook is most easily grasped through contrast with the medieval understanding of the natural world and its physical properties. That understanding rested on a blend of Christian thought with theories derived from ancient Greek writers like Aristotle and Ptolemy.

The explanations given by Aristotle (384–322 B.C.) for the motion of heavy bodies permeated medieval scientific literature. In trying to understand motion, Aristotle had argued simply that it was in the nature of things to move in certain ways. A stone falls because it is absolutely heavy; fire rises because it is absolutely light. Weight is an absolute property of a physical thing; therefore, motion results from the properties of bodies, and not from the forces or laws of motion at work in nature. It follows (logically but incorrectly) that if the medium through which a body falls is taken as a constant, then the speed of its fall could be doubled if its weight were doubled. Only rigorous experimentation could refute this erroneous concept of motion; it was many centuries before such experimentation was undertaken.

Aristotle's physics fitted neatly into his *cosmology,* or world picture. The earth, being the heaviest object, lay stationary and suspended at the center of the universe. The sun, the planets, and the moon revolved in circles around the earth. Aristotle presumed that since the planets were round themselves, always in motion, and seemingly never altered, the most "natural" movement for them should be circular, for it is perfect motion.

Aristotle's physics and cosmology were unified. He could put the earth at the center of the universe and make it stationary because he presumed its absolute heaviness; all other heavy bodies that he had observed fall toward it. He presumed that the planets were made of a fine, luminous ether and held in their circular orbits by luminous spheres, or "tracks." These spheres possessed a certain reality, although invisible to human beings, and hence they came to be known as the crystalline spheres.

Aristotle believed that everything in motion had been moved by another object that was itself in motion—a continuing chain of movers and moved. By inference, this belief led back to some object or being that began the motion. Christian philosophers of the Middle Ages argued that Aristotle's Unmoved Mover must be the God of Christianity. For Aristotle, who had no conception of a personal God or an afterlife of rewards or punishments and who believed that the universe was eternal rather than created at a specific point in time, such an identification would have been meaningless.

Although Aristotle's cosmology never gained the status of orthodoxy among the ancient Greeks, by the second century A.D. in Alexandria, Greek astronomy became codified and then rigid. Ptolemy of Alexandria produced the *Almagest* (A.D. 150), a handbook of Greek astronomy based on the theories of Aristotle. The crucial assumption in the *Almagest* was that a motionless earth stood at the center of the universe (although some Greeks had disputed the notion) and that the planets moved about it in a series of circular orbits, interrupted by smaller circular orbits, called epicycles. The epicycles explained why at certain times a planet was visibly closer to the earth. As Ptolemy put it, if the earth moved, "living things and individual heavy objects would be left behind . . . the earth itself would very soon have fallen completely out of the heavens."[1] By the Late Middle Ages, Ptolemy's handbook had come to represent standard astronomical wisdom. As late as the middle of the seventeenth century, more than a hundred years after the Polish astronomer Nicolaus Copernicus had argued mathematically that the sun was the center of the universe, educated Europeans in most universities still believed that the earth held the central position.

In the thirteenth century, mainly through the philosophical efforts of Thomas Aquinas (1225–1274), Aristotle's thought was adapted to Christian beliefs, often in ingenious ways. Aquinas emphasized that order pervaded nature and that every physical effect had a physical cause. The tendency in Aquinas's thought and that of his followers, who were called scholastics by their seventeenth-century critics, was to search for these causes—again, to ask why things move, rather than how they move. But Aquinas denied that these causes stretched back to infinity. Instead, he insisted that nature proves God's existence; God is the First Cause of all physical phenomena. Despite the scholastic adaptations of Aristotle, the church still regarded Christian Aristotelianism with some suspicion, and in 1277 many of Aristotle's theories were condemned. The condemnation of Aristotle helped to give rise to an Anti-Aristotelian physics, which may have influenced the Scientific Revolution.

Medieval thinkers integrated the cosmology of Aristotle and Ptolemy into a Christian framework that drew a sharp distinction between the world beyond the moon and the earthly realm. Celestial bodies were composed of the divine ether, a substance too pure, too spiritual to be found on earth; heavenly bodies, unlike those on earth, were immune to all change and obeyed different laws of motion than earthly bodies. The universe was not homogeneous but divided into a higher world of the heavens and a lower world of earth. Earth could not compare with the heavens in spiritual dignity, but God had nevertheless situated it in the center of the universe. Earth deserved this position of importance, for only here was the drama of salvation performed. This vision of the universe was to be shattered by the Scientific Revolution.

Also shattered by the philosophy of nature articulated in the seventeenth century was the belief that all reality, natural as well as human, could be described as consisting of *matter* and *form*. Following Aristotle, the scholastics argued that matter was inchoate, lifeless, and indistinguishable; form gave it shape and identity. A table, for instance, possessed a recognizable shape and could be identified because it partook in its form, that of tableness. A human being existed only because the matter of the body was given life by the soul, by its form. This doctrine was central to both medieval philosophy and theology. Important beliefs were justified by it. For example, the church taught that the priest, when performing the sacrament of the Eucharist, had the power to transform bread and wine into the body and blood of Christ. Philosophically, this was possible because, theologians argued, the matter of the bread and wine remained the same (and hence looked the same), but its form was changed by the power of the priest. Similarly, medieval people believed that the king's power resided within him; kingness was part of his essence. So, too, nobility was a quality said to adhere to the person of the nobleman or noblewoman. The mechanical philosophy of Galileo, Boyle, and Newton, which was central to the Scientific Revolution, denied the existence of form. Matter was simply composed of tiny corpuscles, or atoms, which were hard and impenetrable and were governed by the laws of impact or force. Such a conception of nature threatened whole aspects of medieval and even Christian doctrine.

A NEW VIEW OF NATURE

Renaissance Neo-Platonism

Italian Renaissance thinkers rediscovered the importance of the ancient Greek philosopher Plato (see pages 81–86). Plato taught that the philosopher must look beyond the appearances of things to an invisible reality, which is abstract, simple, rational, and best expressed mathematically. For Plato, the greatest achievements of the human mind were mathematics and music; both revealed the inherent harmony and order within nature.

Renaissance Platonists interpreted Plato from a Christian perspective, and they believed that the Platonic search for truth about nature, about God's work, was but another aspect of the search for knowledge about God. The Italian universities and academics became centers where the revival of Plato flourished among teachers and translators, who came to be known as *Neo-Platonists*. Central to their humanist curriculum was the study of philosophy, mathematics, music, Greek and Latin, and in some cases Arabic. Those languages made available the world of pagan, pre-Christian learning and its many different philosophies of nature. The leading thinkers of the Scientific Revolution were all inspired by Renaissance Neo-Platonism. They revered Plato's search for a truth that was abstract and mathematically elegant, and they explored the ancient writers and their theories about nature. Some of the ancients had been atomists; a few had even argued that the sun might be at the center of the universe. They had also invented geometry.

With the impulse to mathematize nature came the desire to measure and experience it. The rediscovery of nature as mappable and quantifiable found expression in the study of the human anatomy, as well as in the study of objects in motion. Renaissance art shows the fruits of this inquiry, for artists tried to depict the human body as exactly as possible and yet to give it ideal form.

In this sense, the revival of artistic creativity associated with the Renaissance is linked to an interest in the natural world and to Neo-Platonism.

Magic and the Search for Nature

The thinkers of the Scientific Revolution also drew on a tradition of magic that reached back to the ancient world. In the first and second centuries A.D., various practitioners and writers elaborated on the mystical and magical approach to nature. Many of these anonymous students of magic were in contact with the Hermetic tradition. They believed that there had once been an ancient Egyptian priest, Hermes Trismegistus, who had possessed secret knowledge about nature's processes and the ultimate forces at work in the universe. In the second century A.D., this magical tradition was written down in a series of mystical dialogues about the universe. When Renaissance Europeans rediscovered these second-century writings, they erroneously assumed the author to be Hermes. Hence, the writings seemed to be even older than the Bible.

This Hermetic literature glorified the mystical and the magical. It stated that true knowledge comes from a contemplation of the One, or the Whole—a spiritual reality higher than, and yet embedded in, nature. Some of these ancient writings argued that the sun was the natural symbol of this Oneness, and such an argument seemed to give weight to a heliocentric picture of the universe. The Hermetic approach to nature also incorporated elements of the Pythagorean and Neo-Platonic traditions, which emphasized the inner mathematical harmony pervading nature. The early modern debt to Hermeticism could therefore be expressed in ways that seem to be contradictory. A follower of Hermeticism might approach nature mathematically, as well as magically. For example, Johannes Kepler (see page 416) was both a fine mathematician and a believer in the magical power of nature. Although not directly influenced by Hermeticism as a system of belief, for much of his life Isaac Newton saw no contradiction in searching for the mathematical laws of nature while practicing alchemy: the illusive search for a way to transform ordinary metals into gold.

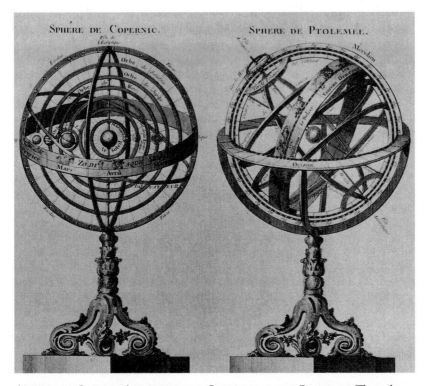

ARMILLARY SPHERES ACCORDING TO COPERNICUS AND PTOLEMY. The spheres reflect the opposing views of the nature of the cosmos that confronted scholars in the sixteenth and early seventeenth centuries. Gradually, Copernicus's heliocentric viewpoint, supported by the discoveries of Kepler, Galileo, and Newton, overturned the Ptolemaic system. (*Smithsonian Institution Libraries*)

The Renaissance followers of Hermes, then, indulged both in what would today be called magic and what would be called science without seeing any fundamental distinction between them. The route that the searcher for nature's wisdom took did not matter as much as the quest itself. Thus, in early modern Europe, the practitioners of alchemy and astrology could also be mathematicians and astronomers, and the sharp distinction drawn today between magic and science—between the irrational and the rational—would not have been made by many of the leading natural philosophers who lived in the sixteenth and seventeenth centuries.

The Renaissance revival of ancient learning contributed a new approach to nature, one that was simultaneously mathematical, experimental, and magical. Although the achievements of modern science depend on experimentation and mathematics, the impulse to search for nature's secrets presumes a degree of self-confidence best exemplified and symbolized by the magician. One of the important byproducts of the Scientific Revolution was that eventually the main practitioners of the new science repudiated magic, largely because of its secretiveness and its associations with popular culture and religion. But this repudiation should not obscure the initial role of magic, among many other factors, as a stimulus to scientific inquiry and enthusiasm.

The Copernican Revolution

Nicolaus Copernicus was born in Poland in 1473. As a young man, he enrolled at the University of Krakow, where he may have come under the influence of Renaissance Platonism, which was spreading outward from the Italian city-states. Copernicus also journeyed to Italy, and in Bologna and Padua he may have become aware of ancient Greek texts containing arguments for the sun being the center of the universe.

Copernicus's interest in mathematics and astronomy was stimulated by contemporary discussions of the need for calendar reform, which required a thorough understanding of Ptolemaic astronomy. The mathematical complexity of the Ptolemaic system troubled Copernicus, who believed that truth was the product of elegance and simplicity. In addition, Copernicus knew that Ptolemy had predecessors among the ancients who philosophized about a heliocentric universe or who held Aristotle's cosmology and physics in little regard. Thus, his Renaissance education gave Copernicus not a body of new scientific truth, but rather the courage to break with traditional truth taught in the universities.

Toward the end of his stay in Italy, Copernicus became convinced that the sun was at the center of the universe. So he began a lifelong task to work out mathematical explanations of how a heliocentric universe operated. Unwilling to engage in controversy with the followers of Aristotle, Copernicus did not publish his findings until 1543, the year of his death, in a work entitled *On the Revolutions of the Heavenly Spheres*. Legend says that his book, which in effect began the Scientific Revolution, was brought to him on his deathbed.

The treatise retained some elements of the Aristotelian-Ptolemaic system. Copernicus never doubted Aristotle's basic idea of the perfect circular motion of the planets or the existence of crystalline spheres within which the stars revolved, and he retained many of Ptolemy's epicycles—orbits within the circular orbits of the sun and planets. But Copernicus proposed a heliocentric model of the universe that was mathematically simpler than Ptolemy's earth-centered universe. Thus, he eliminated some of Ptolemy's epicycles and cleared up various problems that had troubled astronomers who had based their work on an earth-centered universe.

Copernicus's genius was expressed in his ability to pursue an idea—a sun-centered universe—and to bring to that pursuit lifelong dedication and brilliance in mathematics. By removing the earth from its central position and by giving it motion—that is, by making the earth just another planet—Copernicus undermined the system of medieval cosmology and made possible the birth of modern astronomy.

But because they were committed to the Aristotelian-Ptolemaic system and to biblical statements that they thought supported it, most thinkers of the time rejected Copernicus's conclusions. They also raised specific objections. The earth, they said, is too heavy to move. How, some of Copernicus's colleagues asked, can an object falling from a high tower land directly below the point from which it was dropped if the earth is moving so rapidly?

The Laws of Planetary Motion: Tycho and Kepler

Copernicus laid the foundation for the intellectual revolution that overturned the medieval conception of the universe and ushered in modern cosmology. But it fell to other astronomers, who were more observers than philosophers, to fill in the important details. Tycho Brahe (1546–1601) never accepted the Copernican system, but he saw that it presented a challenge to astronomers. Aided by the king of Denmark, Tycho built the finest observatory in Europe. In 1572, he observed a new star in the heavens. Its existence offered a direct and serious challenge to the Aristotelian and scholastic assumption of unalterable, fixed, and hence perfect heavens. To this discovery of what eventually proved to be an exploding star, Tycho added his observations on the comet of 1577. He demonstrated that it moved unimpeded through the areas between the planets and passed right through the crystalline spheres. This finding raised the question of whether such spheres existed, but Tycho himself remained an Aristotelian. Although his devotion to a literal reading of the Bible led Tycho to reject the Copernican sun-centered universe, he did propose an alternative system, in which the planets revolved around the sun, but the sun moved about a motionless earth.

Ultimately, Tycho's fame rests on his skill as a practicing astronomer. He bequeathed to future generations precise calculations about the movements of heavenly bodies. These calculations proved invaluable. They were put to greatest use by Johannes Kepler (1571–1630), a German who collaborated with Tycho during the latter's final years. Tycho bequeathed his astronomical papers to Kepler, who brought to these data a scientific vision that was both experimental and mystical.

Kepler searched persistently for harmonious laws of planetary motion. He did so because he believed profoundly in the Platonic ideal: a spiritual force infuses the physical order; beneath appearances are harmony and unity; and the human mind can begin to comprehend that unity only through *gnosis*—a direct and mystical realization of unity—and through mathematics. Kepler believed that both approaches were compatible, and he managed to combine them. He believed in and practiced astrology (as did Tycho) and throughout his lifetime tried to contact an ancient but lost and secret wisdom.

In the course of his studies and observations of the heavens, Kepler discovered the three basic laws of planetary motion. First, the orbits of the planets are elliptical, not circular as Aristotle and Ptolemy had assumed, and the sun is one focus of the ellipse. Unlike Tycho, Kepler accepted Copernicus's theory and provided proof for it. Kepler's second law demonstrated that the velocity of a planet is not uniform, as had been believed, but increases as its distance from the sun decreases. Kepler's third law—that the squares of the times taken by any two planets in their revolutions around the sun are in the same ratio as the cubes of their average distances from the sun—brought the planets into a unified mathematical system.

The significance of Kepler's work was immense. He gave sound mathematical proof to Copernicus's theory, eliminated forever the use of epicycles, which had saved the appearance of circular motion, and demonstrated that mathematical relationships can describe the planetary system. But Kepler left a significant question unresolved: what kept the planets in their orbits? Why did they not fly out into space or crash into the sun? The answer would be supplied by Isaac Newton, who synthesized the astronomy of Copernicus and Kepler with the new physics developed by Galileo.

Galileo: Experimental Physics

At the same time that Kepler was developing a new astronomy, his contemporary, Galileo Galilei

(1564–1642), was breaking with the older physics of Aristotle. A citizen of Pisa by birth, Galileo lived for many years in Padua. When Galileo lived in Padua, he conducted some of his first experiments on the motion of bodies. Guided by the dominant philosophy of the Italian Renaissance—the revived doctrines of Plato—Galileo believed that beyond the visible world lay certain universal truths, subject to mathematical verification. Galileo insisted that the study of motion entails not only the use of logic (as Aristotle had believed), but also the application of mathematics. For this Late Renaissance natural philosopher, mathematics became the language of nature. Galileo also believed that only after experimenting with the operations of nature can the philosopher formulate the harmonious laws of the universe and give them mathematical expression.

In his mechanical experiments, Galileo discovered that, all other things being equal, bodies of unequal weight will experience a uniform acceleration (due to gravity). He demonstrated that bodies fall with arithmetic regularity. Motion could, therefore, be treated mathematically.

Galileo came very close to perceiving that inertia governs the motion of bodies, but his concept of inertia was flawed. He believed that inertial force was circular. He did not grasp what Newton would later proclaim: that bodies move in a straight line at a uniform velocity unless impeded. But Galileo's contribution was enormous; he had suggested that terrestrial objects could in theory stay in motion forever.

Galileo established a fundamental principle of modern science: the order and uniformity of nature. There are no distinctions in rank or quality between the heavens and earth; heavenly bodies are not perfect and changeless as Aristotle had believed. In 1609, Galileo built a telescope through which he viewed the surface of the moon. The next year, in a treatise called *The Starry Messenger,* he proclaimed to the world that the moon "is not smooth, uniform, and precisely spherical as a great number of philosophers believe it and the other heavenly bodies to be, but is uneven, rough, and full of cavities . . . being not unlike the face of the earth, relieved by chains of mountains and deep valleys."[2] In addition, Galileo noticed spots on the sun, providing further evidence that heavenly objects, like earthly objects, undergo change. There are no

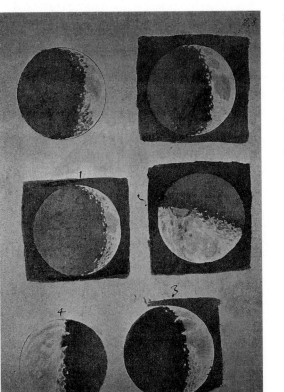

NOTEBOOK SKETCHES OF THE PHASES OF THE MOON BY GALILEO GALILEI, 1609–1610. Galileo saw only shadows when he looked into his telescope. But because he was trained as an artist in the principles of light and dark coloring to emphasize or shorten distance, he knew that what he saw represented real objects, in this case mountains and valleys. Somewhat satirically, he compared the moon to Bohemia. (*Biblioteca Nazionale Centrale, Florence*)

higher and lower worlds; nature is the same throughout. Historians now believe that Galileo was assisted in his observations by his study of drawing and the artistic conventions of the Renaissance. When he saw shadows through his telescope, he assumed that actual bodies were casting them, just as they do on an earthly landscape. The art and science of his age were of a piece.

Through his telescope, Galileo also observed moons around Jupiter—a discovery that helped support the Copernican hypothesis. If Jupiter had moons, then all heavenly bodies did not orbit the earth. The moons of Jupiter removed a fundamental criticism of Copernicus and opened up the possibility that the earth, with its own moon, might be just like Jupiter and that both might in turn revolve around a central point—the sun.

With Galileo, the science of Copernicus and the assault on Aristotle entered a new phase. Priests began to attack Galileo from their pulpits in Florence, backed by teachers within the academic community who routinely taught the old astronomy. These teachers saw a threat to their own power in Galileo's public notoriety and in his following among the laity. A secret group of priests and academics, named the Liga, formed with the express purpose of silencing Galileo; they used Aristotle and the Bible to attack him. Being a friend and courtier of powerful princes, Galileo boldly defied this old elite and championed a new scientific learning for the laity; he proclaimed the new science as a body of learning that required a new elite, freed from the chains of tradition, knowledgeable in mathematics, and committed to experimentation. But in the early seventeenth century, the Catholic church saw danger on every front: Protestants in Germany, recalcitrant people in nearly every state, and laity demanding new schools offering practical education for their children. Now Galileo offered a view of the universe that conflicted with certain scriptural texts.

Historians used to believe that the church attacked Galileo solely because he was a Copernican, that is, because he believed the sun to be at the center of the universe. New evidence from the Vatican archives suggests that the church may also have worried about his theory of matter and his abandonment of the scholastics' view of the relationship between matter and form. That view went to the heart of the doctrine of the Eucharist, and the church saw, rightly, that the new science threatened the philosophical foundations of certain doctrines.

In 1632, Galileo's teachings were condemned, and he was placed under house arrest. These actions cut short the open pursuit of science in many Catholic countries of the seventeenth century. Where the Inquisition was strong, the new science would be viewed as subversive. Censorship worked to stifle intellectual inquiry. By the midcentury, science had become an increasingly Protestant and northern European phenomenon.

THE NEWTONIAN SYNTHESIS: EXPERIMENT, MATHEMATICS, AND THEORY

By 1650, the works of Copernicus and especially of Galileo had dethroned the physics and astronomy of Aristotle and Ptolemy. A new philosophy of nature tied to observation and Neo-Platonism had come into existence; its essence lay in the mathematical expression of physical laws that describe matter in motion. Yet no single overriding law had been articulated that would bring together the experimental successes of the new science, its mathematical sophistication, and its philosophical revolution. This law was supplied by Isaac Newton.

Newton was born in 1642, in Lincolnshire, England, the son of a modest yeoman. Because of his intellectual promise, he obtained a place at Trinity College, Cambridge, and there he devoted himself to natural philosophy and mathematics. Tutors gave him the latest works in philosophy to read; some of these works, in a form of Christian Neo-Platonism, emphasized the operation in the universe of spiritual forces derived from God. Newton's student notebooks survive and show him mastering these texts while also trying to understand the fundamental truths of Protestant Christianity as taught at Cambridge. Combining Christian Neo-Platonism with a genius for mathematics, Newton produced a coherent synthesis of the science of Kepler and Galileo, which eventually captured the imagination of European intellectuals.

In 1666, Newton formulated the mathematics for the universal law of gravitation, and in the same year, after rigorous experimentation, he determined the nature of light. The sciences of physics and optics were transformed. However, for many years, Newton did not publish his discoveries, partly because even he did not grasp the immense significance of his work. Finally, another mathematician and friend, Edmund Halley, persuaded him to publish under the sponsorship of the Royal Society. The result was the *Principia Mathematica* of 1687. In 1704, Newton published his *Opticks* and revealed his theory that light was corpuscular in nature and that it emanated from luminous bodies in a way that scientists later described as waves.

SIR ISAAC NEWTON (1642–1727) BY SIR GODFREY KNELLER. In 1666, Newton's mathematical formulation of the law of universal gravitation and his experiments in the nature of light opened a new stage in human understanding of the physical universe. The poet Alexander Pope expressed Newton's contemporaries' view of his achievements: "Nature, and Nature's Laws lay hid in Night. God said, 'Let Newton be!' and All was Light." (*National Portrait Gallery, London*)

Of the two books, both monumental achievements in the history of science, the *Principia* made the greater impact on contemporaries. Newton offered universal mathematical laws, as well as a philosophy of nature that sought to explain the essential structure of the universe: matter is always the same; if is atomic in structure, and in its essential nature it is dead or lifeless; and it is acted upon by immaterial forces that are placed in the universe by God. Newton said that the motion of matter could be explained by three laws: inertia, that a body remains in a state of rest or continues its motion in a straight line unless impelled to change by forces impressed on it; acceleration, that the change in the motion of a body is proportional to the force acting on it; and that for every action there is an equal and opposite reaction.

Newton argued that these laws apply not only to observable matter on earth, but also to the motion of planets in their orbits. He showed that planets did not remain in their orbits because circular motion was "natural" or because crystalline spheres kept them in place. Rather, said Newton, planets keep to their orbits because every body in the universe exercises a force on every other body, a force that he called *universal gravitation.* Gravity is proportional to the product of the masses of two bodies and inversely proportional to the square of the distance between them. It is operative throughout the universe, whether on earth or in the heavens, and it is capable of mathematical expression. Newton built his theory on the work of other scientific giants, notably Kepler and Galileo. No one before him, however, had possessed the breadth of vision, mathematical skill, and dedication to rigorous observation to combine this knowledge into one grand synthesis.

With Newton's discovery of universal gravitation, the Scientific Revolution reached its zenith. The universe could now be described as matter in motion; it was governed by invisible forces that operated everywhere, both on earth and in the heavens, and these forces could be expressed mathematically. The medieval picture of the universe as closed, earthbound, and earth-centered was replaced by a universe seen to be infinite and governed by universal laws. The earth was now regarded as simply another moving planet.

But what was God's role in this new universe? Newton and his circle labored to create a mechanical world-view dependent on the will of God, and in those efforts they were largely successful. Newton retained a central place for a providential deity that operates constantly in the universe. At one time, Newton believed that gravity was simply the will of God operating on the universe. As he wrote in the *Opticks,* the physical order "can be the effect of nothing else than the wisdom and skill of a powerful everliving agent."[3] Because of his strong religious convictions, Newton allowed his science to be used in the service of the established Anglican church, and his followers argued for social stability anchored in an ordered universe and an estab-

lished church. Newton, a scientific genius, was also a deeply religious thinker committed to the maintenance of Protestantism in England. Among his contemporaries, however, were freethinkers like John Toland (see page 434), who used his ideas to argue that nature can operate on its own, without the assistance of a providential God.

BIOLOGY, MEDICINE, AND CHEMISTRY

The spectacular advances in physics and astronomy in the sixteenth and seventeenth centuries were not matched in the biological sciences. Indeed, the day-to-day practice of medicine throughout western Europe changed little in the period from 1600 to 1700, for much of medical practice relied, as it had since the Middle Ages, on astrology.

Doctors clung to the teachings of the ancient practitioners Galen and Hippocrates. In general, Galenic medicine paid little attention to the discovery of specific cures for particular diseases. As a follower of Aristotle, Galen emphasized the elements that make up the body; he called their manifestations *humors.* A person with an excess of blood was sanguine; a person with too much bile was choleric. Health consisted of a restoration of balances among these various elements, so Galenic doctors often prescribed purges of one sort or another. The most famous of these was bloodletting, but sweating was also a favorite remedy. Taught devotedly in the medical schools of Europe, these methods were often as dangerous as the diseases they sought to cure.

Despite the tenacity of Galenic medicine, sixteenth- and seventeenth-century innovators and reformers did try to challenge and overturn medical orthodoxy. With an almost missionary zeal, Paracelsus (1493–1541), a Swiss-German physician and Hermeticist, introduced the concept of diagnostic medicine. He argued that particular diseases can be differentiated and are related to chemical imbalances. His treatments relied on chemicals and not on bloodletting or the positions of the stars (although he did not discount such influences), and he proclaimed an almost ecstatic vision of human vitality and longevity. In most universities, the faculties of medicine bitterly opposed his views, but by 1650 in England and later in that century in France, Paracelsian ideas had many advocates. Support for Paracelsian medicine invariably accompanied an attack on the traditional medical establishment and its professional monopoly, and it often indicated support for the new science in general. The struggle between Galenists and Paracelsians quickly took on a social dimension; the innovators saw themselves pitted against a medical elite, which, in their opinion, had lost its commitment to medical research and existed solely to perpetuate itself. Eventually, in the eighteenth century, Paracelsian ideas became commonplace.

The medical reforms of the eighteenth century did not rest solely on the Paracelsian approach; they also relied heavily on the experimental breakthroughs made in the science of anatomy. A pioneer in this field was the Belgian surgeon Andreas Vesalius (1515–1564), who published *The Structure of the Human Body* in 1543. Opposing Galenic practice, Vesalius argued for observation and anatomical dissection as the keys to knowing how the human body works. By the late seventeenth century, doctors had learned a great deal about the human body, its structure, and its chemistry.

The study of anatomy yielded dramatic results. In 1628, William Harvey (1578–1657) announced that he had discovered the circulation of blood. Harvey compared the functioning of the heart to that of a mechanical pump, and once again the tendency to mechanize nature, so basic to the Scientific Revolution in physics, led to a significant discovery. Yet the acceptance of Harvey's work was very slow, and the practical uses of his discovery were not readily perceived.

The experimental method in medicine produced other innovations, among them systematic examination not only of corpses, but also of patients. In the late 1600s, the finest doctor of the age, Herman Boerhaave, taught his students in Leiden, in the Netherlands, by taking them on house calls, arguing that nothing in medicine can be known without a careful and rigorous examination of the body. He proclaimed that he was trying to bring the methods and philosophy of the new science to medicine.

Just as Newton applied the theory and method of science to the heavens, his contemporaries on both sides of the English Channel sought to utilize

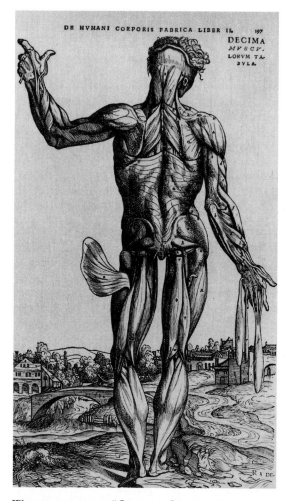

WOODCUT FROM "ON THE STRUCTURE OF THE HUMAN BODY" BY ANDREAS VESALIUS, 1543. Vesalius was a professor at Padua. Originally a follower of Galen's teachings, he carried out many exacting dissections of corpses, which he documented with his vividly realistic drawings. His research led Vesalius to become one of the foremost critics of Galen. (*Royal College of Physicians*)

science in regard to every object we experience. Protestantism inspired them to be aggressive in their assault on scholasticism. Indeed, the most original experimenter of the age, who codified the experimental method as we know it, was a devout English Protestant. Robert Boyle (1627–1691) believed that Aristotle's physics and the philosophy that supported it promoted Catholic teachings and thus amounted to little more than magic. Boyle wanted to abolish the invisible forces on which Catholic theology rested at a time when English Protestants feared a revival of Catholic and absolutist monarchy. He also wished to defeat the magic of what he called "the vulgar," that is, the beliefs of the populace, whose disorder and tendencies to rebellion he feared.

To accomplish these aims, Boyle urged scientists to adopt the zeal of the magicians, but without their secretive practices and their conjuring with spirits. As an alternative to spirits, Boyle advocated the atomic explanation of matter: that matter consists of small, hard, indestructible particles that behave with regularity. According to Boyle, the existence of these particles explained the changes in gases, fluids, and solids.

Boyle pioneered the experimental method with such exciting and accurate results that by the time of his death no serious scientist could attempt chemical experiments without following his guidelines. Thus, the science of chemistry acquired its characteristic experimentalism; it was also based on an atomic theory of matter. But not until late in the eighteenth century was this new discipline applied to medical research.

PROPHETS AND PROPONENTS OF THE NEW SCIENCE

The spectacular scientific discoveries from 1543 to 1687 necessitated a complete rethinking of the social and intellectual role of scientific inquiry. Science needed prophets and social theorists to give it direction and to assess its implications. During the early modern period, three major reformers tried, in disparate ways, to channel science into the service of specific social programs: Giordano Bruno (1548–1600), Francis Bacon (1561–1626), and René Descartes (1596–1650).

Bruno

Giordano Bruno's life is one of the most fascinating and tragic to be found in the turbulent world of the Reformation and Counter Reformation. Born in Italy, Bruno began his mature years as a monk, yet the same church that he set out to serve ended his life by having him burned at the stake. What led him to this cruel fate was his espousal of new religious ideas, which were in fact as old as the second century A.D. but which threatened the beliefs of the church. In Hermetic philosophy, which he believed to be confirmed by Copernicus's heliocentric theory, Bruno found the basis of a new universal religion. He proposed that religion be rooted in the laws found in nature and not rely on supernaturally inspired doctrines taught by the clergy.

Bruno was one of those Late Renaissance reformers who believed that the Hermetic philosophy, with its mystical approach to God and nature, held the key to true wisdom. The Hermetic philosophy accorded the sun a special symbolic role because it infused life into nature. Because of his belief, Bruno accepted Copernicus's sun-centered concept of the universe and began to write and preach about it all over Europe. Indeed, Bruno's fertile imagination, fired by Hermetic mysticism and the new science, led him to be one of the first Europeans to proclaim that the universe is infinite, filled with innumerable worlds. He also speculated that there might be life on other planets.

All of these notions were deemed dangerous by the church. In effect, Bruno was presenting the Hermetic philosophy, coupled with the new science, as an alternative religious vision to both Protestantism and Catholicism. His awed enchantment with the natural order resembles that of later—eighteenth-century—freethinkers who regarded scientific study and contemplation of nature, when combined with a vague sense of the Creator's majesty, as an alternative to organized religious worship. Bruno was a prophet of the new science to the extent that he saw its discoveries as confirming his belief in the wonders of creation.

Bacon

A contrast to Bruno in his lack of mysticism, the decidedly practical and empirical Francis Bacon stands as the most important English proponent of the new science, although not its most important practitioner. Unlike Bruno, Bacon became profoundly suspicious of magic and the magical arts, not because they might not work, but because he saw secrecy and arrogance as characteristic of their practitioners. Bacon was lord chancellor of England under James I, and he wrote about the usefulness of science partly in an effort to convince the crown of its advantages. He wanted science to serve the interests of strong monarchy.

Yet no philosopher of modern science has surpassed Bacon in elevating the study of nature to a humanistic discipline. In the *Advancement of Learning* (1605), Bacon argued that science must be open and all ideas must be allowed a hearing. Science must have human goals: the improvement of humanity's material condition and the advancement of trade and industry, but not the making of war or the taking of lives. Bacon also preached the need for science to possess an inductive methodology grounded in experience; the scientist should first of all be a collector of facts.

Although Bacon was rather vague about how the scientist as a theorist actually works, he knew that preconceived ideas imposed on nature seldom yield positive results. An opponent of Aristotle, Bacon argued that university education should move away from the ancient texts and toward the new learning. As a powerful civil servant, he was not afraid to attack the guardians of tradition. The Baconian vision of progress in science leading to an improvement of the human condition and the security of the state inspired much scientific activity in the seventeenth century, particularly in England.

Descartes

René Descartes, a French philosopher of the first half of the seventeenth century, went to the best French schools and was trained by the Jesuits in mathematics and scholastic philosophy. Yet in his early twenties, he experienced a crisis of confidence. He felt that everything he had been taught was irrelevant and meaningless.

Descartes began to search within himself for what he could be sure was clear and distinct knowledge. All he could know with certainty was the fact of his existence, and even that he knew only because he experienced not his body, but his mind: "I think, therefore I am." From this point of certitude, Descartes deduced God's existence. God exists because Descartes had in his mind an idea of a supreme, perfect being, and, Descartes reasoned, this idea could have been put there only by such a being, not by any ordinary mortal. Therefore, God's existence

ENGRAVING OF RENÉ DESCARTES (1596–1650) TUTORING QUEEN CHRISTINA OF SWEDEN. Descartes was rare among major scientists because he believed passionately in the intelligence of his female followers and correspondents. Rejecting authority, he asserted confidence in the human mind's ability to arrive at truth through its own capacities. (*Jean-Loup Charmet*)

means that the physical world must be real, for no Creator would play such a cruel trick and invent a vast hoax.

For Descartes, the new science meant confidence: in his own mind, the knowability of the physical world, and in mathematics and reason. Scientific thought meant an alternative to everything he associated with the medieval: confusion, disorder, conflict between church and state, fear of the unknown, and magic. Turning his back on the centuries immediately preceding his own, Descartes, possibly as a result of knowing Bacon's ideas for practical science, proclaimed that "it is possible to attain knowledge which is very useful in life, and that, instead of that speculative philosophy which is taught in the schools [that is, scholasticism], we may find a practical philosophy by means of which . . . we can . . . render ourselves the masters and possessors of nature."[4] Descartes was the first person to dream about the capacity of science to control and dominate nature, though he could not imagine its potential to destroy nature.

In order to affirm the existence of anything other than the abstractions of mathematics, Descartes had to proclaim the existence of God and the Universe, largely because both were ideas in his mind. He radically separated matter from spirit, mind from nature, and in the process widened a gap in Western thought that would haunt philosophers for centuries. What if a thinker who understood the implications of Descartes's separation of matter from spirit was to argue that only matter existed? The thinker who did so was Benedict de Spinoza.

Spinoza

Born in Amsterdam of recently immigrated Jewish parents, Benedict de Spinoza (1632–1677) was trained in the classical languages and Hebrew thought. His genius drew him to the new science, and he became an early explicator of Cartesian philosophy. In it he spied a central weakness: its inability to explain the linkage between matter and spirit or to connect God to nature in any meaningful way. Spinoza's solution was radical, logical, and thoroughly heretical to Christian thinkers. He argued that God is Nature, that matter and spirit in effect are one.

To this day, philosophers dispute Spinoza's purpose. Was he an atheist who wanted to do away with the Judeo-Christian conception of God, or was he a mystic who wished to infuse God into Nature? His contemporaries of every religious persuasion (he was expelled from his Amsterdam synagogue) deemed him an atheist and thought that he had become one by reading too much science. Their condemnation made "spinozism" a byword for atheism and freethinking. In the Enlightenment freethinkers and materialists (see page 433–435) would claim that they had been inspired by Spinoza.

The thoughts and visions of Bruno, Bacon, Descartes, and Spinoza revealed the power and importance of scientific knowledge. Science could promote human well-being, as Bacon insisted; it could express mysticism, as in Bruno's case; it could make human beings and nature the foundation of all meaningful knowledge, as Descartes assumed; or it could justify a belief in Nature as God, as it did for Spinoza. Whichever position educated westerners embraced by the late 1600s, science would be used to challenge the traditional authority of the clergy, whether Catholic or fundamentalist Protestant. Why believe in dogmas and texts when nature offered another kind of truth—universal and, just as important, applicable to human problems? For good or ill, the Scientific Revolution gave its followers a sense of power and self-confidence unimagined even by Renaissance proponents of individualism or by the theorists of absolute state power.

SOCIAL FACTORS IN THE SCIENTIFIC REVOLUTION

Historians used to regard the Scientific Revolution as the legacy of a few heroic scientists and philosophers, whose mathematical and experimental genius created a new understanding of nature. However, we now understand more about the role of social and political factors in generating and spreading scientific knowledge.

Perhaps the critical factor in causing the historical phenomenon called the Scientific Revolution was the acceptance and use of the new science by educated elites. Without such acceptance, the science of Galileo, Kepler, Descartes, Boyle, and Newton would have remained the specialized knowledge of the few—or worse still, a suspect, even heretical, approach to nature. Galileo could not have succeeded as much as he did in disseminating his theories (despite the hostility of the church) without his large European following and his many aristocratic patrons, particularly in Florence.

Access to the printing press in Europe was also critical to the acceptance of the new mechanical understanding of nature. Descartes understood that fact when he left France, after the condemnation of Galileo, and published and lived in the Netherlands. Persecution and censorship meant that the new science made far less of an impact in Catholic than in Protestant Europe.

Another social factor favoring acceptance of the new science was the dream of power that mechanical knowledge offered both governments and early promoters of industry. In the seventeenth century, this dream enticed monarchs and states-

Giraudon/Art Resource, NY

MADAME DU CHÂTELET

In the eighteenth century women entered the world of science for the first time, and the most accomplished and famous among these scientists was Madame du Châtelet (1706–1749). She was one of the foremost mathematicians of her era and helped to bring Newtonian science to France. Her translation of Newton's *Principia* remains the only French translation. Her mathematical skill was formidable, as was her ability to convey complex scientific ideas in a readable form. Most importantly, Du Châtelet realized earlier than many French professors that Newton's calculus was superior to the Cartesian system. She and Voltaire were lovers, and both were at the center of the French Enlightenment. In matters scientific, however, he was her pupil. When the first scientific society for women in the world was founded in 1785 in the Dutch Republic, the name of Madame du Châtelet was invoked in its founding documents. As did so many women of her age, she died in childbirth.

men to give their patronage to scientific academies and projects. The achievements of the new science were quickly institutionalized in academies dominated either by the state, as in France, or by the landed and commercial elite, as in England. Founded in the 1660s, the scientific academies, such as the Royal Society in England, became centers for the dissemination of science at a time when many universities, still controlled by the clergy, were hostile to its attack on scholasticism.

The new mechanical learning—not first read in Newton's *Principia*, which was far too technical for most people, but the mechanical information in handbooks and lectures that came after it—first began to be applied in Britain and Scotland during the second half of the eighteenth century. The applied mechanics that improved the steam engine and utilized it in coal mining and water engineering stemmed from Newtonian lectures and books, which proliferated in Britain during the 1700s. The road from the Scientific Revolution leads more directly to the Industrial Revolution than is often realized.

Political factors, too, affected the generation and spread of scientific knowledge. Descartes's emphasis on order and reason can best be understood in relation to the chaos that had plagued French government and society as a result of the French wars of religion. His exposition of the new science stressed its advantages in promoting order and stability and diverting people to the search for mastery over nature rather than having them meddle in state affairs.

But while Descartes struggled to create the philosophical foundations for order and state authority—in effect, for absolutist monarchical government—his Protestant counterparts in England, Boyle and Newton, formulated a philosophy of nature that required the rule of law. They sought order and discipline in nature that could be copied by political elites without the absolute authority of an all-powerful monarch and court. Newton's universe was ruled by law. Whether he intended it or not, the Newtonian universe would become a model for British society and government in the eighteenth century.

THE MEANING OF THE SCIENTIFIC REVOLUTION

The Scientific Revolution was decisive in shaping the modern mentality; it shattered the medieval view of the universe and replaced it with a wholly different world-view. Gone was the belief that a motionless earth lay at the center of a universe that was finite and enclosed by a ring of stars. Gone, too, was the belief that the universe was divided into higher and lower worlds and that different laws of motion operated in the heavens than on earth. The universe was now viewed as a giant machine functioning according to universal laws, which could be expressed mathematically. Nature could be conceptually mastered.

The methodology that produced this view of nature—the new science—played a crucial historical role in reorienting Western thought from medieval theology and metaphysics to the study of physical and human problems. In the Late Middle Ages, most men of learning were Aristotelians and theologians. But by the mid-eighteenth century, knowledge of Newtonian science and the dissemination of useful learning had become the goal of the educated classes. All knowledge, it was believed, could emulate scientific knowledge: it could be based on observation, experimentation, or rational deduction; and it could be systematic, verifiable, progressive, and useful. This new approach to learning used the scientists of the sixteenth and seventeenth centuries as proof that no institution or dogma had a monopoly on truth; the scientific approach would yield knowledge that night, if properly applied for the good of all people, produce a new and better age. Such an outlook gave thinkers new confidence in the power of the human mind to master nature and led them to examine European institutions and traditions with an inquiring, critical, and skeptical spirit. Thus inspired, the reformers of the eighteenth century would seek to create an Age of Enlightenment.

The Scientific Revolution ultimately weakened traditional Christianity. God's role in a mechanical universe was not clear. Newton had argued that God not only set the universe in motion but still intervened in its operations, thus leaving room for miracles. Others retained a place for God as Creator but regarded miracles as limitations on nature's mechanical perfection. Soon other Christian teachings came under attack as contrary to the standards of verification postulated by the new science. Applied to religious doctrines, Descartes's reliance on methodical doubt and clarity of thought and Bacon's insistence on careful observation led thinkers to question the validity of Christian teachings. Theology became a separate and somewhat irrelevant area of intellectual inquiry, not fit for the interests of practical, well-informed people. Not only Christian doctrines, but also various popular beliefs grew suspect. Magic, witchcraft, and astrology, still widespread among the European masses, were regarded with disdain by elite culture. The Scientific Revolution widened the gap between the elite culture of the rich and landed and popular culture. The masses of people remained devoted to some form of traditional Christianity, and the uncertainty of a universe governed by devils, witches, or the stars continued to make sense to peasants and laborers, who remained powerless in the face of nature or the domination of the rich and landed.

In Catholic countries, where the Scientific Revolution began, hostility toward scientific ideas gathered strength in the early 1600s. The mentality of the Counter Reformation enabled lesser minds to exercise their fears and arrogance against any idea they regarded as suspicious. Galileo was caught in this hostile environment, and the Copernican system was condemned by the church in 1616. In Spain and Poland, it was not officially taught until the 1770s.

Consequently, by the midcentury, science had become an increasingly Protestant phenomenon. The major Protestant countries, such as England and the Netherlands, accorded intellectuals greater freedom, and their presses were relatively free. Eventually, science also proved to be more compatible with the Protestant emphasis on individual striving and the mercantile exploitation of nature for material gain.

Gradually, the science of Newton became the science of western Europe: nature mechanized, analyzed, regulated, and mathematicized. As a result of the Scientific Revolution, learned westerners came to believe more strongly than ever that nature could be mastered. Mechanical science—applied to canals, engines, pumps, and levers—became the science of industry. Thus, the Scientific Revolution, operating on both intellectual and commercial levels, laid the groundwork for two major developments of the modern West: the Age of Enlightenment and the Industrial Revolution.

◆ ◆ ◆

NOTES

1. Quoted in Jean D. Moss, *Novelties in the Heavens.* (Chicago: University of Chicago Press, 1993), p. 33.
2. Excerpted in *Discoveries and Opinions of Galileo,* ed. Stillman Drake (Garden City, N.Y.: Doubleday, 1957), p. 28.
3. Excerpted in *Newton's Philosophy of Nature,* ed. H. S. Thayer (New York: Hafner, 1953), p. 177.
4. Excerpted in *Descartes' Philosophical Writings,* ed. Norman Kemp Smith (New York: Modern Library, 1958), pp. 130–131.

SUGGESTED READING

Appleby, J., L. Hunt, and M. Jacob, *Telling the Truth about History* (1994). Discusses the issues raised by the heroic model of science that came out of the Scientific Revolution and relates the issues of today's attitudes toward science.

Brooke, John H., *Science and Religion. Some Historical Perspectives* (1991). A lively, intelligent discussion of the tensions between science and religion since the sixteenth century.

Crosland, M., ed., *The Emergence of Science in Western Europe* (1975). A collection of essays by various authors dealing with all the European countries.

Dobbs, B. J. T., and Margaret C. Jacob, *Newton and the Culture of Newtonianism* (1995). Describes Newton's life and discusses the legacy of his science through the late eighteenth century; intended for students.

Ginsburg, Carlo, *The Cheese and the Worms* (1982). Shows how "ordinary" people understood nature in this period; good reading.

Jacob, Margaret C., ed., *The Politics of Western Science, 1640–1990* (1994). A collection of essays by experts in every field, from the time of Boyle and Newton to the cold war period.

Laudan, Larry, *Science and Relativism. Some Key Controversies in the Philosophy of Science* (1990). Debates some of the implications of being pro or antiscience; intended for students.

Moss, Jean Dietz, *Novelties in the Heavens. Rhetoric and Science in the Copernican Controversy* (1993). The way scientists from Copernicus to Galileo described their discoveries tells us about their beliefs and values.

Schiebinger, Londa, *Nature's Body. Gender in the Making of Modern Science* (1993). Discusses how scientists project their own values on the things they study, from plants to apes and people.

Stewart, Larry, *The Rise of Public Science. Rhetoric, Technology, and Natural Philosophy in Newtonian Britain, 1660–1750* (1992). Despite the long title, a very readable account of how engineers and entrepreneurs took up science and applied it to industry, mining, and transportation.

REVIEW QUESTIONS

1. What was the difference between the scientific understanding of the universe and the medieval understanding of it?

2. Describe the major achievements of Copernicus, Kepler, Galileo, and Newton.

3. How did the practice of medicine change during the Scientific Revolution? Describe the changes.

4. What were Bruno's differences with the church? Describe what happened.

5. Does modern science conform to Francis Bacon's ideals? List these ideals and discuss why it does or does not conform.

6. Was the Scientific Revolution essentially the achievement of a few men of genius, or was the process more complex than that?

7. How did early modern Europeans perceive the new science as it was developing?

8. What was the relationship between science and magic in this period?

9. What role did the Scientific Revolution play in shaping a modern mentality? Why have some people in the late twentieth century become antiscience?

The Age of Enlightenment:
Reason and Reform

*T*he eighteenth century's most exciting intellectual movement is called the Enlightenment. So powerful was its dedication to reason and rational thought that until quite recently the era was sometimes characterized as the Age of Reason. The turn toward what became known by 1750 as the Enlightenment began in the late seventeenth century. Three factors were critically important in this new intellectual ferment: a revulsion against monarchical and clerical absolutism, especially as practiced by Louis XIV in France; a new freedom of publishing and, with it, the rise of a new public and a secular culture, found most dramatically in England and the Dutch Republic; and, not least, the impact of the Scientific Revolution, particularly the excitement generated by Newton's *Principia* (1687).

Newton's work seemed to prove that order and mathematically demonstrable laws were at work in the physical universe. Perhaps a similar order and rationality could be imposed on the social and political institutions. This ideal fired the imagination of the leaders of the Enlightenment, who gradually became known as *philosophes*, simply the French word for "philosophers." But regardless of national origin, the name took hold for thinkers as diverse as the French writer Voltaire, the American scientist and statesman Benjamin Franklin, and the German philosopher Immanuel Kant (1724–1804). The French philosophes were the most outspoken and most radical of the century, and to this day when historians think of the Enlightenment, they think first of France.

Late in the eighteenth century, Kant gave the most succinct definition of the Enlightenment: bringing "light into the dark corners of mind," dispelling ignorance, prejudice, and superstition. Kant went to the heart of one aspect of the

Madame Geoffrin's Salon. (*Giraudon/Art Resource, NY*)

CHRONOLOGY 18.1 The Enlightenment

1685	Revocation of the Edict of Nantes; persecution of Protestants in France
1687	Publication of Newton's *Principia*
1688–89	Revolution in England: the clergy's power is weakened and censorship loosened
1690	Publication of Locke's *Two Treatises of Government*
1717	Founding of the Grand Lodge, London; the beginning of organized Freemasonry
1733	Voltaire publishes *Letters Concerning the English Nation*
1740	Frederick the Great invades Silesia; the War of the Austrian Succession ensues
1748	Hume publishes *An Enquiry Concerning Human Understanding*; Montesquieu publishes *The Spirit of the Laws*
1751	Publication of Diderot's *Encyclopedia* in Paris
1756–1763	Seven Years' War
1762	Rousseau publishes *Émile* and *The Social Contract*
1775	American Revolution
1776	Adam Smith publishes *The Wealth of Nations*
1785	Russian Charter of Nobility; the servitude of the peasants is guaranteed
1787	Dutch Revolution begins
1789	French Revolution

Enlightenment: its insistence that each individual should reason independently, without recourse to the authority of schools, churches, or clergymen.[1]

Being a political moderate and living in Prussia, Kant hoped that the call for self-education and critical thought would mean no disruption of the political order, at least at home. His moderation was typical of most philosophes. Distrusting the uneducated people, these intellectual leaders sought a gradual transformation of the human condition. But there were radical thinkers during the late eighteenth century, such as the American revolutionary Thomas Jefferson (1743–1826) and the feminist Mary Wollstonecraft (1759–1797) who were prepared to endorse an immediate political disruption of the traditional authority of monarchy, aristocracy, fathers, and churchmen. Whether radical or moderate, the philosophes were united by certain key ideas. They believed in the new science, were critical of clergy and all rigid dogma but tolerant of people's right to worship freely, and believed deeply in freedom of the press. They were also willing to entertain, although not necessarily accept, new heresies—such as atheism or the belief that the earth had gradually evolved or the view that the Bible was a series of wise stories but not the literal word of God.

Philosophes were found most commonly in

the major European cities, where they clubbed and socialized in literary and philosophical societies. By the 1770s, Paris had become the center of the Enlightenment, but circles of philosophes could be found in Berlin, Moscow, Budapest, London, The Hague, and, across the Atlantic, in Philadelphia. Their writings spread far and wide because they adopted a new style for philosophical discussion: clear, direct, witty, satirical, even naughty and audacious. At times, they were more like journalists, propagandists, writers of fiction, even pornographers. Now and then, they wrote anonymously, but always they sought to live by their pens. Their success owed much to the growing literacy of urban men and women, a new prosperity that made books affordable, and, not least, the existence of an audience that liked what they had to say. The philosophes' readers, too, were fed up with all vestiges of medieval culture. They resented priestly privileges, protected social classes, monarchical decrees in place of deliberation in representative assemblies, and restrictions on who could manufacture what and where. They had wearied of inequitous taxes designed by bureaucrats who never had to pay them, and indeed of everything that could not be explained rationally.

Appealing to the professional classes, literate merchants, and women with leisure to read, the philosophes opposed the old scholastic learning of the universities, mocked the clergy, and denied the Christian mysteries. They expressed confidence in science and reason, called for humanitarian treatment of slaves and criminals, and played a cat-and-mouse game with censors. Dedicated to freedom of thought and person, they combined these liberal values with a secular orientation and a belief in future progress. The philosophes helped shape, if not define, the modern outlook.

THE FORMATION OF A PUBLIC AND SECULAR CULTURE

In England and the Dutch Republic, by the late seventeenth century, freedom of the press was a practical or a legal reality. During the same period, in 1685, Louis XIV outlawed Protestants from France. Faced with forced conversion or imprisonment, thousands of highly educated Protestants (as well as menial workers) fled to England or the Netherlands. They set up journals and newspapers, formed new clubs, and began a vast international discussion—conducted in French, the language of all well-educated Europeans—aiming it against the injustices of monarchical absolutism and the evils of religious persecution. In journals and newspapers, the reformers endorsed the need for political change.

At the same time, relative freedom of assembly in the cities of western Europe (even in Paris, which was just too big to police) gave rise to a new public and secular sphere: a zone for social life outside the family but not attached to churches or courts. The new public sphere, found in *salons* (gatherings in private homes), coffee houses, and Masonic lodges, as well as in academies for scientific learning like the Royal Society of London, laid the ground for the emergence of the Enlightenment.

All these autonomous and voluntary groups helped create a new secular and public culture. In this new and free mental space, what we now call civil society, people mingled with strangers, politeness and conviviality became norms of behavior, and informal learning flourished. Lecturers gave scientific demonstrations, ordinary men learned to vote for their leaders or to debate publicly, and women met outside the home to discuss novels or politics. Indeed in some of the Parisian salons, women were often the key organizers. By the 1780s throughout Western Europe no town of any size was without a private association, club, and newspaper. In the Dutch Republic, in 1785, the first scientific society founded by and for women met in the town of Middelburg (no larger than about 17,000 souls located in the province of Zeeland). The women chose a freemason and follower of Voltaire to give scientific demonstrations, and they set about learning Newtonian mechanics[2] with such dedication that their society lasted for over 100 years.

Men and women met at these sociable gatherings not because they were relatives, belonged to the same religion, or practiced the same trade or profession, but because they had a common interest in politics, science, the new novels, or simply in self-improvement. Members of these new clubs shared certain characteristics: they were highly literate; they possessed some surplus wealth and leisure time; and, if titled aristocrats, they were not opposed to mixing with bourgeois lawyers, doctors, civil servants, and merchants. Such men and women made the theories of the philosophes come alive. The new societies thus became schools where the literate expanded their universe, learning about the new peoples of the Orient and the Americas and about the Newtonian heavens. In the words of Kant, they dared to think for themselves.

This training in self-governance, self-education, and social criticism helped prepare the way for the liberal revolutions that swept across Europe at the end of the eighteenth and during the first half of the nineteenth century. In the first years of the French Revolution, one of the earliest activities of the revolutionaries was to set up clubs based on equality and fraternity and modeled after the clubs and lodges of the Enlightenment. As the revolutions spread, these societies spread the principles of the French Revolution, among them nationalist fervor. In the nineteenth century every nation had its patriotic clubs, but with them came the demise of the cosmopolitan ideals of the enlightened fraternities and salons.

Salons

Perhaps the most famous of the many new forms of secular culture were the salons, often run by women and mostly found in Paris. Intellectually ambitious women, such as Madame Necker and Madame Geoffrin, organized regular evening receptions in their drawing rooms, where philosophes gathered to discuss ideas in an atmosphere that was civilized, independent of the crown and the nobility, and open. Originally, the salon had been an institution found only in noble homes, where the room designated for leisure activities gave the gathering its name. But the Parisian women and their philosophe friends transformed the custom into gatherings where men and women could educate themselves and where some of the most outrageous ideas of the age could be openly discussed. The habits of luxurious feasting and gaming disappeared and in their place came serious, if somewhat formal, egalitarian conversation.

Salons also developed an international correspondence, with letters from all over Europe being read to the assembled guests. The notion of a republic of letters and the goal of cosmopolitanism were actually experienced in the salons. Some salons, however, excluded women, who were attacked as frivolous and gossipy. The free mixing of women and men always generated controversy in the eighteenth century.

Freemasons

As the search for a science of religion during the Enlightenment came to mean a search for an alternative to traditional beliefs and practices, societies with a ritual and ethical component began to flourish. Among them were the Freemasons, a fraternity that evolved in the late seventeenth century in England and Scotland out of the guilds of stonemasons. In 1717, a group of London gentlemen, many of them very interested in the new science, founded the Grand Lodge, a collection of various Masonic lodges that met in pubs around the city. From that date onward, Freemasonry spread throughout Britain and then onto the Continent. It was often exported by British ambassadors, who brought it in the 1730s to Paris and The Hague and who used membership in the lodges to foster interest in British customs and institutions.

In the lodges, men, and eventually some women, were meant to meet "upon the level," that is, as fraternal equals, to hold elections, and to live under a constitution patterned on the rules that the old lodges had evolved during the seventeenth century. On the Continent, however, such practices as annual elections, representative government within the framework of a constitution, and habits of self-governance were new and experimental. The lodges sought to make their members virtuous, disciplined, and civilized. For some men, this experience came to rival that found in the churches. Philosophes, such as Benjamin Franklin and, late in his life, Voltaire, joined lodges; in some cities, lodges became cultural centers. In Vienna, Mozart was a Freemason and wrote music for his lodge, while in Berlin, Frederick the Great cultivated the lodges, which in turn became centers for the cult of enlightened monarchy.

FREEMASONS' CEREMONY: AN ETCHING C. 1745. Freemasons held initiation ceremonies to formalize their sociability. Some French lodges had altars with sanctuaries, where they placed copies of their constitution. They sought to give religious meaning to the social and the secular. (*Bibliothèque Nationale, Paris*)

By the middle of the eighteenth century, perhaps as many as fifty thousand men belonged to lodges in just about every major European city. British constitutionalism, as well as the old fraternal ideals of equality and liberty, took on new meaning in these private gatherings. In France, in the 1780s, the national Grand Lodge instituted a national assembly of elected representatives, as well as a monthly payment of charity for impoverished brothers. The lodges for women became places where women and men actually talked about the meaning of liberty and equality for their own lives. Many lodges were dominated by the most elite elements in Old Regime society, who found themselves giving allegiance, and often considerable financial support, to a new system of belief and governance that was ultimately incompatible with the principles of birth and inheritance on which their power rested. At the time of the French Revolution, its opponents claimed that the lodges were responsible for the uprising. There was no truth to the claim, which opponents of all reforms and revolutions have often repeated. The subversive quality of the lodges lay not in any conspiracy, but rather in the freedom they allowed for thought, self-governance, and discussion.

Scientific Academies

By the midcentury, there were provincial scientific academies all over the Continent. The first scientific societies had formed in the 1660s, in London and Paris (see page 424). They continued to flourish, but now they were imitated in Turin, Budapest, Berlin, and the small cities of the Dutch Republic, such as Haarlem and Utrecht. All these societies performed experiments of greater or lesser sophistication, listened to learned papers, collected samples, and kept a cabinet of "rarities," with everything in it from rocks to deformed animal bones. Any man (and only rarely a woman visitor) who possessed what the age called curiosity could join the society and try to become a man of science. By the 1770s, these scientific societies served as models for groups specifically interested in the application of scientific knowledge, or in useful learning. The new groups became centers for the reformers and critics of the age, who sought to turn the Enlightenment into a movement for changing society and government.

In Germany and France, where the scientific academies tended to be dominated by aristocratic leadership, new societies with a utilitarian purpose were founded and had to compete with the older societies. As a result, the turn toward the applied and the utilitarian was not as visible as in England and Scotland. In France, the academies became centers for abstract and advanced science and mathematics—for important and original contributions with little practical application. During the French Revolution, however, the academies were reformed to emphasize industrial applications of mechanics and chemistry.

THE SCIENCE OF RELIGION

Christianity Under Attack

No single thread had united Western culture more powerfully than Christianity. Until the eighteenth century, educated people, especially rulers and servants of the state, had to give allegiance to one or another of the Christian churches—however unChristian their actions. The Enlightenment produced the first widely read and systematic assault on Christianity launched from within the ranks of the educated. The philosophes argued that many Christian dogmas defied logic—for example, the conversion of the substance of bread and wine into the body and the blood of Christ during the Eucharist. They also ridiculed theologians for arguing about obscure issues that seemed irrelevant to

the human condition and a hindrance to clear thinking. "Theology amuses me," wrote Voltaire. "That's where we find the madness of the human spirit in all its plenitude." In the same vein, the philosophes denounced the churches for inciting the fanaticism and intolerance that led to the horrors of the Crusades, the Inquisition, and the wars of the Reformation. They viewed Christianity's preoccupation with salvation and its belief in the depravity of human nature, a consequence of Adam and Eve's defiance of God, as barriers to social improvement and earthly happiness.

Skeptics, Freethinkers, and Deists

An early attack on Christian dogma was made by the skeptic Pierre Bayle (1647–1706), who came to distrust Christian dogma and to see superstition as a social evil far more dangerous than atheism. Bayle was a French Protestant forced to flee to the Netherlands as a result of Louis XIV's campaign against Protestants. Although a Calvinist himself, Bayle also ran into opposition from the strict Calvinist clergy, who regarded him as lax on doctrinal matters. He attacked his critics and persecutors in a new and brilliant form of journalism, his *Historical and Critical Dictionary* (1697), which was more an encyclopedia than a dictionary. Under alphabetically arranged subjects and in copious footnotes, Bayle discussed the most recent learning of the day on various matters and never missed an opportunity to ridicule the dogmatic, the superstitious, or the just plain arrogant. In Bayle's hands, the ancient philosophy of skepticism, the doubting of all dogma, was revived and turned into a tool; rigorous questioning of accepted ideas became a method for arriving at new truths. As Bayle noted in his *Dictionary,* "It is therefore only religion that has anything to fear from Pyrrhonism [that is, skepticism]."[3] In this same critical spirit, Bayle, in his dictionary article entitled "David," compared Louis XIV to Goliath. The message was clear enough: great tyrants and the clergy who prop them up should beware of self-confident, independently minded citizens who are skeptical of the claims of authority made by kings and churches and are eager to use their own intellects to search for truth.

Bayle's *Dictionary,* which was in effect the first encyclopedia, had an enormous impact throughout Europe. Its very format captured the imagination of the philosophes. Here was a way of simply, even scientifically, classifying and ordering knowledge. Partly through Bayle's writings, skepticism became an integral part of the Enlightenment approach to religion. It taught its readers to question the clerical claim that God's design governs human events—that "God ordains" certain human actions. Skepticism dealt a serious blow to revealed religion and seemed to point in the direction of "natural" religion, that is, toward a system of beliefs and ethics designed by rational people on the basis of their own needs.

The religious outlook of the philosophes was also colored by late seventeenth- and early eighteenth-century English freethinkers. These early representatives of the Enlightenment used the term *freethinking* to signal their hostility to established church dogmas and their ability to think for themselves. They looked back to the English Revolution of the midcentury for their ideas about government; many English freethinkers were republicans in the tradition established by important figures of the interregnum (see Chapter 16). Indeed, the English freethinkers of the 1690s and beyond helped popularize English republican ideas at home and in the American colonies, where in 1776 these views would figure prominently in the thinking of American revolutionaries.

The freethinkers had little use for organized religion or even for Christianity itself. In 1696, the freethinker John Toland (1670–1722) published a tract, entitled *Christianity Not Mysterious,* in which he argued that any religious doctrine that seemed to contradict reason or common sense—for example, the resurrection of Jesus or the miracles of the Bible—ought to be discarded. Toland also attacked the clergy's power; in his opinion, the Revolution of 1688–89 had not gone far enough in undermining the power of the established church and the king. Toland and his freethinking associates Anthony Collins and Matthew Tindal wanted England to be a republic governed by "reasonable" people who worshiped, as Toland proposed, not a mysterious God but intelligible nature. For Toland, Newton's science made nature intelligible, and he used it as a stick with which to beat at the doctrines of revealed religion.

In science combined with skepticism, freethinking, and anticlericalism, thoughtful critics could find ample reason for abandoning all traditional authority. By 1700, a general crisis of confidence in established authority had been provoked by the works of Bayle, the freethinkers, and philosophers such as Descartes. Once started in England and the Netherlands and broadcast via Dutch and French refugee printers, the Enlightenment quickly became international.

The leaders of the Enlightenment sought to repudiate traditional Christianity and to put in its place a rational system of ethics and philosophy based on scientific truths. Some of the early proponents of the Enlightenment were atheists. They often published clandestinely. A particularly early and outrageous example of their thinking appeared under the title *The Treatise on the Three Imposters* (1719), which identified Jesus, Moses and Muhammad as the imposters. However, most of the philosophes were simply deists, who believed only those Christian doctrines that could meet the test of reason. For example, they considered it reasonable to believe in God, for only with a creator, they said, could such a superbly organized universe have come into being. But, in their view, after God set the universe in motion, he took no further part in its operations. Thus, although deists retained a belief in God the Creator, they rejected clerical authority, revelation, original sin, and miracles. They held that biblical accounts of the resurrection and of Jesus walking on water or waking the dead could not be reconciled with natural law. Deists viewed Jesus as a great moral teacher, not as the Son of God, and they regarded ethics, not faith, as the essence of religion. Rational people, they said, served God best by treating their fellow human beings justly.

David Hume (1711–1776), a Scottish skeptic, attacked both revealed religion and the deists' natural religion. He maintained that all religious ideas, including Christian teachings and even the idea of God, stemmed ultimately from human fears and superstitions. Hume rejected the deist argument that this seemingly orderly universe required a designing mind to create it. The universe, said Hume, might very well be eternal, and the seeming universal order simply a natural condition that requires no explanation. Hume's attack made it impossible to establish a necessary link between a mechanical universe and a creator. As a consequence of Hume's critique, Christian belief rested more than ever before on faith, not reason.

Voltaire the Philosophe

The French possessed a vital tradition of intellectual skepticism going back to the late sixteenth century, as well as a tradition of scientific rationalism exemplified by Descartes. In the early eighteenth century, however, the French found it difficult to gain access to the new literature of the Enlightenment because the French printing presses were among the most tightly controlled and censored in Europe. As a result, a brisk but risky traffic developed in clandestine books and manuscripts subversive of authority, and French-language journals poured from Dutch presses.

As a poet and writer struggling for recognition in Paris, the young François Marie Arouet, known to the world as Voltaire (1694–1778), encountered some of the new ideas that were being discussed in salons in Paris. In the French capital, those educated people who wanted to read books and discuss ideas hostile to the church or to the Sorbonne, the clerically controlled university, had to proceed with caution. Individuals had been imprisoned for writing, publishing, or owning books hostile to Catholic doctrine. Although Voltaire learned something of the new enlightened culture in Paris, it was in 1726, when he journeyed to London, that Voltaire the poet became Voltaire the philosophe.

In England, Voltaire became acquainted with the ideas of John Locke and Isaac Newton. From Newton, Voltaire learned the mathematical laws that govern the universe; he witnessed the power of human reason to establish general rules that seemed to explain the behavior of physical objects. From Locke, Voltaire learned that people should believe only the ideas received from the senses. Locke's theory of learning, his *epistemology*, impressed many of the proponents of the Enlightenment. Again, the implications for religion were most serious: if people believed only what they experienced, they would not accept mysteries and doctrines simply because they were taught by churches and clergy. Voltaire enjoyed considerable freedom of thought in England and saw a religious toleration that contrasted sharply

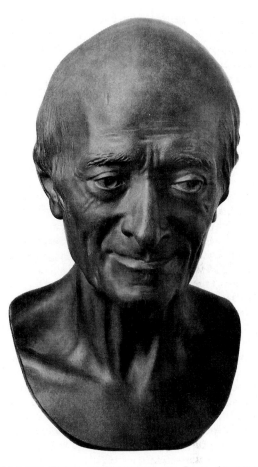

MARBLE BUST OF VOLTAIRE BY JEAN ANTOINE HOUDON, 1781. François Marie Arouet (1694–1778), better known as Voltaire, was the most celebrated mind and wit in Europe. A relentless critic of religious dogmatism and intolerance, he denounced censorship and advised and urged the enlightened despots of Russia and Prussia to use their absolute power to reform society. He attacked his own country's institutions and praised those of England. His literary brilliance was acknowledged even by his enemies; he was the single most effective leader of the French philosophes. (*Musée Fabre, Montpellier*)

with the absolutism of the French kings and the power of the French clergy. He also witnessed a freer mixing of bourgeois and aristocratic social groups than was permitted in France at this time.

Throughout his life, Voltaire fiercely supported the Enlightenment and bitterly criticized churches and the Inquisition. Although his books were banned in France, he probably did more there than any other philosophe to popularize the Enlightenment and to mock the authority of the clergy. In *Letters Concerning the English Nation* (1733), Voltaire wrote about his experiences in England. He offered constitutional monarchy, new science, and religious toleration as models to be followed by all of Europe. In the *Letters,* he praised English society for its encouragement of these ideals. As he put it, "This is the country of sects. An Englishman, as a free man, goes to Heaven by whatever road he pleases."[4] Voltaire never ceased to ridicule the purveyors of superstition and blind obedience to religious authority. In such works as *Candide* (1759) and *Micromegas* (1752), he castigated the clergy, as well as other philosophical supporters of the status quo who would have people believe that this was the best of all possible worlds.

Voltaire was also a practical reformer, who campaigned for the rule of law, a freer press, religious toleration, humane treatment of criminals, and a more effective system of government administration. His writings constituted a radical attack on several aspects of eighteenth-century French society. Yet, like so many philosophes, Voltaire feared the power of the people, especially if goaded by the clergy. He was happiest in the company of the rich and powerful, provided they tolerated his ideas and supported reform. Not surprisingly, Voltaire was frequently disappointed by eighteenth-century monarchs, like Frederick the Great in Prussia, who promised enlightenment but sought mainly to increase their own power and that of their armies.

Perhaps the happiest decision of Voltaire's life was to team up with the scientist and philosophe Madame du Châtelet (1706–1749). Together they read Newton, although she became the more proficient mathematician. Before her death during the birth of their child, Madame du Châtelet made the only French translation of the *Principia,* explicated it, and trained scientists, who took up Newtonian ideas and spread them throughout western Europe.

POLITICAL THOUGHT

With the exception of Machiavelli (see page 310) in the Renaissance and Thomas Hobbes and the republicans during the midcentury English Revo-

lution, the Enlightenment produced the greatest originality in modern political thought witnessed in the West up to that time. Three major European thinkers and a host of minor ones wrote treatises on politics that remain relevant to this day: John Locke, *Two Treatises of Government* (1690); Baron de la Brède et de Montesquieu, *The Spirit of the Laws* (1748); and Jean Jacques Rousseau, *The Social Contract* (1762). All repudiated the divine right of kings and strove to check the power of monarchy; each offered different formulas for achieving that goal. These major political theorists of the Enlightenment were also aware of the writings of Machiavelli and Hobbes and, although often disagreeing with them, borrowed some of their ideas.

During the Renaissance, Machiavelli (d. 1527) had analyzed politics in terms of power, fortune, and the ability of the individual ruler; he did not call in God to justify the power of princes or to explain their demise. Machiavelli had also preferred a republican form of government to monarchy, and his republican vision did not lose its appeal during the Enlightenment. Very late in the century, most liberal theorists recognized that the republican form of government, or at the least the virtues practiced by citizens in a republic, offered the only alternative to the corruption and repression associated with absolute monarchy.

Political thinkers of the Enlightenment were ambivalent toward much of the writing of Thomas Hobbes (1588–1679). All, however, liked his belief that self-interest is a valid reason for engaging in political activity and his refusal to bring God into his system to justify the power of kings. Hobbes said that power did not rest on divine right but arose out of a contract made among men who agreed to elevate the state, and hence the monarch, to a position of power over them. That contract, once made, could not be broken. As a consequence, the power of the government, whether embodied in a king or a parliament, was absolute.

Hobbes published his major work, *Leviathan,* in 1651, soon after England had been torn by civil war; thus, he was obsessed with the issue of political stability. He feared that, left to their own devices, men would kill one another; the "war of all against all"[5] would prevail without the firm hand of a sovereign to stop it. Hobbes's vision of human nature was dark and forbidding. In the state of nature, the original men had lived lives that could only have been "nasty, brutish, and short." Their sole recourse was to set up a power over themselves that would restrain them. For Hobbes, the state was, as he put it, a "mortal god," the only guarantee of peace and stability. He was the first political thinker to realize the extraordinary power that had come into existence with the creation of strong centralized governments. Most Enlightenment theorists, however, beginning with John Locke, denied that governments possessed absolute power over their subjects, and to that extent they repudiated Hobbes. Many European thinkers of the eighteenth century, including Rousseau, also rejected Hobbes's gloomy view that human nature is greedy and warlike. Yet Hobbes lurks in the background of the Enlightenment. He is the first wholly secular political theorist, and he sounded the death knell for theories of the divine right of kings. The Enlightenment theorists started where he left off.

Locke

Probably the most widely read political philosopher during the first half of the eighteenth century was John Locke (1632–1704). Locke came to maturity in the late 1650s, and like so many of his contemporaries, he was drawn to science. Although he became a medical doctor, his major interest lay in politics and political theory. His *Two Treatises of Government* was seen as a justification for the English Revolution of 1688–89 and the notion of government by consent of the people. (Although they were published in 1690, Locke wrote the treatises before the English Revolution; that fact, however, was not known during the Enlightenment.)

Locke's theory, in its broad outlines, stated that the right to govern derived from the consent of the governed and was a form of contract. When people gave their consent to a government, they expected it to govern justly, protect their property, and ensure certain liberties for the propertied. If a government attempted to rule absolutely and arbitrarily—if it violated the natural rights of the individual—it reneged on its contract and forfeited the loyalty of its subjects. Such a government could legitimately be overthrown. Locke believed that a constitutional government that limited the power of rulers was the best defense of property and individual rights. He also

advocated religious toleration for those religious groups whose beliefs did not threaten the state. Locke denied toleration to Catholics because of their association with the Stuarts and to atheists because their oaths to God could not be trusted. He also promoted the necessity for education, particularly for those who saw themselves as the natural leaders of society. And not least, he advocated commerce and trade as one of the foundations of England's national strength.

Late in the eighteenth century, Locke's ideas were used to justify liberal revolutions in both Europe and America. His *Treatises of Government* had been translated into French early in the century by Huguenot refugees. These Protestant victims of French absolutism, persecuted for their religion, saw that the importance of Locke's political philosophy was not simply in his use of contract theory to justify constitutional government; he also asserted that the community could take up arms against its sovereign in the name of the natural rights of liberty and property. Locke's ideas about the foundation of government had greater impact on the Continent and in America during the eighteenth century than in England.

Montesquieu

Baron de la Brède et de Montesquieu (1689–1755) was a French aristocrat who, like Voltaire, visited England late in the 1720s and knew the writings of Locke. Montesquieu had little sympathy for revolutions, but he did approve of constitutional monarchy. His primary concern was to check the unbridled authority of the French kings. In opposition to the Old Regime, Montesquieu proposed a balanced system of government, with an executive branch offset by a legislature whose members were drawn from the landed and educated elements in society. From his writings we derive our notion of government divided into branches. Montesquieu genuinely believed that the aristocracy possessed a natural and sacred obligation to rule and that their honor called them to serve the community. He also sought to fashion a government that channeled the interests and energies of its people, a government that was not bogged down in corruption and inefficiency. In stressing the rule of law and the importance of nonmonarchical authority, Montesquieu became a source for legitimating the authority of representative institutions. Hardly an advocate of democracy, Montesquieu was nonetheless seen as a powerful critic of royal absolutism. His writings, particularly *The Spirit of the Laws,* established him both as a major philosophe who possessed republican tendencies and as a critic of the Old Regime in France. Once again, innovative political thinking highlighted the failures of absolutist government and pointed to the need for some kind of representative assembly in every European country. In addition, Montesquieu's ideas on a balanced system of government found favor in the new American republic.

Rousseau

Not until the 1760s did democracy find its champion: Jean Jacques Rousseau (1712–1778). Rousseau based his politics on contract theory and his reading of Hobbes. For Rousseau, the people choose their government and, in so doing, effectively give birth to civil society. But he further demanded (in contrast to Hobbes) that the contract be constantly renewed and that government be made immediately and directly responsible to the will of the people. *The Social Contract* opened with this stirring cry for reform, "Man is born free; and everywhere he is in chains," and went on to ask how that restriction could be changed. Freedom is in the very nature of man: "to renounce liberty is to renounce being a man, to surrender the rights of humanity and even its duties."[6]

Rousseau's political ideal was the city-state of ancient Greece, where men (but not women) participated actively and directly in politics and were willing to sacrifice self-interest to the community's needs. To the ancient Greek, said Rousseau, the state was a moral association that made him a better person, and good citizenship was the highest form of excellence. In contrast, modern society was prey to many conflicting interests; the rich and powerful used the state to preserve their advantages and power, and the poor and powerless viewed it as an oppressor. Consequently, the obedience to law, the devotion to the state, and the freedom that had characterized the Greek city-state had been lost.

In *The Social Contract,* Rousseau tried to resolve the conflict between individual freedom and the demands of the state. His solution was a small state, modeled after the Greek city-state.

JEAN JACQUES ROUSSEAU ALONE, A SELF-EXILE FROM THE CITY. Rousseau viewed nature and solitude as curative. He also advocated reading for introspection and enlightenment. (*Photographie Bulloz*)

Such a state, said Rousseau, should be based on the *general will:* that which is best for the community, which expresses its common interests. Rousseau wanted laws of the state to coincide with the general will. He felt that people have the wisdom to arrive at laws that serve the common good, but to do so, they must set aside selfish interests for the good of the community. For Rousseau, freedom consisted of obeying laws prescribed by citizens inspired by the general will. The citizens themselves must constitute the lawmaking body; lawmaking cannot be entrusted to a single person or a small group.

In Rousseau's view, those who disobey laws— who act according to their private will rather than in accordance with the general will as expressed in law—degrade themselves and undermine the community. Therefore, government has the right to force citizens to be obedient, to compel them to exercise their individual wills in the proper way. He left the problem of minority rights unresolved.

No philosopher of the Enlightenment was more dangerous to the Old Regime than Rousseau. His ideas were perceived as truly revolutionary: a direct challenge to the power of kings, the power of the church, and the power of aristocrats. Although Rousseau thought that many leaders of the Enlightenment had been corrupted by easy living and the life of the salons, with their attendant aristocrats and dandies, he nevertheless earned an uneasy place in the ranks of the philosophes. In the French Revolution, his name would be invoked to justify democracy, and of all the philosophes, Rousseau would probably have been the least horrified by the early phase of that revolutionary upheaval.

SOCIAL THOUGHT

Rousseau looked upon society as the corrupter of human beings, who, left to their own devices, were inherently virtuous and freedom-loving. A wide spectrum of thinkers in the Enlightenment also viewed society, if not as corrupting, at least as needing constant reform. Some enlightened critics were prepared to work with those in power to bring about social reforms. Other philosophes believed that the key to reform lay not in social and political institutions, but in changing the general mentality through education and knowledge.

Epistemology and Education

Just as Locke's *Two Treatises of Government* helped shape the political thought of the Enlightenment, his *Essay Concerning Human Understanding* (1689) provided the theoretical foundations for an unprecedented interest in education. Locke's view that at birth the mind is blank—a clean slate, or *tabula rasa*—had two important implications. First, if human beings were not born with innate ideas, then they were not, as Christianity taught, inherently sinful. Second, a person's environment was the decisive force in shaping that person's character and intelligence. Nine of every ten men, wrote Locke, "are good or evil, useful or not, [because of] their education." Such a theory was eagerly received by the reform-minded philosophes, who preferred attributing wickedness to faulty institutions, im-

proper rearing, and poor education rather than to a defective human nature.

"Locke has unfolded to man the nature of human reason," Voltaire wrote in his *Letters*. For the Enlightenment, the proper study of humanity addressed the process by which people can and do know. Locke had said that individuals take the information produced by their senses and reflect on it; in that way, they arrive at complex ideas. Aside from an environment promoting learning, education obviously requires the active participation of students. Merely receiving knowledge not tested by their own sense experience is inadequate.

More treatises were written on education during the eighteenth century than in all previous centuries combined. On the Continent, where the clergy controlled many schools and all the universities, the educated laity began to demand state regulation and inspection of educational facilities. This insistence was one practical expression of the growing discontent with the clergy and their independent authority. By the second half of the century, new schools and universities in Prussia, Belgium, Austria, Hungary, and Russia attempted to teach practical subjects suited to the interests of the laity. Predictably, science was given a special place in these new institutions. In France, for all the interest in education on the part of the philosophes, by 1789 probably only 50 percent of the men and about 20 percent of women were literate.

The standards of education for girls and women were appalling. Only a few philosophes, mostly women, and the occasional clergyman who had seen firsthand the poor quality of female education in reading and writing called for reform. But reform did not come till after 1800, when industrialization put more women in the work force and required some literacy. As for higher education, women were excluded, with a few exceptions. Madame du Châtelet in France had studied mathematics with a private tutor; and in Italy, Laura Bassi became the first woman to teach in a European university, at Bologna. In the Netherlands, women founded a scientific academy in 1785. However, these were isolated waves in a sea of indifference.

Generally, Protestant countries were better at ensuring basic literacy and numeracy for boys and probably also for girls. Lutheran Prussia and Presbyterian Scotland excelled in the field of educa-

The Board of Trustees of the National Museums and Galleries on Merseyside, Walker Art Gallery

MARY WOLLSTONECRAFT

One of the founders of modern feminism and a deeply committed defender of liberty, human rights, and the French Revolution, Mary Wollstonecraft (1759–1797) came to maturity in a circle of English radicals. Her friends included Richard Price and Joseph Priestley, and she also knew Thomas Paine. Although she received little formal education, she taught herself languages, made a living as a translator, read Rousseau critically, and began an intellectual odyssey that took her from liberal Protestantism to freethinking and possibly atheism. She went to France during its revolution and wanted to raise her daughter there because she believed that in France she would be freer. By far her most famous book is *The Vindication of the Rights of Women* (1792), a classic statement of women's rights and the causes of prejudice and inequality. With the two hundredth anniversary of Wollstonecraft's famous book, her writings have been revived, and she has been placed at the center of the European Enlightenment as an embodiment of its belief in science and the possibility of human emancipation.

tion, but for very different reasons. In Prussia, Frederick the Great decreed universal public education for boys as part of his effort to surpass the level of technical expertise found in other countries. His educational policy was another example of his using the Enlightenment to increase the power of the central government. In Scotland, the improvements in education were largely sponsored by the established Presbyterian (Calvinist) church. The Protestant universities were by and large more progressive intellectually than their Catholic counterparts. The Jesuits, for instance, resisted teaching the new science. By contrast, medicine at the universities of Edinburgh—along with that of the University of Leiden in the Netherlands—became the most advanced of the century. But ironically, the universities were never at the forefront of the Enlightenment. For the latest ideas, one went to the salons rather than consulted the professors.

That fact fitted in very well with Locke's doctrine that knowledge comes primarily through experience. Rousseau took it up and brought it to its logical conclusion. In *Émile* (1762), he argued that individuals learn from nature, from people, or from things. Indeed, Rousseau wanted the early years of a child's education to be centered on developing the senses, and not spent with the child chained to a schoolroom desk. Later, attention would be paid to intellectual pursuits, and then finally to morality. Rousseau grasped a fundamental principle of modern psychology: the child is not a small adult, and childhood is not merely preparation for adulthood, but a particular stage in human development, with its own distinguishing characteristics.

Rousseau appealed especially to women to be virtuous and to protect their children from social convention, that is, to teach their children about honesty and sentiment. There were problems with Rousseau's educational system. He would make the family the major educational force, and he wanted the products of such education to be cosmopolitan and enlightened individuals, singularly free from superstition and prejudice. However, women (whom Rousseau would confine to the home) were to bear the burden of instilling enlightenment, although they had little experience of the world beyond the family and in France their education was entirely in the hands of nuns.

Rousseau's contradictions, particularly about women, sprang in large measure from his desperate search for an alternative to aristocratic mores and clerical authority. He also shared in the gender bias of his age, although what may seem bias to us may also have reflected his belief that women sought the home as a solace and refuge. Certainly, many women read him critically, but essentially as an ally and defender.

Humanitarianism

Crime and Punishment   No society founded on the principles of the Enlightenment could condone the torture of prisoners and the inhumanity of a corrupt legal system. On those points, all the philosophes were clear, and they had plenty of evidence from their own societies on which to base their condemnation of torture and the inhumanity of the criminal justice system.

Whether an individual was imprisoned for unpaid debts or for banditry or murder, prison conditions differed little. Prisoners were often starved or exposed to disease, or both. In many Continental countries, where torture was still legal, prisoners could be subjected to brutal interrogation or to random punishment. In 1777, English reformer John Howard published a report in England and Wales that documented how prisoners went without food or medical assistance.

To imagine that the enlightened reformers invented the techniques of discipline and punishment—as some philosophers in the twentieth century have thought—denies the historical record. It was the reformers of the Enlightenment who began to agitate against the prison conditions of the day. Even if torture was illegal, as was only the case in England, prison conditions were often as harmful as torture to the physical and mental health of inmates.

Although there is something particularly reprehensible about the torturer, his skills were consciously applauded in many countries during the eighteenth century. Fittingly, the most powerful critique of the European system of punishment came from Italy, where the Inquisition and its torture chambers had reigned with little opposition for centuries. In Milan, during the early 1760s, the Enlightenment had made very gradual inroads, and in a small circle of reformers the practices of the Inquisition and the relationship between church and state in the matter of criminal justice were avidly discussed.

Out of that intellectual ferment came one of the most important books of the Enlightenment: *Of Crime and Punishment* (1764), by the Milanese reformer Cesare Beccaria (1738–1794). For centuries, sin and crime had been wedded in the eyes of the church; the function of the state was to punish crime because it was a manifestation of sin. Beccaria cut through that thicket of moralizing and argued that the church should concern itself with sin; it should abandon its prisons and courts. The state should concern itself with crimes against society, and the purpose of punishment should be to reintegrate the individual into society. Punishment should be swift but intended to rehabilitate.

Beccaria also inquired into the causes of crime. Abandoning the concept of sin, Beccaria, rather like Rousseau, who perceived injustice and corruption in the very fabric of society, regarded private property as the root of social injustice and hence the root of crime. Pointedly, he asked, "What are these laws I must respect, that they leave such a huge gap between me and the rich? Who made these laws? Rich and powerful men. . . . Let us break these fatal connections. . . . let us attack injustice at its source."[7]

Beccaria's attackers labeled him a *socialist*— the first time (1765) that term was used—by which they meant that Beccaria paid attention only to people as social creatures and that he wanted a society of free and equal citizens. In contrast, the defenders of the use of torture and capital punishment, and of the necessity of social inequality, argued that Beccaria's teachings would lead to chaos and to the loss of all property rights and legitimate authority. These critics sensed the utopian aspect of Beccaria's thought. His humanitarianism was not directed toward the reform of the criminal justice system alone;

ENGRAVING, NEWGATE PRISON, EIGHTEENTH CENTURY. Prison conditions during the Age of Enlightenment were appalling. Here, a manacled man struggles with a wheelbarrow, and two others are led off to the gallows. Meanwhile a guard watches over the dungeon filled with bound prisoners, who were as often debtors as criminals.

he sought to restructure society in such a way as to render crime far less prevalent and, whenever possible, to reeducate its perpetrators.

When Beccaria's book and then the author himself turned up in Paris, the philosophes greeted them with universal acclaim. All the leaders of the period—Voltaire, Rousseau, Denis Diderot, and the atheist d'Holbach—embraced one or another of Beccaria's views. But if the criminal justice system and the schools were subject to scrutiny by enlightened critics, what did the philosophes have to say about slavery, the most pernicious of all Western institutions?

Slavery　On both sides of the Atlantic during the eighteenth century, criticism of slavery was growing. At first, it came from religious thinkers like the Quakers, whose own religious version of enlightenment predated the European-wide phenomenon by several decades. The Quakers were born out of the turmoil of the English Revolution, and their strong adherence to democratic ideas grew out of their conviction that the light of God's truth works in every man and woman. Many philosophes on both sides of the Atlantic knew Quaker thought, and Voltaire, who had mixed feelings about slavery, and Benjamin Franklin, who condemned it, admired the Quakers and their principles.

On the problem of slavery, the Enlightenment was strangely ambivalent. In an ideal world—just about all philosophes agreed—slavery would not exist. But the world was not ideal, and given human wickedness, greed, and lust for power,

Voltaire thought that both slavery and exploitation might be inevitable. "The human race," Voltaire wrote in his *Philosophical Dictionary* (1764), "constituted as it is, cannot subsist unless there be an infinite number of useful individuals possessed of no property at all."[8] Diderot thought that slavery was probably immoral but concluded that, given the importance of slavery in the colonies and the fact that the French monarchy provided no leadership in changing the situation, there was no point in trying to abolish slavery at this time. Indeed, not until 1794, and only after agonized debate, did the French government, no longer a monarchy, finally abolish slavery in its colonies.

It must be remembered that political thinkers of the Enlightenment, among them Locke (who condoned slavery) and Montesquieu (whose ideas were used to condone it), rejected God-given political authority and argued for the rights of property holders and for social utility as the foundations of good government. Those criteria, property and utility, played right into the hands of the proslavery apologists. Montesquieu condemned slavery, but that did not stop its apologists from using his ideas about the relationship between hot climates and sloth to justify making Africans into slaves.

Yet the Enlightenment must also be credited with bringing the problem of slavery to the forefront of public discussion in Europe and the American colonies. The utility argument cut both ways. If the principle held, as so many philosophes argued, that human happiness was the greatest good, how could slavery be justified? In his short novel *Candide,* Voltaire has his title character confront the spectacle of a young African who has had his leg and arm cut off merely because it is the custom of a country. Candide's philosophical optimism is shattered as he reflects on the human price paid by this slave, who harvested the sugar that Europeans enjoyed so abundantly. Throughout the eighteenth century, the emphasis placed by the Enlightenment on moral sensibility produced a literature that used shock to emphasize over and over again, and with genuine revulsion, the inhumanity of slavery.

By the second half of the century, a new generation of philosophes launched strongly worded attacks on slavery. With Rousseau in the vanguard, they condemned slavery as a violation of the natural rights of man. In a volume issued in 1755, the great *Encyclopedia* of the Enlightenment, edited by Diderot, condemned slavery in no uncertain terms: "There is not a single one of these hapless souls . . . who does not have the right to be declared free . . . since neither his ruler nor his father nor anyone else had the right to dispose of his freedom."[9] That statement appeared in thousands of copies and various editions of an encyclopedia that was probably the most influential publication resulting from the French Enlightenment. Indeed, French writers led the enlightened attacks on slavery. The Dutch novelist Betje Wolff had to translate French writers when, in 1790, she launched her attack on the Dutch slave trade.

These writers probably tipped the scales to put the followers of the Enlightenment in the antislavery camp. But that victory was clouded by much ambiguous language coming straight from the pens of some of Europe's supposedly most enlightened thinkers and by their prejudice against blacks as non-Europeans.

Social Equality   The humanitarian impulse inevitably entailed taking a cold, hard look at social inequalities, which were very obvious in a century when dress, speech, body gestures, and even smell told all. The poor were visibly underfed; workers wore the costumes of their trade; aristocrats, both men and women, dressed in elaborate wigs, shoes, silks, jewels, and lace. Devout Calvinist women often wore black, and only their rings or headpieces betrayed their social status. How could the ideal of human equality be conceptualized in such a society?

Voltaire despised the lower classes. Kant said that women should feel and not reason: "her philosophy is not to reason, but to sense."[10] Women had few property rights, and the poor had even fewer; the Lockean contract seemed irrelevant to their circumstances. Yet in the American and French Revolutions, the leaders proclaimed human equality as an ideal. But though France freed the slaves in the colonies, it closed down women's political clubs. In the new American republic, slavery remained; women, however, began to take a more active role in civil society. Modern critics condemn the Enlightenment for being duplicitous or inconsistent, but historical reality can only be understood in relation to the backward alternatives offered by absolute monarchs and established churches.

More than any other previous historical movement, the Enlightenment put human equality on the mental agenda of Western societies. Men and women could meet as equals at social gatherings, the new novels could depict the suffering of women at the hands of brutal men or describe the wretched life of the poor, women could travel abroad as never before, and traveling scientific lecturers frequently sought their tuition. Leisure, literacy, public and secular culture, fiery journalism, local newspapers, travelers' reports, even the new and naughty pornography, all attacked the superstitions and contradictions that centuries of custom had enshrined. The new science pointed to a universe where matter was everywhere the same—the atoms are all equal—and it universally obeyed impersonal and impartial laws. The struggle to achieve democratic equality—hence, the dilemma of modern life—first came to the surface in countless acts of reading and conversing in the new enlightened and urban culture.

ECONOMIC THOUGHT

The Enlightenment's emphasis on property as the foundation for individual rights and its search for uniform laws inspired by Newton's scientific achievement led to the development of the science of economics. Appropriately, that intellectual achievement occurred in the most advanced capitalistic nation in Europe, Great Britain. Not only were the British in the vanguard of capitalist expansion; by the third quarter of the eighteenth century, that expansion had also started the Industrial Revolution. Britain's new factories and markets for the manufacture and distribution of goods provided a natural laboratory, where theorists, schooled in the Enlightenment's insistence on observation and experimentation, could watch the ebb and flow of capitalist production and distribution. In contrast to its harsh criticisms of existing institutions and old elites, the Enlightenment on the whole approved of the independent businessman—the entrepreneur. And there was no one more approving than Adam Smith (1732–1790), whose *Wealth of Nations* (1776) became a kind of bible for those who regarded capitalist activity as uniformly worthwhile and never to be inhibited by outside regulation.

Throughout the seventeenth century in England, there had been a long tradition of economic thought. The resulting ideology stressed independent initiative and the freedom of market forces to determine the value of money and the goods it can buy. By 1700, English economic thought was already well ahead of what could be found on the Continent, with the exception of some Dutch writings. That sophistication undoubtedly reflected the complexity of market life in cities like London and Amsterdam.

One important element in seventeenth-century economic thought, as well as in the most advanced thinking on ethics, was the role of self-interest. Far from being considered crude or socially dangerous, it was seen as a good thing, to be accepted and even encouraged. In the mid-seventeenth century, Hobbes took the view that self-interest lay at the root of political action. By the end of the century, Locke argued that government, rather than primarily restraining the extremes of human greed and the search for power, should promote the interests of its citizens. By the middle of the eighteenth century, enlightened theorists all over Europe—especially in England, Scotland, and France—had decided that self-interest was the foundation of all human actions and that at every turn government should aid people in expressing their interests and thus in finding true happiness.

Of course, in the area of economic life, government had for centuries regulated most aspects of the market. The classic economic theory behind such regulation was mercantilism. Mercantilists believed that a constant shortage of riches—bullion, goods, whatever—existed and that governments must so direct economic activity in their states as to compete successfully with other nations for a share of the world's scarce resources. There was also another assumption implicit in mercantilist theory: that money has a "real" value, which governments must protect. The value is not to be determined solely by market forces.

It required enormous faith in the inherent usefulness of self-interest to assert that government should cease regulating economic activity and that the market should be allowed to be free. The doctrine of *laissez faire*—leaving the market to its own devices—was the centerpiece of Adam

MAP 18.1 European Expansion, 1715 ▶

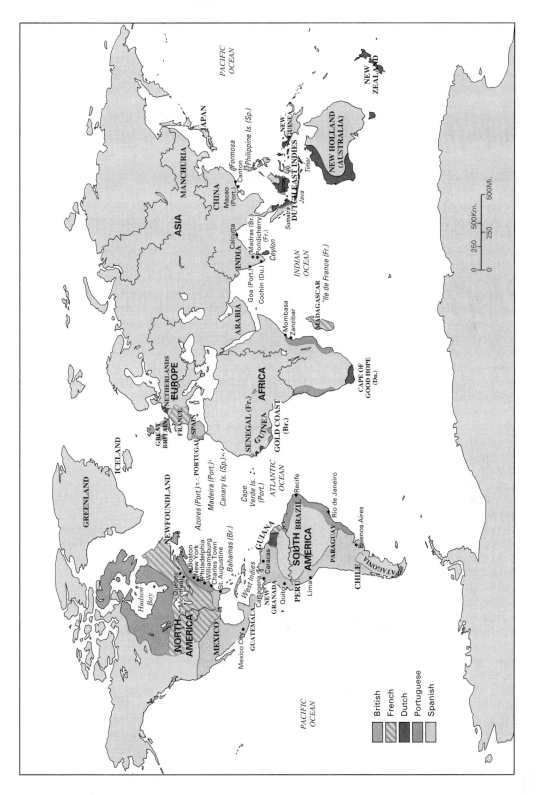

PACIFIC
OCEAN

NEW
ZEALAND

NEW HOLLAND
(AUSTRALIA)

NEW
GUINEA

DUTCH EAST INDIES

JAPAN

MANCHURIA

ASIA

CHINA

Macao
(Port.)

Canton

(Formosa)

Philippine Is. (Sp.)

Borneo

Timor

Java

Sumatra

INDIA

Calcutta

Madras (Br.)

*Pondicherry
(Fr.)*

Ceylon

Goa (Port.)

Cochin (Du.)

*INDIAN
OCEAN*

Île de France (Fr.)

ARABIA

MADAGASCAR

Mombasa

Zanzibar

NETHERLANDS

EUROPE

AFRICA

GUINEA

SENEGAL (Fr.)

GOLD COAST
(Br.)

CAPE OF
GOOD HOPE
(Du.)

GREAT
BRITAIN

FRANCE

SPAIN

PORTUGAL

ICELAND

GREENLAND

NEWFOUNDLAND

Azores (Port.)

Madeira (Port.)

Canary Is. (Sp.)

*Cape
Verde Is.
(Port.)*

*ATLANTIC
OCEAN*

Recife

Rio de Janeiro

Buenos Aires

SOUTH
AMERICA

BRAZIL

PARAGUAY

PATAGONIA

CHILE

PERU

Lima

NEW
GRANADA

Quito

GUIANA

Caracas

Cartagena

Bahamas (Br.)

West Indies

Boston
New York
Philadelphia
Williamsburg
Charles Town
St. Augustine

Quebec
Montreal

*Hudson
Bay*

NORTH
AMERICA

MEXICO

Mexico City

GUATEMALA

PACIFIC
OCEAN

500 Mi.

500 Km.

250

250

British

French

Dutch

Portuguese

Spanish

445

Smith's massive economic study on the origins of the wealth of nations.

As a professor in Glasgow, Scotland, Smith actually went to factories to observe the work. He was one of the first theorists to see the importance of the division of labor in making possible the manufacture of more and cheaper consumer goods. Smith viewed labor as the critical factor in a capitalist economy: the value of money, or of an individual for that matter, rested on the ability to buy labor or the byproducts of labor, namely goods and services. According to *The Wealth of Nations,* "labor is the real measure of the exchangeable value of all commodities."[11] The value of labor is in turn determined by market forces, by supply and demand. Before the invention of money or capital, labor belonged to the laborer, but in the money and market society, which had evolved since the Middle Ages, labor belonged to the highest bidder.

Smith was not bothered by the apparent randomness of market forces, although he was distressed by signs of greed and exploitation. Beneath the superficial chaos of commerce, he saw order—the same order that he saw in physical nature through his understanding of the new science. He used the metaphor of "the invisible hand" to explain the source of this order; by that he probably meant Newton's regulatory God, made very distant by Smith, who was a deist. That hand would invisibly reconcile self-interest to the common or public interest. With the image of the invisible hand, Smith expressed his faith in the rationality of commercial society and laid the first principle for the modern science of capitalist economics. He did not mean to license the oppression of the poor and the laborer. Statements in *The Wealth of Nations* such as "Landlords, like all other men, love to reap where they never sowed" or "Whenever there is great property, there is great inequality"[12] reveal Smith to be a moralist. Yet he knew of no means to stop the exploitation of labor. He believed that its purchase at market value ensured the working of commercial society, and he assumed that the supply of cheap labor was inexhaustible.

British theorists like Smith looked at commerce and industry as the keys to national wealth. But on the Continent most theorists saw agriculture, and not industry, as the engine of wealth and progress. This physiocratic philosophy, as it was called, was particularly commonplace in France, where the richness and diversity of the climate produced fine crops and luxury items such as wine and perfume from flowers and herbs. Despite this relative abundance, physiocratic doctrine reluctantly permitted state intervention to ensure that food would be evenly distributed. Right up to the 1780s, the poor needed and expected such intervention. But because of their dedication to agriculture and the commerce that came with it, few physiocrats foresaw the immense importance that manufacturing and steam power would assume by 1800.

For all their differences, Smith and the French physiocrats shared certain characteristics common to enlightened economic theorists. They wanted to find the laws that regulated economic life; in that search they imitated the successes of the new science. In addition, they believed that progress was possible and that wealth and well-being could be increased for all. Knowledge is progressive; hence, by implication, the human condition also yields to constant improvement. This vision sometimes made the theorists myopic when it came to poverty and the injustice of the market. What they bequeathed to the modern age was a belief in the inevitability of progress wedded to capitalism and free trade—a belief that remains powerful to this day.

THE HIGH ENLIGHTENMENT

More than any other political system in western Europe, the old Regime in France was directly threatened by the doctrines and reforming impulse of the Enlightenment. The Roman Catholic church was deeply entrenched in every aspect of life: landownership, control over the universities and the presses, and access to both the court and, through the pulpit, the people. For decades the church had brought its influence to bear against the philosophes, yet by 1750, the Enlightenment had penetrated learned circles and academies in Paris and the provinces. After 1750, censorship of the press was relaxed by a new censor deeply influenced by Enlightenment ideals. In fact, censorship had produced the opposite of the desired effect: the more irreligious and atheistic the book or manuscript, the more attractive and sought-after it became.

By the 1740s, the fashion among proponents

FRONTISPIECE BY C. N. COCHIN, DIDEROT'S *ENCY-CLOPEDIA,* 1751. Today's scholars still debate the symbolism being used here by Diderot and his fellow authors. Some have seen it as masonic, others emphasize the gendered quality of the scene, with the typical motif of truth represented by a woman. Diderot did believe in women's education, but he had some very stereotypical things to say about them nonetheless. (*Bettmann*)

of the Enlightenment was to seek an encyclopedic format for presenting their ideas. This form of writing was the natural byproduct of the Enlightenment's desire to encompass all learning. After Bayle's *Dictionary,* the first successful encyclopedia was published in England by Ephraim Chambers in 1728, and before too long, a plan was under way for its translation into French. A leading Freemason in France, the Chevalier Ramsay, even advocated that all the Masonic lodges in Europe should make a financial contribution to this effort, but few, if any, responded to the call.

Four aggressive Parisian publishers took up the task of producing the encyclopedia. One of them had had some shady dealings in clandestine litera-

ture, which had acquainted him with the more irreligious and daring philosophes in Paris; that is how he knew the young Denis Diderot (1713–1784), who had spent six months in jail for his philosophical and pornographic writings. Out of that consortium of publishers and philosophes came the most important book of the Enlightenment, Diderot's *Encyclopedia.* Published in 1751 and in succeeding years and editions, the *Encyclopedia* initiated a new stage in the history of Enlightenment publishing. In the process, it brought to the forefront pantheistic and materialistic ideas, which, until that time, only the most radical freethinkers in England and the Netherlands had openly written about. The new era thus ushered in, called the High Enlightenment, was characterized by a violent attack on the church's privileges and the very foundations of Christian belief. From the 1750s to the 1780s, Paris shone as the capital of the Enlightenment. The philosophes were no longer a persecuted minority. Instead, they became cultural heroes. The *Encyclopedia* had to be read by anyone claiming to be educated.

In his preface to the *Encyclopedia,* Diderot's collaborator, Jean D'Alembert (c. 1717–1783), summed up the principles on which it had been compiled. In effect, he wrote a powerful summation of the Enlightenment's highest ideals. He also extolled Newton's science and gave a short description of its universal laws. The progress of geometry and mechanics in combination, d'Alembert wrote in his preface, "may be considered the most incontestable monument of the success to which the human mind can rise by its efforts."[13] In turn, he urged that revealed religion should be reduced to a few precepts to be practiced; religion should, he implied, be made scientific and rational. The *Encyclopedia* itself explicitly followed Bacon's admonition that the scientist should first of all be a collector of facts; in addition, it gave dozens of examples of useful new mechanical devices.

D'Alembert in the preface also praised the epistemology of Locke: all that is known, is known through the senses. He declared that all learning should be catalogued and readily available, that the printing press should enlighten, and that literary societies should encourage men of talent. These societies, he added, "should banish all inequalities that might exclude or discourage men who are endowed with talents that will enlighten others."[14]

During the High Enlightenment, reformers

dwelled increasingly on the Old Regime's inequalities, which seemed to stifle men of talent. The aristocracy and the clergy were not always talented, and seldom were they agitators for enlightenment and reform. Their privileges seemed increasingly less rational. By the 1780s, Paris had produced a new generation of philosophes, for whom Voltaire, Diderot, and Rousseau were aged or dead heroes. But these young authors found the life of the propagandist to be poor and solitary, and they looked at society's ills as victims rather than as reformers. They gained first-hand knowledge of the injustices catalogued so brilliantly by Rousseau in *The Social Contract.*

The High Enlightenment's systematic, sustained, and occasionally violent attacks on the clergy and the irrationality of privilege link that movement with the French Revolution. The link did not lie in the comfortable heresies of the great philosophes, ensconced as they were in the fashionable Parisian salons. Rather, it was to be found in the way those heresies were interpreted by a new generation of reformers—Marat and Robespierre among them—who in the early days of the Revolution used the Enlightenment as a mirror on which they reflected the evils of the Old Order.

EUROPEAN POLITICAL AND DIPLOMATIC DEVELOPMENTS

Warfare

The dreams of the philosophes seemed unable to forestall troublesome developments in power politics, war, and diplomacy. The century was dominated by two areas of extreme conflict: Anglo-French rivalry over control of territory in the New World and hegemony in northern Europe; and intense rivalry between Austria and Prussia over control of central Europe. These major powers, with their imperialistic ambitions, were led by cadres of aristocratic ministers or generals. The Enlightenment did little to displace the war-making role that had belonged to the aristocracy since the Middle Ages.

Yet even in international affairs, there was a growing realization, not unrelated to the propaganda of the philosophes, that extreme power held by one state would threaten the order and stability of the whole of Europe. By the early eighteenth century, every European state identified France, by virtue of its sheer wealth and size, as the major threat to European stability.

By then, France and England were the great rivals in the New World, although colonization had been well under way since the early sixteenth century. Spain had been the first sovereign state to establish an empire in America; located principally in South America and Central America, this empire was based on mining gold and silver, trade, and slaves. The English and the Dutch had followed, first as settlers and then also as slave traders, but their colonies lay to the north—in Virginia, New Amsterdam (later to become New York), and New England. Farther north, the French explored and exploited Canada and the region now known as the midwestern United States. Early in the eighteenth century, the Dutch and the Spanish had largely dropped out of the race for colonies in North America, leaving the field to the French and the English.

By the middle of the eighteenth century, the rivalry of these two powers for territory in the New World increased tension in the Old World. Earlier, the British had sought to contain the French colossus and ensure their historic trading interests in the Low Countries and the Rhineland by allying themselves with the Dutch Republic and the Austrians, who controlled what is today called Belgium. The alliance of the Maritime Powers (Britain and the Netherlands) with Austria provided the balance of power against France for the entire first half of the eighteenth century.

Meanwhile, Prussia under Frederick the Great was entering the ranks of the major powers. In 1740, Frederick launched an aggressive foreign policy against neighboring states and ruthlessly seized the Austrian province of Silesia. The forces of the new Austrian queen, Maria Theresa, were powerless to resist this kind of military onslaught. In two years, Prussia had acquired what was probably the largest territory captured by any Continental European state in that era. Silesia augmented the Prussian population by 50 percent, and Frederick also gained a relatively advanced textile manufacturing area. The Austrians never forgave his transgression.

MAP 18.2 Europe, 1789 ▶

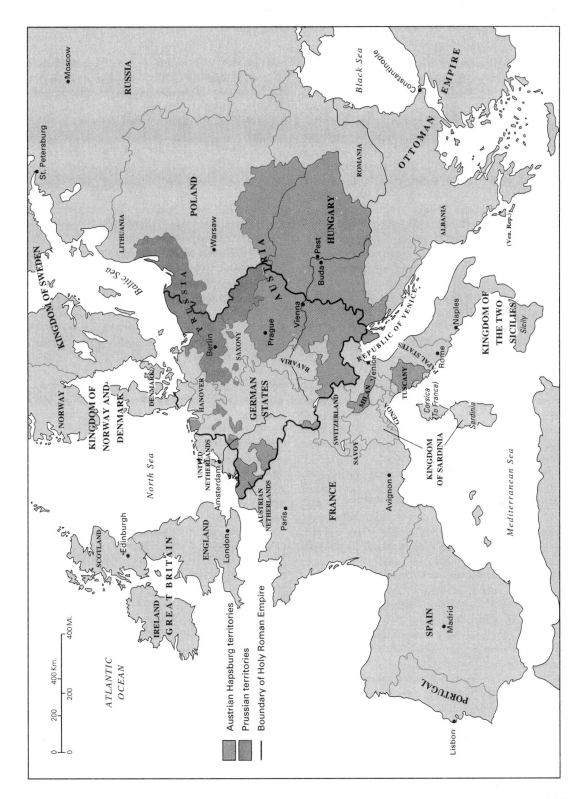

In 1756, Maria Theresa formed an alliance with France against Prussia; the ensuing Seven Years' War (1756–1763) involved every major European power. Austria's alliance with France in 1756, which ended the historic rivalry between France and the House of Hapsburg, is known as the "diplomatic revolution." The Austrians had grown to fear Prussia in the north more than they feared the French. From the Austrian point of view, Prussia had stolen Silesia in 1740, and regaining it was more important than preserving historic rivalries with France. On the French side, King Louis XV longed for an alliance with a Roman Catholic power and for peace in Europe so that France would be better able to wage war against Britain in the New World.

For their part, the British sought an ally in the newer, stronger Prussia, and reneged their traditional ally, Austria. Frederick the Great stood at the head of new state that was highly belligerent yet insecure, for all the European powers had reasons to want to keep Prussia weak and small. The Seven Years' War—which seesawed between the opponents, with French, Austrian, and Russian forces ranged against Frederick's Prussians—changed things little in Europe, but it did reveal the extraordinary power of the Prussian war machine. Prussia joined the ranks of the Great Powers.

Hostilities in North America tipped the balance of power there in favor of the English. From 1754 to 1763, the French and the English fought over their claims in the New World. England's victory in this conflict—which was also part of the Seven Years' War—led ultimately to the American Revolution. England secured its claim to control the colonies of the eastern seaboard, a market that would enrich its industrialists of the next generation enormously—although, from the colonists' point of view, unjustly.

While the major western European powers were growing stronger, some eastern European countries were falling further under the domination of the Ottoman (Turkish) Empire as the result of warfare. Only Hungary decidedly benefited from the wars led by Austria against the Turks. With its new independence finally secured from the Turks in 1718, Hungary entered an era of peace and enlightenment.

Empires and nation-states were the beneficiaries of eighteenth-century war and diplomacy. Only in the Dutch Republic did a little-noticed revolution in 1747–48 provide any indication that the Great Powers or the merchant capitalists had anything to fear from their home populations. The Dutch Revolution was led by men who identified with the Enlightenment and who wanted to reform the institutions of government. Inspired by the restoration of the House of Orange, Amsterdam rose in a democratic rebellion, headed by a coalition of small merchants and minor philosophes. They failed to effect any meaningful changes, but the calls they made for reform and renewal would be heard again in Amsterdam in 1787 and in Paris in 1789. On the latter occasion, the world would listen. For most of the eighteenth century, however, warfare seemed only to confirm the internal security and stability of the ruling monarchs and elites controlling most European states.

Enlightened Despotism

Enlightened despotism, an apparent contradiction in terms, was used as a phrase by the French philosophe Diderot as early as the 1760s. Wherever the philosophes used this phrase, it referred to an ideal shared by many of them: the strong monarch who would implement rational reforms, removing obstacles to freedom and allowing the laws of nature to work, particularly in trade, commerce, and against book censorship. When historians use the term *enlightened despotism,* they generally are describing the reigns of specific European monarchs and their ministers: Frederick the Great in Prussia; Catherine the Great in Russia; Charles III in Spain; Maria Theresa and, to a greater extent, her son Joseph II in Austria; and Louis XV in France.

These eighteenth-century monarchs instituted specific reforms in education, trade, and commerce and against the clergy. This type of enlightened government must be understood in context: these countries developed late relative to the older states of Europe. Prussia, Austria, and Russia had to move very quickly if they were to catch up to the degree of centralization achieved in England and France. And when monarchies in France and Spain also occasionally adopted techniques associated with enlightened despotism, they generally did so to compete against a more advanced rival—for example, France against England and Spain against France.

Austria In the course of the eighteenth century, Austria became a major centralized state as a result of the reforms of Charles VI and his successors (see Chapter 16). Although Catholic and devout at home, Charles allied himself abroad with Protestant Europe against France. In the newly acquired Austrian Netherlands, he supported the progressive and reforming elements in the nobility, which opposed the old aristocracy and clergy.

His daughter Maria Theresa (1740–1780) continued this pattern, and the Austrian administration became one of the most innovative and progressive on the Continent. Many of its leading ministers, like the Comte du Cobenzl in the Netherlands or Gerard van Swieten, Joseph II's great reforming minister, were Freemasons. This movement often attracted progressive Catholics (as well as Protestants and freethinkers), who despised what they regarded as the medieval outlook of the traditional clergy.

Dynastic consolidation and warfare did contribute decisively to the creation of the Austrian state. But in the eighteenth century, the intellectual and cultural forces of the Enlightenment enabled the state to establish an efficient system of government and a European breadth of vision. With these attributes, Austria came to rival (and, in regard to Spain, surpass) the older, more established states in Europe. Frustrated in their German territories, the Austrian Hapsburgs concentrated their attention increasingly on their eastern states. Vienna gave them a natural power base, and Catholic religiosity gradually united the ruling elites in Bohemia and Hungary with their Hapsburg kings. Hapsburg power created a dynastic state in Austria, yet all efforts to consolidate the German part of the empire and to establish effective imperial rule met with failure. Also problematic were Joseph II's interventions in the southern Netherlands. He offended the clergy without winning liberal support. Revolution erupted in Brussels in 1787.

Prussia German unification proceeded very slowly, and even enlightened despotism could not achieve it. Under the most famous and enlightened Hohenzollerns of the eighteenth century, Prussian absolutism (see Chapter 16) acquired some unique and resilient features. Frederick II, the Great (1740–1786), pursued a policy of religious toleration and, in so doing, attracted French Protestant refugees, who had manufacturing and commercial skills. Intellectual dissidents, such as Voltaire, were also attracted to Prussia. Voltaire eventually went home disillusioned with this new Prussian "enlightened despotism," but not before Frederick had used him and in the process acquired a reputation for learning. By inviting various refugees from French clerical oppression, Frederick gave Berlin a minor reputation as a center for Enlightenment culture. But alongside Frederick's courtship of the French philosophes, with their enlightened ideals, there remained the reality of Prussian militarism and the serfdom of its peasants.

Yet the Hohenzollern dynasty succeeded in creating a viable state, built by the labor of its serfs and the power of its Junker-controlled army. This state managed to survive as a monarchy until World War I. By the middle of the eighteenth century, this small nation, of no more than 2.5 million inhabitants, exercised inordinate influence in European affairs because of its military prowess.

Prussian absolutism rested on the nationally conscripted army and the Junker class, and its economy was state-directed and financed. Its court expenses were held to a minimum; most state expenditures went into maintaining an army of 200,000 troops, the largest in relation to population for all Europe.

Russia Russia during the eighteenth century made significant strides, under various monarchs, toward joining the European state system. During the reign of Peter the Great (1682–1725), the Russians established strong diplomatic ties in almost every European capital. In addition, the Russian metal industry became vital to European development. The English, who lacked the forest lands and wood necessary to fire smelting furnaces, grew dependent on Russian-produced iron.

Catherine the Great (1762–1796) consciously pursued policies intended to reflect her understanding of the Enlightenment. These presented contradictions. She entered into respectful correspondence with philosophes but at the same time extended serfdom to the entire Ukraine. She promulgated a new, more secular, educational system and sought at every turn to improve Russian industry, but her policies rested on the aggrandizement of the agriculturally based aristocracy. The Charter of Nobility in 1785 forever guaranteed the aristocracy's right to hold the peasants in servitude. The Enlightenment, as interpreted by this shrewd monarch, completed the tendency to monarchical absolutism that had been well under way since the sixteenth century.

The Effects of Enlightened Despotism

Enlightened despotism was, in reality, the use of Enlightenment principles by enlightened monarchs to enhance the central government's power and thereby their own. These eighteenth-century monarchs knew, in ways their predecessors had not, that knowledge is power; they saw that application of learned theories to policy can produce useful results.

But did these enlightened despots try to create more humanitarian societies, in which individual freedom flourished on all levels? In this area, enlightened despotism must be pronounced a shallow deployment of Enlightenment ideals. For example, Frederick the Great decreed the abolition of serfdom in Prussia, but had no means to force the aristocracy to conform because he desperately needed their support. In the 1780s, Joseph II instituted liberalized publishing laws in Austria, until artisans began reading pamphlets about the French Revolution. The state quickly retreated and reimposed censorship. In the 1750s, Frederick the Great also had loosened the censorship laws, and writers were free to attack traditional religion; however, they were never allowed to criticize the army, the key to Frederick's aggressive foreign policy. Although Catherine the Great gave Diderot a pension, she would hear of nothing that compromised her political power, and her ministers were expected to give her unquestioning service.

Finally, if the Enlightenment means the endorsement of reason over force, and peace and cosmopolitan unity over ruthless competition, then the foreign policies of these enlightened despots were uniformly despotic. The evidence lies in a long series of aggressions, including Frederick's invasion of Silesia in 1740, Austria's secret betrayal of its alliance with the English and Dutch and the ensuing Seven Years' War, and Austria's attempt in the 1770s to claim Bavaria. In short, the Enlightenment provided a theory around which central and eastern European states that were only recently unified could organize their policies. The theory also justified centralization over the power of local elites, grown

comfortable through centuries of unopposed authority. There were no major philosophes who did not grow disillusioned with enlightened monarchs on the rare occasions when their actions could be observed at close range. The Enlightenment did provide new principles for the organization of centralized monarchical power, but centralization with economic rationalization and management did not make their practitioners or beneficiaries any more enlightened. Enlightened despotism was extinguished largely by the democratic revolutions of the late eighteenth century.

THE ENLIGHTENMENT IN EASTERN EUROPE

The impact of the Enlightenment in the countries of eastern Europe varied enormously. Where it made greatest inroads, there we see the subsequent emergence of discernibly modern social and political ideas and aspirations. In Hungary, for example, independence from the Ottoman Empire in 1718 left a country that was still essentially feudal, yet eager for reform and renewal. In the 1720s, peace brought regeneration; the population doubled in the course of the eighteenth century; agricultural techniques were markedly improved; and by the midcentury, the schools and universities had begun to teach the new science. Hungarian Protestants, who had traveled and studied abroad, came home with the ideas of the philosophes. A lay intelligentsia was created, and with it came new literature and drama, as well as Western-style civil society: lodges, salons, clubs, and societies. By 1790, the Enlightenment and the French Revolution had inspired a movement for Hungarian nationalism and against the control of the Austrians and Hapsburgs. But in 1795, its leaders were executed. However, their nationalistic ideals survived well into the nineteenth and twentieth centuries.

In Poland and Lithuania, the influence of the Jesuits remained strong even after they were expelled from other eastern European countries, such as Hungary. In countries such as Poland, where the Catholic clergy continued to control education, the Enlightenment remained a deeply censored, almost underground movement. Yet it did exist and influence educational reform, especially after the expulsion of the Jesuits in 1773. Those who advocated the Enlightenment allied themselves with the monarchy, which they saw as the only force that might be strong enough to oppose the entrenched clergy and aristocracy. The power of Polish nobility had dire historical consequences for the country. No central authority emerged in eighteenth-century Poland comparable in its unifying ability to the monarchs of Prussia, Austria, and Russia. Not once but three times, in 1772, 1793, and 1795, Poland was partitioned by these three potent neighbors, who took portions of it. Some Poles resisted; a Polish nobleman even appealed to Rousseau in 1771 to help draft a constitution for his beleaguered country. The document in which Rousseau expressed his thoughts on Polish government was cautious and judicious, giving power to all the various elements within Polish elite society. The model came to nothing, and the Poles struggle to this day to achieve a cohesive state.

The failure of the Enlightenment to take hold in parts of eastern Europe had far-reaching consequences, with which the people of those countries continue to grapple. In the 1990s, those countries—such as Hungary and the Czech Republic—that experienced the Enlightenment seem to show the greatest cohesiveness in the struggle to create a unified, secular, tolerant, and independent state.

THE AMERICAN REVOLUTION

England's victory over France in the Seven Years' War set in motion a train of events that culminated in the American Revolution. The war had drained the British treasury, and now Britain had the additional expense of paying for troops to guard the new North American territories, which it had gained in the war. As strapped British taxpayers could not shoulder the whole burden, the members of Parliament thought it quite reasonable that American colonists should help to pay the bill; they reasoned that Britain had protected the colonists from the French and was still protecting them in their conflicts with Indians. Thus, new colonial taxes and import duties were imposed. Particularly galling to the colonists were the Stamp Act (which placed a tax on newspapers, playing cards, liquor licenses, and legal documents) and the Quartering Act (which required

colonists to provide living quarters and supplies to English troops stationed in America).

Vigorous colonial protest compelled the British Parliament to repeal the Stamp Act, but new taxes were imposed, raising the price of many everyday articles, including tea. The stationing of British troops in Boston, the center of rebelliousness, worsened tensions. In March 1770, a crisis ensued after a squad of British soldiers fired into a crowd of Bostonians who had been taunting them and pelting them with rocks and snowballs. Five Bostonians died, and six were wounded. A greater crisis occurred in 1773, when Parliament granted the East India Company exclusive rights to sell tea in America. The colonists regarded this as yet another example of British tyranny. When a crowd of Bostonians dressed as Indians climbed aboard East Indian ships and dumped about ninety thousand pounds of tea overboard, the British responded with a series of repressive measures, which included suppressing self-government in Massachusetts and closing the port of Boston.

The quarrel turned to bloodshed in April and June 1775. On July 4, 1776, delegates from the various colonies adopted the Declaration of Independence, written mainly by the philosophe Thomas Jefferson. Applying Locke's theory of natural rights, this document declared that government derives its power from the consent of the governed, that it is the duty of a government to protect the rights of its citizens, and that people have the right to "alter or abolish" a government that deprives them of their "unalienable rights."

Why were the American colonists so ready to revolt? For one thing, they had brought with them a highly idealized understanding of English liberties; long before 1776, they had extended representative institutions to include small property owners, who probably could not have voted in England. The colonists had come to expect representative government, trial by jury, and protection from unlawful imprisonment. Each of the thirteen colonies had an elected assembly, which acted like a miniature parliament; in these assemblies, Americans gained political experience and quickly learned self-government.

Familiarity with the thought of the Enlightenment and the republican writers of the English Revolution also contributed to the Americans' awareness of liberty. The ideas of the philosophes traversed the Atlantic and influenced educated

THE SIGNING OF THE DECLARATION OF INDEPENDENCE, PHILADELPHIA, JULY 4, 1776: DETAIL BY JOHN TRUMBULL. The success of the American Revolution was hailed as a victory of liberty over tyranny. French military and financial support of the Americans led to the bankruptcy of the French monarchy by 1788, a factor that contributed to the French Revolution. The American founding fathers were familiar with the ideas of the Enlightenment, particularly John Locke's theory of natural rights. (*Copyright Yale University Art Gallery*)

Americans, particularly Thomas Jefferson and Benjamin Franklin. Like the philosophes, American thinkers expressed a growing confidence in reason, valued freedom of religion and of thought, and championed the principle of natural rights.

Another source of hostility toward established authority among the American colonists was their religious traditions, particularly Puritanism, which viewed the Bible as infallible and its teachings as a higher law than the law of the state. Like their counterparts in England, American Puritans challenged political and religious authorities who, in their view, contravened God's law. Thus, Puritans acquired two habits that were crucial to the development of political liberty: dissent and resistance. When transferred to the realm of politics, these Puritan tendencies led

Americans to resist authority that they considered unjust.

American victory came in 1783 as a result of several factors. George Washington proved to be a superior leader, able to organize and retain the loyalty of his troops. France, seeking to avenge its defeat in the Seven Years' War, helped the Americans with money and provisions and then in 1778 entered the conflict. Britain had difficulty shipping supplies across three thousand miles of ocean, was fighting the French in the West Indies and elsewhere at the same time, and ultimately lacked commitment to the struggle.

Reformers in other lands quickly interpreted the American victory as a successful struggle of liberty against tyranny. During the Revolution, the various former colonies drew up constitutions

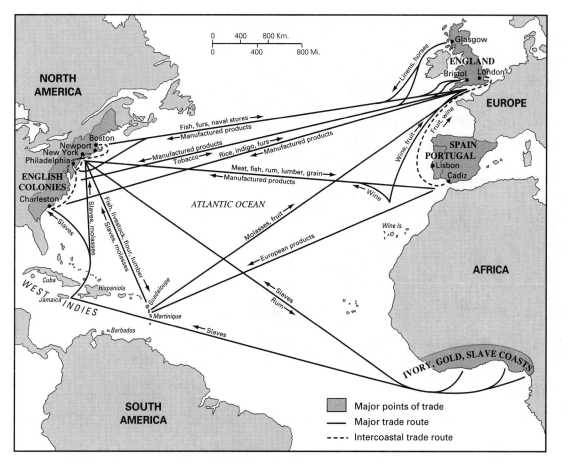

MAP 18.3 Trade Routes Between the Old and New Worlds

based on the principle of popular sovereignty and included bills of rights that protected individual liberty. They also managed, somewhat reluctantly, to forge a nation. Rejecting both monarchy and hereditary aristocracy, the Constitution of the United States created a republic in which power derived from the people. A system of separation of powers and checks and balances set safeguards against the abuse of power, and the Bill of Rights provided for protection of individual rights. To be sure, the ideals of liberty and equality were not extended to all people. Slaves knew nothing of the freedom that white Americans cherished, and women were denied the vote and equal opportunity. But to reform-minded Europeans, it seemed that Americans were fulfilling the promise of the Enlightenment; they were creating a freer and better society.

THE ENLIGHTENMENT AND THE MODERN WORLD

Enlightenment thought was the culmination of a trend begun by Renaissance artists and humanists, who attacked medieval otherworldliness and gave value to individual achievement and the worldly life. It was a direct outgrowth of the Scientific Revolution, which provided a new method of inquiry and verification and demonstrated the power and self-sufficiency of the human intellect. If nature were autonomous—that is, if it operated according to natural laws that did not require divine intervention—then the human intellect could also be autonomous. Through its own powers, it could uncover the general principles that operate in the social world, as well as in nature.

The philosophes sought to analyze nature, government, religion, law, economics, and education through reason alone, without any reference to Christian teachings, and they rejected completely the claims of clerics to a special wisdom. The philosophes broke decisively with the medieval view that the individual is naturally depraved, that heaven is the true end of life, and that human values and norms derive from a higher reality and are made known through revelation. Instead, they upheld the potential goodness of the individual, regarded the good life on earth as the true purpose of existence, and insisted that individuals could improve themselves and their society solely by the light of reason.

In addition, the political philosophies of Locke, Montesquieu, and Rousseau were based on an entirely new (and modern) concept of the relationship between the state and the individual: states should exist not simply to accumulate power, but also to enhance human happiness. From that perspective, monarchy, and even oligarchy not based on merit, began to seem increasingly less useful. And if happiness is a goal, then it must be assumed that some sort of progress is possible in history.

Indeed, the French leaders of the late Enlightenment believed wholeheartedly in the infinite possibility of human progress. If human knowledge is ever increasing and depends only on the ability to sense and experience the world, then surely, they believed, the human condition can constantly improve. Western thought has never entirely relinquished this brave dream.

The philosophes wanted a freer, more humane, and more rational society, but they feared the people and their potential for revolutionary action. As an alternative to revolution, most philosophes offered science as the universal improver of the human condition. Faith in reform without the necessity of revolution proved to be a doctrine for the elite of the salons. In that sense, the French Revolution can be said to have repudiated the essential moderation of philosophes like Voltaire, d'Alembert, and Kant.

However, the Enlightenment established a vision of humanity so independent of Christianity and so focused on the needs and abuses of the society of the time that no established institution, once grown corrupt and ineffectual, could long withstand its penetrating critique. To that extent, the writings of the philosophes point toward the democratic revolutions of the late eighteenth century. To a lesser extent, the writers of the Enlightenment also point toward ideals that remain strong in most democratic Western societies: religious toleration, a disdain for prejudice and superstition, a fear of unchecked political authority, and, of course, a belief in the power of the human mind to recognize the irrational and attempt to correct it.

◆　◆　◆

NOTES

1. "An Answer to the Question: 'What Is Enlightenment?'" in ed. Hans Reiss *Kant's Political Writings* (Cambridge: Cambridge University Press, 1970), pp. 54–60.

2. *Wetten van het Natuurkundig Genootschap, door eenige Dames opgericht, binnen Middelburg den 6 August. 1785. (Rules for the Scientific Society established by women within Middleburg on 6 August 1785)*, Middelburg, [1785], p. 29. The only known copy is to be found in Provincial Library in Zeeland.

3. Pierre Bayle, *Historical and Critical Dictionary*, ed. Richard H. Popkin (New York: Bobbs-Merrill, 1965), p. 195.

4. Voltaire, *Philosophical Letters* (New York: Bobbs-Merrill, 1961), p. 22.

5. Thomas Hobbes, *Leviathan*, ed. C. B. Macpherson (Harmondsworth, England: Penguin, 1977), p. 189.

6. Jean Jacques Rousseau, *The Social Contract and Discourses* (New York: Dutton, 1950), pp. 3, 9.

7. Quoted in Franco Venturi, *Utopia and Reform in the Enlightenment* (Cambridge: Cambridge University Press, 1971), p. 101.

8. Voltaire, *Philosophical Dictionary*, ed. Theodore Besterman (Harmondsworth, England: Penguin, 1974), p. 183.

9. Quoted in David B. Davis, *The Problem of Slavery in Western Culture* (Harmondsworth, England: Penguin, 1970), p. 449.

10. Immanuel Kant, *Beobachtungen* (1900–1919), in *Kants Werke,* ed. Dilthey, 2: 230.

11. Adam Smith, *The Wealth of Nations,* ed. George Stigler (New York: Appleton, 1957), p. 3.

12. Ibid., p. 98.

13. Jean Le Rond d'Alembert, *Preliminary Discourse to the Encyclopedia of Diderot,* trans. Richard N. Schwab (New York: Bobbs-Merrill, 1963), p. 22.

14. Ibid., pp. 101–102.

SUGGESTED READING

Appleby, Joyce, Lynn Hunt, and Margaret Jacob, *Telling the Truth about History* (1994). Part I discusses the meaning of the Enlightenment for the modern age.

Applewhite, Harriet B., and Darline G. Levy, eds., *Women and Politics in the age of the Democratic Revolution* (1990). Lively essays about real women in Europe and America.

Chartier, Roger, *The Cultural Origins of the French Revolution* (1991). A good map through the French Enlightenment; weak on women.

Cranston, Maurice, *Philosophers and Pamphleteers. Political Theorists of the Enlightenment* (1986). A clear, readable account of the major French thinkers.

Darnton, Robert, *The Literacy Underground of the Old Regime* (1982). A collection of essays by a master storyteller.

Gay, Peter, *The Enlightenment, An Interpretation,* 2 vols. (1966–1969). Probably the best synthesis of the period ever written.

Hunt, Lynn, ed., *The Invention of Pornography. Obscenity and the Origins of Modernity* (1993). Pornography arose in the late seventeenth century and was tied to social criticism and eventually to the Enlightenment. It was very different then from what it has subsequently become.

Jacob, Margaret, *Living the Enlightenment: Freemasonry and Politics in Eighteenth-Century Europe* (1991). Examines the new public and secular culture as seen in the lodges throughout western Europe.

Maza, Sarah, *Private Lives and Public Affairs. The Causes Célèbres of Prerevolutionary France* (1993). Shows what the press can do to deflate the authority of kings and aristocrats; fine reading.

Porter, Roy, *The Enlightenment* (1990). The best short introduction now available.

Starobinski, Jean, *Jean-Jacques Rousseau. Transparency and Obstruction* (1971). One of the greatest biographies ever written of the most important philosophe.

REVIEW QUESTIONS

1. What is meant by the Enlightenment? Where did the Enlightenment begin, and what contributed to its spread?

2. Describe the new public sphere and name some of the societies that sprang up within it.

3. Why did Christianity come under attack by deists, skeptics, and freethinkers? What were the sorts of things they said about it?

4. In what ways did Voltaire and Madame du Châtelet exemplify the philosophes?

5. What were the essential characteristics of the political thought of each of the following: Hobbes, Locke, Montesquieu, and Rousseau? Make relevant comparisons and contrasts.

6. Describe Locke's theory of learning. What was its significance for the Enlightenment?

7. How did the philosophes come to terms with the status of slaves and criminals?

8. What were the views of the philosophers on the position of women in society? Did women have an Enlightenment?

9. Did the philosophes approve of capitalism? Explain why or why not.

10. What made the High Enlightenment different from what preceded it? Describe how it differed. How did the *Encyclopedia* exemplify the High Enlightenment?

11. List the major military conflicts of the eighteenth century. Discuss the significance of each.

12. Enlightened despotism was in reality the use of Enlightenment principles by monarchs to enhance the central government's power and thereby their own. Discuss this statement.

13. In what ways was the American Revolution based on Enlightenment principles?

14. The Enlightenment was a pivotal period in the shaping of the modern mentality. Discuss this statement.

PART FOUR

An Age of Revolution: Liberal, National, Industrial

1789–1848

	POLITICS AND SOCIETY	THOUGHT AND CULTURE
1780	French Revolution begins (1789) Declaration of the Rights of Man and of the Citizen (1789)	Kant, *Critique of Pure Reason* (1781) Bentham, *Principles of Morals and Legislation* (1789)
1790	France declares war on Austria (1792) Execution of Louis XVI (1793) Reign of Terror (1793–94) Napoleon seizes power (1799)	Burke, *Reflections on the Revolution in France* (1790) Wollstonecraft, *Vindication of the Rights of Woman* (1792) De Maistre, *Reflections on the State of France* (1796) Wordsworth, *Lyrical Ballads* (1798) Malthus, *Essay on the Principle of Population* (1798)
1800	Battle of Trafalgar—French and Spanish fleets defeated by the British (1805) Napoleon defeats Prussians at Jena (1806) Napoleon defeats Russians at Friedland (1807)	Beethoven, Fifth Symphony (1807–08) Goethe, *Faust* (1808, 1832)
1810	Napoleon invades Russia (1812) Napoleon defeated at Waterloo (1815) Congress of Vienna (1814–15)	Byron, *Childe Harold* (1812)
1820	Revolutions in Spain, Italy, Russia, and Greece (1820–1829)	Shelley, *Prometheus Unbound* (1820) Ricardo, *Principles of Political Economy* (1817) Hegel, *The Philosophy of History* (1822–1831)
1830	Revolutions in France, Belgium, Poland, and Italy (1830–32) Reform in Britain: Reform Act of 1832; slavery abolished within British Empire (1833); Factory Act (1833)	Fourier, *Treatise on Agrarian Domestic Fellowship* (1822) Comte, *Course in Positive Philosophy* (1830–1842)
1840	Irish famine (1845–1849) Revolutions in France, Germany, Austria, and Italy (1848)	Proudhon, *What Is Property?* (1840) De Tocqueville, *Democracy in America* (1835–1840) Gaskell, *Mary Barton* (1848) Marx, *Communist Manifesto* (1848)

CHAPTER 19

The French Revolution: Affirmation of Liberty and Equality

*T*he outbreak of the French Revolution in 1789 stirred the imagination of Europeans. Both participants and observers sensed that they were living in a pivotal age. On the ruins of the Old Order, founded on privilege and despotism, a new era was forming that promised to realize the ideals of the Enlightenment. These ideals included the emancipation of the human personality from superstition and tradition, the triumph of liberty over tyranny, the refashioning of institutions in accordance with reason and justice, and the tearing down of barriers to equality. It seemed that the natural rights of the individual, hitherto a distant ideal, would now become reality, and centuries of oppression and misery would end. Never before had people shown such confidence in the power of human intelligence to shape the conditions of existence. Never before had the future seemed so full of hope.

This lofty vision kindled emotions akin to religious enthusiasm and attracted converts throughout the Western world. "If we succeed," wrote the French poet André Chénier, "the destiny of Europe will be changed. Men will regain their rights and the people their sovereignty."[1] The editor of the Viennese publication *Wiener Zeitung* wrote to a friend: "In France a light is beginning to shine which will benefit the whole of humanity."[2] British reformer John Cartwright expressed the hopes of reformers everywhere: "Degenerate must be that heart which expands not with sentiments of delight at what is now transacting in . . . France. The French . . . are not only asserting their own rights, but they are asserting and advancing the general liberties of mankind."[3]

Drawing by Gerald of the French royal family's refuge in the Assembly Hall after the 1792 sacking of the Tuileries. (*Jean-Loup Charmet*)

Chronology 19.1 The French Revolution

July 1788	Calling of the Estates General
May 5, 1789	Convening of the Estates General
June 17, 1789	Third Estate declares itself the National Assembly
July 14, 1789	Storming of the Bastille
Late July 1789	The Great Fear
August 4, 1789	Nobles surrender their special privileges
June 1791	Flight of Louis XVI
October 1791	Legislative Assembly succeeds the National Assembly
April 20, 1792	Legislative Assembly declares war on Austria
August 10, 1792	Parisians attack the king's palace
September 1792	September Massacres
September 20, 1792	Battle of Valmy
September 21–22, 1792	Abolition of the monarchy
January 21, 1793	Execution of Louis XVI
June 1793	Jacobins replace Girondins as the dominant group in the National Convention
July 28, 1794	Robespierre is guillotined
1795 and 1796	Failed insurrections by the poor of Paris
September 1797	Royalist coup d'état against the Directory is crushed
November 1799	Napoleon seizes power

THE OLD REGIME

Eighteenth-century French society was divided into three orders, or Estates, which were legally defined groupings. The clergy constituted the First Estate, the nobility the Second Estate, and everyone else (about 96 percent of the population) belonged to the Third Estate. The clergy and nobility, totaling about 500,000 out of a population of 26 million, enjoyed special privileges. The social structure of the Old Regime, based on privileges and inequalities sanctioned by law, produced tensions that contributed to the Revolution.

The First Estate

The powers and privileges of the French Catholic church made it a state within a state. As it had done for centuries, the church registered births, marriages, and deaths; collected tithes (a tax on products from the soil); censored books considered dangerous to religion and morals; operated schools; and distributed relief to the poor. Since it was illegal for Protestants to assemble publicly for prayer, the Catholic church enjoyed a monopoly on public worship. Although it owned an estimated 10 percent of the land, which brought in an immense revenue, the church paid no taxes. Instead, it made a "free gift" to the state (the church determined the amount), which was always smaller than direct taxes would have been. Critics denounced the church for promoting superstition and obscurantism, impeding reforms, and being more concerned with wealth and power than with the spiritual message of Jesus.

The clergy reflected the social divisions in France. The upper clergy shared the attitudes and way of life of the nobility from which they sprang. The parish priests, commoners by birth, resented the haughtiness and luxurious living of the upper clergy. In 1789, when the Revolution began, many priests sympathized with the reform-minded people of the Third Estate.

The Second Estate

Like the clergy, the nobility was a privileged order. Nobles held the highest positions in the church, army, and government. They were exempt from most taxes (or used their influence to evade taxes), collected manorial dues from peasants, and owned between one-quarter and one-third of the land. In addition to the income they drew from their estates, nobles were becoming increasingly involved in such nonaristocratic enterprises as banking, finance, commerce, and industry. Many key philosophes—Montesquieu, Condorcet, d'Holbach—were nobles, and nobles were the leading patrons of the arts. Most nobles, however, were suspicious and intolerant of the liberal ideas advanced by the philosophes.

All nobles were not equal; there were gradations of dignity among the 350,000 members of the nobility. Enjoying the most prestige were *nobles of the sword*: families that could trace their aristocratic status back several centuries. Many of these noblemen were officers in the king's army. The highest of the ancient nobles were engaged in the social whirl at Versailles and Paris, receiving pensions and sinecures from the king but performing few useful services for the state. Most nobles of the sword, unable to afford the gilded life at court, remained on their provincial estates, the poorest of them barely distinguishable from prosperous peasants.

Alongside this ancient nobility, a new nobility had arisen, created by the monarchy. To obtain money, reward favorites, and weaken the old nobility, French kings had sold titles of nobility to members of the bourgeoisie and had conferred noble status on certain government offices bought by wealthy bourgeois. Particularly significant were the *nobles of the robe,* who had purchased judicial offices in the parlements—the high law courts—and whose ranks included many former bourgeois.

Opinion among the aristocrats was divided. Influenced by the liberal ideals of the philosophes, some nobles sought to reform France; they wanted to end royal despotism and establish a constitutional government. To this extent, the liberal nobility had a great deal in common with the bourgeoisie. These liberal nobles saw the king's difficulties in 1788 as an opportunity to regenerate the nation under enlightened leadership. When they resisted the king, they claimed that they were attacking despotic rule. But many nobles, concerned with preserving their privileges and honorific status, were hostile to liberal ideals and opposed reform.

The Third Estate

The Third Estate comprised the bourgeoisie, peasants, and urban laborers. Although the bourgeoisie provided the leadership for the Revolution, its success depended on the support given by the rest of the Third Estate.

The Bourgeoisie The bourgeoisie consisted of merchant-manufacturers, wholesale merchants, bankers, master craftsmen, doctors, lawyers, intellectuals, and government officials below the top ranks. Although the bourgeoisie had wealth, it lacked social prestige. A merchant, despite his worldly success, felt that his occupation denied him the esteem enjoyed by the nobility. "There are few rich people who at times do not feel humiliated at being nothing but wealthy," observed an eighteenth-century Frenchman.[4]

Influenced by the aristocratic values of the day

and envious of the nobility's lifestyle, the bourgeosie sought to erase the stigma of common birth and to rise socially by becoming landowners. By 1789, the bourgeoisie owned about 20 percent of the land. Traditionally, some members of the bourgeoisie had risen socially either by purchasing a judicial or political office that carried with it a title of nobility or by gaining admission to the upper clergy and the officer ranks of the army. Access to the nobility remained open throughout the eighteenth century. Nevertheless, since the highest and most desired positions in the land were reserved for the nobility, able bourgeoisie were often excluded, for a variety of reasons: the high cost of purchasing an office, the limited number of new offices created, the resistance of nobles to their advancement, or the hostility of the older nobility toward those recently ennobled. No doubt these men felt frustrated and came to resent a social system that valued birth more than talent. For most of the century, however, the bourgeoisie did not challenge the existing social structure, including the special privileges of the nobility.

By 1789, the bourgeois had many grievances. They wanted all positions in church, army, and state to be open to men of talent regardless of birth. They sought a parliament that would make laws for the nation; a constitution that would limit the king's power and guarantee freedom of thought, a fair trial, and religious toleration; and administrative reforms that would eliminate waste, inefficiency, and interference with business.

"LET'S HOPE THAT THE GAME FINISHES WELL." This political cartoon shows a laboring-class woman carrying smug representatives of the privileged orders on her back. (*Musée de la Ville de Paris*)

The Peasantry The condition of the more than 21 million French peasants was a paradox. On the one hand, they were better off than peasants in Austria, Prussia, Poland, and Russia, where serfdom still predominated. In France, serfdom had largely disappeared; many peasants owned their land, and some were even prosperous. On the other hand, most French peasants lived in poverty, which worsened in the closing years of the Old Regime.

Peasants owned between 30 and 40 percent of the land, but the typical holding was barely large enough to eke out a living. The rising birthrate (between 1715 and 1789, the population may have increased from 18 million to 26 million) led to the continual subdivision of farms among heirs. Moreover, many peasants did not own their own land but rented it from a nobleman or a prosperous neighbor. Others worked as sharecroppers, turning over to their creditors a considerable share of the harvest.

Owning too little land to support themselves, many peasants tried to supplement their incomes. They hired themselves out for whatever employment was available in their region: as agricultural day laborers, charcoal burners, transporters of wine, or textile workers in their own homes. Landless peasants tried to earn a living in such ways. The increasing birthrate resulted in an overabundance of rural wage earners. This worsened the plight of small landowners and reduced the landless to beggary. "The number of our children reduces us to desperation,"[5] was a common complaint of the peasants by 1789.

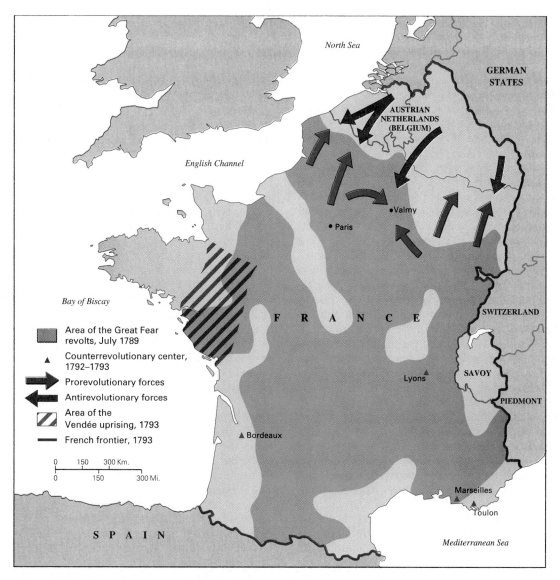

Map 19.1 The French Revolution, 1789–1793

An unjust and corrupt system of taxation weighed heavily on the peasantry. Louis XIV had maintained his grandeur and financed his wars by milking ever more taxes from the peasants, a practice that continued throughout the eighteenth century. An army of tax collectors victimized the peasantry. In addition to royal taxes, peasants paid the tithe to the church and manorial dues to lords.

Although serfdom had ended in most parts of France, lords continued to demand obligations from peasants as they had done in the Middle Ages. Besides performing labor services on the lord's estate, peasants still had to grind their corn in the lord's mill, bake their bread in his oven, press their grapes in his winepress, and give him part of their produce in payment. (Their fees were called *banalities*.) In addition, the lord collected a land rent from peasant proprietors, levied dues on goods at markets and fairs, and exercised exclusive hunting rights on lands tilled by peasants. The last was a particularly onerous right, for the lord's hunting parties damaged crops. Lords were determined to hold on to these privileges not only because of the income they brought, but because they were symbols of authority and social esteem. The peasants, on the other hand, regarded these obligations as hateful legacies of the past from which they derived no benefit.

In the last part of the eighteenth century, lords sought to exact more income from their lands by reviving manorial dues that had not been collected for generations, increasing the rates on existing dues, and contracting businessmen to collect payments from the peasants. These capitalists naturally tried to squeeze as much income as possible from the peasants, making them hate the whole system of manorial obligations even more.

Inefficient farming methods also contributed to the poverty of the French peasants. In the eighteenth century, France did not experience a series of agricultural improvements comparable to those in England. Failure to invest capital in modernizing agricultural methods meant low yields per acre and a shortage of farm animals.

A rise in the price of necessities during the closing years of the Old Regime worked hardship on those peasants who depended on wages for survival. With prices rising faster than wages, only the more prosperous peasants with produce to sell benefited. The great majority of peasants were driven deeper into poverty, and the number of beggars roaming the countryside increased. A poor harvest in 1788–89 aggravated peasant misery and produced an atmosphere of crisis. The granaries were empty; the price of bread, the staple food of the French, soared; and starvation threatened. Hatred of the manorial order and worsening poverty sparked a spontaneous and autonomous peasant revolution in 1789.

Urban Laborers The urban laboring class in this preindustrial age consisted of journeymen working for master craftsmen, factory workers in small-scale industries, and wage earners such as day laborers, gardeners, handymen, and deliverymen, who were paid by those they served. The poverty of the urban poor, like that of the peasant wage earners, worsened in the late eighteenth century. From 1785 to 1789, the cost of living increased by 62 percent, while wages rose only 22 percent. For virtually the entire decade of the

Revolution, urban workers struggled to keep body and soul together in the face of food shortages and rising prices, particularly the price of their staple food, bread. Material want drove the urban poor to acts of violence that affected the course of the Revolution.

Inefficient Administration and Financial Disorder

Eighteenth-century France was in theory an absolute monarchy. The king claimed that his power derived from God, and, unlike Britain, France had no parliament that represented the people and met as a continuous body. The administration of the country was complex, confusing, and ineffective. The practice of buying state offices from the king, introduced as a means of raising money, brought in many incompetent officeholders. "When his Majesty created an office," stated one administrator, "Providence called into being an imbecile to buy it."[6] Tariffs on goods shipped from one French province to another and differing systems of weights and measures hampered trade. No single law code applied to all the provinces; instead, there were overlapping and conflicting law systems based on old Roman law or customary feudal law, which made the administration of justice slow, arbitrary, and unfair. To admirers of the philosophes, the administrative system was an insult to reason. The Revolution would sweep the system away.

Financial disorders also contributed to the weakness of the Old Regime. In the regime's last years, the government could not raise sufficient funds to cover expenses. Servicing the debt incurred during the War of the Austrian Succession (1740–1748) and the Seven Years' War (1756–1763) placed an immense burden on the treasury. This burden reached crisis proportions when France incurred additional expenses by aiding the colonists in the American Revolution. The king's gifts and pensions to court nobles and the extravagant court life further drained the treasury.

Finances were in a shambles, not because France was impoverished, but because it had an inefficient and unjust tax system. Few wealthy Frenchmen, including the bourgeois, paid their fair share of taxes. Because tax revenue came chiefly from the peasants, it was bound to be inadequate. Excise duties and indirect taxes on consumer goods yielded much-needed revenue in the last decades of the Old Regime. However, instead of replenishing the royal treasury, these additional funds were pocketed by rich tax collectors, who, for a fixed payment to the state, had obtained the right to collect these indirect taxes. Although serious, the financial crisis could have been solved if the clergy, nobility, and bourgeoisie paid their fair share of taxes. Some progressive ministers recognized the need for comprehensive reforms, but nobles and clergy resisted them, clinging tenaciously to their ancient privileges. The irresolution of the king and the intrigues, rivalries, and incompetence of his ministers also impeded reform.

The nobles were able to thwart royal will mainly through the parlements. Many parlementaires were originally wealthy bourgeois who had purchased their offices from the state (nobles of the robe). Both the office and status of nobility remained within the family. The Paris parlement and twelve provincial parlements reviewed the judgments of lower courts and registered royal edicts. The parlements had the right to *remonstrate*, that is, to pass judgment on the legality of royal edicts before registering them. If the courts considered the king's new laws at variance with previous legislation or ancient traditions, they would refuse to register them. (Generally, it was the Paris parlement that set the example.) The king could revise the edicts in accordance with the parlements' instructions, or force their registration by means of a *lit de justice*: a solemn ceremony in which the monarch appeared before the court. If the parlementaires stood firm in their resistance, the king might order the arrest of their leaders. Although the king could force his will on the parlements, their bold opposition damaged royal prestige.

With France on the brink of bankruptcy, the king's ministers proposed that the nobility and the church surrender some of their tax privileges. The parlements protested and remonstrated. Some nobles resisted because they were steadfast defenders of noble prerogatives; the more liberal nobles resisted because they saw an opportunity to check absolutism and introduce fundamental reforms that would regenerate the nation.

The resistance of the nobility forced the government, in July 1788, to call for a meeting of the Estates General—a medieval representative assembly, which had last met in 1614—to deal with the financial crisis. The body was to convene in May 1789. Certain that they would dominate the Estates General, the nobles intended to weaken the power of the throne. Once in control of the government, they would introduce financial reforms. But the revolt of the nobility against the crown had unexpected consequences. It opened the way for revolutions by the Third Estate, which destroyed the Old Regime and with it the aristocracy and its privileges.

The Roles of the Enlightenment and the American Revolution

Revolutions are born in the realm of the spirit. Revolutionary movements, says George Rudé, a historian of the French Revolution, require "some unifying body of ideas, a common vocabulary of hope and protest, something, in short, like a common 'revolutionary psychology.'"[7] For this reason, many historians see a relationship between the Enlightenment and the French Revolution. Although the philosophes themselves were not revolutionaries, their attacks on the pillars of the established order helped create a revolutionary psychology. As Henri Peyre observes,

> *Eighteenth-century philosophy taught the Frenchman to find his condition wretched, or in any case, unjust and illogical and made him disinclined to the patient resignation to his troubles that had long characterized his ancestors. . . . The propaganda of the "Philosophes" perhaps more than any other factor accounted for the fulfillment of the preliminary condition of the French Revolution, namely discontent with the existing state of things.*[8]

As the Revolution progressed, its leaders utilized the philosophes' ideas and language to justify their own reform program.

The American Revolution, which gave practical expression to the liberal philosophy of the philosophes, also helped pave the way for the French Revolution. The Declaration of Independence, which proclaimed the natural rights of man and sanctioned resistance against a government that deprived men of these rights, influenced the framers of the Declaration of the Rights of Man and of the Citizen. The United States showed that a nation could be established on the principle that sovereign power derived from the people. The Americans set an example of social equality unparalleled in Europe. In the United States, there was no hereditary aristocracy, no serfdom, and no state church. Liberal French aristocrats, such as the Marquis de Lafayette, who had fought in the American Revolution returned to France more optimistic about the possibilities of reforming French society.

A Bourgeois Revolution?

Because the bourgeois were the principal leaders and chief beneficiaries of the French Revolution, many historians have viewed it, along with the English revolutions of the seventeenth century and the growth of capitalism, as "an episode in the general rise of the bourgeoisie."[9] Those who regard the Revolution as a "bourgeois revolution" argue that in the last part of the eighteenth century it became increasingly difficult for the bourgeoisie to gain the most honored offices in the land. According to this view, in the eighteenth century, a decadent and reactionary aristocracy sought to regain the powers that it had lost under Louis XIV. Through parlements, aristocrats blocked reforms proposed by the king that threatened their privileges, and they united to prevent commoners from entering their ranks. The nobility's determination to safeguard its power and social exclusiveness clashed head on with the aspirations of a wealthy, talented, and progressive bourgeoisie. Finding the path to upward mobility and social dignity barred, the bourgeoisie, imbued with the rational outlook of the Enlightenment, came to perceive nobles as an obstacle to its advancement and the nation's progress. "The essential cause of the Revolution," concludes French historian Albert Soboul, "was the power of a bourgeoisie arrived at its maturity and confronted by a decadent aristocracy holding tenaciously to its privileges."[10] Thus, when the bourgeois found the opportunity during the Revolution, they ended the legal division of France into separate orders.

Recently, some historians have challenged this interpretation. These revisionists argue that before 1789 the nobles and the bourgeoisie did not represent antagonistic classes divided by sharp differences. On the contrary, they were not clearly distinguishable from each other. The bourgeois aspired to noble status, and many nobles were involved in business enterprises—mining, metallurgy, textiles, and overseas trading companies—traditionally considered the province of the bourgeoisie. Abandoning a traditional aristocratic disdain for business, many nobles had aquired the capitalist mentality associated with the middle class. Some nobles also shared with the bourgeois the liberal values of the philosophes and a desire to do away with monarchical despotism and reform France according to rational standards. Thus, French nobles, particularly those who lived in urban centers or had traveled to Britain and the American colonies, were receptive both to new means of livelihood and to progressive ideas. Moreover, the French nobility was constantly infused with new blood from below. During the eighteenth century, thousands of bourgeoisie, through marriage, the purchase of an office that carried with it a title of nobility, or service as local officials—mayors, for example—had some entitlement of nobility. As British historian William Doyle puts it, "the nobility was an open elite, not a hereditary class apart. Nor is it now possible to maintain that this elite grew less open as the eighteenth century went on thanks to some exclusive 'aristocratic reaction.'"[11]

Just prior to 1789, revisionists contend, nobles and prosperous bourgeois were no longer clearly differentiated; the traditional distinctions that had set them apart were now obsolete. France's social elite actually consisted not of a hereditary nobility, but of *notables*—both nobles and bourgeois—distinguished more by wealth than by birth. Bourgeois notables were essentially moderate; they did not seek the destruction of the aristocracy that was accomplished in the opening stage of the Revolution. The elimination of aristocratic privileges was not part of a preconceived bourgeois program, revisionists maintain, but an improvised response to the violent upheavals in the countryside in July and August 1789. Moreover, not until early 1789, when a struggle erupted over the composition of the Estates General (see the next section), did the bourgeoisie start to become conscious of itself as a class with interests that clashed with those of the aristocracy. Until then, both the bourgeoisie and many aristocrats were united around a common and moderate reform program.

Finally, revisionists argue that the nobility was not as decadent or reactionary as traditional accounts would have it. The nobles resisted the king's reforming ministers because they doubted the ability of a despotic and incompetent state to solve the financial crisis. To be sure, there were aristocrats who selfishly wanted to cling to their privileges, but many also aspired to serve the public good by instituting structural changes that would liberate the nation from despotic and inefficient rule and reform its financial and administrative system. It was this desire to institute crucial changes in French political life, say revisionists, that led nobles to press for the convening of the Estates General.

THE MODERATE STAGE, 1789–91

The Clash Between the Nobility and the Third Estate

Frenchmen in great numbers met in electoral assemblies to elect deputies to the Estates General. Churchmen and nobles voted directly for their representatives. Most deputies of the clergy were parish priests, many of them sympathetic to reform. Although the majority of deputies of the Second Estate were conservative country nobles, there was a sizable liberal minority (including some who had fought in the American Revolution), which favored reform; political liberalism was not a monopoly of the bourgeoisie. The representatives from the Third Estate were elected indirectly, with virtually all taxpaying males over the age of twenty-five being eligible to vote. The delegates of the Third Estate consisted predominantly of bourgeois drawn from government service and the professions, including many articulate lawyers.

Each Estate drew up lists of grievances and suggestions *(cahiers de doléances)*. The cahiers from all three orders expressed loyalty to monarchy and church. Many cahiers of the nobility insisted on the preservation of manorial rights and honorific privileges, whereas cahiers prepared by the urban bourgeoisie often demanded the abolition of serfdom, the fees paid by peasants to lords, the lords' courts, and the lords' exclusive hunting rights. On the other hand, cahiers drawn up by liberal nobles agreed with bourgeois demands on many crucial issues. Both groups called

for the establishment of a national assembly that would meet periodically and consent to taxation. Both also wanted a written constitution, financial reforms, including the surrender of tax exemptions, a guarantee of personal liberty, and freedom of the press. There was general agreement that a constitutional government that met regularly to pass laws was preferable to absolute monarchy that ruled by decree. Both reform-minded nobles and bourgeois held great hopes for the regeneration of France and the advancement of liberty.

At this stage, then, with a significant number of nobles sympathetic to reform, there was no inseparable gulf between the Second and the Third Estates. However, it soon became clear that the hopes of reformers clashed with the intentions of many aristocrats. What had started as a struggle between the crown and the aristocracy was turning into something far more significant: a conflict between the two privileged orders on one side and the Third Estate on the other. As one keen observer noted in early 1789, "The public debate has changed. Now the King, despotism, the constitution are merely secondary: it is a war between the Third Estate and the other two orders."[12] One pamphleteer, Abbé Sieyès (1748–1836), expressed the hatred that the bourgeoisie had for the aristocracy. "The privileged order has said to the Third Estate: 'Whatever be your services, whatever be your talents, you shall go thus far and no farther. It is not fitting that you be honored.'" The higher positions in the land, said Sieyès, should be the "reward for talents," not the prerogative of birth. Without the Third Estate, "nothing can progress"; without the nobility, "everything would proceed infinitely better."[13] What triggered the conflict between them was the issue of representation in the Estates General—a medieval assembly divided into the traditional orders of clergy, aristocracy, and commoners.

Formation of the National Assembly

The Estates General convened at Versailles on May 5, 1789, but was stalemated by the question of procedure. Seeking to control the assembly, the nobility insisted that the three Estates follow the traditional practice of meeting separately and voting as individual bodies. Because the two privileged orders were likely to stand together, the

FORMATION OF THE NATIONAL ASSEMBLY, BY JACQUES LOUIS DAVID (DETAIL).
By forming the National Assembly in June 1789, the Third Estate successfully
challenged the nobility and defied the king. In this painting glorifying the event,
aristocrat, clergyman, and commoner embrace before a cheering National Assembly. (*Versailles/Cliche des Musèes Nationaux*)

Third Estate would always be outvoted, two to
one. The delegates from the Third Estate, unwilling to allow the nobility and the higher clergy to
dominate the Estates General, proposed instead
that the three Estates meet as one body and vote by
head. There were some 610 delegates from the
Third Estate; the nobility and clergy together had
an equivalent number. Since the Third Estate could
rely on the support of sympathetic parish priests
and liberal nobles, it would be assured a majority if
all orders met together. As aristocrats and bourgeoisie became more polarized, anti-noble rhetoric
gained a growing audience among all segments of
the Third Estate. Many commoners now saw the
aristocracy as the chief obstacle to reform.

On June 10, the Third Estate broke the stalemate. It invited the clergy and nobility to join

with it in a common assembly; if they refused,
the Third Estate would go ahead without them.
A handful of priests answered the roll call, but
not one noble. On June 17, the Third Estate
made a revolutionary move. It declared itself the
National Assembly. On June 20, locked out of
their customary meeting hall (apparently by accident), the Third Estate delegates moved to a
nearby tennis court and took a solemn oath not
to disband until a constitution had been drawn
up for France. By these acts, the bourgeois delegates demonstrated their desire and determination to reform the state.

Louis XVI commanded the National Assembly
to separate into orders, but the Third Estate held
firm. The steadfastness of the delegates and the
menacing actions of Parisians who supported the

National Assembly forced Louis XVI to yield. On June 27, he ordered the nobility (some had already done so) and the clergy (a majority had already done so) to join with the Third Estate in the National Assembly. The Third Estate had successfully challenged the nobility and defied the king. It would use the National Assembly to institute reforms, including the drawing-up of a constitution that limited the king's power.

But the victory of the bourgeoisie was not yet secure, for most nobles had not resigned themselves to a bourgeois-dominated National Assembly. Recognizing that France was on the threshold of a social revolution that jeopardized their power and status, many nobles now reversed their position of previous years and joined with the king in an effort to crush the National Assembly. Louis XVI, influenced by his wife Queen Marie Antoinette, his brother Comte d'Artois, and court aristocrats, ordered special foreign regiments to the outskirts of Paris and Versailles. He also replaced Jacques Necker, a reform-minded minister, with a nominee of the queen. It appeared that Louis XVI, overcoming his usual hesitancy and vacillation, had resolved to use force against the National Assembly and to stop the incipient revolution. At this point, uprisings by the common people of Paris and peasants in the countryside saved the National Assembly, exacerbated hostilities between the Third Estate and the nobility, and ensured the victory of the forces of reform.

Storming of the Bastille

In July 1789, the level of tension in Paris was high for three reasons. First, the calling of the Estates General had aroused hopes for reform. Second, the price of bread was soaring: in August 1788, a Parisian laborer had spent 50 percent of his income on bread; by July 1789, he was spending 80 percent. The third element in the tension was the fear of an aristocratic plot to crush the National Assembly. Frightened that royal troops would bombard and pillage the city, Parisians searched for weapons.

On July 14, eight hundred to nine hundred Parisians gathered in front of the Bastille, a fortress used as a prison and a despised symbol of royal despotism. They gathered primarily to obtain gunpowder and to remove the cannon

that threatened a heavily populated working-class district. Fearing an attack, the governor of the Bastille, Bernard Jordan de Launay, ordered his men to fire into the crowd; they killed ninety-eight and wounded seventy-three people. When the tables were turned and five cannon were aimed on the main gate of the Bastille, de Launay surrendered. Despite the promise that he would not be harmed, de Launay and five of his men were killed, and their heads were paraded on pikes through the city.

Historians hostile to the French Revolution have long depicted the besiegers of the Bastille as a destructive mob made up of the dregs of society—smugglers, beggars, bandits, degenerates. However, more recent scholarship reveals that the Bastille crowd was not drawn from the criminal elements but consisted almost entirely of small tradesmen, artisans, and wage earners—concerned citizens driven by hunger, fear of an aristocratic conspiracy, and hopes for reform.[14]

The fall of the Bastille had far-reaching consequences: a symbol of the Old Regime had fallen; some court nobles hostile to the Revolution decided to flee the country; the frightened king told the National Assembly that he would withdraw all the troops ringing Paris. The revolutionary act of the Parisians had indirectly saved the National Assembly and with it the bourgeois revolution.

The Great Fear

The uprising of the Parisians strengthened the hand of the National Assembly. Revolution in the countryside also served the interests of the reformers. The economic crisis of 1788–89 had worsened conditions for the peasantry; the price of bread soared, and the number of hungry beggars wandering the roads and spreading terror multiplied. Peasants feared that the beggars would seize their crops, which would soon be ready for harvest. Also contributing to the revolutionary mentality were the great expectations unleashed by the summoning of the Estates General, for like the urban poor, the peasants hoped that their grievances would be remedied. In the spring of 1789, peasants were attacking food convoys and refusing to pay royal taxes, tithes, and manorial dues. These revolutionary outbreaks intensified in the last weeks of July.

STORMING OF THE BASTILLE, JULY 14, 1789. A Parisian crowd stormed the dreaded fortress of the Bastille, long identified with the abuses of the Old Regime. (*Brown Brothers*)

Inflamed by economic misery and stirred by the uprisings of the Parisians, peasants began to burn manor houses and destroy the registers on which their obligations to the lords were inscribed.

The flames of the peasants' insurrection were fanned by rumors that aristocrats were organizing bands of brigands to attack the peasants. The large number of vagrants roaming the countryside helped trigger irrational fears among the peasantry. The mythical army of brigands never materialized, but the Great Fear, as this episode is called, led more peasants to take up arms against the lords. Convinced that aristocrats were plotting to block reforms, the peasants attacked the lords' chateaux with greater fury.

The peasant upheavals in late July and early August, like the insurrection in Paris, worked to the advantage of the reformers. The attacks provided the National Assembly with an opportunity to strike at noble privileges by putting into law what the peasants had accomplished with the

torch—the destruction of feudal remnants. On the night of August 4, 1789, aristocrats, seeking to restore calm in the countryside, surrendered their special privileges: exclusive hunting rights, tax exemptions, monopoly on highest offices, manorial courts, and the right to demand labor services from peasants. The Assembly maintained that "the feudal regime had been utterly destroyed."*

In the decrees of August 5 and 11, the National Assembly implemented the resolutions of August 4. The Assembly also declared that the planned constitution should be prefaced by a declaration of rights. On August 26, it adopted the Declaration of the Rights of Man and of the Citizen.

---

*This was not entirely true. Some peasant obligations were abolished outright. However, for being released from other specified obligations, peasants were required to compensate their former lords. The peasants simply refused to pay, and in 1793 the Jacobins, recognizing reality, declared the remaining debt null and void.

October Days

Louis XVI, cool to these reforms, postponed his approval of the August Decrees and the Declaration of Rights. It would require a second uprising by the Parisians to force the king to agree to the reforms and to nail down the victory of the reformers.

On October 5, 1789, Parisian housewives (and men) marched twelve miles to Versailles to protest the lack of bread to the National Assembly and the king. A few hours later, twenty thousand Paris Guards, a citizen militia sympathetic to the Revolution, also set out for Versailles in support of the protesters. The king had no choice but to promise bread and to return with the demonstrators to Paris. Two weeks later, the National Assembly abandoned Versailles for Paris.

Once again, the "little people" had aided the bourgeoisie. Louis XVI, aware that he had no control over the Parisians and fearful of further violence, approved the August Decrees and the Declaration of the Rights of Man and of the Citizen. Nobles who had urged the king to use force against the Assembly and had tried to block reforms fled the country in large numbers.

Reforms of the National Assembly

With resistance weakened, the National Assembly continued the work of reform begun in the summer of 1789. By abolishing both the special privileges of the nobility and the clergy and the absolutism based on the divine right of kings, the National Assembly completed the destruction of the Old Regime.

1. *Abolition of special privileges.* By ending the special privileges of the nobility and the clergy in the August Decrees, the National Assembly legalized the equality that the bourgeoisie had demanded. The aristocratic structure of the Old Regime, a remnant of the Middle Ages that had hindered the progressive bourgeoisie, was eliminated.

2. *Statement of human rights.* The Declaration of the Rights of Man and of the Citizen expressed liberal and universal goals of the philosophes and the particular interests of the bourgeoisie. To contemporaries, it was a refutation of the Old Regime, a statement of ideals that, if realized, would end longstanding abuses

and usher in a new society. In proclaiming the inalienable right to liberty of person and freedom of religion and thought and to equal treatment under the law, the declaration affirmed the dignity of the individual. It asserted that government belonged not to any ruler, but to the people as a whole, and that its aim was the preservation of the natural rights of the individual. Because the declaration contrasted sharply with the principles espoused by an intolerant clergy, a privileged aristocracy, and a despotic monarch, it has been called the death warrant of the Old Regime.

The declaration expressed the view of the philosophes that people need not resign themselves to the abuses and misfortunes of human existence: through reason, they could improve society. But in 1789, the declaration was only a statement of intent. It remained to be seen whether its principles would be achieved.

3. *Subordination of church to state.* The National Assembly also struck at the privileges of the Roman Catholic church. The August Decrees declared the end of tithes. To obtain badly needed funds, the Assembly in November 1789 confiscated church lands and put them up for sale. In 1790, the Assembly passed the Civil Constitution of the Clergy, which altered the boundaries of the dioceses, reducing the number of bishops and priests, and transformed the clergy into government officials elected by the people and paid by the state.

Almost all bishops and many priests opposed the Civil Constitution. One reason was that the reorganization deprived a sizable number of clergymen of their positions. Moreover, Protestants and nonbelievers could, in theory, participate in the election of Catholic clergy. In addition, the Assembly had issued the decree without consulting the pope or the French clergy as a body. When the Assembly required the clergy to take an oath that they would uphold the Civil Constitution, only about one-half would do so, and many believing Catholics supported the dissenting clergy. The Civil Constitution divided the French and gave opponents of the Revolution an emotional issue around which to rally supporters.

4. *A constitution for France.* In September 1791, the National Assembly achieved the goal at which it had been aiming since June 1789: a constitution limiting the power of the king and guaranteeing all French citizens equal treatment under

the law. Citizens paying less than a specified amount in taxes could not vote. Probably about 30 percent of the males over the age of twenty-five were excluded by this stipulation, and only the more well-to-do citizens qualified to sit in the Legislative Assembly, a unicameral parliament created to succeed the National Assembly. Despite this restriction, suffrage requirements under the constitution of 1791 were far more generous than in Britain.

5. *Administrative and judicial reforms.* The National Assembly sought to reform the chaotic administrative system of France. It replaced the patchwork of provincial units with eighty-three new administrative units, or departments, approximately equal in size. The departments and their subdivisions were allowed a large measure of self-government.

Judicial reforms complemented the administrative changes. A standardized system of courts replaced the innumerable jurisdictions of the Old Regime, and the sale of judicial offices was ended. All judges were selected from graduate lawyers, and citizen juries were introduced in criminal cases. In the penal code completed by the National Assembly, torture and barbarous punishments were abolished.

6. *Aid for business.* The National Assembly put an end to all tolls and duties on goods transported within the country, maintained a tariff to protect French manufacturers, and insisted that French colonies trade only with the mother country. The Assembly also established a uniform system of weights and measures, eliminated the guilds (medieval survivals that blocked business expansion), and forbade workers to form unions or to strike.

By ending absolutism, striking at the privileges of the nobility, and preventing the mass of people from gaining control over the government, the National Assembly consolidated the rule of the bourgeoisie. With one arm, it broke the power of the aristocracy and throne; with the other, it held back the common people. Although the reforms benefited the bourgeoisie, it would be a mistake to view them merely as a selfish expression of bourgeois interests. The Declaration of the Rights of Man and of the Citizen was addressed to all; it proclaimed liberty and equality as the right of all and called upon citizens to treat one another with respect. Both French and foreign intellectuals be-

lieved that the Revolution would lead ultimately to the emancipation of humanity. "The men of 1789," says French historian Georges Lefebvre, "thought of liberty and equality as the common birthright of mankind."[15] These ideals became the core of the liberal-democratic credo that spread throughout much of the West in the nineteenth century.

THE RADICAL STAGE, 1792–94

The Sans-Culottes

Pleased with their accomplishments—equality before the law, careers open to talent, a written constitution, parliamentary government—the men of 1789 wished the Revolution to go no further. But revolutionary times are unpredictable. Soon the Revolution moved in a direction neither anticipated nor desired by the reformers. A counterrevolution, led by irreconcilable nobles and alienated churchmen, gained the support of strongly Catholic peasants. It began to threaten the changes made by the Revolution, forcing the revolutionary leadership to resort to extreme measures.

The discontent of the *sans-culottes**—small shopkeepers, artisans, and wage earners—also propelled the Revolution toward radicalism. Although they had played a significant role in the Revolution, particularly in the storming of the Bastille and the October Days, they had gained little. The sans-culottes, says French historian Albert Soboul, "began to realize that a privilege of wealth was taking the place of a privilege of birth. They foresaw that the bourgeoisie would succeed the fallen aristocracy as the ruling class."[16] Inflamed by poverty and their hatred of the rich, the sans-culottes insisted that it was the government's duty to guarantee them the "right of existence"—a policy that ran counter to the economic individualism of the bourgeoisie. They demanded that the government increase wages, set price controls on food supplies, end food shortages, punish food speculators and profiteers, and deal severely with counterrevolutionaries.

Although most sans-culottes upheld the princi-

---

*Literally, *sans-culottes* means "without culottes" and refers to the people who did not wear the knee breeches that aristocrats wore before the Revolution.

ple of private property, they wanted laws to prevent extremes of wealth and poverty. Socially, their ideal was a nation of small shopkeepers and small farmers. "No one should own more than one workshop or one store," read a sans-culotte petition.[17] Whereas the men of 1789 sought equality of rights, liberties, and opportunities, the sans-culottes expanded the principle of equality to include narrowing the gap between the rich and poor. To reduce economic inequality, the sans-culottes called for higher taxes for the wealthy and the redistribution of land. Politically, they favored a democratic republic in which the common man had a voice.

In 1789, the bourgeoisie had demanded equality with the aristocrats: the right to hold the most honored positions in the nation and an end to the special privileges of the nobility. By the close of 1792, the sans-culottes were demanding equality with the bourgeois. They wanted political reforms that would give the poor a voice in the government and social reforms that would improve their lot.

Foreign Invasion

Despite the pressures exerted by reactionary nobles and clergy on the one hand and discontented sans-culottes on the other, the Revolution might not have taken a radical turn had France remained at peace. The war that broke out with Austria and Prussia in April 1792 exacerbated internal dissensions, worsened economic conditions, and threatened to undo the reforms of the Revolution. It was in these circumstances that the Revolution moved from its moderate stage into a radical one, which historians refer to as the Second French Revolution.

In June 1791, Louis XVI and the royal family, traveling in disguise, fled Paris for the northeast of France to join with *émigrés* (nobles who had left revolutionary France and were organizing a counterrevolutionary army) and to rally foreign support against the Revolution. Discovered at Varennes by a village postmaster, they were brought back to Paris as virtual prisoners. The flight of the king turned many French people against the monarchy, strengthening the position of the radicals who wanted to do away with kingship altogether and establish a republic. But

it was foreign invasion that ultimately led to the destruction of the monarchy.

In the Legislative Assembly, the lawmaking body that had succeeded the National Assembly in October 1791, one group, called the Girondins, urged an immediate war against Austria, which was harboring and supporting the émigrés. The Girondins believed that a successful war would unite France under their leadership, and they were convinced that Austria was already preparing to invade France and destroy the Revolution. Moreover, regarding themselves as crusaders in the struggle of liberty against tyranny, the Girondins hoped to spread revolutionary reforms to other lands to provoke a war of the people against kings.

On April 20, 1792, the Legislative Assembly declared war on Austria. Commanded by the duke of Brunswick, a combined Austrian and Prussian army crossed into France. French forces, short of arms and poorly led (about six thousand of some nine thousand officers had abandoned their command), could not halt the enemy's advance. Food shortages and a counterrevolution in the west increased the unrest. In an atmosphere already charged with tension, the duke of Brunswick issued a manifesto declaring that if the royal family were harmed he would exact a terrible vengeance on the Parisians. On August 10, 1792, enraged Parisians and militia from other cities attacked the king's palace, killing several hundred Swiss guards.

In early September, as foreign troops advanced deeper into France, there occurred an event analogous to the Great Fear of 1789. As rumors spread that jailed priests and aristocrats were planning to break out of their cells to support the duke of Brunswick, Parisians panicked. Driven by fear, patriotism, and murderous impulses, they raided the prisons and massacred eleven to twelve hundred prisoners. Most of the victims were not political prisoners but ordinary criminals.

On September 21 and 22, 1792, the National Convention (the successor to the Legislative Assembly) abolished the monarchy and established a republic. In December 1792, Louis XVI was placed on trial, and in January 1793, he was executed for conspiring against the liberty of the French people. The execution of Louis XVI intensified tensions between the revolutionaries and

THE EXECUTION OF LOUIS XVI. The king died with dignity. His last words were, "I forgive my enemies; I trust that my death will be for the happiness of my people, but I grieve for France, and I fear that she may suffer the anger of the Lord." (*Giraudon/Art Resource, NY*)

the crowned heads of Europe. The uprising of August 10, the September Massacres, the creation of a republic, and the execution of Louis XVI all confirmed that the Revolution was taking a radical turn.

Meanwhile, the war continued. Short of supplies, hampered by bad weather, and possessing insufficient manpower, the duke of Brunswick never did reach Paris. Defeated by superior artillery at Valmy on September 20, 1792, the foreign forces retreated to the frontier, and the armies of the republic took the offensive. By the beginning of 1793, French forces had overrun Belgium (then a part of the Austrian Empire), the German Rhineland, and the Sardinian provinces of Nice and Savoy. To the peoples of Europe, the National Convention solemnly announced that it was waging a popular crusade against privilege and tyranny, against aristocrats and princes.

These revolutionary political and social ideas, the execution of Louis XVI, and, most important, French expansion that threatened the balance of power frightened the rulers of Europe. Urged on by Britain, by the spring of 1793, they formed an anti-French alliance. The allies' forces pressed toward the French borders, endangering the republic.

Counterrevolutionary insurrections further undermined the fledgling republic. In the Vendée, in western France, peasants who were protesting against taxation and conscription and were still loyal to their priests and Catholic tradition, which the Revolution had attacked, took up arms against the republic. Led by local nobles, the peasants of the Vendée waged a guerrilla war for religion, royalism, and their traditional way of life. In some provinces, federalists objecting to the power wielded by the centralized government in Paris also revolted. The republic was unable to exercise control over much of the country.

The Jacobins

As the republic tottered under the weight of foreign invasion, internal insurrection, and economic crisis, the revolutionary leadership grew still more radical. In June 1793, the Jacobins replaced the Girondins as the dominant group in the National Convention. The Girondins favored a government in which the departments would exercise control over their own affairs. The Jacobins, on the other hand, wanted a strong central government, with Paris as the center of power. The Girondins also opposed government interference in business, whereas the Jacobins supported temporary governmental controls to deal with the needs of war and economic crisis. This last point was crucial; it won the Jacobins the support of the sans-culottes.

Both the Girondins and the Jacobins came from the bourgeoisie, but some Jacobin leaders were more willing to listen to the economic and political demands of the hard-pressed sans-culottes. Besides, the Jacobins wanted an alliance with the sans-culottes in order to defend the Revolution against foreign and domestic enemies.

The Jacobins had a further advantage in the power struggle: they were tightly organized, well disciplined, and convinced that only they could save the republic. On June 2, 1793, some eighty thousand armed sans-culottes surrounded the Convention and demanded the arrest of Girondin delegates—an act that enabled the Jacobins to gain control of the government.

The problems confronting the Jacobins were staggering. They had to cope with civil war, particularly in the Vendée, economic distress, blockaded ports, and foreign invasion. They lived with the terrible dread that if they failed, the Revolution for liberty and equality would perish. Only strong leadership could save the republic. It was provided by the Committee of Public Safety. Serving as a cabinet for the Convention, the Committee of Public Safety organized the nation's defenses, formulated foreign policy, supervised ministers, ordered arrests, and imposed the central government's authority throughout the nation. The twelve members of the committee, all ardent patriots and veterans of revolutionary politics, constituted "a government of perhaps the ablest and most determined men who have ever held power in France."[18]

Jacobin Achievements

The Jacobins continued the work of reform. A new constitution, in 1793, expressed Jacobin enthusiasm for political democracy. It contained a new Declaration of Rights, which affirmed and amplified the principles of 1789. By giving all adult males the right to vote, it overcame sansculotte objections to the constitution of 1791. However, the threat of invasion and the revolts caused the implementation of the new constitution to be postponed, and it was never put into effect. Furthermore, by abolishing both slavery in the French colonies and imprisonment for debt and by making plans for free public education, the Jacobins revealed their humanitarianism and their debt to the philosophes.

Jacobin economic policies derived from the exigencies of war. To halt inflation and gain the support of the poor—both necessary for the war effort—the Jacobins decreed the *law of the maximum*, which fixed prices on bread and other essential goods. To win over the peasants, the Ja-

cobins made it easier for them to buy the property of émigré nobles. To equip the Army of the Republic, the Committee of Public Safety requisitioned grain, wool, arms, shoes, and other items from individual citizens, required factories and mines to produce at full capacity, and established state-operated armament and munitions plants.

The Nation in Arms

For the war against foreign invaders, the Jacobins, in an act that anticipated modern conscription, drafted unmarried men between eighteen and twenty-five years of age. They mobilized all the resources of the nation, infused the army with a love for *la patrie* (the nation), and in a remarkable demonstration of administrative skill, equipped an army of more than 800,000 men. In creating the nation in arms, the Jacobins heralded the emergence of modern warfare. Inspired by the ideals of liberty, equality, and fraternity and commanded by officers who had proved their skill on the battlefield, the citizen-soldiers of the republic won decisive victories. In May and June 1794, the French routed the allied forces on the vital northern frontier, and by the end of July, France had become the triumphant master of Belgium.

By demanding complete devotion to the nation, the Jacobin phase of the Revolution also heralded the rise of modern nationalism. In the schools, in newspapers, speeches, and poems, on the stage, and at rallies and meetings of patriotic societies, the French people were told of the glory won by republican soldiers on the battlefield and were reminded of their duties to *la patrie*. "The citizen is born, lives and dies for the fatherland."[19] These words were written in public places for all citizens to read and ponder. The soldiers of the Revolution fought not for money or for a king, but for the nation. "When *la patrie* calls us for her defense," wrote a young soldier to his mother, "we should rush to her.... Our life, our goods, and our talents do not belong to us. It is to the nation, to *la patrie*, to which everything belongs."[20] Could this heightened sense of nationality, which concentrated on the special interests of the French people, be reconciled with the Declaration of the Rights of Man, whose principles were addressed to all humanity? The revolutionaries themselves did not understand the implications of the new force that they had unleashed.

The Republic of Virtue and the Reign of Terror

Robespierre   At the same time that the Committee of Public Safety was forging a revolutionary army to deal with external enemies, it was also waging war against internal opposition. The pivotal personality in this struggle was Maximilién Robespierre (1758–1794). Robespierre, who had served in the National Assembly and was an active Jacobin, was distinguished by a fervent faith in the rightness of his beliefs, a total commitment to republican democracy, and an integrity that earned him the appellation "the Incorruptible."

Robespierre wanted to create a better society founded on reason, good citizenship, and patriotism. In his Republic of Virtue, there would be no kings or nobles; men would be free, equal, and educated; and reason would be glorified and superstition ridiculed. There would be no extremes of wealth or poverty; a person's natural goodness would prevail over vice and greed; and laws would preserve, not violate, inalienable rights. In this utopian vision, an individual's duties would be "to detest bad faith and despotism, to punish tyrants and traitors, to assist the unfortunate, to respect the weak, to defend the oppressed, to do all the good one can to one's neighbor, and to behave with justice towards all men."[21]

A disciple of Rousseau, Robespierre considered the national general will to be ultimate and infallible. Its realization meant the establishment of a Republic of Virtue; its denial meant the death of an ideal and a return to despotism. Robespierre believed that he and his colleagues in the Committee of Public Safety had correctly ascertained the needs of the French people. He was certain that the committee members were the genuine interpreters of the general will, and he felt duty-bound to ensure its realization. He pursued his ideal society with religious zeal. Knowing that the Republic of Virtue could not be established while France was threatened by foreign and civil war, Robespierre urged that enemies of the republic "be prosecuted by all not as ordinary enemies, but as rebels, brigands, and assassins."[22]

To preserve republican liberty, the Jacobins

ROBESPIERRE, AN ENGRAVING BY FIÉSINGER AFTER A DRAWING BY PIERRE-NARCISSE GUÉRIN. To create a Republic of Virtue where men would be free and equal, Maximilién Robespierre considered terror necessary. Fearing that no one was safe from the Terror, members of the Convention ordered Robespierre's arrest and execution. (*Bibliothèque Nationale, Paris*)

made terror a deliberate government policy. Robespierre declared:

> *Does not liberty, that inestimable blessing . . . have the . . . right to sacrifice lives, fortunes, and even, for a time, individual liberties? . . . Is not the French Revolution . . . a war to the death between those who want to be free and those content to be slaves? . . . There is no middle ground; France must be entirely free or perish in the attempt, and any means are justifiable in fighting for so fine a cause.*[23]

With Robespierre playing a key role, the Jacobin leadership attacked those they considered enemies of the republic: Girondins who challenged Jacobin authority; federalists who opposed a strong central government emanating from Paris; counterrevolutionary priests and nobles and their peasant supporters; and profiteers who hoarded food. The Robespierrists also executed Jacques Danton, a hero of the Revolution, who wished to end the terror and negotiate peace with the enemy. The Jacobins even sought to discipline the ardor of the sans-culottes who had given them power. Fearful that sans-culotte spontaneity would undermine central authority and promote anarchy, Robespierrists brought about the dissolution of sans-culotte societies. In addition, they executed radical revolutionaries known as the *enragés* (literally, madmen), who had considerable influence on the Paris sans-culottes. The leaders of the *enragés* threatened insurrection against Jacobin rule and pushed for more social reforms than the Jacobins would allow, including setting limits on incomes and on the size of farms and businesses.

Robespierre and his fellow Jacobins did not resort to the guillotine because they were bloodthirsty or power mad. Instead, they sought to establish a temporary dictatorship in a desperate attempt to save the republic and the Revolution. Deeply devoted to republican democracy, the Jacobins viewed themselves as bearers of a higher faith. Like all visionaries, Robespierre was convinced that he knew the right way and that the new society he envisaged would benefit all humanity. He saw those who impeded its implementation as not just opponents, but sinners who had to be liquidated for the general good.

Special courts were established in Paris and other cities to try suspects. The proceedings were carried on in haste, and most judgments called either for acquittal or execution. In the Vendée, where civil war raged, many of the arrested were executed by firing squads, without trial; some five thousand were loaded onto barges, which were then sunk in the middle of the Loire River.

Ironically, most of the executions took place after the frontiers had been secured and the civil war crushed. In many ways, the Terror was less a means of saving the beleaguered republic and more a way of shaping the new republican society and the new individual in accordance with the radical Jacobin ideology. Perhaps as many as forty thousand people from all segments of society perished during the Terror.

The Jacobins did save the republic. Their regime expelled foreign armies, crushed the feder-alist uprisings, contained the counterrevolutionaries in the Vendée, and prevented anarchy. Without the discipline, order, and unity imposed on France by the Robespierrists, it is likely that the republic would have collapsed under the twin blows of foreign invasion and domestic anarchy.

The Significance of the Terror The Reign of Terror poses fundamental questions about the meaning of the French Revolution and the validity of the Enlightenment conception of the individual. To what extent was the Terror a reversal of the ideals of the Revolution as formulated in the Declaration of the Rights of Man? To what extent did the feverish passions and the fascination with violence demonstrated in the mass executions in the provinces and in the public spectacles in Paris indicate a darker side of human nature, beyond control of reason? Did Robespierre's religion of humanity revive the fanaticism and cruelty of the wars of religion, which had so disgusted the philosophes? Did the Robespierrists, who considered themselves the staunchest defenders of the Revolution's ideals, soil and subvert these ideals by their zeal? The Jacobins mobilized the might of the nation, created the mystique of *la patrie*, and imposed dictatorial rule in defense of liberty and equality; they also legalized and justified terror committed in the people's name. In so doing, were they unwittingly unleashing new forces that, in later years, would be harnessed by totalitarian ideologies consciously resolved to stamp out the liberal heritage of the Revolution? Did 1793 mark a change in the direction of Western civilization: a movement away from the ideals of the philosophes and the opening of an age of violence and irrationalism, which would culminate in the cataclysms of the twentieth century?

The Fall of Robespierre

The Terror had been instituted during a time of crisis and keyed-up emotions. By the summer of 1794, with the victory of the republic seemingly assured, the fear of an aristocratic conspiracy had subsided, the will to punish "traitors" had slackened, and popular fervor for the Terror had diminished. As the need and enthusiasm for the Terror abated, Robespierre's political position weakened.

Opponents of Robespierre in the Convention, feeling the chill of the guillotine blade on their

Giraudon/Art Resource, NY

GRACCHUS BABEUF

In 1796, militant supporters of the poor conspired to overthrow the Directory, which was dominated by moderate bourgeois. Among the plotters was Gracchus Babeuf (1760–1797), whose newspaper, *Tribune of the People,* founded in 1794, shortly after the fall of Robespierre, regularly attacked the government. Made aware of the plot—known as the Conspiracy of the Equals—by informers, the Directory ordered the conspirators rounded up. Most of those indicted were freed, seven were deported, and two, including Babeuf, were executed.

The historical significance of Babeuf and his associates derives not from their inconsequential conspiracy, but from their call to abolish private property and end the division of society into exploiter and exploited. Historians view the conspirators as pre-Marxist socialists who, like their Marxist successors, aspired to seize power in order to radically transform society.

own necks, ordered the arrest of Robespierre and some of his supporters. On July 28, 1794, the tenth of Thermidor according to the new republican calendar, Robespierre was guillotined. Parisian sans-culottes might have saved him, but they made no attempt to do so. With their political clubs dissolved, they lacked the organization needed for an armed uprising. Moreover, the sans-culottes' ardor for Jacobinism had waned. They resented Robespierre for having executed their leaders, and apparently the social legislation instituted by the Robespierrist leadership had not been sufficient to soothe sans-culotte discontent.

After the fall of Robespierre, the machinery of the Jacobin republic was dismantled. Leadership passed to the property-owning bourgeois who had endorsed the constitutional ideas of 1789–91, the moderate stage of the Revolution. The new leadership, known as Thermidoreans until the end of 1795, wanted no more of the Jacobins or of Robespierre's society. They had considered Robespierre a threat to their political power because he would have allowed the common people a considerable

voice in the government. They had also viewed him as a threat to their property because he would have introduced some state regulation of the economy to aid the poor.

The Thermidorean reaction was a counterrevolution. The new government purged the army of officers who were suspected of Jacobin leanings, abolished the law of the maximum, and declared void the constitution of 1793. A new constitution, approved in 1795, reestablished property requirements for voting. The counterrevolution also produced a counterterror, as royalists and Catholics massacred Jacobins in the provinces.

At the end of 1795, the new republican government, the Directory, was burdened by war, a sagging economy, and internal unrest. The Directory crushed insurrections by Parisian sans-culottes, maddened by hunger and hatred of the rich (1795, 1796), and by royalists seeking to restore the monarchy (1797). As military and domestic pressures increased, power began to pass into the hands of generals. One of them, Napoleon Bonaparte, seized control of the gov-

In the spirited defense he gave at his trial, Babeuf often quoted passages from *Tribune of the People*, such as the following, which reveals the socialist character of his thought.

The masses can no longer find a way to go on living; they see that they possess nothing and that they suffer under the harsh and flinty oppression of a greedy ruling class. The hour strikes for great and memorable revolutionary events, already foreseen in the writings of the times, when a general overthrow of the system of private property is inevitable, when the revolt of the poor against the rich becomes a necessity that can no longer be postponed. . . .

Nature has placed everyone under an obligation to work. None may excempt himself from work without committing an antisocial action. Work and its fruits should be common to all. Oppression exists when one man is ground down by toil and lacks the barest necessaries of life, while another revels in luxury and idleness.

It is impossible for anyone, without committing a crime, to appropriate for his own exclusive use the fruits of the earth or of manufacture.

In a truly just social order there are neither rich nor poor. The rich, who refuse to give up their superfluous wealth for the benefit of the poor, are enemies of the people.

None may be permitted to monopolize the cultural resources of society and hence to deprive others of the education essential for their wellbeing. Education is a universal human right.

The purpose of the Revolution is to abolish inequality and to restore the common welfare. The Revolution is not yet at an end, since the wealthy have diverted its fruits, including political power, to their own exclusive use, while the poor in their toil and misery lead a life of actual slavery and count for nothing in the State.*

**The Defense of Gracchus Babeuf*, ed. and trans. John Anthony Scott (New York: Schocken Books, 1972), pp. 45–46.

ernment in November 1799, pushing the Revolution into yet another stage.

THE MEANING OF THE FRENCH REVOLUTION

The French Revolution was a decisive period in the shaping of the modern West. It implemented the thought of the philosophes, destroyed the hierarchical and corporate society of the Old Regime, which was a legacy of the Middle Ages, promoted the interests of the bourgeoisie, and quickened the growth of the modern state.

The Revolution also weakened the aristocracy. With their ancient feudal rights and privileges eliminated, the nobles became simply ordinary citizens. Throughout the nineteenth century, France would be governed by both aristocrats and bourgeois. Property, not noble birth, determined the composition of the new ruling elite—a trend already in evidence before the Revolution.

The principle of careers open to talent gave the bourgeoisie access to the highest positions in the state. Having wealth, talent, ambition, and now opportunity, the bourgeoisie would play an ever more important role in French political life. Throughout the Continent, the reforms of the French Revolution served as a model for progressive bourgeoisie who, sooner or later, would challenge the Old Regime in their own lands.

The French Revolution transformed the dynastic state, on which the Old Regime was based, into the modern state: national, liberal, secular, and rational. When the Declaration of the Rights of Man and of the Citizen asserted that "the source of all sovereignty resides essentially in the nation," the concept of the state took on a new meaning. The state was no longer merely a territory or a federation of provinces; it was not the private possession of the king claiming to be God's lieutenant on earth. In the new conception, the state belonged to the people as a whole, and the individual, formerly a subject, was now a citizen with both rights and duties and was governed by laws that drew no distinction on the basis of birth.

The liberal thought of the Enlightenment found practical expression in the reforms of the Revolution. Absolutism and divine right of monarchy, repudiated in theory by the philosophes, were invalidated by constitutions that set limits on the powers of government and by elected parliaments that represented the governed. By providing for equality before the law and the protection of human rights—habeas corpus, trial by jury, and freedom of religion, speech, and the press—the Revolution struck at the abuses of the Old Regime. Because of violations and interruptions, these gains seemed at times more theoretical than actual. Nevertheless, these liberal ideals reverberated throughout the Continent. During the nineteenth century, the pace of reform would quicken. And with the demands of the sans-culottes for equality with the bourgeois, for political democracy, and for social reform, the voice of the urban poor began to be heard in politics. This phenomenon would intensify with growing industrialization.

At the same time, the Revolution presented a dilemma for bourgeois liberals, who valued reforms promoting liberty and equality but also feared the entrance into politics of the uneducated and unpropertied sans-culottes, with their demand for state intervention in the economy to improve living standards. And bourgeois moderates were haunted by memories of Jacobin radicalism. The Terror was a frightening demonstration of how liberty could degenerate into a new kind of despotism.

By disavowing any divine justification for the monarch's power and by depriving the church of its special position, the Revolution accelerated the secularization of European political life. Sweeping aside the administrative chaos of the Old Regime, the Revolution attempted to impose rational norms on the state. The sale of public offices, which had produced ineffective and corrupt administrators, was eliminated, and the highest positions in the land were opened to men of talent, regardless of birth. The Revolution abolished the peasantry's manorial obligations, which had hampered agriculture, and swept away barriers to economic expansion. It based taxes on income and streamlined their collection. By destroying feudal remnants and eliminating internal tolls and guilds, it speeded up the expansion of a com-

LIBERTY ARMED WITH THE SCEPTER OF REASON STRIKES DOWN IGNORANCE AND FANATICISM, AN ENGRAVING BY JEAN-BAPTISTE CHAPUY, C. 1793. Using a scepter given to her by Reason standing at the left, Liberty strikes down ignorance and fanaticism, usually identified with religion. Many of these prints were produced in 1793 and 1794 when there was a concerted effort to replace traditional Christianity with a civic religion, the Cult of Reason. (*Bibliothèque Nationale, Paris*)

petitive market economy. In the nineteenth century, reformers in the rest of Europe would follow the lead set by France.

The French Revolution also unleashed two potentially destructive forces identified with the modern state: total war and nationalism. These contradicted the rational and universal aims of the reformers as stated in the Declaration of the Rights of Man. Whereas eighteenth-century wars were fought by professional soldiers for limited aims, the French Revolution, says British historian Herbert Butterfield,

> brings conscription, the nation in arms, the mobilization of all the resources of the state for unrelenting conflict. It heralds the age when peoples, woefully ignorant of one another, bitterly uncomprehending, lie in uneasy juxtaposition watching one another's sins with hysteria and indignation. It heralds Armageddon, the giant conflict for justice and right between angered populations each of which thinks it is the righteous one. So a new kind of warfare is born—the modern counterpart to the old conflicts of religions.[24]

The world wars of the twentieth century are the terrible fulfillment of this new development in warfare.

The French Revolution also gave birth to modern nationalism. During the Revolution, loyalty was directed to the entire nation, not to a village or province or to the person of the king. The whole of France became the fatherland. Under the Jacobins, the French became converts to a secular faith preaching total reverence for the nation. "In 1794 we believed in no supernatural religion; our serious interior sentiments were all summed up in the one idea, how to be useful to the fatherland. Everything else . . . was, in our eyes, only trivial. . . . It was our only religion."[25] Few suspected that the new religion of nationalism was fraught with danger. Louis-Antoine de Saint-Just, a young, ardent Robespierrist, was gazing into our own century when he declared: "There is something terrible in the sacred love of the fatherland. This love is so exclusive that it sacrifices everything to the public interest, without pity, without fear, with no respect for the human individual."[26]

The Revolution attempted to reconstruct society on the basis of Enlightenment thought. The Declaration of the Rights of Man and of the Citizen, whose spirit permeated the reforms of the Revolution, upheld the dignity of the individual, demanded respect for the individual, attributed to each person natural rights, and barred the state from denying these rights. It insisted that society and the state have no higher duty than to promote the freedom and autonomy of the individual. "It is not enough to have overturned the throne," said Robespierre; "our concern is to erect upon its remains holy Equality and the sacred Rights of Man."[27] The tragedy of the Western experience is that this humanist vision, brilliantly expressed by the Enlightenment and given recognition in the reforms of the French Revolution, would be undermined in later generations. And, ironically, by spawning total war, nationalism, terror as government policy, and a revolutionary mentality that sought to change the world through coercion and violence, if necessary, the French Revolution itself contributed to the shattering of this vision.

◆ ◆ ◆

NOTES

1. Quoted in G. P. Gooch, *Germany and the French Revolution* (New York: Russell & Russell, 1966), p. 39.

2. Quoted in Ernst Wangermann, *From Joseph II to the Jacobin Trials* (New York: Oxford University Press, 1959), p. 24.

3. Excerpted in Alfred Cobban, ed., *The Debate on the French Revolution* (London: Adam & Charles Black, 1960), p. 41.

4. Quoted in Elinor G. Barber, *The Bourgeoisie in Eighteenth-Century France* (Princeton, N.J.: Princeton University Press, 1967), p. 57.

5. Quoted in C. B. A. Behrens, *The Ancien Régime* (New York: Harcourt, Brace & World, 1967), p. 43.

6. Quoted in Leo Gershoy, *The French Revolution and Napoleon* (New York: Appleton-Century-Crofts, 1933), p. 18.

7. George Rudé, *Revolutionary Europe, 1783–1815* (New York: Harper Torchbooks, 1966), p. 74.

8. Henri Peyre, "The Influence of Eighteenth-Century Ideas on the French Revolution," *Journal of the History of Ideas,* 10 (1949):73.

9. Georges Lefebvre, *The French Revolution from 1793 to 1799,* trans. John Hall Stewart and James Friguglietti (New York: Columbia University Press, 1964), 2:360.

10. Quoted in T. C. W. Blanning, *The French Revolution: Aristocrats Versus Bourgeois?* (Atlantic Highlands, N.J.: Humanities Press, 1987), p. 9.

11. William Doyle, *Origins of the French Revolution* (Oxford University Press, 1980), p. 21.

12. Quoted in Blanning, *French Revolution,* p. 38.

13. Excerpted in John Hall Stewart, ed., *A Documentary Survey of the French Revolution* (New York: Macmillan, 1951), pp. 43–44.

14. See George Rudé, *The Crowd in the French Revolution* (New York: Oxford University Press, 1959).

15. Georges Lefebvre, *The Coming of the French Revolution* (Princeton, N.J.: Princeton University Press, 1967), p. 210.

16. Albert Soboul, *The Parisian Sans-Culottes and the French Revolution, 1793–94,* trans. Gwynne Lewis (London: Oxford University Press, 1964), pp. 28–29.

17. Quoted in Soboul, *Parisian Sans-Culottes,* p. 64.

18. Alfred Cobban, *A History of Modern France* (Baltimore: Penguin, 1961), 1:213.

19. Quoted in Hans Kohn, *Nationalism: Its Meaning and History* (Princeton, N.J.: D. Van Nostrand, 1965), p. 25.

20. Quoted in Carlton J. H. Hayes, *The Historical Evolution of Modern Nationalism* (New York: Richard R. Smith, 1931), p. 55.

21. Excerpted in George Rudé, ed., *Robespierre* (Englewood Cliffs, N.J.: Prentice-Hall, 1976), p. 72.

22. Ibid., p. 57.

23. Excerpted in E. L. Higgins, ed., *The French Revolution* (Boston: Houghton Mifflin, 1938), pp. 306–307.

24. Herbert Butterfield, *Napoleon* (New York: Collier Books, 1962), p. 18.

25. Quoted in Hayes, *Evolution of Modern Nationalism,* p. 55.

26. Quoted in Hans Kohn, *Making of the Modern French Mind* (New York: D. Van Nostrand, 1955), p. 17.

27. Quoted in Christopher Dawson, *The Gods of Revolution* (New York: New York University Press, 1972), p. 83.

Suggested Reading

Blanning, T. C. W. *The French Revolution: Aristocrats Versus Bourgeois?* (1987). Summarizes recent scholarship on the question; a volume in Studies of European History series.

Carr, John L., *Robespierre* (1972). A biography of the revolutionary leader.

Doyle, William, *Origins of the French Revolution* (1980). In recent decades, several historians have challenged the traditional view that the French Revolution was an attempt by the bourgeoisie to overthrow the remnants of aristocratic power and privilege and that it was a victory of a capitalist bourgeois order over feudalism. This book summarizes the new scholarship and argues that the nobility and bourgeoisie had much in common before the Revolution.

———, *The Oxford History of the French Revolution* (1990). A narrative history that incorporates new thinking on the causes and nature of the Revolution.

Forrest, Alan, *The French Revolution* (1995). Social, political, and ideological changes wrought by the Revolution.

Furet, François, and Mona Ozouf, eds., *A Critical Dictionary of the French Revolution* (1989). Articles on many topics pertaining to the Revolution; highly recommended.

Gershoy, Leo, *The Era of the French Revolution* (1957). A brief survey with useful documents.

Gourbet, Pierre, *The Ancien Régime* (1973). A survey of French society from 1600 to 1750.

Higgins, E. L., ed., *The French Revolution* (1938). Excerpts from contemporaries.

Kafker, F. A., and J. M. Laux, *The French Revolution: Conflicting Interpretations* (1976). Excerpts from leading historians.

Lefebvre, Georges, *The French Revolution,* 2 vols. (1962, 1964). A detailed analysis by a master historian.

———, *The Coming of the French Revolution* (1967). A brilliant analysis of the social structure of the Old Regime and the opening phase of the Revolution.

Palmer, R. R., *The Age of the Democratic Revolution,* 2 vols. (1959, 1964). The French Revolution as part of a revolutionary movement that spread on both sides of the Atlantic.

———, *Twelve Who Ruled* (1965). An admirable treatment of the Terror.

Rudé, George, *The Crowd in the French Revolution* (1959). An analysis of the composition of the crowds that stormed the Bastille, marched to Versailles, and attacked the king's palace.

———, *Robespierre: Portrait of a Revolutionary Democrat* (1976). A biography of the revolutionary leader.

Soboul, Albert, *The Sans-Culottes* (1972). An

abridgment of the classic study of the popular movement of 1793–94.

Stewart, J. H., *A Documentary Survey of the French Revolution* (1951). A valuable collection of documents.

Sutherland, D. M. G., *France 1789–1815* (1986). Like Doyle, Sutherland departs from the classic theory of the bourgeois revolution.

REVIEW QUESTIONS

1. What privileges did clergy and nobility enjoy in the Old Regime?

2. What were the grievances of the bourgeoisie, the peasantry, and the urban laborers?

3. Why was France in financial difficulty?

4. Why do some historians regard the French Revolution as a bourgeois revolution? Why do revisionists dispute this view?

5. Identify and explain the significance of the following: the formation of the National Assembly, the storming of the Bastille, the Great Fear, and the October Days.

6. Analyze the nature and significance of the reforms of the National Assembly.

7. What were the grievances of the sans-culottes?

8. Identify and explain the significance of the following: flight of the king, the Brunswick manifesto, and the September Massacres.

9. What were the principal differences between the Jacobins and the Girondins?

10. What were the accomplishments of the Jacobins?

11. How did Robespierre justify the Terror? What meaning do you ascribe to the Terror?

12. Why was the French Revolution a decisive period in the shaping of the West?

CHAPTER *20*

Napoleon:
Subverter and Preserver
of the Revolution

*T*he upheavals of the French Revolution made possible the extraordinary career of Napoleon Bonaparte. This popular general, who gained control over France in 1799, combined a passion for power with a genius for leadership. Under Napoleon's military dictatorship, the constitutional government for which the people of 1789 had fought and the republican democracy for which the Jacobins had rallied the nation seemed lost. Nevertheless, during the Napoleonic era, many achievements of the Revolution were preserved, strengthened, and carried to other lands.

RISE TO POWER

Napoleon was born on August 15, 1769, on the French-ruled island of Corsica, the son of a petty noble. After finishing military school in France, he became an artillery officer; the wars of the French Revolution gave him an opportunity to advance his career. In December 1793, Napoleon's brilliant handling of artillery forced the British to lift their siege of the city of Toulon. Two years later, he saved the Thermidorean Convention from a royalist insurrection by ordering his troops to fire into the riotous mob—the famous "whiff of grapeshot." In 1796, he was given command of the French Army of Italy. His star was rising.

In Italy, against the Austrians, Napoleon demonstrated a dazzling talent for military planning and leadership, which earned him an instant reputation. Having tasted glory, he could never do without it. Since he had experienced only success, nothing seemed impossible. He sensed that he was headed for greatness. Years later, he recalled: "[In Italy] I realized I was a superior being and conceived the ambition of performing great things, which hitherto had filled my thoughts only as a fantastic dream."[1]

Murals at Versailles, showing Napoleon reviewing his troops. (*Agence Photographie de la Reunion des Musees Nationaux*)

CHRONOLOGY 20.1 Napoleon's Career

1796	Napoleon gets command of the French Army of Italy
1798	Battle of the Nile: the British annihilate Napoleon's fleet
November 10, 1799	He helps to overthrow Directory's rule, establishing a strong executive in France
1802	He becomes first consul for life; peace is made with Austria and Britain
March 21, 1804	Civil Code (called Code Napoléon in 1807)
December 2, 1804	Napoleon crowns himself emperor of the French
October 1805	French forces occupy Vienna
October 21, 1805	Battle of Trafalgar: French and Spanish fleets are defeated by the British
December 1805	Battle of Austerlitz: Napoleon defeats Russo-Austrian forces
1806	War against Prussia and Russia
October 1806	Napoleon defeats Prussians at Jena, and French forces occupy Berlin
June 1807	French victory over Russians at Friedland
July 1807	Treaties of Tilsit was signed with Russia and Prussia
1808–1813	Peninsular War: Spaniards, aided by the British, fight against French occupation
September 14, 1812	Grand Army reaches Moscow
October–December 1812	Grand Army retreats from Russia
October 1813	Allied forces defeat Napoleon at Leipzig
1814	Paris is captured, and Napoleon is exiled to Elba
March 20, 1815	Escaping, Napoleon enters Paris and begins "hundred days" rule
June 1815	Defeated at Waterloo, he is exiled to Saint Helena

In November 1797, Napoleon was ordered to plan an invasion of England. Aware that the French navy was weak, he recommended postponing the invasion. He urged instead that an expedition be sent to the Near East to strike at British power in the Mediterranean and British commerce with India, and perhaps to carve out a French empire in the Near East. With more than thirty-five thousand troops, Napoleon set out for Egypt, then a part of the Turkish empire. Although he captured Cairo, the Egyptian campaign was far from a success. At the battle of the Nile (1798), the British, commanded by Admiral Horatio Nelson, annihilated Napoleon's fleet. Deprived of reinforcements and supplies, with his manpower reduced by battle and plague, Napoleon was compelled to abandon whatever dreams he might have had of threatening India. Although the Egyptian expedition was a failure, Napoleon, always seeking to improve his image, sent home glowing bulletins about French victories. To people in France, he was the conqueror of Egypt, as well as of Italy.

Meanwhile, political unrest, financial disorder, and military reversals produced an atmosphere of crisis in France. Napoleon knew that in such times people seek out a savior. A man of destiny must act. Without informing his men, he slipped out of Egypt, avoided British cruisers, and landed in France in October 1799.

Coup d'État

When Napoleon arrived in France, a conspiracy was already under way against the government of the Directory. Convinced that only firm leadership could solve France's problems, some politicians plotted to seize power and establish a strong executive. Needing the assistance of a popular general, they turned to Napoleon, whom they thought they could control. Although the hastily prepared coup d'état was almost bungled, the government of the Directory was overthrown. The French Revolution entered a new stage, that of military dictatorship.

Demoralized by a decade of political instability, economic distress, domestic violence, and war, most of the French welcomed the leadership of a strong man. The bourgeois, in particular, expected Napoleon to protect their wealth and the influence they had gained during the Revolution.

The new constitution (1799) created a strong executive. Although three consuls shared the executive office, the first consul, Napoleon, monopolized power. Whereas Napoleon's fellow conspirators, who were political moderates, sought only to strengthen the executive, Napoleon aspired to personal rule. He captured the reins of power after the coup, and his authority continued to expand. In 1802, he was made first consul for life, with the right to name his successor. And on December 2, 1804, in a magnificent ceremony at the Cathedral of Notre Dame in Paris, Napoleon crowned himself emperor of the French. General, first consul, and then emperor—it was a breathless climb to the heights of power. Napoleon, who once said that he loved "power as a musician loves his violin,"[2] was determined never to lose it.

Napoleon's Character

What sort of man was this on whom the fate of France and Europe depended? Napoleon's complex and mysterious personality continues to baffle biographers. However, certain distinctive characteristics are evident. Napoleon's intellectual ability was impressive. His mind swiftly absorbed and classified details, which his photographic memory stored. With surgical precision, he could probe his way to the heart of a problem while still retaining a grasp of peripheral considerations. Ideas always danced in his head, and his imagination was illuminated by sudden flashes of insight. He could work for eighteen or twenty hours at a stretch, deep in concentration, ruling out boredom or fatigue by an act of will. Napoleon, man of action, warrior par excellence, was in many ways, says Georges Lefebvre, "a typical man of the eighteenth century, a rationalist, a *philosophe* [who] placed his trust in reason, in knowledge, and in methodical effort."[3]

Rationalism was only one part of his personality. There was also that elemental, irresistible urge for action, "the romantic Napoleon, a force seeking to expand and for which the world was no more than an occasion for acting dangerously."[4] This love of action fused with his boundless ambition. Lefebvre continues:

> His greatest ambition was glory. "I live only for posterity," he exclaimed, "death is nothing, but to live defeated and without

CORONATION OF NAPOLEON AND JOSEPHINE BY DAVID. Napoleon crowned himself emperor in a magnificent ceremony. To French émigrés and nobles throughout Europe, he was the "crowned Jacobin" who threatened aristocratic privileges and European stability. (*Louvre © R.M.N.*)

glory is to die every day." His eyes were fixed on the world's great leaders: Alexander who conquered the East and dreamed of conquering the world; Caesar, Augustus, Charlemagne. . . . They were for him examples, which stimulated his imagination and lent an unalterable charm to action. He was an artist, a poet of action, for whom France and mankind were but instruments.[5]

He also exuded an indefinable quality of personality, a charismatic force that made people feel that they were in the presence of a superior man. Contemporaries remarked that his large gray eyes, penetrating, knowing, yet strangely expressionless, seemed to possess a hypnotic power. He was capable of moving men to obedience, to loyalty, and to heroism.

The rationalist's clarity of mind and the romantic's impassioned soul, the adventurer's love of glory and the hero's personal magnetism—these were the components of Napoleon's personality. There was also an aloofness—some would say callousness—that led him to regard people as pawns to be manipulated in the pursuit of his destiny. "A man like me," he once said, "troubles himself little about the lives of a million men."[6]

Napoleon's genius might have gone unheralded and his destiny unfulfilled had it not been for the opportunities created by the French Revolution. By opening careers to talent, the Revolution enabled a young Corsican of undistinguished birth to achieve fame and popularity. By creating a national army and embroiling France in war, it provided a military commander with enormous sources of power. By plunging France into one crisis after another, it opened up extraordinary possibilities for a man with a gift of leadership and an ambition "so intimately linked with my very being that it is like the blood that circulates in my veins."[7] It was the Revolution that made Napoleon conscious of his genius and certain of his destiny.

NAPOLEON AND FRANCE

Living in a revolutionary age, Napoleon had observed firsthand the precariousness of power and
the fleetingness of popularity. A superb realist, he
knew that his past reputation would not sustain
him. If he could not solve the problems caused by
a decade of revolution and war and bind together
the different classes of French people, his prestige
would diminish and his power collapse. The general must become a statesman, and when necessary, a tyrant. His domestic policies, showing the
influence of both eighteenth-century enlightened
despotism and the Revolution, affected every aspect of society and had an enduring impact on
French history. They continued the work of the
Revolution in destroying the institutions of the
Old Regime.

Government: Centralization and Repression

In providing France with a strong central government, Napoleon continued a policy initiated centuries earlier by Bourbon monarchs. The Bour-
bons, however, had not been able to overcome
completely the barriers presented by provinces, local traditions, feudal remnants, and corporate institutions. Napoleon, on the other hand, succeeded
in giving France administrative uniformity. An
army of officials, subject to the emperor's will,
reached into every village, linking together the entire nation. This centralized state suited Napoleon's desire for orderly government and rational
administration, enabled him to concentrate power
in his own hands, and provided him with the taxes
and soldiers needed to fight his wars. To suppress
irreconcilable opponents, primarily die-hard royalists and republicans, Napoleon used the instruments of the police state: secret agents, arbitrary
arrest, summary trials, and executions.

Napoleon also shaped public opinion to prevent hostile criticism of his rule and to promote
popular support for his policies and person. In
these actions, he was a precursor of twentieth-century dictators. Liberty of the press came to an end.
Printers swore an oath of obedience to the emperor, and newspapers were converted into government mouthpieces. Printers were forbidden to
print and booksellers to sell or circulate "anything

which may involve injury to the duties of subjects
toward the sovereign or the interests of the state."[8]
When Napoleon's secretary read him the morning
newspapers, Napoleon would interrupt, "Skip it,
skip it. I know what is in them. They only say what
I tell them to."[9] These efforts at indoctrination
even reached schoolchildren, who were required to
memorize a catechism glorifying the ruler, which
ran, in part, as follows:

> *Q. What are the duties of Christians with
> respect to the princes who govern them, and
> what in particular are our duties toward
> Napoleon I, our Emperor?*
>
> *A. Christians owe to the princes who govern
> them, and we owe in particular to Napoleon I,
> our Emperor, love, respect, obedience, fidelity,
> military service; . . . we also owe him . . .
> prayers for his safety. . . .*
>
> *Q. Why are we bound to all these duties
> towards our Emperor?*
>
> *A. First of all, because God, who creates
> emperors and distributes them according to
> his will, in loading our Emperor with gifts,
> both in peace and war, has established him as
> our sovereign. . . . To honor and to serve our
> Emperor is then to honor and to serve God
> himself.*
>
> *Q. What . . . of those who may be lacking in
> their duty towards our Emperor?*
>
> *A. . . . they would be resisting the order estab-
> lished by God himself and would make them-
> selves worthy of eternal damnation.*[10]

By repressing liberty, subverting republicanism,
and restoring absolutism, Emperor Napoleon reversed some of the liberal gains of the Revolution.
Although favoring equality before the law and
equality of opportunity as necessary for a well-run
state, Napoleon believed that political liberty impeded efficiency and threatened the state with anarchy. He would govern in the interest of the people as an enlightened but absolute ruler.

Religion: Reconciliation with the Church

For Napoleon, who was a deist, if not an atheist,
the value of religion was not salvation, but social

Profile

Roger-Viollet

FRANÇOIS DOMINIQUE TOUSSAINT L'OUVERTURE

In 1791, in the midst of the French Revolution, black slaves on San Domingo, the rich French sugar colony in the West Indies, revolted, murdering their masters, burning down plantations, and crying "Vengeance! Vengeance!" Their hatred of servitude, which had ignited slave revolts in previous decades, was intensified by the ideals of liberty and equality reverberating across the Atlantic.

François Dominique Toussaint L'Ouverture (c. 1743–1803) joined the rebellion and quickly rose to a position of command. Toussaint was the son of a petty African chief from Dahomey who, like millions of other Africans, had been captured in war, sold to westerners, and brought in chains to toil on plantations in the New World. Toussaint, the eldest of eight children, was born in captivity. A remarkable old black taught him French and some Latin and geometry, and his master, recognizing Toussaint's ability, made him first a coachman and then steward of the plantation's

and political cohesion. It promoted national unity and prevented class war. He stated:

> *Society cannot exist without inequality of fortunes, and inequality of fortunes cannot exist without religion. When a man is dying of hunger alongside another who stuffs himself, it is impossible to make him accede to the difference unless there is an authority which says to him God wishes it thus; there must be some poor and some rich in the world, but hereafter and for all eternity the division will be made differently.*[11]

This is what Napoleon probably had in mind when he said: "Men who do not believe in God—one does not govern them, one shoots them."[12]

Napoleon tried to close the breach between the state and the Catholic church, which had appeared during the Revolution. Such a reconciliation would gain the approval of the mass of the French people, who still remained devoted to their faith, and would reassure the peasants and bourgeoisie who had bought confiscated church lands. For these reasons, Napoleon negotiated an agreement with the pope. The Concordat of 1801 recognized Catholicism as the religion of the great majority of the French, rather than as the official state religion (the proposal that the pope desired). The clergy were to be paid and nominated by the state but consecrated by the pope.

In effect, the Concordat guaranteed the reforms of the Revolution. The church did not regain its confiscated lands nor its right to collect the tithe. The French clergy remained largely subject to state control. And by not establishing Catholicism as the state religion, the Concordat did not jeopardize the newly won toleration of Jews and Protestants. Napoleon had achieved his aim. The Concordat

livestock, a position almost never held by a nonwhite.

At the time of the rebellion, 42,000 whites, employing brutal means of repression—whipping, chaining, roasting, and mutilation—dominated 500,000 black slaves, often working them like beasts. Complicating the social structure were mulattos, people of mixed race who were granted French citizenship in 1793 out of fear that they would side with the rebellious black slaves.

Aspiring to eliminate slavery entirely, Toussaint organized an army consisting mainly of illiterate slaves into a fighting force capable of defeating European-trained soldiers. In 1794, the Jacobins abolished slavery over the opposition of the white planters, and Toussaint, who had distinguished himself as a military commander, was appointed assistant governor. Toussaint was also a man of vision, deeply committed to the revolutionary ideals of liberty and equality and to introducing economic, administrative, and educational reforms in San Domingo. Contrary to the wishes of the more radical black officers, he permitted whites and mulattos to hold important positions in the bureaucracy. Toussaint's reluctance to declare independence from France also angered the radicals.

In 1801, two years after he had seized power, Napoleon sent twenty thousand troops to San Domingo to restore slavery and to subdue Toussaint, whose power had increased considerably. The old warrior, having lost none of his skills in guerrilla warfare, was at the point of defeating the French when he proposed peace. The French commander tricked Toussaint into believing that if he retired, France would negotiate a favorable settlement with San Domingo. Shortly after he retired to his farm, Toussaint was arrested and sent to prison in France, where he suffered abuse and humiliation until his death in 1803. In that same year, revolutionaries on the island established the independent state of Haiti, whose foundation Toussaint L'Ouverture had laid.

made his regime acceptable to Catholics and to owners of former church lands.

Law: The Code Napoléon

Under the Old Regime, France was plagued with numerous and conflicting law codes. Reflecting local interests and feudal traditions, these codes obstructed national unity and administrative efficiency. Efforts by the revolutionaries to draw up a unified code of laws bogged down. Recognizing the value of such a code in promoting effective administration throughout France, Napoleon pressed for the completion of the project. The Code Napoléon incorporated many principles of the Revolution: equality before the law, the right to choose one's profession, freedom of religion, protection of property rights, the abolition of serfdom, and the secular character of the state.

The code also had its less liberal side, denying equal treatment to workers in their dealings with employers, to women in their relations with their husbands, and to children in their relations with their fathers. By making wives inferior to their husbands in matters of property, adultery, and divorce, the code reflected both Napoleon's personal attitude and the general view of the times toward women and family stability. Of women, he once said that "the husband must possess the absolute power and right to say to his wife: 'Madam, you shall not go out, you shall not go to the theater, you shall not receive such and such a person: for the children you shall bear shall be mine!'"[13]

Adopted in lands conquered by France, the Code Napoléon helped to weaken feudal privileges and institutions and clerical interference in the secular state. With justice, Napoleon could say: "My true glory is not to have won forty battles. . . . Wa-

NAPOLEON PRESENTING THE LEGION OF HONOR TO ARTISTS, OCTOBER 1808.
Believing that like himself the French cherished glory above all, Napoleon established in 1802 the Legion of Honor, an order of soldiers who had demonstrated valor and of accomplished civilians who had shown special merit. Many French officials and intellectuals attacked the Legion on the grounds that it violated the egalitarian spirit of the Revolution, but many others coveted membership in the Legion. (© R.M.N.)

terloo will erase the memory of so many victories. . . . But what nothing will destroy, what will live forever, is my Civil Code."[14]

Education: The Imperial University

Napoleon's educational policy was in many ways an elaboration of the school reforms initiated during the Revolution. Like the revolutionaries, Napoleon favored a system of public education, with a secular curriculum and minimum church involvement. For Napoleon, education served a dual purpose: it would provide him with capable officials to administer his laws and trained officers to lead his armies; and it would indoctrinate the young in obedience and loyalty. He established the University of France, a giant board of education that placed education under state control. To this day, the French school system, un-

like that in the United States, is strictly centralized, with curriculum and standards set for the entire country.

The emperor did not consider education for girls important, holding that "marriage is their whole destination."[15] In his view, whatever education girls did receive should stress religion. "What we ask of education is not that girls should think but that they should believe. The weakness of women's brains, the instability of their ideas, the place they fill in society, their need for perpetual resignation . . . all this can only be met by religion."[16]

Economy: Strengthening the State

Napoleon's financial and economic policies were designed to strengthen France and enhance his popularity. To stimulate the economy and to retain the favor of the bourgeois, who supported his seizure of power, Napoleon aided industry through tariffs and loans. He fostered commerce (while also speeding up troop movements) by building or repairing roads, bridges, and canals. To protect the currency from inflation, he established the Bank of France, which was controlled by the nation's leading financiers. By keeping careers open to talent, he endorsed one of the key demands of the bourgeoisie during the Revolution. Fearing a revolution based on lack of bread, he provided food at low prices and stimulated employment for the laboring poor. He endeared himself to the peasants by not restoring feudal privileges and by allowing them to keep the land they had obtained during the Revolution.

Napoleon did not identify with the republicanism and democracy of the Jacobins. Rather, by preserving many social gains of the Revolution while suppressing political liberty, he showed himself to be an heir of the enlightened despots. Like the reforming despots, Napoleon admired administrative uniformity and efficiency, hated feudalism, religious persecution, and civil inequality, and favored government regulation of trade and industry. He saw in enlightened despotism a means of ensuring political stability, overcoming the confusion presented by feudal and corporative institutions, avoiding the dangers of democracy, which he equated with mob rule, and strengthening the state militarily.

NAPOLEON AND EUROPE

Although Napoleon's domestic policies gained him wide support, it was his victories on the battlefield that mesmerized the French people and gratified their national vanity. Ultimately, his popularity and his power rested on the sword. In 1802, he declared,

> My power proceeds from my reputation, and my reputation from the victories I have won. My power would fail if I were not to support it with more glory and more victories. Conquest has made me what I am; only conquest can maintain me.[17]

Napoleon, the Corsican adventurer, realized Louis XIV's dream of French mastery of Europe.

NAPOLEON CROSSING THE GREAT ST. BERNARD PASS. Integral to Napoleon's art of war was his ability to move his troops quickly across difficult terrain and surprise his opponents with confounding tactics. (*Bulloz, Paris*)

Between 1805 and 1807, Napoleon decisively defeated Austria, Prussia, and Russia, becoming the virtual ruler of Europe. In these campaigns, as in his earlier successes in Italy, Napoleon demonstrated his greatness as a military commander.

Napoleon's Art of War

Although forgoing a set battle plan in favor of flexibility, Napoleon was guided by certain general principles, which constituted his art of war. He stressed the advantage of "a rapid and audacious attack" in preference to waging defensive war from a fixed position. "Make war offensively; it is the sole means to become a great captain and to fathom the secrets of the art."[18] Warfare could not be left to chance but required mastering every detail and anticipating every contingency. "I am accustomed to thinking out what I shall do three or four months in advance, and I base my calculations on the worst of conceivable circumstances."[19] Every master plan contained numerous alternatives to cover all contingencies.

Surprise and speed were essential ingredients of Napoleonic warfare. Relying heavily on surprise, Napoleon employed various stratagems to confuse and deceive his opponents: providing newspapers with misleading information, launching secondary offensives, and placing a dense screen of cavalry ahead of marching columns to prevent penetration by enemy patrols. Determined to surprise and consequently demoralize the enemy by arriving at a battlefield ahead of schedule, he carefully selected the best routes to the chosen destination, eliminated slow-moving supply convoys by living off the countryside, and inspired his men to incredible feats of marching as they drew closer to the opposing army. In the first Italian campaign, his men drove 50 miles in thirty-six hours; in 1805, against Austria, they marched 275 miles in twenty-three days.

His campaigns anticipated the blitzkrieg, or lightning warfare, of the twentieth century. As the moment of battle neared, Napoleon would disperse his troops over a wide area; the enemy would counter by dividing its forces. Then, by rapid marches, Napoleon would concentrate a superior force against a segment of the enemy's strung-out forces. Here the hammer blow would fall. Employing some troops to pin down the opposing force, he would move his main army to the enemy's rear or flank, cutting off the enemy supply line. Conducted with speed and deception, these moves broke the spirit of the opposing troops. Heavy barrages by concentrated artillery opened a hole in the enemy lines, which was penetrated first by infantry and then by shock waves of cavalry. Unlike the typical eighteenth-century commander, who maneuvered for position and was satisfied with his opponent's retreat, Napoleon sought to annihilate the enemy's army, thereby destroying its source of power.

The emperor thoroughly understood the importance of morale in warfare. "Moral force rather than numbers decides victory," he once said.[20] He deliberately sought to shatter his opponent's confidence by surprise moves and lightning thrusts. He also recognized that he must maintain a high level of morale among his own troops. By sharing danger with his men, he gained their affection and admiration. He inspired his men by appealing to their honor, vanity, credulity, and love of France. "A man does not have himself killed for a few half-pence a day or for a petty distinction," he declared.

"You must speak to the soul in order to electrify the man."[21] This Napoleon could do. It was Napoleon's charisma that led the duke of Wellington to remark: "I used to say of him that his presence on the field made a difference of 40,000 men."[22]

Despite his reputation, Napoleon was not an original military thinker. His greatness lay rather in his ability to implement and coordinate the theories of earlier strategists. Eighteenth-century military planners had stressed the importance of massed artillery, rapid movement, deception, living off the countryside, and the annihilation of the enemy army. Napoleon alone had the will and ingenuity to convert these theories into battlefield victories.

Napoleon also harnessed the military energies generated during a decade of revolutionary war. The Revolution had created a mass army, had instilled in the republican soldier a love for *la patrie,* and had enabled promising young soldiers to gain promotions on the basis of talent rather than birth. Napoleon took this inheritance and perfected it.

The Grand Empire: Diffusion of Revolutionary Institutions

By 1810, Napoleon dominated the Continent, except for the Balkan Peninsula. The Grand Empire comprised lands annexed to France, vassal states, and cowed allies. The French republic had already annexed Belgium and the German Left Bank of the Rhine. Napoleon incorporated several other areas into France: German coastal regions as far as the western Baltic and large areas of Italy, including Rome, Geneva and its environs, Trieste, and the Dalmatian coast. Vassal states in the Grand Empire included five kingdoms ruled by Napoleon's relatives: two kingdoms in Italy and the kingdoms of Holland, Westphalia, and Spain.

Besides the five satellite kingdoms, there were several other vassal states within the Grand Empire. Napoleon formed the Confederation of the Rhine in 1806. Its members, a loose association of sixteen (later eighteen) German states, were subservient to the emperor, as were the nineteen cantons of the Swiss confederation. The Grand Duchy of Warsaw, formed in 1807 from Prussia's Polish lands, was placed under the rule of

Map 20.1 Napoleon's Europe, 1810 ▶

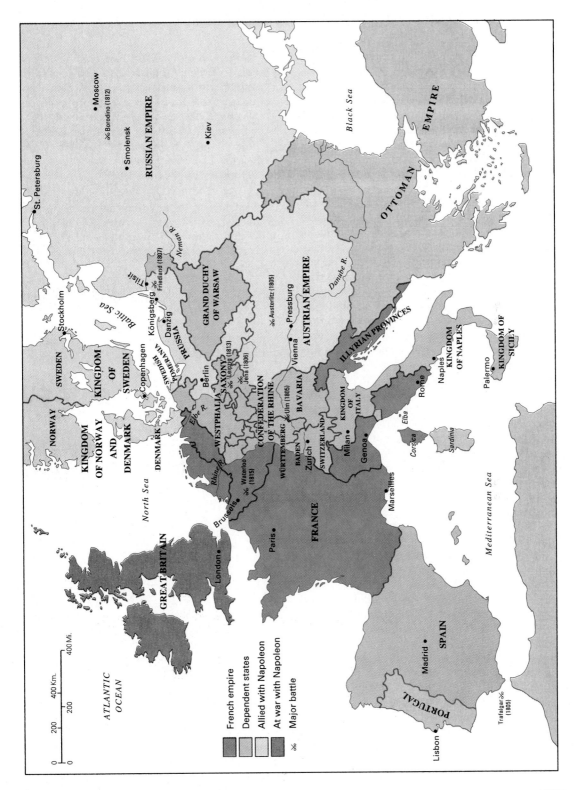

ATLANTIC
OCEAN

400 Mi.

400 Km.

200

200

0

0

French empire

Dependent states

Allied with Napoleon

At war with Napoleon

⚔ Major battle

GREAT BRITAIN

London •

North Sea

NORWAY

KINGDOM
OF NORWAY
AND
DENMARK

DENMARK

SWEDEN

KINGDOM
OF
SWEDEN

Stockholm •

Copenhagen •

Baltic Sea

St. Petersburg •

Moscow •

⚔ Borodino (1812)

• Smolensk

RUSSIAN EMPIRE

• Kiev

Neman R.

Tilsit

⚔ Friedland (1807)

Königsberg •

Danzig

SWEDISH POMERANIA

PRUSSIA

GRAND DUCHY
OF WARSAW

Berlin •

⚔ Leipzig (1813)

SAXONY

⚔ Jena (1806)

WESTPHALIA

Elbe R.

CONFEDERATION
OF THE RHINE

Brussels •

Waterloo ⚔
(1815)

Rhine R.

Paris •

FRANCE

WÜRTTEMBERG

BADEN

Zurich •

SWITZERLAND

⚔ Ulm (1805)

BAVARIA

Vienna •

AUSTRIAN EMPIRE

Pressburg •

⚔ Austerlitz (1805)

Danube R.

OTTOMAN EMPIRE

Black Sea

ILLYRIAN PROVINCES

KINGDOM
OF
ITALY

Milan •

Genoa •

Marseilles •

Corsica

Sardinia

Elba

Rome •

KINGDOM OF NAPLES

Naples •

KINGDOM
OF
SICILY

Palermo •

Mediterranean Sea

SPAIN

Madrid •

PORTUGAL

Lisbon •

Trafalgar ⚔
(1805)

497

the German king of Saxony, one of Napoleon's vassals. Finally, the Grand Empire included states compelled to be French allies—Austria, Prussia, and Russia, as well as Sweden and Denmark.

With varying degrees of determination and success, Napoleon extended the reforms of the Revolution to other lands. His officials instituted the Code Napoléon, organized an effective civil service, opened careers to talent, and equalized the tax burden. Besides abolishing serfdom, manorial payments, and the courts of the nobility, they did away with clerical courts, promoted freedom of religion, permitted civil marriage, pressed for civil rights for Jews, and fought clerical interference in secular matters. They also abolished guilds, introduced a uniform system of weights and measures, eliminated internal tolls, and built roads, bridges, and canals. They promoted secular education and improved public health. Napoleon had launched a Europe-wide social revolution that attacked the privileges of the aristocracy and the clergy—who regarded him as that "crowned Jacobin"—and worked to the advantage of the bourgeoisie. This diffusion of revolutionary institutions weakened the old regimes irreparably in much of Europe and hastened the modernization of nineteenth-century Europe.

Napoleon had a twofold purpose in implementing these reforms: promoting administrative efficiency and winning the support of conquered peoples. He explained his position in a letter to his brother Jerome, ruler of the kingdom of Westphalia.

> *What the people of Germany desire with impatience is that the individuals who are not nobles and who have talents have an equal right to your consideration and to positions; it is that every kind of serfdom and intermediary bonds between the sovereign and the lowest class of people be entirely abolished.*[23]

Pleased by the overhaul of feudal practices and the reduction of clerical power, many Europeans, particularly the progressive bourgeoisie, welcomed Napoleon as a liberator.

But there was another side to Napoleon's rule. The tyrant of Europe turned conquered lands into satellite kingdoms and exploited them for the benefit of France. In a letter to Prince Eugène, viceroy of Italy, Napoleon revealed his policy:

> *All the raw silk from the Kingdom of Italy goes to England. I wish to divert it from this route to the advantage of my French manufacturers: otherwise my silk factories, one of the chief supports of French commerce, will suffer substantial losses. My principle is France first. You must never lose sight of the fact that . . . France should claim commercial supremacy on the continent.*[24]

The satellite states and annexed territories were compelled to provide recruits for Napoleon's army and taxes for his war treasury. Opponents of Napoleon faced confiscation of property, the galleys, and execution.

These methods of exploitation and repression increased hatred for Napoleon and French rule. Subject peoples, including bourgeois liberals who felt that he had betrayed the ideals of the Revolution, came to view Napoleon as a tyrant ready for his downfall.

THE FALL OF NAPOLEON

Aside from the hostility of subject nationals, Napoleon had to cope with the determined opposition of Great Britain. Its subsidies and encouragement kept resistance to the emperor alive. But perhaps Napoleon's greatest obstacle was his own boundless ambition, which warped his judgment. From its peak, the emperor's career soon slid downhill to defeat, dethronement, and deportation.

Failure to Subdue England

Britain was Napoleon's most resolute opponent. It could not be otherwise, for any power that dominated the Continent could organize sufficient naval might to threaten British commerce, challenge its sea power, and invade the island kingdom. Britain would not make peace with any state that sought European hegemony, and Napoleon's ambition would settle for nothing less.

Since he could not make peace with Britain, Napoleon resolved to crush it. Between 1803 and 1805, he assembled an invasion flotilla in the English Channel. But there could be no invasion of Britain while British warships commanded the channel. In 1805, the battle of Trafalgar demonstrated British naval power when Admiral Nelson devastated a combined French and Spanish fleet. Napoleon was forced to postpone his invasion scheme indefinitely.

Unable to conquer Britain by arms, Napoleon decided to bring what he called "the nation of shopkeepers" to its knees by damaging the British economy. His plan, called the Continental System, was to bar all countries under France's control from buying British goods. Although hurt, Britain escaped economic ruin by smuggling goods onto the Continent and increasing trade with the New World. But the Continental System also punished European lands dependent on British imports; hundreds of ships lay idle in European ports, and industries closed down. Though generally supportive of Napoleon's social and administrative reforms, the bourgeoisie turned against him because of the economic distress caused by the Continental System. Furthermore, Napoleon's efforts to enforce the system enmeshed him in two catastrophic blunders: the occupation of Spain and the invasion of Russia.

AND THERE IS NO REMEDY, ETCHING BY FRANCISCO GOYA (1746–1828). Spaniards resisted the installation of Joseph, Napoleon's brother, as king of Spain. Both sides engaged in terrible atrocities in the ensuing Peninsular War. The Spanish painter Francisco Goya captured the war's brutality. (*Philadelphia Museum of Art: SmithKline Beechum Corporation Fund*)

The Spanish Ulcer

An ally of France since 1796, Spain proved a disappointment to Napoleon. It failed to prevent the Portuguese from trading with Britain and contributed little military or financial aid to France's war effort. Napoleon decided to incorporate Spain into his empire; in 1808, he deposed the Spanish ruler, and designated his brother Joseph as king of Spain.

Napoleon believed that the Spanish would rally round the gentle Joseph and welcome his liberal reforms. This confidence was a fatal illusion. Spanish nobles and clergy feared French liberalism; the overwhelmingly peasant population, illiterate and credulous, intensely proud, fanatically religious, and easily stirred up by the clergy, viewed Napoleon as the Devil's agent. Loyal to the Spanish monarchy and faithful to the church, the Spanish fought a "War to the Knife" against the invaders.

Both sides in the Peninsular War displayed extreme cruelty. Wrote one shocked French officer: "At La Carolina we established a hospital and left 167 of our sick and wounded men. That hospital was set afire . . . all were burned alive or horribly massacred. The barbarians believed they had done a glorious thing for God and religion!"[25] Guerrilla bands, aided and encouraged by priests preaching holy war, congregated in mountain hideouts. Striking from ambush, they raided French convoys and outposts, preventing the French from consolidating their occupation and keeping the French forces in a permanent state of anxiety. An invisible army had spread itself over Spain. The war waged by Spanish partisans foreshadowed a twentieth-century phenomenon: the inability of a great power, using trained soldiers and modern weapons, to subdue peasant guerrillas.

Seeking to keep alive the struggle against Napoleon, Britain came to the aid of the Spanish insurgents. The intervention of British troops, commanded by Sir Arthur Wellesley, the future duke of Wellington, led to the ultimate defeat of Joseph in 1813. The "Spanish ulcer" drained Napoleon's treasury, tied down French troops, enabled Britain to gain a foothold on the Continent from which to invade southern France, and inspired patriots in other lands to resist the French emperor.

The German War of Liberation

Anti-French feeling also broke out in the German states. Hatred of the French invaders evoked a feeling of national outrage among some Germans, who up to this time had thought only in terms of their own particular state and prince. Some German intellectuals, using the emotional language of nationalism, called for a war of liberation against Napoleon and, in some instances, for the creation of a unified Germany.

Besides arousing a desire for national independence and unity, the defeat of the Prussians at Jena (1806) and French domination of Germany stimulated a movement for reform among members of the Prussian high bureaucracy and officer corps. To survive in a world altered by the French Revolution, Prussia would have to learn the principal lessons of the Revolution: that aroused citizens fighting for a cause make better soldiers than mercenaries and oppressed serfs and that officers selected for daring and intelligence command better than nobles possessing only a gilded birthright. The reformers believed that the elimination of social abuses would overcome defeatism and apathy and encourage Prussians to serve the state willingly and to fight bravely for national honor. A revitalized Prussia could then deal with the French.

Among the important reforms introduced in Prussia between 1807 and 1813 were the abolition of serfdom, the granting to towns of a large measure of self-administration, the awarding of army commissions on the basis of merit instead of birth, the elimination of cruel punishment in the ranks, and the establishment of national conscription. In 1813, the reform party forced King Frederick William III to declare war on France. The military reforms did improve the quality of the Prussian army. In the War of Liberation (1813), Prussian soldiers demonstrated far more enthusiasm and patriotism than they had at Jena in 1806, and the French were driven from Germany. The German War of Liberation came on the heels of Napoleon's disastrous Russian campaign.

Disaster in Russia

The unsuccessful invasion of Russia in 1812 diminished Napoleon's glory and hastened the collapse of his empire. Deteriorating relations between Russia and France led Napoleon to his fatal decision to attack the eastern giant. Unwilling to permit Russia to become a Mediterranean power, the emperor resisted the tsar's attempts to acquire Constantinople. Napoleon's creation of the Grand Duchy of Warsaw irritated the tsar, who feared a revival of Polish power and resented French influence on Russia's border. Another source of friction between the tsar and Napoleon was Russia's illicit trade with Britain in violation of the Continental System. Napoleon reasoned that if he permitted the tsar to violate the trade regulations, other lands would soon follow and England would never be subdued. No doubt Napoleon's inexhaustible craving for power also compelled him to strike at Russia.

Napoleon assembled one of the largest armies in history: some 614,000 men, 200,000 animals, and 20,000 vehicles. Frenchmen constituted about half of the *Grande Armée de la Russie;* the other soldiers, many serving under compulsion, were drawn from a score of nationalities. The emperor intended to deal the Russians a crushing blow, forcing Tsar Alexander I to sue for peace. But the Russians had other plans: to avoid pitched battles, retreat eastward, and refuse to make peace with the invader. Napoleon would be drawn ever deeper into Russia in pursuit of the enemy.

In June 1812, the Grand Army crossed the Neman River into Russia. Fighting only rear-guard battles and retreating according to plan, the tsar's forces lured the invaders into the vastness of Russia, far from their lines of supply. In September, the Russians made a stand at Borodino, some seventy miles west of Moscow. Although the French won, opening the road to Moscow, they lost forty thousand men and failed to destroy the Russian army, which withdrew in order. Napoleon still did not have the decisive victory with which he hoped to compel the tsar to make peace. At midnight on September 14, the Grand Army, its numbers greatly reduced by disease, hunger, exhaustion, desertion, and battle, entered Moscow. Expecting to be greeted by a deputation of nobles, Napoleon found instead that the Muscovites had virtually evacuated their holy city. To show their contempt for the French conquerors and to deny the French shelter, the Russians set fire to the city, which burned for five days.

Taking up headquarters in Moscow, Napoleon waited for Alexander I to admit defeat and come to terms. But the tsar remained intransigent.

DISASTER IN RUSSIA. Lacking winter provisions, Napoleon's Grand Army abandoned Moscow in October 1812. The retreating French were decimated by hunger, winter, and Russian attacks. (*Musée de l'Armee*)

Napoleon was in a dilemma: to penetrate deeper into Russia was certain death; to stay in Moscow with winter approaching meant possible starvation. Faced with these alternatives, Napoleon was forced to retreat westward to his sources of supply. On October 19, 1812, ninety-five thousand troops and thousands of wagons loaded with loot left Moscow for the long trek back.

In early November came the first snow and frost. Army stragglers were slaughtered by Russian Cossacks and peasant partisans. Hungry soldiers pounced on fallen horses, carving them up alive. The wounded were left to lie where they dropped. Some poor wretches, wrote a French officer, "dragged themselves along, shivering . . . until the snow packed under the soles of their boots, a bit of debris, a branch, or the body of a fallen comrade tripped them and threw them down. Then their moans for help went unheeded. The snow soon covered them up and only low white mounds showed where they lay. Our road was strewn with these hummocks, like a cemetery."[26]

In the middle of December, with the Russians in pursuit, the remnants of the Grand Army staggered across the Neman River into East Prussia. Napoleon had left his men earlier in the month and, traveling in disguise, reached Paris on December 18. Napoleon had lost his army; he would soon lose his throne.

Final Defeat

After the destruction of the Grand Army, the empire crumbled. Although Napoleon raised a new army, he could not replace the equipment, cavalry horses, and experienced soldiers squandered in Russia. Now he had to rely on schoolboys and overage veterans.

Most of Europe joined in a final coalition against France. In October 1813, allied forces from Austria, Prussia, Russia, and Sweden defeated Napoleon at Leipzig; in November, Anglo-Spanish forces crossed the Pyrenees into France.

Finally, in the spring of 1814, the allies captured Paris. Napoleon abdicated and was exiled to the tiny island of Elba, off the coast of Italy. The Bourbon dynasty was restored to the throne of France in the person of Louis XVIII, younger brother of the executed Louis XVI and the acknowledged leader of the émigrés.

Only forty-four years of age, Napoleon did not believe that it was his destiny to die on Elba. On March 1, 1815, he landed on the French coast with a thousand soldiers. Louis XVIII ordered his troops to stop Napoleon's advance. When Napoleon's small force approached the king's troops, Napoleon walked up to the soldiers who blocked the road. "If there is one soldier among you who wishes to kill his Emperor, here I am." It was a brilliant move by a man who thoroughly understood the French soldier. The king's troops shouted, "Long live the Emperor!" and joined Napoleon. On March 20, 1815, Napoleon entered Paris to a hero's welcome. He had not lost his charisma.

Raising a new army, Napoleon moved against the allied forces in Belgium. There the British, led by the duke of Wellington, and the Prussians, led by Field Marshal Gebhard von Blücher, defeated Napoleon at Waterloo in June 1815. Napoleon's desperate gamble to regain power—the famous "hundred days"—had failed. This time the allies sent Napoleon to Saint Helena, a lonely island in the South Atlantic, a thousand miles off the coast of southern Africa. On this gloomy and rugged rock, Napoleon Bonaparte, emperor of France and would-be conqueror of Europe, spent the last six years of his life.

THE LEGEND
AND THE ACHIEVEMENT

"Is there anyone whose decisions have had a greater consequence for the whole of Europe?" asks Dutch historian Pieter Geyl about Napoleon.[27] It might also be asked: is there anyone about whom there has been such a wide range of conflicting interpretations? Both Napoleon's contemporaries and later analysts have seen Napoleon in many different lights.

Napoleon himself contributed to the historical debate. Concerned as ever with his reputation, he reconstructed his career while on Saint Helena. His recorded reminiscences are the chief source of the Napoleonic legend. According to this account, Napoleon's principal aim was to defend the Revolution and consolidate its gains. He emerges as a champion of equality and supporter of popular sovereignty, who destroyed aristocratic privileges, restored order, and opposed religious intolerance. He appears as a lover of peace forced to take up the sword because of the implacable hatred of Europe's reactionary rulers. According to this reconstruction, Napoleon meant to spread the blessings of the Revolution to the Germans, Dutch, Spaniards, Poles, and Italians; he wished to create a United States of Europe, a federation of free and enlightened nations living in peace. Had Napoleon realized this vision of a socially modernized, economically integrated, rationally ruled, and politically unified western Europe, which already shared a common cultural tradition, he would have performed one of the great creative acts in human history.

Undoubtedly, Napoleon did disseminate many gains of the Revolution. Nevertheless, say his critics, this account overlooks much. It ignores the repression of liberty, the subverting of republicanism, the oppression of conquered peoples, and the terrible suffering resulting from his pursuit of glory. The critics see the reminiscences as another example of Napoleonic propaganda.

Although the debate over Napoleon continues, historians agree on two points. First, his was no ordinary life. A self-made man who harnessed the revolutionary forces of the age and imposed his will on history, Napoleon was right to call his life a romance. His drive, military genius, and charisma propelled him to the peak of power; his inability to moderate his ambition bled Europe, distorted his judgment, and caused his downfall. His overweening pride, the hubris of the Greek tragedians, would have awed Sophocles; the dimensions of his mind and the intricacies of his personality would have intrigued Shakespeare; his cynicism and utter unscrupulousness would have impressed Machiavelli. Second, historians agree that by spreading revolutionary ideals and institutions, Napoleon made it impossible for the traditional rulers to restore the Old Regime intact after the emperor's downfall. He had assured not only the destruction of feudal remnants and the secularization of society, but also the transformation of the dynastic state into the modern national state and the prominence of the bourgeoisie.

The new concept of warfare and the new spirit of nationalism also became an indelible part of the European scene. In the course of succeeding generations, the methods of total warfare in the service of a belligerent nationalism would shatter Napoleon's grandiose vision of a united Europe. They would also subvert the liberal humanism that was the essential heritage of the Enlightenment and the French Revolution.

◆　◆　◆

NOTES

1. Quoted in Felix Markham, *Napoleon and the Awakening of Europe* (New York: Collier Books, 1965), p. 27.

2. Excerpted in J. Christopher Herold, ed., *The Mind of Napoleon* (New York: Columbia University Press, 1955), p. 260.

3. Georges Lefebvre, *Napoleon*, trans. J.E. Anderson (New York: Columbia University Press, 1969), 2:65.

4. Ibid., p. 67.

5. Ibid., p. 66.

6. Quoted in David Chandler, *The Campaigns of Napoleon* (New York: Macmillan, 1966), p. 157.

7. Excerpted in Maurice Hutt, ed., *Napoleon* (Englewood Cliffs, N.J.: Prentice-Hall, 1972), p. 3.

8. Excerpted in David L. Dowd, ed., *Napoleon: Was He the Heir of the Revolution?* (New York: Holt, Rinehart, & Winston, 1966), p. 42.

9. Quoted in Felix Markham, *Napoleon* (New York: Mentor Books, 1963), p. 100.

10. Excerpted in Frank Malloy Anderson, ed., *The Constitution and Other Select Documents Illustrative of the History of France* (Minneapolis: H. W. Wilson, 1908), pp. 312–313.

11. Quoted in Robert B. Holtman, *The Napoleonic Revolution* (Philadelphia: Lippincott, 1967), pp. 123–124.

12. Quoted in Holtman, *Napoleonic Revolution*, p. 121.

13. Quoted in Markham, *Napoleon*, p. 97.

14. Excerpted in Dowd, *Napoleon*, p. 27.

15. Quoted in Holtman, *Napoleonic Revolution*, p. 143.

16. Excerpted in Hutt, *Napoleon*, pp. 49–50.

17. R. M. Johnston, ed., *The Corsican: A Diary of Napoleon's Life in His Own Words* (Boston: Houghton Mifflin, 1910) p. 166.

18. Quoted in Chandler, *Campaigns of Napoleon*, p. 145.

19. Ibid.

20. Ibid., p. 155.

21. Ibid.

22. Ibid., p. 157.

23. Quoted in Jacques Godechot, Beatrice F. Hyslop, and David L. Dowd, *The Napoleonic Era in Europe* (New York: Holt, Rinehart, & Winston, 1971), pp. 170, 172.

24. Excerpted in Dowd, *Napoleon*, p. 57.

25. Quoted in Owen Connelly, *The Gentle Bonaparte* (New York: Macmillan, 1968), pp. 110–11.

26. Quoted in J. Christopher Herold, *The Age of Napoleon* (New York: Dell, 1963), p. 320.

27. Pieter Geyl, *Napoleon: For and Against* (New Haven: Yale University Press, 1964), p. 16.

SUGGESTED READING

Chandler, David, *The Campaigns of Napoleon* (1966). An analysis of Napoleon's art of war.

Connelly, Owen, *Napoleon's Satellite Kingdoms* (1965). Focuses on the kingdoms in Naples, Italy, Holland, Spain, and Westphalia, which were created by Napoleon and ruled by his relatives.

———, *The Gentle Bonaparte* (1968). A biography of Napoleon's elder brother; a good treatment of Napoleon's involvement in Spain.

Cronin, Vincent, *Napoleon Bonaparte* (1972). A highly acclaimed biography.

Geyl, Pieter, *Napoleon: For and Against* (1964). A critical evaluation of French writers' views of Napoleon.

Herold, J. Christopher, ed., *The Mind of Napoleon* (1955). Valuable selections from the written and spoken words of Napoleon.

———, *The Horizon Book of the Age of Napoleon* (1965). Napoleon and his times.

Holtman, Robert B., *The Napoleonic Revolution* (1967). A portrait of Napoleon as the revolutionary innovator who influenced every aspect of European life; particularly good on Napoleon the propagandist.

Howarth, David, *Waterloo* (1968). A recreation of the battle as it appeared to those who fought it.

Hutt, Maurice, ed., *Napoleon* (1972). Excerpts from Napoleon's words and the views of contemporaries and later historians.

Lefebvre, Georges, *Napoleon,* 2 vols. (1969). An authoritative biography.

Markham, Felix, *Napoleon* (1963). A first-rate short biography.

———, *Napoleon and the Awakening of Europe* (1965). An exploration of Napoleon's influence on other lands.

REVIEW QUESTIONS

1. What made it possible for Napoleon to gain power?

2. What personality traits did Napoleon exhibit?

3. What principles underlay Napoleon's domestic reforms?

4. What was Napoleon's "art of war"? Describe his tactics.

5. Napoleon both preserved and destroyed the ideals of the French Revolution. Discuss this statement.

6. Why did England feel compelled to resist Napoleon? What were the intent and significance of the Continental System?

7. What was the significance of the Peninsular War?

8. Why did Prussian officials urge reforms? Describe the nature and significance of these reforms.

9. Account for Napoleon's defeat in Russia.

10. Identify and explain the historical significance of the battle of Leipzig and the "hundred days."

11. What were Napoleon's greatest achievements? What were his greatest failures?

12. Why do some people regret that Napoleon did not establish a "United States of Europe"?

CHAPTER *21*

The Industrial Revolution:
The Transformation of Society

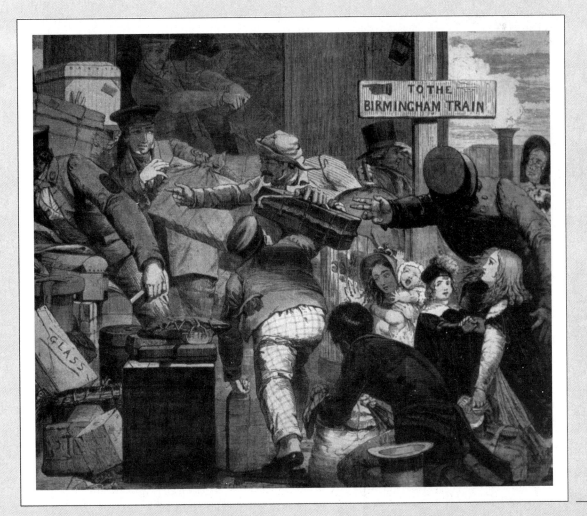

orces at work in the European economy and society in the second half of the eighteenth century had such enormous significance for humanity that the total process of the changes has been called the *Industrial Revolution.* The term refers to the shift from an agrarian, handicraft, labor-intensive economy to one dominated by machine manufacture powered by fossil fuels, by specialization of tasks or division of labor; and by factories, a freer flow of capital, and the concentration of people in cities. These changes took place first in England. Within a generation, however, they had spread to western Europe and the United States, and by the twentieth century they had affected the entire world. For contemporaries, the Industrial Revolution was the result of a series of inventions applied to human tasks. Many early inventions were the laborers' simple alterations of their tools. The features of the Industrial Revolution that stand out today are the increase in agricultural productivity; the new and more efficient ways of organizing tasks to utilize plentiful labor and stretch limited natural resources and capital; and the expanded role of banking.

Industrial progress did not proceed at the same pace everywhere. The changes that began in England in the mid 1700s did not start in France until the French Revolution. From the 1780s to 1850, the social and political turmoil in France had a mixed effect on economic development: in some respects, conflict advanced it; in others, it hindered growth. In the German and Italian states, industrial growth lagged, partly because they were not unified politically. Industry began in Germany during the 1840s, nearly a century after England took off on the road to industrialization. Even after German unification in 1870, when industry grew phenomenally, many aspects of the traditional economy persisted alongside the

Train Station, Birmingham, England. (*National Railway Museum*)

revolutionary industrial changes. In Italy, too, industrialization began slowly. It was hampered by the sharp economic divisions between north and south, the comparative lack of natural resources, and the slow political unification of the peninsula. Eastern Europe did not start industrializing until the 1890s, and, in some cases, not until the twentieth century.

Britain, thus, had stepped out ahead. European states copied its techniques, borrowed and stole its plans, imported its engineers as advisers, borrowed its capital, and carefully studied its politics and society to imitate whatever seemed essential to industrialization. By the second half of the nineteenth century, Germany, France, and the United States had moved into genuine competition with Britain as industrial powers; and Italy, Russia, and Austria-Hungary were being drawn into the Industrial Revolution. Almost inevitably, Europeans and Americans, and eventually people in countries around the globe, were driven to adopt the changes in agriculture and industry that had originated in England. Everywhere, as the economy changed, the conditions of labor and life were profoundly altered. The Industrial Revolution has been truly a revolution without boundaries and, thus far, without an end in sight.

THE ORIGINS
OF THE INDUSTRIAL AGE

Why did the process of industrialization begin in western Europe rather than elsewhere in the world? The reasons are complex and interrelated. From the fifteenth to the eighteenth century, western Europe had accumulated substantial wealth, and this wealth was spread across more classes of people. Improved agriculture in the late Middle Ages, increased population, and the widespread practice of diverse rural handicrafts after the fifteenth century provided the foundations for the relatively rapid expansion of trade, both overseas and on the Continent, in the next two centuries. This expansion resulted from an aggressive search for new markets rather than from new methods of production; it built on the capi-

talist practices of medieval and Renaissance bankers and merchants, and it tapped the wealth of a much larger world than the Mediterranean lands accessible to earlier generations. Thus, the resources of the New World and of Africa, both human and material, fueled Europe's accumulation of wealth.

In the early modern period, the states that had centralized power in the hands of a strong monarch—England, Spain, Portugal, and France, as well as the much less centralized Netherlands—competed for markets, territory, and prestige in ways that contributed to economic expansion. Engaged in fierce military and commercial rivalries, these states, with varying degrees of success, actively promoted industries to manufacture weaponry, uniforms, and ships; they also encouraged commerce for the sake of tax revenues. Thus aided, the growth in commerce nurtured a greatly expanded economy, in which many levels of society took part: owners of large estates, merchant princes, innovative entrepreneurs, the sugar plantation colonials, slave traders, sailors, and peasants.

The growth of commerce freed much of European labor. In Russia and America, however, the promise of profits was an incentive for greater control of labor through serfdom, slavery, and peonage. Western Europe had no state power comparable to that of China or Russia, which kept labor tied to the land. An expanding population in western Europe furnished both labor and consumers for the development of industry.

The Population Explosion

Most of Europe's explosive population growth took place after the middle of the eighteenth century and continued into the nineteenth. In 1800, Europe had about 190 million people; by 1850, 260 million; by 1914, it had 460 million, and some 200 million other Europeans had settled throughout the world.

Population growth might have brought famine, disease, and misery to Europe, as had happened so many times before and has continued to happen in other regions, particularly Asia and Africa. But despite signs of rural destitution and social unrest in the last half of the eighteenth

THE AGRICULTURAL REVOLUTION: THE MCCORMICK REAPER. Harvesting grain by machine released great numbers of laborers from farms to labor in factories and cities. The great demand for labor may explain, in part, the constant search for and investment in mechanical devices for farm and factory in America, a major food exporter even today. (*State Historical Society of Wisconsin*)

century, major changes were taking place in agriculture: a "green revolution" of new crops and new and different ways of utilizing land and labor. These changes increased productivity sufficiently to feed the growing population and to improve the diet of many Europeans.

The population expanded rapidly for several reasons. More efficient agriculture and better food distribution reduced malnutrition, which meant better health, more births, and fewer deaths. With better nutrition, more children survived, grew stronger and taller, could work harder and longer, and were abler intellectually. Women married at younger ages—on the average, as much as three years earlier than before—which was a sign of greater prosperity among farmers and brought an increase in the number of births. The signs of better nutrition and better health included greater height (the average European man was five feet six inches tall in 1900, compared with five feet a century earlier) and a lower age at which girls began to menstruate, which contributed to more births. A decline in the number of deaths was even more important

than the higher birthrate. Population growth, agricultural productivity, and improved nutrition are intertwined phenomena, both causes and results of aspects of industrialization.

The Agricultural Revolution

By the eighteenth century, traditional patterns of farming were breaking up in western Europe. Agriculture became more and more a capitalist enterprise; production was for the market, not for family or village consumption. Many people, aristocrats as well as peasants, persisted in traditional patterns and obligations: the social economy of reciprocity and redistribution. But powerful forces gradually drew most farmers to the marketplace, first in western, then in central, and finally in eastern Europe. Land freed from traditional obligations became just another commodity to be bought, sold, and traded—and managed for profit.

Peasants freed from manorial obligations joined the ranks of entrepreneurs, tenants, or

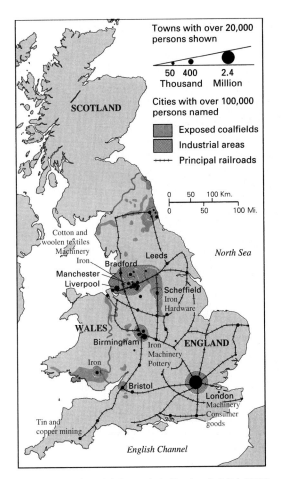

MAP 21.1 Industrial Growth in England, Mid-1800s

The agricultural revolution of the 1700s comprised mainly changes in landholding, soil usage, and animal husbandry; the application of machines to farming would not take place till the end of the nineteenth century. After 1750, the British and Dutch practice of selective breeding of animals became more widespread. Land use grew more efficient. Through convertible husbandry, which cycled land from grain production through soil-restoring crops of legumes and then pasturage, farmers could keep cultivating all their fields and not leave some lands fallow, as had been the practice for centuries. The improved methods gradually extended to the peasantry. However, in some areas within every country, particularly in central and eastern Europe, the old practices continued well into the 1800s.

By the middle of the nineteenth century—after two centuries of increasing agricultural productivity, with little change in technology—the application of technical ingenuity to farming brought steel plows, improved reapers, horse-drawn rakes, and threshers. (The Americans were very inventive in this area; their agricultural machinery formed a substantial part of their manufacturing exports.) These changes greatly increased efficiency and production. They also meant that fewer men and women could produce more food and raw materials.

Britain First

Why was Great Britain the first country to industrialize? What advantages did it possess that other European nations lacked? France, for example, was wealthier, more populous, and possessed an empire equal to England's in trading importance. Its scientific and intellectual life was equal to Britain's as well. The French had a skilled populace, and their government, if anything, was more responsive than Britain's to the need for transportation and communication. It had established schools for technicians and trained civil engineers for public works such as waterworks, canals, roads, and bridges. The French, however, seemed less willing than the British to change traditional ways—methods of agriculture or craft production, for example. The size of the landholdings, which were smaller than

wage laborers—all farming for the market. Undeveloped land was brought under cultivation, and common land used for grazing animals was claimed as private property, generally by great landowners, whose political power gave them an advantage. This process, known as *enclosure,* took place over much of Europe. In England, the greatest acreage of enclosure had occurred in the sixteenth and seventeenth centuries, as powerful landlords increased and consolidated their total holdings. Although a relatively small number of enclosures took place in the eighteenth century, these enclosures and the new agricultural trends displaced farmers, who then moved to urban areas or emigrated to the Americas and Australia.

in England, may have discouraged experimentation. By and large, the French populace lived less well than the English, but it had enough wealth to make an effective demand for products at home. Well into the nineteenth century, the French produced fine goods by hand for the few, rather than cheap goods by machine for the many. As a result of these commercial and cultural differences, French industrialization was slow. A more serious hindrance to industrialization, which France shared with the German and Italian states, was the existence of internal tariffs. England did not have these obstacles to the free flow of goods within the country, and after the union of Scotland with England in 1707, trade flourished throughout the British Isles.

In some ways, the French Revolution, which gave so much political freedom and economic opportunity, perpetuated traditional agricultural and commercial practices. Peasants who acquired land in the Revolution often gained plots so small that the new farming methods were difficult to apply. They followed the old practices and tried to restrict their family size in order to feed themselves. Inefficient small farms did not produce a surplus for the market. Furthermore, political instability made it hard for the French to develop or maintain the optimism and the willingness to take risks that contribute to economic development.

Like France, the Netherlands had sufficient wealth to support industrialization. During the seventeenth century, the Dutch had developed techniques of finance and commerce that every nation tried to imitate. They had a good transportation system, a fine navy, and technical know-how. They were also skilled farmers. However, they lacked natural resources.

Britain, thus, possessed several advantages enabling it to take the lead. First, it had a labor pool of hardworking, skilled farmers who could no longer earn a living for their families on the land. In addition, large and easily developed supplies of coal and iron had given the British a long tradition of metallurgy and mining. In the early stages of industrialization, Britain's river transportation system was supplemented by canals and toll roads (turnpikes), which private entrepreneurs financed and built for profit. The role played by private enterprise in Britain's economic

development was extraordinary and unique in the history of industrialization. No other country relied so completely on private capital resources and individual entrepreneurs for its industrial development. Small wonder, then, that free trade and economic individualism would have so many champions there.

The state did contribute to Britain's industrial revolution, however. British business thrived in a climate favorable to economic expansion—an environment of law, order, and protection of private property. Laws allowed the enclosure of common lands, which pushed the remaining small farmers off the land and permitted the consolidation of large holdings. Parliament chartered businesses, such as toll bridge and canal builders and the East Indies company, which expanded trade routes and enriched the British economy. The freedom of entry into economic activity was remarkable. Entrepreneurs were much less restricted by monopolies, charters, and guilds than they had been in the previous century or than other Europeans were in the eighteenth and nineteenth centuries.

Changes in Technology

The Industrial Revolution brought a change from handicrafts to machine manufacture and from human or animal power to other forms of energy, such as steam and the internal combustion engine. In the long run, these were revolutionary changes, but the first stages of industrialization in any particular trade often resulted from simple changes made by workers as they plied their craft. Such changes involved very little, if any, capital.

Cotton Textiles   Long the home of an important wool trade, Britain jumped ahead in cotton production, the first industry to experience unprecedented growth rates. British cotton production expanded tenfold between 1760 and 1785, and another tenfold between 1785 and 1825. A series of inventions revolutionized the industry and drastically altered the social conditions of the work. In 1733, long before expansion started, a simple invention—John Kay's flying shuttle—made it possible for weavers to double their output. This shut-

WOMAN AT HARGREAVES'S SPINNING JENNY. The cotton textile trade was one of the first to be mechanized. In cottage industries, the whole family contributed to the thread and cloth. Many early inventions were made by the workers themselves, such as Hargreaves's adjustment of his wife's thread-spinning tool. (*Mary Evans Picture Library*)

tle, which could be used in the home, was just an adaptation of a device that had been used in the wool trade for generations. The flying shuttle enabled weavers to produce faster than spinners could spin—until James Hargreaves's spinning jenny, perfected by 1768, allowed an operator to work several spindles at once, powered only by human energy. Within five years, Richard Arkwright applied a water-frame spinning machine, which could be powered by water or animals. Samuel Crompton's spinning mule (1779) powered many spindles, first by human and later by animal and water energy. These changes improved spinning productivity so much that there were bottlenecks in weaving until Edmund Cartwright developed a power loom in 1787. To the end of the century, there was a race to speed up the spinning part of the process and then the weaving part by applying water power to looms or new, larger devices to the jenny.

The much increased demand for cotton set off another chain of events. Eli Whitney's cotton gin of 1793 removed the seeds from raw cotton quickly and cheaply, leading farmers and planta-

tion owners to devote more land to cotton. Within a generation, more laborers were required for the fields and fewer to process the cotton. The higher demand for field labor brought far-reaching changes in the system of slavery, just as the series of inventions caused the shift from the domestic production system to a factory one. Arkwright's water frame made it more efficient to bring many workers together rather than send work out to individuals and families in their own homes. This development was the beginning of the factory system, which, within two or three generations, would revolutionize the conditions of labor. Because water power drove these early machines, mills were located near rivers and streams. Thus, towns grew up where machinery could be powered by water. When steam power became widely applied, laborers could be dispersed, but in fact the factory system generally urbanized labor.

Weavers and spinners—not technicians, engineers, or scientists—invented the simple devices that were modeled after machines already in use. These inventions did not cause the cotton industry's expansion; it resulted from social and

Profile

Spectrum Color Library

The Darby Family

Three generations of an English family of iron manufacturers, the Darby family, developed by trial and error new ways of producing the precious metal of industrialization. Abraham Darby (1677–1717) started as a workman in Coalbrookdale, Shropshire, England and built a blast furnace, trying several ways to cast iron. Though others have claimed the honor, he is believed to be the first to use coke in iron-smelting, replacing the use of charcoal that became too expensive in the 1700s as the English rapidly depleted their forests. Coke made less brittle iron than raw coal because it had less sulphur content. Able to make larger furnaces and superior iron, Darby's product was used for the casting of quality cannon for the Royal Navy.

With Abraham Darby II (1711–1763) coke-smelting became the dominant technique for making cast iron. The industry (still consisting of small firms) began by the mid-1700s to be concentrated in coal-rich regions like Coalbrookdale.

The pride of the family was Abraham III

---

economic demand. However, once begun, the expansion was so great, the demand so urgent, and the potential profits so great that more and more complicated technology was developed. A role emerged for the engineer who was an expert in building or adapting machines and in utilizing different sources of power.

Steam Power The process that took place in textiles over two or three generations was replicated in other industries as well. James Watt, a Scottish engineer, developed the steam engine in the 1760s, but it was too expensive to be widely adapted to production. Women, children, and even men laborers were cheaper than steam-powered machinery. By the 1830s in England, however, as engines and fuel became cheaper, entrepreneurs began to use them and expansion became even more rapid. Because they ran on coal or wood, not water power, steam engines allowed flexibility in locating factories.

By the midcentury, steam power was widely ap-

plied—particularly to transportation—resulting in the incredible rate of change that most people identify with the Industrial Revolution. But during the two previous centuries, increasing productivity, which made possible the accumulation of capital and provisioning of population growth, had been powered by people, animals, and water—an extraordinary feat. With steam, work was revolutionized because weaker, younger, and less-skilled workers could perform the few simple necessary tasks. The shift from male to female and child labor was a radical social change. Moreover, as steam took hold, human participation in the process of manufacture diminished; engines replaced people, and workers became "hands" that drove machines.

The Iron Industry Although steam power meant that employers could hire weaker people to operate machinery, it required machines made of stronger metals to withstand the forces generated by a stronger power source. As in the case of

512

(1750–1791) who built in 1779 the first cast-iron bridge, which still stands after 180 years, a semicircular arch across the Severn River. The story of the Darbys and the bridge symbolizes English industrialization. Another Ironmaster, John Wilkinson, had begun trying to raise the capital to build a bridge, but had failed. Darby designed, cast, and built the bridge. He also laid out half of the total funds required and none of the other half came from government. The Severn bridge was a major technological feat. Darby rebuilt his grandfather's furnaces to cast large enough pieces for a bridge that is 100 feet long with 45-foot-high castings. There are 378 tons of interlocking iron pieces in the bridge, held together with bolts or rivets. It was a marvel which engineers, as well as travelers, from all Europe came to see. It was also a financial marvel: built with private capital, most of which was actually provided by the workman-entrepreneur, who wasn't even incorporated.

textiles, the history of the search for better iron illustrates how developments in one industry prompted change in related industries; it furnishes many examples of trial and error that led to better techniques.

Before the eighteenth century, producing iron had not changed much since the Middle Ages. Abraham Darby took the first step to produce high-quality coke-smelted cast iron in 1709. By the mid-eighteenth century, the quality of cast iron was so high that it began to replace scarce and valuable wood in construction. Another major advance came when ironmakers learned to turn cast iron into wrought iron. But high-quality wrought iron was expensive because the wood to fire the furnaces was so scarce. The English used cheap coal, which contained impurities that made a poor, brittle metal. Henry Cort borrowed a French idea of making a furnace with two separate compartments, one for coal and one for iron, altering the process by puddling (stirring the molten iron) and then rolling it as it cooled. This reduced the impurities and speeded up the process. By the 1780s, trial and error had perfected the production of wrought iron, which became the most widely used metal until steel began to be cheaply produced in the 1860s.

Producing iron required coal. With steam engines, miners could pump water more efficiently and at a much deeper level; the engines also lifted coal up the main shaft to the surface. Rich veins in existing mines became accessible. Britain's production of coal kept pace with the industrial growth it powered; it rose from 16 million tons at the end of the Napoleonic wars to 30 million in 1836 and 65 million in 1856. Greater coal production allowed the continued improvement of iron smelting, as well as many other basic industries.

Then in 1856, Henry Bessemer converted pig iron into steel by removing the impurities in the iron. In the 1860s, William Siemens and Pierre and Émile Martin developed the open-hearth process, which could handle much greater amounts of metal than Bessemer's converter. Steel became so cheap to produce that it quickly replaced iron in building and in industry. The age of steel was born.

Transportation and Communication Changes in mining, metallurgy, textiles, pottery, and farming speeded change in other industries, especially transportation and communication. Revolutionized transportation provided a network that could support expansion. Major road building took place in the eighteenth century in England and in France, and later in the rest of Europe. Both Britain and the United States experienced a boom in canal construction between 1760 and 1820. But canals were quickly outmoded by railroads, which, although more expensive, were more flexible and caught the public imagination. Steam-powered engines began to replace horse-powered railroads in the 1820s. Deeming railroads essential to their strength and unity, Continental governments expended major efforts to develop rail networks, particularly where canals or roads were inadequate. Railroads were so successful that in mid-nineteenth-century England roads became just paths leading to the station. Stations all over Europe looked like palaces. Not until the start of the twentieth century was a complete network of roads considered crucial to public transport in Britain.

Unprecedented amounts of private British capital built Britain's system of roads, canals, railways, and steamships. Continental states were slower to adopt steam transport because they lacked capital and skilled civil engineering. Only France invested a great percentage of private capital in building a Europe-wide transportation system. Various failures of management and inadequate financing led the French government to take control of its railroads, but in most of Europe, state construction and control was the rule. In the United States, Congress gave enormous grants of land to railroad companies to encourage the laying of tracks. Everywhere during the railroad building boom that extended throughout the nineteenth century, financiers invested heavily in railroads. The flow of capital from western Europe, particularly Britain and France, to other lands in Europe and America was an awe-inspiring achievement. The flow of finance across borders and oceans was matched only by the flow of labor, as Europeans and Asians built railroad networks to support the expanding agriculture and industry of the Americas.

Communication changed as spectacularly as transportation. Britain inaugurated the penny post in 1840, making it possible to send a letter to any part of the kingdom for about half an American penny. But the cost of postage was so high elsewhere that letters were rarely written; many letters of the time fill every space on a single sheet of paper because the postage rate was cheapest for one sheet. When the telegraph was invented, it developed rapidly as business demanded cheap and fast communications. The first telegraphic message was sent from Baltimore to Washington, D.C., in 1844. Within seven years, the first undersea cable was laid under the English Channel, and by 1866, transatlantic cable was operating. Although certainly not inexpensive until the last quarter of the nineteenth century, the telegraph was quickly employed by ever-expanding business.

Changes in Finance

The first steps of industrialization—the use of new crop mixes and tools in agriculture and the first changes in spinning and weaving—did not require much capital. Neither did the early adaptations in the iron industry. Subsequent growth,

however—from the spread of factories and the extensive application of machinery in agriculture to the expansion of mining and construction in the cities—required the investment of enormous capital. Railroads and steamship lines were often so expensive that only governments could finance them; even in Belgium, where they were privately financed at first, the king was the major investor. Large capital infusions were also needed to fund the steel industry.

In the earliest stages of industrialization, the owning family was the source of a company's financing, its management, and even its technical innovation. Family firms dominated industry. But outside investment grew with the demand for capital, which rose steadily from 1860 to World War I (1914). In Britain, wealthy merchants and landlords provided investment capital, and low interest rates encouraged borrowing. On the Continent, where the supply of capital was limited, the British became international investors of the first rank, furnishing much of the capital for the industrialization of other nations. French investors, who were sometimes reluctant to invest at home for fear of political instability, financed railroads in central Europe. They were also the major investors in the Suez Canal and in the first canal project in Panama, which failed. Among banking families—including the Barings of London and the Rothschilds of France, England, and Germany—kinship ties joined together large amounts of investment capital. People of the same religion or region would often band together to gather capital for development, as the Protestant and Jewish bankers of France did. These investor groups fueled European industrialization.

Banking, however, was risky business in the nineteenth century; dozens of banks failed in every financial crisis. Lacking insurance for deposits and possessing only limited resources, banks tended to be cautious about risks. They diversified their investments so as not to lose everything in the failure of a single industry. Thus, in any given country, the number of industries able to borrow substantial amounts of capital was limited in the early stages of industrialization. In many countries, bankers preferred safe investments in government debt, a preference that slowed the development of industry.

Financing industry was difficult because there

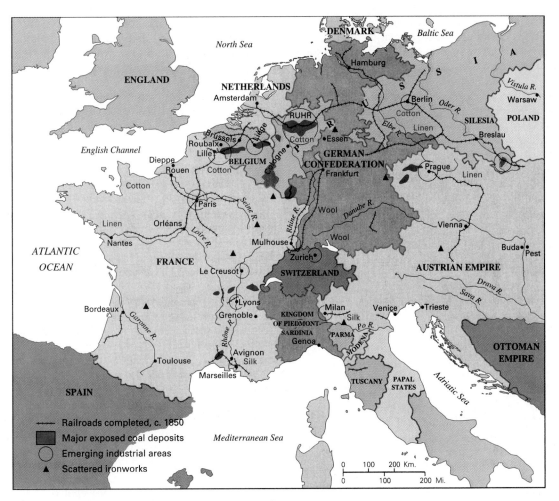

MAP 21.2 Industrial Growth on the Continent, Mid-1800s

was no formal organization to enable a number of people to pool their capital safely. In the existing joint-stock companies, individuals could be held responsible for all the debts of the enterprise. Despite this risk, more and more individuals joined together, retaining the right to transfer their shares without the consent of other stockholders. England was innovative in finance, repealing the laws against joint-stock companies in 1825 and permitting incorporation in 1844. Investors were liable for a corporation's debts only in proportion to the number of shares they owned. This legal change meant that investors endangered only the amount that they had paid for their stock, and not all the funds that they or their family possessed. In 1844, after nearly a century of industrial progress, England had almost 1,000 such companies—with a stock value of £345 million—compared with only 260 in France. In the 1850s, limited liability was applied to the stock of most English businesses, and a little later it was extended to banking and insurance companies. By the 1860s, France, Germany, and the United States permitted limited liability, which released such a flow of savings that it sparked a surge of industrial energy.

Like so much of the Industrial Revolution, solving the problems of organizing, structuring, and managing firms and of acquiring funds for the development of industry was a matter of trial and error, experiment, and innovation. These inventions of the mind and culture were as important to the expanding revolution as the invention of machines.

SOCIETY TRANSFORMED

European society before industrialization was based on kinship. Property, in the form of land, determined social class and social power, which was usually exercised on a local or provincial level. Industrialization brought a new world, with many forms of property and power. Individuals became increasingly important—before the law, in trade, in political thought, and in politics. Ultimately, the nation became more important than the province, region or local area, but even in western Europe, this did not happen for most people until the last quarter of the nineteenth century.

While the foundations of a new society were being laid, much of the old life persisted, particularly during the first half of the nineteenth century. Landed property was still the principal form of wealth, and large landowners continued to exercise political power. From England to Russia, families of landed wealth (often the old noble families) still constituted the social elite. European society remained overwhelmingly rural. Nonetheless, the explosion of cities and industrial towns that accompanied industrialization so overwhelmed contemporaries that they perceived it as a sudden and complete break with the past. For them it was the shattering of traditional moral and social patterns. Some people remembered the past clearly, but others idealized it as a golden age, in which the relations between master and worker had been based on values other than the cash nexus—than wages, hours, and production.

Urbanization

The urbanization of Western society greatly accelerated during the Industrial Revolution. Classical civilization had been urban, and medieval cities had been the centers of commerce and government. But in the nineteenth century, cities became places of manufacture and industry, growing in number, size, and population. Before 1800, about 10 percent of the European population lived in cities (20 percent in Great Britain and the Netherlands, the leading areas of urban living). Only forty-five cities in the *world* had more than 100,000 people. Halfway through the nineteenth century, when 52 percent of the English lived in cities, just 25 percent of the French, 36 percent of the Germans, 7 percent of the Russians, and 10 percent of U.S. inhabitants were urban dwellers. Most of the shift from rural to urban living in the West has occurred in the twentieth century, as industrialization spread. But the increase in Europe's urban population during the 1800s was acute, springing up overnight in some regions: the Midlands in England, the Lowlands in Scotland, the northern plains in France, the German Rhineland, the northeast United States, and parts of northern Italy.

Unlike capital cities, industrial ones, particularly in England, grew rapidly, without planning or much regulation by local or national governments. Government and business were often reluctant to use taxation to finance remedies for poor working and living conditions. Civic pride and private patronage were too weak to combat the effects of unregulated private enterprise. In the rest of Europe, where industrialization came later, states were more willing to regulate industrial and urban development. They also had a bureaucracy for planning and regulation, but such efforts were still inadequate. So much growth with so little planning or control led to cities with minimal sanitation, no street lighting, wretched housing, poor transportation, and scant security. Cities had grown without planning before, but they had not been home and workplace for such large numbers of people, many of them new arrivals. Rich and poor alike suffered in this environment of disease, crime, and ugliness, although the poor obviously bore the brunt of these evils.

Major industrial cities developed similar housing patterns mainly because of the wide disparity in economic and social power between the classes. By the middle of the nineteenth century, the wealthiest inhabitants circled the city's edge and were close to the country, living in "suburbs," which were roomier and cleaner than the city proper. As a general rule, the farther one lived from the central city, the wealthier one was;

URBANIZATION: VIEW OF SHEFFIELD BY WILLIAM IBBIT, 1815. Unlike Manchester, which was a new factory town, springing up from the fields without plan or government at first, Sheffield was an old cutlery manufacturing center which expanded enormously when the introduction of mass production technology brought a new wave of workers. (*Sheffield City Museum*)

the suburban houses were detached (they were not row houses, but stood alone) and usually had gardens. The outer ring of the city itself was the location most preferred by the middle class, and it shared many of the characteristics of the wealthier suburbs. In the city's inner ring were the artisans' dwellings, ranging from middle-class residences to small, attached row houses, perhaps with a small garden. Further down the social scale came workers' row houses, located in the center of industrial towns. Long rows, several stories high, were jammed together as close to the factories as possible, separated from each other by a courtyard. Usually, this yard was a strip of mud or cobblestones, with a pump in the middle that served all the residents adjoining the courtyard. When public transportation developed in the second half of the century, workers' districts dispersed, sometimes to circle great governmental cities, such as London and Paris, where the wealthy monopolized the central city. In industrial cities, the earlier pattern remained, although new workers' housing might be scattered.

Almost universally, those who wrote about industrial cities—England's Manchester, Leeds, and Liverpool, and France's Lyons—described the stench, the filth, the inhumane crowding, the poverty, and the immorality. Novelists Charles Dickens, George Sand, and Émile Zola captured the horrors of urban industrial life and the plight of the poor. In *Bleak House*, Dickens, referring to one of the characters in the novel, warned about the effects of such wretchedness: "There is not an atom of Tom's slime . . . not a wickedness, not a brutality of his committing, but shall work its retribution, through every order of society, up to the proudest of the proud and the highest of the high."[1] Factual parliamentary reports read like the novels when depicting a London row:

> *In the centre of this street there is a gutter into which potato parings, the refuse of vegetable and animal matter of all kinds, the dirty water from the washing of clothes and of the houses are all poured, and where they stagnate and putrefy.*

An 1842 government report from Leeds described the conditions there as follows:

> *Walls unwhitewashed for years, black with the smoke of foul chimneys, without water . . . and sacking for bedclothing, with floors unwashed from year to year, without out-offices [lavatories]. Outside there are streets, raised a foot, sometimes two above the level of the causeway, by the accumulation of years . . . stagnant puddles here and there . . . and excrementitious deposits on all sides as a consequence, undrained, unpaved, unventilated, uncared-for by any authority but the landlord, who weekly collects his miserable rents from his miserable tenants.*

These parliamentary reports helped to mold English public opinion, which was crucial in forcing the regulation of urban building, transportation, sanitation, and public health. On the Continent, the state took a more active role in controlling urban conditions.

Changes in Social Structure

The Industrial Revolution destroyed forever the old division of society into clergy, nobility, and commoners. The development of industry and commerce caused a corresponding development of a bourgeoisie, a middle class comprising people of common birth who engaged in trade and other capitalist ventures. Usually referred to as the middle classes because of the several economic layers, the wealthiest bourgeois were bankers, factory and mine owners, and merchants, but shopkeepers, managers, lawyers, and doctors were included. The middle classes stressed the virtues of work, thrift, ambition, and caution. Their critics believed, however, that the bourgeois perverted these virtues into materialism, selfishness, and callousness. Generally, too, these critics saw the bourgeoisie as culturally smug and bound by convention.

From the eighteenth century on, as industry and commerce developed, the middle class grew in size, first in England and then throughout western Europe. But its larger size did not automatically bring greater power. The Industrial Revolution had begun in a preindustrial, agrarian society dominated by the aristocracy. Throughout the eighteenth and nineteenth centuries, the middle class struggled to end this political, economic, and social discrimination. The bourgeoisie was indeed able to force radical changes, but its members still functioned in a political and social world that had existed long before they gained power and influence.

In the 1800s, as industrial wealth became more important, the middle class gained greater political power and social respectability. By the end of the century, bourgeois politicians held the highest offices in much of western Europe and shared power with aristocrats. In central and eastern Europe, aristocrats maintained their dominance into the twentieth century. Wealthy bourgeois tended to imitate the aristocracy—buying great estates, marrying their daughters to sons of aristocrats—but they were the elite of the new industrial age, not of the Old Regime.

While industrialization may have reduced some barriers between the landed elites and the middle class, it sharpened the distinctions between the middle class and the laboring class. Like the middle class, the laborers encompassed different economic levels: rural laborers, miners, and city workers. Rural laborers included not only farmers, but also "cottage workers." In the 1700s and 1800s, an important segment of production was done in the villages, usually in the home, hence the name "domestic system" for work performed in a domicile or home. A middleman would supply materials to a worker, who wove or spun them at piecework rates. This system preceded factory production, which would undercut these workers' livelihoods and ultimately force their children or grandchildren into urban labor. In the first years of the Industrial Revolution, rural workers responded to the harsh conditions and low wages by destroying machinery and engaging in other acts of violence. Calling themselves "king Ludd's men" (Ludd being the name they gave to their Robin Hood) they raided farms in the night breaking the machines they thought caused their misery.

Many gradations existed among city workers, from artisans to factory workers and servants. Factory workers were the newest and most rapidly growing social group; at midcentury, however, they did not constitute the majority of laboring people in any major city. For example, as late as 1890, they constituted only one-sixth of London's population.

The artisans were the largest group of workers in the cities till the 1850s, and in some places for much longer. They worked in construction, printing, small tailoring or dressmaking establishments, food preparation, and food processing. They also included craftspeople, who produced such luxury items as furniture, jewelry, lace, and velvet. Artisans as a group were distinct from factory workers; their technical skills were difficult to learn, and traditionally their crafts were acquired in guilds, which still functioned as both social and economic organizations. Artisans were usually educated (they could read and write), lived in one city or village for generations, and maintained stable families, often securing places for their children in their craft.

As the Industrial Revolution progressed, artisans had to compete with cheap, factory-produced goods. They began to downgrade their skills by dropping apprenticeship training, forcing journeymen to work longer hours with shoddy materials, and loosening the rules of the guilds. In 1848, artisans, rather than factory workers, were at the forefront of the revolutionary movement as they tried to save themselves from the effects of the Industrial Revolution (see pages 567–572).

The third group of urban workers comprised the servants, who were especially numerous in the capitals. During the first half of the nineteenth century, in cities like Paris and London, where the number of factories was not great, servants outnumbered factory workers. The great increase in domestic labor—a middle-class family employed at least one servant—freed middle-class women from many household chores, so that they could spend more time with their husbands and children or pursue interests in the outside world if they chose to do so.

Working in a middle- or upper-class household, urban servants lived in a world apart from factory workers and artisans; they were often women who had come to the city from the country, where they might also have been servants. They were completely at the mercy of their employers. They might be treated decently or exploited, but they had little recourse when they were abused. Some worked their entire life as servants; some women left service to marry working-class men. (Domestic help could not keep their jobs when they married.) Servants usually had some education. If they married and had a family, they taught their children to read and write and sometimes to observe the manners and values of the household in which the parent had worked. Many historians believe that these servants passed on to their children their own deference to authority and their aspirations to bourgeois status, which may have limited social discontent and radical political activity.

Working-Class Life

Life was difficult for the early factory workers. Usually recent arrivals from agricultural areas, where they had been driven off the land, they had no special skills or traditions of working with others in a craft. Frequently, factory workers moved to the city without their families, leaving them behind until they could afford to support them in town. Other workers were single men or women who could find no jobs as servants or farm laborers in their villages. These people entered rapidly growing industries, where long hours—sometimes fifteen a day—were common. Farming had meant long hours, too, as had the various forms of labor for piecework rates in the home, but the pace of the machine and the routine made factory work oppressive. Once technological advances became an important aspect of industrialization, the machines required highly regulated human labor: generally menial, often dangerous, but definitely routine.

In the mines, steam engines did not chop the coal from the veins; they did not even haul the coal wagons to the main shaft. Men, women, and small children hacked out the coal and sorted it, while horses and mules—and sometimes humans—pulled coal wagons on rails to the main shaft, where steam-powered engines lifted the coal to the surface. The miners labored to keep pace with the machines, literally backbreaking labor. They faced the hazards of cave-ins, explosions, and deadly gas fumes. Deep under the earth's surface, life was dark, cold, wet, and tenuous. Their bodies stunted and twisted, their lungs wrecked, miners labored their lives away in "the pits." Technological advances saved their lives (for example, special lamps that would not

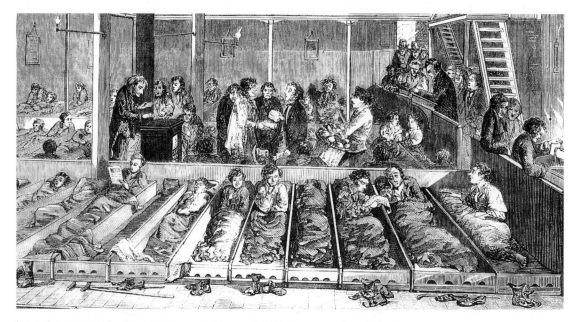

ENGRAVING FROM THE *ILLUSTRATED TIMES*, 1859. As unemployed workers flooded into the great cities of Europe, homelessness became a pressing social problem. Here to keep dry and warm, homeless men sleep in coffins for the living in a factory or prison-like building. These facilities were charitable institutions—not the poor-law workhouses—but they too reflected the common morality of the day that poverty was the fault of the poor, who should learn to help themselves. (*Mansell Collection*)

ignite underground gases), but almost a century passed before their labor was lightened.

Factory workers fared a little better than the miners. Sometimes, compared with their lives in the country, the workers' standard of living rose, particularly if the whole family found work together. The pay for a family might be better than they could have earned for farm labor, though in a rural area they might have been able to supplement earnings with food. But working conditions were terrible, as were living conditions. The factories were dirty, hot, unventilated, and frequently dangerous. Housing was overcrowded, dirty, and badly built. If the workers were unmarried or had left their families in the country, they often lived in barracks with other members of their sex. If they lost their jobs, they also lost their shelter.

Factory workers' lives were depressing. They had few links to their surroundings, and like immigrants to a new country, they lived with hard-

ship and deprivation. In the villages they had left, they had been poor but were socially connected to family, church, and even to local landlords. In the cities, on the other hand, factory workers labored in plants with twenty to a hundred workers and had little contact with their employers; instead, foremen pushed them to work hard and efficiently for long hours to keep up with the machines. They had little time to socialize with other workers; they were fined for talking to one another, as well as for lateness and for many petty infringements. To keep their jobs, they often became competitors. Lacking organization, a sense of comradeship, education, and experience of city life, they found little succor when times were bad.

Yet factory workers did make lives for themselves. They married or entered into some relationship at a younger age than artisans and, on the average, had more children than other classes. A wife and children were an economic asset because they worked to help the family. When workers grew old or were disabled, their children were their only "pension." As mechanization progressed, women and children were generally driven out of the factory labor force, but in the early factory system, they were the mainstay of the industrial process.

Many workers developed a life around the pub, the café, or some similar gathering place, where there were drinks and games and the gossip and news of the day. On Sundays, their one day off, workers drank and danced; absenteeism was so great on Monday that the day was called "holy Monday." Gin drinking was denounced on all sides; workers, their wives, and reformers alike urged temperance. Most workers did not attend church, but when they did, they frequented those churches that tried to reach them—usually not the established churches, which seemed to them to care only about the wealthy. In England, workers attended revivals; the Methodists and other Dissenters welcomed them. The Catholic church had a particularly strong following among the Irish workers. Many workers played sports, and some social organizations grew up around their sporting games. In these and other ways, workers developed a culture of their own—a culture that was misunderstood and often deplored by middle-class reformers.

Industrial workers rarely protested their conditions violently; in some countries they did so more than in others. By and large, the workers endured their lack of political and economic rights. They toiled long hours, were fined for mistakes and even for accidents, were fired at the will of the employer or foreman, and suffered from job insecurity. Yet they rarely broke machines—unlike country laborers, who protested the mechanization of agriculture by burning ricks and machinery in a desperate revolt against "progress." Factory workers had few organizations and no political rights. Although they lacked the traditions and organizations of the craftspeople, they did join with artisans in movements for political rights: the Chartists in England and the republicans in France. When workers protested, they were repressed. Even a peaceful demonstration, during which they sang hymns and prayed, might be disrupted by soldiers and gunfire. Workers who protested lost their jobs and were "blacklisted" (employers circulated their names

so that other employers would not hire them). The law might say that they were equal, but workers were neither wealthy enough nor sufficiently organized to take offending employers to court for violating the law.

Many workers and radicals believed that the only hope for their class lay in unified action through trade unions, mutual aid societies, cooperatives, or political organizations. In England and western Europe, trade unions grew, despite the fact that they were illegal. Unions made some headway in protecting their members from unemployment and dangerous working conditions. But strikes were rarely successful. Often suppressed by force, strikes were usually misunderstood by the general public, which was imbued with individualist and laissez-faire principles and saw strikes as an attack on the businessman's right to carry on trade. Not until the 1870s and 1880s was widespread discontent expressed by militant trade unions (see Chapter 26).

Although workers' political agitation did not achieve its goals in the first half of the nineteenth century, workers made some progress in attaining a minimum of economic security. They formed "friendly" or "mutual aid" societies and cooperatives to help themselves when they were out of work or sick. They paid some dues or took up special collections when one of their members died or was killed on the job. They also created clubs, where they could learn to read and write or someone could read to them or write a letter for them. Self-help organizations often developed into unions; sometimes they were unions in disguise to circumvent the law.

In England, unions were legalized in 1825, but they were forbidden to strike. The law made no special provision for them as it did for corporations; for example, if a union's officer ran away with its treasury, English law did not protect the workers' dues. Small unions were powerless. An 1834 attempt to gain strength by joining all unions together in a Grand National Consolidated Trades Union failed because measures that would help one trade would not necessarily help another. In the 1850s, highly skilled workers joined together in a single craft union, which was a more successful tactic because employers found it difficult to replace a skilled worker. Still, the vast majority of workers were not organized during much of the nineteenth century.

RELIEF AND REFORM

With the onset of industrialization, poverty became an issue. Moralists said that there had always been poor people, but with industrialization, the economic and psychological hardships borne by the work force seemed to increase. Many people believed that the condition of the poor had actually deteriorated in the midst of increased wealth. If machines could produce so much wealth and so many products, why were there so many poor people, living in such misery?

Britain was the first nation to face the worsening condition of the poor. In the eighteenth century, English agricultural laborers had a higher standard of living than their counterparts on the Continent. However, as Britain rapidly industrialized, the changing conditions convinced observers that both rural and urban workers' lives had worsened. Parliamentary reports and investigations by civic-minded citizens documented the suffering for all to read. Many leaders opposed legislative relief because they believed that only increasing economic capacity would end distress. But would the economy expand and benefit the lowliest workers by itself, that is, through laissez faire, or did it need direction from the state? Others, including socialists, utilitarians, and practical reformers, believed that better organization of industry and government would relieve the situation.

The English Factory Acts were a series of measures, beginning in 1802, that limited the hours of those (especially women and children) who labored in mines and factories. By 1833, children under thirteen could work not more than nine hours a day and no one aged thirteen to eighteen could work more than twelve hours or at night. The acts also required children to go to school for two hours a day because reformers thought that one way to protect the children of the poor was to educate them. However, the law neglected to furnish the funds for schools. England was much slower than France or Germany to provide state schools; British private enterprise and charities, rather than government, took the initiative. But controversy erupted among the religious sects about which of them should educate the children, who remained uneducated or self-educated amidst the conflict. Sometimes there were schools for boys and not for girls. It was argued that for moral reasons the sexes should not mix in the classroom, even though they worked side by side in the factory.

In 1847, the working hours of adult males were affected when women and children were no longer permitted to work more than ten hours a day. Many employers switched to a single system of ten hour shifts, but a loophole in the Ten Hours Act allowed some to develop a "relay system" in which children worked intermittently during the day to the total of ten hours. Men could still work as much as sixteen hours. At first, workers resented the regulations because family income declined if children could not work. Gradually, they realized that the humanitarian protection of women and children might make their own lives easier and safer and their wages higher. However, a ten hour day for adult male workers was not enacted until 1874, despite two generations of agitation.

In 1834, a reform of the Poor Law, which dated from the reign of Queen Elizabeth I, tried to differentiate between the "deserving" poor and the "undeserving" poor. The New Poor Law required anyone receiving assistance to live in a prison-like workhouse. Legislators thought only those who were truly needy would submit to the conditions just to receive a meal and shelter. Legislators were proved right. The poor and the unemployed working class hated and feared the workhouse, where families were separated by age and sex, miserably fed, and hired out to manufacturers and farmers for less than the going wage. The poor feared "pauperization." Humanitarians protested these harsh reforms. In the "hungry forties," when want was widespread, there were not enough workhouses for the homeless and the jobless. Forced relegation to the workhouses failed.

In contrast to Britain, on the Continent people more readily accepted the idea that the state could interfere with the market to protect labor. Besides, most states in Europe had larger bureaucracies to enforce regulations and to carry out relief measures. There was concern, however, that too much interference with employers would handicap businesses competing with the English. Governments in Germany, France, and Belgium did not always follow a policy of unrestricted industry, but sometimes they did. Such policies deepened class bitterness.

Historians still debate how bad workers' conditions were in the early stages of industrializa-

THE GREAT EXHIBITION OF 1851 BY DICKINSON. The Crystal Palace exhibit drew enormous crowds from all over Europe to see the products and processes of machine and craft industries. The building itself was a glass palace supported by a cast-iron frame, a construction imitated in many grand railroad terminals, department stores, and auditoriums throughout Europe and the United States. (*By permission of the Houghton Library, Harvard University*)

tion. Workers' testimony of acute distress, particularly in the 1780–1830 period and again in the 1840s, has left a powerful impression of their misery. Their champions—humanitarians, radicals and socialists—defended them from inhuman treatment and dreadful lives. Today historians, dealing with limited statistics or governmental and humanitarian reports, generally conclude that the standard of living actually improved over the eighteenth and early nineteenth centuries. Awareness of higher wages, greater opportunities, and more choices for men and women has led historians to take a more optimistic view of the long-range effects of industrialization than many contemporaries did. There is no denying, however, that the rapidity of change caused great hardships for the workers of all countries. They endured cruel conditions in factories and slums. Craft workers faced competition from machines and displacement; Irish farm laborers and their families starved during the great famine. Emigration to England, British colonies, or the United States might mean escape from starvation, but workers still lived desperately hard lives. As to the workers who did not emigrate, statistical evidence showing an increase in the living standard does not reveal much about the radically reduced quality of life that men, women, and children experienced as they moved from rural communities to urban factories and slums—and to daily insecurity. Their grim experiences were relived by workers in the rest of Europe and the United States later in the century and in many countries in the twentieth century as well.

INDUSTRIALISM IN PERSPECTIVE

Like the French Revolution, the Industrial Revolution helped to modernize Europe. Eventually, it transformed every facet of society and even the natural world. In preindustrial society—Europe in the mid-eighteenth century—agriculture was the dominant economic activity and peasants were the most numerous class. Peasant life centered on the family and the village, which country folk rarely left. The new rational and critical spirit associated with the Enlightenment hardly penetrated rural Europe; there, religious faith, clerical authority, and ancient superstition remained firmly entrenched. The richest and most powerful class was the aristocracy, whose wealth stemmed from land and whose privileges were protected by custom and law. The French Revolution undermined the traditional power structure: king, aristocracy, and clergy.

The Industrial Revolution accelerated the pace of modernization. In time, agricultural villages and handicraft manufacturing were eclipsed in importance by cities and factories. The very geography of the world changed with the construction of dams, canals, roads, railroads, cities, and factories. In the society fashioned by industrialization and urbanization, aristocratic power and values declined. At the same time, the bourgeoisie increased in number, wealth, importance, and power. More and more, a person was judged by talent or income rather than by birth, and opportunities for upward social mobility expanded. In time, the Industrial Revolution became a great force for democratization; during the nineteenth century, first the middle class and then the working class gained the vote.

The Industrial Revolution also hastened the secularization of European life. In the cities, former villagers, separated from traditional communal ties, drifted away from their ancestral religion. Along with urban living, the increase in governments' power over individuals through public education and required military service contributed greatly to the molding of a secular, as well as a nationalistic, society. Modernization did not proceed everywhere at the same pace and with the same thoroughness. Generally, premodern social and institutional forms remained deeply entrenched in eastern and southern Europe and persisted there well into the twentieth century.

Despite the many problems it created, some of which still remain, the Industrial Revolution was a great triumph. Ultimately, it made possible the highest standard of living in human history and created new opportunities for social advancement, political participation, and educational and cultural development. In the second half of the nineteenth century, industrialization widened the gap between the West and the rest of the world in terms of science and technology. Western states were able to extend their power so that virtually the entire globe came under Western dominance by the twentieth century. At the end of the century, the world is still engaged in the process of industrialization, and the process is, indeed, worldwide, encompassing most of the peoples and places of the globe.

◆ ◆ ◆

NOTES

1. Dickens, Charles. *Bleak House* (Middlesex, England: Penguin, 1971), p.683.

SUGGESTED READING

The Cambridge Economic History of Europe, vol. 6 (1965). Includes several fine essays on industrialization by specialists in central and eastern Europe.

Cameron, Rondo, *France and the Economic Development of Europe, 1800–1914* (1975). Emphasizes France's role as investor in the development of the rest of Europe.

Craft, N. F. R., *British Economic Growth During the Industrial Revolution* (1985). Argues that the process of industrialization was much slower and less transforming in the nineteenth century than the phrase Industrial Revolution connotes.

Crouzet, F., *The First Industrialists: The Problem of Origins* (1985).

Deane, Phyllis, *The First Industrial Revolution, 1750–1850* (1965). An excellent introduction.

Floud, Roderick, and Donald McCloskey, *The Eco-*

nomic History of Britain Since 1900, 2 vols. (1981). This work incorporates the latest scholarship on British industrialization.

Halévy, Elie, *A History of the English People in the Nineteenth Century*, vols. 1–3, rev. ed. (1987). A classic and fundamental work.

Himmelfarb, Gertrude, *The Idea of Poverty: England in the Early Industrial Age* (1983). A brilliant history of English social thought focused on the condition of the poor.

Hobsbawm, Eric, *The Age of Revolution: 1789–1848* (1964). *The Age of Capital* (1988). A Marxist survey of this tumultuous period, stressing the connections between economic, social, and political revolution.

Landes, David, *The Unbound Prometheus: Technological Change and Industrial Development in Western Europe from 1750 to the Present* (1969). A classic treatment of a complex subject, beautifully and intelligently written.

Langer, William L., *Political and Social Upheaval: 1832–1852* (1969). An excellent source, with good references and bibliography.

Milward, A. S., *Economic Development of Continental Europe, 1780–1870* (1973).

Sewell, William H., Jr., *Work and Revolution in France: The Language of Labor from the Old Regime to 1848* (1980). A review of labor's involvement in this turbulent period.

Thompson, E. P., *The Making of the English Working Class* (1966). A very readable, dramatic, and enormously influential book.

Webb, R. K., *Modern England from the Eighteenth Century* (1967 and 1980). A balanced, well-written, and well-informed text.

Novels of Special Note

Balzac, Honoré de, *Eugénie Grandet; Père Goriot; César Piroteau*. A great novelist's studies of the decay of human character under social and economic pressures.

Dickens, Charles, *Hard Times; Our Mutual Friend; Oliver Twist; Bleak House*. The great humanitarian's social protest novels.

Disraeli, Benjamin, *Sybil*. A politician's program in novel form.

Eliot, George, *Adam Bede, Middlemarch*.

Gaskell, Elizabeth, *North and South; Mary Barton*. A woman's vision of industrial and social change.

Zola, Émile, *Germinal*. Describes the condition of miners in the 1850s and 1860s. Very interesting to compare with Richard Llewellyn's novel of Welsh miners, *How Green Was My Valley*.

REVIEW QUESTIONS

1. Why did England experience industrialization before the rest of Europe? How did political and social factors influence industrialization in England?

2. How did political and social factors promote or delay industrialization in France, in the German states, and in the Netherlands?

3. How did changes in European agriculture in the early 1800s reflect the impact of capitalism and industrialization?

4. Historians argue about the relative importance of labor, capital, government, technological invention, and natural resources and geography in the process of industrialization. Construct arguments for the primacy of each of these factors.

5. What factors promoted the growth of cities between 1800 and 1860?

6. Historians argue for and against the concept of the Industrial Revolution. What arguments could be made that industrialization is a slow process? What arguments could be made that industrialization as experienced by 1850 was rapid?

7. Which groups were designated middle class and which were considered working class, or lower orders, in nineteenth-century Europe? Why did contemporaries and some historians make the terms plural?

8. Why did organized religion play a decreasing role or a role different from its spiritual one in the lives of working-class people in the mid 1800s?

9. What aspects of working-class life and culture did the middle class try to change in the nineteenth century?

10. How did the law discriminate against and punish the working class during the early stages of industrialization? How did it try to protect this class?

CHAPTER 22

Thought and Culture
in the Early Nineteenth Century

*I*n 1815, the armies of France no longer marched across the Continent, and Napoleon was imprisoned on an island a thousand miles off the coast of Africa. The traditional rulers of Europe, some of them just restored to power, were determined to protect themselves and society from future Robespierres who organized reigns of terror and Napoleons who obliterated traditional states. As defenders of the status quo, they attacked the reformist spirit of the philosophes, which had produced the French Revolution. In *conservatism*, which championed tradition over reason, hierarchy over equality, and the community over the individual, they found a philosophy to justify their assault on the Enlightenment and the Revolution.

But the forces unleashed by the French Revolution had penetrated European consciousness too deeply to be eradicated. One of them was *liberalism*, which aimed to secure the liberty and equality proclaimed by the Revolution. Another was *nationalism*, which sought to liberate subject peoples and unify broken nations.

The early 1800s also saw the flowering of a new cultural orientation. *Romanticism*, with its plea for the liberation of human emotions and the free expression of personality, challenged the Enlightenment stress on rationalism. Although primarily a literary and artistic movement, romanticism also permeated philosophy and political thought, particularly conservatism.

Still another force emerging in the post-Napoleonic period was socialism. Reacting to the problems spawned by the Industrial Revolution, socialists called for creating a new society, based on cooperation rather than on capitalist competition. A minor movement in the era from 1815 to 1848, socialism in its Marxist version became a major intellectual and social force in the last part of the century.

Traveller Looking Over a Sea of Fog, by Caspar David Friedrich. (*Hamburger Kunsthalle*)

ROMANTICISM: A NEW CULTURAL ORIENTATION

The Romantic Movement, which began in the closing decades of the eighteenth century, dominated European cultural life in the first half of the nineteenth. Historians recognize the prominence of romanticism in nineteenth-century cultural life, but the movement was so complex and the differences among the various romantic writers, artists, and musicians so numerous that historians cannot agree on a definition of romanticism. Romantics were both liberals and conservatives, revolutionaries and reactionaries; some were preoccupied with religion and God, while others paid little attention to faith.

Most of Europe's leading cultural figures came under the influence of the Romantic Movement. Among the exponents of romanticism were the poets Shelley, Wordsworth, Keats, and Byron in England; the novelist Victor Hugo and the Catholic novelist and essayist Chateaubriand in France; and the writers A. W. and Friedrich Schlegel, the dramatist and poet Schiller, and the philosopher Schelling in Germany. Caspar David Friedrich in Germany and John Constable in England expressed the romantic mood in art, and Beethoven, Schubert, Chopin, and Wagner expressed it in music.

Exalting Imagination, Intuition, and Feelings

Perhaps the central message of the romantics was that the imagination of the individual should determine the form and content of an artistic creation. This outlook ran counter to the rationalism of the Enlightenment, which itself had been a reaction against the otherworldly Christian orientation of the Middle Ages. The philosophes had attacked faith because it thwarted and distorted reason; romantic poets, philosophers, and artists now denounced the scientific rationalism of the philosophes because it crushed the emotions and impeded creativity.

According to the romantics, the philosophes had turned flesh-and-blood human beings into soulless thinking machines. The philosophes' geometric spirit, which sought to fit all life into a mechanical framework, had diminished and demeaned the individual. Such shallow thinking had stifled imagination and spontaneity, preventing people from realizing their human potential. To be restored to their true nature and made whole again, human beings must be emancipated from the tyranny of excessive intellectualizing; their feelings must be nourished and expressed. Taking up one of Rousseau's ideas, romantics yearned to rediscover in the human soul the pristine freedom and creativity that had been squashed by habits, values, rules, and standards imposed by civilization.

The philosophes had concentrated on people in general, focusing on the elements of human nature shared by all people. The romantics, in contrast, emphasized human diversity and uniqueness: the traits that set one human being apart from others. Discover and express your true self, romantics commanded: cultivate your own imagination; play your own music; write your own poetry; paint your own personal vision of nature; live, love, and suffer in your own way. The philosophes had asserted the mind's autonomy—its capacity to think for itself independent of authority. Romantics, on the other hand, gave primary importance to the autonomy of the personality—the individual's need and right to find and fulfill an inner self. This intense introspection, the individual's preoccupation with human feelings, is the distinguishing feature of romanticism. In the opening lines of his autobiography, *The Confessions,* Jean Jacques Rousseau, a romantic in an age of reason, expressed the passionate subjectivism that was to characterize the Romantic Movement:

> *I am commencing an undertaking, hitherto without precedent and which will never find an imitator. I desire to set before my fellows the likeness of a man in all the truth of nature, and that man myself. Myself alone! I know the feelings of my heart, and I know men. I am not made like any of those I have seen. I venture to believe that I am not made like any of those who are in existence. If I am not better, at least I am different.*[1]

Whereas the philosophes had regarded feelings as an obstacle to clear thinking, to the romantics they were the human essence. People could not

DANTE'S INFERNO: THE WHIRLWIND OF LOVERS BY WILLIAM BLAKE (1757–1827). Blake was a radical Romantic painter and poet who totally rejected the artistic conventions of the past. His religious and political beliefs were as unique as his art; he spent his life trying to convey tormented inward visions. A prolific illustrator, his imaginative genius was stimulated by great literature such as Dante's *Divine Comedy*. (*National Gallery of Art, Washington, D.C. Gift of W.G. Allen*)

live by reason alone, said the romantics. They agreed with Rousseau's words that "For us, to exist is to feel and our sensibility is incontestably prior to our reason."[2] For the romantics, reason was cold and dreary, its understanding of people and life meager and inadequate. Reason could not comprehend or express the complexities of human nature or the richness of human experience. By always dissecting and analyzing, by imposing deadening structure and form, and by demanding adherence to strict rules, reason crushed inspiration and creativity and barred true understanding. "The Reasoning Power in Man,"

wrote William Blake, the British poet, artist, and mystic, is "an Incrustation over my Immortal Spirit."[3]

The avenue to truth for the romantics was spontaneous human emotion rather than the intellect. By cultivating instincts and imagination, individuals could experience reality and discover their authentic selves. The romantics wanted people to feel and to experience—"To bathe in the Waters of Life," said Blake.[4] Or as Johann Goethe, Germany's great poet, wrote in *Faust*, "My worthy friend, gray are all theories, /And green alone Life's golden tree."[5]

Consequently, the romantics insisted that imaginative poets had a deeper insight into life than analytical philosophers. Poetry is a true philosophy, the romantics said; it can do what rational analysis and geometric calculations cannot do—speak directly to the heart, clarify life's deepest mysteries, participate in the eternal, and penetrate to the depths of human nature. To think profoundly, one has to feel deeply, said the romantics. For reason to function best, it must be nourished by the poetic imagination; that alone extricates and ennobles feelings hidden in the soul. "I am certain of nothing but of the holiness of the Heart's affections and the truth of Imagination," wrote John Keats. "O for a Life of Sensations rather than of Thoughts."[6] In his preface to *The Lyrical Ballads* (1798), often called the manifesto of romanticism, William Wordsworth (1770–1850) held that poetry—that is, imagination and feeling—not mathematics and logic, yielded the highest truth.

The Enlightenment mind had been clear, critical, and controlled. It had adhered to standards of esthetics, thought to be universal, that had dominated European cultural life since the Renaissance. That mind stressed technique, form, and changeless patterns and tended to reduce the imagination to mechanical relationships. "Analysis and calculation make the poet, as they make the mathematician," wrote Étienne Condillac, a prominent French philosophe. "Once the material of a play is given, the invention of the plot, the characters, the verse, is only a series of algebraic problems to be worked out."[7] Following in this tradition, Népomucène Lemercier determined that there were twenty-six rules for tragedy, twenty-three for comedy, and twenty-four for the epic; he proceeded to manufacture plays and epics according to this formula.

Romantic poets, artists, and musicians broke with the traditional styles and uniform standards and created new cultural forms and techniques. "We do not want either Greek or Roman Models," Blake declared, "but [should be] just & true to our own Imaginations."[8] Victor Hugo (1802–1885), the dominant figure among French romantics, urged: "Freedom in art! . . . Let us take the hammer to the theories, the poetics [the analysis of poetry] and the systems."[9] Yearning for unhindered self-expression, the romantics believed that one did not learn how to write poetry or paint

pictures by following textbook rules, nor could one grasp the poet's or artist's intent by judging works according to fixed standards. Only by trusting their own feelings could individuals attain their creative potential and achieve self-realization. Hence, the most beautiful works of art were not photographic imitations of nature but authentic and spontaneous expressions of the artist's feelings, fantasies, and dreams. It was the artist's inner voice that gave a work of art its supreme value. Similarly, the romantics were less impressed by Beethoven's constructions than by the intensity and power of his music. Thus, a contemporary of Beethoven's said that his "music moves the levers that open the floodgates of fear, terror, of horror, of pain and arouses the longing for the eternal which is the essence of Romanticism."[10]

The romantics explored the inner life of the mind, which Freud would later call *the unconscious.* "It is the beginning of poetry," wrote Friedrich Schlegel, "to abolish the law and the method of the rationally proceeding reason and to plunge us once more into the ravishing confusion of fantasy, the original chaos of human nature."[11] It was this dimension of the mind—mysterious, primitive, more elemental and more powerful than reason, the wellspring of creativity—that the romantics longed to revitalize and release.

Nature, God, History

The philosophes had viewed nature as a lifeless machine, a giant clock, all of whose parts worked together in perfect precision and harmony. Nature's laws, operating with mathematical certainty, were uncovered by the methodology of science. The romantics rejected this impersonal, mechanical model. Inspired and awed by nature's beauty and majesty, they responded emotionally to nature, and sought a mystical union with it. To the romantics, nature was alive and suffused with God's presence. Nature stimulated the creative energies of the imagination; it taught human beings a higher form of knowledge. As William Wordsworth wrote,

> One impulse from a vernal wood
> May teach you more of man,
> Of moral evil and of good,
> Than all the sages can.[12]

Wordsworth felt that the poet had a unique capacity to know nature. Interaction with nature fostered self-discovery. Thus, Wordsworth saw in nature

> *The anchor of my purest thoughts, the nurse,*
> *The guide, the guardian of my heart, and soul*
> *Of all my moral being.*[13]

For the romantics, the poet's imagination unlocked nature's most important secrets. In perhaps the most impassioned application of this principle, English romantics decried their country's drab factories—the "dark satanic mills," which deprived life of its joy and separated people from nature.

Regarding God as a great watchmaker—a detached observer of a self-operating mechanical universe—the philosophes tried to reduce religion to a series of scientific propositions. Many romantics, on the contrary, viewed God as a spiritual force that inspired people and enriched life, and they deplored the decline of Christianity. The cathedrals and ceremonies, poetic and mysterious, satisfied the esthetic impulse; Christian moral commands, compassionate and just, elevated human behavior to a higher level. Consequently, the romantics condemned the philosophes for weakening Christianity by submitting its dogmas to the test of reason, and they recoiled with anger at the philosophes' relegation of God to the status of a watchmaker. As Samuel Taylor Coleridge (1772–1834), poet and conservative political thinker, wrote: "What indeed but the wages of death can be expected from a doctrine which degrades the Deity into a bland hypothesis, and that the hypothesis of a clockwork-maker . . . a godless nature, and a natureless, abstract God . . . the Sunday name of gravitation."[14] The romantics' call to acknowledge the individual as a spiritual being and to cultivate the religious side of human nature accorded with their aim of restoring the whole personality, which had been fragmented by the philosophes' excessive emphasis on the intellect.

The Middle Ages, too, appeared as a very different era to the philosophes and the romantics. To the former, that period was a time of darkness, when superstition and fanaticism reigned; surviving medieval institutions and traditions served only to bar progress. The romantics, on the other hand, revered the Middle Ages. The

LORD BYRON (1788–1824). One of the leading romantic poets, Byron created the "Byronic hero," a lonely and mysterious figure. His own short life exalted the emotions and the senses. He went to Greece in 1824 to aid the revolutionaries and died there from poor health. (*Stock Montage*)

wars of the French Revolution, Napoleon, and the breakdown of political equilibrium had produced a sense of foreboding about the future. Some sought spiritual security by looking back to the Middle Ages, when Europe was united by a single faith and the fabric of society was intact and strong. To the romantic imagination, the Middle Ages, steeped in religious faith, had nurtured social harmony and abounded with heroic and chivalrous deeds as well as colorful pageantry.

The romantics and the philosophes also diverged in their conception of history. For the philosophes, history served a didactic purpose by providing examples of human folly. Such knowledge helped people prepare for a better future, and for that reason alone history should be studied. To the romantics, a historical period, like an individual, was a unique entity with its own soul. They wanted the historian to portray and analyze the variety of nations, traditions, and institutions that constituted the historical experience, always recognizing what is particular and unique to a given time and place. The romantics' feeling for the uniqueness of phenomena and their appreciation of cultural differences laid the foundation of modern historical scholarship. For they sought to study the specific details of history and culture and to comprehend them in their own terms within the context of their own times.

Searching for universal principles, the philosophes had dismissed folk traditions as peasant superstitions and impediments to progress. The romantics, on the other hand, rebelling against the standardization of culture, saw native languages, songs, and legends as the unique creations of a people and the deepest expression of national feeling. The romantics regarded the legends, myths, and folk traditions of a people as the wellspring of poetry and art and as the spiritual source of that people's cultural vitality, creativity, and identity. Hence, they examined these earliest cultural expressions with awe and reverence. In this way, romanticism helped shape modern nationalism.

The Impact of the Romantic Movement

The romantic revolt against the Enlightenment had an important and enduring impact on European history. By focusing on the creative capacities inherent in the emotions—intuition, spontaneity, instinct, passion, will, empathy—the romantics shed light on a side of human nature that the philosophes had often overlooked or undervalued. By encouraging personal freedom and diversity in art, music, and literature, they greatly enriched European cultural life. Future artists, writers, and musicians would proceed along the path cleared by the romantics. Modern art, for example, owes much to the Romantic Movement's emphasis on the legitimacy of human feeling and to its exploration of the hidden world of dreams and fantasies. The romantic emphasis on feeling sometimes found expression in humanitarian movements that fought slavery, child labor, and poverty. Romantics were among the first to attack the emerging industrial capitalism for subordinating individuals to the requirements of the industrial process and treating them as mere things. By

recognizing the distinctive qualities of historical periods, peoples, and cultures, the romantics helped create the modern historical outlook. By valuing a nation's past, romanticism contributed to modern nationalism and conservatism.

However, the Romantic Movement had a potentially dangerous side: it serves as background to the extreme nationalism of the twentieth century. As Ernst Cassirer points out, the romantics "never meant to politicize but to 'poeticize' the world," and their deep respect for human individuality and national diversity was not compatible with Hitler's racial nationalism. Yet by waging their attack on reason with excessive zeal, the romantics undermined respect for the rational tradition of the Enlightenment and thus set up a precondition for the rise and triumph of fascist movements. Although their intention was cultural and not political, by idealizing the past and glorifying ancient folkways, legends, native soil, and native language, the romantics introduced a highly charged nonrational component into political life. In later generations, romanticism, particularly in Germany, fused with political nationalism to produce "a general climate of inexact thinking, an intellectual . . . dreamworld and an emotional approach to problems of political action to which sober reasoning should have been applied."[15]

The philosophes would have regarded the romantics' veneration of a people's history and traditions as a barbarous regression to superstition and a triumph of myth over philosophy. Indeed, when transferred to the realm of politics, the romantics' idealization of the past and fascination with inherited national myths as the source of wisdom did reawaken a way of thinking about the world that rested more on feeling than on reason. In the process, people became committed to nationalist and political ideas that were fraught with danger. The glorification of myth and the folk community constitutes a link, however unintended, between romanticism and extreme nationalism, which culminated in the world wars of the twentieth century.

GERMAN IDEALISM

The romantics' stress on the inner person also found expression in the school of German philosophy called *idealism*. Idealists did not see the world as something objective, that is, existing independently of individual consciousness. Rather, they held that human consciousness, the knowing subject, builds the world and determines its form. German idealism arose in part as a response to the challenge posed by David Hume (see Chapter 18), the great English empiricist and skeptic.

The Challenge Posed by Hume's Empiricism

Enlightenment thinkers believed that physics and astronomy, epitomized by Newton, provided the kind of certainty that other forms of inquiry, notably theology, could not. But in his *Treatise of Human Nature* (1739–40) and *Enquiry Concerning Human Understanding* (1748), Hume cast doubt on the view that scientific certainty was possible. He demolished the religious argument for miracles and the deist argument for a Creator; he also called into question the very notion of scientific law.

Science rests on the conviction that regularities observed in the past and the present will be repeated in the future: that there does exist an objective reality, which rational creatures can comprehend. Hume, however, argued that science cannot demonstrate a *necessary connection* between cause and effect. Because we repeatedly experience a burning sensation when our fingers have contact with a flame, we assume a cause-and-effect relationship. This is unwarranted, says Hume. All we can acknowledge is that there is a constant conjunction between the flame and the burning sensation.

According to Hume, a thoroughgoing empiricist, sense perception is the only legitimate source of knowledge, and our sense experiences can never prove a necessary connection between what we customarily perceive as cause and effect. We can see things happening, but we cannot see why they happen. Experience tells us only what happens at a particular moment; it cannot tell us with certainty that the same combination of events will be repeated in the future. Based on past experience, the mind expects the flame to burn, but we cannot prove that there is a law at work in nature guaranteeing that a specific cause will produce a specific effect. What we mean by cause and effect is simply something that the

mind, through habit, imposes on our sense perceptions. For practical purposes, we can say that two events are in association with each other, but we cannot conclude with certainty that the second was caused by the first—that natural law is operating within the physical universe. Such a radical empiricism undermines the very foundations of science, so revered by progressive thinkers.

Immanuel Kant

In the *Critique of Pure Reason* (1781), Immanuel Kant (see page 428), the great German philosopher and proponent of Newtonianism and the scientific method, undertook the challenge of rescuing reason and science from Hume's empiricism. Kant rejected Hume's (and Locke's) underlying premise that all knowledge derives from sense experience, which imprints impressions on the mind. The mind, said Kant, is not a *tabula rasa*, a blank slate, passively receiving sense impressions, but an active instrument that structures, organizes, and interprets the multiplicity of sensations coming to it. The mind can coordinate a chaotic stream of sensations because it contains its own inherent logic; it is equipped with several categories of understanding, including cause and effect. These categories are a priori and universal: that is, they are necessary constituents of all human minds and exist independently of and prior to experience.

For Kant, cause and effect has an objective existence; it exists as an a priori component of human consciousness. Because of the way our mind is constituted, we presuppose a relationship of cause and effect in all our experiences with the objects of this world. The mind does not treat the physical world in an arbitrary or random way; it imposes structure and order on our sense experiences. Cause and effect and the other categories of the mind permit us to attribute certainty to scientific knowledge. The physical world must possess certain definite characteristics because these characteristics conform to the categories of the mind. The object, said Kant, must "accommodate itself to the subject."

Kant rescued science from Hume's assault: the laws of science are universally valid. But in the process, Kant made scientific law dependent on the mind and its a priori categories. We see nature in a certain way because of the mental apparatus that we bring to it. The mind does not derive the laws of nature from the physical world. Indeed, the reverse is true. The mind imposes its own laws on nature—on the raw impressions received by the senses—giving the physical world form, structure, and order. By holding that objects must conform to the rules of the human mind, that it is the knowing subject that creates order within nature, Kant gave primacy to the knower rather than to the objects of knowledge. He saw the mind as an active agent, not a passive receptacle for sensations. This "turn in philosophy," which Kant considered as revolutionary as the Copernican theory had been for astronomy, gave unprecedented importance to the inner self, to the active and creative knower.

It is a fundamental principle of Kant's thought that we cannot know ultimate reality. Our knowledge is limited to the phenomenal world, the realm of natural occurrences. We can know only the things that we experience, that is, things as they appear to us through the active intervention of the mind's categories. We can have no knowledge of a thing-in-itself, that is, of an object's ultimate or real nature—its nature as it is independently of the way we experience it, apart from the way our senses receive it. The human mind can acquire knowledge only of that part of reality revealed through sense experience. We can say nothing about the sun's true nature but only describe the way the sun appears to us: that is, our impression of the sun formed by the mind's ordering of our sense experiences of it. Thus, at the same time that Kant reaffirmed the validity of scientific law, he also limited the range of science and reason.

G. W. F. Hegel

Kant had insisted that knowledge of what lies beyond the phenomena—knowledge of ultimate or absolute reality itself—is forever denied us. Georg Wilhelm Friedrich Hegel (1770–1831), another German philosopher, could not accept this. He constructed an all-embracing metaphysical system, which attempted to explain all reality and uncover the fundamental nature and meaning of the universe and human history. In the process, he synthesized the leading currents of thought of his day: the rationalism of the Enlightenment, romanticism, and Kantian philosophy.

Hegel inherited from the philosophes a respect for reason and the conviction that the human intellect can make sense out of nature and human experience—that the universe is intelligible. The romantics taught him to appreciate the wide diversity of human experience and to search for truth in the varieties of cultural life and history rather than in an unchanging natural order. Like the romantics, Hegel held that the scientific method provided only a partial and limited view of reality. He also acquired from the romantics the idea that we should aspire to see things wholly, as an organic unity of interdependent parts, rather than as separate atoms in isolation.

Adopting Kant's notion that the mind imposes its categories on the world, Hegel emphasized the importance of the thinking subject in the quest for truth. However, Kant held that we can have knowledge only of how a thing appears to us, not of the thing-in-itself. Hegel, in contrast, maintained that ultimate reality, total truth, is knowable to the human mind: the mind can comprehend the conceptual truths underlying all existence and can grasp the essential meaning of human experience.

Kant had asserted the essential idealist position that it is the knowing subject that organizes our experiences of the phenomenal world. Hegel went a giant step beyond that by positing the existence of a universal Mind—Absolute Spirit—which differentiates itself in the minds of thinking individuals. He saw Mind, the thing-in-itself, as a universal agent, whose nature can be apprehended through thought.

Absolute Spirit is truth in its totality and wholeness. Plato believed that true reality, the Idea, was static, timeless, and unchanging and existed in a higher, superterrestrial world, apart from the transitory world of phenomena that we observe every day. But Hegel held that ultimate reality was characterized by change and development and was to be found in the concrete world of human experience; in cultural life and political conflicts, the Idea or Spirit becomes actualized. To discover ultimate truth, the mind does not flee from the objects of this world to a higher reality; rather, it aspires to a deeper understanding of existing things.

HEGEL IN HIS STUDY. Georg Wilhelm Friedrich Hegel (1770–1831) constructed a comprehensive philosophical system that sought to explain all reality. His philosophy of history, particularly the theories of dialectical conflict and of progression toward an ultimate end, greatly influenced Karl Marx. (*Bildarchiv Preussischer Kulturbesitz, Berlin*)

Because Hegel viewed Absolute Spirit not as fixed and static, but as evolving and developing, history plays a central role in his philosophical system. History is the development of Spirit in time. In the arena of world history, truth unfolds and makes itself known to the human mind. Like the romantics, Hegel said that each historical period has a distinctive character that separates it from every preceding age and enables us to see it as an organic whole. The art, science, philosophy, religion, politics, and leading events are sufficiently interconnected that the period may be said to possess an organic unity, a historical coherence.

Does history contain an overarching meaning? Are past, present, and future linked together by something more profound, more unifying than random chance? Hegel believed that world history reveals a rational process; an internal principle of order underlies historical change. There is a purpose and an end to history: the unfolding of Absolute Spirit. In the course of history, an immanent Spirit manifests itself; gradually, progressively, and nonrepetitively, it actualizes itself, becoming itself fully. Nations and exceptional human beings, "World-Historical" individuals—Alexander the Great, Caesar, Napoleon—are the vehicles through which Spirit realizes its potentiality and achieves self-consciousness. Hegel's philosophy of history gives meaning, purpose, and direction to historical events. Where is history taking us? What is its ultimate meaning? For Hegel, history is humanity's progress from lesser to greater freedom: "The History of the World is none other than the progress of the consciousness of Freedom . . . [It is] the absolute goal of history."[16]

According to Hegel, Spirit manifests itself in history through a dialectical tension between opposing forces; the struggle between one force (thesis) and its adversary (antithesis) is evident in all spheres of human activity. This clash of opposites gains in intensity, ending in a resolution that unifies both opposing views. Thought and history then enter a new and higher stage, that of synthesis, which, by absorbing the truths within both the thesis and the antithesis, achieves a higher level of truth and a higher stage of history. Soon this synthesis itself becomes a thesis that enters into another conflict with another set of opposing forces. This conflict too is resolved by a still higher synthesis. Thus, the dynamic struggle between thesis and antithesis—sometimes expressed in revolutions and war, and sometimes in art, religion, and philosophy—and its resolution into a synthesis accounts for movement in history. Or, in Hegelian language, Spirit is closer to realization: its rational structure is progressing from potentiality to actuality. The dialectic is the march of Spirit through human affairs. Since Hegel held that freedom is the essence of Spirit, it is through history that human beings progress toward consciousness of their own freedom. They become self-consciously aware of their own self-determination—their ability to regulate their lives rationally according to their own consciousness.

SØREN KIERKEGAARD

Søren Kierkegaard's childhood was marred by pain. Born in Copenhagen in 1813, the youngest of seven children, he suffered from a malformed spine, and within a ten-year period, his mother and five of his brothers and sisters died. In his adult years, he never would be free of melancholy. Influenced by his devout father, young Søren was drawn to religious questions.

Both Feuerbach (see page 586) and Marx attacked Hegelian metaphysics for transcending a naturalistic approach to the human condition. A different kind of objection was raised by Kierkegaard. He assailed Hegel's view that universal truth, the Absolute, is a realizable goal of speculative thought—that through reason we can comprehend the essential nature of reality. Kierkegaard attacked Hegel's system for being too abstract, too

But for individual freedom to be realized, said Hegel, social and political institutions must be rationally determined and organized, that is, the will of the individual must be harmonized with the needs of the community. For Hegel, freedom is not a matter of securing abstract natural rights for the individual, which was the goal of the French Revolution. Rather, true freedom is attained only within the social group. Thus, in Hegel's view, human beings discover their essential character—their moral and spiritual potential—only as citizens of a cohesive political community. This view goes back to the city-states of ancient Greece, which Hegel admired.

Like Rousseau, Hegel sought to bring the individual's free choice into harmony with the needs of society as a whole. Hegel linked freedom to obedience to the state's commands. In the state's laws and institutions, which are manifestations of reason, the objectivization of Spirit, individuals find a basis for rationally determining their own life. In this way, the private interests of citizens become one with common interests of the community. For Hegel, Absolute Spirit, which is also

Ultimate Reason, realizes itself in the state, the highest form of human association. The state joins fragmented individuals together into a community and substitutes a rule of justice for the rule of instincts. It permits individuals to live the ethical life and to develop their human potential. An individual cannot achieve these goals in isolation.

The rationally organized community favored by Hegel was a constitutional monarchy. Yet he also reached the perplexing conclusion that the pinnacle of the consciousness of freedom was to be found in the Germany of his day. Germans recognized the value of monarchical leadership, he said, but also assimilated the Christian principle of the individual's infinite worth.

In deeming the Prussian state, which had an autocratic king, no constitution, no popularly elected parliament, and government-imposed censorship, to be the pinnacle of freedom and the goal for which history had been striving, Hegel's thought reveals a powerful undercurrent of statism—that is, the exaltation of the state and the subordination of the individual to it. For Hegel, the national state

intellectual, and too indifferent to individual human beings, their real existence and individual natures. Kierkegaard was concerned not with human beings in general, but with what it means "that you and I and he are human beings, each one for himself."

For Hegel, truth was something objective and universal, that could be reached through dispassionate speculative thought. Kierkegaard saw it as subjective and personal, reached through passion and commitment: "The thing to do is to find a truth which is true *for me*, to find *the idea for which I can live and die*." According to Kierkegaard, the Hegelian system and indeed all systems fail because they are concerned with objective certainty and humanity in general and not with what truly matters—the individual standing alone and making choices based on passionately held beliefs. It is this experience that brings the individual face to face with God.

The individual does not know God through disinterested reflection, Kierkegaard declared but by making a passionate commitment to him. It is precisely because Christian truths can surpass reason that we must believe.

True Christians, said Kierkegaard, commit themselves to beliefs that are unintelligible. With confidence they plunge into the absurd. But it is this leap of faith that enables Christians to conquer the agonizing feeling that life in its deepest sense is nothingness and to give meaning to their own existence. Faith based on total commitment, said Kierkegaard, is the true avenue of self-discovery. Kierkegaard's thought influenced twentieth-century existentialists (see Chapter 32).

was the embodiment of Universal Reason and the supreme achievement of Absolute Spirit:

> It must . . . be understood that all the worth which the human being possesses—all spiritual reality, he possesses only through the State. . . . Thus only is he fully conscious; thus only is he a partaker of morality—of a just and moral social and political life. For Truth is the unity of the universal . . . and the Universal is to be found in the State, in its laws, its universal and rational arrangements. The state is the Divine Idea as it exists on Earth.[17]

German conservatives used Hegel's idea that existing institutions have a rational legitimacy to support their opposition to rapid change. Existing reality, even if it appears cruel and hateful, is the actualization of Absolute Spirit. Therefore, it is inherently necessary and rational and should not be altered.

Some of Hegel's followers, known as Young Hegelians, interpreted Hegel in a radical sense. They rejected his view that the Prussian state, or any German state, was the goal of world history, the realization of freedom. The Germany of their day, held the Young Hegelians, had not attained a harmony between the individual and society: it was not rationally organized and did not foster freedom. These Young Hegelians saw Hegel's philosophy as a means for radically altering the world to make existing society truly rational. The most important of the radical Young Hegelians was Karl Marx. Marx retained Hegel's overarching principles that history contains an inner logic, that it is an intelligible process, and that a dialectical struggle propels history from a lower stage to a higher stage (see page 589).

CONSERVATISM: THE VALUE OF TRADITION

To the traditional rulers of Europe—kings, aristocrats, and clergy—the French Revolution was a great evil, which had inflicted a near-fatal wound on civilization. As far as they were concerned, the revolutionaries heralded chaos when they executed Louis XVI, confiscated the land of the church, destroyed the special privileges of the aristocracy, and instituted the Reign of Terror. Then the Revolution gave rise to Napoleon, who deposed kings, continued the assault on the traditional aristocracy, and sought to dominate Europe. Disgusted and frightened by the revolutionary violence, terror, and warfare, the traditional rulers sought to refute the philosophes' worldview, which had spawned the Revolution. To them, natural rights, equality, the goodness of man, and perpetual progress were perverse doctrines that had produced the Jacobin "assassins." In conservatism, they found a political philosophy to counter the Enlightenment ideology.

Edmund Burke's *Reflections on the Revolution in France* (1790) was instrumental in shaping conservative thought. Burke (1729–1797), an Anglo-Irish philosopher and statesman, wanted to warn his countrymen of the dangers inherent in the ideology of the revolutionaries. Although writing in 1790, Burke astutely predicted that the Revolution would lead to terror and military dictatorship. To Burke, fanatics armed with abstract ideas divorced from historical experience had dragged France through the mire of revolution. Burke developed a coherent political philosophy, which served as a counterweight to the ideology of the Enlightenment and the Revolution.

The leading conservative theorists on the Continent—more aptly called reactionaries—were Joseph de Maistre (1753–1821) and Vicomte Louis de Bonald (1754–1840). De Maistre, who fled his native Piedmont (northern Italy) in 1792 and again in 1793, after the invasion by the armies of the new French Republic, vociferously denounced the philosophes for undermining belief and authority. He called their activity an "insurrection against God." In *Reflections on the State of France* (1796) and other works, he attacked the philosophes and the French Revolution, which he blamed them for inciting. Committed to authority and order, de Maistre fought any kind of political or religious liberalism. To him, the Revolution was a satanic evil; all its pronouncements must be totally condemned and its roots expunged from the soil of Christian Europe.

Like de Maistre, de Bonald, a French émigré, detested the French Revolution, staunchly de-

fended monarchy, and attacked the rational spirit of the Enlightenment as an enemy of faith. His Catholicism and monarchism are summarized in his famous remark: "When God wished to punish France, he took away the Bourbon from her governance."

Hostility to the French Revolution

Entranced by the great discoveries in science, the philosophes and French reformers had believed that the human mind could also transform social institutions and ancient traditions according to rational models. Progress through reason became their faith. Intent on creating a new future, the revolutionaries abruptly dispensed with old habits, traditional authority, and familiar ways of thought.

To conservatives, who like the romantics venerated the past, this was supreme arrogance and wickedness. They regarded the revolutionaries as presumptuous men who recklessly severed society's links with ancient institutions and traditions and condemned venerable religious and moral beliefs as ignorance. De Maistre called Voltaire the man "into whose hands hell has given all its power."[18] Moreover, the revolutionaries forgot—or never knew—that the traditions and institutions that they wanted to destroy did not belong solely to them. Past generations and, indeed, future generations had a claim on these creations of French genius. By attacking time-honored ways, the revolutionaries had deprived French society of moral leadership and opened the door to anarchy and terror. "You began ill," wrote Burke of the revolutionaries, "because you began by despising everything that belonged to you. . . . When ancient opinions and rules of life are taken away, the loss cannot possibly be estimated. From that moment we have no compass to govern us; nor can we know distinctly to what port we steer."[19]

The philosophes and French reformers had expressed unlimited confidence in the power of human reason to understand and to change society. Although conservatives also appreciated human rational capacities, they recognized the limitations of reason. "We are afraid to put men to live and trade each on his own private stock of reason," said Burke, "because we suspect that this stock in each man is small, and that the individuals would do better to avail themselves of the general bank and capital of nations and of ages."[20] Conservatives saw the Revolution as a natural outgrowth of an arrogant Enlightenment philosophy that overvalued reason and sought to reshape society in accordance with abstract principles.

Conservatives did not regard human beings as good by nature. Human wickedness was not due to a faulty environment, as the philosophes had proclaimed, but was at the core of human nature, as Christianity taught. Evil was held in check not by reason, but by tried and tested institutions, traditions, and beliefs. Without these habits inherited from ancestors, said conservatives, the social order was threatened by sinful human nature.

Because monarchy, aristocracy, and the church had endured for centuries, argued the conservatives, they had worth. The clergy taught proper moral values; monarchs preserved order and property; aristocrats guarded against despotic kings and the tyranny of the common people. All protected and spread civilized ways. By despising and uprooting these ancient institutions, the revolutionaries had hardened the people's hearts, perverted their morals, and caused them to commit terrible outrages on each other and on society.

Conservatives detested attempts to transform society according to a theoretical model. They considered human nature too intricate and social relations too complex for such social engineering. In the conservatives' view, the revolutionaries had reduced people and society to abstractions divorced from their historical settings. Consequently, they had destroyed ancient patterns that seemed inconvenient and had drawn up constitutions based on the unacceptable principle that government derives its power from the consent of the governed.

The art of politics, argued Burke, entails practical reason: pursuing limited and realizable goals for a particular community. The wise statesman, said traditionalists, abhors abstract principles and spurns ideal models. Rather, he values the historical experiences of his nation and is concerned with real people in specific historical situations. He recognizes that institutions and beliefs do not require theoretical excellence; they do not have to meet the test of reason or of nature in order to benefit society. Statesmen who ignore these truisms and strive to reform a commonwealth according to a priori models—political formulas that do not fit the realities of history

and the social order—plunge the nation into anarchy. To Burke, the revolutionaries were zealots who, like the religious radicals during the Reformation, resorted to force and terror in order to create a new man and a new society. In politics, experience is the best teacher and prudence the best method of procedure. Burke warned:

> [I]t is with infinite caution that any man ought to venture upon pulling down an edifice which has answered in any tolerable degree for ages the common purposes of society, or on building it up again, without having models and patterns of approved utility before his eyes.[21]

For conservatives, God and history were the only legitimate sources of political authority. States were not made; rather, they were an expression of the nation's moral, religious, and historical experience. No legitimate or sound constitution could be drawn up by a group assembled for that purpose. Scraps of paper with legal terminology and philosophic visions could not produce an effective government. Instead, a sound political system evolved gradually and inexplicably in response to circumstances. For this reason, conservatives admired the English constitution. It was not a product of abstract thought; no assembly had convened to fashion it. Because it grew imperceptibly out of the historical experience and needs of the English people, it was durable and effective.

Conservatives did not view society as a machine with replaceable parts, but as a complex and delicate organism. Tamper with its vital organs, as the revolutionaries had done, and it would die.

The Quest for Social Stability

The liberal philosophy of the Enlightenment and the French Revolution started with the individual. The philosophes and the revolutionaries envisioned a society in which the individual was free and autonomous. Conservatives, on the other hand, believed that the individual could function well only as part of a social group: family, church, or state. Alone, a person would be selfish, unreliable, and frail. Through membership in a social group, however, individuals learned cooperation and manners. From the conservative perspective, by exalting the individual, the revolutionaries had threatened to dissolve society into disconnected parts. Individualism would imperil social stability, destroy obedience to law, and fragment society into self-seeking isolated atoms.

Holding that the community was more important than the individual, conservatives rejected the philosophy of natural rights. Rights were not abstractions that preceded an individual's entrance into society and pertained to all people everywhere. Rather, the state, always remembering the needs of the entire community and its links to past generations, determined what rights and privileges its citizens might have. There were no "rights of man," only rights of the French, the English, and so forth, as determined and allocated by the particular state.

Conservatives viewed equality as another pernicious abstraction that contradicted all historical experience. Since for conservatives, society was naturally hierarchical, they believed that some men, by virtue of their intelligence, education, wealth, and birth, were best qualified to rule and instruct the less able. They blamed the revolutionaries for uprooting a long-established ruling elite and thus depriving society of effective leaders, causing internal disorder, and paving the way for a military dictatorship.

Whereas the philosophes had attacked Christianity for promoting superstition and fanaticism, conservatives saw religion as the basis of civil society. They were convinced that excess liberty and the weakening of religion had brutalized people and shattered the foundations of society. Catholic conservatives, in particular, held that God had constituted the church and monarchy to check sinful human nature. "Christian monarchs are the final creation of the development of political society and of religious society," said Louis de Bonald. "The proof of this lies in the fact that when monarchy and Christianity are both abolished society returns to savagery."[22]

Conservatism exposed a limitation of the Enlightenment by pointing out that human beings and social relationships are far more complex than the philosophes had imagined. People do not always accept the rigorous logic of the philosopher and are not eager to break with ancient ways, however illogical they appear to the intellect. They often find familiar customs and ancestral religions more satisfying guides to life than the blueprints of philosophers. The granite might of tradition remains an obstacle to the visions of reformers. Conservative theorists warned that revolutionary violence in the pursuit of utopian dreams transforms politics into an ideological crusade that ends in terror and despotism. These warnings bore bitter fruit in the twentieth century.

LIBERALISM: THE VALUE OF THE INDIVIDUAL

The decades after 1815 saw a spectacular rise of the bourgeoisie. Talented and ambitious bankers, merchants, manufacturers, professionals, and officeholders wanted to break the stranglehold of the landed nobility, the traditional elite, on political power and social prestige. They also wanted to eliminate restrictions on the free pursuit of profits.

The political philosophy of the bourgeoisie was most commonly liberalism. While conservatives sought to strengthen the foundations of traditional society, which had been severely shaken in the period of the French Revolution and Napoleon, liberals strove to alter the status quo. Believing in the goodness of human nature and the capacity of individuals to control their own lives, they hoped to realize the promise of the Enlightenment and the French Revolution.

The Sources of Liberalism

In the long view of Western civilization, liberalism is an extension and development of the democratic practices and rational outlook that originated in ancient Greece. Also flowing into the liberal tradition is Judeo-Christian respect for the worth and dignity of the individual endowed by God with freedom to make moral choices. But the immediate historical roots of nineteenth-century liberalism extended back to seventeenth-century England. At that time, the struggle for religious toleration by English Protestant dissenters established the principle of freedom of conscience, which is easily transferred into freedom of opinion and expression in all matters. The Glorious Revolution of 1688 set limits on the power of the English monarchy. In that same century, John Locke's natural-rights philosophy proclaimed that the individual was by nature entitled to freedom, and it justified revolutions against rulers who deprived citizens of their lives, liberty, or property.

The French philosophes also helped shape liberalism. From Montesquieu, liberals derived the theory of the separation of powers and of checks and balances: principles intended to guard against autocratic government. The philosophes had supported religious toleration and freedom of thought, expressed confidence in the capacity of the human mind to reform society, maintained that human beings are essentially good, and believed in the future progress of humanity—all fundamental tenets of liberalism.

The American and French Revolutions were crucial phases in the history of liberalism. The Declaration of Independence gave expression to Locke's theory of natural rights; the Constitution of the United States incorporated Montesquieu's principles and demonstrated that people could create an effective government; and the Bill of Rights protected the person and rights of the individual. In destroying the special privileges of the aristocracy and opening careers to talent, the French National Assembly of 1789 implemented the liberal ideal of equality under the law. It also drew up the Declaration of the Rights of Man and of the Citizen, which affirmed the dignity and rights of the individual, and a constitution that limited the king's power. Both Revolutions explicitly called for the protection of property rights, another basic premise of liberalism.

Individual Liberty

The liberals' primary concern was the enhancement of individual liberty. They agreed with Kant that every person exists as an end in himself or herself and not as an object to be used arbitrarily by others. If uncoerced by government and churches and properly educated, a person could develop into a good, productive, and self-directed human being. People could make their own decisions, base actions on universal moral principles, and respect each other's rights.

Liberals rejected a legacy of the Middle Ages, the classification of the individual as a commoner or aristocrat on the basis of birth. They held that a man was not born into a certain station in life but made his way through his own efforts. Taking

their cue from the French Revolution, liberals called for an end to all privileges of the aristocracy.

In the tradition of the philosophes, liberals stressed the preeminence of reason as the basis of political life. Unfettered by ignorance and tyranny, the mind could eradicate evils that had burdened people for centuries and begin an age of free institutions and responsible citizens. For this reason, liberals supported the advancement of education. They believed that educated people apply reason to their political and social life, and thus they act in ways beneficial to themselves and society and are less likely to submit to tyrants.

Liberals attacked the state and other authorities that prevented the individual from exercising the right of free choice, interfered with the right of free expression, and impeded the individual's self-determination and self-development. They agreed with John Stuart Mill, the British philosopher, that "over his own body and mind, the individual is sovereign . . . that the only purpose for which power can be rightly exercised over any member of a civilized community, against his will, is to prevent harm to others."[23]

The great question confronting nineteenth-century liberals was the relationship between state authority and individual liberty. To guard against the absolute and arbitrary authority of kings, liberals demanded written constitutions that granted freedom of speech, of the press, and of religion; freedom from arbitrary arrest; and the protection of property rights. To prevent the abuse of political authority, liberals called for a freely elected parliament and the distribution of power among the various branches of government. Liberals held that a government that derived its authority from the consent of the governed, as given in free elections, was least likely to violate individual freedom. A corollary of this principle was that the best government is the one that governs least—that is, one that interferes as little as possible with the economic activities of its citizens and does not involve itself in their private lives or their beliefs.

Liberal Economic Theory

Bourgeois liberals thought that the economy, like the state, should proceed according to natural laws rather than the arbitrary fiat of rulers. Adopting the laissez-faire theory of Adam Smith, they argued that a free economy, in which private enterprise was unimpeded by government regulations, was as important as political freedom to the well-being of the individual and the community. When people acted from self-interest, the liberals said, they worked harder and achieved more. Self-interest and natural competitive impulses spurred economic activity and ensured the production of more and better goods at the lowest possible price, thereby benefiting the entire nation. For this reason, the government must neither block free competition nor deprive individuals of their property, which gave them the incentive to work hard and efficiently. The state contributed to the nation's prosperity when it maintained domestic order; it endangered economic development when it tampered with the free pursuit of profits.

Believing that individuals were responsible for their own misfortunes, liberals were often unmoved by the suffering of the poor. Indeed, they used the principle of laissez faire—that government should not interfere with the market—to justify their opposition to humanitarian legislation intended to alleviate the misery of the factory workers. Liberals regarded such social reforms as unwarranted and dangerous meddling with the natural law of supply and demand.

One theorist upholding this view was Thomas R. Malthus (1766–1834), an Anglican cleric and professor of history and political economy. In his *Essay on the Principle of Population* (published in 1798 and then in a second, much enlarged, edition in 1803), Malthus asserted that population grows at a much faster rate than the food supply, resulting in food shortages, irregular employment, lower wages, and high mortality. The poor's distress, said Malthus, was not due to faulty political institutions or existing social and property relations. Its true cause was the number of children they had.

When the wages of labour are hardly sufficient to maintain two children, a man marries and has five or six. He of course finds himself miserably distressed. . . . He accuses his parish. . . . He accuses the avarice of the rich. He accuses the partial and unjust institutions of society. . . . In searching for objects of accusation, he never alludes to the quarter from which all his misfortunes originate. The last person that he would think of accusing is himself.[24]

The state cannot ameliorate the poor's misery, said Malthus; "the means of redress are in their own hands, and in the hands of no other persons whatever."[25] This "means of redress" would be a lowering of the birthrate through late marriages and chastity, but Malthus believed that the poor lacked the self-discipline to refrain from sexual activity. When they receive higher wages, they have more children, thereby upsetting the population-resource balance and bringing misery to themselves and others. The view of poverty as an iron law of nature, which could not be undone by the good intentions of the state through philanthropy, buttressed supporters of strict laissez faire and eased the consciences of the propertied classes. Compassion for the poor was simply a misplaced emotion; government reforms were doomed to fail and higher wages provided no relief. Malthus's theory also flew in the face of adherents of human perfectibility and inevitable progress. Poverty, like disease, was simply a natural phenomenon—a law of nature that could not be eliminated. No wonder his contemporaries called economics "the dismal science."

In *Principles of Political Economy* (1817), David Ricardo (1772–1823) gave support to Malthus's gloomy outlook. Higher wages, said Ricardo, lead workers to have more children, causing an increase in the labor supply. Competition for jobs by an expanding labor force brings down wages. This "iron law of wages" offered bleak prospects for the working poor.

When, however, by the encouragement which high wages give to the increase of population, the number of labourers is increased, wages again fall to their natural price [to a subsistence level] and indeed from a reaction sometimes fall below it. . . . It is a truth which admits not a doubt, that the comforts and well-being of the poor cannot be permanently secured without some regard on their part, or some effort on the part of the legislature, to regulate the increase of their numbers, and to render less frequent among them early and improvident marriages.[26]

Liberals of the early nineteenth century saw poverty and suffering as part of the natural order and beyond the scope of government. They feared that state intervention in the economy to redress social ills would disrupt the free market, threatening personal liberty and hindering social well-being. Thus, on May 13, 1848, an editorial in the *Economist* protesting against a bill before Parliament that sought to improve housing and sanitation declared: "suffering and evil are nature's admonitions; they cannot be got rid of; and the impatient attempts of benevolence to banish them from the world by legislation . . . have always been productive of more evil than good." Government interference, liberals also argued, discouraged the poor from finding work and so promoted idleness. According to liberal political economy, unemployment and poverty stemmed from individual failings.

A particularly glaring example of the coldness and harshness of liberals toward suffering was their response to the Irish famine of 1845–1849. While the Irish were dying of starvation, the liberal leadership in Britain, fearing that government intervention would promote dependence, did little to lessen the suffering. "The more I see of government interference," wrote Sir Charles Wood, chancellor of the Exchequer, "the less I am disposed to trust it, and I have no faith in anything but private capital employed under the individual charge."[27] To some hardhearted liberals, the famine, which killed about 1.5 million people, was simply nature's way of dealing with Ireland's excess population. A dogmatic commitment to laissez faire discouraged British officials from coping humanely and creatively with this disaster.

In the last part of the century, liberals modified their adherence to strict laissez faire, accepting the principle that the state had a responsibility to protect the poor against the worst abuses of rapid industrialization (see pages 594–597).

Liberalism and Democracy

The French Revolution presented a dilemma for liberals. They supported the reforms of the moderate stage: the destruction of the special privileges of the aristocracy, the drawing up of a declaration of rights and a constitution, the establishment of a parliament, and the opening of careers to talent. But they repudiated Jacobin radicalism. Liberals were frightened by the excesses of the Jacobin regime: its tampering with the economy, which, to liberals, violated the rights of private property; its appeal to the "little people," which liberals saw as inviting mob rule; its subjection of the individual to the state, which they regarded as the denial of individual rights; and its use of the guillotine, which awakened the basest human feelings.

Although many liberals still adhered to the philosophy of natural rights, some who were disturbed by the Jacobin experience discarded the theory underlying the reforms of the Revolution. Fearing social disorder as much as conservatives did, these liberals did not want to ignite revolutions by the masses. In the hands of the lower classes, the natural-rights philosophy was too easily translated into the democratic creed that all people should share political power, a prospect that the bourgeois regarded with horror. To them, the participation of commoners in politics meant a vulgar form of despotism and the end of individual liberty. They saw the masses—uneducated, unpropertied, inexperienced, and impatient—as lacking both the ability and the temperament to maintain liberty and protect property.

Few thinkers in the first half of the nineteenth century grasped the growing significance of the masses in politics as did Alexis de Tocqueville (1805–1859), the French political theorist and statesman. In the wake of the French Revolution, de Tocqueville, an aristocrat by birth but a liberal by temperament, recognized that the destruction of aristocracy—a system based on rank—and the march toward democracy could not be curbed. In *Democracy in America* (1835–1840), based on his travels in the United States, de Tocqueville analyzed, with cool detachment and brilliance, the nature, merits, and weaknesses of American democratic society. In contrast to the France of the Old Regime, wrote de Tocqueville, American society had no hereditary aristocracy with special privileges; the avenues to social advancement and political participation were open to all. Arguing that democracy was more just than aristocratic government, de Tocqueville saw it as the political system of the future. But he also recognized the dangers inherent in democracy.

In a democratic society, he noted, people's passion to be equal outweighs their commitment to liberty. Spurred by the ideal of equality, people in a democracy desire the honors and possessions that they deem to be their due. They demand that the avenues to social, economic, and political advancement be opened to all; and they no longer accept the disparity in wealth and position as part of the natural order. However, since people are not naturally equal in ability, many are frustrated and turn to the state to secure for them the advantages that they cannot obtain for themselves. To improve their material well-being, they are willing to sacrifice political liberty. Consequently, democracies face an ever present danger that people, craving equality, will surrender their liberty to a central government if it promises to provide them with property and other advantages.

Granted ever more power by the people, the state would regulate its citizens' lives and crush local institutions that impede centralized control. Liberty would be lost not to the despotism of kings, but to the tyranny of the majority. To prevent democracy from degenerating into state despotism, de Tocqueville urged strengthening institutions of local government, forming numerous private associations over which the state would have no control, protecting the independence of the judiciary, and preserving a free press—all of which promote active and responsible citizenship.

Another danger in a democratic society, said de Tocqueville, is the tendency of the majority to demand conformity of belief. Since the majority's power is absolute and irresistible, the minority fears to stray from the prescribed track.

According to de Tocqueville, democracy also spawns a selfish individualism, which could degenerate into vulgar hedonism. Driven by an overriding concern for possessions and profits, people can lose their taste for political participation and their concern for the public good. If self-interest prevails over a sense of public duty, liberty cannot long endure.

Although recognizing the limitations of democracy, de Tocqueville did not seek to reverse its growth. In this new age that is dawning, he wrote,

all who shall attempt . . . to base freedom upon aristocratic privilege will fail . . . all who

shall attempt to draw and to retain authority within a single class, will fail. . . . All . . . who would establish or secure the independence and the dignity of their fellow-men, must show themselves the friends of equality. . . . Thus the question is not how to reconstruct aristocratic society, but how to make liberty proceed out of that democratic state of society in which God has placed us.[28]

The problems of democracy, declared de Tocqueville, must be resolved without jeopardizing freedom. The task of a democratic society is to temper extreme individualism and unrestrained acquisitiveness by fostering public spirit. Without direct participation by cooperating citizens—that is, without a concern for the common good—democracy faces a bleak future. Freedom depends less on laws than it does on cultivating the sentiments and habits of civic virtue.

Because bourgeois liberals feared that democracy could quash personal freedom as ruthlessly as any absolute monarch, they called for property requirements for voting and officeholding. They wanted political power to be concentrated in the hands of a safe and reliable—that is, a propertied and educated—middle class. Such a government would prevent revolution from below, a prospect that caused anxiety among bourgeois liberals.

When liberals of the early nineteenth century engaged in revolutions, their aims were always limited. Once they had destroyed absolute monarchy and gained a constitution and a parliament or a change of government, they quickly tried to terminate the revolution. When the fever of revolution spread to the masses, liberals either withdrew or turned counterrevolutionary, for they feared the stirrings of the multitude.

Although liberalism was the political philosophy of a middle class generally hostile to democracy, the essential ideals of democracy flowed logically from liberalism. Eventually, democracy became a later stage in the evolution of liberalism because the masses, their political power enhanced by the Industrial Revolution, would press for greater social, political, and economic equality. Thus, by the early twentieth century, many European states had introduced universal manhood suffrage, abandoned property requirements for officeholding, and improved conditions for workers.

But the fears of nineteenth-century liberals were not unfounded. In the twentieth century, the participation of common people in politics has indeed threatened freedom. Impatient with parliamentary procedures, the masses, particularly when troubled by economic problems, have in some instances given their support to demagogues who promised swift and decisive action. The granting of political participation to the masses has not always made people freer. The confidence of democrats has been shaken in the twentieth century by the seeming willingness of common people to trade freedom for state authority, order, economic security, and national power. Liberalism is based on the assumption that human beings can and do respond to rational argument and that reason will prevail over base human feelings. The history of our century shows that this may be an overly optimistic assessment of human nature.

RADICALISM AND DEMOCRACY: THE EXPANSION OF LIBERALISM

In the early 1800s, democratic ideals were advanced by thinkers and activists called radicals. Inspired by the democratic principles expressed in Rousseau's *Social Contract* and by the republican stage of the French Revolution, French radicals championed popular sovereignty—rule by the people. In contrast to liberals, who feared the masses, French radicals trusted the common person. Advocating universal manhood suffrage and a republic, radicalism gained the support of French workers in the 1830s and 1840s.

British radicals, like their liberal cousins, inherited the Enlightenment's confidence in reason and its belief in the essential goodness of the individual. In the 1790s, British radicals expressed sympathy for the French Revolution, approving its concern for natural rights and its attack on feudal privileges. In the first half of the nineteenth century, English radicals sought parliamentary reforms because some heavily populated districts were barely represented in Parliament, while lightly populated districts were overrepresented. They demanded payment for members of Parliament to permit the nonwealthy to hold office; they sought universal manhood suffrage to give the masses representation in Parliament; and

they insisted on the secret ballot to prevent intimidation of and reprisals against voters. Radicals attacked the hereditary aristocracy and fought corruption. Some, like William Cobbett, a crusading journalist, supported the struggle of the working class to improve its condition. He described the workers' penury:

> *A labouring man in England with a wife and only three children, though he never lose a day's work, though he and his family be economical, frugal and industrious in the most extensive sense of these words, is not now able to procure himself by his labour a single meal of meat from one end of the year into the other. Is this a state in which the labouring man ought to be?*[29]

English radicalism embodied the desires of parliamentary reformers for broader political representation and the hopes of the laboring poor for a better life. Two important theorists of the movement were Thomas Paine and Jeremy Bentham.

Thomas Paine

Thomas Paine (1737–1809), responding to Burke's *Reflections on the Revolution in France* with *The Rights of Man* (published in two parts in 1791 and 1792), denounced reverence for tradition, defended the principle of natural rights, and praised as progress the destruction of the Old Regime. Paine shared the conviction of other Enlightenment thinkers that superstition, intolerance, and despotism had interfered with human progress in the past, and he staunchly supported both the American and French Revolutions. To initiate a true age of enlightenment, he said, it is necessary to recognize that "all the great laws of society are laws of nature,"[30] and to reconstitute the social and political order in accordance with these principles inherent in nature. Paine denounced all hereditary monarchy and aristocracy as wretched systems of slavery, which deprived people of their inherent right to govern themselves and exploited them financially in order to raise money for war. The only legitimate government, he claimed, was representative democracy, in which the right of all men to participate was assured. Paine believed that republican governments would be less inclined than hereditary ones to wage war and more concerned with the welfare of the common person.

From Paine, the English radical tradition acquired a faith in reason and human goodness, a skeptical attitude toward established institutions, an admiration for the open and democratic society being shaped in the United States, and a dislike of organized religion. It also gained the belief that the goal of government was the greater happiness of ordinary people and that excluding common people from political participation was unjust.

Jeremy Bentham

In contrast to Paine, Jeremy Bentham (1748–1832) rejected the doctrine of natural rights as an abstraction with no basis in reality, and he regarded the French Revolution as an absurd attempt to reconstruct society according to principles as misguided as those that had supported the Old Regime. Bentham's importance to the English radical tradition derives from the principle of *utility,* which he offered as a guide to reformers. The central fact of human existence, said Bentham, is that human beings seek to gratify their desires, that they prefer pleasure to pain, and that pleasure is intrinsically good and pain bad. In Bentham's view, human beings are motivated solely by self-interest, which they define in terms of pleasure and pain: "Nature has placed mankind under the governance of two sovereign masters, *pain* and *pleasure.* It is for them alone to point out what we ought to do, as well as to determine what we shall do."[31] Consequently, every political, economic, judicial, or social institution and all legislation should be judged according to a simple standard: does it bring about the greatest happiness for the greatest number? If not, it should be swept away.

Bentham believed that he had found an objective and scientific approach to the study and reform of society. By focusing on the necessity for change and improvement on every level of society and by encouraging a careful and objective analysis of social issues, Bentham and his followers, called philosophical radicals, contributed substantially to the shaping of the English reform tradition.

According to Bentham, those in power had always used what they considered the highest principles—God's teachings, universal standards, and

honored traditions—to justify their political and social systems, their moral codes, and their laws. On the basis of these principles, they persecuted and abused people, instituted practices rooted in ignorance and superstition, and imposed values that made people miserable because they conflicted with human nature and the essential needs of men and women. Bentham contended that the principle of utility—that one should act always to derive the greatest happiness for the greatest number of people—permits the reforming of society in accordance with people's true nature and needs. It does not impose unrealistic standards on men and women but accepts people as they are. Utilitarianism, he declared, bases institutions and laws on an objective study of human behavior rather than on unsubstantiated religious beliefs, unreliable traditions, and mistaken philosophical abstractions. Its goal is to propose measures that augment rather than diminish the community's happiness. In his desire to make people happier, Bentham was representative of the humanitarianism of the Enlightenment.

Bentham's utilitarianism led him to press for social and political reforms. The aristocratic ruling elite, he said, were not interested in producing the "greatest happiness of the greatest number" but in furthering their own narrow interests. Only if the rulers came from the broad masses of people would government be amenable to reforms based on the principle of greatest happiness. Thus, he supported extension of the suffrage and a secret ballot and attacked political corruption and clerical control over education. Bentham wanted to do away with the monarchy and the House of Lords and to disestablish the Anglican church. In contrast to laissez-faire liberals, Benthamites argued for legislation to protect women and children in the factories. They also sought to improve sanitation in the cities and to reform the archaic British prison system.

EARLY SOCIALISM: NEW POSSIBILITIES FOR SOCIETY

A new group, called socialists, went further than either the liberals or the radicals. Socialists argued that the liberals' concern for individual freedom and the radicals' demand for extension of the suffrage had little impact on the poverty, oppression, and gross inequality of wealth that plagued modern society. Asserting that the liberals' doctrine of individualism degenerated into selfish egoism, which harmed community life, socialists demanded the creation of a new society based on cooperation rather than on competition. Reflecting the spirit of the Enlightenment and the French Revolution, socialists, like liberals, denounced the status quo for perpetuating injustice and held that people could create a better world. Like liberals, too, they placed the highest value on a rational analysis of society and on transforming society in line with scientifically valid premises, whose truth rational people could grasp. Socialists believed that they had discerned a pattern in human society, which, if properly understood and acted upon, would lead men and women to an earthly salvation. Thus, early socialists were also romantics for they dreamed of a new social order, a future utopia, where each individual could find happiness and self-fulfillment.

The most important early socialist thinkers—Saint-Simon, Fourier, and Owen—espoused a new social and economic system, in which production and distribution of goods would be planned for the general benefit of society. The current organization of society was unjust, for it kept great masses of people in poverty, oppression, and despair. Society was also mismanaged, for people were prevented from working for the common good. The thought of the early socialists influenced Karl Marx and Friedrich Engels, who, in the second half of the nineteenth century, became the most influential formulators and propagators of socialism. (See Chapter 24.) There were also Christian communitarians, who protested the treatment of the poor and the unsettling conditions caused by industrialization. These Christian "socialists" urged believers to share their property and labor and live together in model communities.

Socialists questioned the assumption that society was made up of isolated and self-seeking individuals, and they challenged the laws of economics as formulated by the laissez-faire economists. Denying that human beings fared best as competing individuals, they argued that people achieved more happiness for themselves and for others as members of a cooperative community that lived, worked, and planned together. Some socialists urged voluntary divorce from the larger society. They proposed communes or model factory towns as places to apply the principles of socialism or communitarianism. Some were very perceptive about the nature of industrialization and the future of industrial society. Others romantically longed for the past and created schemes that would preserve the values and ethics of village life as it existed before the Industrial Revolution. All socialists denounced as hollow and hypocritical the liberals' preoccupation with liberty and equality, arguing that to the lower classes devastated by poverty these ideals were merely formal principles. They protected the person and property of the wealthy while the majority were mired in poverty and helplessness.

Saint-Simon: Technocratic Socialism

Descended from a distinguished French aristocratic family, Henri Comte de Saint-Simon (1760–1825) renounced his title during the French Revolution and enthusiastically preached the opportunity for a new society. He regarded his own society as defective and in need of reorganization: the critical philosophy of the Enlightenment had shattered the Old Order, but it had not provided a guide for reconstructing society. Saint-Simon believed that he had a mission to set society right by providing an understanding of the new age being shaped by science and industry. Many of the brightest young people in France believed in his mission.

Saint-Simon argued, however, that just as Christianity had provided social unity and stability during the Middle Ages, so scientific knowledge would bind the society of his time. The scientists, industrialists, bankers, artists, and writers would replace the clergy and the aristocracy as the social elite. Saint-Simon had a romantic love of genius and talent. In the new industrial age, he thought, the control of society must pass to the *industriels*—those who produce or who make it possible to produce. These manufacturers, bankers, engineers, intellectuals, and scientists would harness technology for the betterment of humanity. Saint-Simon's disciples championed efforts to build great railway and canal systems, including the Suez and Panama Canals. His vision of a scientifically organized society led by trained experts was a powerful force among intellectuals in the nineteenth century and

SAINT-SIMONIAN COMMUNITY AT MÉNILMONTANT. Followers of Saint-Simon established this community in a suburb of Paris. It was headed by Father Enfantin, whose iconoclastic theories of love and marriage outraged many people. (*Bibliothèque Nationale, Paris*)

is very much alive today among those who believe in a technocratic society.

Like the philosophes, Saint-Simon valued science, had confidence in the power of reason to improve society, and believed in the certainty of progress according to laws of social development. Also like the philosophes, he attacked the clergy for clinging to superstition and dogma at the expense of society. The essence of Christianity was the golden rule: the sublime command that people should treat each other like brothers and sisters. According to Saint-Simon, the traditional clergy, having placed dogma above moral law, had forfeited its right to lead Europe, just as the aristocracy had before the French Revolution forfeited its right to rule. He called for "a new Christianity" (the title of one of his books) to serve as an antidote to selfish interests and to abjure the narrow nationalism that divided the peoples of Europe.

Saint-Simon's thought reveals several socialist elements: that industrial society constitutes a new stage in history, that unchecked individualism is detrimental to society, and that creative and collective planning is necessary to cope with social ills. He argued, as Marx would later, that liberalism failed to deal with the deprivation of the workers, the real producers of wealth. But a crucial socialist conception was absent from his thought: he did not view society as divided into classes with competing interests that necessitated violent conflict.

Fourier: Psychological Socialism

Another early French socialist was Charles Fourier (1772–1837), who believed, as the romantics did, that society conflicted with the natural needs of human beings and that this tension was responsible for human misery. Only the reorganization of society so that it would satisfy people's desire for pleasure and contentment would end that misery. Whereas Saint-Simon and his followers had elaborate plans to reorganize society on the grand scale of large industries and giant railway and canal systems, Fourier sought to create small communities that would allow men and women to enjoy life's simple pleasures. These communities of about sixteen hundred people, called *phalansteries,* would be organized according to the unchanging needs of human nature.

Fourier was not greatly concerned about the realities of industrialization, and his ideas reflect the artisan society that still existed in France when he was growing up. In the phalansteries, no force would coerce or thwart innocent human drives. All the people would work at tasks that interested them and produce things that brought them and others pleasure. Like Adam Smith, Fourier understood that specialization bred boredom and alienation from work and life. Unlike Smith, he did not believe that vastly increased productivity compensated for the evils of specialization. In the phalansteries, money and goods would not be equally distributed; those with special skills and responsibilities would be rewarded accordingly. This system of rewards conformed to nature because people have a natural desire to be rewarded.

Both Fourier and the Saint-Simonians supported female equality, placing them among the first social thinkers to do so. Fourier did not define female equality merely in political terms. He thought that marriage distorted the natures of both men and women because monogamy restricted their sexual needs and narrowed the scope of their lives to the family alone. Instead, people should think of themselves as part of the family of all humanity. Because married women had to devote all their strength and time to household and children, they had no time or energy left to enjoy life's pleasures. Fourier did not call for the abolition of the family, but he expressed the hope that it would disappear on its own as society adjusted to his theories. Men and women would find new ways of fulfilling themselves sexually, and the community would be organized so that it could care for the children. Fourier's ideas found some acceptance in the United States, where in the 1840s at least twenty-nine communities were founded on Fourierist principles. None, however, lasted more than five or six years.

Owen: Industrial Socialism

In 1799, Robert Owen (1771–1858) became part owner and manager of the New Lanark cotton mills in Scotland. Distressed by widespread mistreatment of workers, Owen resolved to improve the lives of his employees without destroying profits. He raised wages, upgraded working conditions, refused to hire children under ten, and provided workers with neat homes, food, and clothing, all at reasonable prices. He set up schools for children and for adults. In every way,

he demonstrated his belief that healthier, happier workers produced more than less fortunate ones. Like Saint-Simon, Owen believed that industry and technology could enrich humankind if organized according to the proper principles. Heads of state, members of parliaments, and business leaders came from all over Europe to see Owen's factories.

Just like many philosophes, Owen was convinced that the environment was the principal shaper of character: that the ignorance, alcoholism, and crime of the poor derived from bad living conditions. Public education and factory reform, said Owen, would make better citizens of the poor. When Parliament balked at reforms, Owen even urged the creation of a grand national trade union of all the workers in England. In the earliest days of industrialization, with very few workers organized in unions, this dream seemed an impossible one. Owen came to believe that the entire social and economic order must be replaced by a new system based on harmonious group living rather than on competition. He established a model community at New Harmony, Indiana, but it was short-lived. Even in his factory in Scotland, Owen had some difficulty holding on to workers, many of whom were devout Christians and resented his secular ideas and the dancing taught to their children in his schools.

NATIONALISM: THE SACREDNESS OF THE NATION

Nationalism is a conscious bond shared by a group of people who feel strongly attached to a particular land and who possess a common language, culture, and history, marked by shared glories and sufferings. Nationalists contend that one's highest loyalty and devotion should be given to the nation. They exhibit great pride in their people's history and traditions and often feel that their nation has been specially chosen by God or history. They assert that the nation—its culture and history—gives meaning to an individual's life and actions. Like a religion, nationalism provides the individual with a sense of community and with a cause worthy of self-sacrifice. Identifying with the nation's collective achievements enhances feelings of self-worth.

In an age when Christianity was in retreat, nationalism became the dominant spiritual force in nineteenth-century European life. Nationalism provided new beliefs, martyrs, and "holy" days that stimulated feelings of reverence; it offered membership in a community, which satisfied an overwhelming psychological need of human beings for fellowship and identity. And nationalism supplied a mission—the advancement of the nation—to which people could dedicate themselves.

The Emergence of Modern Nationalism

The essential components of nationalism emerged during the French Revolution. The Revolution asserted the principle that sovereignty derived from the nation, from the people as a whole: the state was not the private possession of the ruler but the embodiment of the people's will. The nation-state was above king, church, estate, guild, or province, superseding all other loyalties. The French people must view themselves not as subjects of the king, not as Bretons or Normans, nobles or bourgeois, but as citizens of a united fatherland, *la patrie*. These two ideas—that the people possess unlimited sovereignty and that they are united in a nation—were crucial in fashioning a nationalist outlook.

As the Revolution moved from the moderate to the radical stage, French nationalism intensified. In 1793–94, when the republic was threatened by foreign invasion, the Jacobins created a national army, demanded ever greater allegiance to and sacrifice for the nation, and called for the expansion of France's borders to the Alps and the Rhine. With unprecedented success, the Jacobins used every means—press, schoolroom, and rostrum—to instill a love of country.

The Romantic Movement also awakened nationalist feelings. By examining the language, literature, and folkways of their people, romantic thinkers instilled a sense of national pride in their compatriots. Johann Gottfried Herder (1744–1803), a prominent German writer, conceived the idea of the *Volksgeist*—the spirit of the people. For Herder, each people was unique and creative; each expressed its genius in language, literature, monuments, and folk traditions. Herder did not make the theoretical jump from a spiritual or cultural nationalism to political nationalism; he did not call for the formation of states based on nationality. But his emphasis on the unique culture of a people and his assertion that an individual is defined as a member of a specific culture or nation stimulated a national consciousness among Germans and the various Slavic peoples who lived under foreign rule. Fascination with the Volksgeist prompted intellectuals to investigate the past of their own people, to rediscover their ancient traditions, and to extol their historic language and culture. From this cultural nationalism, it was only a short step to a political nationalism that called for national liberation, unification, and statehood.

The romantics were the earliest apostles of German nationalism. They restored to consciousness memories of the German past, and they emphasized the distinct qualities of the German folk and the special destiny of the German nation. The romantics glorified medieval Germany and valued hereditary monarchy and aristocracy as vital links to the nation's past. They saw the existence of each individual as inextricably bound up with folk and fatherland, and they found the self-realization for which they yearned in the uniting of their own egos with the national soul. To these romantics, the national community was a vital force that gave the individual both an identity and a purpose in life. And the nation stood above the individual; the national spirit linked isolated souls into a community of brethren. In unmistakably romantic tones, poet Ernst Moritz Arndt (1769–1860) urged Germans to unite against Napoleon:

> *German man, feel again God, hear and fear the eternal, and you hear and fear also your Volk [people], you feel again in God the honor and dignity of your fathers, their glorious history rejuvenates itself in you, their firm and gallant virtue reblossoms in you, the whole German Fatherland stands again before you in the august halo of past centuries. No longer Catholics and Protestants, no longer Prussians and Austrians, Saxons and Bavarians, Silesians and Hanoverians, no longer of different faith, different mentality, and different will— be Germans, be one, will to be one by love and loyalty, and no devil will vanquish you.*[32]

Most German romantics expressed hostility to the liberal ideals of the French Revolution. They condemned the reforms of the Revolution for trying to reconstruct society by separating individuals from their national past, for treating them as isolated abstractions. They declared that the German folk spirit should not be polluted by foreign French ideas.

To the philosophes, the state was a human creation providing legal safeguards for the individual. To the romantics, the state was something holy, the expression of the divine spirit of a people; it could not be manufactured to order by the intellect. The state's purpose was not the protection of natural rights or the promotion of economic well-being. Rather, the state was a living organism that linked each person to a sacred past, imbued individuals with a profound sense of community, and subordinated the citizen to the nation.

Nationalism and Liberalism

In the early 1800s, liberals were the principal leaders and supporters of nationalist movements. They viewed the struggle for national rights—the freedom of a people from foreign rule—as an extension of the struggle for the rights of the individual. There could be no liberty, said nationalists, if people were not free to rule themselves in their own land.

Liberals called for the unification of Germany and Italy, the rebirth of Poland, the liberation of Greece from Turkish rule, and the granting of autonomy to the Hungarians of the Austrian Empire. Liberal nationalists envisioned a Europe of independent states based on nationality and popular sovereignty. Free of foreign domination and tyrant princes, these newly risen states would protect the rights of the individual and strive to create a brotherhood of nationalities in Europe.

In the first half of the nineteenth century, few intellectuals recognized the dangers inherent in nationalism or understood the fundamental conflict between liberalism and nationalism. For the liberal, the idea of universal natural rights transcended all national boundaries. Inheriting the cosmopolitanism of the Enlightenment, liberalism emphasized what all people had in common, called for all individuals to be treated equally under the law, and preached toleration. Nationalists, manifesting the particularist attitude of the in-group and the tribe, regarded the nation as the essential fact of existence. Consequently, they often willingly subverted individual liberty for the sake of national grandeur. The liberal sought to protect the rights of all within the state, whereas the nationalist often ignored or trampled on the rights of individuals and national minorities. Liberalism grew out of the rational tradition of the West; nationalism derived from the emotions. Because it fulfilled an elemental yearning for community and kinship, nationalism exerted a powerful hold over human hearts, often driving people to political extremism. Liberalism demanded objectivity in analyzing tradition, society, and history, but nationalism evoked a mythic and romantic past that often distorted history.

In the last part of the nineteenth century, the irrational and mythic quality of nationalism intensified. By stressing the unique qualities and history of a particular people, nationalism promoted hatred between nationalities. By kindling deep love for the past, for community, and for kinship, it often raised emotions to fever pitch. It shattered rational thinking, dragged the mind into a world of fantasy and myth, and introduced extremism into politics. Love of nation became an overriding passion, threatening to extinguish the liberal ideals of reason, freedom, and equality.

◆ ◆ ◆

NOTES

1. Jean Jacques Rousseau, *The Confessions* (New York: Modern Library, 1950), p. 2.

2. Quoted in H. G. Schenk, *The Mind of the European Romantics* (Garden City, N.Y.: Doubleday, 1969), p. 4.

3. William Blake, *Milton*, in *The Poetry and Prose of William Blake*, ed. David V. Erdman (Garden City, N.Y.: Doubleday, 1965), bk. 2, plate 40, lines 34–36.

4. Ibid., plate 41, line 1.

5. Goethe, *Faust*, trans. Bayard Taylor (New York: Modern Library, 1950), pt. 1, sc. 4.

6. Letter of Keats, November 22, 1817, in *The*

Letters of John Keats, ed. Hyder E. Rollins (Cambridge, Mass.: Harvard University Press, 1958), 1:184–185.

7. Quoted in John Herman Randall, Jr., *The Career of Philosophy* (New York: Columbia University Press, 1965), 2:80.

8. Blake, *Milton,* Preface.

9. Quoted in Robert T. Denommé, *Nineteenth-Century French Romantic Poets* (Carbondale: Southern Illinois University Press, 1969), p. 28.

10. Quoted in Frederic Ewen, *Heroic Imagination* (Secaucus, N.J.: Citadel Press, 1984), p. 276.

11. Quoted in Ernst Cassirer, *An Essay on Man* (New York: Bantam Books, 1970), p. 178.

12. From "The Tables Turned," in *The Complete Poetical Works of Wordsworth,* ed. Andrew J. George (Boston: Houghton Mifflin, 1904, rev. ed. 1982), p. 83.

13. From "Lines Composed a Few Miles Above Tintern Abbey," *The Complete Poetical Works of William Wordsworth* (Philadelphia: Porter & Coates, 1851), p. 194.

14. Quoted in R. W. Harris, *Romanticism and the Social Order 1780–1830* (New York: Barnes & Noble, 1969), pp. 223–224.

15. Horst von Maltitz, *The Evolution of Hitler's Germany* (New York: McGraw-Hill, 1973), p. 217.

16. G. W. F. Hegel, *The Philosophy of History,* trans. J. Sibree (New York: Dover, 1956), pp. 19, 23.

17. Ibid., p. 39.

18. George Brandes, *Revolution and Reaction in Nineteenth Century French Literature* (New York: Russell & Russell, reprint ed., n.d.), pp. 106–107.

19. Edmund Burke, *Reflections on the Revolution in France* (New York: Liberal Arts Press, 1955), pp. 40, 89.

20. Ibid., p. 99.

21. Ibid., p. 70.

22. Quoted in Frederick B. Artz, *Reaction and Revolution, 1814–1832* (New York: Harper Torchbooks, 1963), p. 73.

23. John Stuart Mill, *On Liberty,* ed. Currin V. Shields (Indianapolis: Bobbs-Merrill, 1956), chap. 1.

24. Thomas Robert Malthus, *First Essay on Population,* reprinted for the Royal Economic Society (London: Macmillan, 1926), p. 16.

25. Ibid., p. 17.

26. Excerpted in Allan Bullock and Maurice Shock, eds., *The Liberal Tradition from Fox to Keynes* (London: Adam & Charles Black, 1956), pp. 31–32.

27. Quoted in Anthony Arblaster, *The Rise and Decline of Western Liberalism* (Oxford: Basil Blackwell, 1984), p. 258.

28. Alexis de Tocqueville, *Democracy in America,* trans. Henry Reeve (New York: Oxford University Press, 1924), pp. 493–494.

29. Quoted in Raymond Williams, *Culture and Society, 1780–1945* (New York: Columbia University Press, 1983), p. 14.

30. Quoted in Francis Canavan, "Thomas Paine," in *History of Political Philosophy,* eds. Leo Strauss and Joseph Cropsey (Chicago: Rand McNally, 1963), p. 594.

31. Jeremy Bentham, *An Introduction to the Principles of Morals and Legislation,* together with *A Fragment on Government* (London: Basil Blackwell, 1948), chap. 1, sec. 1, p. 125.

32. Quoted in Hans Kohn, *Prelude to Nation-States* (Princeton, N.J.: D. Van Nostrand, 1967), p. 262.

SUGGESTED READING

Arblaster, Anthony, *The Rise and Decline of Western Liberalism* (1984). A critical analysis of liberalism, its evolution and characteristics.

Bullock, Alan, and Maurice Shock, eds., *The Liberal Tradition from Fox to Keynes* (1956). Selections from the works of British liberals, preceded by an essay on the liberal tradition.

Denommé, Robert T., *Nineteenth-Century French Romantic Poets* (1969). The genesis of romanticism in France; an analysis of several French romantic poets.

de Ruggiero, Guido, *The History of European Liberalism* (1927). A classic study.

Epstein, Klaus, *The Genesis of German Conser-*

vatism (1966). An analysis of German conservative thought as a response to the Enlightenment and the French Revolution.

Fried, Albert, and Ronald Sanders, eds., *Socialist Thought* (1964). Selections from the writings of socialist theorists.

Harris, R. W., *Romanticism and the Social Order, 1780–1830* (1969). Involvement of English romantics in social and political questions.

Hayes, Carlton J. H., *Historical Evolution of Modern Nationalism* (1931). A pioneering work in the study of nationalism.

Honour, Hugh, *Romanticism* (1979). A study of the influence of romanticism on the visual arts.

Kohn, Hans, *The Idea of Nationalism* (1961). A comprehensive study of nationalism from the ancient world through the eighteenth century by a leading student of the subject.

———, *Prelude to Nation-States* (1967). The emergence of nationalism in France and Germany.

MacCoby, S., ed., *The English Radical Tradition, 1763–1914* (repr. 1952). Selections from the writings of English radicals.

Manuel, Frank, *The Prophets of Paris* (1962). Good discussions of Saint-Simon and Fourier.

Markham, F. M. H., ed., *Henri Comte de Saint-Simon* (1952). Selected writings.

Poster, Mark, ed., *Harmonian Man* (1971). Selected writings of Fourier.

Schapiro, J. S., *Liberalism: Its Meaning and History* (1958). A useful survey with readings.

Schenk, H. G., *The Mind of the European Romantics* (1966). A comprehensive analysis of the Romantic Movement.

Shafer, B. C., *Faces of Nationalism* (1972). The evolution of modern nationalism in Europe and the non-European world; contains a good bibliography.

Simon, W. M., *French Liberalism 1789–1848* (1972). Selections from the writings of French liberals.

Smith, A. D., *Theories of Nationalism* (1972). The relationship between nationalism and modernization.

Weiss, John, *Conservatism in Europe, 1770–1945* (1977). Conservatism as a reaction to social modernization.

REVIEW QUESTIONS

1. The Romantic Movement was a reaction against the dominant ideas of the Enlightenment. Discuss this statement.

2. What was the significance of the Romantic Movement?

3. How did Kant try to resolve the problem posed by Hume's empiricism? Why did he think his discovery in philosophy was as important as the Copernican theory in astronomy?

4. What was Hegel's view of history? What influence did it have?

5. What were the attitudes of the conservatives toward the philosophes and the French Revolution?

6. "It is with infinite caution that any man ought to venture upon pulling down an edifice which had answered in any tolerable degree for ages the common purposes of society." Discuss how this statement by Burke is representative of the conservative viewpoint.

7. Why did conservatives reject the philosophy of natural rights?

8. What were the sources of liberalism?

9. Contrast the views of early nineteenth-century liberals and conservatives regarding the individual's relationship to society.

10. What fundamental difference existed between French radicals and liberals?

11. What did British radicalism owe to Paine and Bentham?

12. What basic liberal-capitalist doctrines were attacked by early socialists?

13. Why are Saint-Simon, Fourier, and Owen regarded as early socialists?

14. How did the French Revolution and romanticism contribute to the rise of modern nationalism?

15. What is the relationship between nationalism and liberalism?

16. Account for nationalism's great appeal.

CHAPTER 23

Europe, 1815–1848: Revolution and Counterrevolution

uring the years 1815 through 1848, the forces unleashed by the French Revolution clashed with the traditional outlook of the Old Regime. The period opened with the Congress of Vienna, which drew up a peace settlement after the defeat of Napoleon, and closed with the revolutions that swept across most of Europe in 1848.

Much of the Old Regime outside France survived the stormy decades of the French Revolution and Napoleon. Monarchs still held the reins of political power. Aristocrats, particularly in central and eastern Europe, retained their traditional hold on the army and administration, controlled the peasantry and local government, and enjoyed tax exemptions. Determined to enforce respect for traditional authority and to smother liberal ideals, the conservative ruling elites resorted to censorship, secret police, and armed force.

The French Revolution, however, had shown that absolutism could be successfully challenged and feudal privileges abolished. Inspired by the revolutionary principles of liberty, equality, and fraternity, liberals and nationalists continued to engage in revolutionary action.

THE CONGRESS OF VIENNA, 1814–15

Metternich: The Archconservative

After the defeat of Napoleon, representatives of European powers convened in Vienna to draw up a peace settlement. The pivotal figure at the Congress of Vienna was Prince Klemens von Metternich (1773–1859) of Austria, who had organized the coalition that triumphed over Napoleon. A man of the Old Order, Metternich hated the new forces of nationalism and liberalism.

He regarded liberalism as a dangerous disease

The Uprising, by Honoré Daumier (1808–1879). (*The Phillips Collection, Washington, D.C.*)

carried by middle-class malcontents and believed that domestic order and international stability depended on rule by monarchy and respect for aristocracy. The misguided liberal belief that society could be reshaped according to the ideals of liberty and equality, said Metternich, had led to twenty-five years of revolution, terror, and war. In order to restore stability and peace, the old Europe must suppress liberal ideas and quash the first signs of revolution. If the European powers did not destroy the revolutionary spirit, they would be devoured by it.

Metternich also feared the new spirit of nationalism. Because Austria was a multinational empire, it was particularly vulnerable to nationalist unrest. If its many ethnic groups—Poles, Czechs, Magyars, Italians, South Slavs, and Romanians—became infected with the nationalist virus, they would shatter the Hapsburg Empire. A highly cultured, multilingual, and cosmopolitan aristocrat, Metternich considered himself the defender of European civilization. He thought that by arousing the masses and setting people against people nationalism could undermine the foundations of the European civilization that he cherished.

Metternich's critics accuse him of shortsightedness. Instead of harnessing and directing the new forces let loose by the French Revolution, he sought to stifle them. Instead of trying to rebuild and remodel, he sought to prop up dying institutions. Regarding any attempt at reform as opening the door to radicalism and revolution, Metternich refused to make any concessions to liberalism.

Metternich wanted to return to power the ruling families deposed by more than two decades of revolutionary warfare. He also sought to restore the balance of power so that no one country could be in a position to dominate the European continent as France under Napoleon had done. Metternich was determined to end the chaos of the Napoleonic period and restore stability to Europe. There must be no more Napoleons who obliterate states, topple kings, and dream of European hegemony. Although he served the interests of the Hapsburg monarchy, Metternich also had a sense of responsibility to Europe as a whole. He sought a settlement that would avoid the destructiveness of a general war.

The other nations at the Congress of Vienna included Britain, Russia, France, and Prussia. Representing Britain was Robert Stewart, Viscount Castlereagh (1769–1822), the British foreign secretary, who was realistic and empirically minded. Although an implacable enemy of Napoleon, Castlereagh demonstrated mature statesmanship by not seeking to punish France severely. Tsar Alexander I (1777–1825) attended the congress himself. Steeped in Christian mysticism, the tsar wanted to create a European community based on Christian teachings. Alexander regarded himself as the savior of Europe, an attitude that caused other diplomats to view him with distrust. Representing France was Prince Charles Maurice de Talleyrand-Périgord (1754–1838). A devoted patriot, Talleyrand sought to remove from France the stigma of the Revolution and Napoleon. The aging Prince Karl von Hardenberg (1750–1822) represented Prussia. Like Metternich, Castlereagh, and Talleyrand, the Prussian statesman believed that the various European states, besides pursuing their own national interests, should concern themselves with the well-being of the European community as a whole.

Crisis over Saxony and Poland

Two interrelated issues threatened to disrupt the conference and enmesh the Great Powers in another war. One was Prussia's intention to annex the German kingdom of Saxony; the other was Russia's demand for Polish territories. The tsar wanted to combine the Polish holdings of Russia, Austria, and Prussia into a new Polish kingdom under Russian control. Britain and Austria saw such an extension of Russia's power into central Europe as a threat to the balance of power. Metternich declared that he had not fought Napoleon to prepare the way for the tsar. Britain agreed that Russia's westward expansion must be checked.

Prince Talleyrand of France suggested that Britain, Austria, and France conclude an alliance to oppose Prussia and Russia. This clever move by Talleyrand restored France to the family of nations. Now France was no longer the hated enemy but a necessary counterweight to Russia and Prussia. Threatened with war, Russia and Prussia moderated their demands and the crisis ended.

The Settlement

After months of discussion, quarrels, and threats, the delegates to the Congress of Vienna finished

CONGRESS OF VIENNA, 1815, BY JEAN BAPTISTE ISABEY (1767–1855). The delegates to the Congress of Vienna sought to re-establish many features of Europe that existed before the French Revolution and Napoleon. They can be accused of shortsightedness; nevertheless, the balance of power that they formulated preserved international peace. Metternich is standing before a chair at the left. (*The New York Public Library*)

their work. Resisting Prussia's demands for a punitive peace, the allies did not punish France severely. They feared that a humiliated France would only prepare for a war of revenge. Moreover, Metternich continued to need France to balance the power of both Prussia and Russia. France had to pay a large indemnity over a five-year period and submit to allied occupation until the obligation was met.

Although it lost most of its conquests, France emerged with somewhat more land than it possessed before the Revolution. To guard against a resurgent France, both Prussia and Holland received territories on the French border. Holland obtained the southern Netherlands (Belgium);

Prussia gained the Rhineland and part of Saxony, but not as much as the Prussians had desired. Nevertheless, Prussia emerged from the settlement significantly larger and stronger. Russia obtained Finland and a considerable part of the Polish territories, but not as much as the tsar had anticipated; the Congress prevented further Russian expansion into central Europe. The northern Italian province of Lombardy was restored to Austria, which also received adjacent Venetia. England obtained strategic naval bases: Helgoland in the North Sea, Malta and the Ionian Islands in the Mediterranean, the Cape Colony in South Africa, and Ceylon in the Indian Ocean. Germany was organized into a confederation of thirty-eight (later thirty-

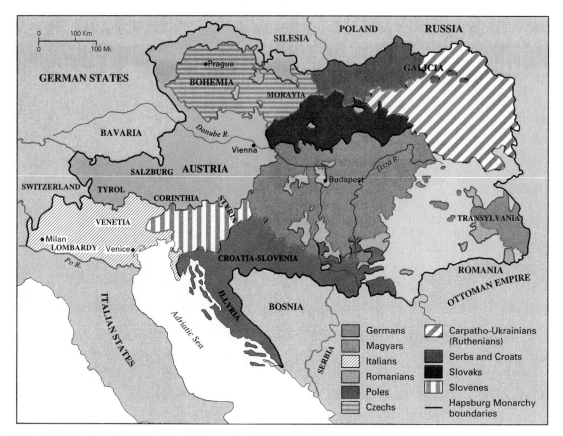

MAP 23.1 Peoples of the Hapsburg Monarchy, 1815

nine) states. Norway was given to Sweden. The legitimate rulers, who had been displaced by the Revolution and the wars of Napoleon, were restored to their thrones in France, Spain, Portugal, the Kingdom of the Two Sicilies, the Papal States, and many German states.

The conservative delegates at the Congress of Vienna have often been criticized for ignoring the liberal and nationalist aspirations of the different peoples and turning the clock back to the Old Regime. Critics have castigated the congress for dealing only with the rights of thrones and not the rights of peoples. But after the experience of two world wars in the twentieth century, some historians today are impressed with the peacemakers' success in restoring a balance of power that effectively stabilized international relations. No one country was strong enough to dominate the Continent; no Great Power was so unhappy that it resorted to war to undo the settlement. Not until the unification of Germany in 1870–71 was the balance of power upset; not until World War I in 1914 did Europe have another general war of the magnitude of the Napoleonic wars.

REVOLUTIONS, 1820–1829

Russia, Austria, Prussia, and Great Britain agreed to act together to preserve the territorial settlement of the Congress of Vienna and the balance of power. After paying its indemnity, France was admitted into this Quadruple Alliance, also known as the Concert of Europe. Metternich intended to use the Concert of Europe to maintain harmony between nations and internal stability

CHRONOLOGY 23.1 Revolution and Reaction

1820	Revolt in Spain
1821	Austria crushes revolts in Italy
1823	French troops crush revolt in Spain
1825	Uprising in Russia crushed by Nicholas I
1829	Greece gains its independence from Ottoman Empire
1830	July Ordinances in France are followed by a revolution, which forces Charles X to abdicate
August 1830	Belgian revolution
October 1830	Belgians declare their independence from Holland, establishing a liberal government
1831	Polish revolution fails
1831–32	Austrian forces crush a revolution in Italy
1832	Reform Act extends suffrage to the middle class in Britain
1848	Year of revolution
February 1848	Revolution in Paris; Louis Philippe abdicates, and France becomes a republic
March 1848	Uprisings in capital cities of the German states lead to liberal reforms
March 18–22, 1848	"Five Glorious Days" in Milan
March 22, 1848	Citizens of Venice declare their freedom from Austria and establish a republic
June 1848	June Days of Paris: revolutionaries are beaten by professional soldiers
August 1848	Constitutional Assembly meets in Vienna; serfdom is abolished
December 1848	Louis Napoleon is elected president of the Second Republic of France
August 1849	Hungarians' bid for independence is crushed by Hapsburg forces, aided by Russian troops

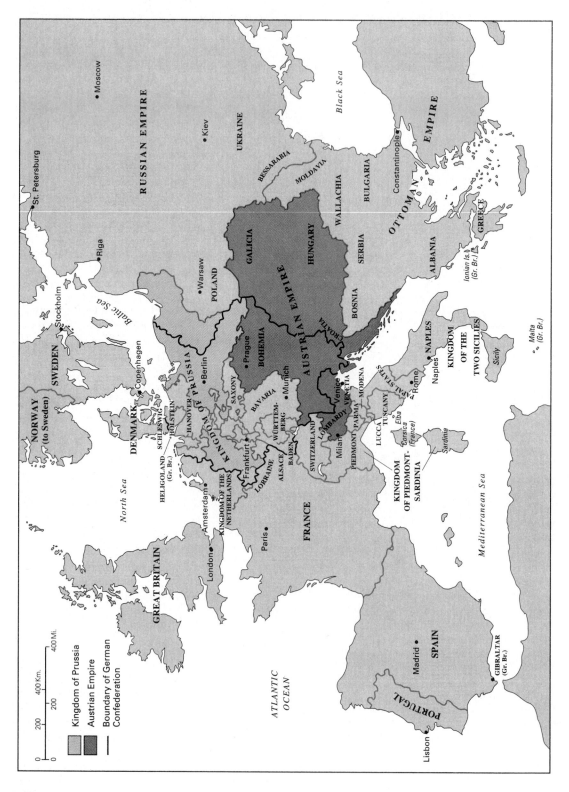

within nations. Toward this end, conservatives in their respective countries censored books and newspapers, imprisoned liberal activists, and suppressed nationalist uprisings.

But repression could not contain the liberal and nationalist ideals unleashed by the French Revolution; nothing could halt the transformation of European society. The first revolution after restoration of the legitimate rulers occurred in Spain in 1820. Fearing that the Spanish uprising, with its quasi-liberal overtones, would inspire revolutions in other lands, the Concert of Europe empowered France to intervene. In 1823, a hundred thousand French troops crushed the revolution.

Revolutionary activity in Italy also frightened the Concert of Europe. In 1821, it authorized Austria to extinguish a liberal uprising in the Kingdom of the Two Sicilies. The Austrians also crushed an uprising in Piedmont, in northern Italy (see Chapter 25). Rulers in other Italian states jailed and executed liberal leaders, and several thousand Italians went into exile.

In both instances, Britain strongly opposed the actions of the alliance. It interpreted the alliance differently than Austria, Prussia, and Russia. The three eastern powers wanted the alliance to smother in the cradle all subversive movements that threatened the Old Order. To Metternich, the central problem of the age was suppressing revolutions, and he regarded the alliance as a means of preserving the status quo. Britain, however, viewed the alliance solely as a means of guarding against renewed French aggression. It did not consider intervention in the domestic affairs of other nations to be in its own interest.

A revolution also failed in Russia. During the Napoleonic wars and the occupation of France, Russian officers were introduced to French ideas. Contrasting French liberal ideas and ways with Russian autocracy, some officers resolved to change conditions in Russia. Like their Western counterparts, they organized secret societies and disseminated liberal ideas within Russia. When Alexander I died, these liberal officers struck. But representing only a fraction of the aristocracy and with no mass following among the soldiers, they had no chance of success. Their uprising in December 1825 was easily smashed by the new tsar,

Nicholas I, and the leaders were severely punished. To prevent Western ideas from infiltrating his realm, Nicholas imposed rigid censorship and organized the Third Section, a secret police force, which spied on suspected subversives. The Decembrists had failed, but their courage would inspire future opponents of tsarist autocracy.

The revolutions in Spain, Italy, and Russia failed, but the Concert of Europe also suffered setbacks. Stimulated by the ideals of the French Revolution, the Greeks revolted against their Turkish rulers in 1821. Although the Turkish sultan was the legitimate ruler, Russia, France, and Britain aided the Greek revolutionaries, for they were Christians, while the Turks were Muslims. Moreover, pro-Greek sentiments were very strong among educated western Europeans, who had studied the literature and history of ancient Greece and viewed the Greeks as struggling to regain their ancestral freedom. Not only the pressure of public opinion, but also the fear of Russian motives led Britain to join in the intervention. If Russia carried out its intention of aiding the Greeks on its own, no doubt the Russian bear would never release Greece from its hug. Britain could not permit this extension of Russian power in the eastern Mediterranean. Despite Metternich's objections, Britain, France, and Russia took joint action against the Turks.

In 1829, Greece gained its independence. The Metternich system, which aimed to preserve the territorial settlements made at Vienna and to protect traditional and legitimate rulers against liberal and nationalist revolutions, had been breached. The success of the Greeks heartened liberals in other lands.

REVOLUTIONS, 1830–1832

After Napoleon's defeat, a Bourbon king, Louis XVIII (1814–1824), ascended the throne of France. Louis XVIII's heart belonged to the Old Regime, but his intellect told him that twenty-five years of revolutionary change could not be undone. Recognizing that the French people would not accept a return to the Old Order, Louis pursued a moderate course. Although his pseudoconstitution, the Charter, declared that the king's power rested on divine right, it acknowledged that citizens possessed fundamental rights: freedom of thought and religion and equal treatment

◄ MAP 23.2 Europe, 1815

LIBERTY LEADING THE PEOPLE, 1830, BY EUGENE DELACROIX (1799–1863).
Early nineteenth-century reformers found their rallying cry in liberty, a legacy of
the French Revolution. In this painting, Delacroix, the leader of French romantic artists, glorifies liberty. (*Louvre/Cliche des Musées Nationaux*)

under the law. It also set up a two-house parliament. But peasants, urban workers, and most
bourgeois could not meet the property requirements for voting.

Aided by competent ministers and committed
to a policy of moderation, Louis XVIII governed
effectively, although he was resisted by diehard
aristocrats, or *ultras*. These aristocrats, many of
them returned émigrés, wanted to erase the preceding twenty-five years of French history and restore the power and privileges of church and aristocracy. Their leader was the king's younger
brother, the Comte d'Artois, who, after Louis's
death in 1824, ascended the throne as Charles X
(1824–1830).

The new government aroused the hostility of
the bourgeoisie by indemnifying the émigrés for
the property they had lost during the Revolution,
by censoring the press, and by giving the church
greater control over education. In the election of
1830, the liberal opposition to Charles X won a
decisive victory. Charles responded with the July

Ordinances, which dissolved the newly elected
Chamber of Deputies; the ordinances also deprived rich bourgeois of the vote and severely
curbed the press.

The bourgeoisie, students, and workers rebelled. They engaged in street demonstrations
and put up barricades. Army regiments that had
deserted Charles joined the rebels. In the fighting
that followed, some two thousand Parisians were
killed.

The insurgents hoped to establish a republic,
but the wealthy bourgeois who took control of the
revolution feared republican radicalism. They offered the throne to the Duc d'Orléans; Charles X
abdicated and went into exile in Britain. The new
king, Louis Philippe (1830–1848), never forgot
that he owed his throne to the rich bourgeois. And
the Parisian workers who had fought for a republic
and economic reforms to alleviate poverty felt betrayed by the outcome, as did the still-disenfran-
chised petty bourgeois.

The Revolution of 1830 in France set off

shock waves in Belgium, Poland, and Italy. The Congress of Vienna had assigned Catholic Belgium to Protestant Holland. From the outset, the Belgians had protested. Stirred by the events in Paris, Belgian patriots proclaimed their independence from Holland. The Dutch could not suppress the insurgents, and the Quadruple Alliance did not act, largely because Russia was tied down by a revolution in Poland. Thus, liberal government was established in Belgium.

Inspired by the uprisings in France and Belgium, Polish students, intellectuals, and army officers took up arms against their Russian overlords. The peasants refused to join the insurrection because the revolutionaries did not promise land reform. The revolutionaries wanted to restore Polish independence, a dream that poets, musicians, and intellectuals had kept alive. Polish courage, however, was no match for Russian might, and Warsaw fell in 1831. The tsar took savage revenge on the revolutionaries; those who failed to escape to the West were executed. Subsequently, the tsar's government made strenuous efforts to impose Russian language and culture on Polish students.

In 1831–32, Austrian forces again extinguished a revolution in Italy. Here, too, revolutionary leaders had failed to stir the great peasant masses to the cause of Italian independence and unity.

THE RISE OF REFORM IN BRITAIN

Although it was the freest state in Europe in the early decades of the nineteenth century, Britain was far from democratic. A constitutional monarchy, with many limits on the powers of king and state, Britain was nonetheless dominated by aristocrats. Landed aristocrats controlled both the House of Lords and the House of Commons—the House of Lords because they constituted its membership and the House of Commons because they patronized or sponsored men favorable to their interests. The vast majority of people, from the middle class as well as from the working class, could not vote. Many towns continued to be governed by corrupt groups. New industrial towns were not allowed to elect representatives to Parliament; often lacking a town organization, they could not even govern themselves effectively.

The social separation of noble and commoner was not as rigid in Britain as on the Continent. Younger sons of aristocrats did not inherit titles and were therefore obliged to make careers in law, business, the military, and the church. The upper and middle classes mingled much more freely than on the Continent, and the wealthiest merchants tended to buy lands, titles, and husbands for their daughters. Nonetheless, Parliament, the courts, local government, the established Anglican church, the monarch—all were a part of a social and political system dominated by aristocratic interests and values. This domination had changed little despite the vast changes in social and economic structure that had taken place in the process of industrialization during the second half of the eighteenth century.

Some members of Parliament urged timely reforms. In 1828, Parliament repealed a seventeenth-century act that in effect barred Catholics and Nonconformists (non-Anglican Protestants) from government positions and from universities. In 1833, slavery was abolished within the British Empire. (The British slave trade had been abolished earlier.) The Municipal Corporations Act (1835) granted towns and cities greater authority over their affairs. This measure created town and city governments that could begin to solve some problems of urbanization and industrialization. These municipal corporations could institute reforms such as sanitation, which Parliament encouraged by passing the first Public Health Act in 1848.

Increasingly, reform centered on extending suffrage and on enfranchising the new industrial towns. Middle-class men, and even workers, hoped to gain the right to vote. Because of population shifts, some sparsely populated regions, called *rotten boroughs,* sent representatives to the House of Commons, while many densely populated factory towns had little or no representation. Often a single important landowner controlled many seats in the Commons. Since voting was public, it made intimidation possible, and candidates frequently tried to influence voters with drinks, food, and even money.

Intense and bitter feelings built up during the campaign for the Reform Bill of 1832. The House of Commons passed the bill to extend suffrage by some 200,000, almost double the number of those who were then entitled to vote.

CARTOON SHOWING THE CONTROVERSY SURROUNDING GREY'S REFORM ACT.
Depicted here are supporters of the Reform Bill of 1832, hacking away at the
rotten system. On the right, opponents of reform seek to preserve the status
quo. (*Hulton Deutsch Collection*)

The House of Lords, however, refused to pass the
bill. There were riots and strikes in many cities,
and mass meetings, both of workers and of the
middle-class, took place all over the country.
King William IV (1830–1837) became convinced,
along with many politicians, that the situation
was potentially revolutionary. To defuse it, he
threatened to increase the number of the bill's
supporters in the House of Lords by creating new
peers. This threat brought reluctant peers into
line, and the bill was passed. The Reform Act of
1832 extended the suffrage to the middle class
and made the House of Commons more representative. The rotten boroughs lost their seats,
which were granted to towns. Suffrage did not
extend to workers, however, because there were
high property qualifications.

During the 1830s and 1840s, reformers called
Chartists agitated for democratic measures, such
as universal manhood suffrage, the secret ballot,
salaries and the abolition of property qualifications for members of Parliament, and annual
elections of Parliament. The Chartists came from
the ranks of both intellectual radicals and workers. Their platform remained the democratic reform program for the rest of the century, long

after the death of Chartism itself at midcentury.
All of the Chartists' demands, except annual elections for members of Parliament, were eventually
realized.

The last political effort by the Chartists was
led by Feargus O'Connor, a charismatic Irish-
man, who organized a mass demonstration to
present a huge petition of six demands to Parliament in 1848. The cabinet ignored the great
charter, which had signatures of at least 2 million
names. The movement died out just as most of
Europe burst into revolution. The working-class
leadership of Chartism turned away from political programs almost exclusively to economic activity, such as trade unions, which could bring
immediate benefits to workers.

Unlike the continental states, England avoided
revolution. British politicians thought that it was
because they had made timely reforms in the
1830s and 1840s, and that belief itself became a
force in political life. Whenever times were hard,
there were always political leaders who would
say that the remedy was reform and that reform
would prevent revolution. The political experience of the first half of the nineteenth century
laid the foundation for British parliamentary

practices, which came to be the model of liberal, progressive, and stable politics. Britain was the symbol for all those who argued for reform rather than revolution. In the rest of Europe in 1848, however, such arguments were meeting with little success.

THE REVOLUTIONS OF 1848: FRANCE

In 1848, often called *the year of revolution,* uprisings for political liberty and nationhood took place throughout Europe. The economic crisis of the previous two years had intensified political and national unrest. Food riots broke out in many places. The decimation of the potato crop by disease and of the grain harvest by drought had caused terrible food shortages. Furthermore, a financial crisis precipitated by overspeculation had caused business failures, unemployment, and reduced wages. The common people blamed their governments for their misery and sought redress. Doubtless, economic hardship aggravated discontent with the existing regimes. But "it was the absence of liberty," concludes historian Jacques Droz, "which . . . was most deeply resented by the peoples of Europe and led them to take up arms."[1]

The February Revolution

An uprising in Paris set in motion the revolutionary tidal wave that was to engulf much of Europe in 1848. The Revolution of 1830 had broken the back of the ultras in France. There would be no going back to the Old Regime. But King Louis Philippe and his ministers, moderates by temperament and philosophy, had no intention of going forward to democracy. A new law in 1831 broadened the franchise from fewer than 100,000 voters to 248,000 by 1846. Even so, only 3 percent of adult males qualified to vote.

The government of Louis Philippe was run by a small elite, consisting of wealthy bourgeois bankers, merchants, and lawyers, as well as aristocrats who had abandoned the hope of restoring the Old Regime. This ruling elite championed the revolutionary ideas of equal treatment under the law and of careers open to talent but feared

democracy and blocked efforts to broaden the franchise. When the poorer bourgeoisie protested against the limited franchise, which still excluded professionals and small tradesmen, François Guizot, the leading minister, arrogantly proclaimed: "Get rich, then you can vote." The ruling elite had become a selfish, entrenched oligarchy, unresponsive to the aspirations of the rest of the nation. Articulate intellectuals denounced the government for its narrow political base and voiced strong republican sentiments. To guard against republicanism and as a reaction to repeated attempts to assassinate the king, the government cracked down on radical societies and newspapers.

Radical republicans, or democrats, wanted to abolish monarchy and grant all men the vote. They had fought in the Revolution of 1830 but were disappointed with the results. Patriots and romantics, who looked back longingly on the glory days of Napoleon, also hated Louis Philippe's government. These French nationalists complained that the king, who dressed like a businessman and pursued a pacifist foreign policy, was not fit to lead a nation of patriots and warriors. Under Louis Philippe, they said, France could not realize its historic mission of liberating oppressed nationalities throughout Europe.

The strongest rumblings of discontent, barely heeded by the ruling elite, came from the laboring poor. Many French workers, still engaged mainly in pre–Industrial Revolution occupations, were literate and concerned with politics; they read the numerous books and newspapers that denounced social injustice and called for social change. Artisans and their families had participated in the great revolutionary outbreaks of 1789 and had defended the barricades in 1830. Like their sans-culotte forebears, they favored a democratic republic that would aid the common people. They felt betrayed by the regime of Louis Philippe, which had brought them neither political representation nor economic reform.

The few factory workers and the artisans in small workshops were becoming attracted to socialist thinkers who attacked capitalism and called for state programs to deal with poverty. Louis Blanc, a particularly popular socialist theorist, denounced capitalist competition and demanded that the government establish cooperative workshops. Owned by the workers themselves, these workshops would assure employment for the jobless.

A poor harvest in 1846 and an international financial crisis in 1847, which drastically curtailed French factory production, aggravated the misery of the laboring poor. Prevented by law from striking, unable to meet the financial requirements for voting, and afflicted with unemployment, the urban workers wanted relief. Alexis de Tocqueville, in a speech before the Chamber of Deputies on January 29, 1848, captured the mood of the working class:

> *Do you not hear them repeating unceasingly that all that is above them is incapable and unworthy of governing them; that the present distribution of goods throughout the world is unjust; that property rests on a foundation which is not an equitable foundation? And do you not realize that when such opinions take root, when they spread in an almost universal manner, when they sink deeply into the masses, they are bound to bring with them sooner or later, I know not when nor how, a most formidable revolution?*
>
> *This, gentlemen, is my profound conviction: I believe that we are at this moment sleeping on a volcano. I am profoundly convinced of it.*[2]

The government, however, steadfastly refused to pass reforms. Its middle-class opponents sidestepped regulations against political assemblies and demonstrations by gathering at large banquets to protest. When the government foolishly tried to block future banquets, students and workers took to the streets in February 1848, denouncing Guizot and demanding reforms. Barricades began to go up. Attempting to defuse an explosive situation, Louis Philippe dismissed the unpopular Guizot. But the barricades, commanded by republicans, did not come down, and the antigovernment demonstrations continued. When soldiers, confused by a shot that had perhaps gone off accidentally, fired directly into a crowd and killed fifty-two Parisians, the situation got out of hand. Unable to pacify the enraged Parisians, Louis Philippe abdicated. France became a republic, and the people of Paris were jubilant.

The June Days: Revolution of the Oppressed

Except for one workingman, the leadership of the provisional government established in February consisted of bourgeois. The new leaders were committed to political democracy, but only some, notably the socialist Louis Blanc, favored social reforms. Most of the ministers had little understanding of or sympathy for the plight of the laboring poor, and they viewed socialist ideas as a threat to private property. Although they considered it a sacred duty to fight for the rights of the individual, they did not include freedom from hunger and poverty among these rights. The middle class saw itself as separate from the laboring poor by reason of occupation and wealth. To the bourgeoisie, the workers were dangerous creatures, "the wild ones," "the vile mob."

Meanwhile, workers who could find jobs labored twelve and fourteen hours a day under brutalizing conditions. In some districts, one out of three children died before the age of five. Everywhere in France, beggars, paupers, prostitutes, and criminals were evidence of the struggle to survive.

The urban poor were desperate for jobs and bread. Socialist intellectuals, sympathetic to the plight of the workers, proposed that the state organize producer cooperatives run by workers. Some wanted the state to take over insurance companies, railroads, mines, and other key industries. To the property owners of all classes, such schemes smacked of madness.

The middle-class leaders of the new republic gave all adult males the vote and abolished censorship; however, their attempts to ease the distress of the urban poor were insincere and halfhearted. The government limited the workday to ten hours and legalized labor unions, but it failed to cope effectively with unemployment. The socialist Louis Blanc called for the creation of producer cooperatives in order to guarantee employment for the city poor. The republic responded by establishing national workshops, which provided some employment on public works projects. Most workers, however, received wages for doing nothing. Drawn by the promise of work, tens of thousands of laborers left the provinces for Paris, swelling the ranks of the unemployed. The national workshops provided work, food, and medical benefits for some of the unemployed. But to the workers, this was a feeble effort to deal with their monumental distress. To the property-owning peasantry and bourgeoisie, the national workshops were a hateful concession to socialism and a waste of government funds. They viewed the workshops as nests of working-class radicalism, where plans were being hatched to change the economic system and seize their property.

For their participation in the February uprising against Louis Philippe, the workers had obtained meager benefits. When the government closed the workshops, working-class hostility and despair turned to open rebellion. Again, barricades went up in the streets of Paris.

The June Revolution in Paris was unlike previous uprisings in France. It was a revolt against poverty and a cry for the redistribution of property; as such, it foreshadowed the great social revolutions of the twentieth century. The workers stood alone. To the rest of the nation, they were barbarians attacking civilized society. Aristocrats, bourgeois, and peasants feared that no one's property would be safe if the revolution succeeded. From hundreds of miles away, Frenchmen flocked to Paris to crush what they considered to be the madness within their midst.

Although they had no leaders, the workers showed remarkable courage. Women and children fought alongside men behind the barricades. After three days of vicious street fighting and atrocities on both sides, the army extinguished the revolt. Some 1,460 lives had been lost, including four generals. The June Days left deep scars on French society. For many years, workers would never forget that the rest of France had united against them; the rest of France would remain terrified of working-class radicalism.

In December 1848, the French people, in overwhelming numbers, elected Louis Napoleon—nephew of the great emperor—president of the Second Republic. They were attracted to the magic of Louis Napoleon's name, and they expected him to prevent future working-class disorders. The election, in which all adult males could vote, demonstrated that most Frenchmen were socially conservative; they were unsympathetic to

THE BARRICADE, BY ADOLPHE HERVIER. Although this painting is supposed to capture a precise moment: six o'clock in the evening, June 24, 1848, it is symbolic of the revolutions that erupted that year in France, Germany, and the Austrian empire. (*Photo Jean-Loup Charmet*)

working-class poverty and deeply suspicious of socialist programs.

THE REVOLUTIONS OF 1848: GERMANY, AUSTRIA, AND ITALY

Like an epidemic, the fever of revolution that broke out in Paris in February raced across the Continent. Liberals, excluded from participation in political life, fought for parliaments and constitutions; many liberals were also nationalists who wanted unity or independence for their nations. Some liberals had a utopian vision of a new Europe of independent and democratic states. In this vision, reactionary rulers would no longer stifle individual liberty; no longer would a people be denied the right of nationhood.

The German States: Liberalism Defeated

After the Congress of Vienna, Germany consisted of a loose confederation of thirty-nine independent states, of which Austria and Prussia were the most powerful. Jealous of their independence and determined to preserve their absolute authority, the ruling princes detested liberal and nationalist ideals. In the southern German states, which had been more strongly influenced by the French Revolution, princes did grant constitutions and establish parliaments to retain the loyalty of their subjects. But even in these states, the princes continued to hold the reins of authority.

The German nationalism that had emerged during the French occupation intensified during the restoration (the post-Napoleonic period), as intellectuals, inspired in part by the ideas of the romantics, insisted that Germans, who shared a common language and culture, should also be united politically. During the restoration, the struggle for German unity and liberal reforms continued to be waged primarily by students, professors, writers, lawyers, and other educated people. The great mass of people, knowing only loyalty to their local prince, remained unmoved by appeals for national unity.

The successful revolt against Louis Philippe, hostility against absolute princes, and an economic crisis combined to produce uprisings in the capital cities of the German states in March 1848. Throughout Germany, liberals clamored for constitutions, parliamentary government, freedom of thought, and an end to police intimidation. Some called for the creation of a unified Germany governed by a national parliament and headed by a constitutional monarch. The poor joined the struggle. The great depression of the 1840s had aggravated the misery of the German peasant and urban masses, and as the pressures of hunger and unemployment worsened, their discontent exploded into revolutionary fervor.

In the spring of 1848, downtrodden artisans, who faced severe competition from the new factories, served as the revolution's shock troops. Unable to compete with the new machines, arti-

sans saw their incomes fall and their opportunities for work decrease. For example, skilled weavers working at home earned far less than factory hands, and some unemployed craftsmen were forced to take factory jobs, which they regarded as a terrible loss of status. These craftsmen wanted to restrict the growth of factories, curtail capitalist competition, and restore the power of the guilds, which had given them security and status.

Having lost hope that the absolute princes would aid them, craftsmen gave their support to bourgeois liberals, who, without this support, could not challenge the throne or wrest power from the aristocrats. In many German states, the actions of the embittered urban craftsmen determined the successful outcome of the insurrections. (The factory workers in the emerging industries, on the other hand, showed no enthusiasm for revolution, despite the appeals of radical socialists.) Adding to the discomfort of the ruling princes was rioting in the countryside by peasants, goaded by crop failure, debt, and oppressive demands from the aristocracy.

Terrified that these disturbances would lead to anarchy, the princes made concessions to the liberals, whom they previously had censored, jailed, and exiled. During March and April 1848, the traditional rulers in Baden, Württemberg, Bavaria, Saxony, Hanover, and other states replaced reactionary ministers with liberals, eased censorship, established jury systems, framed constitutions, formed parliaments, and ended peasant obligations to lords.

In Prussia, tensions between the army and Berliners exploded into violence. Unable to subdue the insurgents, the army urged bombarding the city with artillery. Frederick William IV opposed the idea and ordered the troops to leave Berlin. The insurgents had won the first round. The Prussian king, like the other German princes, had to agree to the formation of a parliament and the admission of prominent liberals into the government.

But the triumph of the liberals in Prussia and the other German states was not secure. Although reforms liberalized the governments of the German states, the insurrections had not toppled the ruling dynasties. Moreover, the alliance between the bourgeois and the artisans was tenuous. The artisans' violence frightened the property-owning middle class, which sought only moderate political reforms, preferably through peaceful means. In addition, the middle class saw restoration of the guild system as a reactionary economic measure.

Liberals took advantage of their successes in Prussia and other German states to form a national assembly charged with the task of creating a unified and liberal Germany. Representatives from all the German states attended the assembly, which met at Frankfurt. The delegates, including many articulate lawyers and professionals, came predominantly from the educated middle class; only a handful were drawn from the lower classes. After many long debates, the Frankfurt Assembly approved a federation of German states. The German union would have a parliament and would be headed by the Prussian king. Austria, with its many non-German nationalities, would be excluded from the federal union. Some radical democrats wanted to proclaim a German republic, but they were an ineffective minority. Most delegates were moderate liberals, who feared that universal (male) suffrage and the abolition of monarchy would lead to plebeian rule and the destruction of the social order. The deputies selected Frederick William as emperor of the new Germany, but the Prussian king refused; he would never wear a crown given to him by common people during a period of revolutionary agitation.

While the delegates debated, the ruling princes recovered from the first shock of revolution and ordered their armies to crush the revolutionaries. The February Revolution in Paris had shown European liberals that authority could be challenged successfully; the June Days, however, had shown the authorities that revolutionaries could be beaten by professional soldiers. Moreover, the German middle class, frightened by lower-class agitation and unsympathetic to the artisans' demands to restrict capitalism and restore guilds, was losing its enthusiasm for revolution, and so, too, were the artisans. The disintegration of the alliance between middle-class liberals and urban artisans deprived the revolutionaries of mass support. A revival of the Old Order would not face much resistance.

In Prussia, a determined Frederick William ordered his troops to reoccupy Berlin. In March, the citizens of Berlin had fought against the king's troops, but in November, no barricades went up in Berlin. Prussian forces also assisted the other German states in crushing the new parliaments. The masses of workers and peasants did not fight to save the liberal governments, which fell one by one. A small minority of democrats resisted, particularly in Baden; many of these revolutionaries died in the fighting or were executed.

German liberalism had failed to unite Germany or to create a constitutional government dominated by the middle class. Liberalism, never securely rooted in Germany, was discredited. In the following decades, many Germans, identifying liberalism with failure, turned to authoritarian Prussia for leadership in the struggle for unification. The fact that authoritarians hostile to the spirit of parliamentary government eventually united Germany had deep implications for future German and European history.

Austria: Hapsburg Dominance

The Hapsburg (Austrian) Empire, the product of dynastic marriage and inheritance, had no common nationality or language; it was held together only by the reigning Hapsburg dynasty, its army, and its bureaucracy. The ethnic composition of the empire was enormously complex. The Germans dominated; concentrated principally in Austria, they constituted about 25 percent of the empire's population. The Magyars predominated in the Hungarian lands of the empire. The great bulk of the population consisted of Slavs: Czechs, Poles, Slovaks, Slovenes, Croats, Serbs, and Ruthenians. In addition, there were Italians in northern Italy and Romanians in Transylvania. The Hapsburg dynasty, aided by the army and the German-dominated civil service, prevented the multinational empire from collapsing into anarchy.

Metternich, it is often said, suffered from a "dissolution complex": he understood that the new forces of nationalism and liberalism could break up the Austrian Empire. Liberal ideas could lead Hapsburg subjects to challenge the authority of the emperor, and nationalist feelings could cause the different peoples of the empire to rebel against German domination and Hapsburg rule. To keep these ideas from infecting Austrian subjects, Metternich's police imposed strict cen-

FRANCIS PALACKY

Hulton Deutsch Collection

Francis Palacky (1798–1876), Czech historian and statesman, is regarded by the Czech people as the founder of their nation. Palacky was a leader in the "Czech renaissance," a cultural revival in the first half of the nineteenth century. At that time, Czech writers began to use the Czech language as a vehicle of literary expression. (Hitherto German had been the dominant literary language.) This facilitated the Czechs' discovery of their historical past and helped to shape a national identity.

During the revolution of 1848, Palacky became the political spokesman for his people, advocating the right of the Czech nation to exist along with the other small nations of Austria in a federation of Danubian nations under the jurisdiction of the Hapsburg Empire. He participated in the Constituent Assembly, which met in Vienna in 1848, to draft a constitution for the Empire. After months of deliberation, the assembly was disbanded by the Emperor's army.

After the revolution, Palacky concentrated on completing his monumental *History of the Czech Nation.* The entire project occupied him over forty

sorship, spied on professors, and expelled from the universities students caught reading forbidden books. Despite Metternich's political police, the universities still remained hotbeds of liberalism.

In 1848, revolutions spread throughout the Austrian Empire, starting in Vienna. Aroused by the abdication of Louis Philippe, Viennese liberals denounced Hapsburg absolutism and demanded a constitution, relaxation of censorship, and restrictions on the police. The government responded hesitantly and with limited force to the demonstrations of students and workers, and many parts of Vienna fell to the revolutionaries. The authorities used force that was strong enough to incense the insurrectionists and create martyrs but not strong enough to subdue them. Confused and intimidated by the revolutionaries, the government allowed freedom of the press, ac-

cepted Metternich's resignation, and promised a constitution. The Constitutional Assembly was convened and in August voted the abolition of serfdom. At the same time that the Viennese insurgents were tasting the heady wine of reform, revolts in other parts of the empire—Bohemia, Hungary, and northern Italy—added to the distress of the monarchy.

But the revolutionaries' victory was only temporary, and the defeat of the Old Order only illusory; the Hapsburg government soon began to recover its balance. The first government victory came with the crushing of the Czechs in Bohemia. In 1848, Czech nationalists wanted the Austrian Empire reconstructed along federal lines that would give the Czechs equal standing with Germans. The Czechs called for a constitution for Bohemia and equal status for the Czech lan-

years. In the introduction he wrote, "From my youth I have known no higher goal than to provide my beloved nation with a portrait of its past, in which, as in a mirror, it could recognize itself and remember what its needs are."

Palacky revered the ideals of the Enlightenment and supported the reforms of the French Revolution calling for constitutional government and protection of individual rights. The nationalism he advocated was liberal and cosmopolitan, not exclusive and intolerant. In contrast to many nineteenth-century nationalists who descended into a world of irrational and dangerous myths, Palacky's love of the Czech nation was circumscribed by a respect for humanity and reason. He wanted the Czechs, whom he regarded among the forerunners of the Enlightenment, to take their place in the modern age as an independent nation among the progressive nations of the world.

Palacky's liberal nationalism inspired twentieth-century Czech democrats, including Thomas Masaryk, Eduard Benes, and more recently, Vaclav Havel.

guage in all official business. In June, students and destitute workers engaged in violent demonstrations, which frightened the middle and upper classes—both Czech and German. General Alfred zu Windischgrätz bombarded Prague, the capital of Bohemia, into submission and reestablished Hapsburg control.

In October 1848, the Hapsburg authorities ordered the army to bombard Vienna. Against the regular army, the courageous but disorganized and divided students and workers had little hope. Imperial troops broke into the city, overcame resistance, and executed several of the revolutionary leaders. In March 1849, the Hapsburg leadership replaced the liberal constitution drafted by the popularly elected Constitutional Assembly with a more conservative one, drawn up by its own ministers.

The most serious threat to the Hapsburg realm came from the Magyars in Hungary. Some 12 million people lived in Hungary, 5 million of whom were Magyars. The other nationalities comprised South Slavs (Croats and Serbs) and Romanians. The upper class consisted chiefly of Magyar landowners, who enjoyed tax exemptions and other feudal privileges. Drawn to liberal and modern ideas and fearful of peasant uprisings, some Hungarian nobles pressed for an end to serfdom and the tax exemptions of the nobility. Louis Kossuth (1802–1894), a member of the lower nobility, called for both social reform and a deepening of national consciousness. The great landowners, determined to retain their ancient privileges, resisted liberalization.

Led by Kossuth, the Magyars demanded local autonomy for Hungary. Hungary would remain within the Hapsburg Empire but would have its own constitution and national army and would control its own finances. The Hungarian leadership introduced liberal reforms: suffrage for all males who could speak Magyar and owned some property, freedom of religion, freedom of the press, the termination of serfdom, and the end of the privileges of nobles and church. Within a few weeks, the Hungarian parliament changed Hungary from a feudal to a modern liberal state.

But the Hungarian leaders' nationalist dreams towered above their liberal ideals. The Magyars intended to incorporate lands inhabited by Croats, Slovaks, and Romanians into their state (Magyars considered these lands an integral part of historic Hungary) and to transform these peoples into Hungarians. As historian Hugh Seton-Watson has written,

Kossuth and his friends genuinely believed that they were doing the non-Hungarians a kindness by giving them a chance of becoming absorbed in the superior Hungarian culture. To refuse this kindness was nationalist fanaticism; to impose it by force was to promote progress. The suggestion that Romanians, Slovaks, or Serbs were nations, with a national culture of their own, was simply ridiculous nonsense.[3]

In the spring of 1849, the Hungarians renounced their allegiance to the Hapsburgs and proclaimed Hungary an independent state, with Kossuth as president.

The Hapsburg rulers took advantage of the ethnic animosities inside and outside Hungary. They encouraged Romanians and Croats to resist the new Hungarian government. When Hapsburg forces moved against the Magyars, they were joined by an army of Croats, whose nationalist aspirations had been flouted by the Magyars. (The Slovaks fought alongside the Magyars.) Emperor Francis Joseph, who had recently ascended the Hapsburg throne, also appealed to Tsar Nicholas I for help. The tsar complied, fearing that a successful revolt by the Hungarians might lead the Poles to rise up against their Russian overlords. The Hungarians fought with extraordinary courage but were overcome by superior might. Kossuth and other rebel leaders went into exile; about one hundred rebel leaders were executed. Thus, through division and alliance, the Hapsburgs prevented the disintegration of the empire.

Italy: Continued Fragmentation

Italian nationalists, eager to end the humiliation of Hapsburg occupation and domination and to unite the disparate states into a unified and liberal nation, also rose in rebellion in 1848. Revolution broke out in Sicily six weeks before the February Revolution in Paris. Bowing to the revolutionaries' demands, King Ferdinand II of Naples granted a liberal constitution. The grand duke of Tuscany, King Charles Albert of Piedmont-Sardinia, and Pope Pius IX, ruler of the Papal States, also felt compelled to introduce liberal reforms.

Then the revolution spread to the Hapsburg lands in the north. The citizens of Milan, in Lombardy, built barricades and stood ready to fight the Austrian oppressor. When the Austrian soldiers attacked, they were fired on from nearby windows. From rooftops, Italians hurled stones and boiling water. After "Five Glorious Days" (March 18–22) of street fighting, the Austrians withdrew. The people of Milan had liberated their city. On March 22, the citizens of Venice declared their city free of Austria and set up a republic. King Charles Albert, who hoped to acquire Lombardy and Venetia, declared war on Austria. Intimidated by the insurrections, the ruling princes of the Italian states and Hapsburg Austria had lost the first round.

But soon everywhere in Italy the forces of reaction recovered and reasserted their authority. The Austrians defeated the Sardinians and reoccupied Milan, and Ferdinand II crushed the revolutionaries in the south. Revolutionary disorders in Rome had forced Pope Pius IX to flee in November 1848; in February 1849, the revolutionaries proclaimed Rome "a pure democracy with the glorious title of the Roman Republic." Heeding the pope's call for assistance, Louis Napoleon attacked Rome, destroyed the infant republic, and allowed Pope Pius to return. The last city to fall to the reactionaries was Venice, which the Austrians subjected to a merciless bombardment. After six weeks, the Venetians, weakened by starvation and cholera, surrendered. Reactionary princes still ruled in Italy; the Hapsburg occupation persisted in the north. Italy was still a fragmented nation.

THE REVOLUTIONS OF 1848: AN ASSESSMENT

The revolutions of 1848 in central Europe and Italy began with much promise, but they all ended in defeat. The revolutionaries' initial success was due less to their strength than to the governments' hesitancy to use their superior force. The reactionary rulers overcame their paralysis, however, and moved decisively to smash the revolutions. The courage of the revolutionaries was no match for regular armies. Thousands were killed and imprisoned; many fled to America.

Class divisions weakened the revolutionaries in central Europe. The union between middle-class liberals and workers, which brought success in the opening stages of the revolutions, was only temporary. Bourgeois liberals favoring political reforms—constitution, parliament, and protection of basic rights—grew fearful of the laboring poor, who demanded social reforms, that is, jobs and bread. To the bourgeois, the workers were a mob, driven by dark instincts. When the workers engaged in revolutionary violence, a terrified middle class deserted the cause of revolution or joined the old elites in subduing the workers.

MAP 23.3 Europe's Age of Revolutions ▶

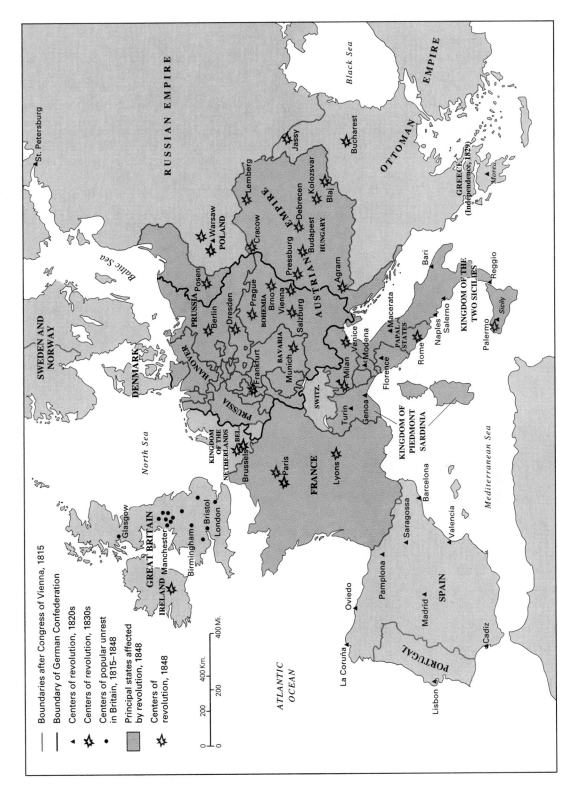

RUSSIAN EMPIRE

Black Sea

OTTOMAN EMPIRE

GREECE
(Independence, 1829)

Morea

St. Petersburg

Baltic Sea

Jassy

Bucharest

Lemberg

Warsaw
POLAND

Cracow

Kolozsvar

Debrecen

Blaj

AUSTRIAN EMPIRE

Posen

PRUSSIA

Berlin

Dresden

Prague

BOHEMIA

Brno

Budapest
HUNGARY

Pressburg

Vienna

Agram

Bari

HANOVER

Salzburg

KINGDOM OF THE
TWO SICILIES

Frankfurt

BAVARIA

Munich

Venice

Modena

Macerata

PAPAL
STATES

Salerno

Reggio

Sicily

SWEDEN AND
NORWAY

DENMARK

North Sea

Florence

Rome

Naples

Palermo

SWITZ.

Milan

Turin

Genoa

KINGDOM OF
PIEDMONT
SARDINIA

KINGDOM
OF THE
NETHERLANDS

BEL.

Brussels

PRUSSIA

Paris

Lyons

FRANCE

Glasgow

Bristol

London

Birmingham

Manchester

GREAT BRITAIN

IRELAND

Mediterranean Sea

Barcelona

Saragossa

Valencia

Pamplona

Madrid

SPAIN

Oviedo

La Coruña

Cadiz

PORTUGAL

Lisbon

ATLANTIC
OCEAN

Boundaries after Congress of Vienna, 1815

Boundary of German Confederation

Centers of revolution, 1820s

Centers of revolution, 1830s

Centers of popular unrest
in Britain, 1815–1848

Principal states affected
by revolution, 1848

Centers of
revolution, 1848

400 Mi.

400 Km.

200

200

0

0

573

Intractable nationalist animosities helped to destroy all the revolutionary movements against absolutism in central Europe. In many cases, the different nationalities hated each other more than they hated the reactionary rulers. Hungarian revolutionaries dismissed the nationalist yearnings of the South Slavs and Romanians living in Hungary, who in turn helped the Hapsburg dynasty to extinguish the nascent Hungarian state. The Germans of Bohemia resisted Czech demands for self-government and the equality of the Czech language with German. When German liberals at the Frankfurt Convention debated the boundary lines of a united Germany, the problem of Prussia's Polish territories emerged. In 1848, Polish patriots wanted to recreate the Polish nation, but German delegates at the convention, by an overwhelming majority, opposed returning the Polish lands seized by Prussia in the late eighteenth century. In addressing his fellow delegates, Wilhelm Jordan described the Poles as a people "which does not possess the same measure of human content as is given to the German kind" and denounced those Germans who would permit their kinsmen to live under Polish rule as traitors to their people. Then he justified Germany's claim to the Polish lands:

> It is high time for us to wake up . . . to a healthy national egoism . . . which places the welfare and honor of the fatherland above everything else. . . . Frankly, the rules of theoretical justice never seem more pitiful to me than when they presume to fix the fate of nations. . . . No, I admit without blinking, our right is no other than the right of the stronger, the right of conquest.[4]

Before 1848, democratic idealists envisioned the birth of a new Europe of free people and liberated nations. The revolutions in central Europe showed that nationalism and liberalism were not natural allies and that nationalists were often indifferent to the rights of other peoples. Disheartened by these nationalist antagonisms, John Stuart Mill, the English liberal statesman and philosopher, lamented that "the sentiment of nationality so far outweighs the love of liberty that the people are willing to abet their rulers in crushing the liberty and independence of any people not of their race or language."[5] In the Revolutions of 1848, concludes British historian Lewis Namier, "'nationality', the passionate creed of the intellectuals, invades the politics of central and east-central Europe, and with 1848 starts the Great European War of every nation against its neighbors."[6]

The liberal and nationalist aims of the revolutionaries were not realized, but liberal gains were not insignificant. All French men obtained the right to vote; serfdom was abolished in Austria and the German states; and parliaments, dominated, to be sure, by princes and aristocrats, were established in Prussia and other German states. In later decades, liberal reforms would spread. These reforms would be introduced peacefully, for the failure of the revolutions of 1848 convinced many people, including liberals, that popular uprisings were ineffective ways of changing society. The Age of Revolution, initiated by the French Revolution of 1789, had ended.

◆ ◆ ◆

NOTES

1. Jacques Droz, *Europe Between Revolutions, 1815–1848* (New York: Harper Torchbooks, 1967), p. 248.

2. *The Recollections of Alexis de Tocqueville*, trans. Alexander Teixeira de Mattos (Cleveland: Meridian Books, 1969), pp. 11–12.

3. Hugh Seton-Watson, *Nations and States* (Boulder, Colo.: Westview Press, 1977), p. 162.

4. Quoted in J. L. Talmon, *Political Messianism: The Romantic Phase* (New York: Praeger, 1960), p. 482.

5. Quoted in Hans Kohn, *Nationalism: Its Meaning and History* (Princeton, N.J.: Van Nostrand, 1965), pp. 51–52.

6. Lewis Namier, *1848: The Revolution of the Intellectuals* (Garden City, N.Y.: Doubleday, Anchor, 1964), p. 38.

SUGGESTED READING

Deak, Istvan, *The Lawful Revolution* (1979). A review of the Hungarian revolution.

Droz, Jacques, *Europe Between Revolutions* (1967). A fine survey of the period 1815–1848.

Duveau, Georges, *1848: The Making of a Revolution* (1967). France in 1848.

Fasel, George, *Europe in Upheaval: The Revolutions of 1848* (1970). A good introduction.

Fejtö, François, ed., *The Opening of an Era: 1848* (1973). Articles by eminent historians.

Langer, W. L., *Political and Social Upheaval, 1832–1852* (1969). Another volume in *The Rise of Modern Europe* series; rich interpretation.

Robertson, Priscilla, *Revolutions of 1848* (1960). Vividly portrays events and personalities.

Sigmann, Jean, *1848: The Romantic and Democratic Revolutions in Europe* (1970). A useful survey.

Sperber, Jonathan, *The European Revolution, 1848–1851* (1994). A recent comprehensive overview.

Stearns, Peter N., *1848: The Revolutionary Tide in Europe* (1974). Strong on social factors.

Talmon, J. L., *Romanticism and Revolt* (1967). Forces shaping European history, 1815 to 1848.

Webb, R. K., *Modern England from the Eighteenth Century to the Present* (1968). A balanced, well-informed book.

REVIEW QUESTIONS

1. What was Metternich's attitude toward the French Revolution? Toward Napoleon?

2. How did the Congress of Vienna violate the principle of nationalism? What did it accomplish?

3. Between 1820 and 1832, where were revolutions suppressed, and how? Where were revolutions successful, and why?

4. How did Parliament respond to demands for economic and political reforms from 1815 to 1848?

5. What was the significance of the June Days?

6. Why did the revolutions of 1848 fail in the German states, the Austrian Empire, and Italy?

7. What were the liberal gains in 1848? Why were liberals and nationalists disappointed?

PART FIVE

An Age of Contradiction: Progress and Breakdown

1848–1914

	POLITICS AND SOCIETY	THOUGHT AND CULTURE
1850	Second Empire in France (1852–1870) Commodore Perry opens Japan to trade (1853) Crimean War (1853–1856) Unification of Italy (1859–1870)	Stowe, *Uncle Tom's Cabin* (1851–52) Dickens, *Hard Times* (1854) Flaubert, *Madame Bovary* (1856) Darwin, *Origin of Species* (1859) Mill, *On Liberty* (1859)
1860	Civil War in the United States (1861–1865) Bismarck in power in Germany (1862–1890) Unification of Germany (1866–1871) Settlement of 1867 splits Hapsburg territories into Austria and Hungary Reform Bill of 1867 in Great Britain Opening of Suez Canal (1869)	Hugo, *Les Misérables* (1862) Marx, *Capital* (1867) Dostoevski, *The Idiot* (1868–69) Tolstoy, *War and Peace* (1863–1869) Mill, *The Subjection of Women* (1869)

1870	Franco-Prussian War (1870–71)
	Third Republic in France (1870–1940)
	Serbs gain independence from Ottoman Turks
	   (1878)
		Impressionism in art (1860–1886): Manet,
		   Monet, Pissaro, Degas, Renoir
		Darwin, *The Descent of Man* (1871)
		Nietzsche, *The Birth of Tragedy* (1872)
		Ibsen, *A Doll's House* (1879)

1880	French fight Chinese over Indochina
	   (1883–85)
	Berlin Conference on Africa (1884)
	Reform Bill of 1884 in Great Britain
		Postimpressionism in art (1880s–1890s):
		   Cézanne, Gauguin, van Gogh, Munch,
		   Matisse
		Zola, *The Experimental Novel* (1880)
		Spencer, *The Man Versus the State* (1884)
		Nietzsche, *The Anti-Christ* (1888)

1890	Dreyfus affair in France (1894–1906) Sino-Japanese War (1894–95) Spanish-American War (1898) Battle of Omdurman in the Sudan (1898) Boer War in South Africa (1899–1902)	Le Bon, *The Crowd* (1895) Chamberlain, *The Foundations of the Nine- teenth Century* (1899) Bernstein, *Evolutionary Socialism* (1899) Durkheim, *Suicide* (1897)

1900	Boxer Rebellion in China (1900)
	Roosevelt Corollary (1904)
	Russo-Japanese War (1904–05)
	Anglo-French Entente Cordiale (1904)
	Anglo-Russian Entente (1907)
	Congo declared a Belgian colony (1908)
	Mexican Revolution (1911)
		Freud, *The Interpretation of Dreams* (1900)
		Cubism in art: Picasso, Braque
		Abstract art: Mondrian, Kandinsky,
		   Duchamp
		Planck: quantum theory (1900)
		Lenin, *What Is To Be Done?* (1902)
		Einstein: theory of relativity (1905)
		Weber, *The Protestant Ethic and the Spirit of
		   Capitalism* (1904–05)
		Sorel, *Reflections on Violence* (1908)

CHAPTER 24

Thought and Culture
in the Mid-Nineteenth Century:
Realism and Social Criticism

*T*he second half of the nineteenth century was marked by great progress in science, a surge in industrialism, and a continuing secularization of life and thought. The principal intellectual currents of the century's middle decades reflected these trends. Realism, positivism, Darwinism, Marxism, and liberalism all reacted against romantic, religious, and metaphysical interpretations of nature and society and focused on the empirical world. In one way or another, each movement derived from and expanded the Enlightenment tradition. Adherents of these movements relied on careful observation and strove for scientific accuracy. This emphasis on objective reality helped stimulate a growing criticism of social ills; for despite unprecedented material progress, reality was often sordid, somber, and depressing. In the last part of the century, reformers, motivated by an expansive liberalism, a socially committed Christianity, or both, pressed for the alleviation of social injustice.

REALISM AND NATURALISM

Realism, the dominant movement in art and literature in the mid 1800s, opposed the romantic veneration of the inner life and romantic sentimentality. The romantics exalted passion and intuition, let their imaginations transport them to a medieval past, which they deemed idyllic, and sought subjective solitude amid nature's wonders. Realists, on the other hand, turned their attention to the actual world and concentrated on social conditions, contemporary manners, and the familiar details of everyday life. With clinical detachment and meticulous care, they analyzed how people looked, worked, and behaved.

Like scientists, realist writers and artists carefully investigated the empirical world. For example, Gustave Courbet (1819–1877), who exem-

The Stone Breakers, (1849) by Gustave Courbet. (*Bildarchiv Foto Marburg/Art Resource, NY*)

plified realism in painting, sought to practice what he called a "living art." He painted common people and commonplace scenes: laborers breaking stones, peasants tilling the soil or returning from a fair, a country burial, wrestlers, bathers, family groups. In a matter-of-fact style, without any attempt at glorification, realist artists also depicted floor scrapers, rag pickers, prostitutes, and beggars. Gustave Flaubert (1821–1880), said of *Madame Bovary,* his masterpiece of realist literature: "Art ought . . . to rise above personal feelings and nervous susceptibilities! It is time to give it the precision of the physical sciences by means of a pitiless method."[1] Émile de Vogüé, a nineteenth-century French writer, described realism as follows:

> They [realists] have brought about an art of observation rather than of imagination, one which boasts that it observes life as it is in its wholeness and complexity with the least possible prejudice on the part of the artist. It takes men under ordinary conditions, shows characters in the course of their everyday existence, average and changing. Jealous of the rigour of scientific procedure, the writer proposes to instruct us by a perpetual analysis of feelings and of acts rather than to divert us or move us by intrigue and exhibition of the passions. . . . The new art seeks to imitate nature.[2]

Romantic writers had written lyrics, for lyric poetry is the language of feeling. The realists' literary genre was the novel because it lends itself admirably to depicting human behavior and social conditions. Realist novels were often serialized in the inexpensive newspapers and magazines, which the many newly literate common people could read. Thus, the commoners' interests helped shape the novels' content. Seeking to portray reality as it is, realist writers frequently dealt with social abuses and the sordid aspects of human behavior and social life.

In his large output of novels, Honoré de Balzac (1799–1850) described how social and economic forces affected people's behavior. Another Frenchman, Eugène Sue, gave harrowing accounts of slum life and crime in his serialized novel, *Les Mystères de Paris* (1842–43). George Sand (a woman writing under a male pen name) portrayed the married woman as a victim in *Indi-*

ana (1832). A reviewer praised the book for presenting

> a true, living world, which is our world . . . characters and manners just as we can observe them around us, natural conversations, scenes in familiar settings, violent, uncommon passions, but sincerely felt or observed and such as are still aroused in many hearts, under the apparent uniformity and monotonous frivolity of our lives.[3]

Many regard Gustave Flaubert's *Madame Bovary* (1856) as the quintessential realistic novel; it tells the story of a self-centered wife, who shows her hatred for her devoted, hardworking, but dull husband by committing adultery. Commenting on the realism of *Madame Bovary,* one critic notes that it "represents an obsession with description. Details are counted one by one, all are given equal value, every street, every house, every room, every book, every blade of grass is described in full."[4]

At the midcentury in Russia, Ivan Turgenev, in *Sketches* (1852), depicted his homeland's rural conditions and expressed compassion for the brutally difficult life of serfs. In *War and Peace* (1863–1869), Leo Tolstoy vividly described the manners and outlook of the Russian nobility and the tragedies that attended Napoleon's invasion of Russia. In *Anna Karenina* (1873–1877), he probed class divisions and the complexities of marital relationships. Fyodor Dostoevski's *Crime and Punishment* (1866), a psychological novel, offered penetrating insights into human behavior.

Among English writers, Elizabeth Gaskell, the wife of a Unitarian minister in Manchester, dealt compassionately with the plight of industrial workers in her *Mary Barton* (1848) and *North and South* (1855). The novels of Charles Dickens—*Bleak House* (1853), *Hard Times* (1854), and several others—detailed the squalor of life, the hypocrisy of society, and the drudgery of labor in British industrial cities.

Literary realism evolved into naturalism when writers tried to demonstrate a causal relationship between human character and the social environment: that certain conditions of life produced predictable character traits in human beings. The belief that the law of cause and effect governed human behavior reflected the immense prestige

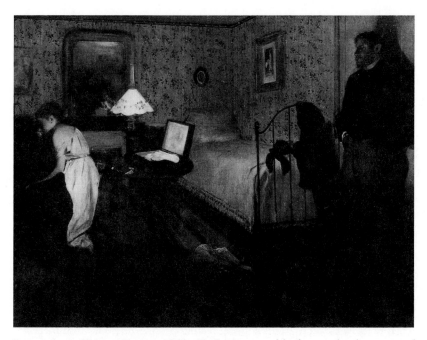

INTERIOR BY EDGAR DEGAS, 1868–69. Set in a world of poor shopkeepers and clerks, *Thérèse Raquin* (1867) was Émile Zola's first great success as a naturalist novelist. This Degas painting depicts the sexual tension and violent emotions which Zola sought to uncover in his work. (*Philadelphia Museum of Art, The Henry P. McIlhenny Collection in Memory of Francis P. McIlhenny*)

attached to science in the closing decades of the nineteenth century.

The leading naturalist novelist, Émile Zola (1840–1902), had an immense confidence in the scientific method and was convinced that it applied to literature as well. According to Zola, the novelist should proceed like a scientist performing an experiment. The "experimental novel," he wrote, shows "the reciprocal effect of society on the individual and the individual on society." It shows "man living in social conditions produced by himself, which he modifies daily, and in the heart of which he himself experiences a continual transformation." This type of novel, Zola claimed,

> is a consequence of the scientific evolution of the century; it continues and completes physiology, which itself leans for support on chemistry and medicine; it substitutes for the study of the abstract and the metaphysical man the study of the natural man, governed by physical and chemical laws, and modified by the influences of his surroundings; it is in one word the literature of our scientific age, as the classical and romantic literature corresponded to a scholastic and theological age.[5]

In his own novels, Zola probed the slums, brothels, mining villages, and cabarets of France, examining how people were conditioned by the squalor of their environment. *Germinal* (1885), his greatest novel, graphically renders the terrible toil and drudgery endured by coal miners.

Naturalism was not restricted to the novel or to France. The leading naturalist playwright, Henrik Ibsen (1828–1906)—a Norwegian—examined with clinical precision the commercial and professional classes, their personal ambitions and family relationships. His *Pillars of Society* (1877) scrutinizes bourgeois social pretensions and hypocrisy. In *A Doll's House* (1879), he took up a theme that shocked the late-nineteenth-century bourgeois audience: a woman leaving her husband to seek a more fulfilling life.

In striving for a true-to-life portrayal of human behavior and the social environment, realism and naturalism reflected attitudes shaped by science, industrialism, and secularism, which stressed the importance of the external world. The same outlook gave rise to positivism in philosophy.

POSITIVISM

In the nineteenth century, science and technology continued to make astonishing strides. Combined with striking economic progress, these advances led many westerners to believe that a golden age was on the horizon. Viewing science as the highest achievement of the mind, intellectuals sought to apply the scientific method to other areas of thought. They regarded this method as a reliable way to approach all problems. Even history could be studied scientifically, they insisted, and society could be reorganized to conform with scientific laws of social development. Marxism was one attempt to fashion a science of society; another attempt was *positivism*.

According to the positivists, although people's knowledge of nature was vastly expanding, their understanding of society was deficient. This deficiency could be remedied by applying a strict empirical approach to the study of society. The philosopher must proceed like a scientist, carefully assembling and classifying data and formulating general rules that demonstrate regularities in the social experience. Such knowledge, based on concrete facts, would provide the social planner with useful insights. Positivists rejected metaphysics, which, in the tradition of Plato, tried to discover ultimate principles through reason alone, rather than through observation of the empirical world. For positivists, any effort to go beyond the realm of experience to a deeper reality would be a mistaken and fruitless endeavor. They restricted human knowledge only to what could be experienced and saw the method of science as the only valid approach to knowledge.

A leading figure in the emergence of positivism was Auguste Comte (1798–1857), an engineer with scientific training. Comte served as secretary to Saint-Simon (see page 547) until their association, punctuated by frequent quarrels,

ended in 1824. But much of Saint-Simon's thought found its way into Comte's philosophy. Like Saint-Simon (and Marx), Comte called for a purely scientific approach to history and society: only by a proper understanding of the laws governing human affairs could society, which was in a state of intellectual anarchy, be rationally reorganized. He shared with Saint-Simon the view that the Enlightenment and the French Revolution had shattered the Old Regime but had not replaced it with new institutions and a new ideology; remedying this failure was the pressing need of the age.

Comte called his system positivism because he believed that it rested on sure knowledge derived from observed facts and was therefore empirically verifiable. Like others of his generation, he believed that scientific laws underlay human affairs and could be discovered through the methods of the geologist and the chemist: that is, through recording and systematizing observable data. "I shall bring factual proof," he said, "that there are just as definite laws for the development of the human race as there are for the fall of a stone."[6]

One of the laws that Comte believed he had discovered was the "law of the three stages." The human mind, he asserted, had progressed through three broad historical stages: theological, metaphysical, and scientific. In the theological stage, the most primitive of the three, the mind found a supernatural explanation for the origins and purpose of things, and society was ruled by priests. In the metaphysical stage, which included the Enlightenment, the mind tried to explain things through abstractions, such as "nature," "equality," "natural rights," or "popular sovereignty," which rested on hope and belief rather than on empirical investigation. The metaphysical stage was a transitional period between the infantile theological stage and the highest stage of society, the scientific, or positive, stage. In this culminating stage, the mind breaks with all illusions inherited from the past, formulates laws based on careful observation of the empirical world, and reconstructs society in accordance with these laws. People remove all mystery from nature and base their social legislation on laws of society similar to the laws of nature discovered by Newton.

Showing more insight than the philosophes, who tended to dismiss religion as a superstition and obsolete, Comte recognized that religion performs indispensable psychological and social functions. It is a powerful unifying force and a necessary outlet for human emotional needs. He therefore attempted to fashion a new religion for a new age: the Religion of Humanity, in which the veneration of the human race would supersede Christian teachings.

Because Comte advocated the scientific study of society, he is regarded as the principal founder of sociology; indeed, he coined the term. Comte's effort inspired many thinkers to collect and analyze critically all data pertaining to social phenomena. Émile Durkheim (see pages 693–694), a pioneer in the science of sociology, declared his indebtedness to Comte and, despite criticisms of Comte's work, recommended it as a superb introduction to the study of sociology. In trying to make the study of civilization an exact science, the English historian Henry T. Buckle (1821–1862), for example, looked at human culture as a product of climate, soil, and food; consequently, he thought that the achievements of western Europe were due to a favorable environment and the backwardness of Russia and Africa to an unfavorable one. Buckle believed that rigorous laws operated in the social world and that they could be best uncovered through statistical studies.

Although Comte attacked the philosophes for delving into abstractions instead of fashioning laws based on empirical knowledge, he was also influenced by the spirit of eighteenth-century philosophy. Like the philosophes, he valued science, criticized supernatural religion, and believed in progress. In this way, he accepted the Enlightenment's legacy, including the empirical and antitheological spirit of Diderot's *Encyclopedia* and Montesquieu's quest for historical laws governing society. Comte also acknowledged his debt to Condorcet, who saw intellectual and social progress as an inevitable condition of humanity.

DARWINISM

Many contributed to the steady advance of science in the nineteenth century. In 1808, John Dalton, an English chemist, formulated the modern atomic theory. In 1831, an English chemist and physicist, Michael Faraday, discovered the principle of electromagnetic induction, on which

A CARICATURE OF DARWIN. Darwin's theory of evolution created much controversy and aroused considerable bitterness. In this caricature, the apelike Darwin, holding a mirror, is explaining his theory of evolution to a fellow ape. (*Hulton Picture Company/Bettmann Archive*)

the electric generator and electric motor are based. In 1847, Hermann von Helmholtz, a German physicist, formulated the law of conservation of energy, which states that the total amount of energy in the universe is always the same; energy that is used up is not lost but is converted into heat. In 1887, another German physicist, Heinrich Hertz, discovered electromagnetic waves—a discovery that later made possible the invention of radio, television, and radar. Almost two decades earlier, in 1869, Dmitri Mendeleev, a Russian chemist, constructed a periodic table for the elements, which helped to make chemistry more systematic and mathematical. In 1861, Louis Pasteur, a French scientist, initiated a revolution in medicine by proving that some diseases were caused by microbes, and he devised vaccines to prevent them.

Perhaps the most important scientific advance was the theory of evolution formulated by Charles Darwin (1809–1882). An English naturalist, Darwin did for biology what Newton had done for physics: he made it an objective science based on general principles. The Scientific Revolution of the seventeenth century had given people a new conception of space; Darwin radically altered our conception of time and biological life, including human origins.

Natural Selection

During the eighteenth century, almost all people had adhered to the biblical account of creation contained in Genesis. God had instantaneously created the universe and the various species of animal and plant life. He had given every river and mountain a finished and permanent form and made each species of animal and plant distinct from every other species. God had designed the bird's wings so that it could fly, the fish's eyes so that it could see under water, and human legs so that people could walk. All this, it was believed, had occurred some five or six thousand years ago.

Gradually, this view was questioned. In 1794, Erasmus Darwin, the grandfather of Charles Darwin, published *Zoonomia, or the Laws of Organic Life,* which offered evidence that the earth had existed for millions of years before the appearance of people and that animals experienced modifications, which they passed on to their offspring. Nearly forty years later, Sir Charles Lyell published his three-volume *Principles of Geology* (1830–1833), which showed that the planet had evolved slowly over many ages.

In December 1831, Charles Darwin sailed as a naturalist on the HMS. *Beagle,* which surveyed the shores of South America and some Pacific islands. During the five-year expedition, Darwin collected and examined specimens of plant and animal life; he concluded that many animal species had perished, that new species had

emerged, and that there were links between extinct and living species.

Influenced by Lyell's achievement, Darwin sought to interpret distant natural occurrences by means of observable processes that were still going on. He could not accept that a fixed number of distinct and separate species had been instantaneously created a mere five thousand years ago. In the *Origin of Species* (1859), and the *Descent of Man* (1871), Darwin used empirical evidence to show that the wide variety of animal species was due to a process of development over many millennia, and he supplied a convincing theory that explained how evolution operates.

Darwin adopted the Malthusian idea (see page 542) that the population reproduces faster than the food supply, causing a struggle for existence. Not all infant organisms grow to adulthood; not all adult organisms live to old age. The principle of *natural selection* determines which members of the species have a better chance of survival. The offspring of a lion, giraffe, or insect are not exact duplications of their parents. A baby lion might have the potential for being slightly faster or stronger than its parents; a baby giraffe might grow up to have a longer neck than its parents; an insect might have a slightly different color.

These small and random variations give the organism a crucial advantage in the struggle for food and against natural enemies. The organism favored by nature is more likely to reach maturity, to mate, and to pass on its superior qualities to its offspring, some of which will acquire the advantageous trait to an even greater degree than the parent. Over many generations, the favorable characteristic becomes more pronounced and more widespread within the species. Over millennia, natural selection causes the death of old species and the creation of new ones. Very few of the species that dwelt on earth 10 million years ago still survive, and many new ones, including human beings, have emerged. People themselves are products of natural selection, evolving from earlier, lower, nonhuman forms of life.

Darwinism and Christianity

Like Newton's law of universal gravitation, Darwin's theory of evolution had revolutionary consequences in areas other than science. Evolution challenged traditional Christian belief. To some, it undermined the infallibility of Scripture and the conviction that the Bible was indeed the Word of God. Natural selection could explain the development of the organic world without reference to any divine design or ultimate purpose. Indeed, supernatural explanations of the origin of species now seemed superfluous and an obstacle to a scientific understanding of nature.

Darwin's theory touched off a great religious controversy between outraged fundamentalists, who defended a literal interpretation of Genesis, and advocates of the new biology. One theologian declared, "If the Darwinian theory is true, Genesis is a lie, the whole framework of the book of life falls to pieces, and the revelation of God to man, as we Christians know it, is a delusion and a snare."[7] A Methodist publication contended: "We regard this theory, which seeks to eliminate from the universe the immediate, ever-present, all pervasive action of a living and personal God, which excludes the possibility of the supernatural and the miraculous . . . as practically destructive of the authority of divine revelation, and subversive of the foundation of religion and morality."[8] In time, most religious thinkers tried to reconcile evolution with the Christian view that there was a Creation and that it had a purpose. These Christian thinkers held that God created and then directed the evolutionary process, that modifications within a species were made by an intelligent creator.

Darwinism ultimately helped end the practice of relying on the Bible as an authority in questions of science, completing a trend initiated by Galileo. Darwinism thus contributed to the waning of religious belief and to a growing secular attitude which dismissed or paid scant attention to the Christian view of a universe designed by God and a soul that rises to heaven. For many, the conclusion was inescapable: nature contained no divine design or purpose, and the human species itself was a chance product of impersonal forces. The core idea of Christianity—that people were children of God participating in a drama of salvation—rested more than ever on faith rather than reason. Some even talked openly about the death of God. The notion that people are sheer accidents of nature was shocking. Copernicus had deprived people of the comforting belief that the earth had been placed in the center of the universe just for them; Darwin deprived them of the privilege of being God's special creation, thereby contributing to the feeling of anxiety that characterizes the twentieth century.

Social Darwinism

Darwin's theories were extended by others beyond the realm in which he had worked. Social thinkers, who recklessly applied Darwin's conclusions to the social order, produced theories that had dangerous consequences. Social Darwinists—those who transferred Darwin's scientific theories to social and economic issues—used the terms "struggle for existence" and "survival of the fittest" to buttress an often brutal economic individualism and political conservatism. Successful businessmen, they said, had demonstrated their fitness to succeed in the competitive world of business. Their success accorded with nature's laws and therefore was beneficial to society. Thus, American industrialist Andrew Carnegie (1835–1919) wrote in *The Gospel of Wealth* (1900):

> We accept and welcome . . . the concentration of business, industrial and commercial, in the hands of a few and the law of competition . . . as being, not only beneficial, but essential to the future progress of the race. . . . We start, then, with a condition of affairs under which the best interests of the race are promoted, but which inevitably gives wealth to the few.[9]

Those who lost out in the socioeconomic struggle demonstrated their unfitness. Traditionally, failure had been ascribed to human wickedness or to God's plan. Now it was attributed to an inferior hereditary endowment.

Using Darwin's model of organisms evolving and changing slowly over tens of thousands of years, conservatives insisted that society, too, should experience change at an unhurried pace. Instant reforms conflicted with nature's laws and wisdom and resulted in a deterioration of the social body.

The application of Darwin's biological concepts to the social world, where they did not apply, also buttressed imperialism, racism, nationalism,

Profile

Photo AKG London

LUDWIG FEUERBACH

Ludwig Feuerbach (1804–1872), a German philosopher and theologian, criticized Hegel, and indeed all traditional philosophy, for harboring a religious world-view. In his *Essence of Christianity* (1841), Feuerbach argued that the starting point of philosophy should be the human being and the material world, not God. "Religion is the dream of the human mind," he said, and God is a human creation, a product of human feelings and wishes. Human beings believe in the divine because they seek assistance from it in life and fear death.

Feuerbach treated religion as an expression of mythical thinking and God as an unconscious projection of human hopes, fears, and self-doubts. Christianity diminishes human beings in order to affirm God, said Feuerbach; Christians deny their own worth and goodness that they might ascribe

and militarism—doctrines that preached relentless conflict. Social Darwinists insisted that nations and races were engaged in a struggle for survival in which only the fittest survive and deserve to survive. Karl Pearson, a British professor of mathematics, stated in *National Life from the Standpoint of Science* (1900):

> *History shows me only one way, and one way only in which a higher state of civilization has been produced, namely the struggle of race with race, and the survival of the physically and mentally fitter race. . . . The path of progress is strewn with the wrecks of nations; traces are everywhere to be seen of the [sacrifice] of inferior races, and of victims who found not the narrow way to perfection. Yet these dead people are, in very truth, the stepping stones on which mankind has arisen to the higher intellectual and deeper emotional life of today.[10]*

"We are a conquering race," said U.S. Senator Albert J. Beveridge. "We must obey our blood

and occupy new markets, and if necessary, new lands."[11] "War is a biological necessity of the first importance," claimed the Prussian general Friedrich von Bernhardi in *Germany and the Next War* (1911).[12]

Darwinian biology was used to promote the belief in Anglo-Saxon (British and American) and Teutonic (German) racial superiority. Social Darwinists attributed to racial qualities the growth of the British Empire, the expansion of the United States to the Pacific, and the extension of German power. The domination of other peoples—American Indians, Africans, Asians, Poles—was seen as the natural right of the superior race. British naturalist Alfred Russel Wallace, who arrived at the theory of evolution independently of Darwin, wrote in 1864:

> *The intellectual and moral, as well as the physical qualities of the European are superior; the same power and capacities which have made him rise in a few centuries from the condition of the wandering savage . . . to his present state of culture and advancement . . .*

all value to God. The human being, weak and self-hating,

> sets God before him as the antithesis of himself. . . . God is the infinite, man the finite being; God is perfect, man imperfect; God eternal, man temporal; God almighty, man weak; God holy, man sinful. God and man are extremes: God is the absolutely positive, the sum of all realities; man the absolutely negative. . . .
>
> But in religion man contemplates his own latent nature. Hence it must be shown that this antithesis, this differencing of God and man, with which religion begins, is a differencing of man with his own nature.*

Religion, said Feuerbach, is a form of self-alienation, for human beings diminish their humanity when they invest their finest qualities in a nonexistent God and reserve their worst qualities for themselves. God represents the ex-ternalization of an idealized human being. When individuals measure themselves against this God-ideal, they see only miserable, contemptible, and worthless creatures. "To enrich God, man must become poor; that God may be all, man must become nothing. . . . [M]an is wicked, corrupt, incapable of good; but, on the other hand, God is the only good—the Good Being."† Humanity liberates itself, said Feuerbach, when it rejects God's existence and religion's claim to truth. He declared that it was his aim to change the friends of God into friends of human beings and the seekers of heaven into active, productive, and life-affirming individuals.

---

*Ludwig Feuerbach, *The Essence of Christianity*, trans. George Eliot (New York: Harper Torchbooks, 1957), p. 33.
†Ibid, pp. 26–28.

> enable him when in contact with savage man, to conquer in the struggle for existence and to increase at his expense.[13]

The theory of evolution was a great achievement of the rational mind, but in the hands of the Social Darwinists it served to undermine the Enlightenment tradition. Whereas the philosophes emphasized human equality, Social Darwinists divided humanity into racial superiors and inferiors. The philosophes believed that states would increasingly submit to the rule of law to reduce violent conflicts; Social Darwinists, on the other hand, regarded racial and national conflict as a biological necessity, a law of history, and a means of progress. In propagating a tooth-and-claw version of human and international relations, Social Darwinists dispensed with the humanitarian and cosmopolitan sentiments of the philosophes and distorted the image of progress. Their views promoted territorial aggrandizement and military buildup and led many to welcome World War I. The Social Darwinist notion of the struggle of races for survival became a core doc-trine of the Nazi party after World War I and provided the "scientific" and "ethical" justification for genocide.

MARXISM

The failure of the revolutions of 1848 and a growing fear of working-class violence led liberals to abandon revolution and to press for reforms through the political process. In the last part of the nineteenth century, Marxists and anarchists became the chief proponents of revolution. Both liberalism and Marxism shared common principles derived from the Enlightenment. Their adherents believed in the essential goodness and perfectibility of human nature and claimed that their doctrines rested on rational foundations. They wanted to free individuals from accumulated superstition, ignorance, and prejudices of the past and to fashion a more harmonious and rational society. Both liberals and Marxists believed in social progress and valued the full realization of human talents.

587

KARL MARX WITH HIS DAUGHTER. Interpreting history in economic terms, Marx predicted that socialism would replace capitalism. He called for the proletariat to overthrow capitalism and to establish a classless society. (*Culver Pictures*)

Despite these similarities, the differences between liberalism and Marxism are profound. The goal of Marxism—the seizure of power by the working class and the destruction of capitalism—was inimical to bourgeois liberals; so, too, was the Marxist belief that violence and struggle were the essence of history, the instruments of progress, the vehicle to a higher stage of humanity. Liberals, who placed the highest value on the individual, held that through education and self-discipline people could overcome inequality and poverty. Marxists, on the other hand, insisted that without a transformation of the economic system individual effort by the downtrodden would amount to very little.

Karl Marx (1818–1883) was born of German-Jewish parents (both descendants of prominent rabbis). To save his job as a lawyer, Marx's father converted to Protestantism. Enrolled at a university to study law, Marx switched to philosophy. In 1842, he was editing a newspaper, which was soon suppressed by the Prussian authorities for its outspoken ideas. Leaving his native Rhineland, Marx went to Paris, where he met another German, Friedrich Engels (1820–1895), who was the son of a prosperous textile manufacturer. Marx and Engels entered into a lifelong collaboration and became members of socialist groups. In February 1848, they published the *Communist Manifesto,* which called for a working-class revolution to overthrow the capitalist system. Forced to leave France in 1849 because of his political views, Marx moved to London, where he spent the rest of his life.

Although supported by Engels, Marx was continually short of funds, and at times he and his wife and daughters lived in dreadful poverty. In London, Marx spent years writing *Capital*—a study and critique of the modern capitalistic economic system, which, he predicted, would be destroyed by a socialist revolution.

A Science of History

As did other thinkers influenced by the Enlightenment, Marx believed that human history, like the operations of nature, was governed by scientific law. Marx was a strict materialist; rejecting all religious and metaphysical interpretations of both nature and history, he sought to fashion an empirical science of society. He viewed religion as a human creation—a product of people's imagination and feelings and a consolation for the oppressed. The happiness it brought he considered an illusion. Real happiness would come, said Marx, not by transcending the natural world but by improving it. Rather than deluding oneself by seeking refuge from life's misfortunes in an imaginary world, one must confront the ills of society and reform them. This last point is crucial. "The philosophers have only *interpreted* the world in different ways; the point is to *change it.*"[14]

The world could be rationally understood and changed, said Marx. People were free to make their own history, but to do so effectively, they must comprehend the inner meaning of history: the laws governing human affairs in the past and operating in the present. Marx adopted Hegel's view that history was not an assortment of unrelated and disconnected events, but a progressive development, which, like the growth of a plant, proceeded ineluctably according to its own inner laws (see page 535). For both Hegel and Marx, the historical process was governed by objective and rational principles. Marx also adopted Hegel's view that history advanced dialectically: that the clash of opposing forces propelled history into a higher stage.

However, Marx also broke with Hegel in crucial ways. For Hegel, it was the dialectical clash of opposing ideas that moved history into the next stage. For Marx, it was the clash of classes representing conflicting economic interests— what is called dialectical materialism—that accounted for historical change and progress. In Hegel's view, history was the unfolding of the Absolute Spirit, and a higher stage of development was produced by the synthesis of opposing ideas. According to Marx, Hegel's system failed because it was too metaphysical. It transcended the known world and downgraded reality to a mere attribute of Spirit. Marx saw Hegel's abstract philosophy as deflecting attention from the real world and its problems, which cried out for understanding and solution; it was a negation of life. For Marx, history was explainable solely in terms of natural processes—empirically verifiable developments.

As it is often said, Marx turned Hegel upside down. Hegel began with metaphysical consciousness—the Idea, Spirit, or God—which unfolded itself in human existence. Human beings and the human situation were attributes or emanations of the universal Idea, whose self-actualization gave essential meaning to the historical process. For Marx, the real relation of thought to human life was the exact reverse. The starting point and ultimate significance of history was to be found in the human social and economic environment, the natural conditions of life; thought was a product of these conditions. Marx valued Hegel's insight that history is a progressive and purposeful process, but he criticized Hegel for embedding this insight in metaphysical-theological fantasy. Hegel, said Marx, had made a mystical principle the real subject of history and thought. But, in truth, it is the "real man," the person who lives in and is conditioned by the objective world, the

only true reality, who is the center of history. History is not Spirit aspiring to self-actualization but people becoming fully human, fulfilling their human potential. The moving forces in history, said Marx, were economic and technological factors: the ways in which goods were produced and wealth distributed. They accounted for historical change and were the basis of all culture—politics, law, religion, morals, and philosophy. "The history of humanity," he concluded, "must therefore always be studied and treated in relation to the history of industry and exchange."[15]

According to Marx, material technology—the methods of cultivating land and the tools for manufacturing goods—determined society's social and political arrangements and its intellectual outlooks. For example, the hand mill, the loose yoke, and the wooden plow had given rise to feudal lords, whereas power-driven machines had spawned the industrial capitalists. As material technology expanded, it came into conflict with established economic, social, and political forms, and the resulting tension produced change. Thus, feudal patterns could not endure when power machinery became the dominant mode of production. Consequently, medieval guilds, communal agriculture, and even the domestic production of goods gave way to free labor, private property, and the factory system of manufacturing. As Marx put it, the expansion of technology triggered a change from feudal social and economic relationships to capitalist ones. Ultimately, the change in economic-technological conditions would become the cause for great political changes.

This process was most clearly demonstrated by the French Revolution. Radical changes in the economic foundations of society had taken place since the Middle Ages without corresponding political changes. However, the forces of economic change could not be contained in outdated political forms. In France, this tension exploded into revolution. Whatever their conscious intentions, said Marx, the bourgeois leaders of the French Revolution had scattered feudal remnants to the wind; they had promoted free competition and commercial expansion and transferred power from the landed aristocracy to the leaders of finance and industry. Not every revolutionary change in history is explosive, according to Marx, but whenever major economic changes take place, political and social changes must follow.

Class Conflict

Throughout history, said Marx, there has been a class struggle between those who own the means of production and those whose labor has been exploited to provide wealth for this upper class. This dialectical, or opposing, tension between classes has pushed history forward into higher stages. In the ancient world, when wealth was based on land, the struggle was between master and slave, patrician and plebeian; during the Middle Ages, when land was still the predominant mode of production, the struggle was between lord and serf. In the modern industrial world, two sharply opposed classes were confronting each other: the capitalists owning the factories, mines, banks, and transportation systems, and the exploited wage earners (the proletariat).

The class with economic power also controlled the state, said Marx and Engels. That class used political power to protect and increase its property and to hold down the laboring class. "Thus the ancient State was above all the slaveowners' state for holding down the slaves," said Engels, "as a feudal State was the organ of the nobles for holding down the . . . serfs, and the modern representative State is the instrument of the exploitation of wage-labor by capital."[16]

According to Marx and Engels the class that controlled material production also controlled mental production: that is, the ideas held by the ruling class became the dominant ideas of society. These ideas, presented as laws of nature or moral and religious standards, were regarded as the truth by oppressor and oppressed alike. In reality, however, these ideas merely reflected the special economic interests of the ruling class. Thus, said Marx, bourgeois ideologists would insist that natural rights and laissez faire were laws of nature having universal validity. But these "laws" were born of the needs of the bourgeoisie in its struggle to wrest power from an obsolete feudal regime and to protect its property from the state. Similarly, nineteenth-century slaveholders convinced themselves that slavery was morally right: that it had God's approval and was good for the slave. Slave owners and capitalist employers alike may have defended their labor systems by citing universal principles that they thought were true, but in reality their systems rested on a simple economic consideration: slave labor was good for the pocketbook of the slave owner, and wage labor was good in the same way for the capitalist.

The Destruction of Capitalism

Under capitalism, said Marx, workers knew only poverty. They worked long hours for low wages, suffered from periodic unemployment, and lived in squalid, overcrowded dwellings. Most monstrous of all, they were forced to send their young children into the factories. In *Capital*, Marx quotes a British official who declared in 1860:

> *Children of nine or ten years are dragged from their squalid beds at two, three, or four o'clock in the morning and compelled to work for a bare subsistence until ten, eleven, or twelve at night, their limbs wearing away, their frames dwindling, their faces whitening, and their humanity absolutely sinking into a stone-like torpor, utterly horrible to contemplate.*[17]

Capitalism also produced another kind of poverty, according to Marx: poverty of the human spirit. Under capitalism, the factory worker was reduced to a laboring beast, performing tedious and repetitive tasks in a dark, dreary, dirty cave—an altogether inhuman environment, which deprived people of their human sensibilities. Unlike the artisans in their own shops, factory workers found no pleasure and took no pride in their work; they did not have the satisfaction of creating a finished product that expressed their skills. Work, said Marx, should be a source of fulfillment for people. It should enable people to affirm their personalities and develop their potential. By treating people not as human beings but as cogs in the production process, capitalism alienated people from their work, from themselves, and from one another. Marx wrote:

> *[T]he worker . . . does not fulfil himself in his work but denies himself, has a feeling of misery rather than well-being, does not develop freely his mental and physical energies but is physically exhausted and mentally debased. . . . His work is not voluntary but imposed, forced*

labour. It is not the satisfaction of a need, but only a means for satisfying other needs. Its alien character is clearly shown by the fact that as soon as there is no physical or other compulsion it is avoided like the plague. . . .

. . . [T]he more the worker expends himself in work, . . . the poorer he becomes in his inner life, and the less he belongs to himself. . . . The worker puts his life into the object, and his life then belongs no longer to himself but to the object.[18]

Marx further asserted that capitalism dehumanized not only the workers, but the capitalists as well. Consumed by greed and a ruthless competitiveness, they abused workers and each other and lost sight of life's true meaning: the fulfillment of the individual's creative potential. Marx's view of the individual owed much to the Western humanist tradition, which aspired to shape self-sufficient and productive human beings who strive to develop their intellectual, esthetic, and moral capacities and relate to others as subjects, not as objects. By reducing people to commodities and human relations to a cash nexus, said Marx, capitalism thwarted the realization of this humanist vision.

Marx believed that capitalist control of the economy and the government would not endure forever. The capitalist system would perish just as the slave society of the ancient world and the feudal society of the Middle Ages had perished. For Marx, the destruction of capitalism was inevitable; it was necessitated by the law of historical materialism. From the ruins of a dead capitalist society, a new socioeconomic system, socialism, would emerge.

Marx predicted how capitalism would be destroyed. Periodic unemployment would increase the misery of the workers and intensify their hatred of capitalists. Small businesspeople and shopkeepers, unable to compete with the great capitalists, would sink into the ranks of the working class, greatly expanding its numbers. Society would become polarized into a small group of immensely wealthy capitalists and a vast proletariat, poor, embittered, and desperate. The monopoly of capital by the few would become a brake on the productive process. Growing increasingly conscious of their misery, the workers—aroused, educated, and organized by com-

munist intellectuals—would revolt. "Revolution is necessary," said Marx, "not only because the *ruling* class cannot be overthrown in any other way, but also because only in a revolution *can the class which overthrows it* rid itself of the accumulated rubbish of the past and become capable of reconstructing society."[19] The working-class revolutionaries would smash the government that helped the capitalists maintain their dominance. Then they would confiscate the property of the capitalists, abolish private property, place the means of production in the workers' hands, and organize a new society. The *Communist Manifesto* ends with a ringing call for revolution:

The Communists . . . openly declare that their ends can be attained only by the forcible overthrow of all existing social conditions. Let the ruling classes tremble at a Communist revolution. The proletarians have nothing to lose but their chains. They have a world to win.
Workingmen of all countries, unite![20]

Marx did not say a great deal about the new society that would be ushered in by the socialist revolution. With the destruction of capitalism, the distinction between capitalist and worker would cease and with it the class conflict. No longer would society be divided into haves and have-nots, oppressor and oppressed. Since this classless society would contain no exploiters, there would be no need for a state, which was merely an instrument for maintaining and protecting the power of the exploiting class. Thus, the state would eventually wither away. The production and distribution of goods would be carried out through community planning and communal sharing, replacing the capitalist system of competition. People would work at varied tasks, rather than being confined to one form of employment, just as Fourier had advocated (see page 548).

A revolutionary change in the conditions of life, Marx predicted, would produce a radical transformation of the human being. No longer debased by the self-destructive pursuit of profit and property and no longer victims of capitalist exploitation, people would become finer human beings—altruistic, sensitive, cooperative, and creative. United with others in a classless society free of exploitation and no longer divided by divergent interests, individuals would become truly communal and truly free beings (surpassing the merely political freedom achieved in the bourgeois state)—that is, they would become truly human.

Marxism's Appeal and Influence

Marxism had immense appeal for both the downtrodden and intellectuals. It promised to end the injustices of industrial society; it offered explanations that claimed the certainty of science for all the crucial events of history; and it assured adherents that history guaranteed the triumph of their cause. Far from being a scientific system, however, Marxism had the features of a religious myth. It had adapted and secularized several Judeo-Christian themes: an apocalyptic struggle between good and evil brings history to an end; humanity's messianic hopes are realized when human beings, emancipated from the slavery of exploitation, undergo spiritual regeneration and fulfill the promise of their human nature; and militant proletarians serve as the agents of salvation. Ultimately faith, not science, assures the triumph of the proletariat and the redemption of humanity. The writings of Marx (and later those of Lenin and Mao) became official dogma for the faithful. Those who deviated were branded as heretics and condemned for their sins. As Robert Tucker notes, it was this religious quality in Marxism that attracted many people to its cause:

> Like medieval Christianity, Marx's system undertakes to provide an integrated all-inclusive view of reality, an organization of all significant knowledge in an interconnected whole, a frame of reference within which all possible questions of importance are answered. . . .
> This, of course, indicates a source of his system's appeal to some modern men in whom the hold of traditional religion has loosened but the craving for an all-inclusive world-view remains alive and strong.[21]

Marx's influence grew during the second wave of industrialization in the closing decades of the nineteenth century, when class bitterness between the proletariat and the bourgeoisie seemed to worsen. Many workers thought that liberals and conservatives had no sympathy for their plight and that the only way to improve their lot was through socialist parties.

The emphasis Marx placed on economic forces has immeasurably broadened the perception of historians, who now explore the economic factors in historical developments. This approach has greatly expanded our understanding of Rome's decline, the outbreak of the French Revolution and the American Civil War, and other crucial developments. Marx's theory of class conflict has provided social scientists with a useful tool for analyzing social process. His theory of alienation has been adapted by sociologists and psychologists. Of particular value to social scientists is Marx's insight that the ideas people hold to be true and the values they consider valid often veil economic interests. On the political level, both the socialist parties of western Europe, which pressed for reform through parliamentary methods, and the communist regimes in Russia and China, which came to power through revolution, claimed to be heirs of Marx.

Critics of Marx

Critics point out serious weaknesses in Marxism. The rigid Marxist who tries to squeeze all historical events into an economic framework is at a disadvantage. Economic forces alone will not explain the triumph of Christianity in the Roman Empire, the fall of Rome, the Crusades, the French Revolution, modern imperialism, World War I, or the rise of Hitler. Economic explanations fall particularly flat in trying to account for the emergence of modern nationalism, whose appeal, resting on deeply ingrained emotional needs, crosses class lines. Most great struggles of the twentieth century have not been between classes but between nations.

Many of Marx's predictions or expectations have not materialized. Workers in Western lands did not become the oppressed and impoverished working class that Marx had described in the mid-nineteenth century. Because of increased productivity and the efforts of labor unions and reform-minded governments, Western workers improved their lives considerably, so that they now enjoy the highest standard of living in history. The tremendous growth of a middle class of professionals, civil service employees, and small-business people belies Marx's prediction that capitalist society would be polarized into a small group of very rich capitalists and a great mass of destitute workers. Marx believed that socialist revolutions would break out in the advanced industrialized lands. But the socialist revolutions of the twentieth century have occurred in underdeveloped, predominantly agricultural states. The state in communist lands, far from withering away, grew more centralized, powerful, and oppressive. In no country where communist revolutionaries seized power have people achieved the liberty that Marx desired. Nor, indeed, have communists been able to sustain a viable economic system. The phenomenal collapse of communist regimes in the former Soviet Union and Eastern Europe in recent years testifies to Marxism's failure. All these failed predictions and expectations seem to contradict Marx's claim that his theories rested on an unassailable scientific foundation.

ANARCHISM

Anarchism was another radical movement that attacked capitalism. Like Marxists, anarchists denounced the exploitation of workers and the coercive authority of government and envisioned a stateless society. Only by abolishing the state, said anarchists, could the individual live a free and full life. To achieve these ends, a small number of anarchists advocated revolutionary terrorism; others, like the great Russian novelist Leo Tolstoy, rejected all violence. These anarchists sought to destroy the state by refusing to cooperate with it.

Pierre Joseph Proudhon

Anarchists drew inspiration from Pierre Joseph Proudhon (1809–1865), a self-educated French printer and typesetter. Proudhon criticized social theorists who devised elaborate systems that regimented daily life, conflicted with human nature, and deprived people of their personal liberty. He desired a new society that maximized individual freedom. He looked back longingly to preindus-

trial society, which he saw as free of exploitation and corruption and of great manufacturers and financiers. He respected the dignity of labor and wanted to liberate workers from the exploitation and false values of industrial capitalism. An awakened working class would construct a new moral and social order.

Proudhon believed that people would deal justly with one another, respect one another, and develop their full potential in a society of small peasants, shopkeepers, and artisans. Such a society would not require a government; government only fosters privilege and suppresses freedom:

> To be governed is to be watched over, inspected, spied on, directed, legislated at, regulated, docketed, indoctrinated, preached at, controlled . . . censored, ordered about, by men who have neither the right nor the knowledge nor the virtue. To be governed means to be, at each operation, at each transaction, at each movement . . . registered, controlled, taxed . . . hampered, reformed, rebuked, arrested. It is to be, on the pretext of the general interest, taxed, drilled . . . exploited . . . repressed, fined, abused. . . . That's government, that's its justice, that's its morality.[22]

Proudhon was less a theorist than a man who could express passionately the disillusionment and disgust with the new industrial society that was developing in Europe.

Mikhail Bakunin

Anarchism had a particular appeal in Russia, where there was no representative government and no way, other than petitions to the tsar, to legally redress injustice. A repressive regime, economic backwardness, a youth movement passionately committed to improving the lives of the masses, and a magnetic leader, Mikhail Bakunin (1814–1876), all contributed to shaping the Russian anarchist tradition. Bakunin was a man of action who organized and fought for revolution and set an example of revolutionary fervor. The son of a Russian noble, he left the tsar's army to study philosophy in the West, where he was attracted to the ideas of Proudhon and Marx. He was arrested for participating in the

German revolution of 1848 and turned over to tsarist officials. He served six years in prison and was then banished to Siberia, from which he escaped in 1861.

Bakunin devoted himself to organizing secret societies that would lead the oppressed in revolt. Whereas Marx held that revolution would occur in the industrial lands through the efforts of a class-conscious proletariat, Bakunin wanted all oppressed people to revolt, including the peasants (the vast majority of the population in central and eastern Europe). Toward this end, he favored secret societies and terrorism.

Marx and Bakunin disagreed on one crucial issue of strategy. Marx wanted to organize the workers into mass political parties; Bakunin, on the other hand, held that revolutions should be fought by secret societies of fanatic insurrectionists. Bakunin feared that after the Marxists overthrew the capitalist regime and seized power, they would become the new masters and exploiters, using the state to enhance their own power. They would, said Bakunin, become a "privileged minority . . . of *ex-workers,* who, once they become rulers or representatives of the people, cease to be workers and begin to look down upon the toiling people. From that time on they represent not the people but themselves and their claims to govern the people."[23] Therefore, said Bakunin, once the workers capture the state, they should destroy it forever. Bakunin's astute prediction that a socialist revolution would lead state power to intensify rather than disappear has been borne out in the twentieth century.

Anarchists engaged in acts of political terrorism, including the assassination or attempted assassination of heads of state and key ministers, but they never waged a successful revolution. They failed to reverse the trend toward the concentration of power in industry and government, which would characterize the twentieth century.

LIBERALISM IN TRANSITION

In the early 1800s, European liberals were preoccupied with protecting the rights of the individual against the demands of the state. They championed laissez faire because they feared that state interference in the economy to redress social evils would threaten individual rights and the free market, which they thought were essential to personal liberty. They also favored property requirements for voting and officeholding because they were certain that the unpropertied and uneducated masses lacked the wisdom and experience to exercise political responsibility.

In the last part of the century, liberals began—not without reservation and qualification—to support extended suffrage and government action to remedy the abuses of unregulated industrialization. This growing concern for the welfare of the laboring poor coincided with and was influenced by an unprecedented proliferation of humanitarian movements on both sides of the Atlantic. Nurtured by the Enlightenment, as well as Christian teachings, reform movements called for the prohibition of child labor, schooling for the masses, humane treatment for prisoners and the mentally ill, equality for women, the abolition of slavery, and an end to war. By the beginning of the twentieth century, liberalism had evolved into liberal democracy, and laissez faire had been superseded by a reluctant acceptance of social legislation and government regulation. But from beginning to end, the central concern of liberals remained the protection of individual rights.

John Stuart Mill

The transition from laissez-faire liberalism to a more socially conscious and democratic liberalism is seen in the thought of John Stuart Mill (1806–1873), a British philosopher and statesman. Mill's *On Liberty* (1859) is the classic statement of individual freedom: that the government and the majority have no right to interfere with the liberty of another human being whose actions do no injury to others.

Mill regarded freedom of thought and expression, the toleration of opposing and unpopular viewpoints, as a necessary precondition for the shaping of a rational, moral, and civilized citizen. When we silence an opinion, said Mill, we hurt present and future generations. If the opinion is correct, "we are deprived of the opportunity of exchanging error for truth." If the opinion is wrong—and of this we can never be entirely certain—we "lose the clearer perception and livelier impression of truth produced by its collision

GUSTAVE COURBET (1819–1877): PROUDHON AND HIS DAUGHTERS. Pierre Joseph Proudhon condemned the new industrial society, which he believed restricted workers and spread poverty. He sought a society that would maximize individual freedom. His call for freedom influenced many social thinkers and was adopted by nineteenth-century anarchists. (*Giraudon/Art Resource, NY*)

with error."[24] Therefore, government has no right to force an individual to hold a view

> *because it will be better for him to do so, because it will make him happier, or because in the opinions of others, to do so would be wise, or even right. These are good reasons for remonstrating with him, or reasoning with him, or persuading him, or entreating him, but not for compelling him or visiting him with any evil in case he do otherwise.[25]*

Mill would place limits on the power of government, for in an authoritarian state citizens cannot develop their moral and intellectual potential. Although he feared the state as a threat to indi-

vidual liberty, Mill also recognized the necessity for state intervention to promote individual self-development: the expansion of individual moral, intellectual, and esthetic capacities. For example, he maintained that it was permissible for the state to require children to attend school against the wishes of their parents, to regulate hours of labor, to promote public health, and to provide workers' compensation and old age insurance.

In *Considerations on Representative Government* (1861), Mill endorsed the active participation of all citizens, including the lower classes, in the political life of the state. However, he also proposed a system of plural voting in which education and character would determine the number of votes each person was entitled to cast. In

CHILD MINE LABOR, REPORT OF A PARLIAMENTARY COMMISSION OF INQUIRY, 1842. In 1842 the British Parliament passed the Mines Act, prohibiting employment of girls and boys under the age of ten in coal mines. This report, detailing children being forced to drag sledge tubs through narrow tunnels, among other abuses, convinced Parliament to act. Further legislation regulating safety and labor practices in the coal industry followed after 1850. (*Hulton Deutsch Collection*)

this way Mill, a cautious democrat, sought to protect the individual from the tyranny of a politically unprepared majority.

Thomas Hill Green

The leading late-nineteenth-century figures in the shaping of a new liberal position in Britain were Thomas Hill Green (1836–1882), an Oxford University professor; D. G. Ritchie (1853–1903), who taught philosophy at Oxford and Saint Andrews; J. A. Hobson (1858–1940), a social theorist; and L. T. Hobhouse (1864–1929), an academic who also wrote for the *Manchester Guardian*. In general, these thinkers argued that laissez faire protected the interests of the economically powerful class and ignored the welfare of the nation. For example, Green valued private property but could not see how this principle helped the poor. "A man who possesses nothing but his powers of labor and who has to sell these to a capitalist for bare daily maintenance, might as well . . . be denied rights of property altogether."[26]

Green argued that the do-nothing state advocated by traditional laissez-faire liberalism condemned many citizens to destitution, ignorance, and despair. The state must preserve individual liberty and at the same time secure the common good

by promoting conditions favorable for the self-development of the majority of the population.

Liberalism, for Green, encompassed more than the protection of individual rights from an oppressive government. A truly liberal society, he said, gives people the opportunity to fulfill their moral potential and human capacities. And social reforms initiated by the state assisted in the realization of this broader conception of liberty. Green and other advocates of state intervention contended that the government has a moral obligation to create social conditions that permit individuals to make the best of themselves. Toward that end, the state should promote public health, ensure decent housing, and provide for education. The uneducated and destitute person cannot be morally self-sufficient or a good citizen, Green and other progressives argued.

Green and his colleagues remained advocates of capitalism but rejected strict laissez faire, which, they said, benefited only a particular class at the expense of the common good. Overcoming a traditional liberal mistrust of state power, they assigned the state a positive role in improving social conditions and insisted that state actions need not threaten individual freedom.

In general, by the beginning of the twentieth century, liberals in Britain increasingly acknowledged the need for social legislation. The foundations for the British welfare state were being laid. On the Continent, too, social welfare laws were enacted. To be sure, the motives behind such legislation were quite diverse and often had little to do with liberal sentiments (see Chapter 26). Nevertheless, in several countries liberalism was expanding into political and social democracy, a trend that would continue in the twentieth century.

Herbert Spencer: Rejection of State Intervention

Many traditional liberals regarded state intervention—"creeping socialism," they called it—as a betrayal of the liberal principle of individual freedom. They held to the traditional liberal view that the plight of the downtrodden was not a legitimate concern of the state. The new liberalism, they argued, would make people dependent on the state, thereby stifling industriousness, self-reliance, and thrift. Paternalistic government would cripple the working class morally by turning them into "grown-up babies."

In *The Man Versus the State* (1884), British philosopher Herbert Spencer rejected the idea "that evils of all kinds should be dealt with by the State." The outcome of state intervention, he said, is that "each member of the community as an individual would be a slave to the community as a whole . . . and the slavery will not be mild."[27] Committed to a philosophy of extreme individualism, Spencer never abandoned the view that the state was an evil and oppressive institution. He favored a society in which government would play the smallest role possible and individual freedom would be maximized, for when the power of the state is extended, however well-intentioned the motive, the freedom of the individual is restricted.

Spencer's extreme laissez faire and "rugged individualism" led him to oppose various forms of government intervention, including factory inspection, sanitary laws, pure food and drug requirements, a state postal system, compulsory public education, and public relief for the poor. "The function of Liberalism in the past was that of putting a limit to the powers of kings," he declared. "The function of true Liberalism in the future will be that of putting a limit to the powers of Parliament."[28]

A thoroughgoing Social Darwinist, Spencer saw the poor as incapable, weak, imprudent, and lazy—unfit to compete in the struggle for existence. For Spencer, state action was always misguided, for it tampered with nature's laws. "Instead of diminishing suffering, it eventually increases it. It favours the multiplication of those worst fitted for existence, and, by consequence, hinders the multiplication of those best fitted for existence—leaving, as it does, less room for them."[29] Government assistance creates an attitude of dependency among the poor; because they expect things to be done for them, they do not do things for themselves.

FEMINISM: EXTENDING THE PRINCIPLE OF EQUALITY

Another example of the expansion of liberalism was the emergence of feminist movements in western Europe and the United States. Feminists insisted that the principles of liberty and equality expressed by the philosophes and embodied in the French Declaration of the Rights of Man and of the Citizen and the American Declaration of Independence be applied to women. Thus, Olympe de Gouges's *Declaration of the Rights of Women* (1791), modeled after the Declaration of the Rights of Man and of the Citizen (1789), the French Revolution's tribute to Enlightenment ideals, stated: "Woman is born free and remains equal to man in rights. . . . The aim of every political association is the preservation of the natural . . . rights of man and woman."[30] Mary Wollstonecraft's *Vindication of the Rights of Woman* (see page 440), written under the influence of the French Revolution, protested against the prevailing subordination and submissiveness of women and the limited opportunities afforded them to cultivate their minds. She considered it an act of tyranny for women "to be excluded from a participation of the natural rights of mankind."[31] And in 1837, English novelist and economist Harriet Martineau observed: "One of the fundamental principles announced in the Declaration of Independence is that governments derive their just power from the consent of the governed. How can the political condition of women be reconciled with this?"[32]

In the United States, in the 1830s, Angelina

and Sarah Grimké spoke in public—something women rarely did—against slavery and for women's rights. In 1838, Sarah Grimke published *Letters on the Equality of the Sexes and the Condition of Women,* where she stated emphatically: "Men and women were Created Equal: they are both moral and accountable beings, and whatever is *right* for man to do is *right* for women. . . . How monstrous, how anti-Christian, is the doctrine that woman is to be dependent on man!"[33] The Woman's Suffrage Movement, holding its first convention in 1848 in Seneca Falls, New York, drew up a Declaration of Statements and Principles, which broadened the Declaration of Independence: "We hold these truths to be self-evident: that all men and women are created equal." The document protested "that woman has too long rested satisfied in the circumscribed limits which corrupt customs and a perverted application of the Scriptures have marked out for her" and called for the untiring effort of both men and women to secure for women "an equal participation with men in the various trades, professions, and commerce."[34]

In their struggle for equality, feminists had to overcome deeply ingrained premises about female inferiority and deficiencies. Even the philosophes, who often enjoyed the company of intelligent and sophisticated women in the famous salons, continued to view women as intellectually and morally inferior to men. Some philosophes, notably Condorcet, who wrote *Plea for the Citizenship of Women* (1791), argued for female emancipation, but they were the exception. Most philosophes concurred with Hume, who held that "nature has subjected" women to men and that their "inferiority and infirmities are absolutely incurable."[35] Rousseau, who believed that nature had granted men power over women, regarded traditional domesticity as a woman's proper role.

I would a thousand times rather have a homely girl, simply brought up, than a learned lady and a wit who would make a literary circle of my house and install herself as its president. A female wit is a scourge to her husband, her children, her friends, her servants, to everybody. From the lofty height of her genius, she scorns every womanly duty, and she is always trying to make a man of herself.[36]

Nevertheless, by clearly articulating the ideals of liberty and equality, the philosophes made a women's movement possible. The growing popularity of these ideals could not escape women, who measured their own position by them. Moreover, by their very nature, these ideals were expansive. Denying them to women would ultimately be seen as an indefensible contradiction.

Opponents of women's rights argued that feminist demands would threaten society by undermining marriage and the family. An article in the *Saturday Review,* an English periodical, declared that "It is not the interest of States . . . to encourage the existence of women who are other than entirely dependent on man as well for subsistence as for protection and love. . . . Married life is a woman's profession."[37] And in 1870, a member of the House of Commons wondered "what would become, not merely of woman's influence, but of her duties at home, her care of the household, her supervision of all those duties and surroundings which make a happy home . . . if we are to see women coming forward and taking part in the government of the country."[38] This concern for the family combined with a traditional biased view of woman's nature, as one writer for the *Saturday Review* revealed:

The power of reasoning is so small in women that they need adventitious help, and if they have not the guidance and check of a religious conscience, it is useless to expect from them self-control on abstract principles. They do not calculate consequences, and they are reckless when they once give way, hence they are to be kept straight only through their affections, the religious sentiment and a well-educated moral sense.[39]

In contrast to most of their contemporaries, some prominent men did support equal rights for women. "Can man be free if woman be slave?"[40] asked Shelley, who favored female suffrage. So too did Bentham and political economist William Thompson, who wrote *Appeal of One Half of the Human Race* (1825). John Stuart Mill thought that differences between the sexes (and between the classes) were due far more to education than to inherited inequalities. Believing that all people—women as well as men—should be able to develop their talents and intellects as fully as possible, Mill was an early champion of female equality, including women's suffrage. In 1867, Mill, as a member of Parliament, proposed that the suffrage be extended to women (the proposal was rejected by a vote of 194 to 74).

In 1851, Mill had married Harriet Taylor, a long-time friend and a recent widow. An ardent feminist, Harriet Mill influenced her husband's thought. In *The Subjection of Women* (1869), Mill argued that male dominance of women constituted a flagrant abuse of power. He described female inequality as a single relic of an old outlook that had been exploded in everything else. It violated the principle of individual rights and hindered the progress of humanity:

> . . . *the principle which regulates the existing social relations between the two sexes—the legal subordination of one sex to the other—is wrong in itself, and now one of the chief hindrances to human improvement . . . it ought to be replaced by a principle of perfect equality, admitting no power or privilege on the one side, nor disability on the other.*[41]

Mill considered it only just that women be admitted to all the functions and occupations until then reserved for men. The struggle for female rights became a major issue in several lands at the end of the nineteenth century and the beginning of the twentieth.

◆ ◆ ◆

NOTES

1. Quoted in George J. Becker, *Master European Realists of the Nineteenth Century* (New York: Ungar, 1982), pp. 30–31.

2. Cited in Damian Grant, *Realism* (London: Methuen, 1970), pp. 31–32.

3. Cited in F. W. J. Hemmings, ed., *The Age of Realism* (Atlantic Highlands, N.J.: Humanities Press, 1978), p. 152.

4. Quoted in Leonard J. Davis, "Gustave Flaubert," in *The Romantic Century*, eds. Jacques Barzun and George Stade, vol. 7 of *European Writers* (New York: Charles Scribner's Sons, 1985), p. 1382.

5. Émile Zola, *The Experimental Novel*, trans. Belle M. Sherman (New York: Haskell House, 1964), pp. 20–21, 23.

6. Quoted in Ernst Cassirer, *The Problem of Knowledge*, trans. William H. Woglom and Charles W. Hendel (New Haven, Conn.: Yale University Press, 1950), p. 244.

7. Quoted in Andrew D. White, *A History of the Warfare of Science with Theology in Christendom* (New York: Appleton, 1896), 1:71.

8. Excerpted in Richard Olson, ed., *Science as Metaphor* (Belmont, Calif.: Wadsworth, 1971), p. 124.

9. Andrew Carnegie, *The Gospel of Wealth* (New York: Century, 1900), pp. 4, 11.

10. Karl Pearson, *National Life from the Standpoint of Science* (London: Adam & Charles Black, 1905), pp. 21, 64.

11. Quoted in H. W. Koch, "Social Darwinism in the 'New Imperialism,'" in *The Origins of the First World War*, ed. H. W. Koch (New York: Taplinger, 1972), p. 341.

12. Ibid., p. 345.

13. Quoted in John C. Greene, *The Death of Adam* (New York: Mentor Books, 1961), p. 313.

14. Karl Marx, *Theses on Feuerbach*, excerpted in *Karl Marx: Selected Writings in Sociology and Social Philosophy*, eds. T. B. Bottomore and Maximilien Rubel (London: Watts, 1956), p. 69.

15. Karl Marx, *The German Ideology* (New York: International Publishers, 1939), p. 18.

16. Friedrich Engels, *The Origin of the Family, Private Property & the State,* in Emile Burns, *A Handbook of Marxism* (New York: Random House, 1935), p. 330.

17. Karl Marx, *Capital* (Chicago: Charles H. Kerr, 1912), 1:268.

18. Karl Marx, *Economic and Philosophical Manuscripts,* in *Karl Marx: Early Writings,* ed. T. B.

Bottomore (New York: McGraw-Hill, 1963), pp. 122, 124–125.

19. Marx, *German Ideology,* p. 69.

20. Karl Marx, *Communist Manifesto,* trans. Samuel Moore (Chicago: Henry Regnery, 1954), pp. 81–82.

21. Robert Tucker, *Philosophy and Myth in Karl Marx* (Cambridge: Cambridge University Press, 1972), p. 22.

22. Quoted in James Joll, *The Anarchists* (New York: Grosset & Dunlap, 1964), pp. 78–79.

23. Excerpted in G. P. Maximoff, ed., *The Political Philosophy of Bakunin* (Glencoe, Ill.: The Free Press, 1953), p. 287.

24. John Stuart Mill, *On Liberty* (Boston: Ticknor & Fields, 1863), p. 36.

25. Ibid., p. 22.

26. Thomas Hill Green, *Lectures on the Principles of Political Obligation* (Ann Arbor, Mich.: The University of Michigan Press, 1967), p. 219.

27. Herbert Spencer, *The Man Versus the State* (London: Watts, 1940), pp. 34, 49–50.

28. Ibid., p. 152.

29. Quoted in Anthony Arblaster, *The Rise and Decline of Liberalism* (London: Basil Blackwell, 1984), p. 290.

30. Excerpted in Eleanor S. Riemer and John C. Fout, eds., *European Women: A Documentary History, 1789–1945* (New York: Schocken Books, 1980), pp. 63–64.

31. Mary Wollstonecraft, *Vindication of the Rights of Woman* (London: Dent, 1929), pp. 11–12.

32. Excerpted in Gayle Graham Yates, ed., *Harriet Martineau on Women* (New Brunswick, N.J.: Rutgers University Press, 1985), p. 134.

33. Excerpted in Miriam Schneir, ed., *Feminism: The Essential Historical Writings* (New York: Vintage Books, 1972), pp. 40–41.

34. Ibid., pp. 76, 82.

35. Quoted in Bonnie S. Anderson and Judith P. Zinsser, *A History of Their Own* (New York: Harper & Row, 1988), 2:113.

36. Jean Jacques Rousseau, *Emile,* trans. Barbara Foxley (London: Dent, Everyman's Library, 1974), p. 370.

37. Quoted in J. A. and Olive Banks, *Feminism and Family Planning in Victorian England* (Liverpool: Liverpool University Press, 1965), p. 43.

38. Ibid., p. 46.

39. Ibid., p. 47.

40. Percy Bysshe Shelley, "The Revolt of Islam," canto 2, stanza 43, in *The Complete Poetical Works Of Percy Bysshe Shelley,* ed. Thomas Hutchinson (London: Oxford University Press, 1929), p. 63.

41. John Stuart Mill, *The Subjection of Women,* in *On Liberty, Etc.* (London: Oxford University Press, 1924), p. 427.

SUGGESTED READING

Andreski, Stanislav, ed., *The Essential Comte* (1974). An excellent collection of excerpts from Comte's works.

Becker, George, J., *Master European Realists of the Nineteenth Century* (1982). Discussions of Flaubert, Zola, Chekhov, and other realists.

Bullock, Alan, and Maurice Shock, eds., *The Liberal Tradition* (1956). Well-chosen selections from the writings of British liberals; the introduction is an excellent survey of liberal thought.

de Ruggiero, G., *The History of European Liberalism* (1927). A good starting point for a study of the subject.

Farrington, Benjamin, *What Darwin Really Said* (1966). A brief study of Darwin's work.

Grant, Damian, *Realism* (1970). A very good short survey.

Greene, J. C., *The Death of Adam* (1961). The impact of evolution on Western thought.

Hemmings, F. W. J., ed., *The Age of Realism* (1978). A series of essays exploring realism in various countries.

Hofstadter, Richard, *Social Darwinism in American Thought* (1955). A classic treatment of the impact of evolution on American conservatism, imperialism, and racism.

Joll, James, *The Anarchists* (1964). A fine treatment of anarchists, their lives and thought.

McLellan, David, *Karl Marx: His Life and Thought* (1977). A highly regarded biography.

———, ed., *Karl Marx: Selected Writings* (1977). A balanced selection of Marx's writings.

Manuel, Frank E., *The Prophets of Paris* (1965). Contains a valuable chapter on Comte.

Matthews, Betty, ed., *Marx: A Hundred Years On* (1983). A collection of eleven essays by noted authorities.

Nochlin, Linda, *Realism* (1971). The nature of realism; realism in art.

Richter, Melvin, *The Politics of Conscience* (1964). A study of Thomas Hill Green and his age.

Tucker, Robert, *The Marxian Revolutionary Idea* (1969). Marxism as a radical social philosophy.

———, *Philosophy and Myth in Karl Marx* (1972). Relationship of Marxist thought to German philosophy. Good treatment of Marx's early writings.

———, ed., *The Marx-Engels Reader* (1972). An anthology of Marx's essential writings.

REVIEW QUESTIONS

1. How did realism differ from romanticism?

2. Realism and naturalism reflected attitudes of mind shaped by science, industrialism, and secularism. Discuss this statement.

3. What was the relationship between positivism and science?

4. What was Comte's "law of the three stages"?

5. The theory of evolution had revolutionary consequences in areas other than science. Discuss this statement.

6. Why were Social Darwinist theories so popular?

7. What did Marx have in common with the philosophes of the Enlightenment?

8. What did Marx's philosophy of history owe to Hegel? How did it diverge from Hegel?

9. What relationship did Marx see between economics and politics?

10. What relationship did Marx see between economics and thought?

11. Why did Marxism attract followers?

12. Discuss Marx's historical importance.

13. What weaknesses in Marxism have critics pointed out?

14. Why was Marx convinced that capitalism was doomed? How would its destruction happen?

15. Why did Proudhon hate government?

16. In what ways did Bakunin and Marx differ?

17. Relate the theories of Mill, Green, and Spencer to the evolution of liberalism. Draw relevant comparisons and contrasts.

18. The feminist movement was an outgrowth of certain ideals that emerged during the course of Western history. Discuss this statement.

19. What arguments were used by opponents of equal rights for women?

CHAPTER 25

The Surge of Nationalism: From Liberal to Extreme Nationalism

*T*he revolutions of 1848 ended in failure, but nationalist energies were too powerful to contain. In 1867, Hungary gained the autonomy it had sought in 1848, and by 1870, the unification of both Italy and Germany was complete.

The leading architects of Italian and German unification were not liberal idealists or romantic dreamers of the type who had fought in the revolutions of 1848; they were tough-minded practitioners of *Realpolitik*, "the politics of reality." Shrewd and calculating statesmen, they respected power and knew how to wield it; focusing on the actual world, they dismissed ideals as illusory, noble sentiments that impeded effective action. Realpolitik was the political counterpart of realism and positivism. All three outlooks shared the desire to view things coldly and objectively as they are, rather than as idealists would like them to be.

Nationalism, gaining in intensity in the last part of the nineteenth century, was to become the dominant spiritual force in European life. Once Germany was unified, Pan-Germans sought to incorporate Germans living outside the Reich into the new Germany and to build a vast overseas empire. Russian Pan-Slavs dreamed of bringing the Slavs of eastern Europe under the control of "Mother Russia." Growing increasingly resentful of Magyar and German domination, the Slavic minorities of the Hapsburg Empire agitated for recognition of their national rights. In the late 1800s, nationalism became increasingly belligerent, intolerant, and irrational, threatening both the peace of Europe and the liberal-humanist tradition of the Enlightenment.

William I of Prussia, German Emperor in the Hall of Mirrors at Versailles, 1871. (*The Mansell Collection*)

CHRONOLOGY 25.1 Unification of Italy

1821	Austria suppresses Carbonari rebellion
1831–32	Austria suppresses another Carbonari insurrection
1832	Mazzini forms Young Italy
March 1848	Austrians are forced to withdraw from Milan and Venice
November 1848	Liberal revolution forces Pope to flee Rome
1848–49	Austria reasserts its authority in Milan and Venice; Louis Napoleon crushes revolutionaries in Rome
1858	Napoleon III agrees to help Piedmont-Sardinia against Austria
1859	War between Piedmont-Sardinia and Austria: Piedmont obtains Lombardy from Austria; Parma, Modena, Tuscany, and Romagna vote to join with Piedmont
1860	Garibaldi invades Kingdom of the Two Sicilies
March 17, 1861	Victor Emmanuel of Piedmont is proclaimed king of Italy
1866	Italy's alliance with Prussia against Austria results in annexation of Venetia by Italy
1870	Rome is incorporated into the Italian state and unity is achieved

THE UNIFICATION OF ITALY

In 1848, liberals had failed to drive the Austrians out of Italy and to unite the Italian nation. By 1870, however, Italian unification had been achieved. But the movement for unification had faced many obstacles.

Forces for and Against Unity

In 1815, Italy consisted of several separate states. In the south, a Bourbon king ruled the Kingdom of the Two Sicilies; the pope governed the Papal States in central Italy; Hapsburg Austria ruled Lombardy and Venetia in the north; and Hapsburg princes subservient to Austria ruled the duchies of Tuscany, Parma, and Modena. Piedmont in the northwest and the island of Sardinia were governed by an Italian dynasty, the House of Savoy. Besides all these political divisions, Italy was divided economically and culturally. Throughout the peninsula, attachment to the local region was stronger than devotion to national unity. Economic ties between north and south were weak; inhabitants of the northern Italian cities felt little closeness to Sicilian peasants. Except for the middle class, most Italians clung to the values of the Old Regime. Believing that society was ordered by God, they accepted without question rule by prince and pope and rejected the values associated with the French Revolution and the Enlightenment. To these traditionalists, national unity was also hateful. It would deprive the pope of his control over central Italy, introduce liberal ideas that would undermine clerical and aristocratic authority, and depose legitimate princes.

During the wars of the French Revolution, France had occupied Italy. The French eliminated many barriers to trade among the Italian states. They built roads, which improved links between the various regions, and they introduced a standard system of law over most of the land. The French had also given the Italian states constitutions, representative assemblies, and the concept of the state as a community of citizens.

The Italian middle class believed that expelling foreign rulers and forging national unity would continue the process of enlightened reform initiated by the French occupation and that this process would promote economic growth. Merchants and manufacturers wanted to abolish taxes on goods transported from one Italian state to another; they wanted roads and railways built to link the peninsula together; and they wanted to do away with the numerous systems of coinage and weights and measures, which complicated business transactions. Italians who had served Napoleon as local officials, clerks, and army officers resisted the restoration of clerical and feudal privileges, which denied them career opportunities.

Through novels, poetry, and works of history, an expanding intellectual elite awakened interest in Italy's glorious past. It insisted that a people who had built the Roman Empire and had produced the Renaissance must not remain weak and divided, their land occupied by Austrians. These sentiments appealed particularly to university students and the middle class. But the rural masses, illiterate and preoccupied with the hardships of daily life, had little concern for this struggle for national revival.

Failed Revolutions

Secret societies kept alive the hopes for liberty and independence from foreign rule in the period after 1815. The most important of these societies was the Carbonari, which had clubs in every state in Italy. In 1820, the Carbonari, its members drawn largely from the middle class and the army, enjoyed a few months of triumph in the Kingdom of the Two Sicilies. Supported by the army and militia, they forced King Ferdinand I to grant a constitution and a parliamentary government. But Metternich feared that the germ of revolution would spread to other countries. Supported by Prussia and Russia, Austria suppressed the constitutional government in Naples and another revolution, which broke out in Piedmont. In both cases, Austria firmly fixed an absolute ruler on the throne. In 1831–32, the Austrians suppressed another insurrection by the Carbonari, in the Papal States. During these uprisings, the peasants had given little support; indeed, they seemed to side with the traditional rulers.

After the failure of the Carbonari, a new generation of leaders emerged in Italy. One of them, Giuseppe Mazzini (1805–1872), dedicated his life to the creation of a united and republican Italy— a goal he pursued with extraordinary moral intensity and determination. Mazzini was both a romantic and a liberal. As a liberal, he fought for republican and constitutional government and held that national unity would enhance individual liberty. As a romantic, he sought truth through heightened feeling and intuition and believed that an awakened Italy would lead to the regeneration of humanity. Mazzini believed that just as Rome had provided law and unity in the ancient world and the Roman pope had led Latin Christendom during the Middle Ages, so a third Rome, a newly united Italy, would usher in a new age of free nations, personal liberty, and equality. This era would represent great progress for humanity: peace, prosperity, and universal happiness would replace conflict, materialism, and self-interest. Given to religious mysticism, Mazzini saw a world of independent states founded on nationality, republicanism, and democracy as the fulfillment of God's plan.

After his release from prison for participating in the insurrection of 1831, Mazzini went into exile and founded a new organization, Young Italy. Consisting of dedicated revolutionaries, many of them students, Young Italy was intended to serve as the instrument for the awakening of Italy and the transformation of Europe into a brotherhood of free peoples. This sacred struggle, said Mazzini, demanded heroism and sacrifice.

Mazzini believed that a successful revolution must come from below—from the people, moved by a profound love for their nation. They must overthrow the Hapsburg princes and create a democratic republic. The Carbonari had failed, he said, because they had staged only local uprisings and had no overall plan for the liberation and unification of Italy. This could be achieved only by a revolution of the masses. Mazzini had great charisma, determination, courage, and eloquence; he was also a prolific writer. His idealism attracted the intelligentsia and youth and kept alive the spirit of national unity. He infused the *Risorgimento,* the movement for Italian unity, with spiritual intensity.

Mazzini's plans for a mass uprising against Austria and the princes failed. In 1834, a band of Mazzini's followers attempted to invade Savoy from bases in Switzerland. But everything went wrong, and the invasion collapsed. Other setbacks occurred in 1837, 1841, and 1843–44. During the revolutions of 1848, however, Italian liberal-nationalists enjoyed initial successes (see page 572). In Sicily, revolutionaries forced King Ferdinand to grant a liberal constitution. The rulers of Tuscany and Piedmont-Sardinia promised constitutions. After five days of fighting, revolutionaries drove the Austrians out of Milan in Lombardy. The Austrians were also forced to evacuate Venice, where a republic was proclaimed. The pope fled Rome, and Mazzini was elected to an executive office in a new Roman Republic. However, the forces of reaction, led by Hapsburg Austria, regained their courage and authority, and crushed the revolutionary movements one by one. French troops dissolved the infant Roman Republic and restored Pope Pius IX to power. Italy remained divided, and Austria still ruled the north.

Cavour and Victory over Austria

The failure of the revolutions of 1848 contained an obvious lesson: that Mazzini's approach, an armed uprising by aroused masses, did not work. It failed because the masses were not deeply committed to the nationalist cause and the revolutionaries were no match for the Austrian army. Italian nationalists now hoped that the Kingdom of Piedmont-Sardinia, ruled by an Italian dynasty, would expel the Austrians and lead the drive for unity. Count Camillo Benso di Cavour (1810–1861), the chief minister of Piedmont-Sardinia, became the architect of Italian unity.

Unlike Mazzini, Cavour was neither a dreamer nor a speechmaker, but a cautious and practical politician who realized that mass uprisings could not succeed against Austrian might.

Moreover, mistrusting the common people, he did not approve of Mazzini's goal of a democratic republic. Cavour had no precise plan for unifying Italy. His immediate aim was to increase the territory of Piedmont by driving the Austrians from northern Italy and incorporating Lombardy and Venetia into Piedmont-Sardinia. But this expulsion could not be accomplished without allies, for Austria was a great power and Piedmont a small state. To improve Piedmont's image in foreign affairs, Cavour launched a reform program to strengthen the economy. He reorganized the currency, taxes, and the national debt; in addition, he had railways and steamships built, fostered improved agricultural methods, and encouraged new businesses. Within a few years, Piedmont had become a progressive modern state.

In 1855, Piedmont joined England and France in the Crimean War against Russia. Cavour had no quarrel with Russia but sought the friendship of Britain and France and a chance to be heard in world affairs. At the peace conference, Cavour was granted an opportunity to denounce Austria for occupying Italian lands.

After the peace conference, Cavour continued to encourage anti-Austrian feeling among Italians and to search for foreign support. He found a supporter in Napoleon III (1852–1870), the French emperor, who hoped that a unified northern Italy would become an ally and client of France.

In 1858, Cavour and Napoleon III reached a secret agreement. If Austria attacked Piedmont, France would aid the Italian state. Piedmont would annex Lombardy and Venetia and parts of the Papal States. For its assistance, France would obtain Nice and Savoy from Piedmont. With this agreement in his pocket, Cavour cleverly maneuvered Austria into declaring war (he did so by strengthening Piedmont's army and encouraging volunteers from Austrian-controlled Lombardy to join it), for it had to appear that Austria was the aggressor.

Supported by French forces and taking advantage of poor Austrian planning, Piedmont conquered Lombardy and occupied Milan. But Napoleon III quickly had second thoughts. If Piedmont took any of the pope's territory, French Catholics would blame their own leader. Even

VICTOR EMMANUEL AND GARIBALDI AT THE BRIDGE OF TEANO, 1860. The unification of Italy was the work of the romantic liberal Giuseppe Mazzini, the practical politician Count Cavour, and the seasoned revolutionary Giuseppe Garibaldi. Selflessly, Garibaldi turned over his conquests in the south to Victor Emmanuel in 1861. (*Scala/Art Resource, NY*)

more serious was the fear that Prussia, suspicious of French arms, would aid Austria. For these reasons Napoleon III, without consulting Cavour, signed an armistice with Austria. Piedmont would acquire Lombardy, but no more. An outraged Cavour demanded that his state continue the war until all northern Italy was liberated, but King Victor Emmanuel of Piedmont accepted the Austrian peace terms.

The victory of Piedmont-Sardinia, however, proved greater than Cavour had anticipated. During the conflict, patriots in Parma, Modena, Tuscany, and Romagna (one of the Papal States) had seized power. These new revolutionary governments voted to join with Piedmont. Neither France nor Austria would risk military action to thwart Piedmont's expansion. In return for Napoleon III's acquiescence, Piedmont ceded Nice and Savoy to France.

Garibaldi and Victory in the South

Piedmont's success spurred revolutionary activity in the Kingdom of the Two Sicilies. In the spring of 1860, some one thousand red-shirted adventurers and patriots led by Giuseppe Garibaldi (1807–1882) landed in Sicily. They were determined to liberate the land from its Bourbon ruler, and they succeeded.

An early supporter of Mazzini, Garibaldi had been forced to flee Italy to avoid arrest for his revolutionary activities. He spent thirteen years in South America, where he took part in revolutionary movements. There he learned the skills of the revolutionary's trade and toughened his body and will for the struggle that lay ahead.

Garibaldi held exceptional views for his day. He supported the liberation of all subject nationalities, female emancipation, the right of workers to organize, racial equality, and the abolition of capital punishment. But the cause of Italian national unity was his true religion. Whereas Cavour set his sights primarily on extending Piedmont's control over northern Italy, Garibaldi dedicated himself to the creation of a unified Italy.

Garibaldi returned to Italy just in time to fight in the revolution of 1848. He was an extraordinary leader, who captivated the hearts of the people and won the poor and illiterate to the cause of Italian nationality. A young Italian artist who fought beside Garibaldi in 1849 said of his commander:

> I shall never forget that day when I first saw him on his beautiful white horse. He reminded us of . . . our Savior . . . everyone said the same. I could not resist him. I went after him; thousands did likewise. He only had to show himself. We all worshipped him. We could not help it.[1]

After the liberation of Sicily in 1860, Garibaldi invaded the mainland. He occupied Naples without a fight and prepared to advance on Rome. In this particular instance, Garibaldi's success confirmed Mazzini's belief that a popular leader could arouse the masses to heroic action.

Cavour feared that an assault on Rome by Garibaldi would lead to French intervention. Napoleon III had pledged to defend the pope's lands, and a French garrison had been stationed in Rome since 1849. Moreover, Cavour considered Garibaldi too impulsive and rash, too attracted to republican ideals, and too popular to lead the struggle for unification.

Cavour persuaded Napoleon III to approve an invasion of the Papal States by Piedmont to head off Garibaldi. A papal force offered only token opposition, and the Papal States of Umbria and the Marches soon voted for union with Piedmont, as did Naples and Sicily. Refusing to trade on his prestige with the masses to fulfill personal ambition, Garibaldi turned over his conquests to Piedmont's King Victor Emmanuel, who was declared king of Italy in 1861.

Italian Unification Completed

Two regions still remained outside the control of the new Italy: the city of Rome, ruled by the pope and protected by French troops; and Venetia, occupied by Austria. Cavour died in 1861, but the march toward unification continued. During the conflict between Prussia and Austria in 1866, Italy sided with the victorious Prussians and was rewarded with Venetia. During the Franco–Prussian War of 1870, France withdrew its garrisons from Rome; much to the anger of the pope, Italian troops marched in, and Rome was declared the capital of Italy.

THE UNIFICATION OF GERMANY

In 1848, German liberals and nationalists, believing in the strength of their ideals, had naively underestimated the power of the conservative Old Order. After the failed revolution, some disenchanted revolutionaries retained only a half-hearted commitment to liberalism or embraced conservatism; others fled the country, weakening the liberal leadership. All liberals came to doubt the effectiveness of revolution as a way to transform Germany into a unified state; all gained a new respect for the realities of power. Abandoning idealism for realism, liberals now thought that German unity would be achieved through Prussian arms, not liberal ideals.

Prussia, Agent of Unification

During the late seventeenth and eighteenth centuries, Prussian kings had fashioned a rigorously trained and disciplined army. The state bureaucracy, often staffed by ex-soldiers, perpetuated the military mentality. As the chief organizations in the state, the army and the bureaucracy drilled into the Prussian people a respect for discipline and authority.

The Prussian throne was supported by the Junkers. These powerful aristocrats, who owned vast estates farmed by serfs, were exempt from most taxes and dominated local government in their territories. The Junkers' commanding position made them officers in the royal army, diplomats, and leading officials in the state bureaucracy. The Junkers knew that a weakening of the king's power would lead to the loss of their own aristocratic prerogatives.

In France in the late 1700s, a powerful and

CHRONOLOGY 25.2 Unification of Germany

1815	Formation of the German Confederation
1834	Establishment of the Zollverein under Prussian leadership
1848	Failure of the liberals to unify Germany
1862	Bismarck becomes chancellor of Prussia
1864	Austria and Prussia defeat Denmark in a war over Schleswig-Holstein
1866	Seven Weeks' War between Austria and Prussia: Prussia emerges as the dominant power in Germany and organizes the North German Confederation
1870–71	Franco-Prussian War
January 18, 1871	William I becomes German kaiser

politically conscious middle class had challenged aristocratic privileges. The Prussian monarchy and the Junkers had faced no such challenge, for the Prussian middle class at that time was small and without influence. The idea of the rights of the individual did not deeply penetrate Prussian consciousness, nor did it undermine the Prussian tradition of obedience to military and state authority.

Reforms from Above The reform movement that began after Napoleon had completely routed the Prussians at Jena arose from distress at the military collapse and at the apathy of the Prussian population. High bureaucrats and military men demanded reforms that would draw the people closer to their country and king. These leaders had learned the great lesson of the French Revolution: a devoted citizen army fights more effectively than oppressed serfs. To imbue all classes with civic pride, the reformers abolished hereditary serfdom, gave the urban middle class a greater voice in city government, laid the foundations for universal education, and granted full citizenship to Jews. To improve the army's morale, they eliminated severe punishments and based promotions on performance rather than birth.

But the reformers failed to give Prussia a constitution and parliamentary institutions. The middle class still had no voice in the central government. Monarchical power persisted, and the economic, political, and military power of the Junkers remained unbroken. Thus, liberalism had an unpromising beginning in Prussia. In France, the bourgeoisie had instituted reforms based on the principles of liberty and equality; in Prussia, the bureaucracy introduced reforms to strengthen the state, not to promote liberty. A precedent had been established: reform in Prussia would come from conservative rulers, not from the efforts of a middle class aroused by liberal ideals.

In 1834, under Prussian leadership, the German states, with the notable exception of Austria, had established the *Zollverein,* a customs union, which abolished tariffs between the states. The customs union stimulated economic activity and promoted a desire for greater unity. Businessmen, particularly, felt that having thirty-nine states in Germany was an obstacle to economic progress. The Zollverein provided the economic foundations for the political unification of Germany, and it led many Germans to view Prussia, not Austria, as the leader of the unification movement.

Liberals' Failure During the restoration, the ideas of legal equality, political liberty, and careers open to talent found favor with the Prussian bourgeoisie. Like the French bourgeois of the Old Regime, Prussian bankers, manufacturers, and

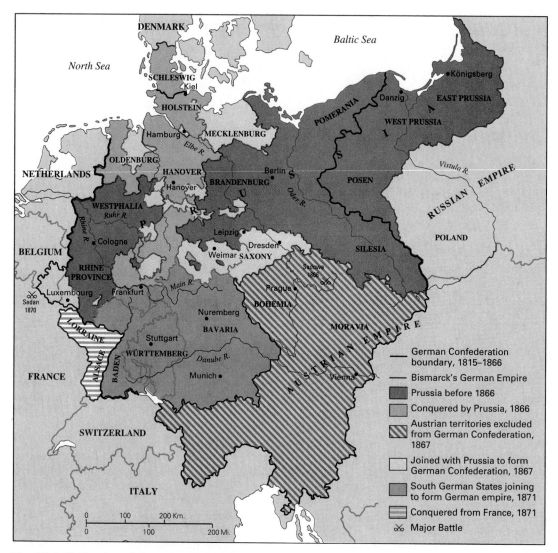

MAP 25.1 Unification of Germany, 1866–1871

lawyers hated a system that denied them social recognition and political influence but rewarded idle sons of the nobility with the best positions. They also denounced government regulations and taxes, which hampered business, and they loathed the rigorous censorship, which stifled free thought. The peasants and artisans, concerned with economic survival, respectful of tradition, and suspicious of new ideas, had little comprehension of or sympathy for liberal principles.

During the revolution of 1848, liberals failed to wrest power from the monarchy and aristoc-

racy and create a unified Germany. Frederick William IV (1840–1861) had refused the crown offered him by the Frankfurt Assembly (see page 569). The Prussian monarch could not stomach German unity created by a revolution of commoners. But a German union fashioned and headed by a conservative Prussia was different and proved attractive to Frederick William. In 1849, Prussia initiated a diplomatic campaign toward this end. Austria resisted this maneuver because it was determined to retain its preeminence in German affairs. Faced with Hapsburg resistance, Prussia renounced its plans for a German union and agreed to the reestablishment of the German Confederation (see page 558). This political humiliation taught Frederick William an obvious lesson: before Prussia could extend its hegemony over the other German states, Austrian influence in German affairs would have to be eliminated.

Bismarck and the Road to Unity

In 1858, Frederick William IV, by then mentally deranged, surrendered control of the government to his brother, who became William I (1861–1888), king of Prussia, when Frederick William died. William also regarded Austria as the chief barrier to the extension of Prussian power in Germany. This was one reason why he called for a drastic reorganization of the Prussian army. But the liberals in the lower chamber of the Prussian parliament blocked passage of the army reforms, for they feared that the reforms would greatly increase the power of the monarchy and the military establishment. Unable to secure passage, William withdrew the reform bill and asked the lower chamber for additional funds to cover government expenses. When parliament granted these funds, he used the money to institute the army reforms. Learning from its mistake, the lower chamber would not approve the new budget in 1862 without an itemized breakdown.

A conflict had arisen between the liberal majority in the lower chamber and the crown. If the liberals won, they would, in effect, establish parliamentary control over the king and the army. At this critical hour, King William asked Otto von Bismarck (1815–1898) to lead the battle against parliament.

Descended on his father's side from an old aristocratic family, Bismarck was a staunch supporter of the Prussian monarchy and the Junker class and a devout patriot. He yearned to increase the territory and prestige of his beloved Prussia and to protect the authority of the Prussian king, who, Bismarck believed, ruled by the grace of God. Liberals were outraged by Bismarck's domineering and authoritarian manner and his determination to preserve monarchical power and the aristocratic order. Set on continuing the reorganization of the army and deter-

OTTO VON BISMARCK. Bismarck (1815–1899) the Iron Chancellor, was instrumental in unifying Germany. A conservative, he resisted parliament's efforts to weaken the monarch's power. Here he is portrayed in his youth before becoming chancellor. (*Photo AKG London*)

mined not to bow to parliamentary pressure, Bismarck ordered the collection of taxes without parliament's approval—an action that would have been unthinkable in Britain or the United States.

When the lower chamber continued to withhold funds, Bismarck dismissed the chamber, imposed strict censorship on the press, arrested outspoken liberals, and fired liberals from the civil service. The liberals protested against these arbitrary and unconstitutional moves, but they did not use force. Since the army fully supported the government and there was no significant popular support for challenging the government, an armed uprising would have failed. What led to a resolution of the conflict was Bismarck's extraordinary success in foreign affairs.

Wars with Denmark and Austria To Bismarck, a war between Austria and Prussia seemed inevitable, for only by removing Austria from German affairs could Prussia extend its dominion over the other German states. Bismarck's first move, however, was not against Austria but against Denmark. The issue that led to the war in 1864 was enormously complex. Simplified, the issue was that Bismarck (and German nationalists) wanted to free the two duchies of Schleswig and Holstein from Danish control. Both territories, which contained a large number of Germans, had been administered by Denmark, but in 1863, Schleswig was incorporated into the Danish realm. Hoping to prevent Prussia from annexing the territories, Austria joined Prussia as an ally. After Denmark's defeat, Austria and Prussia tried to decide the ultimate disposition of the territories. What Austria wanted was a joint Austrian and Prussian occupation of the disputed regions. But the negotiations broke down. Bismarck used the dispute to goad Austria into war. The Austrians, on their side, were convinced that Prussia must be defeated for Austria to retain its influence over German affairs.

In the Austro-Prussian war of 1866, Prussia, with astonishing speed, assembled its forces and overran Austrian territory. At the battle of Sadowa (or Königgrätz), Prussia decisively defeated the main Austrian forces and the Seven Weeks' War ended. Prussia took no territory from Austria, but the latter agreed to Prussia's annexation of Schleswig and Holstein and a number of small German states. Prussia, moreover, organized a confederation of North German states, from which Austria was excluded. In effect, Austria was removed from German affairs, and Prussia became the dominant power in Germany.

The Triumph of Nationalism and Conservatism over Liberalism The Prussian victory had a profound impact on political life within Prussia. Bismarck was the man of the hour, the great hero who had extended Prussia's power. Most liberals forgave Bismarck for his authoritarian handling of parliament. The liberal press, which had previously denounced Bismarck for running roughshod over the constitution, now lionized him. Prussians were urged to concentrate on the glorious tasks ahead and put aside the constitutional struggle, which, in contrast, appeared petty and insignificant.

Bismarck recognized the great appeal of nationalism and used it to expand Prussia's power over other German states and strengthen Prussia's voice in European affairs. By heralding his state as the champion of unification, Bismarck gained the support of nationalists throughout Germany. In the past, the nationalist cause had belonged to the liberals, but Bismarck appropriated it to promote Prussian expansion and conservative rule.

Prussia's victory over Austria, therefore, was a triumph for conservatism and nationalism and a defeat for liberalism. The liberal struggle for constitutional government in Prussia collapsed. The Prussian monarch retained the right to override parliamentary opposition and act on his own initiative. In 1848, Prussian might had suppressed a liberal revolution; in 1866, liberals, beguiled by Bismarck's military triumphs, gave up the struggle for responsible parliamentary government. They had traded political freedom for Prussian military glory and power.

The capitulation of Prussian liberals demonstrated the essential weakness of the German liberal tradition. German liberals displayed a diminishing commitment to the principles of parliamentary government and a growing fascination with power, military triumph, and territorial expansion. Bismarck's words, written in 1858, turned out to be prophetic: "Exalt his self-esteem toward foreigners and the Prussian forgets whatever bothers him about conditions at home."[2] The liberal dream of a united Germany had been preempted by conservatives. Enthralled by Bismarck's achievement, many liberals abandoned liberalism and threw their support behind the authoritarian Prussian state. And Germans of all classes acquired an adoration for Prussian militarism and for the power state, with its Machiavellian guideline that all means are justified if they result in the expansion of German power. In 1848, German liberals had called for "Unity and Freedom." What Bismarck gave them was unity and authoritarianism.

War with France Prussia emerged from the war with Austria as the leading power in the North German Confederation; the Prussian king controlled the armies and foreign affairs of the states within the confederation. To complete the unification of Germany, Bismarck would have to draw the South German states into the new confederation. But the South German states, Catholic and hostile to Prussian authoritarianism, feared being absorbed by Prussia.

Bismarck hoped that a war between Prussia and France would ignite the nationalist feelings of the South Germans, causing them to overlook the differences that separated them from Prussia. Napoleon III, the emperor of France, was not averse to war either. The creation of a powerful North German Confederation had frightened the French, and the prospect that the South German states might one day add their strength to the new Germany was terrifying. Both France and Prussia had parties that advocated war.

A cause for war arose over the succession to the vacated Spanish throne. Under strong consideration was Prince Leopold of Hohenzollern–Sigmaringen, a distant relative of King William of Prussia. France vehemently opposed the candidacy of Leopold, for his accession might lead to Prussian influence being extended into Spain. William, seeking to preserve the peace, urged Prince Leopold to withdraw his name from consideration.

The French ambassador then demanded that William give formal assurance that no Hohenzollern would ever again be a candidate for the Spanish crown. William refused. In a telegram sent from Ems to Berlin, he informed Bismarck of his conversation with the French ambassador. With the support of high military leaders, Bismarck edited the telegram. The revised version gave the impression that the Prussian king and the French ambassador had insulted each other. Bismarck wanted to inflame French feeling against Prussia and arouse German opinion against France. He succeeded. In both Paris and Berlin, crowds of people, gripped by war fever, demanded satisfaction. When France declared a general mobilization, Prussia followed suit; Bismarck had his war.

With the memory of the great Napoleon still strong, the French expected a quick victory. But the poorly prepared and incompetently led French army could not withstand the powerful Prussian military machine. The South German states, as Bismarck had anticipated, came to the aid of Prussia. Quickly and decisively routing the French forces and capturing Napoleon III, the Prussians went on to besiege Paris. Faced with starvation, Paris surrendered in January 1871. France was compelled to pay a large indemnity and to cede to Germany the border provinces of Alsace and Lorraine—a loss that French patriots could never accept.

The Franco-Prussian War completed the unification of Germany. On January 18, 1871, at Versailles, the German princes granted the title of German kaiser (emperor) to William I. A powerful nation had arisen in central Europe. Its people were educated, disciplined, and efficient; its industries and commerce were rapidly expanding; its army was the finest in Europe. Vigorous, confident, and intensely nationalistic, the new German Empire would be eager to play a greater role in world affairs. No nation in Europe was a match for the new Germany. Metternich's fears had been realized: a Germany dominated by Prussia had upset the balance of power. The unification of Germany created fears, tensions, and rivalries that would culminate in world war.

NATIONALITY PROBLEMS IN THE HAPSBURG EMPIRE

In Italy and Germany, nationalism had led to the creation of unified states; in Austria, nationalism eventually caused the destruction of the centuries-old Hapsburg dynasty. A mosaic of different nationalities, each with its own history and traditions, the Austrian Empire could not survive in an age of intense nationalism. England and France had succeeded in unifying peoples of different ethnic backgrounds, but they did so during the Middle Ages, when ethnic consciousness was still rudimentary. The Austrian Empire, on the other hand, had to weld together and reconcile antagonistic nationalities when nationalistic consciousness was high. The empire's collapse in the final stages of World War I was the culmination of years of antagonism between its different peoples.

In the first half of the nineteenth century, the Germans, constituting less than one-quarter of the population, were the dominant national group in the empire. But Magyars, Poles, Czechs, Slovaks, Croats, Romanians, Ruthenians, and Italians were experiencing national self-awareness. Poets and writers who had been educated in

Latin, French, and German began to write in their mother tongue and extol its splendor. By searching their past for glorious ancestors and glorious deeds, writers kindled pride in their native history and folklore and aroused anger against past and present injustices.

In 1848–49, the Hapsburg monarchy had extinguished the Magyar bid for independence, the Czech revolution in Prague, and the uprisings in the Italian provinces of Lombardy and Venetia. Greatly alarmed by these revolutions, the Austrian power structure resolved to resist pressures for political rights by strengthening autocracy and tightening the central bureaucracy. German and Germanized officials took over administrative and judicial duties formerly handled on a local level. An expanded secret police stifled liberal and nationalist expressions. The various nationalities, of course, resented these efforts at centralization and repression.

Magyarization

The defeats by France and Piedmont in 1859 and by Prussia in 1866 cost Austria its two Italian provinces. The defeat by Prussia also forced the Hapsburg monarchy to make concessions to the Magyars, the strongest of the non-German nationalities; for without a loyal Hungary, the Hapsburg monarchy could suffer other humiliations. The Settlement of 1867 split the Hapsburg territories into Austria and Hungary. The two countries retained a common ruler, Francis Joseph (1848–1916), who was emperor of Austria and king of Hungary. Hungary gained complete control over its internal affairs: the administration of justice and education. Foreign and military affairs, as well as common financial concerns, were dealt with by a ministry consisting of delegates from both lands.

With the Settlement of 1867, Magyars and Germans became the dominant nationalities in the empire. The other nationalities felt that the German-Magyar political, economic, and cultural domination blocked their own national aspirations. Nationality struggles in the half-century following the Settlement of 1867 consumed the energies of the Austrians and Hungarians. In both lands, however, the leaders failed to solve the problem of minorities, a failure that ulti-

mately led to the dissolution of the empire during the last weeks of World War I.

The nationality problems in Hungary differed substantially from those in Austria. Constituting slightly less than half the population of Hungary, the Magyars were determined to retain their hegemony over the other minorities: Romanians, Slovaks, Ruthenians, Serbs, Croats, and Jews. In the first phase of their national struggle, the Hungarians had sought to liberate their nation from German domination. In the second phase, after 1867, the landholding aristocracy, which ruled Hungary, tried to impose the Magyar language and traditions on the other nationalities. Non-Magyars who learned the Magyar language and considered themselves Hungarians could participate as equals in Hungarian society. Those who resisted were viewed as traitors and conspirators and faced severe penalties. Non-Magyars were largely excluded from voting and virtually barred from government jobs, which were reserved for Magyars or those who had adopted Magyar language and culture.

The government tightly controlled the non-Magyar peoples. It suppressed their cultural organizations and newspapers, and the great majority of public schools, even in predominantly non-Magyar regions, carried on instruction largely in Magyar. Protests by the nationalities against this forced Magyarization often led to jail sentences. The repressive measures strengthened the Slavs' and Romanians' hatred of the regime. At the same time, however, Magyarization brought economic and cultural opportunities. Jews in particular accepted the Magyar government and took advantage of what it offered.

But nationality movements within Hungary constituted less of a threat to the preservation of the Austro-Hungarian Empire than did Magyar nationalism itself. The Independence party, whose influence grew after 1900, began to demand a complete end to the link with Austria and the "cursed common institutions."

German Versus Czech

The Austrian population of the Dual Monarchy was made up of Germans (one-third) and Slavs (two-thirds). Hungary strove to forge a unified state by assimilating the non-Magyars; Austria,

THE YOUNG CZECH PARTY DEMONSTRATING IN THE AUSTRIAN PARLIAMENT, 1900. The Hapsburg Empire was burdened by conflicts between its different nationalities. In Bohemia, Czechs and Germans often engaged in violent confrontations as Czechs pressed for recognition of their language and rights. (*Osterreichische Nationalbibliothek*)

on the other hand, made no deliberate effort to Germanize the Slavs. It did not try to make German the official language of the state or to dissociate non-Germans from their native traditions. In Austria, elementary school students were usually taught in their mother tongues. The state acknowledged the equal right of all the country's languages in the schools, in administration, and in public life.

But the nationality problem was aggravated by the haughty attitude of the German Austrians, who considered themselves culturally superior to the Slavic peoples. Neither the Germans nor the Magyars would allow the Czechs and the South Slavs the same control over domestic affairs that had been granted the Magyars in the Settlement of 1867. The Germans believed that they had a historic mission to retain their dominance, an attitude that clashed with the Slavs' growing national consciousness. And the Slavic masses were not only aroused by nationalism but, with the spread of liberal-democratic ideas, were also gaining the vote.

The most serious conflict occurred in Bohemia between the Germans and the Czechs, the largest group of Slavs. The Czechs had the highest literacy rate in the Dual Monarchy, and Bohemia had become the industrial heartland of the empire. The emergence of a Czech university and Czech youth associations and the growth of Czech literature stimulated the development of a national consciousness. Championed by a growing middle class, which had made considerable economic and cultural gains, nationalism among the Czechs of Bohemia intensified in the final decades of the nineteenth century. Between the Czechs and the Germans there was great animosity.

Concentrated primarily in the Sudetenland, the German Bohemians regarded themselves as culturally and morally superior to the Czechs and wanted to preserve their predominance in the government's administration. Considering the Czech language fit only for peasants and servants, the Sudeten Germans deemed it ridiculous that Czech be placed on an equal level with the German tongue. The two groups argued over whether street signs and menus should be written in German or Czech. Czech nationalists wanted the same constitutional independence that had been granted to the Hungarians; Sudeten Germans demanded that Austria remain a centralized state governed by a German-dominated bureaucracy. Violent demonstrations, frenzied oratory, and strident editorials fanned the flames of hatred. A mounting resentment against the Czechs and a growing admiration for Bismarck's new Germany led some Austrian Germans, particularly the Sudeten Germans, to seek union with Germany. Georg von Schönerer, the leader of the Austrian Pan-German movement, denounced both Slavs and Jews as racial inferiors and called for the creation of a Greater Germany.

The clash between Czechs and Germans turned uglier when in 1897 a new prime minister, Count Casimir Badeni, required government officials in Bohemia to know both the German and the Czech languages. This requirement was no hardship for Czech officials, since most of them already knew German. Few German officials, however, knew Czech or cared to learn it. Riots broke out in various cities, German and Czech deputies in parliament engaged in fistfights, and the emperor was forced to dismiss Badeni. Eventually, the reform was dropped, but Czech-German hostilities remained intense.

South Slavs

The problem of the South Slavs in Austria—Serbs, Croats, and Slovenes—differed from that of the Czechs. No Czech state served as a magnet for the Czechs living within Austria, whereas in the Kingdom of Serbia (which gained full independence from the Ottoman Turks in 1878), the South Slavs had a foreign state to encourage their nationalist hopes. Serbian nationalists dreamed of extending their rule over their ethnic cousins, the South Slavs of Austria-Hungary. The Hapsburg monarchy viewed this vision of a Greater Serbia as a threat to its existence. This conflict between Serbia and Austria-Hungary was to trigger World War I.

The awakening of nationalism in the multiethnic Austro-Hungarian Empire raised the specter of dissolution. Could the forces of unity—the army, the bureaucracy, and loyalty to the Haps-

burg dynasty—contain the centrifugal forces that threatened to shatter the empire into separate parts? A restructuring of the Dual Monarchy into a federated state that would give equality to the Slavs might have eased the pressures within the empire, particularly since only extremists among the minorities were calling for independence. But the leading statesmen resisted the Slavs' demands. At the end of World War I, the empire was fractured into separate states based on nationality.

THE RISE OF RACIAL NATIONALISM

In the first half of the nineteenth century, nationalism and liberalism went hand in hand. Liberals sought both the rights of the individual and national independence and unification. Liberal nationalists believed that a unified state free of foreign subjugation was in harmony with the principle of natural rights, and they insisted that love of country led to love of humanity. "With all my ardent love of my nation," said Francis Palacky, a Czech patriot, "I always esteem more highly the good of mankind and of learning than the good of the nation."[3] Addressing the Slavs, Mazzini declared: "We who have ourselves arisen in the name of our national right, believe in your right, and offer to help you to win it. But the purpose of our mission is the permanent and peaceful organization of Europe."[4]

As nationalism grew more extreme, however, its profound difference from liberalism became more apparent. The extreme nationalism of the late nineteenth and early twentieth centuries contributed to World War I and to the rise of fascism after the war. It was the seedbed of totalitarian nationalism.

Concerned exclusively with the greatness of the nation, extreme nationalists rejected the liberal emphasis on political liberty. They attacked parliamentary government as a barrier to national unity and greatness and maintained that authoritarian leadership was needed to meet national emergencies. The needs of the nation, they said, transcended the rights of the individual. Extreme nationalists also rejected the liberal ideal of equality. Placing the nation above everything, nationalists accused national minorities of corrupt-

CELEBRATION OF THE UNVEILING OF THE STATUE OF HERMANN (ARMINIUS) AT THE SITE OF TEUTOBERGER WALD. The Franco-Prussian War (1870–1871) brought German unity and intensified nationalist feelings. German nationalists glorified the traditions and deeds of their ancient ancestors who overran the Roman Empire. Depicted here is the unveiling of the statue erected in 1875 for Arminius, a tribal chieftain, who had defeated a Roman force in 9 A.D. German nationalism, which grew more extreme in succeeding decades, helped give rise to the world wars of the twentieth century. (*Bildarchiv Preussischer Kulturbesitz*)

ing the nation's spirit; and they glorified war as a symbol of the nation's resolve and will. In the name of national power and unity, they persecuted minorities at home and stirred up hatred against other nations. They also increasingly embraced militaristic, imperialistic, and racist doctrines. At the founding of the Nationalist Association in Italy in 1910, one leader declared:

> *Just as socialism teaches the proletariat the value of class struggle, so we must teach Italy the value of international struggle. But international struggle is war? Well, then, let there be war! And nationalism will arouse the will for a victorious war, . . . the only way to national redemption.*[5]

Interpreting politics with the logic of emotions, extreme nationalists insisted that they had a sacred mission to regain lands once held in the Middle Ages, to unite with their kinfolk in other lands, or to rule over peoples considered inferior. They organized patriotic societies, denounced national minorities, particularly Jews, and created a cult of ancestors and a mystique of blood, soil, and a sacred national past. In these ancestral traditions and attachments, the nationalist found a higher reality akin to religious truth. Loyalty to the nation-state was elevated above all other allegiances. The ethnic state became an object of religious reverence; the spiritual energies that formerly had been dedicated to Christianity were now channeled into the worship of the nation-state. In 1902, Friedrich Paulsen, a German philosopher, warned of nationalism's threat to reason and morality:

> *A supersensitive nationalism has become a very serious danger for all the peoples of Europe; because of it, they are in danger of losing the feeling for human values. Nationalism, pushed to an extreme, just like sectarianism, destroys moral and even logical consciousness. Just and unjust, good and bad, true and false, lose their meaning; what men condemn as disgraceful and inhuman when done by others, they recommend in the same breath to their own people as something to be done to a foreign country.*[6]

By the beginning of the twentieth century, conservatives had become the staunchest advocates of nationalism, and the nationalism preached by conservative extremists was stripped of Mazzinian ideals of liberty, equality, and the fellowship of nations. Landholding aristocrats, generals, and clergy, often joined by big industrialists, saw nationalism as a convenient instrument for gaining a mass following in their struggle against democracy and socialism. Championing popular nationalist myths and dreams and citing Social Darwinist doctrines, a newly radicalized right hoped to harness the instinctual energies of the masses, particularly the peasants and the lower middle class—shopkeepers, civil servants, and white-collar workers—to conservative causes. Peasants viewed liberalism and Marxism as threats to traditional values, while the lower bourgeoisie feared the proletariat. These people were receptive to the rhetoric of ultranationalists, who denounced democracy and Marxism as threats to national unity and Jews as aliens who endangered the nation. Nationalism was presented as a victory of idealism over materialism and as the subordination of class and personal interests to the general good of the nation.

Volkish Thought

Extreme nationalism was a general European phenomenon, but it was especially dangerous in Germany. Bismarck's triumphs lured Germans into a dream world. Many started to yearn for the extension of German power throughout the globe. The past, they said, belonged to France and Britain; the future, to Germany.

The most ominous expression of German nationalism (and a clear example of mythical thinking) was *Volkish* thought.[7] (*Volk* means "folk" or "people.") German Volkish thinkers sought to bind together the German people through a deep love of their language, traditions, and fatherland. These thinkers felt that Germans were animated by a higher spirit than that found in other peoples. To Volkish thinkers, the Enlightenment and parliamentary democracy were foreign ideas that corrupted the pure German spirit. With fanatical devotion, Volkish thinkers embraced all things German: the medieval past, the German landscape, the simple peasant, and the village. They denounced the liberal-humanist tradition of the West as alien to the German soul.

Among the shapers of the Volkish outlook was Wilhelm von Riehl (1823–1897), a professor at the University of Munich. He contrasted the artificiality of modern city life with the unspoiled existence in the German countryside. Berthold Auerbach (1812–1882) glorified the peasant as the ideal German. Paul de Lagarde (1827–1891), a professor of oriental languages, called for a German faith, different from Christianity, that would unite the nation; he saw the Jews as enemies of Germany. Julius Langbehn (1851–1907) lauded a mystical and irrational life force as superior to reason and held that the Jews corrupted the German spirit.

Volkish thought attracted Germans frightened by all the complexities of the modern age: industrialization, urbanization, materialism, class conflicts, and alienation. Seeing their beloved Germany transformed by these forces of modernity, Volkish thinkers yearned to restore the sense of community, which they attributed to the preindustrial age. Only by identifying with their sacred soil and sacred traditions could modern Germans escape from the evils of industrial society. Only then could the different classes band together in an organic unity.

The Volkish movement had little support from the working class, which was concerned chiefly with improving its standard of living. It appealed mainly to farmers and villagers, who regarded the industrial city as a threat to native values and a catalyst for foreign ideas; to artisans and small shopkeepers, threatened by big business; and to scholars, writers, teachers, and students, who saw in Volkish nationalism a cause worthy of their idealism. The schools were leading agents for the dissemination of Volkish ideas.

Volkish thinkers looked back longingly to the Middle Ages, which they viewed as a period of social and spiritual harmony and reverence for national traditions. They also glorified the ancient Germanic tribes that overran the Roman Empire; they contrasted their courageous and vigorous German ancestors with the effete and degenerate Romans. A few tried to harmonize ancient Germanic religious traditions with Christianity.

Such attitudes led Germans to see themselves as a heroic people fundamentally different from and better than the English and French. It also led them to regard German culture as unique—innately superior to, and, indeed, contravening, the humanist outlook of the Enlightenment. Like their romantic predecessors, Volkish thinkers claimed that the German people and culture had a special destiny and a unique mission. They pitted the German soul against the Western intellect—feeling and spirit against a drab rationalism. To be sure, the Western humanist tradition had many supporters in Germany, but the counterideology of Volkish thought was becoming increasingly widespread.

Racist doctrines had a special appeal for Volkish thinkers. Racist ideologues saw race as the key to history. They maintained that not only physical features, but also moral, esthetic, and intellectual qualities distinguished one race from another. In their view, a race demonstrated its vigor and achieved greatness when it preserved its purity; intermarriage between races was contamination that would result in genetic, cultural, and military decline. Like their Nazi successors, Volkish thinkers claimed that the German race was purer than, and therefore superior to, all other races. Its superiority was revealed in such physical characteristics as blond hair, blue eyes,

and fair skin: all signs of inner qualities lacking in other races. German racists claimed that Germans were descendants of ancient Aryans.* They held that the Aryans were a superior race and the creators of European civilization and that the Germans had inherited their superior racial qualities.

Volkish thinkers embraced the ideas of Houston Stewart Chamberlain (1855–1927), an Englishman whose fascination with Germanism led him to adopt German citizenship. In *The Foundations of the Nineteenth Century,* published in 1899, Chamberlain asserted in pseudoscientific fashion that races differed not only physically, but also morally, spiritually, and intellectually, and that the struggle between races was the driving force of history. He attributed Rome's decline to the dilution of its racial qualities through the intermixing of races. The blond, blue-eyed, long-skulled Germans, possessing the strongest strain of Aryan blood and distinguished by an inner spiritual depth, were the true ennoblers of humanity—both physically superior and bearers of a higher culture. Chamberlain denied that Christ was a Jew, hinting that he was of Aryan stock. As agents of a spiritually empty capitalism and divisive liberalism, the Jews, said Chamberlain, were undermining German society. Materialistic, cowardly, and devious, they were the very opposite of the idealistic, heroic, and faithful Germans. Chamberlain's book was enormously popular in Germany. Pan-German and other Volkish-nationalist organizations frequently cited it. Kaiser William II called *Foundations* a "Hymn to Germanism" and read it to his children.

Chamberlain's racist and anti-Semitic views make him a spiritual forerunner of Nazism, and he was praised as such by Alfred Rosenberg, the leading Nazi racial theorist in the early days of Hitler's movement. Joseph Goebbels, the Nazi propagandist, hailed Chamberlain as a "pathbreaker" and "pioneer" after meeting him in 1926. In 1923, Chamberlain, then sixty-eight years old, met Hitler, whose movement was still

---

*The Aryans emerged some four thousand years ago, probably between the Caspian Sea and India. An Aryan tongue became the basis of most European languages. Intermingling with others, the Aryans lost their identity as a people.

in its formative stage. Chamberlain subsequently praised Hitler as the savior of the Reich, and Hitler visited Chamberlain on his deathbed and attended his funeral.

German racial nationalists insisted that as a superior race Germans had a right to dominate other peoples, particularly the "racially inferior" Slavs of eastern Europe. The Pan-German Association, whose membership included professors, schoolteachers, journalists, lawyers, and aristocrats, spread racial and nationalist theories and glorified war as an expression of national vitality. A statement from the association's journal sums up its philosophy:

> *The racial-biological ideology tells us that there are races that lead and races that follow. Political history is nothing but the history of struggles among the leading races. Conquests, above all, are always the work of the leading races. Such men can conquer, may conquer, and shall conquer.*[8]

Anti-Semitism: The Power and Danger of Mythical Thinking

German racial nationalists singled out Jews as the most wicked of races and a deadly enemy of the German people. Anti-Semitism, which was widespread in late-nineteenth-century Europe, affords a striking example of the perennial appeal, power, and danger of mythical thinking—of elevating to the level of objective truth ideas that have no basis in fact but provide all-encompassing, emotionally satisfying explanations of life and history. By manufacturing the myth of the wicked Jew, the radical right confirmed the insight proffered by the political philosopher Georges Sorel (see pages 689–690): that people are moved and united by myths that offer simple, clear, and emotionally gratifying resolutions to the complexities of the modern world. Anti-Semitic organizations and political parties sought to deprive Jews of their civil rights, and anti-Semitic publications proliferated. The radical right saw Jew-hatred as a popular formula for mobilizing and uniting all social classes—a precondition for strengthening the nation and destroying liberal democracy.

In 1886, Edouard Drumont, a French journal-

THE PROTOCOLS OF THE ELDERS OF ZION. This infamous forgery, commissioned by the Russian secret police, became an international bestseller and contributed to outrages against Jews. Anti-Semitic organizations continue to publish and circulate it today. The picture is the actual cover of a French edition of the *Protocols*, c. 1934. (*The Wiener Library, London*)

ist, published *Jewish France*, which argued that the Jews, racially inferior and believers in a primitive religion, had gained control of France. The book sold more than a million copies. Drumont blamed the Jews for introducing capitalism, materialism, and greed into France. Like medieval Christian anti-Semites, Drumont accused Jews of deicide and of using the blood of slaughtered Christian children for ritual purposes. (In rural France, the accusation of ritual murder, a deranged survival of the Middle Ages, still persisted, at times fomented by the clergy.) During the anti-Semitic outbursts accompanying the Dreyfus affair (see page 645), when the French right was shouting "Death to the Jews," Drumont's newspaper (founded with Jesuit funds) tried to inflame public opinion with sensational polemics against the Jews. It blamed all the ills of France on the Jews, called for their expulsion from the country, and predicted that they would be massacred.

Romania barred most Jews from holding office and from voting, imposed various economic restrictions on them, and limited their admission into secondary schools and universities. The Romanian government even financed an international congress of anti-Semites, which met in Bucharest in 1886.

Russia placed a quota on the number of Jewish students admitted to secondary schools and higher educational institutions, confined Jews to certain regions of the country, and, "to purify the sacred historic capital," expelled around twenty thousand Jews from Moscow. Some government officials encouraged and even organized *pogroms* (mob violence) against Jews. Between 1903 and 1906, pogroms broke out in 690 towns and villages, most of them in the Ukraine, traditionally a hotbed of anti-Semitism. (Ukrainian folksongs and legends glorified centuries-old massacres of Jews.) The attackers looted, burned, raped, and murdered, generally with impunity. In Russia, and several other lands, Jews were put on trial for the old libel of ritual murder.

In Germany and Austria, hatred of the Jews developed into a systematic body of beliefs. As historian Hans Kohn says, "Germany became the fatherland of modern anti-Semitism; there the systems were thought out and the slogans coined. German literature was the richest in anti-Jewish writing."[9] Like conservatives in other lands, German conservatives deliberately fanned the flames of anti-Semitism to win the masses over to conservative causes. The Christian Social Workers' party, founded in 1878 by Adolf Stöcker, a prominent Protestant preacher, engaged in anti-Semitic agitation in order to recruit the lower bourgeoisie to the cause of the Protestant church and the Prussian monarchy. In German-speaking Austria, Karl Lueger, a leader of the Christian Socialist party, founded by conservative German nationalists, exploited anti-Semitism to win elec-

tions in overwhelmingly Catholic Vienna. Georg von Schönerer, founder of the German National party in Austria, wanted to eliminate Jews from all areas of public life.

Anti-Semitism and the success of the Italians, Germans, Serbians, and others in achieving political independence stirred nationalist feelings among Jews. Jewish nationalism took the form of Zionism—a movement advocating the return of Jews to Palestine, their historic homeland. A key figure in the emergence of Zionism was Theodor Herzl (1860–1904), an Austrian journalist, who was horrified by the anti-Semitism he witnessed in Paris during the Dreyfus trial. In *The Jewish State* (1896), he argued that the creation of a Jewish state was the best solution to the Jewish question. In 1897, in Switzerland, the first Zionist World Congress called for the establishment of a Jewish homeland in Palestine, which was then a province of the Turkish empire.

Anti-Semitism had a long and bloodstained history in Europe, stemming both from an irrational fear and hatred of outsiders with noticeably different ways and from the commonly accepted myth that the Jews as a people were collectively and eternally cursed for rejecting Christ. Christians saw Jews as the murderers of Christ—an image that provoked terrible anger and hatred.

During the Middle Ages, people believed and spread incredible tales about Jews. They accused Jews of torturing and crucifying Christian children in order to use their blood for religious ceremonies, poisoning wells to kill Christians, worshiping the Devil, and organizing a secret government that conspired to destroy Christianity. Jews were thought to be physically different from other people; they were said to have tails, horns, and a distinctive odor. Serving to propagate this myth was the decision of the Fourth Lateran Council (1215), which required Jews to wear a distinguishing mark on their clothing.

Although some medieval popes and bishops condemned these fables and sought to protect Jews from mob violence, the lower clergy and popular preachers spread the tales to the receptive masses. Periodically, mobs humiliated, tortured, and massacred Jews, and rulers expelled them from their kingdoms. Often barred from owning land and excluded from the craft guilds, medieval Jews concentrated in trade and money-

Profile

THEODOR HERZL

Theodor Herzl (1860–1904), the founder of modern Zionism, was born in Budapest and received a law degree from the University of Vienna. Giving up law, he turned to writing stories and plays and working as a journalist. At the time of the Dreyfus trial—when an innocent Jewish army officer was railroaded and humiliated by the army and reviled by anti-Semites—Herzl was Paris correspondent for a prominent Viennese newspaper. Greatly distressed by French anti-Semites, who were shouting "Death to the Jews," Herzl became convinced that European Jews would never escape persecution. In *The Jewish State* (1896), he argued that security for Jews could be guaranteed only by a separate national state for Jews in their historic homeland.

lending—occupations that frequently earned them greater hostility. By the sixteenth century, Jews in a number of lands were forced by law to live in separate quarters of the town, called *ghettos*. Medieval Christian anti-Semitism, which depicted the Jew as vile and Judaism as repulsive, fertilized the soil for modern anti-Semitism.

In the nineteenth century, under the aegis of the liberal ideals of the Enlightenment and the French Revolution, Jews gained legal equality in most European lands. They could leave the ghetto and participate in many activities that had been closed to them. Traditionally an urban people, the Jews, who were concentrated in the leading cities of Europe, took advantage of this new freedom and opportunity. Motivated by the fierce desire of outsiders to prove their worth and aided by deeply embedded traditions that valued education and family life, many Jews achieved striking success as entrepreneurs, bankers, lawyers, journalists, doctors, scientists, scholars, and performers. For example, in 1880, Jews, who constituted about 10 percent of the Viennese

population, accounted for 38.6 percent of the medical students and 23.3 percent of the law students in Vienna. Viennese cultural life before World War I was to a large extent shaped by Jewish writers, artists, musicians, critics, and patrons. All but one of the major banking houses were Jewish. By the early 1930s, German Jews, who constituted less than 1 percent of the population, accounted for 10.9 percent of the doctors, 10.7 percent of the dentists, 5.1 percent of the editors and authors, and 16.3 percent of the lawyers. Thirty percent of the Nobel prize winners in Germany were Jews.

But most European Jews—peasants, peddlers, and laborers—were quite poor. Perhaps five thousand to six thousand Jews of Galicia in Austria-Hungary died of starvation annually, and many Russian Jews fled to the United States to escape from desperate poverty. But the anti-Semites saw only "Jewish influence," "Jewish manipulation," and "Jewish domination." Aggravating anti-Semitism among Germans was the flight of thousands of Russian Jews into Austria and Germany. Poor,

We are a people—one people. We have honestly endeavored to merge ourselves in the social life of surrounding communities and to preserve only the faith of our fathers. We are not permitted to do so. In vain are we loyal patriots . . . ; in vain do we strive to increase the fame of our native land in science and art, or her wealth by trade and commerce. In countries where we have lived for centuries we are still cried down as strangers. . . . I think we shall not be left in peace. . . . [O]ld prejudices against us still lie deep in the hearts of people. . . . I say that we cannot hope for a change in the current . . . feeling. . . . The nations in whose midst Jews live are all either covertly or openly Anti-Semitic. . . . Palestine is our ever-memorable historic home. The very name of Palestine would attract our people with a force of marvellous potency.*

Herzl organized the first Zionist World Congress, which met in Basel, Switzerland in 1897. He was elected president of the World Zionist Organization, a position he held until his death in 1904, at the age of forty-four. Herzl had little success in winning heads of state and Jewish bankers to the Zionist cause, but he did manage to make the Zionist movement into a recognized international organization. His drive and vision—"If you will it, it is no fairy tale"—inspired many Jews, particularly among the poor and persecuted Jewish masses of Russia and Poland, to struggle for the creation of a Jewish state in the land of Israel.

*Theodor Herzl, *The Jewish State* (New York: American Zionist Emergency Council, 1946), pp. 76–77, 85, 96.

speaking a different language (Yiddish, a form of medieval German that was unfamiliar to nineteenth-century Germans), and having noticeably different customs, these Jews offended Germans and triggered primitive fears and hates.

Like other bourgeois, the Jews who were members of the commercial and professional classes gravitated toward liberalism. Moreover, as victims of persecution, they naturally favored societies that were committed to the liberal ideals of legal equality, toleration, the rule of law, and equality of opportunity. As strong supporters of parliamentary government and the entire system of values associated with the Enlightenment, the Jews became targets for conservatives and Volkish thinkers, who repudiated the humanist and cosmopolitan outlook of liberalism and professed a militant nationalism. According to German historian Karl Dietrich Bracher, "Anti-Semitism was a manifestation of a rejection of the 'West' with which the Jews were identified . . . because the Enlightenment and democracy were essential preconditions for their acceptance and progress."[10]

Anti-Semites invented a mythical evil to be blamed for all the social and economic ills caused by the rapid growth of industries and cities and for all the new ideas that were undermining the Old Order. Their anxieties and fears concentrated on the Jews, to whom they attributed everything they considered to be wrong with the modern age, all that threatened the German Volk.

The thought processes of Volkish anti-Semites demonstrate the mind's monumental capacity for irrational thinking. In the mythical world of Volkish thinkers, Jews were regarded as foreign intruders who could never be loyal to the fatherland; as a lower form of humanity that could infect and weaken the German race and debase its culture; and as international conspirators who were plotting to dominate Germany and the world. This latter accusation was a secularized and updated version of the medieval myth that Jews were plotting to destroy Christendom. In an extraordinary display of irrationality, Volkish thinkers held that Jews throughout the world were gaining control over political parties, the press, and the economy in order to dominate the planet.

The myth of a Jewish world conspiracy found its culminating expression in the notorious forgery, the *Protocols of the Elders of Zion*. The *Protocols* was written in France in the 1890s by an unknown author in the service of the Russian secret police, which sought to justify the tsarist regime's anti-Semitic policies. The forger concocted a tale of an alleged meeting of Jewish elders in the Jewish cemetery of Prague. In these eerie surroundings, the elders plot to take over the world. First published in Russia in 1903, the *Protocols* was widely distributed after World War I and widely believed. Influenced by the *Protocols*, Russian anti-Semites interpreted the communist Revolution of 1917 as an attempt by Jews to subjugate Christian Russia. German anti-Semites regarded the *Protocols* as convincing evidence that the Jews were responsible for starting World War I, for Germany's defeat, and for the revolution that toppled the monarchy. Nazi propagandists exploited the *Protocols* to justify their quest for power. Even after the *Protocols* was exposed as a blatant forgery, it continued to be translated and distributed. For anti-Semites, the myth of a Jewish world-conspiracy had become an integrating principle; it provided satisfying answers to the crucial questions of existence.

In the Middle Ages, Jews had been persecuted and humiliated primarily for religious reasons. In the nineteenth century, national-racial considerations supplemented the traditional, biased Christian perception of Jews and Judaism. However, whereas Christian anti-Semites believed that, through conversion, Jews could escape the curse of their religion, racial anti-Semites, who used the language of Social Darwinism, said that Jews were indelibly stained and eternally condemned by their biological makeup. Their evil and worthlessness derived from inherited racial characteristics, which could not be altered by conversion. As one anti-Semitic deputy stated in a speech before the German Reichstag in 1895,

If one designates the whole of Jewry, one does so in the knowledge that the racial qualities of this people are such that in the long run they cannot harmonize with the racial qualities of the Germanic peoples and that every Jew who at this moment has not done anything bad

may nevertheless under the proper conditions do precisely that, because his racial qualities drive him to do it. . . . the Jews . . . operate like parasites . . . the Jews are cholera germs.[11]

The Jewish population of Germany was quite small. In 1900, it was only about 497,000, or 0.95 percent of the total population of 50,626,000. Jews were proud of their many contributions to German economic and intellectual life; they considered themselves patriotic Germans and regarded Germany, a land of high civilization, as an altogether desirable place to live—a place of refuge in comparison to Russia, where Jews lived in terrible poverty and suffered violent attacks. German Jews, who felt that they already had a homeland, had little enthusiasm for Zionism.

German anti-Semitic organizations and political parties failed to get the state to pass anti-Semitic laws, and by the early 1900s, these groups had declined in political power and importance. But the mischief had been done. In the minds of many Germans, even in respectable circles, the image of the Jew as an evil and dangerous creature had been firmly planted. It was perpetuated by the schools, youth groups, the Pan-German Association, and an array of racist pamphlets and books. Late-nineteenth-century racial anti-Semites had constructed an ideological foundation on which Hitler would later build his movement. In words that foreshadowed Hitler, Paul de Lagarde said of the Jews: "One does not have dealings with pests and parasites; one does not rear them and cherish them; one destroys them as speedily and thoroughly as possible."[12]

It is, of course, absurd to believe that a nation of 50 million was threatened by a half-million citizens of Jewish birth, or that the 11 million Jews of the world (by 1900) had organized to rule the planet. The Jewish birthrate in Germany was low, the rate of intermarriage high, and the desire for complete assimilation into German life great. Within a few generations, the Jewish community in Germany might well have disappeared. Moreover, despite the paranoia of the anti-Semites, the German Jews and the Jews in the rest of Europe were quite powerless. There were scarcely any Jews in the ruling circles of governments, armies, civil services, or heavy industries. As events were to prove, the Jews, with no army or state and dwelling in lands where many despised them, were the weakest of peoples. But the race mystics, convinced that they were waging a war of self-defense against a satanic foe, were impervious to rational argument. Anti-Semites, said Theodor Mommsen, the great nineteenth-century German historian, would not listen to

logical and ethical arguments. . . . They listen only to their own envy and hatred, to the meanest instincts. Nothing else counts for them. They are deaf to reason, right, morals. One cannot influence them. . . . [Anti-Semitism] is a horrible epidemic, like cholera—one can neither explain nor cure it.[13]

Racial nationalism, a major element in nineteenth-century intellectual life, attacked and undermined the Enlightenment tradition. Racial nationalists denied equality, scorned toleration, dismissed the idea of the oneness of humanity, and made myth and superstition vital forces in political life. They distorted reason and science to demonize and condemn an entire people and to justify humiliation and persecution. They presented a dangerous racial ideology, fraught with unreason and hate, as something virtuous and idealistic. That many people, including the educated and the enlightened, accepted these racial doctrines was an ominous sign for Western civilization. It made plain the tenuousness of the rational tradition of the Enlightenment and showed how receptive the mind is to dangerous myths, and how easily human behavior can degenerate into inhumanity.

◆ ◆ ◆

NOTES

1. Quoted in Christopher Hibbert, *Garibaldi and His Enemies* (Boston: Little, Brown, 1965), p. 45.

2. Quoted in Otto Pflanze, *Bismarck and the Development of Germany: The Period of Unification* (Princeton, N.J.: Princeton University Press, 1963), p. 232.

3. Quoted in Hans Kohn, *Pan-Slavism* (Notre Dame, Ind.: University of Notre Dame Press, 1953), pp. 66–67.

4. Quoted in Kohn, *Pan-Slavism*, p. 44.

5. Cited in Edward R. Tannenbaum, *1900: The Generation Before the Great War* (Garden City, N.Y.: Doubleday, 1976), p. 337.

6. Quoted in Friedrich Meinecke, *The German Catastrophe* (Boston: Beacon Press, 1963), pp. 23–24.

7. This discussion is based largely on the works of George L. Mosse, particularly *The Crisis of German Ideology* (New York: Grosset & Dunlap Universal Library, 1964).

8. Cited in Horst von Maltitz, *The Evolution of Hitler's Germany* (New York: McGraw-Hill, 1973), p. 33.

9. Hans Kohn, *Nationalism: Its Meaning and History* (Princeton, N.J.: Van Nostrand, Anvil Books, 1955), p. 77.

10. Karl Dietrich Bracher, *The German Dictatorship*, trans. Jean Steinberg (New York: Praeger, 1970), p. 36.

11. Quoted in Raul Hilberg, *The Destruction of the European Jews* (Chicago: Quadrangle, 1967), pp. 10–11.

12. Quoted in Helmut Krausnick, Hans Buchheim, Martin Broszat, and Hans-Adolf Jacobsen, *Anatomy of the SS State,* trans. Richard Barry et al. (London: William Collins Sons, 1968), p. 9.

13. Quoted in Peter G. J. Pulzer, *The Rise of Political Anti-Semitism in Germany and Austria* (New York: Wiley, 1964), p. 299.

SUGGESTED READING

Beales, Derek, *The Risorgimento and the Unification of Italy* (1971). A comprehensive overview, followed by documents.

Hamerow, T. S., *Restoration, Revolution, Reaction* (1958). An examination of economics and politics in Germany, 1815–1871, stressing the problems caused by the transition from agrarianism to industrialism.

———, ed., *Otto von Bismarck* (1962). A collection of readings from leading historians.

Hibbert, Christopher, *Garibaldi and His Enemies* (1965). A vivid portrait of the Italian hero.

Holborn, Hajo, *A History of Modern Germany, 1840–1945* (1969). A standard reference work.

Jászi, Oscar, *The Dissolution of the Habsburg Monarchy* (1961). Originally published in 1929, this volume examines how nationalist animosities contributed to the dissolution of the Hapsburg monarchy.

Katz, Jacob, *From Prejudice to Destruction* (1980). A survey of modern anti-Semitism; views modern anti-Semitism as an outgrowth of traditional Christian anti-Semitism.

Kohn, Hans, *Nationalism: Its Meaning and History* (1955). A concise history of modern nationalism by a leading student of the subject.

Mack Smith, Denis, ed., *Garibaldi* (1969). A collection of readings: Garibaldi as he saw himself, how his contemporaries saw him, and how nineteenth- and twentieth-century historians have viewed him; preceded by a valuable introduction.

Mosse, George L., *Toward the Final Solution* (1978). An analysis of European racism.

———, *The Crisis of German Ideology* (1964). Explores the dark side of German nationalism; an excellent study of Volkish thought.

Pauley, B. F., *The Habsburg Legacy, 1867–1939* (1972). A good brief work on a complex subject.

Pflanze, Otto, *Bismarck and the Development of Germany* (1963). An excellent study of the political history of Germany from 1815 to 1871.

Pulzer, Peter G. J., *The Rise of Political Anti-Semitism in Germany and Austria* (1964). Relationship of anti-Semitism to changing socioeconomic conditions; impact of anti-Semitism on politics.

Rodes, John E., *The Quest for Unity: Modern Germany, 1848–1970* (1971). A good survey of German history.

REVIEW QUESTIONS

1. What forces worked for and against Italian unity?

2. Mazzini was the soul, Cavour the brains, and Garibaldi the sword in the struggle for the unification of Italy. Discuss their participation in and contributions to the struggle.

3. Why is it significant that Prussia rather than the Frankfurt Assembly served as the agent of German unification in 1848?

4. Prussia's victory over Austria was a triumph for conservatism and a defeat for liberalism. Discuss this statement.

5. What was the significance of the Franco-Prussian War for European history?

6. In the Hapsburg Empire, nationalism was a force for disunity. Discuss this statement.

7. To whom did Volkish thought appeal? Describe why.

8. Why is racial nationalism a repudiation of the Enlightenment tradition and a regression to mythical thinking?

9. What is the relationship between medieval and modern anti-Semitism?

10. Anti-Semites attributed to Jews everything that they found repellent in the modern world. Discuss this statement.

11. Anti-Semitism demonstrates the immense power and danger of mythical thinking. Discuss this statement.

CHAPTER 26

The Industrial West: Responses to Modernization

T he quickening pace of industrialization—the "second industrial revolution"—gave momentum to the modernization of European states from 1870 to World War I. The spread of mechanized industry to every European state, though not to every part of these nations, made it possible to deliver vastly increased quantities of goods, produced by the new technology, which was powered by new forms of energy. It also raised new groups to authority and wealth and distributed some of the benefits of productivity among the people. With the material benefits of a mass-producing society surrounding them, it is small wonder that many Europeans came to believe in the inevitability of progress. And those who were still left out of the consuming society struggled for their share.

The mechanization of basic and primary goods industries that had moved western Europe to the fore had proceeded slowly and very unevenly in the first half of the nineteenth century. This time lag allowed traditional economic production and social forms to persist. By the midcentury, only Britain had become predominantly urban and an importer of food; yet even Britain retained many aspects of its earlier social relations. Throughout Europe, the old power structures of rural, agrarian, privileged society endured, resisting and repressing the new and emerging forces and reshaping basic institutions to deal with them. Those who held power in each nation reacted differently, according to their nations' institutions, the rapidity of change, and their ideologies.

Western European governments responded to the major changes wrought by industrialization with state building—a modern term, which means strengthening the central power over diverse interests, regions, classes, and even nationalities. Governments developed the machinery to include and to control great numbers of citizens.

Krupp Metalworks Factory, Essen, Germany, 1861.
(*Photo by Charles Phelps Cushing*)

CHRONOLOGY 26.1 Europe in the Age of Industrialization

1845–47	Great famine in Ireland
1851	Louis Napoleon Bonaparte overthrows the Second Republic, becoming Emperor Napoleon III
1860s	Irish movement for republican form of government (the Fenians); Civil War in the United States; unification movements in German and Italian states; Dual Monarchy in Austria-Hungary
1861	Kingdom of Italy is formed; Tsar Alexander II emancipates the serfs and institutes reforms in Russia
1863	Emancipation of slaves in the United States
1864	Marx founds the First International Workingmen's Association
1867	Second Reform Bill passes, doubling the English electorate
1870–71	Franco-Prussian War; Paris Commune; creation of the German Empire
1873	Great Depression; the Kulturkampf in Germany
1875	German Social Democratic party founded
1880s	Parnell leads the Irish home rule movement
1881	Tsar Alexander II is assassinated
1884	Reform Bill granting suffrage to most English men is passed
1889	Second International Workingmen's Association is founded
1894–1906	The Dreyfus affair in France
1909	Lloyd George introduces "people's budget"
1911	Power of House of Lords limited by act of Parliament

The experience of the unification movements led some governments to encourage popular expressions of nationalism. No longer fearing the democratic and radical aspects of nationalism, leaders saw it as a way of absorbing masses of previously excluded people. The state's power grew enormously as government affected the lives of ordinary citizens through military conscription, public education, broad taxation, and, in some places, social legislation.

By concentrating factory workers in cities and loosening traditional regional ties, industrialization facilitated the trends toward centralization. Civil wars, unification movements, and struggles for political representation usually ended with even greater power in the hands of the government. A new balance of classes and regions in the modern centralized state was achieved through repression of dissent, regionalism, and tradition. The American Civil War, the suppression of the

Irish struggle for home rule, the subjection of southern Italy to the north, the repression of Catholics and socialists in unified Germany, and the persecution of minorities in tsarist Russia all illustrate this process.

Industrialization affected international affairs as well. National power was no longer measured by population, area, and the size of the army. The amount of coal and iron production, the mileage and tonnage of railways and navies, the mechanization of industry, and the skill of the populace became important components of national power. Production, trade, foreign markets, and political empires altered the balance of power, changing the positions of France, Russia, and Austria. The industrial might of Germany and the United States would be decisive in the scale of world power in the generation before 1914.

THE ADVANCE OF INDUSTRY

Industry had developed on the foundation of cheap labor and plentiful agricultural commodities, which were made even more easily and cheaply available by the development of a relatively inexpensive transportation and communication system. It took more than a century for that foundation to be built, but by the middle of the nineteenth century, it was in place for almost all of Europe and parts of the Americas. A new economic world was built so rapidly that many historians see this radical change as a second industrial revolution. It brought radically new forms of business and labor organization, the massive accumulation of capital, scientific and technological advances, and new modes of marketing, distribution and production. What followed was economic growth and prosperity such as the world had never seen before. The apparently limitless change and growth fostered a mentality of expendability: people could be replaced, raw materials replenished, nature rearranged, and even homelands exchanged. To many, anything seemed possible.

A look back to the midcentury provides a measure of the second industrial revolution. Most people were still farmers and much of industry produced tools and materials for farming.

Even in Britain, where industrialization had advanced the most, there were more domestic servants than factory workers and twice as many agricultural laborers as textile and clothing workers. Large factories were few; handicrafts still flourished. Electricity was too fragile to power lighting or drive machines. Steel was so expensive to manufacture that it was treated almost as a precious metal. Sailing ships still outnumbered steamships, and horses carried more freight than trains. On-the-job training was more common than schooling. Construction and machine making were a result of trial and error, not architectural and engineering knowledge.

This situation changed radically in two spurts: the first between 1850 and 1870, and the second after the Great Depression of 1873, from the 1890s until World War I. During the first spurt, most of Europe and America consolidated earlier industrialization and spread it to previously untouched areas. The shift to machine production became permanent. The use of steam power spread, and other forms of energy, as well as more sophisticated tools, were introduced. The concentration of factory workers in industrial cities and the developing urbanization of production spurred many social changes: the growth of unions; the passage of social legislation, especially laws dealing with hours and conditions of labor; and, through government action, some reduction in water pollution, housing, and improvements in sanitation. In the more advanced industrial areas, the social organization of the workplace changed, as did the management and finance of enterprise.

During the second spurt, in the 1890s, the major industrial countries, particularly Germany and the United States, began concentrating heavy industry in large firms, capitalized by specialist banks. Cartels and monopolies—groups of companies joined together so that they could fix prices and giant firms able to dominate entire industries nationally and internationally—drastically altered the scale of development. Monopolies, run by boards of directors, some professional managers, and financiers, operated far-flung enterprises of enormous mechanized factories, manned by unskilled, low-paid, often seasonal workers. These industrial giants were able to control the output, price, and distribution of commodities; they were able to dominate

GARE ST.-LAZARE, PARIS: ARRIVAL OF A TRAIN, 1877 BY CLAUDE MONET (1840–1926). The mania for railroads which captured the British and French in the 1840s ended with those nations, Europe, and much of America, crisscrossed with railroad track. The craze fostered industrial growth in all directions. Artists of many movements—realist, naturalist, impressionist, postimpressionist, futurist—depicted the train. (*Courtesy of the Harvard University Art Museums, Fogg Art Museum, Bequest—Collection of Maurice Wertheim, Class of 1906*)

smaller firms, finance and control research and development, utilize scientific advances, and expand far beyond their national frontiers.

Giant firms welded alliances with specialized banks all over Europe in the post-1890 period. The "captains of industry"—the owners or managers of these large firms—possessed such extraordinary economic power that they often commanded political power as well. In much of Europe such men were ennobled. The railroad barons of Britain and the United States are early examples of this great power. In the United States, bankers and entrepreneurs could order politicians to represent their interests as "the oil senator" or "the railroad senator." The scale of these operations and the dynamic personalities of such powerful entrepreneurs—men who could "cause" depressions or "own" cities—fascinated the public and obsessed their critics. Without drawing much notice, small business expanded

along with big business. The second industrial revolution was a broad movement, not limited to monopolies or cartels.

The rapid growth and the powerful figures in great industries obscured for contemporaries the fact that economic development was extremely uneven, even in advanced industrial states. Industrialized Britain included rural, backward Ireland, which furnished foodstuffs and laboring people but shared few benefits of industrialization. The Irish desire for autonomy was fueled as much by this economic deprivation as by cultural and religious difference. The central, southern, and eastern parts of Europe were also backwater areas, with some large-scale industries, until 1914. Economic oppression in these regions went hand in hand with repression of minority nationalities.

Governments built or subsidized "essential" industries (broadly defined to include transportation, communication, national banks, and the production of war goods), which had been state enterprises for a long time. Britain alone had developed according to laissez-faire policies, although the United States and France experimented with free trade at times. In other sectors, the eastern empires remained economically and socially backward: overwhelmingly agricultural, with craftspeople manufacturing in consumer-oriented, small-scale operations of textiles and food processing. Even Germany, a major power, had megacartels such as the Krupp works alongside handicraft labor. The very uneven development contributed to the political conflicts and social animosities.

Industrial wealth was just as unevenly and unequally distributed. The rise in workers' standard of living and the improvement in conditions of labor did not narrow the gap between the workers and the owners, or between city and rural laborers. Indeed, if anything, the gap widened. The middle class gained political and social influence comparable to its economic power in western Europe. In the Continental empires—Russia, Austria, Hungary, and Germany—social discrimination against the bourgeoisie remained long after economic and political barriers dropped. The bourgeoisie used the state to advance business and inhibit labor. At the same time, the decline of traditional groups—artisans and peasantry—as factory skills replaced craft skills on a national scale, increased the labor supply just when the introduction of heavy equipment reduced the total numbers of workers and replaced women and children with men. What some men gained in personal wages, they lost in family income, unless their wives could enter domestic service or become pieceworkers, seamstresses, or laundresses. The state required their children to be trained in schools for occupations the economy demanded. These changes would have a powerful impact on political movements at the end of the nineteenth century.

Technological Takeoff

Technology revolutionized production in undreamed of ways. It increased the productivity of goods and services at the rate of multiplication, not addition. The practical applications of scientific research and engineering to production, transportation, and communication began to pay high dividends just around the middle of the century, replacing the trial-and-error tinkering of the artisan or inventor. By 1900, German firms in electrical, chemical, and mechanical industries commonly hired engineers and applied scientists, whose job was to solve technical problems and produce new commodities, including artificial ones, of dyestuffs, fertilizers, and fuels. The Americans were not far behind, and they, in particular, applied scientific methods to the "science of management," which was taught in professional business schools by the end of the century. The result was a veritable "takeoff" of technology: each discovery opened up a new runway down which industries could travel, and the new technologies were continually building feeder paths from one runway to another.

This industrial takeoff, connecting industries and technological and scientific advances, can be illustrated by examining a few key industries, which commanded the overall economy—railroads, communications, and energy production—as they grew in Britain, western Europe and the United States. Railroads became the engine of industrial growth in Britain, stimulating the demand for coal and iron, gravel, wood and tar, engineering training, and electronic signaling. A century of iron metallurgy, capped by the Bessemer and Siemens processes that made quality steel cheaply and abundantly, provided suitable materials for railroads and construction. Stronger steel machinery allowed wider application of steam in mines, construction, and other industries. The amount of capital needed for further industrial development called for technical innovation in the uses and acquisition of funds. The public, as well as the investors, was thrilled by railroads which had the aura of progress that canals and roads did not. In Britain and the rest of western Europe, at first many railroad firms competed. Those railroad moguls who could draw in the greatest amounts of capital soon swallowed up their rivals, acquiring immense personal and corporate fortunes.

In countries that lacked moguls, government stepped in to amass the capital, build railroads, take over failing ones, and subsidize private builders by land or monopoly grants. It did so to foster commerce, maintain military power, and strengthen the central authority. Government rewarded loyal supporters with contracts or, if bankruptcy threatened, bailouts, in order to ease economic hardship with jobs or bring separatist regions closer to the center of power. In France, Paris was the hub; all tracks led there, further centralizing the country. Trains turned peasants into Frenchmen, drawing them into a national market and lessening regional loyalties. In the German and Italian states, too, railroads contributed to unification. The citizens' vision widened—just as the economic markets did—to include the nation and beyond.

North America and Eurasia were the most transformed by railroads. In the United States, there were more miles of railway (176,000) by 1870 than in all of Europe. The transcontinental railroad offered an avenue into vast unsettled areas. Canada's railroad did likewise. In Russia in the 1890s, the Trans-Siberian Railroad carried millions of settlers east to the desolate stretches of central Asia. Britain linked up the various regions of the Indian subcontinent by railroad track.

Shipping paralleled the epic expansion of railroads. In 1850, steam-powered ships constituted only 5 percent of the world's tonnage; by 1893, the figure had risen to half of all tonnage. The shift brought changes in marine technology, such as the replacement of iron with steel and the substitution of screw propellers for the paddle wheels that moved riverboats. In 1870, 4.5 million tons of goods were shipped by sailboat and less than a million tons by steamship; by 1881, the tonnage was about equal; and by 1885, steam surpassed sail. By 1913, steam carried 11 million tons of goods and sail only 800,000. By the 1880s the whole world was open to cheap, plentiful goods, products which often could swamp local crafts, allowing European industry to make money abroad, as well as at home.

Steam power fueled the massive increase in productivity from the midcentury on, but its monopoly was broken at the turn of the century. Electricity became more competitive, powering whole industries and lighting great cities. Then two German engineers, Gottlieb Daimler and Karl Benz, perfected the internal combustion engine fueled by petroleum products and applied it to a car. By 1901 an engineer at Daimler Works had produced a luxury automobile which was named for Daimler's daughter Mercedes. The American Henry Ford (1863–1947) produced his Model T for the "ordinary man" in 1908, and by 1914 his mass-production, conveyor belt assembly line techniques revolutionized industrial production. The automobile age was born; engines would be powered by liquid fuels, not steam. The invention of the diesel engine by another German in 1897 meant that cheaper, more efficient fuel could be used on giant cargo ships, warships, and luxury liners. The automobile industry became the symbol of the American industrial system.

In communications, the invention of the telegraph stimulated industrial expansion for more than a generation. At the time, the undramatic but rapid improvement of postal services was much more important to industrial growth than the spectacular inventions like the telephone and the radio. Development costs were so prohibitive for the telephone (invented by Alexander Graham Bell in 1876) and the wireless, or radio (invented by Guglielmo Marconi in 1895) that it took twenty-five years after their invention for either device to be widely used, even in industrial countries. As soon as costs were cut, however, communications grew exponentially.

Advances in electronics illustrate a general trend of the second half of the nineteenth century. After a long lag, the Scientific and the Industrial Revolutions joined forces. Inventions played a greater and more visible role in the late-nineteenth-century industrial expansion than they had in the much slower, more cumulative earlier growth. More than half a century elapsed between Michael Faraday and James Maxwell's discovery of the fundamentals of electricity and the inventions of Thomas Edison, Bell, and Marconi. In a much shorter span of time—by the end of the century—electricity was providing power for lights, for urban and suburban trains, and for some factory engines.

This same trend was also evident in industrial chemistry, which revolutionized many products. In 1850, almost all industrial materials were the ones people had been using for centuries: wood, stone, cotton, wool, flax, hemp, leather, and the base metals such as copper, iron, lead, and tin and their alloys. Even dyes and rugs were the products of plants or animals. However, from the middle of the century onward, building on the general framework provided by John Dalton's theory of molecular structure and Dmitri

PAINTING OF THE BOWERY BY LOUIS SONTAG, 1895. New York City street scene bursting with the commercial energies and activity as the night is lighted by blazing electricity. The painting puts pushcarts, trolleys, horse-drawn cabs, and trains side by side, as it does the classic architecture of the theater and the four-storey buildings housing shops and families on the Bowery. The life of the city throbs with the energy of modern technology. (*Museum of the City of New York #32.275.2. Gift of William B. Miles*)

Mendeleev's classification of elements by valence, chemists discovered new elements and perfected formulas for alloys and other combinations. Dyes and coal-tar products (such as liquid fuel), aspirin and other drugs, saccharin, and disinfectants were developed. By 1900, Germany was the center of applied chemistry, an important segment of that country's industrial expansion.

In medicine, too, the marriage of science and technology produced miraculous progeny. The discovery of anesthetics and antiseptics in the 1850s and the passionate insistence on cleanliness by the English surgeon Joseph Lister made it possible for many more patients to survive surgery and hospitalization. The discovery and isolation of disease-causing bacteria by Louis Pasteur, a French chemist, made it possible to pinpoint the causes of some diseases, to isolate or quarantine the diseased, and to immunize or inoculate the healthy against disease. By the end of the century, researchers had identified the causes of several killer diseases: typhoid, tuberculosis, cholera, tetanus, diphtheria, and leprosy. Science had exposed poor sanitation and squalor as the breeders of disease, and industrialized countries worked harder and more efficiently than before to ameliorate these conditions. Death rates dropped precipitously; life expectancy increased,

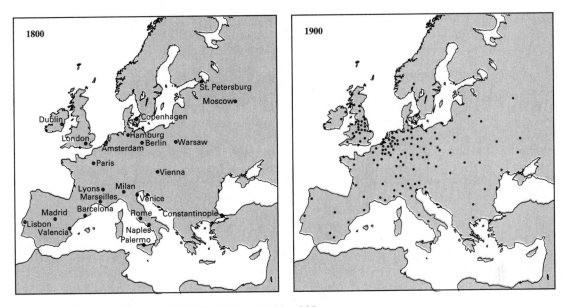

MAP 26.1 European Cities of 100,000 or More, 1800–1900

as did population numbers. In the more industrialized nations, the birthrate declined though the population rose, because many people believed that large families lowered their standard of living and because they knew about health measures and birth control. In all, each advance forced political and social change, and the changes in the political and social power of individuals, groups, and nations pushed industrial and commercial development still further.

Accelerated Urbanization

The force of rapid industrial development brought with it the urbanization of northwestern Europe and the United States. Cities became more numerous, larger, and more densely populated. Industrial cities joined governmental and commercial centers in drawing people from rural life and labor, to mix with those who were city born and bred. By 1850, the majority of England's population lived in cities; most Germans did not until the twentieth century. Although not an industrial city, London had become a megalopolis of 5 million people by 1880 and was home to 7 million by 1914. Paris increased from 2 to 3 million between 1850 and World War I. Berlin, a city of only half a million in 1866,

reached 2 million by World War I. There were just three German cities of more than 100,000 on the eve of unification, but by 1903 there were fifteen.

By the end of the century, the first steps in sanitation, public water supply, policing, public transport, street laying and widening, and construction and regulating of housing and commercial property had been taken in most of western Europe. Cities differed as did nations, but industrial ones seemed to grow more alike. New professions of urban planner, transport engineer, and sanitation engineer joined the well-meaning, civic-minded urban-dwelling men and women volunteers who tried to alleviate the worst effects of urban industrial living.

The draw of the factory and the drama of the train brought village and rural people to the city, where they acclimated to the urban environment. Responding to the various pressures of education, the press, and patriotic campaigns, they became conscious of national loyalties and slowly moved away from regional, class, and religious allegiances.

Industrialization and urbanization played a much more important part in national integration than did government campaigns to create homogeneity. Often the success of minority cultural resistance to the pressures for integration depended on the relative economic backwardness of the area. As industrialization and urbanization proceeded, maintaining traditional loyalties became more and more difficult. There were exceptions, however. Industrialization heightened minority identity among such peoples as the Czechs in Austria-Hungary and the Basques in Spain.

In contrast to northwestern Europe, discontented peasants rejected national integration in Russia, the Balkans and parts of the Austro-Hungarian Empire, the Iberian peninsula, and southern Italy. In these economically backward areas, peasants who held small pieces of land barely eked out a living; landless peasants labored on great estates for landlords, who paid them little. In eastern Europe, the agricultural sector produced for export rather than for home consumption, which meant that the peasants' standard of living (food and steady employment) sometimes declined.

Labor's Responses

Three trends were evident in western Europe by the 1890s: the union organization of unskilled workers by industry, rather than by craft; recruitment of labor to socialist or labor parties; and labor's attempt to make the general public aware of the needs of the poorest workers. In England in 1888, for example, women and girls who worked in match factories, where phosphorus endangered their lives, went on strike and won better conditions. It was usually difficult to win over the public, which was imbued with individualist, property-protecting values and often felt that labor did not have the good of the country in mind. But sweatshop female labor gained the attention of the press and the public, which deplored the miserable conditions and wages of women workers. Other workers called sympathy strikes. When impoverished British dockworkers struck in 1889, they were rescued from sure defeat by the support of Australian and American dockworkers, who knew how vulnerable the union of these rough-and-ready men actually was.

The giant enterprises of the second wave of industrialization required great armies of unskilled workers. These laborers did not fit in the trade or craft unions organized during the prosperous middle years of the nineteenth century. From the 1880s on, skilled craftspeople, trained factory workers, and organized union workers watched as machines and unskilled workers—often foreigners, minorities, or displaced peasants—took their places. They also watched labor standards, quality of goods, and wages decline. The long struggle to organize and to gain legal recognition for unions seemed to have been in vain if the new technology made their skills obsolete. The new unskilled laborers worked for low pay, usually by the day or by the job, if they were lucky enough (or shared enough of their wages with the foreman) to be chosen to work. When workers had low pay, irregular work, and minimal skills, unions (which depended on control of the labor supply) seemed almost impossible to organize. The corporate giants, competing vigorously for markets, actually cooperated to defeat attempts at unionization. They used their political power to keep the union movement weak. Conditions were terrible, the hours were long, and work remained irregular and low-paying in the new industries.

Workers used their suffrage to pressure government for reform. Beginning in the 1860s and 1870s, they demanded union recognition and legislation for minimum wages, maximum hours, and better working conditions. They pushed governments to deal with the social consequences of industrialization and urbanization. Governments paid attention. In the 1880s, Bismarck instituted reforms (see page 646), and by 1914, Britain, France, Austria, Italy, Denmark, and Switzerland provided some benefits for sick, injured, and elderly workers. In some countries, such as the United States, workers voted for the same political parties that other classes voted for. In other countries, such as Britain, workers at first followed that policy and then organized a separate party pledged to their interests. In France, Germany, and Italy, workers were drawn to socialist parties, calling for the end of capitalism; in Italy, Spain, and parts of France even more radical, anarchist parties gained support.

Over the years from 1850 to 1914, workers' lives improved thanks to trade-union organization, government intervention in the economy, and the general increase in productivity brought on by industrialization. In the first period of consolidation, from 1850 to 1870s, the standard of

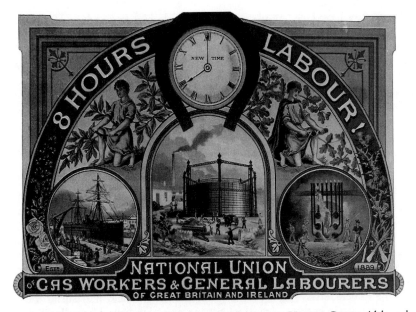

GAS WORKERS AND GENERAL LABOURERS NATIONAL UNION CARD. Although the earliest "unions" were "friendly societies" or remnants of craft guilds, once legalized by parliament, trade unions grew rapidly. This card reflects the campaign for the eight-hour workday. The artist has indicated both the processing of coal to gas and the pride of labor. The pictures of ships, gas tanks, and gas-extracting tubes, like many photographs of the period, illustrate the tools of the trade. The vegetables and flowers in the borders and the laborers surrounding the clock link their labor with that of ancient humanity. (*R.B. Fleming*)

living of many workers, both skilled craftspeople and factory hands, went up. Labor protected itself with craft unions and social clubs to help in times of short labor; it set aside money for sickness and accidents. Later, workers responded to structural changes in the economy by organizing on an industrywide basis and voting for candidates who were sympathetic to their plight.

Still, workers faced problems and inequities that drew them to socialist parties, which strove for state control of industry and worker control of government and workplace. Most workers—and their families—lived in overcrowded, bleak tenements, without central heating or running water. They worked long hours—as much as fifty-five per week in trades where governments restricted the length of the workweek, and from seventy to seventy-five in unregulated trades. Their jobs were exhausting and monotonous. They suffered from malnutrition, diseases (partic-

ularly tuberculosis), and lack of medical care. Because of inadequate treatment, women often died in childbirth. Laborers in heavy industry, particularly miners and dockworkers, commonly experienced job accidents that maimed and killed. Socialists believed that these conditions were due to the capitalist profit system, which exploited and impoverished workers and enriched the owners.

Socialist parties, which by the 1890s were influenced by Marx and his followers (see Chapter 24), grew phenomenally in Germany and rapidly in much of the rest of Europe, reflecting changes in the industrial sector. Even Russia, which was scarcely industrial, had a Marxist socialist party. However, socialists were divided about tactics for change. Their views depended on their ideology and their country's political environment. Some socialists, insisting that they were "orthodox" Marxists, believed that socialist-led revolution was the necessary first step for change; they included

Wilhelm Liebknecht and August Bebel of Germany and Jules Guesde of France. Others—"revisionist" Marxists—argued that Marx's predictions and theory needed to be adapted to new conditions, such as an improving standard of living and universal manhood suffrage. Two "revisionists," in Germany, Eduard Bernstein, and in France, Jean Jaurès, urged socialists to use the political and economic system to build socialism without revolution. Even in England, where Marxism had not gained much influence, the 1880s saw the birth of the Independent Labour party.

In the decade before 1914, the real standard of living for workers in western Europe dropped as the cost of living rose by as much as 10 percent. A wave of strikes, often punctuated by violence, swept through every industrial and industrializing country. Strikes, such as the dock strikes in London and Liverpool, the railroad workers' strike in France, and the miners' strikes in England and France, were put down violently. Labor was convinced that since industrialists were so strong, even with the vote it would not be able to improve its position. The social welfare measures provided only minimum assistance—much less than organized labor provided for itself. The socialist parties and trade union congresses, which belonged to the Second International (successor to Marx's First International Workingmen's Association), annually voted for the "hard line" of revolutionary activity to bring about socialism, despite great debate among the members.

The revolutionary position was internationalist as well, urging workers to support one another across national frontiers. Many middle- and upper-class Europeans feared organized labor and thought it unpatriotic. It was difficult, at the time, to predict how workers would act in a national emergency, but many workers were patriotic, despite the anti-militarist and anti-imperialist declarations of their socialist leadership.

Great Britain: An Industrial Model

In 1850, England appeared to be the most modern and progressive of states. It had made phenomenal industrial progress, and most of its peo-

ple began to share a higher standard of living in the era of free trade after 1847. The British elite, as well as foreigners, believed England to be the model parliamentary government: it balanced an incomparable degree of political liberty with economic and social reforms, and so avoided the extremes of revolution and reaction that other nations experienced in the nineteenth century. Political parties competed with one another to govern and, in the competition, reformed evils and extended membership in the political community to previously excluded groups.

That was the appearance of Victorian England. The reality differed. "Country gentlemen" dominated British politics: titled aristocrats manned the cabinets and commanded the army and navy. Great social mobility existed, but the wealthy industrialists, merchants, and entrepreneurs had to acquire a gentleman's manners to become influential in political and social life. A gentleman's manners, or "good breeding," were expected for the civil service, for any public and private promotion, and for social acceptance.

Reform and Progress

The effect of almost a century of industrial and commercial changes—and some fortuitous events, like the discovery of gold in California and Alaska increasing the money supply—brought prosperity and a sense of well-being, which shaped the politics of the time. Two men of quite different personalities and values were the central political figures of this period: William E. Gladstone (1809–1898), a pious, sober man and an orator whose speeches inspired people on issues of taxes and revenues, and Benjamin Disraeli (1804–1881), a flamboyant personality, a novelist and a dreamer who talked of the greatness of empire. Gladstone, the Liberal, saw politics as the struggle between the forces of good and evil and believed that God had chosen him to carry out the divine will. Disraeli, the Conservative, thought politics a fascinating game and loved the role of courtier to Queen Victoria. Their competition stimulated reform and laid down the rules of the parliamentary game for others to admire and imitate.

In the Reform Bill of 1867, Gladstone moved to extend the suffrage but failed to get the bill passed. He resigned, according to the custom of cabinet responsibility (by which the cabinet must resign if it fails to pass its measures). Then Disraeli proposed giving the vote to the great majority of city workers—many more than Gladstone had envisioned. The Conservatives carried the measure, and suddenly the electorate was doubled. Liberals and Conservatives alike had feared democracy, yet in a moment it had become a reality. Disraeli claimed that he was not afraid because the Conservative social program and imperialistic foreign policy would attract the poor.

The prospect of uneducated voters pushed Parliament to require compulsory elementary education. Gladstone's Reform Bill of 1884 passed, enfranchising rural laborers; now most English men could vote. Women and many Irishmen still could not, but belief grew that it was only a matter of time before democracy would include even them.

Britain's prosperity provided an environment for political and social reform, but the complacent assumption of slow and steady progress was undermined in the severe depression of 1873. Industrial rivalry with Germany and the United States and the inability to resolve the Irish problem led many to question whether the sense of well-being could revive. Would "country gentlemen" be able to admit women, the Irish, and workers into the political community? Would Britain remain the model of an industrial liberal nation? Could it become truly democratic?

Social and Political Unrest

Labor Discontent In the generation after the Chartists' democratic demands were ignored, labor militance subsided. Unlike most of Europe, England had legalized unions. Skilled laborers improved their working conditions through union membership; they created the strongest labor movement in Europe in the stable, prosperous middle decades. However, after the depression of 1873, in England, as in all the countries of Europe, technology altered conditions in whole industries, leading in the 1880s to a rise in militant industrial unions, termed "new unions."

Unlike their Continental brothers, British workers on the whole had never been attracted to socialism, especially Marxism. Working-class socialists (Utopian Owenites and Nonconformist, dissenting Christians) managed to express their protests against injustice within the Liberal party. In the 1880s, widespread poverty and new trends in industry—particularly monopolies, cartels, and foreign competition—led some labor leaders to urge greater militance and an English brand of socialism. One of them was J. Kier Hardie, a colorful speaker who insisted on wearing his worker's cap and jacket when he took his seat in the House of Commons to represent a poor Welsh mining district. He created the Independent Labour party in 1893 to fight for workers' interests. Sometimes in alliance with middle-class socialists, such as the Fabians, sometimes with Liberals, he and other union leaders hammered out a political and economic program, which developed into a platform for a separate Labour party.

The Labour party might never have grown without the Taff Vale decision (1901). The courts awarded damages to an employer picketed by a union. If workers could be fined for picketing or other actions "restraining trade," their unions could be broken. They would lose the gains of half a century at a time when they wanted what German workers got in the 1880s: protection against unemployment and old age. Labor took to politics. In 1906, amidst a Liberal landslide, the new Labour party gained twenty-nine members—a small number but enough to gain necessary reforms whenever Conservatives and Liberals were almost evenly balanced.

The turn of the century saw a wave of labor violence in Britain at the same time that the Liberals carried the Peoples' Budget to fund social legislation. The stagnant wages and rising prices meant the standard of living for workers actually declined, reinforcing worker discontent. Miners, dockworkers, and railway workers urged alliance and a general strike of all workers between 1911–12. A long coal strike in 1912 involved a million and a half workers and ended only with government intervention. Both traditional and new unions of unskilled industrial labor grew more militant on the eve of the first World War.

The Irish Question The great famine of 1845–47 brought unparalleled suffering to the Irish: a million of them died and another million emigrated. Parliament's response to this major catastrophe was repression. The sufferers saw

England as callously indifferent to their plight, and they were filled with hatred for the English. A revolutionary republican terrorist group, the Fenians, was born. Throughout the prosperous 1860s, this group's struggle for Irish independence disrupted British stability and parliamentary politics. Hoping for reconciliation, Gladstone staked the Liberal party's future on Irish reform. In 1869, he ended the taxes that the Catholic Irish paid for a church—the Anglican church—that they did not attend. He also got Parliament to pass a land act, which forced landlords to compensate evicted tenant farmers for any improvements they had made on the land. Until then, renters had no incentive to improve land or farm buildings, which meant that Irish farmers were not producing enough food.

These reforms might have appeased the Irish had they been made in the 1840s and 1850s. By the 1880s, they were too late; the issue had become *home rule* (self-government within the British Empire). Despite the reforms, which alleviated some of the worst injustices, Irish Protestants (called Anglo-Irish) still held economic power and social privilege. In the House of Commons, the Irish, led by Charles Stewart Parnell, formed a separate bloc to force the Conservatives and the Liberals to reckon with the issue of home rule. The Irish used every known parliamentary tactic, and invented some new ones, to secure a separate legislature and executive for Ireland. (The Irish had had no parliament of their own since the union with England and Scotland in 1801.) Even though they denounced violence, Parnell's supporters were hurt by terrorism. Gladstone urged home rule, but his party split over the issue, and as public passions were aroused by terrorist acts, Parliament enacted extreme measures, suspending trial by jury and many other liberties in Ireland. At the end of his career, Gladstone knew that he had failed in his most important task: reconciliation with the Irish. Even independence after World War I would not bring about reconciliation.

Women's Suffrage Other issues threatened the forms of parliamentary government that Gladstone and Disraeli had developed. Like the Irish question and labor militance, the issue of women's suffrage was explosive. In the campaign for it, as feminist tactics and government repression steadily escalated in violence.

POSTER PUBLISHED BY THE ARTISTS' SUFFRAGE LEAGUE, DESIGNED BY EMILY HARDING ANDREWS, C. 1908. This suffragette poster illustrates the fact that British women could not vote in the early twentieth century. The cap and gown of the woman college graduate does not help her find the key which will release her from the imprisoning categorization with felons and the mentally ill, who couldn't vote for parliament either. Women were leaders in local government, where they were in charge of schools, orphanages, and hospitals, but were unable to vote for members of the House of Commons until after World War I. (*Library of Congress*)

Women were allowed to vote for and serve on school and local government boards. In both arenas, they were very active; indeed, they were the backbone of school boards and the charity organizations that were responsible for poverty relief. But despite their peaceful petitions, the right to vote for members of the House of Commons was denied them.

Some feminists thought that women should concentrate on self-improvement and on legal efforts to raise their status in society. Others found that approach too slow and proposed radical action to reach equality. Still others concluded that the political road was the wrong one to take; if women wanted to be free, they needed to liberate themselves economically and socially from their dependence on men. Many Liberals and some Labourites favored women's suffrage; however, women were advised by the leader of the Liberals "to keep on pestering . . . but exercise the virtue of patience." For the women who found this advice patronizing and whose patience was running out, a family of feminists advocated a more militant course of action. Emmeline Pankhurst and her daughters Sylvia and Christabel urged demonstrations, invasions of the House of Commons, destruction of property, and hunger strikes. They did not urge these dramatic measures all at once, but when their petitions and demands were ignored, they moved to more and more shocking actions: breaking windows, starting fires in mailboxes, and chaining themselves to the gates at Parliament. As a gesture of protest, in 1913, one militant suffragette killed herself by jumping in front of the king's horse at the races.

When feminists were arrested for violating the law, they staged hunger strikes. Ugly situations resulted, with the police force-feeding the demonstrators and subjecting them to ridicule and rough treatment. Often the police would release half-starved feminists and, when they had recovered their health, reimprison them. Ridiculed, humiliated, and punished—but above all, legally ignored—the feminists refused to accept the passive role that a male-dominated society had assigned them. When women played a major part on the home front in World War I, many of the elite changed their minds, and in 1918, women over thirty years of age were enfranchised. Finally, in 1928, women gained the right to vote on the same terms as men, that is, they had to be twenty-one years old and to have six months' residency. The World War had already brought the right to vote for women in the United States, Australia, New Zealand, Germany, and the Soviet Union.

Britain on the Eve of War

Between 1906 and 1911, the Liberals, led by David Lloyd George (1863–1945) and the then Liberal Winston Churchill (1874–1965), introduced a series of important social measures. Aided by the Labour party, they enacted a program of old-age pensions, labor exchanges to help the unemployed find work, unemployment and health insurance (a program deeply influenced by Bismarckian social legislation), and minimum wages for certain industries. Parliament also repealed the Taff Vale decision. In the process, however, a constitutional crisis developed between the Liberals, who had Labour support, and the Conservatives, who dominated the House of Lords.

When Lloyd George introduced the "people's budget" of 1909, the House of Lords refused to accept it, even though the House of Commons was traditionally responsible for financial measures. In the people's budget, social legislation was to be financed by raising the income tax and by levying heavier inheritance taxes ("death duties") and "unearned" income taxes on rents, investments, and increases in the value of land. All of these taxes were directed at the wealthy and the privileged. The Liberals waged an all-out political fight with the lords, whom they called "diehards" and "last ditchers" for their intransigence. Many lords saw their struggle as the defense of Britain and its empire against the Liberals' "socialist" campaign.

Lloyd George sarcastically described the dukes as "five hundred men, ordinary men, chosen accidentally from among the unemployed." During the bitter campaign for the budget, class antagonisms, unacknowledged for a couple of generations, were freely expressed, but the people's budget was finally passed. Later, the Parliament Act of 1911 stipulated that the House of Lords could only delay the passage of a bill that the Commons wanted, not prevent it. The machinery for democratic government in Britain was in place.

The continuing bitter struggle for Irish home rule made the explosive environment in prewar Britain still more volatile. The House of Lords, dominated by Tory imperialists (disciples of Disraeli's vision of imperial greatness), used every possible tactic against home rule but could not prevent its passage once the Parliament Act of 1911 became law. The Liberals (disciples of Gladstone) pushed for home rule, but their opponents were so angry that they refused to accept

Parliament's decision. For them the British Empire was too important to be broken up by party politics, elections, and mere majority rule.

Outside Parliament, militant groups took the law into their own hands. The situation was more violent and revolutionary than in Gladstone's day. Irish Catholic extremists, such as the Irish Republican Brotherhood and the Gaelic League, pressed for full independence; among the Protestant Irish (Ulstermen), the Ulster Volunteers recruited a large private army and openly trained it for revolution if home rule should be enacted. Gangs smuggled guns, soldiers fired on demonstrators, and civil war seemed close. English Tory leaders threatened mutiny. One went so far as to review eighty thousand volunteer soldiers willing to fight against Parliament and to urge English soldiers to support Protestant rebellion in Ireland.

In 1914, when Great Britain declared war on Germany, Ireland was uppermost in British minds. With the onset of war, women and labor suspended their militant campaigns, pledging their loyalty to king and country "for the duration." Many Irish fought for Britain in World War I, but the deferred promise of home rule angered many others, who continued their struggle for independence. In 1916, the Easter Rebellion, an Irish insurrection led by Sir Roger Casement, was suppressed and its leaders executed. Lloyd George negotiated a settlement that was carried out after the war: Ireland was divided, the south gaining self-government, and the northern six counties of Ulster remaining a part of the United Kingdom.

The bitter conflicts of prewar Britain showed the cracks in the country's self-image as a stable, liberal, constitutional regime. Parliamentary liberal government proved itself able to conduct and win a grueling world war, but issues of empire and depression would try the constitutional forms again as excluded groups fought for full participation in a democracy.

FRANCE: DEMOCRATIC OR AUTHORITARIAN?

The political fortunes of France in the nineteenth century were very different from Britain's. Virtually each generation faced revolution and reaction, swinging from democratic revolution to authoritarian stability, from active participation of the people to rule by a single man or small group of men. Late to industrialize, France proceeded much more slowly than Germany or the United States, and this greatly affected its place in international affairs.

Another Bonaparte

The personality and politics of Louis Napoleon Bonaparte (1808–1873), nephew of Napoleon I, dominated France at the midcentury. By an overwhelming majority, in an election in which all French males could vote, Bonaparte was elected president of the Second French Republic, which a democratic and social revolution had established in 1848. Within three years, he had made himself dictator and ratified his destruction of the republic by a plebiscite. This vote and subsequent elections were usually rigged. He made himself the second emperor Bonaparte.

Bonaparte outraged liberals and republicans, including Alexis de Tocqueville and Victor Hugo, as well as much of the working class, but most of the other French citizens accepted the "little Napoleon." Many thought that Louis Bonaparte's politics—a mix of democratic, socialist, nationalist, and authoritarian ideas—promised national glory, strong leadership, and social progress. Bonaparte seemed a man who could unite all the French classes and groups.

The 1850s were a period of prosperity, confidence, and political apathy, particularly when compared with the radical 1840s. The general inflation and economic growth helped Bonaparte, who spoke Saint-Simonian language of state-sponsored canal and railroad building on cheap credit from government banks. He also expressed concern for the plight of the workers, whose suffering became acute as industrialization took hold in France. Construction projects on cheap credit may have been regarded by liberals as socialistic, but few socialists were, in fact, willing to claim Bonaparte as one of theirs. Many voters, however, saw him as more sympathetic to the masses than the predominantly middle-class governments before him had been.

Thus, Bonaparte combined the appearance of democracy—elections by universal manhood suffrage, plebiscites, a press, and intellectual debate—with economic expansion, which was beneficial to the bourgeois and the workers. At the same time, he suppressed legislative opposition, censored the press, rarely convened the parliament, and manipulated both elections and debate. He chose his close friends and his relatives as advisers and administrators.

His government was popular among property owners, including the majority of peasants, business groups, and Roman Catholics (all had feared the social change demanded by workers in 1848). They favored stability at home and expansion abroad and approved of the economic development stimulated by railroad construction and the rebuilding of Paris.

In the 1860s, Bonaparte loosened the controls on the press and the legislature, legalized strikes and granted workers a limited right to unionize. When in 1869 many members of the opposition were elected, Napoleon III accepted a new constitution with liberal safeguards for individual liberties, which made his role in government much like that of Queen Victoria: a constitutional parliamentary monarch.

Was Napoleon III, after all, a liberal who wanted first to establish his power and then to give France reforms? Or did he take after the great Napoleon, being more concerned with his personal power and glory and only succumbing to liberalism because he feared revolution?

After the Fall

Defeat in the Franco-Prussian War brought down Bonaparte's empire. Frustration with defeat and hatred of the Prussian invaders led the people of Paris to rise up against the armistice signed by the provisional government—the politicians who had replaced Napoleon III. The Paris Commune (1871) began as a patriotic refusal to accept defeat and a rejection of the corrupt Second Empire. Ultimately, the Communards (those who fought the Prussians and created a radical republican government) challenged property owners, including the peasantry.

When the provisional government agreed to peace terms with Germany, it also demanded payment of the rent and debts not collected in France during the war. The Communards refused to obey. They differed greatly in their programs: They included the followers of Pierre Joseph Proudhon (see page 593), groups of republican and socialist veterans of the Revolution of 1848 who came together liberated from prisons, emerged from hiding, and returned from exile, and disciples of Auguste Blanqui, an old insurrectionist. For two months in the spring of 1871, the revolutionaries ruled Paris, The Jacobins of 1793 and the radicals of June 1848 were their heroes. Then Adolphe Thiers, head of the provisional government and the man who had accepted Bismarck's peace terms for lifting the Prussian siege, ordered a French siege of Paris. The fighting was bitter and desperate, with many acts of terrorism and violence. Both sides in this civil war set fires that destroyed large parts of the city they loved. The Communards were defeated and dealt with as traitors: twenty thousand men and women were executed without trial, and those who were tried received harsh sentences of death, life imprisonment, and transportation to prison colonies.

The Commune became legendary. Across Europe, governing classes were terrified by the hatred that they imagined the masses to feel. But most Communards were ardent French patriots, not international revolutionaries. Their desperate economic plight, rather than some ideological commitment to the abolition of private property, had driven them to action. Nevertheless, many of the governing elite decided that the people should be ruled with an iron fist.

International revolutionaries, both socialists and anarchists, thought that they saw a radicalization of the people in the desperate acts of the Communards. These revolutionaries were convinced that the political leaders of other countries would be just as brutal as Thiers had been. The masses, said revolutionaries like Marx, must perfect their organizations for insurrections and violent seizure of power. Workers must learn to be as ruthless as Thiers. Other radicals, appalled by the bloodbath, argued for using the ballot box and organizing political parties. In their view, the power of the modern state had become too great for insurrection to lead to revolution, as it had in 1789, 1830, and 1848.

The Paris Commune and its brutal suppression by the government dramatized existing distinctions among the French and intensified the

AFTER THE FALL; LAROQUETTE PRISONERS BEFORE THE FIRING SQUAD. The repression of the Paris Commune, which resisted the French provisional government when it tried to make peace with the Prussians, was a brutal bloodbath with atrocities on both sides. When it was over, almost 8,000 were sent into exile, 5,000 imprisoned and fined, and many executed. Few could have predicted that the republic established then would survive to World War II. (*Bettmann Archive*).

hatred between social groups. With the empire defeated and the Commune suppressed, law and order were reestablished under a harsh peace treaty. Burdened by an indemnity and the loss of Alsace and part of Lorraine and embittered by the experience of war and civil war, France slowly rebuilt its national unity and regained its place in Europe.

A Republic by Default

No one expected that the government born from the next few years of political crisis would be the longest-lasting republic in the history of France (1870–1940). The monarchists formed the most numerous and most powerful political group;

they seemed to offer stability and order without the dangers of radical, or even liberal, republicanism. But there were *two* conflicting monarchist parties: the Legitimists and the Orléanists. The Orléanists agreed to compromise, but the Legitimists refused to accept the tricolor, which symbolized the liberties won in the French Revolution.

Disunity among the monarchists made France a republic by default. With no king willing to rule, the republicans gained power. Somewhat in imitation of the British system, the republican government comprised a powerful bicameral legislature—a senate and a chamber of deputies, which resembled the House of Commons—and a prime minister, who had to have its support. The president was a figurehead; republicans wanted no new Napoleon to rise and overthrow the regime. Unlike Britain, France had many political parties, which expressed the differences among the French, but also exaggerated rather than modified them. No one party had sufficient strength within parliament to provide strong leadership. Prime ministers resigned in rapid succession; cabinets rose and fell frequently, giving the impression of a state without direction. Political life seemed to consist of wheeling and dealing; however, in the process, legislation was enacted that made elementary education free and compulsory and legalized trade unions. The Third Republic survived, but not without major crises.

Threats to the Third Republic

In the 1880s, scandals and corruption threatened to destroy the republic. Opposition centered on a dashing general, Georges Boulanger (1837–1891), whose popularity reminded many of Napoleon III. Was France to swing back to authoritarianism? But Boulanger lost his nerve at the moment when he was expected to seize power. He fled to Belgium, where he committed suicide on the grave of his former mistress.

Almost immediately, another scandal was exposed. Several republican deputies were implicated in a giant stock swindle involving the financing of the construction of the Panama Canal. They had taken bribes, then tried to cover this up. The low level of public morality shocked the people. Many came to view all politics as immoral, whereas others saw immorality specifically in democratic politics. Neither attitude helped build a republican morality.

The crisis that tore France in two for over a decade, the Dreyfus affair, came close on the heels of the Boulanger affair and the Panama Canal scandals. In 1894, Captain Alfred Dreyfus, an Alsatian-Jewish artillery officer, was wrongly accused of treason—of having sold secrets to the Germans. He was condemned to life imprisonment on Devil's Island. Anti-Semitic elements joined with the Republic's opponents, including the army, the clergy, and monarchists, to block every attempt to clear Dreyfus. In the beginning, few people defended him; the vast majority felt that the honor of France and the army was at

stake. Then individuals, mainly radical republicans, came to his defense, including the writers Anatole France and Émile Zola and the future republican leader Georges Clemenceau, along with university students. They protested and demonstrated, insisting on a retrial and a revision of the verdict. After many humiliations, Dreyfus was finally cleared in 1906.

When the radical republicans won the election, they launched a fierce campaign to root out the anti-republicans. The radicals attacked the church, expelled religious orders, and confiscated their property. They tried to replace the influence of the parish priest with that of the district schoolmaster. Complete separation of church and state was ordered, making France a secular state. The Dreyfus case had exposed and exacerbated the problems of French society.

France on the Eve of War

Despite progress in the middle of the nineteenth century, French economic development lagged. France had fewer and smaller industries than Britain or Germany, and more French people lived in rural areas or in small communities. In general, industry, trade unions, and socialist groups tended to be decentralized rather than national; artisans were much more influential than proletarians. For a generation after the suppression of the Paris Commune, French labor was markedly antipolitical. Its leadership was broken and dispersed within France or in exile. Militants argued against cooperating with the republic or with any bourgeois government.

In the 1880s, both trade unionism and political parties with a socialist program made headway toward social reform through democratic parliamentary institutions. France was very slow, however, to enact social measures such as pensions and regulations governing working conditions, wages, and hours. These measures, which might have improved the lives of ordinary people, were regarded by the ruling elite as socialism and by the socialists as token offerings to buy off workers. Radical syndicalism (which advocated bringing industries and government under the control of workers) and even anarchism had many supporters among both workers and intellectuals. Instead of engaging in politics they

JEAN JAURÈS

Jean Jaurès (1859–1914) was the most important socialist in the Third French Republic. A brilliant student, he advanced to the highest ranks of the university. He soon tired of teaching philosophy, however, and chose politics. He was the youngest member elected to the Chamber of Deputies. Deeply concerned about workers' problems, Jaurès was convinced that capitalism was creating a new feudalism in which the rich controlled the society. He led a socialist party convinced that only the working class struggled for justice and that their struggle could win over others.

Jaurès brought liberal republicans and social-

---

waged economic war against the state. A wave of strikes beginning in 1909 ended the following year, when the government suppressed a national railway strike by conscripting strikers. Not surprisingly, socialists, syndicalists, and anarchists were all suspicious of politics and politicians.

France was a troubled country, and the Third Republic was not a popular regime. The church, the army, socialism, and even memories of the monarchy and the empire inspired deeper passions than the Republic, which survived only because its enemies were divided. France approached World War I as a deeply divided country; few would have believed that the war would reveal a united French nation.

GERMANY: WELDING AN EMPIRE

The German Empire that Bismarck, the Prussian patriot, created enabled Prussia to control all the German states. The king of Prussia was emperor

and his "Iron Chancellor" was responsible only to him. In foreign policy, all roads led to Berlin's Brandenburg Gate, behind which Bismarck decided the great issues. He was the man of the hour for German conservatives and liberals alike; he shaped the political environment for the next generation.

The Bismarckian Constitution

Bismarck's constitution, like that of Napoleon III, was hardly liberal, although it granted universal manhood suffrage and allowed the Reichstag (lower house) to discuss all topics. The government was federal, the twenty-four states had some powers, but foreign affairs and defense were in the hands of the emperor and his chancellor. Aristocrats staffed the military, the foreign service, and the top echelon of the bureaucracy; they rejected contact with the bourgeoisie and the lower bureaucrats. The German kaiser, unlike the British monarch, had considerable control over

ists together for social reforms. He championed Alfred Dreyfus and argued that socialists had just as much at stake as liberals in questions of justice. Jaurès and French workers joined with intellectuals and students in demonstrating for and demanding a fair trial and freedom for the convicted Jewish officer. Many socialists refused to take part in parliamentary politics; they thought Jaurès a bourgeois politician because he had been a university professor and never a worker. But those credentials brought a wide range of support as Jaurès campaigned vigorously for reforms that French workers still had not won. In 1905 the socialist parties of France joined together under his leadership during a time of strikes and repression. On the international scene, in the Second International, Jaurès was brilliant in his opposition to war, calling for all workers, not just French ones, to refuse to fight should their governments become belligerents.

In the last days before World War I, Jaurès was assassinated by a French nationalist fanatic who was afraid that the great speaker would convince his socialist followers to resist the war.

French workers—even socialists—defended their country in 1914 believing it to be the most democratic nation.

lawmaking, foreign affairs, the army, and the navy.

The German Empire did not have Britain's two-party system, cabinet responsibility, or guarantees of civil liberties. The Reichstag's control over Bismarck was the refusal to pass the budget, an extreme measure that the politicians were usually unwilling to take. Only the king-emperor could remove the chancellor or the cabinet members from office. German liberalism was less concerned with these issues than with those of the common good. Bismarck, who believed that political parties were merely interest groups incapable of making policy for the country, weakened liberal and democratic elements. That Germany remained an authoritarian state had significant consequences for the future.

Bismarck's Kulturkampf

To Bismarck, the Catholics and the socialists were internationalists who did not place the interests of Germany first. Almost 40 percent of Germany was Roman Catholic. Taking advantage of a split in the Catholic church over the question of papal infallibility, and of the prejudice stimulated by that doctrine among non-Catholics, Bismarck began to persecute Catholics. The *Kulturkampf* (struggle for culture) was a series of laws passed in 1873 that tried to subject the church to the state. The laws discriminated against the Jesuits and required state supervision of the church and training of priests in state schools. Catholics had to be married by the state. Churchmen who refused to accept these laws were imprisoned or exiled. German liberals did not defend Catholic civil liberties.

Persecution only strengthened the German Catholics' loyalty to their church, however; the Catholic Center party gained support. Prussian conservatives, though Protestant, resented Bismarck's anticlerical policy, which could hurt Lutherans as well as Catholics. With the succession of Leo XIII to the papacy in 1878, Bismarck quietly opened negotiations for peace with the church.

Bismarck Versus the Socialists

In the late 1870s, Bismarck attacked the socialists. Ferdinand Lassalle (1825–1864), a charismatic lawyer-reformer who had the support of workers and trade unionists and influence with Bismarck himself, formed a German Workers' Association, which he hoped would join patriotism to unionism. Marx and his followers August Bebel and Wilhelm Liebknecht scoffed at Lassalle's program. They opposed attempts to get support from the emperor, the military, or the bureaucracy. Nevertheless, there were more Lassalleans than Marxists, so in 1875 they joined forces to create a German socialist party. The compromises made by socialist groups mattered little because Bismarck intended to separate workers from their leaders and to crush the socialists. He was sure the liberals would fail to defend the socialists too.

Bismarck knew how to manipulate public opinion. When, in 1878, two attempts were made on the emperor's life, Bismarck demanded that the socialists be suppressed. In reality, the socialists, few in number, were not a threat; their immediate practical program was a demand for civil liberties and democracy in Germany. Only the narrowest of conservative views would have labeled the socialists as dangerous, but many in Germany, particularly the Prussian Junker class, held such a narrow view. Once again the liberals did not oppose Bismarck. Special legislation outlawed subversive organizations and authorized the police to ban meetings and newspapers. The Social Democratic party, like the Catholic Center party before, survived the persecution. It grew stronger and better disciplined as the liberals grew weaker, discredited by their unwillingness to act.

Bismarck's policy was not merely repressive. He tried to win the workers with social legislation. Like many conservatives, he was disturbed by the effects of industrialization, which had developed at a rapid pace in the 1850s and 1860s. Germany was the first state to enact a program of social legislation which included insurance against sickness, disability, accidents, and old age. The employer, the state, and the worker each contributed small amounts to an insurance fund. Many people called the legislation *state socialism*. Like socialists in every other nation, German socialists vehemently debated whether they should cooperate with the state or try to use the state's power to enact socialism. These debates greatly overestimated the power of the socialists to change the German state.

Despite Bismarck's attempts to woo them, the German working class supported the Social Democratic party. It was a party and a way of life; its members belonged to the many socialist political organizations, youth and women's divisions, athletic leagues, and cultural societies. On the eve of World War I, union membership was roughly 3 million, and the Social Democratic party was the largest single party in Germany. The socialists talked revolution, but the unions and many party members favored policies of gradual reform. Great numbers of German workers were patriotic, even imperialistic, and thought their government deserved their loyalty.

Germany on the Eve of War

By the century's end, Germany had caught up with, and in some areas surpassed, the British in industrial productivity. When Kaiser William II (1889–1918) ascended the throne, Germany possessed the most extensive sector of large-scale, concentrated industrial and corporate capitalism of any Great Power, with the largest and most powerful unions.

Germany's industrial growth was uneven, however. Although the heavy industries were quickly developing into giant monopolies or cartels, and mining and railroads were state-owned and state-operated, the rapidity of expansion from craft to giant monopoly in some industries was more important than the percentage of the German economy controlled by such industries. Many small firms were operating as well, and large-scale agricultural producers, particularly in the eastern regions, were still very powerful. Large unions had arisen to deal with the monopolies, but workers in smaller firms were still organized by craft.

The population rose one-third in the single generation of 1882 to 1902, but the industrial work force increased by 180 percent in that time; it constituted 35 percent of the active labor force of 27 million people. Many of these people were called directly from the farm to work in heavily concentrated industries in alien urban environments. Only the peasants in Russia or peasant-

1. Joseph Mallard William Turner. *The Burning of the Houses of Parliament.* 1834
(Philadelphia Museum of Art)

Art of the Nineteenth
and Twentieth Centuries

The nineteenth century was one of great change in every facet of modern life. Industrialization, nationalism, revolution, and unification were but a few of the themes that dominated society in every country in the Western world. As we have seen in every century, the visual arts also underwent great changes. During this period, a number of art movements informed painting, sculpture, architecture, and the minor arts as well. In some instances, the movements evolved alongside

political and social change; in other cases, art movements grew as a response, a counter-proposal to the political powers that ruled.

One of the greatest differences that sets nineteenth century art apart from works that came before was the realization that "things do not always have to appear the way they are." In other words, artists were beginning to move away from representational art, pursuing instead a course that will bring them far along the road to abstraction. So far that by the

2. Paul Cézanne. *Madame Cézanne in the Conservatory* (Metropolitan Museum of Art, NY)

beginning of the twentieth century, images bear almost no resemblance to the objects from which they are drawn.

The work of Joseph Mallard William Turner (1775–1851) has its roots in the Romantic movement, which began in Europe at the end of the eighteenth century. As we have seen, however, Romanticism cannot be looked at as a single movement, but one with a number of strands. Turner's Romanticism—taking into account both the Picturesque and the Sublime favored especially by British Romantics—has its basis in historicism. He often portrayed historical, literary, or contemporary events in paintings that hinted at his earlier training as a watercolorist. His images have a translucence and lightness that owe much to the techniques used by that medium.

Turner's *The Burning of the Houses of Parliament* (1834) (Figure 1) illustrates a contemporary event. Britain's seat of government, badly damaged by a conflagration in the

3.Georges Seurat. *Sunday Afternoon on the Island of La Grande Jatte.* (Art Institute of Chicago)

autumn of 1834, is depicted in an almost dream-like haze. Unlike works of earlier periods, the canvas is not meticulously rendered with photographic accuracy. Instead, the artist strives to give an impression, a feeling of the confusion and passion of the event. The people crowding the river bank, the boats on the water, even the Houses of Parliament themselves are recognizable, but not particularly realistic. What is real is the feeling Turner is able to convey. One can almost smell the smoke and feel the heat of the flames.

Art movements of the mid and late nineteenth century include Impressionism, a style that began in France and gained popularity in Europe and in the newest emerging art center, the United States. A host of artists responded to the tenets of the Impressionist movement, which heralded changes in color, in line, and in style. One hallmark of Impressionists was their urge to paint *en plein air*, in nature—to take

their easels out of the confining studio atmosphere and to set them down in fields, in meadows, and anywhere else they could experience nature and put it on canvas.

Art historians describe the Impressionist movement as a revolution in color, in part because Impressionist painters did not laboriously mix their paints on palettes, but on the canvas itself, often juxtaposing colors and letting the human eye do the mixing. But the Impressionist movement, and the post-Impressionists who followed also heralded a revolution in line, in dimension, and in painting itself. No longer were artists confined to a studio; no longer were they confined to the subject matter presented to them within the studio setting. They were free to paint as they wished, where they wished, and to use the canvas as they saw fit.

The artists who followed, called Post-Impressionists, are not as united a group as the

4. Vincent van Gogh. *The Starry Night.* (Museum of Modern Art, NY)

In his brief career, Georges Seurat (1859–1891) was able to take the lessons of the Impressionists and give them a new twist. He, too, shared the Impressionists' love of color, and worked at using color in a whole new way. Called pointillism, the technique used by Seurat required meticulous brush control and a deep understanding of the mechanics of color. Seurat's first pointillist work, *Sunday Afternoon on the Island of La Grande Jatte* (1884–1886) (Figure 3) illustrates the care with which the artist rendered his images.

Seurat's canvas, which more often than not was preceded by a great many sketches and drawings suggesting the manner in which he hoped to execute the final work, comprises literally millions of tiny individual dots and strokes of pure color, applied such that the viewer's eye blends them into their final form. In a way, pointillism heralds the digitization of images used in video art today. Just as pixels of pure color are combined to render television or video images, so too did Seurat render images over a hundred years ago, and without benefit of computer or other high-tech devices.

If a student were asked to name the most famous painter of the nineteenth century, he or she would most likely choose Vincent van Gogh (1853–1890). The subject of biography, music, and endless fascination, Van Gogh could be classified either as a Post-Impressionist or as an Expressionist, although it is probable that neither term would find favor with the artist himself. Van Gogh's career spanned only ten years—even less time than that of Seurat— and some art historians call him the greatest Dutch artist since Vermeer and other painters of the seventeenth century.

Van Gogh's strengths lie in his use of color and his understanding of the medium of oil paint. His thickly applied brush stokes add light and shadow to his luminous canvases. One of his most famous paintings, *The Starry Night* (1889) (Figure 4) is filled with an incredible feeling of energy and motion. With a moon as bright as the sun and individual stars reflected in their own halos of energy, the starry night is not one of calm reflection. Instead it is an

Impressionists. Generally, speaking, the term "Post-Impressionist" can be applied to almost any artist who worked after the 1880s. Usually the artist had an Impressionist phase but then went beyond it to experiment further not only with color. but with form and space as well.

The work of Paul Cézanne (1839–1906) represents some of the best of the Post-Impressionist era. He is best known for his still lifes, but his portraits are also important reminders of the developments in the visual arts during the nineteenth century. The portrait of his wife, entitled *Madame Cézanne in the Conservatory* (c. 1880) (Figure 2) illustrates many of the qualities of a Post-Impressionist work—overlapping brush strokes create depth and volume; their rhythmic patterning add texture to the flat canvas. Cézanne seems to be working at once in a realistic genre and an Impressionist one—the face of the subject is rendered realistically, as is the tree behind her and some other elements of the composition. At the same time, her hands, her dress, and other aspects of the background are Impressionistic. The blending of styles, the experimentation with different vantage points and different elements that go into the overall composition, demonstrate the phase of experimentation common to many artists of this period.

5. Henri Rousseau. *The Sleeping Gypsy.* (Museum of Modern Art, NY)

image of emotion and expression, foretelling perhaps the fate of the artist, whose own emotions were governed by mental distress strong enough to lead him to take his own life.

Among the other "-isms" that defined art in the late nineteenth century was Primitivism, a movement "discovered" by progressive artists like Pablo Picasso who sought the unusual in the world around him. Picasso looked to various sources for his inspiration, including Africa and the Far East. He also championed other artists who worked outside of the main stream.

One such artist was Henri Rousseau, (1844–1910), who would today probably be described as a folk artist, since he was never trained formally and began his career later in life. Rousseau's work is difficult to pigeonhole. It is naive, but it possesses a mysterious quality that defies that categorization. As an example, one need only look at his *The Sleeping Gypsy* (1897) (Figure 5). Here is a work that defies all of the rules of painting. It is primitive in style and in subject matter; at the same time it is sophisticated in rendering and technique. The artist knew how to use paint; he also knew how to convey a sense of serenity tinged with an essence of mystery.

No single style predominates in the twentieth century. Instead, it was—and is—a period of great experimentation and great changes.

One of the most important movements of the early decades of the twentieth century was Abstraction. There is no way to define Abstraction in simple terms. It may be easier to define it visually. One of the champions of the Abstract movement was Pablo Picasso (1881–1974). His *Les Demoiselles d'Avignon* (1907) (Figure 6) takes the female form and redefines it. This is not the *Aphrodite of Knidos;* nor is it Boucher's *Venus.* These female forms are reductive—angular distortions of female bodies, hinting at a number of cultural cross-currents. While some may see suggestions of the Classical in the forms of the three women to the left, there are also echoes of African sculpture; and indeed Picasso was influenced by all of these styles. But Picasso was also inventive and sophisticated. His work reduced the visual to its abstract elements. The changes in his style over his long and productive career indicate his

6. Pablo Picasso. *Les Demoiselles d'Avignon*. (Musem of Modern Art, NY. Copyright ARS, New York)

receptiveness to influences from non-Western and non-industrialized cultures as well as his own Western heritage.

The genre of abstraction pioneered by Picasso is called Cubism. A host of Cubist followers, many of whom developed their own distinct Cubist sub-categories, followed. Marc Chagall (1887–1985), a Russian painter whose works often strongly reflected his Jewish roots, worked in a Cubist style that combined fantasy and reality. His *I and the Village* (1911) (Figure 7) combines elements of Russian and Jewish folk tales with Cubist renderings of scenes from everyday life.

By World War I, avante garde artists had experimented with a multitude of abstract styles. At the Armory Show in New York City in 1913, many abstract painters made their debut on the North American continent.

Generally favorably received by the art community (although not as welcomed by the average viewer) abstract painting began to gain a foothold outside of Europe. Given the disfavor with which the National Socialists in Germany viewed nonrepresentational art, it was a good thing that America was willing to welcome avant garde artists and their work.

In 1939, the Nazis got rid of—either by auction or by destruction—many of the most famous abstract works in German museums. Some pieces were sold to museums or collectors in other European cities, only to fall once again under the strict anti-abstract sentiments of the Nazis as the war progressed; other works, and artists, were able to be saved in the United States.

Art during and after World War II continued to be a compendium of various themes and movements. Not every artist worked in the abstract; some preferred to stick to realism. Still others painted in a style that came to be known as Abstract Expressionism.

The art of Piet Mondrian (1872–1944) may summarize the path taken by many abstract artists whose careers spanned both world wars. Mondrian, a Dutch painter, began his career working with representational images. He soon began to strip away all the elements of the representational, however, replacing reality with abstraction and reducing his canvases to simple, rhythmical, almost mathematically precise shapes and primary colors. He described his own work as Neo-Plasticism; the works themselves suggest strict rules for balancing horizontal and vertical; color and space.

One of Mondrian's last works, his *Broadway Boogie-Woogie* (1942–43) (Figure 8) amply illustrates the flatness and geometric precision of his Neo-Plastic vision. Although the canvas comprises only three colors and is separated only into horizontal and vertical space, it nonetheless possesses a rhythmic sense that reveals great skill and a comprehension of the use of space and color.

However, not all art of the twentieth century is purely abstract and without any grounding whatsoever in reality; some of the best representational art of any period also belongs to the twentieth century. The work of the American Edward Hopper (1882–1967) illustrates that realists also had a place in this era. His haunting *Nighthawks* (1942) (Figure 9), painted the same year as Mondrian completed *Broadway Boogie-Woogie*, shows the reality of loneliness and placed Hopper in the school of Social Realists, who painted true-to-life images of the world around them, even if what they painted was not the most beautiful. Hopper painted images of diners, of barber shops, of movie theaters, not cathedrals or temples. He used light and shadow as skillfully as Rembrandt ; he also did not lose sight of the common in his quest for subject matter.

7. Marc Chagall. *I and the Village.* (Museum of Modern Art, NY. Copyright ARS New York)

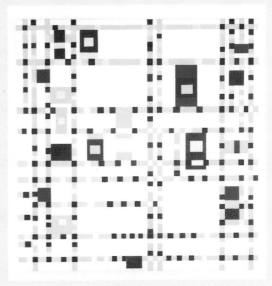

8. Piet Mondrian. *Broadway Boogie-Woogie.* (Museum of Modern Art, NY)

9. Edward Hopper. *Nighthawks*. (Art Institute of Chicago)

10. Jackson Pollock. *Convergence*. (Albright Knox Art Gallery, Buffalo)

After World War II, a plethora of styles emerged, the best known of which was probably Abstract Expressionism. Art historians cite the realities of the post-World War II era—the aftermath of the atom bomb, the Cold War—as the impetus for a number of movements or sub-groups of Abstract Expressionism. One of

these movements, the work of the Action Painters, is best represented by the work of the American Jackson Pollock (1912–1956), whose first action painting was completed in 1950. His technique consisted of pouring and spattering his colors on the canvas, instead of using a brush or palette knife to apply them. His *Convergence* (1952) (Figure 10) may at first appear to be merely an accident, a canvas used as a drop cloth. But each application of color was done in a controlled and studied manner. The artist knew exactly what he was doing every time he dripped, sprayed, or splattered his canvas.

As many post-1950 styles existed as did pre-1950 styles. As the century progresses, each artist feels even more freedom of expression, however, each artist is also subjected to a more and more critical audience. We as viewers feel freer in our ability to criticize and our desire to understand the artist and the work that she or he creates.

immigrants in the United States experienced comparable dislocation. The conflicts between traditional sources of political and social power and the new organizations of industry and labor contributed to great social dissatisfaction.

The constitution was a peculiar mixture of aristocratic Prussian power in the upper house and democratic universal male suffrage, which was manipulated to iliberal ends. Bismarck's opportunistic maneuvers against Catholics, liberals, and socialists had undermined the development of a viable parliamentary government. The bureaucracy, the military, and the chancellor remained out of the reach of the voting populace. The Social Democrats were the one party that campaigned for chancellor responsibility, that is, for legislative power to reject the chancellor. They urged passage of many democratic measures. Their political leaders called for revolution but worked to win from the government those measures that would improve everyday life. In 1914, the most highly industrialized and powerful European nation, with the largest and most successful socialist party, was nevertheless subject to a political regime that preserved aspects of an absolute monarchy.

ITALY: UNFULFILLED EXPECTATIONS

Italian nationalists expected greatness from the unification of their country, so long conquered, plundered, divided, and ruled by absolute princes. But the newly unified Italy faced serious problems. An overwhelmingly Roman Catholic country, it was split by religious controversy. Liberals and republicans wanted a secular state, with civil marriage and public education, which was anathema to the church. Another divisive factor was Italy's long tradition of separate and rival states—an extreme version of the regional conflicts of most states. Many Italians doubted that the central government would deal justly with every region. Furthermore, few Italians could participate in the constitutional monarchy. Of the 27 million citizens, only about 2 million could vote, even after the reforms of 1881, which tripled the electorate. Liberals could point out that almost every literate male could vote, but this achievement was small conso-

lation to those who had fought for unification but now were denied voting privileges because they did not pass a literacy test.

Among Italian workers, cynicism about the government was so deep that many turned to radical movements, which advocated the rejection of authority and the tactics of terrorism, assassination, and general strikes. Disgust with parliamentary government led the workers to believe that direct action would gain more than elections and parties. Other alienated Italians included peasants in some rural areas, particularly in the south. They were so isolated from the national political and economic life that traditional patterns of loyalty to the local landowner, now also a political leader, persisted. Catholic, loyal to their landlord, and bitterly unhappy with their economic situation, they saw few signs of the new state aside from taxation and conscription.

The ruling elite brushed aside Italy's difficult social and economic problems. It concentrated instead on issues more easily expressed to an inexperienced political nation: nationalism, foreign policy, and military glory. The politicians trumpeted Italy's ambitions for Great Power status to justify military expenditures beyond the means of such a poor state. They presented Italy's scramble for African and Mediterranean territories as the solution to all its social ills. Exploiting others would pay for badly needed social reforms, and the raw materials gained would fuel industrialization. None of these promises came true, which deepened the cynicism of a disillusioned people. As a foreign and as a domestic policy, this pursuit of glory was too costly for the fragile nation.

Before World War I, Italy was deeply divided politically. A wave of strikes and rural discontent gave sufficient warning to political leaders so that they declared neutrality, deciding, unlike Russia, not to risk the shaky regime by entering the war. But the appeals of expansionism were too great for them to maintain this policy.

THE UNITED STATES: DEMOCRATIC GIANT

Within a generation after its bloody Civil War (1861–65), fought to prevent the dissolution of the union, the United States moved into the rank

PHOTO OF A NEW YORK SWEAT SHOP BY JACOB RIIS. The latter half of the nineteenth century saw a proliferation of "sweat shops." Adults and children alike, often immigrants, labored long hours in appalling conditions for little pay. (*The Bettmann Archive*)

of giant industrial powers, then to the status of a Great Power, and by the end of World War I, to world leadership.

Around the middle of the nineteenth century, the United States was essentially a producer of primary goods or raw materials. From the time the country was founded, it was a nation of farmers. European free labor plus Southern slaves made up the labor force. The standard of living of the farming majority was high enough—particularly when compared with that of their European counterparts—to spur the development of a domestic market for consumer goods. Thus, the northeastern part of the country became a manufacturing region, based on craft industries. Advancing the domestic market beyond basic goods was as slow a process as in France or most of central Europe, but the expansion of agriculture westward extended that base. It laid the founda-

tion for the more rapid expansion and development of industry after the Civil War.

Despite the immigration from Europe and the great numbers of slaves, there was a steady labor shortage, which may have contributed to a cultural characteristic of Americans: that they were open to new technology of any sort. But even when labor-saving inventions became available, Americans, like most Europeans, were slow to apply them because they were costly, and capital was even scarcer than labor. Until the Civil War, the economy was primarily mercantile. The merchant was the commercial cement bonding the many small artisans, farmers, and exporters.

In many ways, the early industrialization of the United States resembled that of Britain. Unskilled European and rural laborers furnished the manpower for New England textile mills, just as Irish and rural laborers had done for England. A single government, able to provide a stable framework for commerce, maintained tariffs to keep out British competition for an early period, but, like Britain, was noninterventionist—both unwilling and unable to regulate private enterprise. As in Britain, it was the growth of a large internal market for cheap, standardized goods that encouraged entrepreneurs to take the risks of investment and production on a large scale. Even more than the British, perhaps because of the much larger market for cheap goods, Americans took to machines, with standardized and interchangeable parts, which could produce such goods. (Eli Whitney, who invented the cotton gin, got his start in the production of interchangeable parts for handguns.) Unlike Britain, however, the United States was dependent on an influx of capital (most of it from Britain)—a dependence that continued even after the Civil War, when great sectors of the American economy moved from the work of artisans to modern concentrated industry.

After the Civil War, American industrialization gained momentum. Its industrial power rested on the sheer scale of industry, on the exploitation of the continent's resources as private property, and on the extension of agriculture and transportation across the continent. The other crucial factors were a cheap labor force and substantial foreign investment in large-scale corporations in heavy industries, such as coal mining and iron and steel manufacture. On both the regional and the national level, government encouraged free enterprise by treating the nation's resources as commodities that could be claimed by individuals and corporations. It also fostered railroad building, tariff regulation, and free immigration—all of which contributed to the construction of an industrial giant in the northeast segment of the country.

In other areas, however, government took a laissez-faire stance. Urbanization, with its concomitant social problems, accompanied industrialization. American politicians were much less inclined to support social legislation, including pensions and minimum wages, than their European counterparts. There was no Bismarckian or Churchillian social legislation in the land of individual free enterprise. Yet the United States had less labor strife until the end of the century. One reason was that workers shared the dream of entrepreneurial success much more than their European peers. Another reason was the fact that class solidarity was difficult to de-velop among varied ethnic groups of different cultures and languages. Each new immigrant group (and later the rural blacks) entered at the bottom, supplying cheap and competitive labor and experiencing the violent reactions of their fellow workers from other ethnic groups. Established workers, already assimilated, were able to prohibit Asian immigration at the end of the century, after Chinese workers had built the transcontinental railroad.

Labor conflict did flare up, however, in the decade before World War I. Generally, workers voted for one of the two major parties, but in the election of 1912 more than a million voted for the Socialist candidate. Not all of these voters were the "foreigners" or recent immigrants that contemporaries pretended. Many Americans were critical of the money power of giant cartels and monopolies. Theodore Roosevelt of the Republicans and Woodrow Wilson of the Democrats both called for restrictions of monopolies, or trusts. Unrestricted competition, which gave some people an unfair advantage, upset many Americans.

While restricting immigration, Americans were expanding their frontiers in the Spanish-American War of 1898, annexing Puerto Rico, the Philippines, and Guam and controlling Cuba. For the most part, American imperialism did not express itself by annexing territories. Instead, what the Americans sought, starting in the 1890s, was an "Open Door": that is, access for their goods and their traders in all the markets of the world, and particularly in the Pacific.

By 1914, the American market was the largest, most homogeneous, and most rapidly growing in the world. The United States was the largest industrial nation, producing more steel and coal than any other country. It was also the world's leader in automobiles, farming technology, electricity, and petroleum sectors. Its labor was the most productive and had the highest standard of living. The United States had achieved this position in a little more than a generation. Its economic power led it to military action and ultimately to political and diplomatic leadership.

A GOLDEN AGE?

To thoughtful Europeans living in 1915, after a year of World War I, the nineteenth century must have seemed a golden era. They might have viewed it as a period of unparalleled peace and progress, full of the promise of all that well-meaning people considered modern: liberal institutions and democratic movements, autonomous nations, scientific and industrial progress, and individual human development. The century that had just ended seemed one of progress in the production of goods, the alleviation of want, the development of technology, and the application of science to industry and medicine.

Part of that progress, in most minds, was the extension of constitutional and liberal government and the expression of humanitarian concern for others. Serfdom had been abolished in Europe; so had slavery in the United States and Brazil. Europeans spoke of self-government as a right. The importance of democracy had been acknowledged, and in most of Europe, universal manhood suffrage was in effect before the outbreak of the war.

The world had become smaller, more interdependent, and more cosmopolitan. Many westerners were better educated and probably better fed, housed, and clothed than their counterparts in preceding eras. Europe was at the height of its power in the nineteenth century. European productive capacities had reached out to most areas of the world, and European culture was brilliant—whether considered in the aggregate, or individually as German, French, English, or Italian culture.

Yet people looking back from the vantage point of 1915 must have realized, too, that something had gone wrong in the nineteenth century. Authoritarian governments persisted in central, eastern, and southern Europe. Traditional institutions and groups still exercised their privileges at the expense of others, often by brutally repressing opposition, especially regional and minority loyalties. Doubts had been stirred when the revolutions of 1848 had failed to reconcile national and class conflicts. Perhaps the bitter reaction to 1848, the harsh reality of the midcentury wars of unification, and the building of the centralized state had perverted the ideals of liberal government and individual freedom. Many doubted the wisdom of democratic government as they saw the passions of the masses manipulated by cynical leadership. Perhaps the ideals of liberal government, individual freedom, national autonomy, and economic progress were not equally suited to every situation.

In the last part of the nineteenth century and the first part of the twentieth, liberal-democratic ideals fell prey to authoritarianism, extreme nationalism, imperialism, class conflict, and racism. But despite world war, mass destruction, and the manipulation of humanity in the name of nationalist passions, these ideals would survive and spread.

◆ ◆ ◆

SUGGESTED READING

Anderson, Bonnie, and Judith Zinsser, *A History of Their Own: Women in Europe from Prehistory to the Present,* vol. 2 (1988). Best survey to date of the movement for women's independence.

Blake, R., *Disraeli* (1967). An excellent one-volume biography.

Blackbourn, David, and Geoff Eley. *The Peculiarities of German History* (1984). Critically examines traditional assumptions regarding Bismarck's Germany.

Craig, Gordon, *Politics of the Prussian Army* (1955). A very valuable study with important implications for German and European history.

Eyck, Erich, *Bismarck and the German Empire* (1950). A classic liberal critical biography; an abridgment of a larger work.

Ford, Colin, and Brian Harrison, *A Hundred Years Ago* (1983). An excellent social history of Britain, with fine photographs.

Hays, Samuel P., *American Political History as Social Analysis: Essays by Samuel P. Hays (1980).* Relevant social and political reflections on post–Civil War United States.

Hobsbawm, Eric, *The Age of Capital* (1988). A Marxist interpretation of mid-nineteenth-century Europe.

Holborn, Hajo, *History of Modern Germany, 1840–1945,* vol. 3 (1969). A definitive work.

Johnson, D., *France and the Dreyfus Affair* (1967). The best of many books on the controversial affair.

Joll, James, *Europe Since 1870* (1973). A valuable

general survey, particularly good on socialism in the individual nations.

Kemp, Tom, *Industrialization in Nineteenth-Century Europe* (1985). Readable general survey incorporating recent scholarship.

Mack Smith, Denis, *Italy: A Modern History*, rev. ed. (1969). An excellent survey, with emphasis on the theme of the failure of Italy to develop viable liberal institutions or economic solutions.

Mayer, Arno, *The Persistence of the Old Regime* (1981). His theme is the survival of traditional Europe until World War I.

Mosse, W. E., *Liberal Europe, 1848–1875* (1974). A comparative history of Europe in the liberal era.

Nelson, Daniel, *Managers and Workers: Origins of New Factory System in the United States 1880–1920.* (1975). An Intelligent examination of the industrial growth that made the United States a great power.

O'Brien, C. C., *Parnell and His Party, 1880–90* (1957). A good book on this important Irish leader.

Seton-Watson, Christopher, *Italy from Liberalism to Fascism* (1981). An excellent survey of Italian history.

Sheehan, J. J., *German Liberalism in the Nineteenth Century* (1978). Challenges accepted opinions on the failures of German liberalism.

Stansky, P., *Gladstone: A Progress in Politics* (1981). Stresses the importance of Gladstone as an effective statesman.

Stedman Jones, Gareth, *Outcast London* (1971). An excellent study of British social problems and policy at the end of the century.

Weber, E., *Peasants into Frenchmen: Modernization of Rural France, 1870–1914* (1976). Describes the most important aspects of nation building.

Wehler, Hans, *The German Empire 1871–1918* (1986). A revisionist analysis in keeping with Blackbourn and Eley.

Wright, Gordon, *France in Modern Times,* 2nd ed. (1974). A good survey of the entire period.

REVIEW QUESTIONS

1. Why was England seen by many as the model liberal nation in the middle decades of the nineteenth century?

2. How did the competition between political parties promote reform in Victorian England?

3. How did the Reform Bill of 1867 usher in a new era in British politics?

4. In England, the middle class and the workers often worked together for reform in the period from 1860 to 1914. In France they rarely did. Why?

5. How did Napoleon III's domestic policies lead some people to view him as a liberal, even a socialist, and others to see him as a conservative?

6. What was the general crisis of liberalism after 1870?

7. How did the conservatives attempt to win over the masses after 1870?

8. Historians disagree about the merits of the Bismarckian legacy to Germany. Discuss evidence for this disagreement.

9. Nationalism created a consensus supporting those who unified Germany and Italy for almost a generation after 1870. What economic, social, and political conflict seemed to undermine that consensus before World War I? Discuss this changed view of nationalism.

10. On the eve of World War I, most of the European states were threatened by a crisis, either political or social. Discuss the threat of revolution or social change among the Great Powers on the eve of the war.

11. What were the factors that raised the United States to a Great Power by 1914?

12. How were economic and social conditions connected to political crises in the Great Powers in the era before World War I?

CHAPTER 27

Western Imperialism:
Global Dominance

*I*n the last two decades of the nineteenth century, European nations very rapidly laid claim to great portions of the world's surface. Russia and the United States pushed to the end of their continent and beyond. Westerners exploited the weakness of Japanese and Chinese dynasties, forcing commercial connections and the cession of treaty ports and territory to gain economic and political advantage in the Far East. They separated one by one the territories of the Ottoman Turkish ruler. In the second half of the century, the British deprived India of all semblance of independence, ruling it directly or indirectly through puppet princes. They grabbed most of Africa, seizing goods, annexing territories, and carving out empires if local rulers were too weak or too self-interested to prevent it. Latin American development and prosperity became absolutely dependent on Europe and the United States, despite nominal political independence.

From about 1880 to 1914, Europeans confronted each other, willing to fight over stretches of desert or rain forest that they could scarcely locate on the map. Asians and Africans who could not resolve conflicts among themselves found their lives controlled and their lands occupied. Even those who were able to unite could not counter Western military and technological superiority.

European domination of most of the world continued until after World War II. The impact of imperialism—the domination by a country of the political, economic, or cultural life of another country, region, or people—contributed to both world wars and to the conflicting ideologies and crises of the cold war. But it also played a part in to the establishment of the interdependent global economy and culture that we have today.

Lithograph by Joseph Keppler showing the other world powers fighting over China. (*Library of Congress*)

CHRONOLOGY 27.1 Expansion of Western Dominance

1830	The French move into Algeria
1839–1842	Opium War: the British defeat the Chinese, annexing treaty ports in China and opening them to Western trade
1853	Commodore Perry, with U.S. naval forces, opens Japan to trade
1857–58	Sepoy Mutiny; Britain replaces the East India Company and governs India directly
1867	Mexicans led by Juárez execute Emperor Maximilian; Meiji Restoration in Japan
1869	Opening of Suez Canal
1876	Stanley sets up posts in the Congo for Leopold II of Belgium
1878	Congress of Berlin: Great Powers meet to prevent Russia from upsetting the balance of power in the Near East
1878–1881	British and Russian troops occupy Afghanistan
1881	The French take control of Tunisia
1882	Britain occupies Egypt
1883–85	The French fight the Chinese to claim Indochina
1884	Berlin Conference on Africa
1894–95	Sino-Japanese War: the British, Russians, and French intervene to take away Japan's gains
1896	Ethiopians defeat Italian invaders at Adowa
1898	Spanish-American War: the United States annexes the Philippines and Puerto Rico and occupies Cuba; the battle of Omdurman
1899–1902	Boer War between the British and the Afrikaners
1900	Boxers rebel against foreign presence in China
1904–1905	Russo-Japanese War: the Japanese defeat the Russians
1911	Mexican Revolution; Manchu dynasty is overthrown in China, a republic formed, and Sun Zhongshan (Sun Yat-sen) becomes its president; civil war breaks out in China
1919	Britain grants a legislative assembly in India; Gandhi's passive resistance movement broadens in response to the Amritsar Massacre; Kemal Atatürk emerges as the Turkish national leader; League of Nations mandate system established

EMERGENCE OF THE NEW IMPERIALISM

From the long perspective, European history has been one of expansion. It has also been a history of a struggle for domination of others—from the sixteenth-century explorations, conquests, and settlements of the Americas and the aggressive inroads in Southeast Asia and Africa for lucrative trade in spices, silks, luxury goods, and slaves to the eighteenth-century wars over trade and claims to colonies. By the early 1800s, however, the old slaving stations in Africa had declined, as had the Caribbean sugar trade and the mines of Central and South America. Revolutionary wars had liberated the United States and Latin America and seemed to usher in a new era of trade and investment without political control. For most of the nineteenth century Europeans—at least those engaged in the growth of industry and the development of the nation—showed little interest in adding to the remnants of colonial empires. Advocates of free trade argued that commerce would go to whichever country could produce the best goods most cheaply. Efforts to add colonies would be better expended in improving industry, they said. They also hoped that Europeans had grown too civilized to fight over trade networks. European liberals, in particular, believed that a major war would destroy the livelihoods of too many people because commerce was so interdependent.

Meanwhile, European influence over the rest of the world grew as European nations industrialized, world trade expanded, drawing previously untouched peoples into the network of supply and demand of raw materials, finished goods, and capital. The expanson of world trade and the spread of Western ideas and technology continued even without any extensions of political empires. Masses of European immigrants made new homes in North and South America, Australia, and New Zealand.

Suddenly, however, in the last decades of the century, Europeans switched abruptly from commercial penetration to active conquest, political control, and exploitation of previously unclaimed and, in many ways, untouched territories. Why did Europeans strive to claim and control the entire world?

Conflicting Interpretations

Some historians suggest that the new imperialism (to differentiate it from the *colonialism* of settlement and trade of the 1500s and 1600s) was a direct result of industrialization. With intensified economic activity and competition, Europeans struggled for raw materials, markets for their manufactured goods, and places to invest their capital for higher rates of return. In the late 1800s, many politicians and industrialists believed that annexing overseas territories was the only way for their nations to ensure the economic necessities for their people. Trusting the free market might mean triumph for competitor states. Captains of industry defended the search for new empires to their sometimes reluctant governments and compatriots, predicting dire economic consequences if their countries failed to get their share of the world markets.

Historians today, however, point out that most of the areas claimed by Europeans and Americans were not profitable sources of raw materials or wealthy enough to be good markets. For Europeans and Americans, the primary trading and investment venues were Europe and America rather than Asia or Africa. Some individual businesses made colonial profits, but most colonies proved unprofitable for the Western taxpayer. Between 1865 and 1914, for example, only 39 percent of British investment went to lands of the empire outside the British Isles, 28 percent of that amount going to the self-governing dominions. The average rate of return did not surpass that from home investments. In general, the colonies did not attract surplus European population that could contribute to the mother country's economy. The United States drew most of the European emigrants, who also streamed to Australia, Canada, New Zealand, and South America—lands already dominated by westerners. Two-thirds of British emigrants went outside the empire, mostly to the United States. Italians certainly did not migrate to Italy's African territories, and the French scarcely migrated at all.

The economic justifications of imperialism are inseparable from the intensely nationalistic ones. Policymakers hoped that possession of empires would solve economic problems, which were particularly pressing after the crash of 1873, and join together disparate social groups with pride in national power. The newly unified states, Germany and Italy, demanded colonies as recognition of their Great Power status; leaders in those two nations were convinced that Britain's standing depended on colonies and naval power. They were aware of the heavy tax burden on British subjects, the expenses of empire, and the greatly increased possibility of war with rival nations or resistant subjects. Nevertheless, these leaders chose an imperial course. Having lost ingloriously to Prussia in 1870, France also turned its attention overseas, hoping to recoup prestige and to add to its manpower and wealth for future European struggles. Many leaders hoped that imperialism would win them the loyalty of their own people. Some argued that the well-being of the workers depended on colonies. Others argued from strength: Americans, who had built one of the world's great industrial powers after the Civil War, trumpeted their achievements by defeating the once-imperial Spain in Cuba and the Philippines. Still others urged imperialism from weakness. Economically backward Russia pushed east to the Pacific and south toward India for ports and resources to develop its commerce and industry. In the 1890s, Japan announced that it had joined the world's Great Powers by attacking China for control of Korea's raw materials and markets. Thus, both economically powerful states and struggling ones turned to imperialism.

On the eve of World War I, many socialists, including Vladimir Lenin, a revolutionary Marxist who would become one of the leaders of the Russian Revolution in 1917, argued that imperialism was inevitable in a highly advanced capitalist country. He asserted that capitalist nations maintained their monopolistic economy and their political system by exploiting the less-developed world. Monopoly capitalism was condemned to periodic depressions due to lack of materials, markets, and capital, he said. Unless the governments of capitalist countries could ensure high wages and profits for their own people by exploiting colonial peoples, working-class revolutions would break out. Powerful business interests also pushed their governments to the verge of war to safeguard their profits. At the same time, Lenin said, imperialism greatly accelerated both the development of capitalism and opposition to it among the victims of imperialism in Asia,

Africa, and Latin America. He predicted that the struggle for empire would end in war between the Great Powers, which would draw the colonies into European affairs even faster than the operations of the market.

The nationalistic competition among the Europeans led them, for a time, to extend their power struggles to Africa and Asia. Far away from their European boundaries, leaders acquired territories for strategic reasons or sometimes just to keep competitors from doing so. For example, Britons reasoned that they had to keep the Germans from gaining a foothold in the Middle East because it might open the Indian Ocean—and the British-dominated Indian subcontinent—to them. They had to keep the Russians out of Afghanistan *to protect India*. Bismarck actually encouraged the French to expand in Africa, knowing full well that this course would bring them into conflict with the Italians and the British Empire and thus distract their attention from Alsace and Lorraine, which Germany had taken in 1870. The overseas expansion would divide the French people into imperialists and anti-imperialists, creating another political rift to weaken the French government. After Bismarck's dismissal, however, when Germany began expanding its navy, Britain allied with its colonial rival France.

The British liked to think that they were merely defending an empire they already possessed. They defined enormous amounts of territory and water as essential to the defense of their Indian colony. Nations with less extensive or less lucrative empires saw Britain as their primary rival for the spoils of imperialism—for "a place in the sun," as the Germans liked to phrase it. In Russia, a small clique of nobles and officers urged expansion, knowing that a move into Asia would bring Russia into conflict with Britain. Later, such a move would mean confronting the Japanese. Since the conflicts between Europeans were played out in Asia and Africa, perhaps for a while they helped keep Europe itself relatively peaceful. In the long run, however, the tense atmosphere of imperialism—the militarism and the racism—contributed to a more devastating conflict in Europe, World War I, which engaged the empires as well.

The most extreme ideological expression of nationalism and imperialism was Social Darwin-

ROMAN CATHOLIC MISSIONARIES FROM FRANCE. Hats for the tropical sun are a special adaptation of the traditional robes or habits of French nuns working in Madagascar (Malagasay Republic) at the turn of the century. Catholics and Protestant denominations from every European nation strove for converts among the various African peoples with varying degrees of success. (*Roger-Viollet*)

ism (see Chapter 24). Social Darwinists vigorously advocated the acquisition of empires, saying that strong nations—by definition, those that were successful at expanding industry and empire—would survive and that others would not. To these elitists, all white men were more fit than nonwhites to prevail in the struggle for dominance, but among Europeans, some nations were deemed more fit than others for the competition. Usually, Social Darwinists thought their own nation the best, which sparked their competitive enthusiasm, but some feared that their people were incapable of the endurance and sacrifice necessary to win. Their fears did not tame their imperialism, however, as they called for colonies to test and train the people for the struggles ahead. Social Darwinists were blatantly racist; they even applied racial terms to their own lower class. When working-class men proved physically unfit

to serve in the Boer War, British imperialists became advocates of health and education reforms to improve the British "race." In the popular mind, the concepts of evolution justified the exploitation of "lesser breeds without the law" by superior races. This language of race and conflict, of superior and inferior people, had wide currency in the Western states.

Not all advocates of empire were Social Darwinists. Some did not think of themselves as racists. In fact, they believed that the extension of empire, law, order, and industrial civilization would raise "backward peoples" up the ladder of evolution and civilization to equality. In the nineteenth century, in contrast to the seventeenth and eighteenth centuries, Europeans, except for missionaries, rarely adopted the customs or learned the languages of local people. They had little sense that other cultures and other peoples had

PHOTOGRAPH OF EUROPEANS AND WARRIORS AND MUSICIANS IN BORNEO,
C. 1885. Fascinated by the exotic, European travelers made use of the new tech-
nology of photography to record their itineraries throughout various colonies.
(*Royal Anthropological Society*)

merit and deserved respect. Clearly, the European attitude toward other cultures had changed.

Many westerners believed that it was their duty as Christians to set an example and to educate others. Missionaries were the first to meet and learn about many peoples and the first to develop writing for those without a written language. Christian missionaries were ardently opposed to slavery, and throughout the century they went to unexplored African regions to preach against slavery, which was still carried on by Arab and African traders. But even missionaries, thought preaching would not end the enslavement of those Africans who were vanquished in tribal wars. Some, like Livingstone, hoped an expanding European economy would bring Africa to the world market.

Some of the passion for imperialism was sparked by interest in exotic places. At the end of the eighteenth century, the expeditions of Mungo

Park, a Scottish explorer, on the Niger River in West Africa stimulated the romantic imagination. The explorations of David Livingstone in the Congo Basin and of Richard Burton and John Speke (who raced with each other and with Livingstone to find the source of the Nile River) fascinated many Europeans during the second half of the nineteenth century. In the early 1800s, expeditions were a matter of adventure and scientific curiosity; they often included explorers from several countries. After the midcentury, national prestige became a goal in these forays. Sponsored by national geographic and exploratory societies and encouraged by their nation's military, explorers captured the public imagination in much the same way that astronauts do today. Individualist personalities, who seemed larger than life to their contemporaries, often saw exploration as an escape from a humdrum or stultifying existence at home.

Individuals and nations competed to find the

highest mountain, the longest river, the highest waterfall, and the land never before seen by white men. Such challenges called men and women away from their ordinary lives, if not to experience, then at least to dream of, adventure. The mass press—the media of the day—was filled with stories of exotic peoples and customs, European bravery, and self-sacrificing heroes. The fiction of English authors Rudyard Kipling (1865–1936) and H. Rider Haggard (1856–1925) and their many inferior imitators stimulated the passion for faraway places and unknown peoples. They helped shape the attitudes of the next generation. Kipling wrote: "Take up the White Man's Burden—/Send forth the best ye breed—/Go bind your sons to exile/To serve your captives' need." He also wrote of the Indian Gunga Din, whose death in faithful service in battle to his white masters won him their respect. Until twentieth-century writers like Joseph Conrad, George Orwell, Olive Schreiner, and E. M. Forster, authors usually depicted heroism and glory and rarely described the exploitation, cruelty, and abuses of empire.

A Global Economy

The Western economy became truly global by the end of the nineteenth century, thanks to new markets, new technology, and overseas trade and investment, although some areas remained untouched and undeveloped. As the Western powers industrialized, small, backward European countries also exploited raw materials and markets in the rest of the world. In many parts of Europe, even the working classes and the peasantry could buy goods from faraway places that had previously been available only to the very wealthy.

The underdeveloped areas of the world, in turn, found markets for their crops and were able to buy European goods—at least the wealthy could. But being part of the world economy also made these areas subject to the smallest tremors on the European and American stock exchanges and to changing fashions of consumption. Participation in the world market brought wealth to a few people, but it meant hardship for many, as well as loss of traditional customs and social relationships.

Increasing crop production to satisfy European and American markets often created problems. Producing for the Western market meant turning land that had grown food for families over to export crops like coffee or indigo, thus reducing the food supply; it often meant consolidation of small peasant holdings in the hands of richer peasants or landlords. Thus, market forces drove the poorer peasants off the land, into debt to the landlord or to the usurer, and into cities. For most of the nineteenth century, the peasants felt bonded to their traditional masters, but in the twentieth century, they came to see themselves as enslaved by foreigners who either controlled the government or the world market. The passionate desire to escape this bondage has fueled revolutionary movements throughout the world.

Economic interdependence operated to the great advantage of Europeans and Americans. As early as the beginning of the twentieth century, the world economy enriched the lives of consumers and made their lives easier. Many Europeans and Americans dressed in Egyptian cotton, Australian wool, Chinese silk, and Argentinian leather and consumed Chinese tea or Colombian coffee; some had homes or offices furnished in hardwoods from Burma, Malaya, or Africa. Westerners could purchase all these goods, and many more, at prices so favorable that many luxury items became available to those who were not rich. Europeans and Americans could travel anywhere, using gold or easily available foreign currency, exchanged at a rate almost always favorable to them. They could invest their money in the raw materials or the government bonds of virtually any area of the world and expect a good return. They also expected their investments to be secure and their property and person to be protected. Non-Western political authorities unable to guarantee that security, for whatever reason, risked intervention, perhaps occupation, by European or American forces. In some non-Western areas, the governors had to grant *extraterritoriality,* or the right of Europeans to trial by their own laws in foreign countries. Europeans often also lived a segregated and privileged life in quarters, clubs, and whole sections of foreign lands or cities closed to native inhabitants.

Control and Resistance

Changing technology widened the gap between industrialized states and Asia and Africa. Europeans possessed the enormous power of industry and of military technology, and European nation-states could mobilize the support of all their citizens. These facts made it unlikely that a non-European country or people could successfully resist an industrialized European state intent on conquest. Yet Ethiopia was able to resist Italy's incursions, North Africans kept the French on the defensive in Algeria and Morocco, and the Japanese held off potential invaders.

Europeans established varying degrees of political control over much of the rest of the world. Control could mean outright annexation and the governing of a territory as a colony. In this way, Germany controlled Tanganyika (East Africa) after 1886, and Britain ruled much of India. Control could also mean status as a protectorate, in which the local ruler continued to rule but was directed, or "protected," by a Great Power. In this way, the British controlled Egypt after 1882 and maintained authority over their dependent Indian princes, and France guarded Tunisia. There were also spheres of influence, where, without military or political control, a European nation had special trading and legal privileges that other Europeans did not have. At the turn of the century, the Russians and the British, each recognizing the other's sphere of influence divided Persia (Iran). Some peoples were so completely dependent on foreigners to buy their goods or to loan money that they seemed politically independent only in the most technical sense. They dared take no action that might upset their economic connections, not even action that might ease their debt crisis.

Nevertheless, many non-Europeans resisted American and European economic penetration and political control in varied ways, and the very process of resistance shaped their history and their self-awareness. In many areas, such as the Ottoman Empire, China, and Japan, ruling governments found ways of limiting the political influence of Western trading interests. Some countries tried, as Egypt did, to seek economic independence through modernization.

These forms of resistance were carried out by rulers who could command loyal subjects. Other resisters—individuals, groups, and regional communities—sometimes retained traditional ways, rejecting Western education and secularization and often renewing institutions, particularly religious ones, that were falling into disuse when the Europeans arrived. Such resistance became a statement of both national and individual identity. A few of the many instances of such resistance include the Sudanese Muslims' holy war led by the Mahdi Mohammed Ahmed against both Egyptian fellow Muslims, who were regarded as agents of the European nonbelievers, and the Europeans; the Boxer Rebellion in China; and the Sepoy Mutiny in India. Still other resisters reacted with strongly nationalistic feelings and fought to strengthen the nationalism of their people, sometimes even going to Western universities, military schools, and factories to master the West's advanced technology. Mohandas Gandhi, Jawaharlal Nehru, Sun Yatsen (Sun Zhongshan), Chiang Kai-shek (Jiang Jieshi), and Kemal Atatürk are some famous leaders of national resistance to the West.

In most cases, however, efforts at resistance brought non-European peoples more firmly under Western control. When their interests were threatened, Europeans generally responded by annexing the offending region or establishing a protectorate. Resistance continued, nonetheless: whole peoples in Africa moved from place to place to escape European religion, taxes, and laws; and insurgent mountain people in Indochina and Algeria evaded French cultural influence or restricted it to the coastline.

Europeans might dominate the ruler and perhaps the ruling elite, and they might make entire sectors of the economy dependent on their trade. They could also see the influence of their ideas and language on the youth and observe the decline of local traditions. But the level of European power differed in each area, and in many places Europeans were never fully in control. Each region has had a different history of European intervention. Nevertheless, Western domination seemed, to westerners and nonwesterners alike, a relentless force.

EUROPEAN DOMINATION OF ASIA

India, China, and Japan were powerful kingdoms when the first European traders arrived in the age of exploration. For several hundred years, there

MAP 27.1 Asia in 1914 ▶

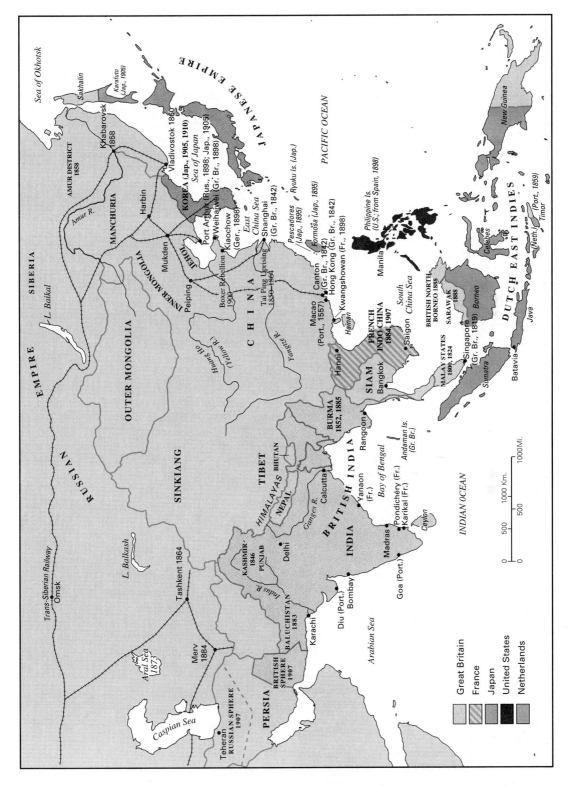

were trading connections in which the European was the weaker party, dependent on the goodwill and interest of the Asians. In China and India, native craftspeople produced goods superior to European products, so Asians had little reason to trade with the West, whereas Europeans had many incentives for commerce with the East. The Asian kingdoms possessed a sense of cultural unity arising from tradition and from loyalty to the great religious and ethical systems of Hinduism, Buddhism, Islam, and Confucianism. When, as a result of industrialization in the nineteenth century, the Europeans came in much greater numbers with greater power, the Chinese and Mogul empires were weakened by internal problems. Indian, Chinese, and Japanese cultural loyalties were not nationalism as Europeans knew it, but within a short time, resentment of European domination developed into national feeling, unifying diverse social and religious communities.

India

The history of the Indian subcontinent is a long one of a series of invasions, from Alexander the Great in the fourth century B.C. to the British in the eighteenth century. When Italian, Portuguese and Spanish merchants came as traders, admirers, and imitators to the Mogul Empire, they found it ruled by a dynasty of highly advanced, wealthy, and religiously tolerant Muslim princes. When the British arrived in the eighteenth century, also as traders, the empire was disintegrating because the Muslim zealot Aurangzeb Alamgir (1658–1707) had launched a holy war, which would tear apart Hindus and Muslims, as well as Sikhs, for half a century. The rivalries of powerful native princes, each of whom wished to succeed the emperor, worked to foreign advantage. India fell prey to the Europeans, and by the end of the century the British cleared out their rivals one by one. India had become the jewel of the British Empire, the most completely governed Asian state.

British Rule British rule was indirect at first. The British East India Company was a regulated chartered monopoly enterprise under the control of Parliament, which actually did little to control

it until the Sepoy Mutiny of 1857–58. (The Indians call this massive act of resistance the Great Rebellion.) This major popular uprising joined Muslim and Hindu soldiers with some native princes, who finally perceived that the British, rather than neighboring princes, were the true threat to their authority. Peasants, who were victims of both their local landlords and the market, also participated in the uprising. In a fierce war, the British, with the aid of faithful troops from the Punjab, repressed the uprising. The British ruled some states through dependent Indian princes, but about two-thirds of the subcontinent was ruled directly by about a thousand British officials. Unlike the Chinese and the Japanese, the peoples of India lost all semblance of independence.

At first the men of the East India Company had mixed with the Indians, often marrying local women and adopting their customs and languages. But the British community felt so threatened by the uprising that it took all the authority it could into its hands and maintained a social and legal separation from Indians. The civil service was entirely British, trained in England and sent out to govern according to English law and customs. Later, an elite of Indians, educated in English and trained in law and administration, became part of the civil service. Along with soldiers drawn from the peoples with a military tradition, the Indian civil service (about 4,000 Europeans and half a million Indians in 1900) ruled some 300 million Indians of almost 200 language groups, and several religions, races, and cultures, living in territories that today are India, Pakistan, and Bangladesh (and for a while Myanmar, or Burma). The British allowed native princes who followed British policies to rule in their territories. Thus, the British created a powerful state with a single system of law, administration and language. The subcontinent had some political unity, an English-educated elite, and a focus of discontent—a common resentment of British control.

India also acquired a modern railroad and communications system and an economy in which a segment was geared to meet the needs of the world market. The rest of the economy tried to supply local and regional demands. The railroad linked areas of food surplus, reducing the incidence and impact of local famines, which, to-

MAHARAJA MADHAV RAO SCINDIA AND THE PRINCE OF WALES AFTER THE HUNT IN INDIA, 1905. The British governed about one fourth of India through the traditional princely rulers. The Maharaja Madhav Rao Scindia is shown here as the quintessential English aristocrat after the hunt, surrounded by the kill. A Westernized high society sent their sons to London for education and the sports of gentlemen. The British partook of and staged elaborate ceremonies symbolically honoring their princely allies, as here the Prince of Wales (later George V) hunted with the Maharaja on his visit to Gwalior. (*The Royal Commonwealth Society*)

gether with warfare, had plagued India's history. Population increased as fewer people died of starvation and lives were saved with public projects of sanitation, hygiene, water and flood control, and Western medicine.

British rule ended the century of war and disorder, which had followed the disintegration of the Mogul Empire; but it did not end the control that local landlords and usurers had over the lives of peasants. Many observers believe that the Indian masses did not benefit from economic progress because landlords demanded payments, which the poor could not pay. Moneylenders cheated the poor. In addition, the increase in population more than matched the increase in food. Even if there were no starvation, for most people malnutrition became the rule. What further aggravated the situation, these critics claim, was that the British flooded the Indian market with cheap, machine-produced English goods,

which drove native artisans out of business or even deeper into debt. Such detrimental consequences were not unique to India; they could be noted in many areas where the market economy and European rule disrupted traditional arrangements.

The racism that excluded the Indian elite from British clubs, hotels, and social gatherings and from top government positions alienated the leaders whom British rule created or co-opted. Many of the older elite of princes and landlords who may have profited from British connections resented the lack of respect for Indian traditions and culture. Educated Indians, demanding equality and self-government, created the Indian National Congress in the 1880s. However, this organization was not national, because its members were upper-class Hindus, and not a congress, because it had no representative authority. At first the Congress party demanded representation for

Indians; later it sought home rule, or equal self-government within the British Empire. Ultimately, it organized masses of Indians to gain independence.

The Anticolonial Campaign Resistance to colonialism grew in militance throughout Asia when the Japanese defeated the Russians in 1904–1905. Radical Indian nationalists were inspired as well. Similarly, World War I brought greater solidarity among Indians, who, though opposed to British rule, had been far from united. Muslims had founded the Muslim League to speak for their minority community. (Many Hindus believed that the British favored the Muslims as part of a divide-and-conquer strategy.) The Indian elite found grounds for cooperation among the disparate communities, but the masses continued to be divided by differences of religion, class, and culture. These differences made Indian self-government seem distant even to the Britons who wanted it.

In 1919, partly in response to agitation and partly as a reward for Indian loyalty during the war, the British granted India a legislative assembly representing almost a million of the 300 million people in the subcontinent. An elaborate scheme allotted representation by groups (that is, to Hindus, Muslims, Europeans, Anglo-Indians, and Sikhs) and by economic and social functions (that is, to rural, urban, university, landholding, and commercial classes). Although the British gave only some powers to this assembly, they appeared to acknowledge the principle of self-government.

At this very time, however, agitation and unrest became most bitter. At Amritsar in the Punjab, a British officer commanded his Gurkha troops to fire into a peaceful demonstration until their ammunition was exhausted; 379 Indians died and 1,200 were wounded. Women and children were among the victims. The government punished the officer, but the British community in India gave him a fortune, honoring him for what he had done. The massacre and British behavior stung Indians to action—even those Indians who had advocated self-government within the British Empire.

Out of this feverish period emerged a gentle but determined revolutionary leader, Mohandas K. Gandhi (1869–1948). He had led resistance to the vicious system of racial discrimination in South Africa and, in the process, developed a doctrine of civil disobedience and nonviolent resistance. He believed that Indians would overthrow British rule through self-discipline and love of one another. His was a spiritually uplifting message, and a shrewd political tactic as well. Gandhi called on the Indian elite to give up their privileges, resign their positions, boycott British schools, and boycott all foreign goods. Freeing India required mass support as well as sacrifice. Gandhi rallied this support dramatically with "the march to the sea": a mass refusal to pay taxes on salt. Thrown in prison, Gandhi and his followers fasted for spiritual discipline. Their tactic also threatened the British with the possibility that the confined leaders would starve to death, setting off more civil disturbances. Gandhi promoted the boycott of foreign goods by spinning cotton and wearing simple native dress. To gain independence, he was even willing to sacrifice the higher standard of living that an industrial economy could bring to India. Most important, he was able to join traditional religious and cultural beliefs with political tactics to inspire Indians with nationalism.

Independence finally came after World War II had exhausted Britain's resources, reduced its power, and stirred much of the world to struggle against racism and for liberty and democracy. There was no war between Britain and India—an accomplishment that many credit to the strength of Gandhi's moral leadership. But even his leadership could not prevent the partition of the country into Muslim Pakistan and predominantly Hindu India. Nor could it prevent bloody communal massacres and his own death at the hands of a Hindu nationalist assassin.

China

European intervention in China was very different. For centuries, Europeans had admired China for its wealth, art, and culture, and even for its imperial government, which ruled through mandarins (men who passed tests of Chinese learning). Unlike India, China excluded foreigners, whether they were missionaries, traders, or soldiers and sailors, in an effort to preserve the traditional ruling class, economy, and beliefs by shielding them from Christianity, Western science, and secular ideologies.

When the British defeated the Chinese in the Opium War of 1839–1842, the Manchu dynasty was forced to open trade with the West. Before the war, such commerce had been limited—controlled by native monopolists to whom the emperor had granted trading privileges. When the Chinese destroyed Indian opium being traded by the East India Company, the British aggressively asserted their right to free trade. In the subsequent war, Britain seized several trading cities along the coast, including Hong Kong. In the Treaty of Nanking (1842), the British insisted on determining the tariffs that the Chinese might charge them. Furthermore, British subjects in China would have the right to be tried according to their own law (the right of extraterritoriality). These provisions undermined the emperor's ability to control the foreigners in his country.

Defeat forced the emperor to change. He drew on China's mandarins to revitalize the Manchu bureaucracy, clean up the official corruption, which weighed heavily on the poorest taxpayers, and strengthen China against westerners. Nevertheless, widespread economic discontent led to the Taiping Rebellion of 1850–1864. This uprising seriously threatened the dynasty, which was able to suppress the rebels only with Western assistance. Britain and France extorted additional concessions. They forced the emperor to allow Chinese people to emigrate to become cheap, exploited labor in South Africa and the United States.

For a time, the Europeans seemed content with trading rights in coastal towns and preferential treatment for their subjects. But the Sino-Japanese War of 1894–95, which Japan won easily, encouraged the Europeans to mutilate China. Britain, France, Russia, and Germany all scrambled for concessions, protectorates, and spheres of influence. China might have been carved up like Africa; however, each Western nation resisted any partition that might give an advantage to a rival. To ensure American interests in China, the United States proclaimed the "Open Door" policy: that trade should be open to all and that the Great Powers should respect the territorial integrity of China. Whether the American action had any part in restraining the Western powers from partitioning China is unclear. The important treaty ports had already been apportioned and market capitalism, the most powerful threat to China's independent status, continued to make major inroads.

Chinese traditionalists organized secret societies to expel foreigners and punish those Chinese who accepted westernization. Usually, these societies opposed the Manchu dynasty, which had tried to institute reforms that would undermine traditional China. Sometimes, though, they allied themselves with it. In 1900, encouraged by Empress Tzu-hsi, the Society of Righteous and Harmonious Fists (called the Boxers by Europeans) attacked foreigners throughout the north of China. An international army of Europeans, Japanese, and Americans suppressed the rebellion, seized Chinese treasures, and forced China to pay an indemnity. They also made China agree to the stationing of foreign troops on its soil.

Chinese discontent with the dynasty deepened, and unrest and nationalistic opposition to the foreigners increased. When the Japanese defeated Russia in 1905, many Chinese argued that the only way to protect their country was to imitate the West, as the Japanese had done. Growing nationalism led to a boycott of American goods in 1905 to protest U.S. restrictions on Chinese immigrants. In 1911, nationalist revolutionaries, particularly strong among soldiers, workers, and students, overthrew the Manchu and declared a republic. Sun Zhongshan (Sun Yat-sen, 1866–1925) returned to China to become the first president of the republic and the head of the Nationalist party.

Espousing the Western ideas of democracy, nationalism, and social welfare (the three principles of the people, as Sun called them), the republic struggled to establish its authority over a China torn by civil war and ravaged by foreigners. Russia was claiming Mongolia and Britain, Tibet. Japan posed a danger as well. In addition, the northern warlords resisted any attempt to strengthen the republic's army because it might diminish their power. However, in the south, the republic more or less maintained control.

After Sun's death, the Guomindong (Kuomintang), under the authoritarian leadership of Jiang Jieshi (Chiang Kai-shek, 1887–1975), tried to westernize by using the military power of the state and introducing segments of a modern economic system. But faced with civil war, attacked from both the right and the communist left under Mao Zedong (Mao Tse-tung, 1893–1976), and by the Japanese after 1931, the Guomindong made slow progress. A divided China continued to be at the mercy of outside interests until after World War II.

COMMODORE PERRY AND THE U.S. SQUADRON MEETING JAPANESE IMPERIAL COMMISSIONERS AT YOKOHAMA, 1854. Commodore Matthew Perry had opened Japan, against its will, to the West the preceding year. With the Meiji Restoration of 1867, a strong central government pushed Japan until it became one of the top ten industrial nations by 1900. Japan's imperialistic expansion brought it into conflict with China, Russia, and the Western imperialist powers. (*Culver Pictures*)

Japan

Like China, Japan was forced open by the West. The Japanese had chosen isolation. However, by the 1850s, as in India and China, social dissension within Japan and foreign pressure combined to force the country to admit outside trade. In 1853, Commodore Matthew C. Perry sailed into Tokyo Bay, making a show of American strength and compelling the Japanese to sign treaties that granted westerners extraterritoriality and control over tariffs. Like China, Japan succumbed to superior technological power.

A flood of violence ensued. The warrior nobility, the samurai, who feared for their social status, attacked foreigners and murdered members of their own government. They thought that trade would enhance the status of merchants, a social class they despised. In response to samurai bel-

ligerence, a fleet of U.S. and European ships attacked, destroying important Japanese fortresses. A group of samurai seized the government, determined to preserve Japan's independence. This takeover—the Meiji Restoration of 1867—returned power to the emperor, or Meiji, from the feudal aristocracy, which had ruled in his name for almost seven hundred years.

The new government enacted a series of reforms, turning Japan into a powerful modern centralized state. Large landowners gave their estates to the emperor in exchange for compensation and high-level positions in the government. All classes were made equal before the law. As in France and Germany, universal military service was required, which diminished social privilege and helped to imbue Japanese of all classes with nationalism. The Japanese modeled their constitution on Bismarck's: there was a bicameral diet, or parliament, but the emperor kept authority. His ministers governed in his name, without much control by the parliament.

The Meiji regime introduced modern industry and economic competition. The Japanese visited factories all over the West and hired westerners to teach industrial skills. The government, like central and eastern European governments, built defense industries, backed heavy industry and mining, and developed a modern communication system of railroads, roads, and telegraph. State moneys and government initiative created this economic development. The government encouraged competitive consumer industries as well. During the 1880s, it sold factories to wealthy family monopolies, the *zaibatsu,* which came to dominate the Japanese economy. Industry in Japan adopted traditional Japanese values and emphasized cooperation more than competition, paternalism rather than individualism, and deference rather than conflict. Westerners regarded the close cooperation of government and powerful families as something peculiar to the Japanese (neither capitalist nor socialist). Within little more than a generation of the Meiji Restoration, Japan moved from economic backwardness to a place among the top ten industrial nations. To underdeveloped countries, Japan became a model of a nation that borrowed from the West, yet preserved its traditional values and social structure.

By 1900, Japan had ended the humiliating treaties with the West and had become an imperialist power in its own right. It had won Taiwan and Korea in its war with China in 1894–95, although the Great Powers intervened, forcing the Japanese to return some of the spoils of victory while they themselves grabbed greater spheres of influence from the helpless Chinese. Their self-serving maneuvering infuriated the Japanese. Finally, in 1904, conflict over influence in Manchuria brought Japan and Russia to war, which Japan won. The victory of an Asian power over a Western power had a tremendous impact on Asian nationalists. If Japan could unite its people through nationalism and strong leadership, others should be able to do likewise. Japan's victory inspired anti-Western and nationalist movements throughout Asia.

In World War I, Japan fought on the side of the Allies and emerged as the most powerful Asian state. It took over the former German holdings north of the equator, except for Germany's sphere of influence in China. (U.S. President Woodrow Wilson blocked that move at the Paris peace conference.) In the 1920s, the prosperous economy strengthened the middle class and increased the importance of the working class, reinforcing democratic institutions. But Japan's dependence on foreign trade meant that the nation was hard hit by the Great Depression of 1929, when the major states subjected its trade to tariffs. The depression weakened the elements that contributed to peace, stability, and democracy in Japan and strengthened the militarist and fascist groups, which were set on imperialism in Manchuria and China.

To Asians in the 1930s, Japan seemed to champion Asian racial equality and to oppose Western imperialism. Many leaders of nationalist movements in Burma, India, Indochina, and Indonesia were attracted for a time by Japan's pose. World War II, however, brought Japanese occupation and exploitation, not freedom and equality for Asians.

Southeast and Central Asia

As China, India, and the Ottoman Empire lost their ability to control their border territories, European states tried to grab them. Indochina, Tibet, Korea, Burma, Afghanistan, and Persia found themselves the objects of Great Power competition. The ensuing struggles for domination of Southeast Asia, Central Asia, and the Middle East all involved conflicts between the Great Powers, between the declining or disintegrating traditional empires, and among the social forces of the region.

In Southeast Asia, the French claimed Indochina (Vietnam, Laos, and Kampuchea today) in a war with China (1883–85). The French parliament threw out the government that had waged war for a faraway and not obviously valuable territory but annexed the territory nonetheless. A prosperous agricultural country, Indochina traded mostly with other Asian countries and very little with France. Some may have profited from the colony—merchants, civil servants, soldiers, priests, and scholars—but as a whole, France was indifferent to its new acquisition.

The French might have expanded into Siam (Thailand) and the British might have moved there from their base in Burma (Myanmar). Neither

Wide World Photos

ATATÜRK

A Young Turk military officer, Mustafa Kemal, emerged from the wave of revolutionary national upheavals that washed across eastern Europe and Asia even before World War I. Born in Saloniki, a predominantly Greek part of the Ottoman Empire, Kemal was an ardent Turkish nationalist. He joined the military and played an important part in the struggle to overthrow the Ottoman sultan Abd Al-Hamid in 1909. But overthrowing the sultan failed to create a republic or allow Kemal to emerge as the national leader.

The pro-German forces in the Empire allied with the Central Powers in World War I. Kemal defeated the British in the battle of Gallipoli. When Turkey was beaten in Syria by British and Arab troops, Kemal was able to keep his army together, a victory of sorts.

Totally committed to making Turkey a republic with himself the leader of a modern state, Kemal and many other Turkish nationalists refused to accept the Turkish government's surrender to the Al-

---

of the two Great Powers was willing to let the other take over Siam. In 1904, however, fear of Germany led Britain and France to put colonial differences aside. Siam, like Turkey in the Middle East, was able to play the powers off against each another and to preserve some territorial integrity.

Elsewhere in Southeast Asia, the United States and Germany challenged British and French pre-eminence. During the Spanish-American War, the Americans seized and annexed the Philippines and Guam. (Although the war was ostensibly fought to free Cuba, the first battle took place at Manila Bay.) Once taken, the islands proved difficult to pacify. Germany, the United States, Britain, and France laid claim to various other Pacific islands, where they built naval stations to symbolize their presence in the East. Throughout the period, the Netherlands maintained its holdings in the East Indies (Indonesia)—the remnant of the once-great

seventeenth-century Dutch empire. Even colonies began to acquire colonies, as New Zealand and Australia pushed claims to Borneo and Tasmania, and, after World War I, to German colonies south of the equator. They had some economic reasons for staking these claims, but asserting their national identity was equally important.

As France and Britain competed in Southeast Asia, and Japan and the great European powers in northern China and Korea, Russia and Britain opposed one another in central Asia. Russia's moves south into Afghanistan and Persia (Iran), both of which bordered India, alarmed the British. They believed that a hostile force on the Indian border might inspire rebellious Indians. After 1889, Britain and Russia vied in lending the shah money to build a railroad to Teheran. The Russians were then borrowing money from the French for their own industrialization, but to create a dependency in Persia, they were willing to

lies or the territorial demands of Italy, Greece, and the British- and French-backed Arabs. Kemal organized a national army, threw out the allies, abolished the sultanate, and declared the republic.

As president of the republic, Atatürk (the father of the republic) established institutions which looked like a democracy, including a parliament and a bureaucracy. Like Lenin in Russia, however, he allowed only one party. There could be no opposition to rapid modernization through mass adult education, secularization, and industrialization. A nationalist, rather than a socialist, he tried to industrialize with private enterprise, but when that floundered he pushed state development of basic industries through a central bank. Born a Moslem, he demanded the complete separation of religion from government, banning the fez and veil. Like the fascist movements which arise in the 1920s and 1930s, intense nationalism motivated the people's enormous sacrifices to build a powerful state in Turkey.

borrow more. The British moved to stop the Russians, whose aim appeared to be the acquisition of a warm-water port on the Persian Gulf—too close to India for British comfort. The years 1878–1881 and 1884–85 saw British and Russian troops engaged in Afghanistan, both trying to dominate the routes to the subcontinent.

The Russians took advantage of Britain's involvement in the Boer War (see page 676) to advance into Persia, Tibet, and Afghanistan. In 1904, the British moved into Tibet to prevent the ruling Dalai Lama's tutor from negotiating special trade agreements with the Russians, even though the total volume of trade would have been infinitesimally small. Within two years, Russia and Britain, afraid of the rise of Germany, were willing to compromise. The Russians agreed to leave the British puppet ruler of Afghanistan alone. Persia would be divided into three zones: one in the north for the Russians, one in the south for the British, and one for the Persians in the middle, to keep the two powers separate.

This resolution of difficulties made British and Russian cooperation in Europe possible. An important piece in the system of alliances that led to World War I was in place. It had tremendous impact on Persia as well. Torn between Britain and Russia, Persia maintained neither independence nor stability. Its situation was further complicated after World War I, when its vast reserves of oil became valuable to the Great Powers. Reza Shah of the Pahlavi family gained control of Persia in 1925 and abolished the special privileges that had been granted to foreigners. In 1934, the shah granted the concession over the Bahrain Islands to the American firm of Standard Oil, thinking that foreigners whose interests seemed to be merely economic might be more easily controlled than foreigners with geopolitical designs. Yet as British power receded in the area during and after World War II, U.S. power took its place.

The Ottoman Empire

The Ottoman Empire once spanned three continents. Throughout the nineteenth century, its territories were the scene of Great Power conflict in North Africa, Europe, and Asia. At the turn of this century, traditional Anglo-Russian rivalry over the "sick man of Europe," as Turkey was called, was overshadowed by Britain's rivalry with Germany.

The origins of the Anglo-German conflict seemed quite innocent, and certainly not political. In the context of a generation of German economic and political expansion in the area, however, the British responded negatively to a business venture of a group of German financiers who proposed a railroad from central Turkey to Baghdad, on the Tigris River, with a connection down the Euphrates River to Basra and the Persian Gulf. Because the proposed new railroad would further open Turkey and its empire to the world market, the sultan was enthusiastic and offered to subsidize the project by guaranteeing the bonds and profits for the syndicate. The German backers of the railroad offered British and French investment groups a 25 percent share each, with 25 percent control to the Turks; the Germans kept the final quarter for themselves.

The British government, however, refused to allow British businessmen to invest in the railroad. Politics dominated economics; the British feared German ascendancy in an area so close to India and the Suez Canal. The repercussions of British action were far-reaching. A group of nationalistic Turkish officers denounced the sultan because they saw that one by one the border territories of the Ottoman Empire were being taken by the Europeans or were declaring their independence. Reforms within the ruling elite alone seemed insufficient to the Young Turks, who tried to make a stronger central government. Britain's action, together with German naval expansion, aggravated Anglo-German relations. The Germans came to see the British as their number one rival. In World War I, the Ottomans sided with the Germans, partly because of German influence over a generation of the Turkish elite and partly out of fear of the Russian presence in the Caucasus and the Black Sea areas.

Throughout World War I, the Allies secretly negotiated the division of the Ottoman Empire. Hoping to weaken its contribution to the German war effort, Britain sponsored Arab independence movements in the Arabian peninsula and in the territories that are today Iraq, Syria, Lebanon, Jordan, and Israel. In the Balfour Declaration of 1917, the British also promised the Zionists a Jewish homeland in Palestine.

When the war was over, the Turks, led by Mustafa Kemal Atatürk, refused to accept the dismemberment of Turkish-speaking territory, although they did accept the loss of Arab lands. The Turks drove the Allies out of Anatolia, declared a republic in 1923 under Atatürk's presidency, and moved the capital to Ankara, far away from the cosmopolitan city of Constantinople (Istanbul). Turkey, which became a secular state, was no longer the spiritual leader of millions of Muslims throughout the world. During Atatürk's presidency (1923–1938), the Turkish government banned traditional practices, such as veils for women, harems, and polygamy. European education and ideas flourished in the new republic. The conflict between the modern and the traditional in Turkey was resolved by war and revolution in favor of modern nationalism.

Among the Arabs, several forces fostered the desire for national self-determination, which grew during and after World War I. Britain schemed for a while to establish a puppet Muslim caliph but was rebuffed. The Arab chiefs welcomed British aid against the Turks but deeply resented British intervention in their spiritual and local political affairs. They suspected that the Europeans were primarily interested in the area's oil. Arab nationalism, once encouraged against the Ottomans, could not be controlled when the Turks ceased to be a power. As nationalism developed, it often combined with religion to foment opposition, which plagued the imperialists between the world wars and afterward.

THE SCRAMBLE FOR AFRICA

The most rapid European expansion took place in Africa. As late as 1880, European nations ruled only a tenth of the continent. By 1914, Europeans had claimed all of Africa except Liberia (a small territory of freed slaves from the United States) and Abyssinia (Ethiopia), which had successfully held off Italian invaders at Adowa in 1896. The only Great Powers that did not play a part in carving up Africa were Russia, Austria-Hungary, and the United States.

European powers had occasionally been involved in Africa early in the nineteenth century. The French had moved into Algeria in 1830. During the Napoleonic wars, the British had gained Cape Town in South Africa, a useful provisioning place for trading ships bound for India and the East. Dutch cattlemen and farmers (Boers), who had settled in the Cape Town area starting in the mid-seventeenth century, refused to accept the British abolition of slavery in 1833. To get away from the British, they had moved northward in a migration called the Great Trek (1835–37), warring with native tribes along the way. The Boers aggressively asserted their independence from the British and by 1880 were firmly established in the territory they had taken in the interior, the Transvaal and the Orange Free State.

In general, though, until the 1870s, Great Power interest in Africa seemed marginal and likely to decline even further. Then the astounding activities of Leopold II, king of Belgium, changed the picture. In 1876, as a private entrepreneur, he formed the International Association

MAP 27.2 Africa in 1914 ▶

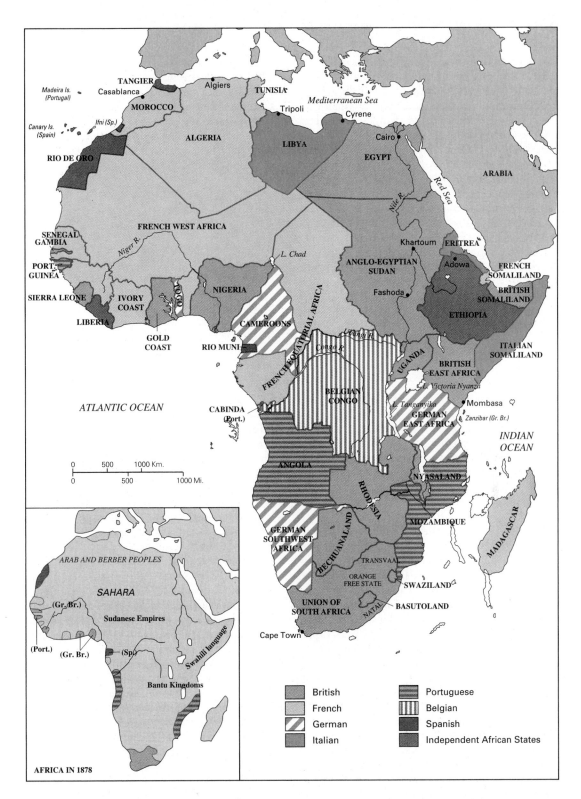

Madeira Is.
(Portugal)

TANGIER
Casablanca
Algiers
TUNISIA
Mediterranean Sea
Tripoli
Cyrene

Canary Is.
(Spain)
Ifni (Sp.)
MOROCCO
Cairo

ALGERIA
LIBYA
EGYPT

RIO DE ORO
ARABIA

Nile R.

FRENCH WEST AFRICA
Niger R.
L. Chad

SENEGAL
GAMBIA
Khartoum
ERITREA
FRENCH
SOMALILAND

PORT.
GUINEA
ANGLO-EGYPTIAN
SUDAN
Adowa
BRITISH
SOMALILAND

SIERRA LEONE
IVORY
COAST
NIGERIA
Fashoda

LIBERIA
TOGO
ETHIOPIA

GOLD
COAST
CAMEROONS
FRENCH EQUATORIAL AFRICA
ITALIAN
SOMALILAND

RIO MUNI
Ubangi R.

Congo R.
UGANDA
BRITISH
EAST AFRICA

ATLANTIC OCEAN
CABINDA
(Port.)
BELGIAN
CONGO
L. Victoria Nyanza
Mombasa

L. Tanganyika
GERMAN
EAST AFRICA
Zanzibar (Gr. Br.)

INDIAN
OCEAN

0   500   1000 Km.
ANGOLA

0   500   1000 Mi.
NYASALAND

RHODESIA
MOZAMBIQUE

MADAGASCAR

GERMAN
SOUTHWEST
AFRICA
BECHUANALAND

TRANSVAAL

ORANGE
FREE STATE
SWAZILAND

UNION OF
SOUTH AFRICA
NATAL
BASUTOLAND

Cape Town

ARAB AND BERBER PEOPLES

SAHARA
(Gr. Br.)

Sudanese Empires

(Port.)
(Gr. Br.)
(Sp.)

Swahili language

Bantu Kingdoms

AFRICA IN 1878

	British		Portuguese
	French		Belgian
	German		Spanish
	Italian		Independent African States

673

for the Exploration and Civilization of Central Africa. Leopold sent Henry Stanley (1841–1904) to the Congo River basin to establish trading posts, sign treaties with the chiefs, and claim the territory for the association. Stanley, an adventurer and a newspaper reporter who had fought on both sides of the American Civil War, had earlier led an expedition to central Africa in search of David Livingstone, the popular missionary–explorer who was believed to be in danger. When Stanley found Livingstone in 1871, the human interest adventure story delighted thousands of readers. For men like Stanley, Leopold's private development efforts promised profit and adventure. For the Africans, they promised brutal exploitation. The French responded to Leopold's actions by immediately establishing a protectorate on the north bank of the Congo. The scramble for African territory was on.

The Berlin Conference

A scramble threatened European stability, and so Bismarck and Jules Ferry, the premier of France, called an international conference in Berlin in 1884 to lay some ground rules for the development of Africa south of the Sahara. Leopold (as an individual, not as the king of Belgium) was declared the personal ruler of the Congo Free State. The Congo basin was made a free trade zone for merchants of every nation.

The Berlin Conference established the rule that a European country had to occupy territory in order to claim it. This led to a mad race to the interior of Africa; it was a field day for explorers and soldiers. As Europeans rushed to claim territory, they ignored both natural and cultural frontiers. Even today, the map of Africa reveals many straight (and thus artificial) boundary lines rather than the irregular lines of natural boundaries, such as rivers and mountains.

The nations at the conference had also agreed to stop slavery and the slave trade in Africa, which was still practiced by Arabs and Africans. Before long, however, the Congo Association was trying to turn a profit with practices as vicious as those of the African slave traders. Edward D. Morel, an English humanitarian, and Roger Casement, an Irish national hero who was at the time a British civil servant, waged a vigorous campaign against

Leopold for the Aborigines' Protection Society. They produced evidence that slavery, mutilation, brutality, and murder were commonly practiced to force blacks to work for the rubber plantations in the Congo. In response to the outcry of world public opinion, the Belgian parliament declared the territory a Belgian colony in 1908, putting an end to Leopold's private enterprise.

Britain in Africa

Great Britain's activities in Africa exemplify the complicated motives, operations, and results of European imperialism. In the second half of the nineteenth century, Britain maintained only a few outposts along the coast of West Africa; even its hold on South Africa appeared to be loosening. From time to time, the British navy interfered with slave traders in Africa, but overall British interest there was minimal. In principle, Britain rejected empire.

Egypt   Eventually, however, local conditions in Egypt, including the construction of the Suez Canal, led to British occupation. For a generation (1805–1847), Mohammed Ali, governor of Egypt, had struggled for his independence from the sultan of the Ottoman Empire. Thereafter, strong *khedives* (Turkish governors), with British and French support, had maintained Egypt's autonomy. But foreign investment and influence grew, as successive khedives spent lavishly, trying to maintain and modernize themselves. Egypt fell deeply into debt to Europeans. The building of the Suez Canal (1859–1869), in which the khedive and British and French capitalists were the principal stockholders, brought the country to the verge of bankruptcy. In the long run, the existence of the canal promised Egypt trade and contact with the world economy, but its cost brought immediate disaster. When European creditors demanded cuts in the army as a way for Egypt to pay its debts, Egyptian soldiers rebelled. The combination of probable national bankruptcy and the khedive's apparent inability to keep law and order was a sufficient pretext to bring the British in as "protectors" in 1882.

The canal was important to the British as a waterway to India, but it was a mere investment to the French. When the British invited them to

THE BATTLE OF OMDURMAN, 1898. A romanticized oil painting depicts the British lancers at the battle of Omdurman in heroic terms. The Muslim fundamentalists who followed the Mahdi in his attempts to expel the Egyptians and British from the Sudan were massacred in 1898 by General Kitchener. As many as 11,000 dervishes were killed, but the British suffered only slight casualties. Paintings such as this fed the public hunger for heroism and thirst for exotic places. (*Eileen Tweedy/E.T. Archive*)

join in the invasion, the French could not do so for domestic political reasons. Still, they deeply resented the British action; patriotic organizations vehemently protested the "insult" to French national honor. Meanwhile, British citizens hired ships to watch the naval bombardment of Egyptian ports as if war were a fireworks display.

Prime Minister Gladstone, a "little Englander" (one who opposed empire), promised to withdraw British troops once the situation stabilized. Every day that the British remained, Egyptian discontent mounted against them, threatening the stability of markets, investments, and even of government. Egyptian opposition took two irreconcilable forms. Some Egyptians wanted a strong government and army so that they could throw the British out. Others hated all modernization because it drew Egypt further away from Islam. As the British became entrenched, vain attempts at resistance grew more violent.

Not only did the British not withdraw from Egypt; they moved farther south. In the Sudan, devout Muslims were waging holy war against Egyptian authority because they resented foreign, non-Muslim influence over the khedive. The British were trying to strengthen the khedive's authority so that taxes would be collected, Egypt's budget balanced, and debts paid. An English general led ten thousand of the khedive's troops against the Sudanese Muslim followers of the Mahdi. The Egyptians were annihilated. Costly occupation without stability angered British financiers. While Gladstone's Liberal party argued against further action in the Sudan, public opinion demanded action.

In 1885, Gladstone sent General Charles "Chinese" Gordon, famous for suppressing the Taiping Rebellion, as an observer to the Sudan. Gordon and the garrison were killed at Khartoum. Gordon's head was severed and placed on a pike. An enraged public accused Gladstone of having martyred the famous hero by forbidding him to wage war though sending him to the war zone to take charge. Gladstone refused to annex the Sudan, but in 1898, when the Conservatives were in power, General Herbert Kitchener was sent there, and his men, armed with machine guns, mowed down charging Muslims at Omdurman. The casualties were reported to be eleven thousand Muslims and twenty-eight Britons, which many Britons felt was appropriate revenge for Gordon's death.

The battle of Omdurman was an ugly victory, and 1898 became a year of ugly confrontations and dubious victories for the British Empire. Immediately after the battle, British forces confronted a French exploratory mission under the command of Major Jean Baptiste Marchand at Fashoda in the Sudan. The French had marched from West Africa to the Sudan en route to Somaliland on the Red Sea in order to lay claim to territory from one side of Africa to the other. The British were moving south from Egypt and north from Kenya into the same territory. In the diplomatic crisis that followed, Britain and France were brought to the brink of war, and public passions were inflamed. Too divided by the Dreyfus affair at home (see Chapter 26) to risk a showdown with Britain, the French cabinet ordered Marchand to retreat.

French public opinion was outraged; the newspapers were filled with hatred of the British. Behind the scenes, however, French diplomats began to negotiate with Britain to reconcile their two nations' ambitions. France could not challenge both Germany across the Rhine and Britain in Africa and Asia. The British, facing problems in Egypt and the Sudan, as well as mounting troubles in South Africa, also realized their limits. "Splendid isolation" was risky business if the whole world could be your battlefield and each of the Great Powers your enemy.

South Africa   Nothing underlined Britain's isolation and the widespread distrust of British motives more than the Boer War, which began in 1899. British relations with the settlers of the Boer territories of the Transvaal and the Orange Free State had been difficult since the Great Trek. They were aggravated by the discovery of rich deposits of gold and diamonds in Boer territory.

The opposing leaders in these territories were strong and unyielding. Paul Kruger (1825–1904), the Boer president of the Transvaal, wanted independence, power, and access to the sea for the Boers. He aimed to restrict the foreign prospectors, who were flooding into Boer territory by the thousands. The prime minister of Cape Colony, Cecil Rhodes (1853–1902), was a British subject who had made a fortune in diamonds and gold in South Africa. He acquired Rhodesia (Zimbabwe), a sizable and wealthy territory, for Britain. He dreamed of British red coloring the map of Africa from Cape Town to Cairo, and he built a railroad from the Cape to Rhodesia.

In 1895, Rhodes's close friend Leander Jameson led about six hundred armed men into the Transvaal to spark an uprising against Kruger, an event that would give the British a pretext to invade. The raid failed and both men were disgraced; Rhodes was censured by Parliament. Joseph Chamberlain, the imperialist colonial secretary in the British cabinet, was accused of complicity in the conspiracy but acquitted. When Kaiser William II of Germany impetuously sent President Kruger a congratulatory telegram, the British took the diplomatic insult as symptomatic of their isolation. Accustomed to the opposition of France in every corner of the globe, they now had to face the fact that Germany opposed them too.

Everything about the Boer War was unfortunate for the British. The Boers were formidable opponents—farmers by day and commandos by night, armed with the latest French and German rifles. Hatred for the British in the press of other European countries was almost universal. The war was exceptionally costly in both money and lives; it roused many Britons to a hysterical patriotism. At the same time, anti-imperialism gained strength. Humanitarians in London found some British tactics shameful; to deal with their stubborn foe, for example, the British herded, or "concentrated," whole settlements of Boers into compounds surrounded by barbed wire. The British won the major battles but faced stiff guerrilla resistance.

The nasty war ended in 1902. Hoping to live together in peace with the Boers, the British drew up a conciliating settlement, making many concessions to the Boers, including the right to use their own language, Afrikaans (English remained the official language), and the offer of amnesty to any Boer who would swear allegiance to the British king. But the settlement that appeared to be generous and just to the belligerents boded ill for other people who were not involved in the war: the majority black population of South Africa. In fact, Boer autonomy meant that the government in London could do little to protect the rights of black Africans in the Boer territories. Few safeguards for blacks were written into the treaty or the constitution of the new Union of South Africa.

The Costs of Colonialism

The cost of imperialism in Africa seemed high not only to the British and French, but to other imperialists as well. The Italians' defeat at Adowa (1896) by Ethiopians belied Italian dreams of empire and national glory. Victory would not have alleviated Italy's economic problems, although it might have reduced political discontent. Germans could take little heart from their African acquisitions—Southwest Africa (Namibia), Southeast Africa (Tanzania, but not Zanzibar, which was British), the Cameroons, and Togo. The German colonies were the most efficiently governed (critics said the most ruthlessly controlled), but because they were costly to govern, they yielded few benefits other than pride of ownership. The Belgians obviously gained no prestige from the horrors perpetrated in the Congo. Serious thinkers, contemplating the depths to which Europeans would sink in search of fortune and fame, began to suggest that barbarity characterized the Europeans more than the Africans. The Europeans seemed to be the moral barbarians, as novelist Joseph Conrad and others pointed out. For the most part, honor was fleeting and profits illusory in these new African empires.

Yet it appeared that Europeans might go to war with each other for African lands with few people and fewer resources. Such a war promised to be more deadly than the colonial conflicts between the technologically superior Europeans and the Africans and Asians. Germany expressed its aggressive imperialism in a naval arms race with the British, which threatened the latter's power and national self-image. The "Teutonic cousins" eyed each other with deepening suspicion. This tension contributed to the alliances that the Great Powers made in the decade before World War I.

LATIN AMERICA

Early in the nineteenth century, Latin American colonists rebelled against Spain to gain political independence. Their rebellion was part of the same era of democratic revolution as the American Revolution in 1776 and the French Revolution in 1789. The colonists, who were active in trade, were encouraged by Britain and the United States, both of which wanted a free hand for their commerce. British Prime Minister George Canning and U.S. President James Monroe issued warnings to the Concert of Europe (Russia, Austria, Prussia, Great Britain, and France) not to intervene in or colonize the Americas. For the entire nineteenth century, Latin America was the object of European trade and immigration. Argentina, Brazil, Chile, and the other countries took in Irish, Germans, Italians, eastern Europeans and Spaniards; like the United States, they became primarily immigrant nations. (A few nations—Mexico and Peru, for example—resisted the Atlantic migration, preserving an Amerindian or mestizo society.)

Europeans also invested heavily in all the Americas. Britain and, to a lesser degree, France, were the dominant economic powers in Latin America; they cooperated commercially with local merchants, loaned money, and arranged treaties favorable to the business interests of their citizens. Toward the end of the 1800s, the United States became a powerful presence in the Caribbean islands and Latin America.

Both the Europeans and the local merchants and landowners exploited the lower classes. Brazil relied on African slave labor to produce for European markets; it was, in fact, the last American nation to abolish slavery. Native Indians were pushed off their lands in Argentina, Brazil, and Chile just as ruthlessly as in North America.

Europe dominated the Western Hemisphere culturally. In Latin America a small, wealthy

SLAVES DRYING COFFEE ON A PLANTATION IN TERREIROS, RIO DE JANEIRO, C. 1882. Brazilian slaves toiled to produce one of its main exports to the world market. The world economy, which began with the Commercial Revolution, emerged full force with the Age of Imperialism, as more and more resources of the non-European world were produced, bought, and sold for overseas consumption. (*Photograph by Marc Ferrez; courtesy of Gilberto Ferrez*)

upper class benefited from its connection with Europe and imitated Continental culture. At Manaus in the Amazon region, rich South Americans built an ornate opera house, resembling Milan's La Scala, from profits of rubber farms worked by enslaved Indians. Wealthy North Americans lived like the British gentry, using the profits of cotton or coffee labor. In Buenos Aires, Rio de Janeiro, and Santiago, merchants discussed the latest European intellectual fad. Upper-class South and North Americans sent their children to Europe to attend school and to acquire "culture" before they entered business, agriculture, and government in their native lands. In these matters, the Latin American elite behaved much the same as the westernizers among the elite of India, the Middle East, or Southeast Asia. In both Latin and North America, however, some people felt that New World countries must develop their own cultures, not imitate Britain or France, and significant cultures did evolve.

The wealthy classes in Latin America de-pended on Europe for trade as well as culture. They became indebted to Europeans for funds to support their governments and build their railroads. For their part, the Europeans were content to gain the profits from commerce without direct colonization. If political dissension threatened to interfere with peaceful trade, Europeans had ways of letting the merchant class know the costs of that dissension. In general, dependent merchants maintained the conditions that Europeans thought were desirable for business. When the rules of free trade were violated, European vessels might blockade harbors or seize custom-houses. But unlike the British in Egypt, Europeans in the Americas usually withdrew their troops or ships as soon as they had enforced their will.

An exception to this general policy of nonintervention was Napoleon III's attempt in 1867 to conquer Mexico and to install an Austrian archduke (Maximilian) on a bogus throne. The Mexicans, led by Benito Juárez (1806–1872), resisted the French invasion. Napoleon thought better of his dreams of easy glory and abandoned the campaign, which was undertaken more to please members of his military than the French business community. The Mexicans captured and executed Emperor Maximilian, and the experience intensified Mexican nationalism.

Latin Americans were sheltered from direct European imperialism by the business interests of Britain and the United States, but they had little protection against the aggressions of the latter. By the end of the nineteenth century, the United States was able to push the British aside and energetically pursue its own interests, first in the Caribbean and Central America and then throughout Latin America. Growing economic power brought the United States into the field of Great Powers. After the Spanish-American War (1898), the United States occupied Cuba and annexed Puerto Rico and the Philippines; it also restated the Monroe Doctrine, which prohibited colonization of the Americas by foreign nations but did not inhibit U.S. expansionism. In the Roosevelt Corollary (1904), the United States announced that Europeans could not intervene in the Western Hemisphere even to protect their citizens or their business interests. Such intervention was too often the pretext for imperial control in one form or another, which the United States felt would jeopardize its interests.

Yet U.S. citizens continued to interfere freely in Latin American affairs. They engineered the secession of Panama from Colombia in 1903 to obtain the rights to build the Panama Canal on favorable terms. The United States intervened repeatedly in the Caribbean, sending marines to occupy the Dominican Republic, Haiti, Nicaragua, and the port of Veracruz in Mexico. Seizing customs revenues for payment of debts, and threatening Latin American governments, American "gunboat diplomacy" replaced English and French commercial power in northern Latin America. Like Britain, the United States used force to maintain its interests, while at the same time articulating a policy of free competition for trade and commerce—of open doors around the world, including Latin America.

In many ways, U.S. behavior resembled European imperialism. Like the European nations that acquired bases in China, the United States took Guantanamo Bay in Cuba, Fonseca in Nicaragua,

and the Canal Zone in Panama, which was originally leased to the United States in perpetuity. Like European businesses, U.S. entrepreneurs invested so heavily in underdeveloped areas that they frequently controlled governments and ruling elites. In 1923, 43 percent of all U.S. foreign investment went to Latin America, 27 percent to Canada, 22 percent to Europe (at a time when the United States was underwriting German recovery from World War I), and 8 percent to Asia and Africa. Foreign investment may have been a mere fraction of total American wealth, but it was significant to important segments of the national economy.

The United States practiced "dollar diplomacy" (exercising political influence over nations through economic investment), as Europeans had done in Morocco, Tunisia, Egypt, Persia, Turkey, and China. Corrupt members of dictatorial regimes in Latin America borrowed money from the United States for national development or for their own personal use. When repayment was not forthcoming, the United States treated these governments like private companies in default, sending in U.S. marines to take customs, taxes, and treasuries until debts were repaid. The United States put the customs revenues of Haiti (1915) and Santo Domingo (1904, 1916–1924) into receivership, just as the British and French had done to Egyptian customs. In Central America, the United States controlled the governments as puppet or client states, just as the European countries directed the governments of the Middle East or Central Asia. And early in the twentieth century, U.S. influence over Mexico under the presidency of Porfirio Diaz (1876–1880, 1884–1911) was very similar to German and British controls over the Ottoman Empire.

The Latin American response to U.S. imperial actions resembled Asian and African responses to European imperialism. The strongest challenge to U.S. interests before World War I came with the Mexican Revolution in 1911. Its leaders, Emiliano Zapata, Victoriano Huerta, and Francisco "Pancho" Villa, differed in their motives for the overthrow of Diaz, but together they upset Mexican-U.S. relations. Zapata's goal was to break up great estates and give them to the peasantry; Huerta, who was encouraged by the British, hoped to strengthen Mexico by increasing foreign investment in industry. In 1916, Villa angered the

United States by killing several U.S. engineers and making a raid across the border. President Woodrow Wilson, who was at that time offering to mediate between the warring European states, ordered U.S. troops into Mexico to pursue Villa. Thus, while Wilson was preaching self-determination of European nations and sympathetically concerned with the wrongs done to the weak by the strong on the Continent, he was also violating the sovereignty of Mexico, which was torn by civil war.

After World War I, relations between the United States and Latin America remained troubled, particularly during the Great Depression of 1929, which had devastating effects on the countries that had begun to industrialize and build an export market. Only recently have U.S.-Latin American relations substantially improved.

THE LEGACY OF IMPERIALISM

World War I was a turning point in the history of imperialism, although neither mother countries nor colonies seemed aware of it at the time. Britain and France divided the German colonial spoils and replaced Turkish power in the Middle East. Both empires were at their peak in 1919, and even more than before the war, leaders in both countries thought colonies essential to the well-being of their nations—for prestige, for manpower, and for trade.

But the origins of decolonization also date from the postwar era. Wilson and Lloyd George, who championed national self-determination at Versailles, may have meant their slogans to apply to Europeans, not to the colonial world, but many intellectuals, both in the colonies and in Europe, argued that the principle of self-determination should also apply to Asians and Africans. Liberal democrats in the West began to talk of training the colonies for eventual self-government or independence. In France, democrats talked of French citizens of all colors within the empire. In the colonies, forces for independence grew. Intellectuals in the colonies for whom the democrats' timetable for equality or for self-government was too slow found leadership in the anti-imperialist campaign of Lenin and the Bolsheviks.

Less than three decades later, World War II exhausted the European colonial powers. It depleted their soldiery, their financial resources, and their willingness to wage war against their rebellious colonies. During this war, the Allies relied on colonies for labor, soldiers, bases, and supplies. Colonies and British Commonwealth states like Australia made giant strides toward industrialization to meet the Allies' demand for supplies. At the very moment that colonies were most important to their mother countries, they were taking steps toward greater economic independence. Furthermore, the inability of the Europeans to avoid the war's slaughter and the racist destruction of the Jews undercut any moral authority westerners might have claimed. For British and French citizens, the postwar task was to realize peace, democracy, and social welfare at home. For many, this meant that the colonies, or at least some of them, would have to have self-determination, perhaps even independence. The question was not *if* there would be self-determination, but *when, where,* and *how* it would occur.

Today, almost a century after the rapid division of the world among the European and U.S. powers and decades after the decolonization of most of the world, the results of imperialism persist. Imperialism has left a legacy of deep animosity in the countries of Asia, Africa, and Latin America. Although most nations have political independence, Western economic and cultural domination still exists and often influences the policies of autonomous governments. Much of the world is still poor and suffers from insufficient capital, unskilled leaders, and unstable governments. Many people in these poor areas believe that their countries' condition has resulted from a century of Western exploitation. They also believe that any political turmoil in their areas is due to the fact that the superpowers regard the areas as strategic to their interests or important in their ideological power struggle.

Many people in the non-Western world, which some people call the Third World, believe that imperialism explains the poverty of their nations and describes the rapaciousness of European and American business. Imperialism has been a source of great bitterness to former colonial peoples not only because of its economic exploitation, but also because of its encouragement of racism and callous disregard of other cultures. Thus, non-Western nationalism has often possessed anti-Western elements. Today, European nations and the United States must deal in areas of economics and politics with nations acutely conscious of their nationhood and quick to condemn any policy that they perceive as imperialistic.

Imperialism also helped spread many aspects of Western civilization and culture around the globe. The influence of Western ideas, institutions, technologies, and economic practices is apparent everywhere. English and, to some extent,

French are international languages. African and Asian lands have adopted and adapted democracy, parliamentary and party government, socialism, and national boundaries left by Western powers. Today, industrialization, business, and science are truly global. Intellectuals speak of a global village, so closely connected is the community of ideas shared by leading Africans, Asians, and Latin Americans with Europeans and North Americans.

◆ ◆ ◆

SUGGESTED READING

Baumgart, Winfried, *Imperialism* (1982). A critical examination of arguments and issues.

Brodie, Fawn, *Devil Drives: A Life of Sir Richard Burton* (1967). A fine biography of the great explorer.

Brunschwig, Henri, *French Colonialism: 1871–1914. Myths and Realities* (trans. 1964). His general thesis is similar to that of Robinson, Gallagher, and Denny (see below); one of the best books on French imperialism.

Headrick, Daniel, *The Tools of Empire* (1981) and *Tentacles of Progress: Technological Transfer in the Age of Imperialism, 1850–1940* (1988). Interesting argument for the role of technology in imperialism.

Henderson, W. O., *Studies in German Colonial History* (1963). Several interesting essays on this topic, which is difficult to research in English sources.

Hobsbawm, Eric, *The Age of Empire* (1988). The third volume in his Marxist interpretation.

Hobson, J. A., *Imperialism: A Study* (1902). This book and those of Luxemburg and Lenin (see below) are the primary sources for the highly controversial theoretical analysis of capitalism as inherently imperialist.

Jeal, Tim, *Livingstone* (1974). A very readable biography of a fascinating life, with good background on Africa.

Langer, William, *European Alliances and Alignments, 1871–1890* and *Diplomacy of Imperialism, 1890–1902*, 2 vols. (1950). Indispensable sources for information about imperialism from the perspective of diplomatic history.

Lenin, V. I., *Imperialism: The Highest Stage in Capitalism* (1917).

Luxemburg, Rosa, *The Accumulation of Capital* (trans. 1963).

May, Ernest, *Imperial Democracy* (1961). American expansionism discussed more thoroughly and less controversially than is usual.

Moorehead, A., *The White Nile* (1971). The adventurous explorers.

Morris, J., *Pax Britannica* (1968). Well-written, exciting narrative.

Packenham, Thomas, *The Scramble for Africa* (1991). Colorful narrative history.

Porter, Bernard, *The Lion's Share: A Short History of British Imperialism, 1850–1970* (1975). A good survey history.

Robinson, R. E., John Gallagher, and Alice Denny, *Africa and the Victorians: The Official Mind of Imperialism* (1961). An essential book for this fascinating subject; well written, controversial, emphasizing politics.

Thornton, A. P., *The Imperial Idea and Its Enemies: A Study in British Power,* 2nd ed. (1985). An interesting study of the ideas and policies of British imperialism.

REVIEW QUESTIONS

1. How did industrialization change Europeans' relations with China, India, and Japan?

2. Why did imperialism grow after 1880? What rationalizations for European expansion were usually offered at the end of the nineteenth century?

3. What examples are there of successful resistance to Western imperialism?

4. How did imperialism fit in with the European alliance system? How did it cause it? How did imperialism undermine European stability under the alliance system?

5. What were the obstacles preventing Indian independence?

6. Why were Japan and China able to withstand imperialist expansion?

7. Why was Africa divided up in such a brief time?

8. How did imperialism threaten world peace in the early twentieth century?

9. How did competition for empire between England, France, and Russia make their friendship on the eve of World War I seem unlikely in 1900?

10. How was Turkey able to maintain itself in the nineteenth century against the encroachments of Europeans? How did Turkey respond to European threats in the twentieth century?

11. What problems in the Middle East and Central Asia appear to have been resolved because Russia was defeated in World War I?

CHAPTER 28

Modern Consciousness:
New Views of Nature,
Human Nature,
and the Arts

he modern mentality may be said to have passed through two broad phases: early modernity and late modernity. Formulated during the era of the Scientific Revolution and the Enlightenment, early modernity stressed confidence in reason, science, human goodness, and humanity's capacity to improve society for human betterment. Then in the late nineteenth and early twentieth centuries, a new outlook took shape. Late modern thinkers and scientists achieved revolutionary insights into human nature, the social world, and the physical universe; and writers and artists opened up hitherto unimagined possibilities for artistic expression.

These developments produced a shift in European consciousness. The mechanical model of the universe, which had dominated the Western outlook since Newton, was altered. The Enlightenment view of human rationality and goodness was questioned, and the belief in natural rights and objective standards governing morality came under attack. Rules of esthetics that had governed the arts since the Renaissance were discarded. Shattering old beliefs, late modernity left Europeans without landmarks—without generally accepted cultural standards or agreed-on conceptions about human nature and life's meaning.

The late modern period was marked by extraordinary creativity in thought and the arts. Yet imaginative and fruitful as these changes were for Western intellectual and cultural life, they also helped create the disoriented, fragmented, and troubled era that is the twentieth century.

IRRATIONALISM

Some late-nineteenth-century thinkers challenged the basic premises of the philosophes and their nineteenth-century heirs. They repudiated the En-

Evening on Karl Johan Street, by Edvard Munch. (*Bettmann Archive*)

lightenment conception of human rationality, stressing instead the irrational side of human behavior. Regarding reason as sovereign, the philosophes had defined human beings by their capacity to think critically; now thinkers saw blind strivings and animal instincts as the primary fact of human existence. To these thinkers, it seemed that reason exercised a very limited influence over human conduct. Impulses, drives, instincts—all forces below the surface—determined behavior much more than did logical consciousness. Like the romantics, proponents of the nonrational placed more reliance on feeling, spontaneity, and intuition than on reason. They belittled the intellect's attempt to comprehend nature and society, praised outbursts of the irrational, and, in some instances, exalted violence.

The new insights into the irrational side of human nature and the growing assault on reason had immense implications for political life. In succeeding decades, these currents of irrationalism would become ideologized and politicized by unscrupulous demagogues, who sought to mobilize and manipulate the masses. The popularity of fascist movements, which openly denigrated reason and exalted race, blood, action, and will, demonstrated the naiveté of nineteenth-century liberals, who believed that reason had triumphed in human affairs.

Nietzsche

The principal figure in the dethronement of reason and the glorification of the irrational was the German philosopher Friedrich Nietzsche (1844–1900). Nietzsche's writings are not systematic treatises but rather collections of aphorisms, often containing internal contradictions. Consequently, his philosophy lends itself to misinterpretation and misapplication, as manifested by Nazi theorists, who distorted Nietzsche to justify their theory of the German master race.

Nietzsche attacked the accepted views and convictions of his day as a hindrance to a fuller and richer existence. He denounced social reform, parliamentary government, and universal suffrage, ridiculed the vision of progress through science, condemned Christian morality, and mocked the liberal belief in man's essential goodness and rationality. According to Nietzsche,

man must understand that life, which is replete with cruelty, injustice, uncertainty, and absurdity, is not governed by rational principles. There exist no absolute standards of good and evil whose truth can be demonstrated by reflective reason. There is only naked man living in a godless and absurd world.

Modern bourgeois society, said Nietzsche, was decadent and enfeebled—a victim of the excessive development of the rational faculties at the expense of will and instinct. Against the liberal-rationalist stress on the intellect, he urged recognition of the dark, mysterious world of instinctual desires, the true forces of life. Smother the will with excessive intellectualizing, and you destroy the spontaneity that sparks cultural creativity and ignites a zest for living. The critical and theoretical outlook destroyed the creative instincts. For man's manifold potential to be realized, he must stop relying on the intellect and nurture again the instinctual roots of human existence.

Christianity, with all its prohibitions, restrictions, and demands to conform, also crushes the human impulse for life, said Nietzsche. Christian morality must be obliterated, for it is fit only for the weak, the slave. The triumph of Christianity in the ancient world, said Nietzsche, was a revolution of the lowest elements of society, the meek, the weak, and the ignoble, who sought to inherit the earth from their aristocratic superiors. It was nothing less than an attempt of the resentful slave and the slavelike plebeians to prevent their aristocratic superiors from expressing their heroic natures and to strike back at the noble spirits whom they envied. They did so by condemning as evil the very traits that they lacked—strength, power, assertiveness, and a zest for life—and by making their own base, wretched, and life-negating values the standard of all things. Then they saddled with guilt all those who deviated from the standard. This transvaluation of values engineered by Christianity, said Nietzsche, led to a deterioration of life and culture. In *The Anti-Christ* (1888), Nietzsche wrote:

> *Christianity has waged a war to the death against this higher type of man. . . . Christianity has taken the side of everything weak, base, ill-constituted, it has made an ideal out of opposition to the . . . instincts of strong life. . . . Christianity is a revolt of everything that*

FRIEDRICH NIETZSCHE (1844–1900) WITH HIS WIFE. Possessing the intuitive genius of a great poet, Nietzsche grasped the crucial problem afflicting the modern European soul: What path should the individual take in a world where God is dead? Nietzsche's answer to this question—the superman who creates his own values—lent itself to considerable misinterpretation and distortion and had little constructive social value. (*Photo AKG London*)

crawls along the ground directed against that which is elevated.[1]

Although the philosophes had rejected Christian doctrines, they had largely retained Christian ethics. Unlike the philosophes, however, Nietzsche did not attack Christianity because it was contrary to reason. He attacked it because, he said, it gave man a sick soul. It was life-denying. Blocking the free and spontaneous exercise of human instincts, it made humility and self-abnegation virtues and pride a vice. In short, Christianity extinguished the spark of life. This spark of life, this inner yearning that is man's true essence, must again burn.

"God is dead," Nietzsche proclaimed. God is man's own creation. Christian morality is also dead. There are no higher worlds, no transcendental or metaphysical truths, no morality derived from God or nature, and no natural rights, scientific socialism, or inevitable progress. All the old values and truths have lost their intelligibility. The death of God and all transcendental truth can mean the liberation of man, insisted Nietzsche. Man can surmount *nihilism* (the belief that moral and social values have no validity); he can create new values and achieve self-mastery. He can overcome the deadening uniformity and mediocrity of modern civilization. He can undo democracy and socialism, which have made masters out of cattlelike masses, and surmount the shopkeeper's spirit, which has made man soft and degenerate. European society lacks heroic figures; everyone belongs to a vast herd, but there are no shepherds.

According to Nietzsche, Europe could be saved only by the emergence of a higher type of man, the *superman* or *overman*, who would not be held back by the egalitarian rubbish preached by democrats and socialists. "A declaration of war on the masses by *higher* man is needed," said Nietzsche, to end "the dominion of *inferior* men." Europe requires "the annihilation of *suffrage universal,* i.e., the system through which the lowest natures prescribe themselves as laws for the higher."[2] Europe needs a new breed of rulers, a true aristocracy of masterful men. The superman is a new kind of man who breaks with accepted morality and sets his own standards. He does not repress his instincts but asserts them. He destroys old values and asserts his prerogative as master. Free of Christian guilt, he proudly affirms his own being; dispensing with Christian "thou shalt not," he instinctively says "I will." He dares to be himself. Because he is not like other people, traditional definitions of good and evil have no meaning for him. He does not allow his individuality to be stifled. He makes his own values, those that flow from his very being.

The superman grasps that "the most fundamental desire in man [is] his drive for power,"[3] that human beings crave and strive for power ceaselessly and uncompromisingly. This will to power governs everyday life and is the determining factor in political life. The enhancement of power brings supreme enjoyment: "The love of power is the demon of men. Let them have everything—health, food, a place to live, entertainment—they are and remain unhappy and low-spirited; for the demon waits and waits and will be satisfied. Take everything from them and satisfy this and they are almost happy—as happy as men and demons can be."[4]

The German philosopher Arthur Schopenhauer (1788–1860) had declared that beneath the conscious intellect is the will, a striving, demanding, and imperious force, which is the real determinant of human behavior. Schopenhauer held that the intellect is merely a tool of an alogical and irrational will. Life is an endless striving to fulfill ceaseless desires. Blind animal impulses, not the capacity for rational choice, are a human being's true essence. Schopenhauer sought to repress the will. He urged people to stifle desires and retreat into quietude to escape from life's agonies.

Nietzsche learned from Schopenhauer to appreciate the unconscious strivings that dominate human behavior, but he rejected Schopenhauer's negation of the will, his flight from life. Instead, Nietzsche called for the heroic and joyful assertion of the will and the affirmation of life in order to redeem life from nothingness.

Supermen cast off all established values. Free of all restrictions, rules, and codes of behavior imposed by society, they create their own values. They burst upon the world propelled by that something that urges people to want, take, strike, create, struggle, seek, dominate. They know that life is purposeless, but live it laughingly, instinctively, fully. Supermen are people of restless energy who enjoy living dangerously, have contempt for meekness and humility, and dismiss humanitarian sentiments; they are noble warriors, hard and ruthless. Only a new elite, which distances itself from the masses and holds in contempt the Christian belief that all people are equal before God, can save European society from decadence.

The influence of Nietzsche's philosophy is still a matter of controversy and conjecture. Perhaps better than anyone else, Nietzsche grasped the crucial problem of modern society and culture: that with the "death of God" traditional moral values had lost their authority and binding power. In a world where nothing is true, all is permitted. Nietzsche foresaw that the future, an age without values, would be violent and sordid,

and he urged individuals to face themselves and life free of illusion, pretense, and hypocrisy. Nietzsche is also part of a general nineteenth-century trend that sought to affirm the human being and earthly aspirations rather than God or salvation.

But no social policy could be derived from Nietzsche's heroic individualism, which taught that "there are higher and lower men and that a single individual can . . . justify the existence of whole millennia."[5] Nietzsche thought only of great individuals, humanity's noblest specimens, who overcome mediocrity and the artificiality of all inherited values. The social community and social injustice did not concern him. "The weak and ill-constituted shall perish: first principle of our philanthropy. And one shall help them to do so."[6] Surely, these words offer no constructive guidelines for dealing with the problems of modern industrial civilization.

Likewise, Nietzsche had no constructive proposals for dealing with the disintegration of rational and Christian certainties. Instead, his vitriolic attack on European institutions and values helped to erode the rational foundations of Western civilization. This assault appealed immensely to intellectuals in central Europe, who saw Nietzsche's philosophy as liberating an inner energy. In addition, many young people, attracted to Nietzsche, welcomed World War I; they viewed it as an esthetic experience and thought that it would clear a path to a new heroic age. They took Nietzsche's words literally: "A society that definitely and *instinctively* gives up war and conquest is in decline."[7]

Nazi theorists tried to make Nietzsche a forerunner of their movement. They sought philosophical sanction for their own thirst for power, contempt for the weak, ruthlessness, and glorification of action, as well as for their cult of the heroic and their Social Darwinistic revulsion for human equality. Recasting Nietzsche in their own image, the Nazis saw themselves as Nietzsche's supermen: members of a master race, who, by force of will, would conquer all obstacles and reshape the world according to their own values. Some German intellectuals were drawn to Nazism because it seemed a healthy affirmation of life, the life with a new purpose, for which Nietzsche called.

Nietzsche himself, detesting German nationalism and militarism, scoffed at the notion of German racial superiority, disdained (despite some unfortunate remarks) anti-Semitism, and denounced state worship. He would have abhorred Hitler and been dismayed at the twisting of his idea of the will to power into a prototype fascist principle. The men that he admired were passionate but self-possessed individuals, who, by mastering their own chaotic passions, would face life and death courageously, affirmatively, and creatively. Such men make great demands on themselves. Nevertheless, as Janko Lavrin points out, "Practically all the Fascist and Nazi theories can find some support in Nietzsche's texts, provided one gives them the required twist."[8] Nietzsche's extreme and violent denunciation of Western democratic principles, including equality, his praise of power, and his call for the liberation of the instincts, as well as his elitism, which denigrates and devalues all human life that is not strong and noble, and his spurning of humane values, provided a breeding ground for violent, antirational, antiliberal, and inhumane movements. His philosophy, which included loose talk about the virtues of pitiless warriors, the breeding of a master race, and the annihilation of the weak and the ill is conducive to a politics of extremes that knows no moral limits.

Dostoevski

Like Nietzsche, the Russian novelist and essayist Fyodor Dostoevski (1821–1881) attacked the fundamental outlook of the Enlightenment, particularly as expressed by liberals and socialists. In contrast to their view that human beings are innately good, responsive to reason's promptings, and capable of constructing the good society through reason, Dostoevski perceived human beings as inherently depraved, irrational, and rebellious.

In *Notes from Underground* (1864), the narrator (the Underground Man) rebels against the efforts of rationalists, humanists, positivists, liberals, and socialists to define human nature according to universal principles and to reform society so as to promote greater happiness. He rebels against science and reason, against the entire liberal and socialist vision. He does so in the name of human subjectivity: the uncontainable, irrepressible, whimsical, and foolish human will.

Human nature, says the Underground Man, is too volatile, too diversified, to be schematized by the theoretical mind.

For the Underground Man, there are no absolute and timeless truths that precede the individual and to which the individual should conform. There is only a terrifying world of naked wills vying with one another. In such a world, people do not necessarily seek happiness, prosperity, and peace—all that is good for them, according to "enlightened" thinkers. To the rationalist who aims to eliminate suffering and deprivation, Dostoevski replies that some people freely choose suffering and depravity because it gratifies them—for some, "even in a toothache there is enjoyment"—and they are repelled by wealth, peace, security, and happiness. They do not want to be robots in a rigorously regulated social order that creates a slot for everything, and they consider excessive intellectualizing—"overacute consciousness"—a disease that keeps them from asserting their autonomy, their "independent choice."

> [I]t seems that something that is dearer to almost every man than his greatest advantages must really exist . . . for which, if necessary, a man is ready to act in opposition to all laws, that is, in opposition to reason, honor, peace, prosperity. . . . One's own free unfettered choice, one's own fancy, however wild it may be, one's own fancy worked up at times to frenzy—why that is that very "most advantageous advantage" which we have overlooked, which comes under no classification and through which all systems and theories are continually being sent to the devil. . . . What man needs is simple independent *choice*, whatever that independence may cost and wherever it may lead.[9]

It is this irrational will that defines the individual's uniqueness and leads him to resist the blueprints drawn up by social theorists. If individuals do not act out of enlightened self-interest—if they constantly act contrary to their own reasoned interests—then what hope is there for social planners desirous of creating the "good" society?

The Underground Man maintains that by following irrational impulses and engaging in irrational acts, human beings assert their individuality; they prove that they are free. The Underground Man is totally free. He struggles to define his existence according to his own needs rather than the standards and values created by others. For him, freedom of choice is a human being's most priceless possession, and it derives not from the intellect, but from impulses and feelings that account for our essential individuality. He considers the "rational faculty" as "simply one-twentieth of all my faculties of life"; life is more than reasoning, more than "simply extracting square roots."[10]

In rejecting external security and liberal and socialist concepts of progress—in aspiring to assert his own individuality even if this means acting against his own best interests—the Underground Man demonstrates that a powerful element of irrationality underlies human nature.

Bergson

Another thinker who reflected the growing preoccupation with the nonrational was Henri Bergson (1859–1941), a French philosopher of Jewish background. Originally attracted to positivism, Bergson turned away from the positivistic claim that science could explain everything and fulfill all human needs. Such an emphasis on the intellect, said Bergson, sacrifices spiritual impulses, imagination, and intuition and reduces the soul to a mere mechanism.

The methods of science cannot reveal ultimate reality, Bergson insisted. European civilization must recognize the limitations of scientific rationalism. Intuition, whereby the mind achieves an immanent relationship with the object, becomes one with it, tells us more about reality than the method of analysis employed by science. Entering into the object through an intuitive experience is an avenue to truth that is closed to the calculations and measurements of science. Although not based on scientific procedures, the method of intuition is a superior means to knowledge, Bergson claimed.

To his admirers, Bergson's philosophy liberated the person from the constraints of positivism, mechanism, and materialism. It also showed the creative potential of intuition, the mystical experience, and the poetic imagination: those forces of life that resist categorization by the scientific mind. A protest against modern technology and bureaucracy—against all the features of mass society that seemed to stifle individual uniqueness and spontaneity—it was an attempt to reaffirm the primacy of the individual in an increasingly mechanized and bureaucratic world. The popularity of Bergson's philosophy with its depreciation of reason, symptomized the unsuspected strength and appeal of the nonrational—another sign that people were searching for new alternatives to the Enlightenment worldview.

Sorel

Nietzsche and Dostoevski proclaimed that irrational forces constitute the essence of human nature; Bergson held that a nonrational intuition provides insights unattainable by the scientific mentality. The French social theorist Georges Sorel (1847–1922), who had given up engineering to follow intellectual pursuits, recognized the political potential of the nonrational. Like Nietzsche, Sorel was disillusioned with contemporary bourgeois society, which he considered decadent, unheroic, and life-denying. Whereas Nietzsche called for the superman to rescue society from decadence and mediocrity, Sorel placed his hopes in the proletariat, whose position made them courageous and virile. He saw them as bearers of higher values: as noble and determined producers struggling against exploiters and parasites.

Sorel wanted workers to destroy the existing bourgeois-liberal-capitalist order and rejuvenate society by infusing it with dynamic and creative energy and a sense of moral purpose. The overthrow of decadent bourgeois society would be accomplished through a general strike: a universal work stoppage, which would bring down governments and give power to the workers. Sorel applauded violence, for it intensified the revolutionaries' dedication to the cause and spurred them to acts of heroism. It also accorded with his general conception that life is an unremitting battle and that history is a perpetual conflict between decay and vitality, between passivity and action. In his view, struggle purified, invigorated, and promoted creative change.

Sorel saw the general strike as having the appeal of a great myth. What was important was not that the general strike actually take place, but that its image stir all the anticapitalist resentments of the workers and inspire them to carry out their revolutionary responsibilities. Sorel understood the extraordinary potency of myth: it structures and intensifies feelings, unifies people, elicits total commitment, and incites heroic action. Because they appeal to the imagination and the emotions, myths are an effective way of organizing the masses, buoying up their spirits, and moving them to revolt. By believing in the myth of the general strike, workers would soar above the moral decadence of bourgeois society and bear the immense sacrifices that their struggle called for.

Like Marx, Sorel believed that the goals of the worker could not be achieved through peaceful parliamentary means. He, too, wanted no reconciliation between bourgeois exploiters and oppressed workers. The only recourse for workers was direct action and violence. However, Marx considered violence simply as a means to a revolutionary end and would dispense with it once the end was achieved. Regarding violence as sublime—a means of restoring grandeur to a flabby world—Sorel valued it as an end in itself.

Sorel's condemnation of liberal democracy and his conviction that fabricated myths could serve as a powerful political weapon found concrete expression in the fascist movements after World War I. Sorel heralded the age of mass political movements committed to revolutionary violence and of myths manufactured by propaganda experts determined to destroy the liberal-rational tradition of the Enlightenment.

FREUD: A NEW VIEW OF HUMAN NATURE

In many ways, Sigmund Freud (1856–1939), an Austrian-Jewish physician who spent most of his adult life in Vienna, was a child of the Enlightenment. Like the philosophes, he identified civilization with reason and regarded science as the avenue to knowledge. But in contrast to the philosophes, Freud focused on the massive power and influence of nonrational drives. Marx had argued that, although people believe that they think freely, in truth their beliefs and thoughts re-

FREUD AND HIS DAUGHTER, ANNA, 1912. Sigmund Freud (1856–1939), the father of psychoanalysis, penetrated the world of the unconscious in a scientific way. He concluded that powerful drives govern human behavior more than reason does. His explorations of the unconscious produced an image of the human being that broke with the Enlightenment's view of the individual's essential goodness and rationality. (*Mary Evans Picture Library*)

flect the ideology of the ruling class. Freud, too, believed that our conscious thoughts are determined by hidden forces—namely, unconscious impulses.

Whereas Nietzsche glorified the irrational and approached it with a poet's temperament, Freud recognized its potential danger. He sought to comprehend it scientifically and wanted to regulate it in the interests of civilization. Unlike Nietzsche, Freud did not belittle the rational but always sought to salvage respect for reason. In a letter to the Austrian novelist Stefan Zweig, Freud wrote that the essential task of psychoanalysis was "to struggle with the demon" of irrationality in a "sober way," to make it "a comprehensible object of science."[11] By "a sober way," he meant the scientific method, not Bergson's intuition or Nietzsche's inspired insights.

Freud held that people are not fundamentally rational; human behavior is governed primarily by powerful inner forces, which are hidden from consciousness. Within the human mind, intense mental activity takes place that is independent of and unknown to consciousness. Primitive drives, strivings, and thoughts influence our behavior, often without our awareness, so that we may not know the real reasons for our actions. Freud considered not just the external acts of a person, but also the inner psychic reality underlying human behavior.

Freud, of course, did not discover the unconscious. Romantic poets had sought the wellspring of creativity in a layer of mind below consciousness. The Greek tragedians, Shakespeare, Schopenhauer, Nietzsche, and Dostoevski, among others, had all penetrated the tangled world of the passions and marveled at its elemental power. Freud, who believed that artistic and literary creativity ultimately derives from primal instincts rooted in the unconscious, paid tribute to creative writers' intuition: "they are apt to know of a whole host of things between heaven and earth of which our philosophy has not yet let us dream. In their knowledge of the mind they are far in advance of us everyday people, for they draw upon sources which we have not yet opened up for science."[12] He described Nietzsche as a philosopher "whose guesses and intuitions often agree in the most astonishing way with the laborious findings of psychoanalysis."[13] Freud's great achievement was to explore the unconscious methodically and systematically with the tools and temperament of a scientist.

After graduating from medical school, Freud specialized in the treatment of nervous disorders. His investigations led him to conclude that childhood fears and experiences, often sexual in nature, accounted for neuroses: disorders in thinking, feeling, and behavior that interfere with everyday acts of personal and social life. Neuroses can take several forms, including hysteria, anxiety, depression, obsessions, and so on. So painful and threatening were these childhood emotions and experiences that his patients banished them from conscious memory to the realm of the unconscious. To understand and treat neurotic behavior, Freud said, it is necessary to look behind overt symptoms and bring to the surface emotionally charged experiences and fears—childhood traumas—that lie buried in the unconscious, along with primitive impulses.

Freud probed the unconscious by urging his patients to say whatever came to their minds. This procedure, called free association, rests on the premise that spontaneous and uninhibited talk reveals a person's underlying preoccupations, his or her inner world, and the "demons" that are at the root of the person's emotional distress. A second avenue to the unconscious is the analysis of dreams. An individual's dreams, said Freud, reveal his or her secret wishes, often socially unacceptable desires, and frightening memories. Finding them too painful to bear, we lock up these wishes and memories in the deepest dungeons of the unconscious. But even in their cages, the demons remain active, continuing to haunt us and to generate conflicts. Our distress is real and even excruciating, but we do not know its source.

The *id,* the subconscious seat of the instincts, said Freud, is "a cauldron full of seething excitations," which constantly demand gratification. The id is primitive and irrational. It knows no values; it has no awareness of good and evil. Unable to endure tension, it demands sexual release, the termination of pain, or the cessation of hunger. When the id is denied an outlet for its instinctual energy, people become frustrated, angry, and unhappy. Gratifying the id is our highest pleasure. But the full gratification of instinctual demands is detrimental to civilized life.

Freud postulated a harrowing conflict between the relentless strivings of our instinctual nature and the requirements of civilization. In Freud's view, civilization requires the renunciation of instinctual gratification and the mastery of animal instincts, a thesis he developed in *Civilization and Its Discontents* (1930). Although Freud's thoughts in this work were, no doubt, influenced by the great tragedy of World War I, the main theme could be traced back to his earlier writings. Human beings derive their highest pleasure from sexual fulfillment, said Freud, but unrestrained sexuality drains off psychic energy needed for creative artistic and intellectual life; it also directs energies away from work needed to preserve communal life. Hence society, through the family, the priest, the teacher, and the police, imposes rules and restrictions on our animal nature. But this is immensely painful. People are caught in a tragic bind. Society's demand for the denial of full instinctual gratification causes frustration; equally distressing, the violation of society's rules under the pressure of instinctual needs evokes feelings of guilt. Either way, people suffer; civilized life simply entails too much pain for people. It seems that the price we pay for civilization is neurosis. Most people cannot endure the amount of instinctual renunciation that civilization requires. There are times when our elemental human nature rebels against all the restrictions and "thou shalt nots" demanded by society, against all the misery and torment imposed by civilization.

"Civilization imposes great sacrifices not only on man's sexuality, but also on his aggressivity,"[14] said Freud. People are not good by nature, as the philosophes had taught; on the contrary, they are "creatures among whose instinctual endowments is to be reckoned a powerful share of aggressiveness." Their first inclination is not to love their neighbor but to "satisfy their aggressiveness on him, to exploit his capacity for work without compensation, to use him sexually without his consent, to seize his possessions, to humiliate him, to cause him pain, to torture and to kill him."[15] Man is wolf to man, concluded Freud. "Who has the courage to dispute it in the face of all the evidence in his own life and in history?"[16] Civilization "has to use its utmost efforts in order to set limits to man's aggressive instincts," but "in spite of every effort these endeavors of civilization have not so far achieved very much."[17] People find it difficult to do without "the satisfaction of this inclination to aggression."[18] When circumstances are favorable, this primitive aggressiveness breaks loose and "reveals man as a savage beast to whom consideration towards his own kind is something alien."[19] For Freud, "the inclination to aggression is an original self-subsisting disposition in man," and it "constitutes the greatest impediment to civilization." Civilization attempts "to combine single human individuals and after that families, then races, peoples and nations into one great unity. . . . But man's natural aggressive instinct, the hostility of each against all and of all against each, opposes this program of civilization."[20] Aggressive impulses

drive people apart, threatening society with disintegration. For Freud, an unalterable core of human nature is ineluctably in opposition to civilized life. To this extent, everyone is potentially an enemy of civilization.

Freud's awareness of the irrational and his general pessimism regarding people's ability to regulate it in the interests of civilization did not lead him to break faith with the Enlightenment tradition, for Freud did not celebrate the irrational. He was too aware of its self-destructive nature for that. Civilization is indeed a burden, but people must bear it, for the alternative is far worse. In the tradition of the philosophes, Freud sought truth based on a scientific analysis of human nature and believed that reason was the best road to social improvement. Like the philosophes, he was critical of religion, regarding it as a pious illusion—a fairy tale in conflict with reason. Freud wanted people to throw away what he believed was the crutch of religion: to break away from childlike dependency and stand alone.

Also like the philosophes, Freud was a humanitarian who sought to relieve human misery by making people aware of their true nature, particularly their sexuality. He wanted society to soften its overly restrictive sexual standards because they were injurious to mental health. As a practicing psychiatrist, he tried to assist his patients in dealing with emotional problems. Freud wanted to raise to the level of consciousness hitherto unrecognized inner conflicts that caused emotional distress. One enduring consequence of the Freudian revolution is the recognition of the enormous importance played by childhood in the shaping of the adult's personality. The neurotic disorders that burden adults begin in early childhood. Freud urged that we show greater concern for the emotional needs of children.

Yet Freud also differed from the philosophes in crucial ways. Dismissing the Christian doctrine of original sin as myth, the philosophes had believed human nature to be essentially good. If people took reason for their guide, evil could be eliminated. Freud, on the other hand, asserted, in secular and scientific terms, a pessimistic view of human nature. He saw evil as rooted in human nature rather than as a product of a faulty environment. Education and better living conditions would not eliminate evil, as the philosophes had expected, nor would abolition of private property, as Marx had declared. The philosophes venerated reason; it had enabled Newton to unravel nature's mysteries and would permit people to achieve virtue and reform society. Freud, who wanted reason to prevail, understood that its soft voice had to compete with the thunderous roars of the id. Freud broke with the optimism of the philosophes. His awareness of the immense pressures that civilization places on our fragile egos led him to be generally pessimistic about the future.

Unlike Marx, Freud had no vision of utopia. He saw the crude and destructive character of human nature as an ever present obstacle to harmonious social relations. That Freud was hounded out of Vienna by the Nazis and his four sisters were murdered by them simply for being Jewish is a telling footnote to his view of human nature, the power of the irrational, and the fragility of civilization.

SOCIAL THOUGHT: CONFRONTING THE IRRATIONAL AND THE COMPLEXITIES OF MODERN SOCIETY

The end of the nineteenth century and the beginning of the twentieth mark the great age of sociological thought. The leading sociological thinkers of the period all regarded science as the only valid model for correct thinking, and all claimed that their thought rested on a scientific foundation. They struggled with some of the crucial problems of modern society: How can society achieve coherence and stability when the customary associations and attachments that had characterized village life had been ruthlessly dissolved by the rapidly developing industrial-urban-capitalist order and when religion no longer united people? What are the implications of the nonrational for political life? How can people preserve their individuality in a society that is becoming increasingly regimented? In many ways, twentieth-century dictatorships were responses to the dilemmas of modern society analyzed by these social theorists. And twentieth-century dictators would employ these social theorists' insights into group and mass psychology for the purpose of gaining and maintaining power.

Durkheim

Émile Durkheim (1858–1917), a French scholar of Jewish background and heir to Comte's positivism, was an important founder of modern sociology. Like Comte, he considered scientific thought to be the only valid model for modern society. A crucial element of Durkheim's thought was the effort to show that the essential ingredients of modern times—secularism, rationalism, and individualism—threaten society with disintegration. In traditional society, the social order was derived from God, and a person's place and function were assigned by God and determined by birth. Modern people, however, captivated by the principle of individualism, do not accept such restraints, said Durkheim. Instead, they seek to uplift themselves and demand that society allow them the opportunity. In the process, they reject or ignore the restraints that society must impose if it is to function. Their attitude leads to anarchy. Durkheim wanted to prevent modern society from disintegrating into a disconnected mass of self-seeking, antagonistic individuals. Like Rousseau, he held that the individual becomes fully human only as a member of a community.

The weakening of those traditional ties that bind the individual to society constituted, for Durkheim, the crisis of modern society. Without collective values and common beliefs, he felt, society was threatened with disintegration and the individual with disorientation. To a Western world intrigued by scientific progress, Durkheim emphasized the spiritual malaise of modern society. Modern people, said Durkheim, suffer from *anomie*—a collapse of values. They do not feel integrated into a collective community and find no purpose in life. In *Suicide* (1897), Durkheim maintained that "the exceptionally high number of voluntary deaths manifests the state of deep disturbances from which civilized societies are suffering and bears witness to its gravity."[21] The high level of boredom, anxiety, and pessimism also evidence the pathology of modern society. Modern people are driven to suicide by intense competition and the disappointment and frustration resulting from unfulfilled expectations and a lack of commitment to moral principles. People must limit their aspirations and exercise discipline over their desires and passions. They must stop wanting more. Religion once spurred people to view restraint and the renunciation of desires as virtues, but it can no longer do so.

Durkheim approved of modernity, but he noted that modern ways have not brought happiness or satisfaction to the individual. Modern scientific and industrial society requires a new moral system, which would bind the various classes into a cohesive social order and help overcome the feelings of restlessness and dissatisfaction tormenting people. Like Saint-Simon, Durkheim called for a rational and secular system of morals to replace Christian dogma, which had lost its power to attract and to bind. If a rational and secular replacement for Christianity is not found, society would run the risk of dispensing with moral beliefs altogether, and it could not endure such a vacuum. Like the positivists, Durkheim insisted that the new moral beliefs must be discovered through the methods of science.

Durkheim hoped that occupational and professional organizations—updated medieval guilds—would integrate the individual into society and provide the moral force capable of restraining the selfish interests of both employer and worker. By curbing egoism, fostering self-discipline, and promoting altruism, these organizations could provide substitutes for religion.

Durkheim focused on a crucial dilemma of modernity. On the one hand, modern urban civilization has provided the individual with unparalleled opportunities for self-development and material improvement. On the other, the breakdown of traditional communal bonds caused by the spread of rationalism and individualism has produced a sense of isolation and alienation. In modern mass society, the individual feels like an outsider, a condition that has been exacerbated by the decline of Christianity. Twentieth-century totalitarian movements sought to integrate these uprooted and alienated souls into new collectivities: a proletarian state based on workers' solidarity or a racial state based on blood and soil.

Pareto

Like Comte, Vilfredo Pareto (1848–1923), an Italian economist and sociologist, aimed to construct a system of sociology on the model of the physical sciences. His studies led him to conclude that social behavior does not rest primarily on reason, but rather on nonrational instincts and sentiments. These deeply rooted and essentially changeless feelings are the fundamental elements in human behavior. Although society may change, human nature remains essentially the same. Whoever aims to lead and to influence people must appeal not to logic, but to elemental feelings. Most human behavior is nonrational; nonlogical considerations also determine the beliefs that people hold. Like Marx and Freud, Pareto believed that we cannot accept a person's word at face value; we find the real cause of human behavior in human instincts and sentiments. People do not act according to carefully thought-out theories. They act first from nonlogical motivations and then construct a rationalization to justify their behavior. Much of Pareto's work was devoted to studying the nonrational elements of human conduct and the various beliefs invented to give the appearance of rationality to behavior that derives from feeling and instinct.

Pareto divided society into two strata: the elite and the masses. Elites have always existed, said Pareto, because human beings are unequal by nature and because the goods that all people seek cannot be shared equally. Because struggle is a general law of life, elites and masses will exist in all societies. Thus, Pareto rejected as naive Marx's vision of the end of the class struggle.

In the tradition of Machiavelli, Pareto held that a successful ruling elite must, with cunning, and if necessary with violence, exploit the feelings and impulses of the masses to its own advantage. Democratic states, he said, delude themselves in thinking that the masses are really influenced by rational argument. A staunch opponent of parliamentary democracy, Pareto predicted that new political leaders would emerge who would master the people through propaganda and force, appealing always to sentiment rather than to reason. To this extent, Pareto was an intellectual forerunner of fascism, which preached an authoritarian elitism. Mussolini praised Pareto and proudly claimed him as a source of inspiration. The extent to which Pareto, who died one year after Mussolini came to power, welcomed the fascist regime is a matter of conjecture. But the triumph of fascism did seem to confirm his convictions that democracy was ready to collapse and that a small minority of determined men, willing to use violence, could gain control of the state if the holders of power were reluctant to counter with force.

Le Bon

Gustave Le Bon (1841–1931), a French social psychologist, concentrated on mass psychology as demonstrated in crowd behavior, a phenomenon of considerable importance in an age of accelerating industrialization and democratization. "The substitution of the unconscious action of crowds for the conscious activity of individuals is one of the principal characteristics of the present age,"[22] Le Bon declared in the preface to *The Crowd* (1895). In the past, said Le Bon, rivalries between monarchs dominated Europe's political stage; "the opinion of the masses scarcely counted, and most frequently did not count at all."[23] But Europe has experienced a great transformation. In this new age, he said, the masses organized in socialist parties and unions, are starting to determine the destinies of nations.

Le Bon applied the term *crowd* to a large group of people in which individuality is submerged in the mass and the individual loses control over his or her ideas and emotions. A psychological crowd could be a street mob, a political party, or a labor union. An agglomeration of individuals "presents new characteristics very different from those of the individuals composing it. The sentiments and ideas of all the persons in the gathering take one and the same direction, and their conscious personality vanishes."[24] The crowd acquires a collective mind, in which critical thinking is swamped and "unconscious qualities obtain the upper hand."[25] Becoming increasingly intolerant and fanatical, the crowd member "descends several rungs in the ladder of civilization. Isolated, he may be a cultivated individual; in a crowd, he is a barbarian—that is, a creature acting by instinct."[26] Crowd behavior demonstrates convincingly that "the part played by the unconscious in all our acts is immense and that played by reason very small."[27] In a contest with sentiment, human reason is utterly powerless.

Le Bon also discussed the leaders of crowds and their means of persuasion. "A crowd is a servile flock that is incapable of ever doing without a master," he stressed. Leaders "are more frequently men of action than thinkers"; they are "morbidly nervous, excitable, . . . bordering on madness." Fanatically committed to their beliefs, they do not respond to logical argument. The masses, "always ready to listen to the strong-willed man,"[28] respond to the intensity of the leader's faith.

Both Mussolini and Hitler, who deliberately sought to seduce, manipulate, and dominate the masses, absorbed Le Bon's ideas, which had become commonplace in the early twentieth century. "I don't know how many times I have reread *Psychologie des Foules [The Crowd]*," declared Mussolini. "It is an excellent work to which I frequently refer."[29] Hitler's analysis of the crowd—"sober reasoning determines their thoughts far less than emotion and feeling"—restates many of Le Bon's observations.

Weber

Probably the most prominent social thinker of the age, the German academic Max Weber (1864–1920) was a leading shaper of modern sociology. In Weber's view Western civilization, unlike the other civilizations of the globe, had virtually eliminated myth, mystery, and magic from its conception of nature and society—the "disenchantment of the world," Weber called it. Most conspicuous in Western science, this process of rationalization, or "calculated action," was also evident in politics, law, and economics. Weber considered Western science to be an attempt to understand and master nature through reason, and Western capitalism, an attempt to organize work and production in a rational manner. The Western state has a rational written constitution, rationally formulated law, and a bureaucracy of trained government officials, which administers the affairs of state according to rational rules and regulations. Justice is not dispensed by wise elders but proceeds from codified law and established procedures.

The question of why the West, and not China or India, engaged in this process of rationalization intrigued Weber, and much of his scholarly effort went into answering it. Weber showed how various religious beliefs have influenced people's understanding of nature, shaped their values, social and political institutions, and economic behavior, and contributed to or blocked the development of rationalism. Weber's most famous thesis is that Protestantism, which saw work as a religious duty, a "calling," and hedonism as a sin, and which demanded a rational planning of one's life in accordance with God's will, produced an outlook compatible with the requirements of capitalism. Capitalism, said Weber, is not a thirst for money, a merely acquisitive desire that has been exhibited since the early days of civilization. The distinguishing feature of capitalism is the rational organization of all business activities, including the labor force, so that profits are continuous and calculable. The Protestant ethic gave religious approval to methodical and patient work and to saving and reinvesting, for it saw worldly success as a sign of God's approval.

Weber understood the terrible paradox of reason. Reason accounts for brilliant achievements in science and economic life, but it also despiritualizes life by ruthlessly eliminating centuries-old traditions, denouncing deeply felt religious beliefs as superstition, and regarding human feelings and passions as impediments to clear thinking. While giving people knowledge, the process of disenchantment has also made them soulless and their life meaningless. This is the dilemma of modern individuals, said Weber. Science cannot provide people with a purpose for living, and the burgeoning of bureaucracy in government, business, and education stifles individual autonomy. The process of secularization and rationalization has fostered self-liberation, for it enabled human beings to overcome illusions and take control of the environment and themselves. But it is also a means of self-enslavement, for it produces institutions—giant bureaucracies—that depersonalize life. Modern officials, said Weber, are emotionally detached. Concerned only with the efficient execution of tasks, they employ reason in a cold and calculating way; such human feelings as compassion and affection are ruled out as hindrances to effectiveness. In the name of efficiency, people are placed in "steel cages," depriving them of their autonomy.

> It is horrible to think that the world could one day be filled with nothing but those little cogs, little men clinging to little jobs and striving towards bigger ones. . . . This passion for bureaucracy . . . is enough to drive one to despair. . . . That the world should know no men but these: it is in such [a process] that we

> are already caught up, and the great question is, therefore, not how we can promote and hasten it, but what can we oppose to this machinery in order to keep a portion of mankind free from this parceling-out of the soul, from this supreme mastery of the bureaucratic way of life.[30]

The prospect existed that people would refuse to endure this violation of their spiritual needs and would reverse the process of disenchantment by seeking redemption in the irrational. Weber himself, however, was committed to the ideals of the Enlightenment and to perpetuating the rational scientific tradition, which he felt was threatened by bureaucratic regimentation on the one hand and irrational human impulses on the other.

Like Freud, Weber was aware of the power of the nonrational in social life. One expression of the irrational that he analyzed in considerable depth was the charismatic leader who attracts people by force of personality. His analysis of this phenomenon throws light on the popularity of twentieth-century dictators and demagogues. Charismatic leaders may be religious prophets, war heroes, or others who possess this extraordinary ability to attract and dominate others. People yearn for charismatic leadership, particularly during times of crisis. The leader claims a mission—a sacred duty—to lead the people during the crisis. The leader's authority rests on the people's belief in the mission and their faith in the leader's extraordinary abilities; a common allegiance to the charismatic leader unites the community.

THE MODERNIST MOVEMENT

Breaking with Conventional Modes of Esthetics

At the same time as Freud and social thinkers were breaking with the Enlightenment view of human nature and society, artists and writers were rebelling against traditional forms of artistic and literary expression, which had governed European cultural life since the Renaissance. Rejecting both classical and realist models, they subordinated form and objective reality to the inner life—to feelings, imagination, and the creative process. Their experimentations produced a great cultural revolution, called *modernism,* which still profoundly influences the arts. In some ways, modernism was a continuation of the Romantic Movement, which had dominated European culture in the early nineteenth century. Both movements subjected to searching criticism cultural styles that had been formulated during the Renaissance and had roots in ancient Greece.

Even more than romanticism, modernism aspired to an intense introspection—a heightened awareness of self—and saw the intellect as a barrier to the free expression of elemental human emotions. Modernist artists and writers abandoned conventional literary and artistic models and experimented with new modes of expression. The consequence of their bold venture, wrote the literary critic and historian Irving Howe, was nothing less than the "breakup of the traditional unity and continuity of Western culture."[31]

Like Freud, modernist artists and writers probed beyond surface appearances for a more profound reality hidden in the human psyche. Writers such as Thomas Mann, Marcel Proust, James Joyce, August Strindberg, D. H. Lawrence, and Franz Kafka explored the inner life of the individual and the psychopathology of human relations. They dealt with the predicament of men and women who rejected the values and customs of their day, and they depicted the anguish of people burdened by guilt, torn by internal conflicts, and driven by an inner self-destructiveness. Besides showing the overwhelming might of the irrational and the seductive power of the primitive, they also broke the silence about sex that had prevailed in Victorian literature.

From the Renaissance through the Enlightenment and into the nineteenth century, Western esthetic standards had been shaped by the conviction that the universe embodied an inherent mathematical order. A corollary of this conception of the outer world as orderly and intelligible was the view that art should imitate reality. According to sociologist Daniel Bell, from the Renaissance on, art was seen as "a mirror of nature, a representation of life. Knowledge was a reflection of what was 'out there' . . . a copy of what was seen."[32] Since the Renaissance, artists had deliberately made use of laws of perspective and proportion; musicians had used harmonic chords, which brought rhythm and melody into a unified

whole; and writers had produced works according to a definite pattern, which included a beginning, middle, and end.

Modernist culture, however, acknowledged no objective reality of space, motion, and time that has the same meaning for all observers. Rather, reality can be grasped in a variety of ways; a multiplicity of frames of reference apply to nature and human experience. Consequently, reality is the way the viewer apprehends it to be through the prism of the imagination. "There is no outer reality," said the modernist German poet Gottfried Benn, but "only human consciousness, constantly building, modifying, rebuilding new worlds out of its own creativity."[33] Modernism is concerned less with the object itself than with how the artist transforms it, with the sensations that an object evokes in the artist's inner being, and with the meaning that the artist's imagination imposes on reality. "Conscientious and exact imitation of nature does not create a work of art," wrote Emil Nolde, a German expressionist painter. "A work becomes a work of art when one re-evaluates the values of nature and adds one's own spirituality."[34] Bell makes this point in reference to painting:

> *Modernism . . . denies the primacy of an outside reality, as given. It seeks either to rearrange that reality, or to retreat to the self's interior, to private experience as the source of its concerns and aesthetic preoccupations. . . . There is an emphasis on the self as the touchstone of understanding and on the activity of the knower rather than the character of the object as the source of knowledge. . . . Thus one discerns the intentions of modern painting . . . to break up ordered space . . . to bridge the distance between object and spectator, to "thrust" itself on the viewer and establish itself immediately by impact.*[35]

Dispensing with conventional forms of esthetics, which stressed structure and coherence, modernism propelled the arts onto uncharted seas. Recoiling from the middle-class, industrial civilization that prized rationalism, organization, clarity, stability, and definite norms and values, modernist writers and artists were fascinated by the bizarre, the mysterious, the unpredictable, the primitive, the irrational, and the formless. Writers,

UPI/Bettmann

ISADORA DUNCAN

Isadora Duncan (1877–1927), a pioneer of modern dance, wanted dancing to consist of natural and flowing movements, which accorded with the body's structure and the pull of gravity. She maintained that classical ballet precluded fluid motion because it relied on set numbers, frozen poses, and starts and stops. Moreover, since toe dancing is unnatural, ballet caused deformed muscles and bones. Ballet technique rests on the principle that the body's center of gravity is at the base of the spine. Holding that the center of gravity lay in the solar plexus, Duncan stressed moving with the upper torso leaning forward and the limbs following.

Besides having them master the art of natural movement, Duncan wanted dancers to express freely the full range of human emotions. Toward this end, she created dances to music—not specifically composed for the dance—of great composers, including Bach, Beethoven, Berlioz, Schubert, Chopin, Johann Strauss, and Tchaikovsky.

Born in San Francisco, Duncan first gained fame dancing in Europe. Her innovations im-

for example, experimented with new techniques to convey the intense struggle between the conscious and the unconscious and to connote the aberrations and complexities of human personality and the irrationality of human behavior. In particular, they devised a new way, the stream of consciousness, to exhibit the mind's every level—both conscious reflection and unconscious strivings—and to capture how thought is punctuated by spontaneous outbursts, disconnected assertions, random memories, hidden desires, and persistent fantasies. In music, Arnold Schoenberg experimented with primitive rhythms and Igor Stravinsky with atonality. When Stravinsky's ballet *The Rite of Spring* was performed in Paris in 1913, the theater audience rioted to protest the composition's break with tonality, its use of primitive, jazzlike rhythms, and its theme of ritual sacrifice.

The modernist movement, which began near the end of the nineteenth century, was in full bloom be-

fore World War I and would continue to flower in the postwar world. Probably the clearest expression of the modernist viewpoint is found in art.

Modern Art

In the late nineteenth century, artists began to turn away from the standards that had characterized art since the Renaissance. The history of modern painting begins with impressionism, a movement spanning the period 1860 to 1886. No longer committed to depicting how an object appears to the eye, artists searched for new forms of expression. They boldly strove to expand or break with the traditional formulas of composition (arrangement of visual elements) and the treatments of color and light. The impressionist movement was centered in Paris, and its leading figures were Edouard Manet, Claude Monet,

pressed many critics. One wrote: "She has discovered entirely new movements of the human body. . . . This is, in fact, the magnificently free dance of nymphs on a Greek chalice where the feet carry the slender body with breathtaking ease."* Another critic stated: "Miss Duncan's dancing . . . seems to spring spontaneously into being, to be the instinctive translation of the rhythm and . . . the mood of the music . . . in wholly natural movement. . . . [Her dancing is] as fluid as are sound and light. . . . [It] knows no rule and it has no customs except for those she imposes."†

Later in her career, Duncan choreographed dances based on political and social issues. For example, during World War I, her performance of the "Marseillaise," the stirring French national anthem, in which she bared her breast in defiance of the enemy, moved the French audience to tears and frenzied cheers. When she lived in the Soviet Union, she composed dances glorifying the cause of workers.

Duncan's personal life was as unconventional as her dancing. She had two children out

of wedlock, one with Gordon Craig, a prominent figure in the theater, and the other with Paris Singer, a scion of the sewing machine family. Duncan married the brilliant Soviet poet Sergei Esenin and for a while lived in the Soviet Union.

Duncan's life was marred by tragedy. Her children, aged six and three, drowned when the stalled vehicle they were sitting in suddenly rolled into the Seine. A third child, also born out of wedlock, died a few hours after birth. Her husband, Esenin, hanged himself in the very hotel room in Leningrad where he and Duncan had first made love. And Duncan, like her two children, died in a freak car accident, when the red shawl draped around her shoulders was caught in the car's axle, breaking her neck.

*Quoted in Fredrika Blair, *Isadora* (New York: McGraw-Hill, 1986), pp. 57–58.
†Quoted in ibid., pp. 190–191.

Camille Pissaro, Edgar Degas, and Pierre Auguste Renoir. Taking Pissaro's advice—"Don't proceed according to rules and principles but paint what you observe and feel"—impressionists tried to give their own immediate and personal impression of an object or an event. They tried to capture how movement, color, and light appeared to the eye at a fleeting instant.

Intrigued by the impact that light has on objects, impressionists left their studios for the countryside, where they painted nature under an open sky. They used bold colors and drew marked contrasts between light and dark to reflect how objects in intense sunlight seem to shimmer against their background.

Besides landscapes, the impressionists painted railways, bridges, and boulevards. They also painted people—in dance halls, cafés, theaters, and public gardens. Impressionistic painters wanted to portray life as it was commonly experienced in a rapidly industrializing and urbanizing world. And they always tried to convey their momentary impression of an event or figure.

In the late 1880s and the 1890s, several artists went beyond impressionism. Called postimpressionists, they further revolutionized the artist's sense of space and color. Even more than the impressionists, they sought to make art a vivid emotional experience and to produce a personal impression of reality rather than a photographic copy of objects.

One of the luminaries of this later movement, Paul Cézanne (1839–1906) came to Paris, the center of the Western art world, from the South of France. In 1882, he returned to the region of his birth, where he painted its natural scenery. By rigorously analyzing his own perception of objects, he made his way of seeing them the real subject of his paintings. When depicting objects in a group, Cézanne deliberately distorted perspective,

THE STARRY NIGHT, BY VINCENT VAN GOGH (1853–1890). Son of a Dutch pastor, Van Gogh served for a time as a lay preacher before devoting himself entirely to art. He was given to wide mood swings—from extreme agitation to melancholy. His tumultuous temperament found expression in his paintings. *The Starry Night* conveys Van Gogh's personal impression of a night sky. (*Collection, The Museum of Modern Art, New York. Acquired through the Lillie P. Bliss Bequest*)

subordinating the appearance of an individual object to the requirements of the total design. Cézanne tried to demonstrate that an object, when placed together with other objects, is seen differently than when it stands alone. His concern with form and design influenced the cubists.

No longer bound by classical art forms, artists examined non-Western art, searching there for new forms of beauty and new ways of expression. The large number of artifacts and art objects from Asia, Africa, and the Pacific area coming into European capitals as souvenirs of imperialist ventures sparked interest in non-Western art, as did the finds of anthropologists and ethnographers. Paul Gauguin (1848–1903) saw beauty in carvings and fabrics made by such technologically backward people as the Marquesans. He also discovered that art did not depend on skilled craftsmanship for its power. Very simple,

even primitive, means of construction could produce works of great beauty.

A successful Parisian stockbroker, Gauguin abandoned the marketplace for art. He came to view bourgeois civilization as artificial and rotten. By severing human beings from the power of their own feelings, industrial civilization blunted the creative expression of the imagination and prevented people from attaining a true understanding of themselves. For these reasons, Gauguin fled to Tahiti. On this picturesque island, which was largely untouched by European ways, he hoped to discover humanity's original nature, without the distortion and corruption of modern civilization.

The postimpressionists produced a revolution not only of space, but also of color, as exemplified by Vincent van Gogh (1853–1890). The son of a Dutch minister, van Gogh was a lonely, tortured, and impetuous soul. For a short period, he served as a lay preacher among desperately poor coal miners. When he moved to Paris in 1886, van Gogh came under the influence of the French impressionists. Desiring to use color in a novel way—his own way—van Gogh left Paris for the Mediterranean countryside, where he hoped to experience a new vision of sunlight, sky, and earth. Van Gogh used purer, brighter colors than artists had used before. He also recognized that color, like other formal qualities, could itself act as a language. He believed that the "real" color of an object does not necessarily express the artist's experience. Artists, according to van Gogh, should seek to paint things not as they are, but as the artists feel them. *The Starry Night* (see page 700) conveys his vision of a night sky not with tiny points of lights, but with exploding and whirling stars in a vast universe, overwhelming the huddled dwellings built by human beings. The foreboding dark cypress intrudes into the sky's turbulence of intense yellow lights.

Practically unknown in his lifetime, van Gogh's art became extremely influential soon after his death. One of the first artists to be affected by his style was the Norwegian Edvard Munch (1863–1944), who discovered van Gogh's use of color while in Paris. In *The Dance of Life,* for example, Munch used strong, simple lines and intense color to explore unexpressed sexual stresses and conflicts. In *The Scream,* he deliberately distorted the human face and the sky, ground, and water to portray terror.

After the postimpressionists, art moved still further away from reproducing an exact likeness of a physical object or human being. Increasingly, artists sought to penetrate the deepest recesses of the unconscious, which they saw as the source of creativity and the abode of a higher truth. Paul Klee, a prominent twentieth-century artist, described modern art as follows:

> *Each [artist] should follow where the pulse of his own heart leads. . . . Our pounding heart drives us down, deep down to the source of all. What springs from this source, whether it may be called dream, idea or phantasy—must be taken seriously. . . .* [36]

In Germany, the tendency to use color for its power to express psychological forces continued in the work of artists known as the German expressionists. In Ernst Ludwig Kirchner's (1880–1938)

Reclining Nude of 1909, strong, acid yellows and greens evoke feelings of tension, stress, and isolation. Kirchner also used bold, rapid lines to define flat shapes, a technique borrowed from folk art and from non-Western native traditions.

In France, another group of avant-garde artists, the *fauves* (wild beasts), used lines, color, and form with great freedom to create new means of personal expression. Henri Matisse (1869–1954), the leading fauvist painter, freed color from every restriction. He painted broad areas with stunning pigment unrelated to the real colors of the subject. His novel use of color and design aroused a violent reaction. After examining the works of the fauves, a French critic wrote: "What is presented here . . . has nothing to do with painting; some formless confusion of colors, blue, red, yellow, green, the barbaric and naive spirit of the child who plays with the box of colors he has just got as a Christmas present." [37] Rebelling against new currents in painting, critics failed to recognize the originality and genius of the fauves.

Between 1909 and 1914, a new style, called *cubism,* was developed by Pablo Picasso (1881–1973) and Georges Braque (1882–1963). They explored the interplay between the flat world of the canvas and the three-dimensional world of visual perception. Like the postimpressionists, they sought to paint a reality deeper than what the eye sees at first glance. Cubist art presents objects from multiple viewpoints. The numerous fragmentary images of cubist art make one aware of the complex experience of seeing. One art historian describes cubism as follows: "The cubist is not interested in usual representational standards. It is as if he were walking around the object he is analyzing, as one is free to walk around a piece of sculpture for successive views. But he must represent all these views at once." [38]

The colors used in early cubist art are deliberately banal, and the subjects represented are ordinary objects from everyday life. Picasso and Braque wanted to eliminate eye-catching color and intriguing subject matter so that the viewer would focus on the process of *seeing* itself.

In *Les Demoiselles d'Avignon,* Picasso painted five nudes. In each instance, the body is distorted in defiance of classical and Renaissance standards of beauty. The masklike faces show Picasso's debt to African art and, along with the angular shapes, deprive the subjects of individuality and personal-

HARMONY IN RED BY HENRI MATISSE (1908). In this early example of French Fauvism, Matisse (1869–1954) broke away from the representational painting of his predecessors and set the tone for much of twentieth-century expressive painting. His sparing use of line, color, and rhythmic motifs transforms the visual surface into brilliant designs and established a new pictorial language. (*The State Hermitage Museum, St. Petersburg*)

ity. The head of the squatting figure combines a profile with a full face: Picasso's attempt to present multiple aspects of an object at the same time.

Throughout the period 1890 to 1914, avant-garde artists were de-emphasizing subject matter and stressing the expressive power of such formal qualities as line, color, and space. It is not surprising that some artists finally began to create work that did not refer to anything seen in the real world. Piet Mondrian (1872–1944), a Dutch artist, came to Paris shortly before World War I. There he saw the cubist art of Picasso and Braque. The cubists had compressed the imaginary depth in their paintings so that all the objects seemed to be contained within a space only a few inches deep. They had also reduced subject matter to insignificance. It seemed to Mondrian that the next step was to get rid of subject matter entirely. His painting *Broadway Boogie Woogie*, for example, is de-

void of representational content. Looking at Mondrian's paintings is a kinesthetic experience, as one senses the delicate interplay of balances and counterweights within the painting and within the viewer. By eliminating from his painting any reference to the visible world, Mondrian helped to inaugurate abstract art.

Another founder of abstract art was Wassily Kandinsky (1866–1944), a Russian residing in Germany. Kandinsky gradually removed all traces of the physical world from his paintings, creating a nonobjective art that bears no resemblance to the natural world. In declaring that he "painted . . . subconsciously in a state of strong inner tension,"[39] Kandinsky explicitly expressed a distinguishing quality of modern Western art: the artist's private inner experience of the world.

The revolution in art that took place near the turn of the century is reverberating still. After

LES DEMOISELLES D'AVIGNON BY PABLO PICASSO (1907). Picasso's painting exemplified new trends in art. Defying classical and Renaissance standards, his work distorts the human form. Rather than conform with the conventions of traditional representation, Picasso aimed to interpret visual reality in accord with his own sensibilities. (*Collection, The Museum of Modern Art, New York. Aquired through the Lillie P. Bliss bequest.*)

nearly a hundred years, these masters of modern art continue to inspire with their passion and vision. By breaking with the Renaissance view of the world as inherently orderly and rational, modern artists opened up new possibilities for artistic expression. They exemplified the growing power and appeal of the nonrational in European life.

MODERN PHYSICS

Until the closing years of the nineteenth century, the view of the universe held by the Western mind rested largely on the classical physics of Newton. It included the following principles: (1)

time, space, and matter were objective realities, existing independently of the observer; (2) the universe was a giant machine, whose parts obeyed strict laws of cause and effect; (3) the atom, indivisible and solid, was the basic unit of matter; (4) heated bodies emitted radiation in continuous waves; and (5) through further investigation, it would be possible to gain complete knowledge of the physical universe.

Between the 1890s and the 1920s, this view of the universe was shattered by a second Scientific Revolution. The discovery of x-rays by Wilhelm Konrad Roentgen in 1895, of radioactivity by Henri Bequerel in 1896, and of the electron by J. J. Thomson in 1897 led scientists to abandon the conception of the atom as a solid and indivisible particle. Rather than resembling a billiard ball, the atom consists of a nucleus of tightly packed protons, separated from orbiting electrons by empty space.

In 1900, Max Planck, a German physicist, proposed the quantum theory, which holds that a heated body does not radiate energy in a continuous unbroken stream, as had been believed, but in intermittent spurts, or jumps, called quanta. Planck's theory of discontinuity in energy radiation challenged a cardinal principle of classical physics: that action in nature was strictly continuous.

In 1905, Albert Einstein, a German-Swiss physicist of Jewish lineage, substantiated and elaborated Planck's theory by suggesting that all forms of radiant energy—light, heat, x-rays—moved through space in discontinuous packets of energy. Then, in 1913, Niels Bohr, a Danish scientist, applied Planck's theory of energy quanta to the interior of the atom and discovered that the Newtonian laws of motion could not fully explain what happened to electrons orbiting an atomic nucleus.

As physicists explored the behavior of the atom further, it became apparent that its nature was fundamentally elusive and unpredictable. They soon observed that radioactive atoms threw off particles and transformed themselves from atoms of one element into atoms of an entirely different element. But the transformation of a single atom in a mass of radioactive material could not be predicted according to inexorable laws of cause and effect. For example, it is known that over a period of 1,620 years half the atoms of the element radium decay and transform themselves into atoms of another element. It is impossible, however, to know when a particular atom in a lump of radium will undergo this transformation. Scientists can make accurate predictions only about the behavior of an aggregate of radium atoms. The transformation of any given radium atom is the result of random chance rather than of any known physical law. The fact that we cannot predict when a particular radioactive atom will decay calls into question the notion of classical physics that physical nature proceeds in an orderly fashion in accordance with strict laws of cause and effect.

Newtonian physics says that, given certain conditions, we can predict what will follow. For example, if an airplane is flying north at four hundred miles per hour, we can predict its exact

ALBERT EINSTEIN (1879–1955). Einstein was a principal architect of modern physics. Forced to flee Nazi Germany because of his Jewish ancestry, he became a United States citizen. He was appointed to the Institute for Advanced Study at Princeton, New Jersey. (*Wide World Photos*)

position two hours from now, assuming that the plane does not alter its course or speed. Quantum mechanics teaches that in the subatomic realm we cannot predict with certainty what will take place; we can only say that, given certain conditions, it is *probable* that a certain event will follow. This principle of uncertainty was developed in 1927 by the German scientist Werner Heisenberg, who showed that it is impossible to determine at one and the same time both an electron's precise speed and its position. Science writer Alan E. Nourse explains:

> [Heisenberg showed] *that the very act of attempting to examine an electron any more closely in order to be* more *certain of where it was and what it was doing at a given instant* would itself alter where the electron was and what it was doing at the instant in question. *Heisenberg, in effect, was saying that in dealing with the behavior of electrons and other elementary particles the laws of cause and effect do not and cannot apply, that all we can do is make predictions about them on the*

*basis of probability and not a very high degree
of probability at that. . . . the more certain we
try to become about a given electron's position at a given instant, the wider the limits of
probability we must accept with regard to
what its momentum [speed] is at the same
time, and vice versa. The more closely either
one property of the electron or the other is examined, the more closely we approach certainty with regard to one property or the
other, the more wildly uncertain the other
property becomes. And since an electron can
really only be fully described in terms of both
its position and its momentum at any given instant, it becomes utterly impossible to describe
an electron at all in terms of absolute certainties. We can describe it only in terms of uncertainties or probabilities.*[40]

In the small-scale world of the electron, we enter
a universe of uncertainty, probability, and statistical relationships. No improvement in measurement techniques will dispel this element of
chance and provide us with complete knowledge
of the universe.

Although Einstein could not accept that a complete comprehension of reality was unattainable,
his theory of relativity was instrumental in shaping
modern physics. It altered classical conceptions of
space and time. Newtonian physics had viewed
space as a distinct physical reality, a stationary
and motionless medium through which light traveled and matter moved. Time was deemed to be a
fixed and rigid framework, the same for all observers and existing independently of human experience. For Einstein, however, neither space nor
time had an independent existence, and neither
could be divorced from human experience. When
asked to explain briefly the essentials of relativity,
Einstein replied: "It was formerly believed that if
all material things disappeared out of the universe,
time and space would be left. According to the relativity theory, however, time and space disappear
together with the things."[41]

Contrary to all previous thinking, relativity theory holds that time differs for two observers traveling at different speeds. Imagine twin brothers involved in space exploration, one as an astronaut,
the other as a rocket designer who never leaves
earth. The astronaut takes off in the most advanced
spaceship yet constructed, one that achieves a speed

close to the maximum attainable in our universe—
the speed of light. After traveling several trillion
miles, the spaceship turns around and returns to
earth. According to the experience of the ship's oc-
cupant, the whole trip took about two years. But
when the astronaut lands on earth, he finds totally
changed conditions. For one thing, his brother has
long since died, for according to earth's calendars
some two hundred years have elapsed since the
rocket ship set out on its journey. Such an occur-
rence seemed to defy all commonsense experience,
yet experiments supported Einstein's claims.

Motion, too, is relative. The only way we can
describe the motion of one body is to compare it
with another moving body. This means that there
is no motionless, absolute, fixed frame of reference anywhere in the universe. Science writer
Isaac Asimov illustrates Einstein's theory of the
relativity of motion:

*Suppose we on the earth were to observe a
strange planet ("Planet X"), exactly like our
own in size and mass, go whizzing past us at
163,000 miles per second relative to ourselves.
If we could measure its dimensions as it shot
past, we would find that it was foreshortened
by 50 per cent in the direction of its motion. It
would be an ellipsoid rather than a sphere and
would, on further measurement, seem to have
twice the mass of the earth.*

*Yet to an inhabitant of Planet X, it would
seem that he himself and his own planet were
motionless. The earth would seem to be moving past him at 163,000 miles per second, and
it would appear to have an ellipsoidal shape
and twice the mass of his planet.*

*One is tempted to ask which planet would
really be foreshortened and doubled in mass,
but the only possible answer is: that depends
on the frame of reference.*[42]

In his famous equation, $E = mc^2$, Einstein
showed that matter and energy are not separate
categories but two different expressions of the same
physical entity. The source of energy is matter, and
the source of matter is energy. Tiny quantities of
matter could be transformed into staggering
amounts of energy. The atomic age was dawning.

The discoveries of modern physics transformed the world of classical physics. Whereas
nature had been regarded as something outside

the individual—an objective reality existing independently of ourselves—modern physics teaches that our position in space and time determines what we mean by reality and that our very presence affects reality itself. When we observe a particle with our measuring instruments, we are interfering with it, knocking it off its course; we are participating in reality. Nor is nature fully knowable, as the classical physics of Newton had presumed. Uncertainty, probability, and even mystery are inherent in the universe.

We have not yet felt the full impact of modern physics, but there is no doubt that it has been part of a revolution in human perceptions. As Jacob Bronowski, a student of science and culture, concludes,

> *One aim of the physical sciences has been to give an exact picture of the material world. One achievement of physics in the twentieth century has been to prove that that aim is unattainable. . . . There is no absolute knowledge. . . . All information is imperfect. We have to treat it with humility. That is the human condition; and that is what quantum physics says. . . . The Principle of Uncertainty . . . fixed once and for all the realization that all knowledge is limited.*[43]

That we cannot fully comprehend nature must inevitably make us less certain about our theories of human nature, government, history, and morality. That scientists must qualify and avoid absolutes has no doubt made us more cautious and tentative in framing conclusions about the individual and society. Like Darwin's theory of human origins, Freud's theory of human nature, and the transformation of classical space by modern artists, the modifications of the Newtonian picture by modern physicists contributed to the sense of uncertainty and disorientation that characterizes the twentieth century.

THE ENLIGHTENMENT TRADITION IN DISARRAY

Most nineteenth-century thinkers carried forward the spirit of the Enlightenment, particularly in its emphasis on science and its concern for individual liberty and social reform. In the tradition of the philosophes, nineteenth-century thinkers regarded science as humanity's greatest achievement and believed that through reason society could be reformed. The spread of parliamentary government and the extension of education, along with the many advances in science and technology, seemed to confirm the belief of the philosophes in humanity's future progress.

But at the same time, the Enlightenment tradition was being undermined. In the early nineteenth century, the romantics revolted against the Enlightenment's rational-scientific spirit in favor of human will and feelings. Romantic nationalists valued the collective soul of the nation—ancient traditions rooted in a hoary and dateless past—over reason and individual freedom. Conservatives emphasized the limitations of reason and attacked the political agenda of the Enlightenment and the French Revolution.

In the closing decades of the century, the Enlightenment tradition was challenged by Social Darwinists, who glorified violence and saw conflict between individuals and between nations as a law of nature. They considered the right of the powerful to predominate to be a right of nature. Echoing Sorel, several thinkers trumpeted the use of force in social and political controversies. A number of thinkers, rejecting the Enlightenment view of people as fundamentally rational, held that subconscious drives and impulses govern human behavior more than reason does. Several of these thinkers urged celebrating and extolling the irrational, which they regarded as the true essence of human beings and life. They glorified an irrational vitality, which transcended considerations of good and evil. "I have always considered myself a voice of what I believe to be a greater renaissance—the revolt of the soul against the intellect—now beginning in the world," wrote the Irish poet William Butler Yeats.[44] German advocates of "life philosophy" explicitly called the mind "the enemy of the soul."

Even theorists who studied the individual and society in a scientific way pointed out that below a surface of rationality lies a substratum of irrationality, which constitutes a deeper reality. The conviction was growing that reason was a puny instrument in comparison with the volcanic strength of nonrational impulses, that these impulses pushed people toward destructive behavior and made political life precarious, and that the nonrational did not bend very much to education. The Enlightenment's image of the autonomous individual who makes rational decisions after weighing the choices (a fundamental premise of liberalism and democracy) no longer seemed tenable. Often the individual was not the master of his or her own person; human freedom was limited by human nature.

Other theorists argued that ideas of right, truth, and justice do not have an independent value. Rather, they are merely tools used by elites in their struggle to gain and maintain power. Opponents of liberalism and democracy utilized the theory of elites advanced by Pareto, as well as the new stress on human irrationality, as proof that the masses were incapable of self-government and that they had to be led by their betters. Many intellectuals of the right employed the new social theories to devalue the individualist and rational bases of liberal democracy bequeathed by the Enlightenment.

At the beginning of the twentieth century, the dominant mood remained that of confidence in Europe's future progress and in the values of European civilization. However, certain disquieting trends were already evident; they would grow to crisis proportions in succeeding decades. Although few people may have realized it, the Enlightenment tradition was in disarray.

The thinkers of the Enlightenment believed in an orderly, machinelike universe; the operation of natural law and natural rights in the social world; objective rules that gave form and structure to artistic productions; the essential rationality and goodness of the individual; and science and technology as instruments of progress. This coherent world-view, which had produced an attitude of certainty, security, and optimism, was in the process of dissolution by the early twentieth century. The commonsense Newtonian picture of the physical universe, with its inexorable laws of cause and effect, was altered; the belief in natural rights and objective standards governing morality was undermined; and rules and modes of expression that were at the very heart of Western esthetics were abandoned. Confidence in human rationality and goodness weakened. Furthermore, science and technology were accused of forging a mechanical, bureaucratic, and materialistic world, which stifled intuition and feelings, thereby diminishing the self. To redeem the self, some thinkers urged a heroic struggle, which could easily be channeled into a primitive nationalism and martial crusades. This radical attack on the

moral and intellectual values of the Enlightenment—the denunciation of reason, exaltation of force, quest for the heroic, and yearning for a new authority—constitutes the intellectual background of the fascist movements that emerged after World War I. Holding the Enlightenment tradition in contempt and fascinated by power and violence, many people, including intellectuals, would exalt fascist ideas and lionize fascist leaders.

Thus, in the early twentieth century, the universe no longer seemed an orderly system, an intelligible whole, but something fundamentally inexplicable. Human nature, too, seemed intrinsically unfathomable and problematic. To the question "Who is man?" Greek philosophers, medieval scholastics, Renaissance humanists, and eighteenth-century philosophes had provided a coherent and intelligible answer. By the early twentieth century, Western intellectuals no longer possessed a clear idea of who the human being was. Individuals had become strangers to themselves, and life seemed devoid of an overriding purpose. Nietzsche sensed this:

> Disintegration characterizes this time, and thus uncertainty: nothing stands firmly on its feet or on a hard faith in itself; one lives for tomorrow as the day after tomorrow is dubious. Everything on our way is slippery and dangerous, and the ice that still supports us has become thin: all of us feel the warm, uncanny breath of the thawing wind; where we still walk, soon no one will be able to walk.[45]

This radical new disorientation led some intellectuals to feel alienated from Western civilization and even hostile toward it. At the beginning of the twentieth century, says Dutch historian Jan Romein, "European man, who only half a century earlier had believed he was about to embrace an almost totally safe existence, and paradoxically enough did so in many ways, found himself before the dark gate of uncertainty."[46]

When the new century began, most Europeans were optimistic about the future, some even holding that European civilization was on the threshold of a golden age. Few suspected that European civilization would soon be gripped by a crisis that threatened its very survival. The powerful forces of irrationalism, which had been celebrated by Nietzsche, analyzed by Freud, and creatively expressed in modernist culture, would erupt with devastating fury in twentieth-century political life, particularly in the form of extreme nationalism and racism, which extolled violence. Disoriented and disillusioned people searching for new certainties and values would turn to political ideologies that openly rejected reason, lauded war, and scorned the inviolability of the human person. Dictators, utilizing the insights into the unconscious and the nonrational offered by Freud and social theorists, succeeded in manipulating the minds of the masses to an unprecedented degree.

These currents began to form at the end of the nineteenth century, but World War I brought them together in a tidal wave. World War I accentuated the questioning of established norms and the dissolution of Enlightenment certainties and caused many people to regard Western civilization as dying and beyond recovery. The war not only exacerbated the spiritual crisis of the preceding generation, but also shattered Europe's political and social order. It gave birth to totalitarian ideologies that nearly obliterated the legacy of the Enlightenment.

◆ ◆ ◆

NOTES

1. Friedrich Nietzsche, *Twilight of the Idols and The Anti-Christ*, trans. R. J. Hollingdale (New York: Penguin, 1972), pp. 117–118.

2. Friedrich Nietzsche, *The Will to Power*, trans. Walter Kaufmann and R. J. Hollingdale, ed. Walter Kaufmann (New York: Vintage Books, 1968), pp. 458–459.

3. Ibid., pp. 383–384.

4. Quoted in R. J. Hollingdale, *Nietzsche* (London: Routledge & Kegan Paul, 1973), p. 82.

5. Nietzsche, *Will to Power*, p. 518.

6. Nietzsche, *Anti-Christ*, p. 116.

7. Nietzsche, *Will to Power*, p. 386.

8. Janko Lavrin, *Nietzsche* (New York: Charles Scribner's Sons, 1971), p. 113.

9. Fyodor Dostoevski, *Notes from Underground and The Grand Inquisitor*, trans. Ralph E. Matlaw (New York: Dutton, 1960), pp. 20, 23.

10. Ibid., p. 25.

11. Quoted in Peter Gay, *Freud: A Life for Our Time* (New York: W. W. Norton, 1988), p. xvii.

12. Sigmund Freud, "Delusions and Dreams in Jensen's 'Gradiva,'" trans. James Strachey, in *The Standard Edition of the Complete Psychological Work of Sigmund Freud*, 2nd ed. (London: The Hogarth Press, 1959), 9:8.

13. Sigmund Freud, "An Autobiographical Study," in *Standard Edition*, 20:60.

14. Sigmund Freud, *Civilization and Its Discontents* (New York: Norton, 1961), p. 62.

15. Ibid., p. 58.

16. Ibid.

17. Ibid., p. 59.

18. Ibid., p. 61.

19. Ibid., p. 59.

20. Ibid., p. 69.

21. Émile Durkheim, *Suicide: A Study in Sociology*, trans. John Spaulding and George Simpson (New York: The Free Press, 1951), p. 391.

22. Gustave Le Bon, *The Crowd: A Study of the Popular Mind* (New York: Viking, 1960), p. 3.

23. Ibid., pp. 14–15.

24. Ibid., p. 23.

25. Ibid., p. 30.

26. Ibid., p. 32.

27. Ibid., p. 7.

28. Ibid., p. 118.

29. Quoted in Robert A. Nye, *The Origin of Crowd Psychology* (Beverly Hills, Calif.: Sage, 1975), p. 178.

30. Quoted in Robert Nisbet, *The Social Philosophers* (New York: Crowell, 1973), p. 441.

31. Irving Howe, ed., *The Idea of the Modern in Literature and the Arts* (New York: Horizon Press, 1967), p. 16.

32. Daniel Bell, *The Cultural Contradictions of Capitalism* (New York: Basic Books, 1976), p. 110.

33. Quoted in Howe, *Idea of the Modern*, p. 15.

34. Excerpted in Herschel B. Chipp, ed., *Theories of Modern Art* (Berkeley: University of California Press, 1968), p. 146.

35. Bell, *Cultural Contradictions,* pp. 110, 112.

36. Paul Klee, *On Modern Art,* trans. Paul Findlay (London: Faber & Faber, 1948), p. 51.

37. Quoted in Alfred H. Barr, Jr., ed., *Masters of Modern Art* (New York: Museum of Modern Art, 1954), p. 46.

38. John Canaday, *Mainstreams of Modern Art* (New York: Holt, 1961), p. 458.

39. Quoted in G. H. Hamilton, *Painting and Sculpture in Europe, 1880–1940* (Baltimore: Penguin Books, 1967), p. 133.

40. Alan E. Nourse, *Universe, Earth, and Atom* (New York: Harper & Row, 1969), pp. 554–555, 560.

41. Quoted in A. E. E. McKenzie, *The Major Achievements of Science* (New York: Cambridge University Press, 1960), 1:310.

42. Isaac Asimov, *Asimov's Guide to Science* (New York: Basic Books, 1972), pp. 354–355.

43. Jacob Bronowski, *The Ascent of Man* (Boston: Little, Brown, 1973), p. 353.

44. Quoted in Roland N. Stromberg, *Redemption by War* (Lawrence: Regents Press of Kansas, 1982), p. 65.

45. Nietzsche, *Will to Power,* p. 40.

46. Jan Romein, *The Watershed of Two Eras,* trans. Arnold J. Pomerans (Middletown, Conn.: Wesleyan University Press, 1978), p. 658.

SUGGESTED READING

Baumer, Franklin, *Modern European Thought* (1977). A well-informed study of modern thought.

Bradbury, Malcolm, and James McFarlane, eds., *Modernism, 1890–1930* (1974). Essays on various phases of modernism; valuable bibliography.

Gay, Peter, *Freud: A Life for Our Times* (1988). A highly recommended study.

Hamilton, G. H., *Painting and Sculpture in Europe, 1880–1940* (1967). An authoritative work .

Hollingdale, R. J., *Nietzsche* (1973). A lucid study.

Hughes, H. Stuart, *Consciousness and Society* (1958). Good on social thinkers.

Kaufmann, Walter, *Nietzsche* (1956). An excellent analysis of Nietzsche's thought.

Masur, Gerhard, *Prophets of Yesterday* (1961). Studies in European culture, 1890–1914.

Monaco, Paul, *Modern European Culture and Consciousness, 1870–1980* (1983). A useful survey.

Nelson, Benjamin, ed., *Freud and the Twentieth Century* (1957). A valuable collection of essays.

Roazen, Paul, *Freud's Political and Social Thought* (1968). The implications of Freudian psychology.

Rosenthal, Bernice, ed., *Nietzsche in Russia* (1986). Essays detailing Nietzsche's impact on Russian thought; good introduction by the editor.

Stromberg, Roland N., *An Intellectual History of Modern Europe* (1975). A fine text.

Zeitlin, I. M., *Ideology and the Development of Sociological Theory* (1968). Examines in detail the thought of major shapers of sociological theory.

REVIEW QUESTIONS

1. What were Nietzsche's attitudes toward Christianity and democracy?

2. Why were the Nazis drawn to Nietzsche's thought?

3. What does Dostoevski's Underground Man mean when he says that life is more than "simply extracting square roots"?

4. How did Bergson reflect the growing irrationalism of the age?

5. How did Sorel show the political potential of the nonrational?

6. In what way was Freud a child of the Enlightenment? How did he differ from the philosophes?

7. For Durkheim, what constituted the crisis of modern society? How did he try to resolve it?

8. What do you think of Pareto's judgment that the masses in a democratic state are not really influenced by rational argument?

9. According to Gustave Le Bon, how are individuals transformed once they become part of a crowd? How does the leader sway the crowd?

10. For Weber, what was the terrible paradox of reason?

11. What were the standards of esthetics that had governed Western literature and art since the Renaissance? How did the modernist movement break with these standards?

12. Describe the view of the universe held by westerners around 1880. How was this view altered by modern physics?

13. In what ways was the Enlightenment tradition in disarray by the early twentieth century?

PART SIX

World Wars and Totalitarianism: The West in Crisis

1914–1945

	POLITICS AND SOCIETY	THOUGHT AND CULTURE
1910	World War I (1914–1918) United States declares war on Germany (1917) Bolshevik Revolution in Russia (1917) Wilson announces his Fourteen Points (1918) Treaty of Versailles (1919)	Bohr: Quantum theory of atomic stucture (1913) Stravinsky, *The Rite of Spring* (1913) Pareto, *Treatise on General Sociology* (1916) Spengler, *The Decline of the West* (1918, 1922) Dadaism in art (1915–1924) Barth, *The Epistle to the Romans* (1919)
1920	Mussolini seizes power in Italy (1922) First Five-Year Plan starts rapid industrialization in the Soviet Union (1928) Forced collectivization of agriculture in the Soviet Union (1929) Start of the Great Depression (1929)	Wittgenstein, *Tractatus Logico-Philosophicus* (1921–22) Eliot, *The Waste Land* (1922) Cassirer, *The Philosophy of Symbolic Forms* (1923–1929) Mann, *The Magic Mountain* (1924) Surrealism in art (c. 1925) Hitler, *Mein Kampf* (1925–26) Hemingway, *The Sun Also Rises* (1926) Benda, *The Treason of the Intellectuals* (1927) Heidegger, *Being and Time* (1927) Lawrence, *Lady Chatterley's Lover* (1928) Remarque, *All Quiet on the Western Front* (1929)
1930	Hitler becomes chancellor of Germany (1933) Hitler sends troops into the Rhineland (1936) Rome-Berlin Axis (1936) Stalin orders mass purges in the Soviet Union (1936–38) Spanish Civil War (1936–1939) Franco establishes a dictatorship in Spain (1939) Nazi-Soviet Non-Aggression Pact (1939) German troops invade Poland: World War II begins (1939)	Freud, *Civilization and Its Discontents* (1930) Ortega y Gasset, *The Revolt of the Masses* (1930) Jaspers, *Man in the Modern Age* (1930) Jung, *Modern Man in Search of a Soul* (1933) Toynbee, *A Study of History* (1934–1961) Keynes, *The General Theory of Employment, Interest, and Money* (1936) Steinbeck, *The Grapes of Wrath* (1939)
1940	Germany invades Belgium, Holland, Luxembourg, and France (1940) Japan attacks Pearl Harbor: United States enters war against Japan and Germany (1941) War in Europe ends (1945) United States drops atomic bombs on Japan; Japan surrenders (1945)	Hemingway, *For Whom the Bell Tolls* (1940) Koestler, *Darkness at Noon* (1941) Fromm, *Escape from Freedom* (1941) Camus, *The Stranger* (1942) Sartre, *Being and Nothingness* (1943) Orwell, *Animal Farm* (1945)

World War I:
The West in Despair

*P*rior to 1914, the dominant mood in Europe was one of pride in the accomplishments of Western civilization and confidence in its future progress. Advances in science and technology, the rising standard of living, the spread of democratic institutions, and Europe's position of power in the world all contributed to a sense of optimism, as did the expansion of social reform and the increase in literacy for the masses. Furthermore, since the defeat of Napoleon, Europe had avoided a general war, and since the Franco-Prussian War (1870–71), the Great Powers had not fought one another. Reflecting on the world he knew before World War I, historian Arnold Toynbee recalled that his generation

> expected that life throughout the World would become more rational, more humane, and more democratic and that, slowly, but surely, political democracy would produce greater social justice. We had also expected that the progress of science and technology would make mankind richer, and that this increasing wealth would gradually spread from a minority to a majority. We had expected that all this would happen peacefully. In fact we thought that mankind's course was set for an earthly paradise, and that our approach towards this goal was predestined for us by historical necessity.[1]

Few people recognized that the West's outward achievements masked an inner turbulence, which was propelling Western civilization toward a cataclysm. The European state system was failing. By 1914, national states, answering to no higher power, were fueled by an explosive nationalism and were grouped into alliances that faced each other with ever mounting hostility. Nationalist passions, overheated by the popular press

The British cavalry passing the ruins of a church in Belgium. (*Courtesy of the Trustees of the Imperial War Museum*)

and expansionist societies, poisoned international relations. Nationalist thinkers propagated pseudoscientific racial and Social Darwinist doctrines, which glorified conflict and justified the subjugation of other peoples. Committed to enhancing national power, statesmen lost sight of Europe as a community of nations sharing a common civilization. Caution and restraint gave way to belligerency in foreign relations.

The failure of the European state system was paralleled by a cultural crisis. Some European intellectuals attacked the rational tradition of the Enlightenment and celebrated the primitive, the instinctual, and the irrational. Increasingly, young people felt drawn to philosophies of action that ridiculed liberal bourgeois values and viewed war as a purifying and ennobling experience. Colonial wars, colorfully portrayed in the popular press, ignited the imagination of bored factory workers and daydreaming students and reinforced a sense of duty and an urge for gallantry among soldiers and aristocrats. These "splendid" little colonial wars helped fashion an attitude that made war acceptable, if not laudable. Yearning to break loose from their ordinary lives and to embrace heroic values, many Europeans regarded violent conflict as the highest expression of individual and national life.

"This peace is so rotten", complained a young German writer, George Heym, in 1912, longing for "a war, even an unjust one."[2] That same year, a survey of French students between the ages of eighteen and twenty-five found

> the most cultivated elite among [them] find in warfare an aesthetic ideal. . . . These young men impute to it all the beauty with which they are in love and of which they have been deprived in ordinary life. Above all, [W]ar, in their eyes is the occasion for the most noble of virtues . . . energy, mastery, and sacrifice for a cause which transcends ourselves."[3]

The popular historian Heinrich von Treitschke (1834–1896), whose lectures influenced many students who were to rise to positions of importance in the German army and administration, expressed the prevailing mood: "Those who preach the nonsense about everlasting peace do not understand the life of the [German] race. . . . [T]o banish war from history would be to banish all progress."[4]

Although technology was making warfare more brutal and dangerous, Europe retained a romantic illusion about combat. "Even if we end in ruin it was beautiful," exclaimed General Erich von Falkenhayn, the future chief of the German general staff, at the outbreak of World War I.[5]

Although Europe was seemingly progressing in the art of civilization, the mythic power of nationalism and the primitive appeal of conflict were driving European civilization to the abyss. Few people recognized the potential crisis—certainly not the statesmen whose reckless blundering allowed the Continent to stumble into war.

AGGRAVATED NATIONALIST TENSIONS IN AUSTRIA-HUNGARY

On June 28, 1914, a young terrorist, with the support of the secret Serbian nationalist society called Union or Death (more popularly known as the Black Hand), murdered Archduke Francis Ferdinand, heir to the throne of Austria-Hungary. Six weeks later, the armies of Europe were on the march; an incident in the Balkans had sparked a world war. An analysis of why Austria-Hungary felt compelled to attack Serbia and why the other powers became enmeshed in the conflict shows how explosive Europe was in 1914. And nowhere were conditions more volatile than in Austria-Hungary, the scene of the assassination.

With its numerous nationalities, each with its own national history and traditions and often conflicting aspirations, Austria-Hungary stood in opposition to nationalism, the most powerful spiritual force of the age. Perhaps the supranational Austro-Hungarian Empire was obsolete in a world of states based on the principle of nationality. Dominated by Germans and Hungarians, the empire remained unable either to satisfy the grievances or to contain the nationalist aims of its numerous minorities, particularly the Czechs and South Slavs (Croats, Slovenes, and Serbs).

The more moderate leaders of the ethnic minorities did not call for secession from the empire. Nevertheless, heightened agitation among several nationalities, which worsened in the decade before 1914, greatly perturbed Austrian leaders. The fear that the empire would be torn apart by rebellion caused Austria to react strongly to any country that fanned the nationalist feelings of its Slavic minorities. This policy increased the tensions between Austria and small Serbia, which had gained its independence from the Ottoman Empire in 1878.

Captivated by Western ideas of nationalism, the Serbs sought to create a Greater Serbia by uniting with their racial kin, the 7 million or so South Slavs living in the Hapsburg Empire. The shrill appeals by Serbian nationalists made Austrian leaders fear that the South Slavs might press for secession. Some of these leaders, notably Foreign Minister Count Leopold von Berchtold and Field Marshal Franz Conrad von Hötzendorf, urged the destruction of Serbia to eliminate the threat to Austria's existence.

Another irritant to Austria-Hungary was Russian Pan-Slavism, which called for the solidarity of Russians with their Slavic cousins in eastern Europe—Poles, Czechs, Slovaks, South Slavs, and Bulgarians. Pan-Slavism was based on a mystic conception of the superiority of Slavic civilization to Western civilization and of Russia's special historic mission to liberate its kin from Austrian and Turkish rule. Although Russian Pan-Slavs were few and did not dictate foreign policy, they constituted a significant pressure group. Moreover, their provocative and semireligious proclamations frightened Austria-Hungary, which did not draw a sharp line between Pan-Slavic aspirations and official Russian policy.

The tensions stemming from the multinational character of the Austro-Hungarian Empire in an age of heightened nationalist feeling set off the explosion in 1914. Unable to solve its minority problems and fearful of Pan-Slavism and Pan-Serbism, Austria-Hungary felt itself in a life-or-death situation. This sense of desperation led it to lash out at Serbia after the assassination of Archduke Francis Ferdinand.

THE GERMAN SYSTEM OF ALLIANCES

Perhaps the war might have been avoided, or at least limited to Austria and Serbia, if Europe in 1914 had not been split into two hostile alliance systems. Such a situation contains inherent dangers. Counting on the support of its allies, a country might pursue a more provocative and reckless course and be less conciliatory during a crisis. Furthermore, a conflict between two states might spark a chain reaction that draws in the other powers, transforming a limited war into a general war. That is what happened after the assassination. This dangerous alliance system originated with Bismarck and the Franco-Prussian War.

The New German Empire

With its unification in 1870–71, Germany became an international power of the first rank, upsetting the balance of power in Europe. For the first time since the wars of the French Revolution, one nation was in a position to dominate the European continent. How a united and powerful Germany would fit into European life was the crucial problem in the decades following the Franco-Prussian War.

To German nationalists, unification both fulfilled a national dream and pointed to an even more ambitious goal: extending German power in Europe and the world. As the nineteenth century drew to a close, German nationalism became more extreme. Believing that Germany must either grow or die, nationalists pressed the government to build a powerful navy, acquire colonies, gain a much greater share of the world's markets, and expand German interests and influence in Europe. Sometimes these goals were expressed in the language of Social Darwinism: nations are engaged in an eternal struggle for survival and domination.

Militant nationalists preached the special destiny of the German race and advocated German expansion in Europe and overseas. Decisive victories against Austria (1866) and France (1871), the formation of the German Reich, rapid indus-

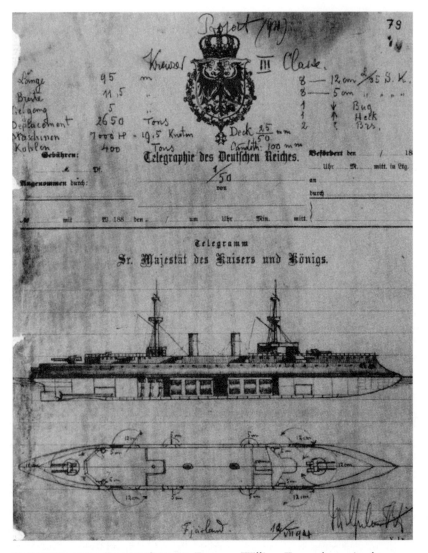

BLUEPRINT FOR A BATTLE CRUISER. Emperor William II was determined to construct a great navy that would challenge Britain's naval supremacy. Above is his sketch for a battle cruiser. (*Bildarchiv Militärarchiv, Freiburg*)

trialization, and the impressive achievements of German science and scholarship had molded a powerful and dynamic nation. Imbued with great expectations for the future, Germans became increasingly impatient to see the fatherland gain its "rightful" place in world affairs—an attitude that alarmed non-Germans.

Bismarck's Goals

Under Bismarck, who did not seek additional territory but wanted only to preserve the recently achieved unification, Germany pursued a moderate and cautious foreign policy. One of Bismarck's goals was to keep France isolated and friendless. Deeply humiliated by its defeat in the Franco-Prussian War and the loss of Alsace and Lorraine, France found its nationalists yearning for a war of revenge against Germany. Victor Hugo expressed the "sacred anger" of the French: "France will have but one thought: to reconstitute her forces, gather her energy, . . . raise her young generation to form an army of the whole people. . . . Then one day she will be irresistible. Then she will take back Alsace-Lorraine."[6] Even though the French government, aware of Germany's strength, was unlikely to initiate a conflict, the issue of Alsace-Lorraine increased tensions between the two countries. Annexing the French provinces proved to be a serious blunder on Germany's part, for it made reconciliation impossible.

Bismarck also hoped to prevent a war between Russia and Austria-Hungary, since it could lead to German involvement, the breakup of Austria-Hungary, and Russian expansion in eastern Europe. To maintain peace and Germany's existing borders, Bismarck forged complex alliances. In the decade of the 1880s, he created the Triple Alliance, consisting of Germany, Austria-Hungary, and Italy, as well as an alliance with Russia.

A major weakness marred Germany's alliance system, however; Austria and Russia were potential enemies. Austria feared Russian ambitions in the Balkans and felt threatened by Russian Pan-Slavs. Bismarck knew that an alliance with Austria was essentially incompatible with Germany's treaty obligations to Russia. But he hoped that the arrangement would enable him to exercise a moderating influence over both eastern powers and prevent a war from erupting and upsetting the status quo. Besides, the treaty with Russia deprived France of a valuable ally.

Bismarck conducted foreign policy with restraint. He formed alliances not to conquer new lands, but to protect Germany from aggression by either France or Russia. His aim was to preserve order and stability in Europe, not to launch war. However, when the young Kaiser William II (1888–1918) ascended the German throne, he clashed with the aging prime minister, and in 1890, Bismarck was forced to resign. Lacking Bismarck's diplomatic skills, his cool restraint, and his determination to keep peace in Europe, the new German leaders pursued a belligerent and imperialistic foreign policy in the ensuing decades.

The first act of the new leadership was to let the treaty with Russia lapse, allowing Germany to give full support to Austria, which was deemed a more reliable ally. Whereas Bismarck had warned Austria to act with moderation and caution in the Balkans, his successors not only failed to hold Austria in check, but actually encouraged Austrian aggression. This proved fatal to the peace of Europe.

THE TRIPLE ENTENTE

Fear of Germany

When Germany broke with Russia in 1890, France was quick to take advantage of the situation. Worried by Germany's increasing military strength, expanding industries, growing population, and alliance with Austria and Italy, France eagerly courted Russia as an ally. The French government urged its bankers to invest in Russia, supplied weapons to the tsar, and arranged for the French and Russian fleets to exchange visits. In 1894, France and Russia entered into an alliance; the isolation forced on France by Bismarck had ended.

Germany's growing military might also alarmed Great Britain. In addition, Germany had become a potent trade rival and strove to become a great colonial power as well—a goal demanded by German nationalists. But what troubled Britain most was Germany's decision to build a great navy, for it could interfere with British overseas trade or even blockade the British Isles. Germany's naval program was the single most important reason that Britain moved closer first to France and then to Russia. Germany's naval construction, designed to increase its stature as a Great Power but not really necessary for its security, was one indication that German leaders had abandoned Bismarck's policy of good sense. Eager to add the British as an ally and demonstrating superb diplomatic skill, France moved to end long-standing colonial disputes with Britain. The Entente Cordiale of 1904 accomplished this conciliation. England had emerged from its self-imposed isolation.

Although the Franco-British understanding heightened German anxiety, Germany doubted that France and England, who had almost gone to war in 1898 in the Sudan, had overcome their deep animosities. Consequently, Chancellor Bernhard von Bülow (1849–1929) decided to test the Entente Cordiale by provoking a crisis in Morocco. Von Bülow chose Morocco because earlier the British had resisted French imperialist designs there. He prodded a reluctant Kaiser William II to visit the Moroccan port of Tangier, a sign that Germany would support the Moroccan sultan against France. In January 1906, at the conference held in Algeciras, Spain, to resolve the crisis, Germany suffered defeat. Britain sided with France, which was given special rights in Morocco. Germany's efforts to disrupt the Anglo-French Entente Cordiale had failed; the two former enemies demonstrated their solidarity.

Eager to counter Germany's Triple Alliance with a strong alliance of their own, French diplomats now sought to ease tensions between their Russian ally and their new British friend. Two events convinced Russia to adopt a more conciliatory attitude toward Britain: a disastrous and unexpected defeat in the Russo-Japanese War of 1904–1905 and a working-class revolution in 1905. Shocked by defeat, its army bordering on disintegration, its workers restive, Russia was now receptive to settling its imperial disputes with Britain over Persia, Tibet, and Afghanistan, a decision encouraged by France. In the Anglo-Russian Entente of 1907, as in the Anglo-French Entente Cordiale of 1904, the former rivals conducted themselves in a conciliatory, if not friendly, manner. In both instances, what engendered this spirit of cooperation was fear of Germany; both agreements represented a triumph for French diplomacy. The Triple Entente, however, was not a firm alliance, for there was no certainty that Britain, traditionally reluctant to send its troops to the Continent, would give more than diplomatic support to France and Russia in case of a showdown with Germany.

Europe was now broken into two hostile camps: the Triple Entente of France, Russia, and Britain and the Triple Alliance of Germany, Austria-Hungary, and Italy. The costly arms race and the maintenance of large standing armies by all the states except Britain served to increase fear and suspicion between the alliances.

German Reactions

Germany denounced the Triple Entente as a hostile anti-German coalition designed to encircle and crush Germany. To survive, Germany must break this ring. In the past, German arms had achieved unification; German military might would also end this threat to the fatherland. Considering Austria-Hungary as its only reliable ally, Germany resolved to preserve the power and dignity of the Hapsburg Empire. If Austria-Hungary fell from the ranks of the Great Powers, Germany would have to stand alone against its enemies. At all costs, Austria-Hungary must not be weakened.

This assessment, however, suffered from dangerous miscalculations. First, Germany overstressed the hostile nature of the Triple Entente. In reality, France, Russia, and Britain drew closer together not to wage aggressive war against Germany, but to protect themselves against burgeoning German military, industrial, and diplomatic power. Second, by linking German security to Austria, Germany greatly increased the chance of war. Growing more and more fearful of Pan-Serbism and Pan-Slavism, Austria might well decide that only a war could prevent its empire from disintegrating. Confident of German support, Austria would be more likely to resort to force; afraid of any diminution of Austrian power, Germany would be more likely to support Austria. In contrast to Bismarck, the new leadership did not think in terms of restraining Austria but of strengthening it, by war if necessary.

THE DRIFT TOWARD WAR

The Bosnian Crisis

After 1908, several crises tested the competing alliances, pushing Europe closer to war. Particularly significant was the Bosnian affair, for it contained many of the ingredients that eventually ignited the war in 1914. The humiliating defeat by Japan in 1905 had diminished Russia's stature as a Great Power. The new Russian foreign minister, Alexander Izvolsky, hoped to gain a diplomatic triumph by compelling the Ottoman Turks to allow Russian warships to pass through the Dardanelles, fulfilling a centuries-old dream of extending Russian power into the Mediterranean. Izvolsky hoped that England and France, traditional opponents of Russia's Mediterranean ambitions but now Russia's allies, would not block the move. But certainly Austria would regard it as a hostile act.

Russia made a deal with Austria: if Austria would support Russia's move to open the Dardanelles, Russia would permit Austrian annexation of the provinces of Bosnia and Herzegovina. Officially a part of the Ottoman Empire, these provinces had been administered by Austria-Hungary since 1878. The population consisted mainly of ethnic cousins of the Serbs. A formal annexation would certainly infuriate the Serbs, who hoped one day to make the region part of a Greater Serbia. In 1908, Austria proceeded to annex the provinces, but Russia met stiff resistance from England and France when it presented its case for opening the strait to Russian warships. Austria had gained a diplomatic victory, while Russia suffered another humiliation. Even more enraged than Russia, Serbia threatened to invade Bosnia to liberate its cousins from Austrian oppression. The Serbian press proclaimed that Austria-Hungary must perish if the South Slavs were to achieve liberty and unity. A fiery attitude also prevailed in Vienna: Austria-Hungary could not survive unless Serbia was destroyed.

During this period of intense hostility between Austria-Hungary and Serbia, Germany supported its Austrian ally. To keep Austria strong, Germany would even agree to the dismemberment of Serbia and to its incorporation into the Hapsburg Empire. As a result of this crisis, Austria and Germany coordinated battle plans in case a conflict between Austria and Serbia involved Russia and France. Unlike Bismarck, who tried to hold Austria in check, German leadership now coolly envisioned an Austrian attack on Serbia, and just as coolly offered German support if Russia intervened.

Balkan Wars

The Bosnian crisis pushed Germany and Austria closer together, brought relations between Austria and Serbia to the breaking point, and inflicted another humiliation on Russia. The first Balkan War (1912) continued these trends. The Balkan states of Montenegro, Serbia, Bulgaria,

MAP 29.1 The Balkans, 1914

and Greece attacked a dying Ottoman Empire. In a brief campaign, the Balkan armies captured the Turkish empire's European territory, with the exception of Constantinople. Because it was on the victorious side, landlocked Serbia gained the Albanian coast and thus a long-desired outlet to the sea. Austria, however, was determined to keep its enemy from reaping this reward, and Germany, as in the Bosnian crisis, supported its ally. Unable to secure Russian support, Serbia was forced to surrender the territory, which in 1913 became the state of Albania.

During a five-year period, Austria-Hungary had twice humiliated Serbia. Russia shared these humiliations, for it had twice failed to help its small Slavic friend and had been denied access to the Dardanelles at the time of the Bosnian crisis. Incensed Serbian nationalists accelerated their campaign of propaganda and terrorism against Austria. Believing that another humiliation would irreparably damage its prestige, Russia vowed to back Serbia in its next confrontation with Austria. And Austria had reached the end of its patience with Serbia. Emboldened by German encouragement, Austria wanted to end the

CHRONOLOGY 29.1 World War I

June 28, 1914	Archduke Francis Ferdinand of Austria is assassinated at Sarajevo
August 4, 1914	The Germans invade Belgium
August 1914	Russians invade East Prussia: are defeated by Germans at the battle of Tannenberg
September 1914	The first battle of the Marne saves Paris
April 1915–January 1916	Gallipoli campaign: Allies withdraw after suffering 252,000 casualties
May 1915	Italy enters war on Allies' side
Spring 1915	Germany launches offensive that forces Russia to abandon Galicia and most of Poland
February 1916	General Pétain leads French forces at Verdun; Germans fail to capture the fortress town
June 1916	Russians suffer more than a million casualties in an offensive against Austrian lines
July–November 1916	Battle of the Somme: Allies suffer 600,000 casualties
January 1917	Germany launches unrestricted submarine warfare
April 6, 1917	United States declares war on Germany

Serbian threat once and for all. Thus, the ingredients for war between Austria and Serbia, a war that might easily draw in Russia and Germany, were present. Another incident might well start a war. It came on June 28, 1914.

Assassination of Francis Ferdinand

Archduke Francis Ferdinand (1863–1914), heir to the throne of Austria, was sympathetic to the grievances of the South Slavs and favored a policy that would place the Slavs on an equal footing with Hungarians and Germans within the Hapsburg Empire. If such a policy succeeded, it could soothe the feelings of the Austrian Slavs and reduce the appeal of a Greater Serbia, the aim of the Black Hand.

On June 28, 1914, Francis Ferdinand was as-sassinated while making a state visit to Sarajevo, the capital of Bosnia. Gavrilo Princip, a young revolutionary who was part of a team of Bosnian terrorists, fired two shots at close range into the archduke's car. Francis Ferdinand and his wife died within fifteen minutes. The conspiracy was organized by Dragutin Dimitrijevic, chief of intelligence of the Serbian army, who was linked to the Black Hand.* By killing the archduke, the terrorists hoped to bring to a boiling point tensions within the Hapsburg Empire and prepare the way for revolution.

---

*Serbia's prime minister, Nikola Pasic, learned of the plot and, through the Serbian envoy in Vienna, tried to get Austria to cancel Francis Ferdinand's visit. The Austrians, however, were not told of a specific assassination attempt, for Pasic did not want to admit that such an act of terrorism was being plotted on Serbian soil.

May 1917	General Pétain restores French army's morale and discipline
July–November 1917	British defeat at Passchendaele
Fall 1917	Italian defeat at Caporetto
November 1917	Bolsheviks take power in Russia
January 1918	U.S. President Woodrow Wilson announces his Fourteen Points
March 1918	Russia signs Treaty of Brest-Litovsk, losing territory to Germany and withdrawing from the war
March 21, 1918	Germans launch a great offensive to end the war
June 3, 1918	Germans advance to within fifty-six miles of Paris
August 8, 1918	British victory at Amiens
October 1918	Turks are forced to withdraw from the war after several British successes
November 3, 1918	Austria-Hungary signs armistice with the Allies
November 11, 1918	Germany signs armistice with the Allies, ending World War I
January 1919	Paris Peace Conference
June 28, 1919	Germany signs Treaty of Versailles

Feeling that Austria's prestige as a Great Power and indeed its very survival as a supranational empire were at stake, key officials, led by the foreign minister, Count Leopold von Berchtold, decided to use the assassination as a pretext to crush Serbia. For many years, Austrian leaders had yearned for war with Serbia in order to end the agitation for the union of the South Slavs. Now, they reasoned, the hour had struck. But war with Serbia would require Germany's approval. Believing that Austria was Germany's only reliable ally and that a diminution of Austrian power and prestige threatened German security, German statesmen decided to support Austria and encouraged it to take up arms against Serbia. Both Germany and Austria wanted a quick strike to overwhelm Serbia before other countries were drawn in.

Germany Abets Austria

Confident of German backing, on July 23 Austria presented Serbia with an ultimatum and demanded a response within forty-eight hours. The terms of the ultimatum were so harsh that it was next to impossible for Serbia to accept them. This reaction was the one that Austria intended, as it sought a military solution to the crisis rather than a diplomatic one. But Russia feared that an Austrian conquest of Serbia was just the first step in an Austro-German plan to dominate the Balkans. Such an extension of German and Austrian power in a region close to Russia was unthinkable to the tsar's government. Moreover, after suffering repeated reverses in foreign affairs, Russia would not tolerate another humiliation. As Germany had

721

HEIR TO AUSTRIA'S THRONE IS SLAIN WITH HIS WIFE BY A BOSNIAN YOUTH TO AVENGE SEIZURE OF HIS COUNTRY

Francis Ferdinand Shot During State Visit to Sarajevo.

TWO ATTACKS IN A DAY

Archduke Saves His Life First Time by Knocking Aside a Bomb Hurled at Auto.

SLAIN IN SECOND ATTEMPT

Lad Dashes at Car as the Royal Couple Return from Town Hall and Kills Both of Them.

LAID TO A SERVIAN PLOT

Heir Warned Not to Go to Bosnia, Where Populace Met Him with Servian Flags.

AGED EMPEROR IS STRICKEN

Shock of Tragedy Prostrates Francis Joseph—Young Assassin Proud of His Crime.

Archduke Francis Ferdinand and his Consort the Duchess of Hohenberg
Slain by Assassin's Bullets.

ASSASSINATION OF ARCHDUKE FRANCIS FERDINAND. Headline from *The New York Times* reporting the assassination. (*Stock Montage*)

resolved to back its Austrian ally, Russia determined not to abandon Serbia.

Serbia responded to Austria's ultimatum in a conciliatory manner, agreeing to virtually all Austrian demands. But it refused Austrian officials entry to investigate the assassination. Having already decided against a peaceful settlement, Austria insisted that rejecting one provision meant rejecting the entire ultimatum, and it ordered the mobilization of its army.

This was a crucial moment for Germany. Would it continue to support Austria, knowing that an Austrian attack on Serbia would most likely bring Russia into the conflict? Determined not to desert Austria and believing that a showdown with Russia was inevitable anyway, the German war party continued to urge Austrian action against Serbia. They argued that it was better to fight Russia in 1914 than a few years later, when the tsar's empire would be stronger. The war party claimed that Germany's superior army could defeat both Russia and France, that Britain's army was too weak to make a difference, and that, in any case, Britain might remain

neutral. Although Germany would have preferred a limited war, involving only Austria and Serbia, the idea of a general war did not dismay it. Indeed, the prospect of a war with Russia and France exhilarated some military leaders and statesmen. The defeat of Germany's enemies would break the ring of encirclement, increase German territory, and establish Germany as the foremost power in the world.

On July 28, 1914, Austria declared war on Serbia. Russia, with the assurance of French support, proclaimed partial mobilization aimed at Austria alone. But the military warned that partial mobilization would throw the slow-moving Russian war machine into total confusion if the order had to be changed suddenly to full mobilization. Moreover, the only plans the Russian general staff had drawn up called for full mobilization, that is, for war against both Austria and Germany. Pressured by his generals, the tsar gave the order for full mobilization on July 30. Russian forces would be arrayed against Germany as well as Austria.

Because the country that struck first gained the advantage of fighting according to its own plans rather than having to improvise in response to the enemy's attack, generals tended to regard mobilization by the enemy as an act of war. Therefore, when Russia refused a German warning to halt mobilization, Germany, on August 1, ordered a general mobilization and declared war on Russia. Two days later, Germany also declared war on France, believing that France would most likely support its Russian ally. Besides, German battle plans were based on a war with both Russia and France; therefore, a war between Germany and Russia automatically meant a German attack on France.

When Belgium refused to allow German troops to march through Belgian territory into France, Germany invaded the small nation, which brought Britain, pledged to guarantee Belgian neutrality, into the war. Britain could never tolerate German troops directly across the English Channel in any case, nor could it brook German mastery of western Europe. A century before, Britain had fought Napoleon to prevent France from becoming master of Europe; now it would fight Germany for the same reason. Additionally, British and French military and naval commands had entered into joint planning, which linked the two powers more closely. Should France be attacked, Britain would be unlikely to stay neutral.

The Question of Responsibility

The question of whether any one power was mainly responsible for the war has intrigued historians. In assessing blame, historians have focused on Germany's role. German historian Fritz Fischer argues that Germany's ambition to dominate Europe was the underlying cause of the war. Germany encouraged Austria to strike at Serbia knowing that an attack on Serbia could mean war with Russia and its French ally. Believing that it had the military advantage, Germany was willing to risk such a war. Hence, "her leaders must bear a substantial share of the historical responsibility for the outbreak of general war in 1914."[7]

Attracted by Social Darwinist and militarist doctrines, continues Fischer, Germany sought to become the foremost economic and political power in Europe and to play a far greater role in world politics; to achieve this goal, it was willing to go to war. Fischer supports his position by pointing to Germany's war aims, drawn up immediately after the outbreak of war, which called for the annexation of neighboring territories and the creation of satellite states. Fischer's critics stress, however, that Social Darwinism and militarism enthralled other nations besides Germany and that this was not peculiarly German, but rather part of a general European sickness. They argue further that Germany would have preferred a limited war between Austria and Serbia and before the war had no plans to dominate Europe.

Historians also attribute blame to the other powers. Austria bears responsibility for its determination to crush Serbia and for its insistent avoidance of a negotiated settlement. Serbia's responsibility stems from pursuing an aggressive Pan-Serbian policy, which set it on a collision course with Austria-Hungary. In 1913, Sir Fairfax Cartwright, the British ambassador to Vienna, warned: "Serbia will some day set Europe by the ears, and bring about a universal war on the Continent. I cannot tell you how exasperated people are getting here at the continual worry which that little country causes to Austria."[8] Russia bears responsibility for instituting general mobilization, thereby turning a limited war between Austria-Hungary and Serbia into a European war; France, for failing to restrain Russia and indeed for encouraging its ally to mobilize; and England, for failing to make clear that it would support its allies. Had Germany seen plainly that Britain would intervene, it might have been more cautious.

Some historians, dismissing the question of responsibility, regard the war as an obvious sign that European civilization was in deep trouble. Viewed in the broad perspective of European history, the war marked a culmination of dangerous forces in European life: the glorification of power; the fascination with violence, and the nonrational; the general dissatisfaction and disillusionment with bourgeois society; and, above all, the explosive nationalism. It also underscored the diminishing confidence in the capacity of reason to solve the problems created by the Industrial Revolution and pointed to the flaws and perils of the alliance system.

WAR AS CELEBRATION

When war was certain, an extraordinary phenomenon occurred. Crowds gathered in capital cities, demonstrating their allegiance to the fatherland and their readiness to fight. Even socialists, who had pledged their loyalty to an international workers' movement, devoted themselves to their respective nations. War and its violence seemed to offer an escape from the dull routine of classroom, job, and home and from the emptiness, drabness, and mediocrity of bourgeois society—from "a world grown old and cold and weary," as Rupert Brooke, a young British poet, put it.[9] To some, war was a "beautiful . . . sacred moment" that satisfied an "ethical yearning."[10] More significantly, the outpouring of patriotic sentiments demonstrated the immense power that nationalism exerted over the European mind. Nationalism welded millions of people into a collectivity ready to commit body and soul to the nation, especially during its hour of need. For decades, state-directed education had indoctrinated youth with nationalist attitudes, beliefs, and myths designed to promote social cohesion. This training had proved extraordinarily successful.

In Paris, men marched down the boulevards

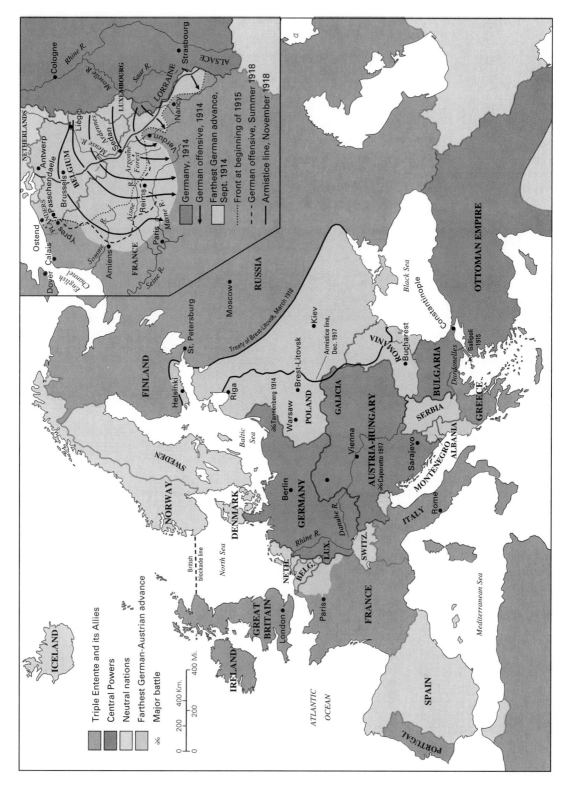

Triple Entente and its Allies
Central Powers
Neutral nations
Farthest German-Austrian advance
✗ Major battle

0 200 400 Km.
0 200 400 Mi.

ICELAND

NORWAY
SWEDEN
FINLAND
Helsinki •
St. Petersburg •
Moscow •
RUSSIA

Treaty of Brest-Litovsk, March 1918

DENMARK
North Sea
British blockade line

IRELAND
GREAT BRITAIN
London •

ATLANTIC OCEAN

NETH.
BELG.
LUX.
Rhine R.
GERMANY
Berlin •
Danube R.
SWITZ.
Riga •
Tannenberg 1914
Warsaw •
POLAND
Brest-Litovsk •
Kiev •
Armistice line, Dec. 1917
GALICIA
Vienna •
AUSTRIA-HUNGARY
Caporetto 1917
ROMANIA
Bucharest •
SERBIA
Sarajevo •
MONTENEGRO
ALBANIA
BULGARIA
GREECE
Black Sea
Constantinople •
Dardanelles
Gallipoli 1915
OTTOMAN EMPIRE

Paris •
FRANCE
Rome •
ITALY
Mediterranean Sea

SPAIN
PORTUGAL

Inset map legend:

Germany, 1914
German offensive, 1914
Farthest German advance, Sept. 1914
Front at beginning of 1915
German offensive, Summer 1918
Armistice line, November 1918

Cologne •
Rhine R.
Moselle R.
Saar R.
LORRAINE
Strasbourg •
ALSACE
NETHERLANDS
Antwerp •
Passchendaele •
BELGIUM
Liège •
LUXEMBOURG
Sedan •
Meuse R.
Ardennes
Argonne Forest
Nancy •
Verdun •
Brussels •
Ostend •
FLANDERS
Ypres •
Dover •
Calais •
English Channel
Amiens •
Somme R.
Aisne R.
Reims •
Marne R.
Paris •
FRANCE
Seine R.

724

singing the stirring words of the French national anthem, the "Marseillaise," while women showered young soldiers with flowers. A participant recollected: "Young and old, civilians and military men burned with the same excitement. . . . thousands of men eager to fight would jostle one another outside recruiting offices, waiting to join up. . . . The word 'duty' had a meaning for them, and the word 'country' had regained its splendor."[11] Similarly, a German newspaper editorialized, "It is a joy to be alive. We wished so much for this hour. . . . The sword which has been forced into our hand will not be sheathed until our aims are won and our territory extended as far as necessity demands."[12] Writing about those momentous days, the British mathematician-philosopher Bertrand Russell recalled his horror and "amazement that average men and women were delighted at the prospect of war. . . . [T]he anticipation of carnage was delightful to something like ninety per cent of the population. I had to revise my views on human nature."[13]

Soldiers bound for battle acted as though they were going off on a great adventure. "My dear ones, be proud that you live in such a time and in such a nation and that you . . . have the privilege of sending those you love into so glorious a battle," wrote a young German law student to his family.[14] The young warriors yearned to do something noble and altruistic, to win glory, and to experience life at its most intense.

The martial mood also captivated many of Europe's most distinguished intellectuals. They shared Rupert Brooke's sentiments: "Now God be thanked Who has matched us with His hour,/ And caught our youth, and wakened us from sleeping."[15] In November 1914, Thomas Mann (see page 804) the distinguished German writer, saw the war as "purification" and "liberation." "How could . . . the soldier in the artist," he asked, "not praise God for the collapse of a peaceful world with which he was fed up, so exceedingly fed up."[16] To the prominent German historian Friedrich Meinecke, August 1914 was "one of the great moments of my life which suddenly filled my soul with . . . the profoundest joy."[17]

Some intellectuals also welcomed the war be-cause it unified the nation in a spirit of fraternity and self-sacrifice, which overcame the sense of individual isolation. Stefan Zweig (1881–1942), an Austrian writer, recalled how news of the war was greeted in Vienna:

> *As never before, thousands and hundreds of thousands felt what they should have felt in peace time, that they belonged together. . . . All differences of class, rank, and language were flooded over at that moment by the rushing feeling of fraternity. Strangers spoke to one another in the streets, people who had avoided each other for years shook hands, everywhere one saw excited faces. Each individual experienced an exaltation of his ego . . . he had been incorporated into the mass . . . and his person, his hitherto unnoticed person, had been given meaning.*[18]

War, in the view of some intellectuals, would spiritually regenerate the nation. It would resurrect glory, nobility, and heroism; it would awaken a spirit of self-sacrifice and give life an overriding purpose; it would rid the nation of its spiritual and racial impurities. From the war would emerge a higher civilization, morally reborn.

Thus, a generation of European youth marched off to war joyously, urged on by their teachers and cheered by their delirious nations. It must be emphasized, however, that both the soldiers who went off to war singing and the statesmen and generals who welcomed war or did not try hard enough to prevent it expected a short, decisive, and gallant conflict. Few envisioned what World War I turned out to be: four years of barbaric, senseless slaughter. The cheers of chauvinists, deluded idealists, and fools drowned out the words of those who realized that Europe was stumbling into darkness. "The lamps are going out all over Europe," said British Foreign Secretary Edward Grey. "We shall never see them lit again in our lifetime."

STALEMATE IN THE WEST

On August 4, 1914, the German army invaded Belgium. German war plans, drawn up years earlier, chiefly by General Alfred von Schlieffen,

◀ MAP 29.2 World War I, 1914–1918

TRENCH WARFARE, BRITISH TROOPS GOING "OVER THE TOP" DURING THE BATTLE OF THE SOMME. The soldiers still had to cross "No Man's Land" and get through the barbed wire in front of the enemy's trenches. (*Popperfoto*)

called for the army to swing through Belgium to outflank French border defenses, envelop the French forces, and destroy the enemy by attacking its rear. With the French army smashed and Paris isolated, German railroads would rush the victorious troops to the eastern front to reinforce the small force that had been assigned to hold off the Russians. The German military felt certain that the spirit and skill of the German army would ensure victory over the much larger Russian forces. But everything depended on speed. France must be taken before the Russians could mobilize sufficient numbers to invade Germany. The Germans were confident that they would defeat France in two months or less.

French strategy called for a headlong attack into Alsace and Lorraine. Inspired by Napoleon's stress on offensive warfare and convinced of French soldiers' unconquerable will and irresistible nerve, the French army prepared its soldiers only for offensive warfare. The field regulations proclaimed: "Battles are . . . struggles of morale. Defeat is inevitable as soon as the hope of conquer-

ing ceases to exist. Success comes . . . to him whose will is firmest and morale strongest."[19]

The French doctrine proved an instant failure. Although bayonet charges against machine-gun emplacements demonstrated the valor of French soldiers, they also revealed the incompetence of French generals. Making no effort at concealment or surprise and wearing striking red and blue uniforms, French soldiers were perfect targets. Marching into concentrated fire, they fell like pins. Everywhere the audacious attack was failing, but French generals, beguiled by the mystique of the offensive, would not change their tactics. In the first six weeks of the war, the French suffered an astounding 385,000 casualties, including 100,000 dead.

German success was not complete, however. Moving faster than anticipated, the Russians invaded East Prussia, which forced General Helmuth von Moltke to transfer troops from the French front, hampering the German advance. By early September, the Germans had reached the Marne River, forty miles from Paris. With their capital at their backs, the regrouped French forces, aided by the British, fought with astounding courage. Meanwhile, the Germans were exhausted by long marches and had outrun their supplies. Moreover, in their rush toward Paris, they had unknowingly exposed their flank, which the French attacked. The British then penetrated a gap that opened up between the German armies, forcing the Germans to retreat. The first battle of the Marne had saved Paris. Now the war entered a new and unexpected phase: the deadlock of trench warfare.

For four hundred miles across northern France, from the Alps to the North Sea, the opposing sides constructed a vast network of trenches. These trenches had underground dugouts, and barbed wire stretched for yards before the front trenches as a barrier to attack. Behind the front trenches were other lines, to which soldiers could retreat and from which support could be sent. Between the opposing armies lay "no man's land," a wasteland of mud, shattered trees, torn earth, and broken bodies. Trench warfare was a battle of nerves, endurance, and courage, waged to the constant thunder of heavy artillery. It was also butchery. As attacking troops climbed over their trenches and advanced bravely across no man's land, they were decimated by heavy artillery and chewed up by machine-gun fire. If they did penetrate the front-line trenches of the enemy, they were soon thrown back by a counterattack.

Despite a frightful loss of life, little land changed hands. So much heroism, sacrifice, and death achieved nothing. The generals ordered still greater attacks to end the stalemate; this only increased the death toll, for the advantage was always with the defense, which possessed machine guns, magazine rifles, and barbed wire. Tanks could redress the balance, but the generals, committed to old concepts, did not make effective use of them. And whereas the technology of the machine gun had been perfected, the motorized tanks often broke down. Gains and losses of land were measured in yards, but the lives of Europe's youth were squandered by the hundreds of thousands. In 1915, for example, France launched numerous attacks against German lines but never gained more than three miles in any one place. Yet these small gains cost France 1,430,000 casualties.

In 1915, neither side could break the dead-lock. Hoping to bleed the French army dry and force its surrender, the Germans in February 1916 attacked the town of Verdun, which was protected by a ring of forts. They chose Verdun because they knew the French could never permit a retreat from this ancient fortress. The Germans hoped that France, compelled to pour more and more troops into battle, would suffer such a loss of men that it would be unable to continue the war. However, the leadership of General Henri Philippe Pétain, the tenacity of the French infantry, and the well-constructed concrete and steel forts enabled the French to hold on. When the British opened a major offensive on July 1, the Germans had to channel their reserves to the new front, relieving the pressure on Verdun. Verdun was World War I's bloodiest battle. France and Germany suffered more than a million casualties.

At the end of June 1916, the British, assisted by the French, attempted a breakthrough at the Somme River. On July 1, after seven days of intense bombardment intended to destroy German defenses, the British climbed out of their trenches and ventured into no man's land. But German positions had not been destroyed. Emerging from their deep dugouts, German machine gunners fired repeatedly at the British, who had been ordered to advance in rows. Marching into concentrated machine-gun fire, few British troops ever made it across no man's land. Out of 110,000 who attacked, 60,000 fell dead or wounded, "the heaviest loss ever suffered in a single day by a British army or by any army in the First World War," observes British historian A. J. P. Taylor.[20] Some reached the German wire, only to become entangled in it. The Germans killed them with rifle fire and bayonets. For days the wounded lay in no man's land, their shrieks unheeded.

After this initial disaster, commonsense and a concern for human life demanded that the attack be called off, but the generals continued to feed soldiers to the German guns. When the battle of the Somme ended in mid November, Britain and France had lost more than 600,000 men; yet the military situation remained essentially unchanged.

In December 1916, the new commander in chief of the French forces, General Robert Nivelle, ordered another mass attack for April 1917.

Photo AKG London

MANFRED FRIEHERR VON RICHTHOFEN (THE "RED BARON")

During World War I, airplanes were first used to gather intelligence about enemy positions. To thwart these reconnaissance planes, the other side sent up its own planes, arming pilots first with revolvers and grenades and later with machine guns. Thus aerial combat was born. The daredevil pilots who dueled in the air captured the imagination of the people back home, and their exploits were widely publicized in the press.

The most famous ace of the war was Manfred Frieherr von Richthofen (1892–1918). Known as the "Red Baron" because he painted his plane scarlet so that both friend and foe could identify it, Richthofen is credited with shooting down eighty Allied aircraft. Richthofen's parents were typical Junker landowners, and Manfred, following in his father's footsteps, pursued a military career. Learning to fly in 1915, he soon was given command of a squadron of fighter pilots. An enthusiastic huntsman, Richthofen confessed that shooting down Al-

---

The Germans discovered the battle plans on the body of a French officer and withdrew to a shorter line on high ground, constructing the strongest defense network of the war. Although he knew that the French had lost the element of surprise, Nivelle went ahead with the offensive, which proved to be another bloodbath. Sometimes the fire was so intense that the French could not make it out of their own trenches. Although French soldiers fought with courage, the situation was hopeless. Still Nivelle persisted with the attack; after ten days, French casualties numbered 187,000.

The soldiers could endure no more. Spontaneous revolts, born of despair and military failure, broke out in rest areas as soldiers refused to return to the slaughter ground. In some instances, they shouted "Peace" and "To hell with the war." Mobs of soldiers seized trains to reach Paris and stir up the population against the war.

Mutineers took control of barracks and threatened to fire on officers who interfered. The mutiny spread to the frontlines as soldiers told their officers that they would defend the trenches but not attack. The French army was disintegrating. "The slightest German attack would have sufficed to tumble down our house of cards and bring the enemy to Paris," recalled a French officer.[21]

General Pétain, the hero of Verdun, replaced the disgraced Nivelle. To restore morale, Pétain granted more leave, improved the quality of food, made the rest areas more comfortable, and ordered officers to demonstrate a personal concern for their men. He visited the troops, listened to their complaints, and told them that France would engage in only limited offensives until the United States, which had just entered the war, reinforced the Allies in large numbers. These measures, combined with imprisonments and execu-

lied planes satisfied his passion for the hunt and a compulsive need for glory.

In drawing comparisons between German and Allied pilots, he stressed the superiority of the Germans' "aggressive spirit," which he believed he exemplified. He noted some of that spirit in the English pilots as well, ascribing it to their "German blood."

The Frenchman lies in wait for his prey to surprise him in a trap. That is hard to do in the air. Only a beginner will let himself be taken unawares. Ambush does not work, for one cannot hide and the inqvisible airplane has not yet been invented. Now and then, however, the Gallic blood rages in him and he launches an attack, but it is comparable to carbonated soda. For a moment there is an awful lot of spirit that suddenly goes flat. He is lacking in tenacious endurance.

The Englishman, on the other hand, shows some of his Germanic blood. These sportsmen take readily to flying, but they lose themselves in sport. They have enough amusement looping, diving, flying upside-down and demonstrating similar stunts for our men in the trenches. This would make a good impression during the Johannistal Sportsweek, but the men in the trenches are not as appreciative. *

April 1917 was a particularly successful month for Richthofen. He shot down twenty-one British planes, including four in one day, and was promoted to captain. One year later, in a furious dogfight above the Somme involving more than twenty German and British planes, the Red Baron's plane was hit by a Canadian pilot. When Australian soldiers reached the crashed plane, they found the Red Baron dead, his nose and jaw crushed from having smashed into the machine-gun butts in front of him. (Since the Australians on the ground were also firing at his plane, it is not certain who inflicted the fatal bullet.)

---

*Manfred Frieherr von Richthofen, *The Red Baron*, trans. Peter Kilduff (Garden City, N.Y.: Doubleday, 1969), p. 67.

tions, restored discipline. The Germans, unaware of the full magnitude of the mutiny, had not put pressure on the front. By the time the Germans attacked, Pétain had revitalized the army.

OTHER FRONTS

While the western front hardened into a stalemate, events moved more decisively on the eastern front. In August 1914, according to plan, the bulk of the German army invaded France, hoping for a speedy victory, while a small force defended the eastern frontier against Russia. Responding to French requests to put pressure on Germany, the Russians, with insufficient preparation, invaded East Prussia. Defeated at the battle of Tannenberg (August 26–30, 1914), the Russians withdrew from German territory, which remained inviolate for the rest of the war.

Meanwhile, Germany's ally Austria was having no success against Serbia and Russia. Germany had to come to Austria's rescue. In the spring of 1915, the Germans made a breakthrough that forced the Russians to abandon Galicia and most of Poland. But Germany did not gain the decisive victory it had sought. Although badly battered, Russia remained in the war, forcing Germany to fight on two fronts.

In June 1916, the Russians launched an offensive, opening a wide breach in the Austrian lines. However, a German counteroffensive forced a retreat and cost the Russians more than a million casualties. Russia's military position deteriorated and its domestic unrest worsened.

In March 1917, food shortages and disgust with the great loss of life exploded into a spontaneous revolution. The tsar abdicated. Dominated by liberals, the new government opted to continue the war, despite the weariness of the Russian masses. In

RED CROSS OR **IRON CROSS?**

WOUNDED AND A PRISONER OUR SOLDIER CRIES FOR WATER. THE GERMAN "SISTER" POURS IT ON THE GROUND BEFORE HIS EYES. THERE IS NO WOMAN IN BRITAIN WHO WOULD DO IT. THERE IS NO WOMAN IN BRITAIN WHO WILL FORGET IT.

BRITISH PROPAGANDA POSTER. The warring countries employed propaganda to strengthen the resolve of the soldiers and civilians on the "home front." (*Stock Montage*)

November 1917, a second revolution brought to power the Bolsheviks, or communists, who promised "Peace, Land, Bread" (see Chapter 30). In March 1918, the Bolsheviks ended Russia's role in the war by signing the punitive Treaty of Brest-Litovsk, in which Russia surrendered Poland, the Ukraine, Finland, and the Baltic provinces.

Some major battles involved belligerents who joined the conflict after August 1914—notably, the Ottoman Turks and the Italians. Intent on seizing the Dardanelles, the Allies met fierce Turkish resistance on the Gallipoli Peninsula (the Turks sided with the Germans). The Gallipoli campaign (1915–16) cost the Allies 252,000 casualties, and they had gained nothing. In 1917, the Italians—neutral until May 1915, when they joined the Allies—were badly defeated by a combined German and Austrian force at Caporetto. Germany and Austria took some 275,000 prisoners.

THE COLLAPSE OF THE CENTRAL POWERS

American Entry

The year 1917 seemed disastrous for the Allies. The Nivelle offensive had failed, the French army had mutinied, a British attack at Passchendaele did not bring the expected breakthrough and added some 300,000 casualties to the list of butchery, and the Russians, torn by revolution and gripped by war weariness, were close to making a separate peace. But there was one encouraging development for the Allies. In April 1917, the United States declared war on Germany.

From the outset, America's sympathies lay with the Allies. To most Americans, Britain and France were democracies, threatened by an autocratic and militaristic Germany. These sentiments were reinforced by British propaganda, which depicted the Germans as cruel "Huns." Since most war news came to the United States from Britain, anti-German feeling gained momentum. What precipitated American entry was the German decision of January 1917 to launch a campaign of unrestricted submarine warfare. To deprive Britain of war supplies and to starve it into submission, the Germans resolved to torpedo both enemy and neutral ships in the war zone around the British Isles. Since the United States was Britain's principal supplier, American ships became a target of German submarines.

Angered by American loss of life and materiel and by the violation of the doctrine of freedom of the seas, and fearful of a diminution of prestige if the United States took no action, President Woodrow Wilson (1856–1924) pressed for American entry. Also at stake was American security, which would be jeopardized by German domination of western Europe. As Secretary of State Robert Lansing wrote in a private memorandum just before American entry, "The Allies must *not* be beaten. It would mean the triumph of Autocracy over Democracy; the shattering of all our moral standards; and a real, though it may seem remote, peril to our independence and institutions."[22]

In initiating unrestricted submarine warfare,

Germany gambled that the United States, even if it became a belligerent, could not intervene in sufficient numbers quickly enough to make a difference. The Germans lost their gamble. The United States broke diplomatic relations with Germany immediately on learning of the submarine campaign. Three weeks later, the British turned over to the Americans a message sent by German Foreign Secretary Arthur Zimmerman to the German ambassador in Mexico City and deciphered by British code experts. In the Zimmerman telegram, Germany proposed that in case of war between Germany and the United States Mexico should join Germany as an ally; in return, Mexico would receive Texas, New Mexico, and Arizona. This fantastic proposal further exacerbated anti-German feeling in the United States. As German submarines continued to attack neutral shipping, President Wilson, on April 2, 1917, urged Congress to declare war on Germany, which it did on April 6.

Although the United States may have entered the war to protect its own security, President Wilson told the American people and the world that the United States was fighting "to make the world safe for democracy." With America's entry, the war was transformed into a moral crusade: an ideological conflict between democracy and autocracy. In January 1918, Wilson enunciated American war aims in the Fourteen Points, which called for territorial changes based on nationality and the application of democratic principles to international relations. An association of nations would be established to preserve peace; it would conduct international relations with the same respect for law as was evidenced in democratic states. In nationalism and democracy, the two great legacies of the nineteenth century, Wilson placed his hope for the future peace of the world.

Germany's Last Offensive

With Russia out of the war, General Erich Ludendorff prepared for a decisive offensive before the Americans could land sufficient troops in France to help the Allies. A war of attrition now favored the Allies, who could count on American supplies and manpower. Without an immediate and decisive victory, Germany could not win the war. Ludendorff hoped to drive the British forces back to the sea, forcing them to withdraw from the Continent. Then he would turn his full might against the French.

On March 21, 1918, the Germans launched the *Kaiserschlacht*—the "Emperor's Battle"— which was intended to bring victory in the west. In a predawn attack on the British trenches, they breached the enemy lines, and the British retreated. Expanding their offensive, the Germans now sought to split the British and French forces by capturing Amiens, the Allies' major communications center, and to drive the British back to the channel ports.

Suddenly, the deadlock had been broken; it was now a war of movement. Within two weeks, the Germans had taken some 1,250 square miles. But British resistance was astonishing, and the Germans, exhausted and short of ammunition and food, called off the drive. A second offensive against the British in April also had to be called off, as the British contested every foot of ground. Both campaigns depleted German manpower while the Americans were arriving in great numbers to strengthen Allied lines and uplift morale.

At the end of May, Ludendorff resumed his offensive against the French. Attacking unexpectedly, the Germans broke through and by June 3 advanced to within fifty-six miles of Paris. General John Pershing, head of the American forces, cabled Washington that "the possibility of losing Paris has become apparent."[23] But the offensive was already winding down as reserves braced the French lines. In the battle of Belleau Wood (June 6–25, 1918), the Americans checked the Germans. There would be no open road to Paris.

In mid July, the Germans tried again, crossing the Marne River in small boats. By August 3, the second battle of the Marne ended with the Germans being forced back over the river. Although they had thrown everything they had into their spring and summer offensives, it was not enough. The Allies had bent, but reinforced and encouraged by American arms, they did not break. Now they began to counterattack. On August 8, the British, assisted by the French and using tanks to great advantage, broke through east of Amiens. Ludendorff called August 8 "the black day of the German Army." The kaiser himself declared to his generals: "We have nearly reached the limit of our powers of resistance. The war must be ended."[24] The Allies, their confidence surging, continued to attack with great success in August and September.

Meanwhile, German allies, deprived of support from a hard-pressed Germany, were unable to cope. An Allied army of French, Britons, Serbs, and Italians compelled Bulgaria to sign an armistice on September 29. Shortly afterward, British successes in the Middle East forced the Turks to withdraw from the war. In the streets of Vienna, people were shouting "Long live peace! Down with the monarchy!" The Austro-Hungarian Empire was rapidly disintegrating into separate states based on nationality.

By early October, the last defensive position of the Germans crumbled. The army's spirit collapsed as well, and war-weary soldiers increasingly refused orders to return to the front. Fearing an Allied invasion of Germany, Ludendorff wanted an immediate armistice. But he needed to find a way to obtain favorable armistice terms from President Wilson and to shift the blame for the lost war from the military and the kaiser to the civilian leadership. Cynically, he urged the creation of a popular parliamentary government in Germany. But events in Germany went further than the general had anticipated. Whereas Ludendorff sought a limited monarchy, the shock of defeat and hunger sparked a revolution that forced the kaiser to abdicate.

On November 11, the new German Republic signed an armistice ending the hostilities. At 11 A.M., the soldiers from both sides walked into no man's land and into a new day. A newspaper correspondent with the British army in France wrote: "Last night for the first time since August in the first year of the war, there was no light of gunfire in the sky, no sudden stabs of flame through darkness, no spreading glow above black trees where for four years of nights human beings were smashed to death. The Fires of Hell had been put out."[25]

THE PEACE CONFERENCE

Wilson's Hope for a New World

In January 1919, representatives of the Allied powers assembled in Paris to draw up peace terms; President Wilson was also there. The war-weary masses turned to Wilson as the prophet who would have the nations beat their swords into plowshares. In Paris, 2 million people lined the streets to cheer Wilson and throw bouquets; his carriage passed under a huge banner proclaiming "Honor to Wilson the Just." In Rome, hysterical crowds called him the god of peace; in Milan, wounded soldiers sought to kiss his clothes; in Poland, university students spoke his name when they shook hands with each other.

For Wilson, the war had been fought against autocracy. He hoped that a peace settlement based on liberal-democratic ideals would sweep away the foundations of war. Wilson proclaimed his message with a spiritual zeal that expressed his Presbyterian background and his faith in American democracy.

None of Wilson's principles seemed more just than the idea of self-determination: the right of a people to have its own state, free of foreign domination. In particular, this goal meant (or was interpreted to mean) the return of Alsace and Lorraine to France, the creation of an independent Poland, a readjustment of the frontiers of Italy to incorporate Austrian lands inhabited by Italians, and an opportunity for Slavs of the Austro-Hungarian Empire to form their own states. Although Wilson did not demand the liberation of all colonies, the Fourteen Points did call for "a free, open-minded and absolutely impartial adjustment of all colonial claims" and a territorial settlement "made in the interest and for the benefit of the population concerned."

Aware that a harshly treated Germany might well seek revenge, engulfing the world in another cataclysm, Wilson insisted that there should be a "peace without victory." A just settlement would encourage a defeated Germany to work with the victorious Allies in building a new Europe. But on one point he was adamant: Prussian militarism, which he viewed as a principal cause of the war, must be eliminated.

To preserve peace and to help remake the world, Wilson urged the formation of a League of Nations, an international parliament to settle disputes and discourage aggression. Wilson wanted a peace of justice to preserve Western civilization in its democratic and Christian form.

Problems of Peacemaking

But how could such moralistic proclamations translate into concrete peace provisions? "Obvi-

WILSON AND CLEMENCEAU ARRIVE AT VERSAILLES, JUNE 28, 1919. The idealism of President Wilson (left) clashed with Premier Clemenceau's (center) determination to enhance France's security. (*Hulton Deutsch Collection*)

ously, no mortal man this side of the millennium could have hoped to bring about all the things that the world came to expect of Wilson," concludes American historian Thomas A. Bailey. "Wilson's own people were bound to feel disillusioned; the peoples of the neutral and Allied countries were bound to feel deceived; and the peoples of the enemy countries were bound to feel betrayed."[26]

Wilson's negotiating position had also been undermined by the Republican party's victory in the congressional elections of November 1918. Before the election, Wilson had appealed to the American people to elect Democrats as a vote of confidence in his diplomacy. But instead Americans sent twenty-five Republicans and fifteen Democrats to the Senate. Although the Republicans' success apparently stemmed from local and national, rather than international, issues, the outcome diminished Wilson's prestige at the conference table. In the view of his fellow negotiators, Wilson was trying to preach to Europe while he lacked the support of his own country. Since the Senate must ratify any

American treaty, European diplomats worried that what Wilson agreed to the Senate might reject, which is precisely what happened.

It has been suggested that Wilson's very presence at the conference table may have diminished his prestige. As president of the nation that had rescued the Allies and as initiator of a peace program that held the promise of a new world, Wilson occupied a position of honor, from which he could exert considerable influence and authority. But by attending the conference in person and haggling with the other representatives, he was knocked from his lofty pedestal and became all too human. "Messiahs tend to arouse less enthusiasm the more they show themselves," notes Bailey; "the role requires aloofness and the spell of mystery."[27]

Another obstacle to Wilson's peace program was France's demand for security and revenge. Nearly the entire war on the western front had been fought on French territory. The country mourned the loss of half its young men. Many French industries and farms had been ruined. Particularly galling to the French was the flooding of mines and the general destruction of property carried out by the Germans just before they left France at the war's end. Viewing the Germans as savages, vandals, and assassins, many in France were skeptical of Wilson's idealism. France's representative at the conference table, Georges Clemenceau (1841–1929), did not share Wilson's hope for a new world or his confidence in the future League of Nations. Instead, he demanded that Germany be severely punished and its capacity to wage war destroyed. He wanted guarantees that the wars of 1870–71 and 1914–1918 would not be repeated. The war had shown that without the help of Britain and the United States, France would have been at the mercy of Germany. Because there was no certainty that these states would again aid France, Clemenceau wanted to use his country's present advantage to cripple Germany.

The intermingling of European nationalities was a further barrier to Wilson's program since no one could create a Europe completely free of minority problems; some nationalities would always feel that they had been treated shabbily. And the various nationalities were not willing to moderate their demands or lower their aspirations. "To most Europeans," states German-American historian Hajo Holborn, "the satisfaction of their national dreams was an absolute end even when their realization violated the national determination of others."[28] For example, the Fourteen Points called for the creation of an independent Poland, with secure access to the sea. But between Poland and the sea lay territory populated by Germans. Giving this land to Poland would violate German self-determination; denying it to Poland would mean that the new country had little chance of developing a sound economy. No matter what the decision, one people would regard it as unjust. Similarly, to provide the new Czechoslovakia with defensible borders, it would be necessary to give it territory inhabited principally by Germans. This, too, could be viewed as a denial of German self-determination, but not granting the area to Czechoslovakia would mean that the new state would not be able to defend itself against Germany.

Secret treaties drawn up by the Allies during the war also interfered with Wilson's program. These agreements, dividing up German, Austrian, and Ottoman territory, did not square with the principle of self-determination. For example, to entice Italy into entering the war, the Allies had promised it Austrian lands that were inhabited predominantly by Germans and Slavs. Italy was not about to repudiate its prize because of Wilson's principles.

Finally, the war had aroused great bitterness, which persisted after the guns had been silenced. Both the masses and their leaders demanded retribution and held exaggerated hopes for territory and reparations. In such an atmosphere of postwar enmity, the spirit of compromise and moderation could not overcome the desire for spoils and punishment. A century earlier, when the monarchs had defeated Napoleon, they sought a peace of reconciliation with France. But setting aside their hatreds proved harder for democratic statesmen and nations than it had been for despotic monarchs and aristocratic diplomats.

The Settlement

After months of negotiations, often punctuated by acrimony, the peacemakers hammered out a settlement. Five treaties made up the Peace of

MAP 29.3 Post-World War I: Broken Empires and Changed Boundaries ▶

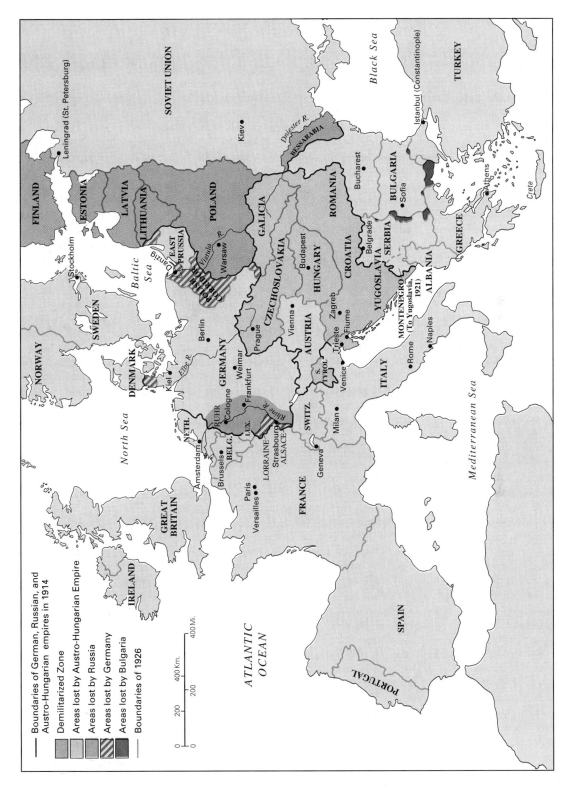

Boundaries of German, Russian, and
Austro-Hungarian empires in 1914

Demilitarized Zone

Areas lost by Austro-Hungarian Empire

Areas lost by Russia

Areas lost by Germany

Areas lost by Bulgaria

Boundaries of 1926

0   200   400 Km.

0   200   400 Mi.

ATLANTIC
OCEAN

NORWAY

SWEDEN

FINLAND

ESTONIA

LATVIA

LITHUANIA

SOVIET UNION

Leningrad (St. Petersburg)

Kiev

POLAND

Danzig

EAST PRUSSIA

Warsaw

Vistula R.

GALICIA

BESSARABIA

Dniester R.

Black Sea

ROMANIA

Bucharest

BULGARIA

Sofia

Istanbul (Constantinople)

TURKEY

GREECE

Athens

Crete

SERBIA

YUGOSLAVIA

Belgrade

CROATIA

MONTENEGRO
(To Yugoslavia,
1921)

ALBANIA

Naples

Rome

ITALY

Venice

S. TYROL

Trieste

Fiume

Zagreb

HUNGARY

Budapest

AUSTRIA

Vienna

CZECHOSLOVAKIA

Prague

Berlin

GERMANY

Weimar

Frankfurt

Cologne

RUHR

Rhine R.

Elbe R.

Kiel

DENMARK

Stockholm

Baltic Sea

North Sea

NETH.

Amsterdam

Brussels

BELG.

LUX.

LORRAINE

ALSACE

Strasbourg

Paris

Versailles

FRANCE

SWITZ.

Geneva

Milan

Mediterranean Sea

SPAIN

PORTUGAL

GREAT BRITAIN

IRELAND

735

Paris: one each with Germany, Austria, Hungary, Bulgaria, and Turkey. Of the five, the Treaty of Versailles, which Germany signed on June 28, 1919, was the most significant.

France regained Alsace and Lorraine, the territory lost to Germany in the Franco-Prussian War of 1870–71. The Treaty of Versailles also barred Germany from placing fortifications in the Rhineland. The French military had wanted to take the Rhineland from Germany and break it up into one or more republics under French suzerainty. The Rhine River was a natural defensive border; one had only to destroy the bridges to prevent a German invasion of France. With Germany deprived of this springboard for invasion, French security would be immensely improved. Recognizing that the German people would never permanently submit to the amputation of the Rhineland, which was inhabited by more than 5 million Germans and contained key industries, Wilson and British Prime Minister David Lloyd George (1863–1945) resisted these French demands. They did not want to create an Alsace-Lorraine in reverse by awarding France a region that was overwhelmingly German. Nor could Wilson ever agree to such a glaring violation of the principle of self-determination.

Faced with the opposition of Wilson and Lloyd George, Clemenceau backed down and agreed instead to Allied occupation of the Rhineland for fifteen years, the demilitarization of the region, and an Anglo-American promise of assistance if Germany attacked France in the future. This last point, considered vital by France, proved useless. The alliance went into effect only if both the United States and Britain ratified it. Since the Security Treaty did not get past the U.S. Senate, Britain also refused to sign it. France had made a great concession on the Rhineland issue but received nothing in exchange. The French people felt that they had been duped and wronged.

A related issue concerned French demands for annexation of the coal-rich Saar Basin, which adjoined Lorraine. By obtaining this region, France would weaken Germany's military potential and strengthen its own. France argued that this would be just compensation for the deliberate destruction of the French coal mines by the retreating German army at the end of the war. But here, too, France was disappointed. The final compro-

mise called for a League of Nations commission to govern the Saar Basin for fifteen years, after which the inhabitants would decide whether their territory would be ceded to France or returned to Germany.

In eastern Germany, in certain districts of Silesia that had a large Polish population, a plebiscite determined the future of the region. As a result, part of Upper Silesia was ceded to Poland. The settlement also gave Poland a corridor cut through West Prussia and terminating in the Baltic port of Danzig, and Danzig itself was declared an international city to be administered by a League of Nations commission. The Germans would never resign themselves to this loss of territory that separated East Prussia from the rest of Germany.

The victorous nations were awarded control of German and Ottoman colonies. However, these nations held the colonies not outright, but as mandates under the supervision of the League, which would protect the interests of the native peoples. Thus, the division of Ottoman and German colonies represented a compromise between traditional imperialism and Wilsonian idealism. The mandate system implied the ultimate end of colonialism, for it clearly opposed the exploitation of colonial peoples and asserted independence as the rightful goal for subject nations.

To strip Germany of any offensive capacity, the settlement abolished the German general staff and forbade military conscription in Germany. The German army was limited to a hundred thousand volunteers and deprived of heavy artillery, tanks, and warplanes. The German navy was limited to a token force, which did not include submarines.

The issue of war reparations (compensation) caused great bitterness between Wilson and his French and British adversaries. The American delegation wanted the treaty to fix a reasonable sum that Germany would have to pay and specify the period of years allotted for payment. But no such items were included; they were left for future consideration. The Treaty of Versailles left Germany with an open-ended bill, which would probably take generations to pay; nor had the Allies considered Germany's capacity to pay. Wilson had lost on the issue of reasonable reparations.

Moreover, Article 231, which preceded the reparation clauses, placed sole responsibility for the war on Germany and its allies. The Germans responded to this accusation with contempt.

In separate treaties, the conference dealt with the dissolution of the Hapsburg Empire. In the closing weeks of the war, the Austro-Hungarian Empire had crumbled as the various nationalities proclaimed their independence from Hapsburg rule. In most cases, the peacemakers ratified with treaties what the nationalities had already accomplished in fact. Serbia joined with Austro-Hungarian lands inhabited by South Slavs to become Yugoslavia. Czechoslovakia arose from the predominantly Czech and Slovak regions of Austria. Hungary, which broke away from Austria to become a separate country, had to cede considerable land to Romania and Yugoslavia. Austria had to turn over to Italy the South Tyrol, which was inhabited by 200,000 Austrian Germans. This clear violation of the principle of self-determination greatly offended liberal opinion. Deprived of its vast territories and prohibited from union with Germany, the new Austria was a third-rate power.

Assessment and Problems

The Germans unanimously denounced the Treaty of Versailles, for in their minds the war had ended not in German defeat but in a stalemate. They regarded the armistice as the prelude to a negotiated settlement among equals, based on Wilson's call for a peace of justice. Instead, the Germans were barred from participating in the negotiations. And they viewed the terms of the treaty as humiliating and vindictive—designed to keep Germany militarily and economically weak. What standard of justice, they asked, allowed the Allies to take the German colonies, reduce the German military to a pitiful size without disarming themselves, ban Germany from the League of Nations, and saddle the country with impossible reparations? Why should Germany lose approximately one-eighth of its territory and one-tenth of its population? Why should the Allies blame the war on Germany; provide for the self-determination of Poles while precluding the union of German-speakinsg Austria with Germany; hand over to Italy some 200,000 Austrian Germans; place Germans under Polish rule; and declare the German port of Danzig a free city?

The Germans protested that, when the United States entered the war, Wilson had stated that the enemy was not the German people, but their government. Surely, the Germans now argued, the new German democracy should not be punished for the sins of the monarchy and the military. To the Germans, the Treaty of Versailles was not the dawning of the new world that Wilson had promised, but an abomination—a vile crime.

War-weary, torn by revolutionary unrest, and desperately short of food, with its economy in disarray and with the Allies poised to invade, the new German Republic had no choice but to sign the treaty. However, the sentiments of the German people were clearly and prophetically expressed by the Berlin *Vorwärts*, the influential Social Democratic newspaper: "We must never forget it is only a scrap of paper. Treaties based on violence can keep their validity only so long as force exists. Do not lose hope. The resurrection day comes."[29]

Critics in other lands also condemned the treaty as a punitive settlement, warning that it would only exacerbate old hatreds and fan the flames of German nationalism. The treaty's defenders, however, insisted that had Germany won the war, it would have imposed a far harsher settlement on the Allies. They pointed to German war aims, which called for the annexation of parts of France and Poland, the reduction of Belgium and Romania to satellites, and German expansion in central Africa. They pointed also to the Treaty of Brest-Litovsk, which Germany compelled Russia to sign in 1918, as an example of Germany's ruthless appetite. An insatiable Germany gained 34 percent of Russia's population, 32 percent of its farmland, 54 percent of its industrial enterprises, and 89 percent of its coal mines. Furthermore, they noted that the peace settlement did reflect Wilson's principles: the new map of Europe was the closest approximation of the ethnic distribution of its peoples that Europe had ever known.

What is most significant about the Treaty of Versailles is that it did not solve the German problem. Germany was left weak but unbroken—its industrial and military power only temporarily contained, its nationalist fervor undiminished. The real danger in Europe was German unwillingness to accept defeat or surrender the dream of expansion.

Would France, Britain, and the United States enforce the treaty against a resurgent Germany? The war had demonstrated that an Allied victory depended on American intervention. But in 1920, the U.S. Senate, angry that Wilson had not taken Republicans with him to Paris and fearing that membership in the League of Nations would involve America in future wars, refused to ratify the Treaty of Versailles. Britain, feeling guilty over the treatment of Germany, lacked the will for enforcement and even came to favor treaty revision. The responsibility for preserving the settlement therefore rested primarily with France, which was not encouraging. The Paris peace settlement left Germany resentful but potentially powerful, and to the east lay small and weak states, some of them with sizable German minorities, that could not check a rearmed Germany.

THE WAR AND EUROPEAN CONSCIOUSNESS

"There will be wars as never before on earth," predicted Nietzsche. World War I bore him out. Modern technology enabled the combatants to kill with unprecedented efficiency; modern nationalism infused both civilians and soldiers with the determination to fight until the enemy was totally beaten. Exercising wide control over its citizens, the modern state mobilized its human, material, and spiritual resources to wage total war. As the war hardened into a savage and grueling fight, the statesmen did not press for a compromise peace but rather demanded ever more mobilization, ever more escalation, and ever more sacrifices.

The Great War profoundly altered the course of Western civilization, deepening the spiritual crisis that had produced it. How could one speak of the inviolability of the individual when Europe had become a slaughterhouse, or of the primacy of reason when nations permitted the slaughter to go unabated for four years? How could the mind cope with this spectacle of a civilization turning against itself, destroying itself in an orgy of organized violence? A young French soldier, shortly before he was killed at Verdun, expressed the disillusionment that gripped the soldiers in the trenches: "Humanity is mad! It must be mad to do what it is

doing. What a massacre! What scenes of horror and carnage, I cannot find words to translate my impressions. Hell cannot be so terrible. Men are mad!"[30] The war, said British poet Robert Graves, provoked an "inward scream" that still reverberates. Now only the naive could believe in continuous progress. Western civilization had entered an age of violence, anxiety, and doubt.

World War I was a great turning point in the history of the West. The war left many with the gnawing feeling that Western civilization had lost its vitality and was caught in a rhythm of breakdown. It seemed that Western civilization was fragile and perishable, that Western people, despite their extraordinary accomplishments, were never more than a step or two away from barbarism. Surely, any civilization that could allow such senseless slaughter to last four years had entered its decline and could look forward to only the darkest of futures.

European intellectuals were demoralized and disillusioned. The orderly, peaceful, rational world of their youth had been destroyed. The Enlightenment world-view, weakened in the nineteenth century by the assault of romantics, Social Darwinists, extreme nationalists, race mystics, and glorifiers of the irrational, was now disintegrating. The enormity of the war had shattered faith in the capacity of reason to deal with crucial social and political questions. It appeared that civilization was fighting an unending and seemingly hopeless battle against the irrational elements in human nature and that war would be a continuous phenomenon in the twentieth century.

Scientific research had produced more efficient weapons to kill and maim Europe's youth. The achievements of Western science and technology, which had been viewed as a boon for humanity and the clearest testament to the superiority of European civilization, were called into question. Confidence in the future gave way to doubt. The old beliefs in the perfectibility of humanity, the blessings of science, and ongoing progress now seemed an expression of naive optimism. As A. J. P. Taylor concludes,

The First World War was difficult to fit into the picture of a rational civilization advancing by ordered stages. The civilized men of the twentieth century had outdone in savagery the barbarians of all preceding ages, and their civ-

KÄTHE KOLLWITZ: THE SURVIVORS (1922). With an estimated ten million dead and twenty-one million wounded, World War I shattered the hope that western Europe had been making continuous progress toward a rational and enlightened civilization. (*National Gallery of Art, Washington, D.C., Rosenwald Collection © Estates of Käthe Kollwitz, VAGA, New York 1991*)

ilized virtues—organization, mechanical skill, self-sacrifice—had made war's savagery all the more terrible. Modern man had developed powers which he was not fit to use. European civilization had been weighed in the balance and found wanting.[31]

Western civilization had lost its spiritual center. The French writer Paul Valéry summed up

the mood of a troubled generation, for whom the sun seemed to be setting on the Enlightenment.

The storm has died away, and still we are restless, uneasy as if the storm were about to break. Almost all the affairs of men remain in a terrible uncertainty. We think of what has disappeared, and we are almost destroyed by what has been destroyed; we do not know what will be born, and we fear the future, not without reason. We hope vaguely, we dread precisely; our fears are infinitely more precise than our hopes; we confess that the charm of life is behind us. There is no thinking man . . . who can hope to dominate this anxiety, to escape from this impression of darkness. . . . But among all these injured things is the Mind. The Mind has indeed been cruelly wounded; its complaint is heard in the hearts of intellectual men; it passes a mournful judgment on itself. It doubts itself profoundly.[32]

This disillusionment heralded a loss of faith in liberal-democratic values that contributed to the widespread popularity of fascist ideologies in the postwar world. Having lost confidence in the power of reason to solve the problems of the human community, in liberal doctrines of individual freedom, and in the institutions of parliamentary democracy, many people turned to fascism as a simple saving faith. Far from making the world safe for democracy, as Wilson and other liberals had hoped, World War I gave rise to totalitarian movements, which would nearly destroy democracy.

The war produced a generation of young people who had reached their maturity in combat. Violence had become a way of life for millions of soldiers hardened by battle and for millions of civilians aroused by four years of propaganda. The astronomical casualty figures—some 10 million dead and 21 million wounded—had a brutalizing effect. Violence, cruelty, suffering, and even wholesale death seemed to be natural and acceptable components of human existence. The sanctity of the individual seemed to be liberal and Christian claptrap.

The fascination with violence and contempt for life persisted in the postwar world. Many returned veterans yearned for the excitement of battle and the fellowship of the trenches—what one French soldier called "the most tender human experience." After the war, a young English officer recalled: "There was an exaltation, in those days of comradeship and dedication, that would have come in few other ways."[33] A fraternal bond united the men of the trenches. But many veterans also shared a primitive attraction to war's fury. A Belgian veteran expressed it this way:

The plain truth is that if I were to obey my native animal instincts—and there was little hope for anything else while I was in the trenches—I should enlist again in any future war, or take part in any sort of fighting, merely to experience again that voluptuous thrill of the human brute who realizes his power to take away life from other human beings who try to do the same to him. What was first accepted as a moral duty became a habit and the habit . . . had become a need.[34]

The brutalizing effect of the war is evident in this statement by a German soldier, for whom the war never ended:

People told us that the War was over. That made us laugh. We ourselves are the War. Its flame burns strongly in us. It envelops our whole being and fascinates us with the enticing urge to destroy. We . . . marched onto the battlefields of the postwar world just as we had gone into battle on the Western Front: singing, reckless, and filled with the joy of adventure as we marched to the attack; silent, deadly, remorseless in battle.[35]

The Great War's veterans made ideal recruits for extremist political movements that glorified action and promised to rescue society from a decadent liberalism.

Both Hitler and Mussolini, themselves ex-soldiers imbued with the ferocity of the front, knew how to appeal to veterans. The lovers of violence and the harbingers of hate who became the leaders of fascist parties would come within a hairsbreadth of destroying Western civilization. The intensified nationalist hatreds following World War I also helped fuel the fires of World War II. The Germans vowed to regain lands lost to the Poles; some Germans dreamed of a war of revenge. Italy, too, felt aggrieved because it had not received more territory from the dismembered Austro-Hungarian Empire.

However, while the experience of the trenches led some veterans to embrace an aggressive militarism, others were determined that the horror should never be repeated. Tortured by the memory of the Great War, European intellectuals wrote pacifist plays and novels and signed pacifist declarations. In the 1930s, an attitude of "peace at any price" discouraged resistance to Nazi Germany in its bid to dominate Europe.

World War I was total war; it encompassed the entire nation and had no limits. States demanded total victory and total commitment from their citizens. They regulated industrial production, developed sophisticated propaganda techniques to strengthen morale, and exercised ever greater control over the lives of their people, organizing and disciplining them like soldiers. This total mobilization of nations' human and material resources provided a model for future dictators. With ever greater effectiveness and ruthlessness, dictators would centralize power and manipulate thinking. The first indication that the world would never be the same again, and perhaps the most important consequence of the war, was the Russian Revolution in 1917 and the Bolshevik seizure of power.

◆ ◆ ◆

NOTES

1. Arnold Toynbee, *Surviving the Future* (New York: Oxford University Press, 1971), pp. 106–107.

2. Quoted in Roland N. Stromberg, *Redemption by War* (Lawrence: The Regents Press of Kansas, 1982), p. 24.

3. Excerpted in John W. Boyer and Jan Goldstein, eds., *Twentieth Century Europe,* vol. 9 of *University of Chicago Readings in Western Civilization,* ed. John W. Boyer and Julius Kirshner (Chicago: University of Chicago Press, 1987), p. 26.

4. Heinrich von Treitschke, *Politics,* excerpted in *Germany's War Mania* (New York: Dodd, Mead, 1915), pp. 222–223.

5. Quoted in James Joll, "The Unspoken Assumptions," in *The Origins of the First World War,* H. W. Koch, ed. (New York: Taplinger, 1972), p. 325.

6. Quoted in Barbara Tuchman, *The Guns of August* (New York: Macmillan, 1962), pp. 46–47.

7. Fritz Fischer, *Germany's Aims in the First World War* (New York: Norton, 1967), p. 88.

8. Quoted in Joachim Remak, *The Origins of World War I* (New York: Holt, 1967), p. 135.

9. Rupert Brooke, "Peace," in *Collected Poems of Rupert Brooke* (New York: Dodd, Mead, 1941), p. 111.

10. Quoted in Joachim C. Fest, *Hitler* (New York: Harcourt Brace Jovanovich, 1973), p. 66.

11. Roland Dorgelàs, "After Fifty Years," excerpted in *Promise of Greatness,* ed. George A. Panichas (New York: John Day, 1968), pp. 14–15.

12. Quoted in Tuchman, *The Guns of August,* p. 145.

13. Bertrand Russell, *The Autobiography of Bertrand Russell, 1914–1944* (Boston: Little, Brown, 1951, 1956), 2:4–6.

14. Quoted in Robert G. L. Waite, *Vanguard of Nazism* (New York: Norton, 1969), p. 22.

15. Brooke, "Peace," p. 111.

16. Quoted in Peter Gay, *Freud: A Life for Our Time* (New York: Norton), p. 348.

17. Quoted in Koch, *Origins of the First World War,* p. 318.

18. Stefan Zweig, *The World of Yesterday* (New York: Viking, 1970), p. 223.

19. Quoted in Tuchman, *Guns of August,* p. 51.

20. A. J. P. Taylor, *A History of the First World War* (New York: Berkeley, 1966), p. 84.

21. Quoted in Richard M. Watt, *Dare Call It Treason* (New York: Simon & Schuster, 1963), p. 215.

22. Quoted in Daniel M. Smith, *The Great Departure* (New York: Wiley, 1965), p. 20.

23. Quoted in S. L. A. Marshall, *The American Heritage History of World War I* (New York: Dell, 1966), p. 334.

24. Quoted in John Terraine, *To Win a War: 1918, the Year of Victory* (Garden City, N.Y.: Doubleday, 1981), p. 102.

25. Excerpted in Louis L. Snyder, ed., *Historic*

Documents of World War I (Princeton: Van Nostrand, 1958), p. 183.

26. Thomas A. Bailey, *Woodrow Wilson and the Lost Peace* (Chicago: Quadrangle Books, 1963), p. 29.

27. Ibid., p. 209.

28. Hajo Holborn, *The Political Collapse of Europe* (New York: Alfred A. Knopf, 1966), p. 102.

29. Quoted in Bailey, *Woodrow Wilson*, p. 303.

30. Quoted in Alistair Horne, *The Price of Glory* (New York: Harper, 1967), p. 240.

31. A. J. P. Taylor, *From Sarajevo to Potsdam* (New York: Harcourt, Brace & World, 1966), pp. 55–56.

32. Paul Valéry, *Variety* (New York: Harcourt, Brace, 1927), pp. 27–28.

33. Quoted in Modris Eksteins, *Rites of Spring: The Great War and the Birth of the Modern Age* (New York: Doubleday Anchor Books, 1989), p. 232.

34. Quoted in Eric J. Leed, *No Man's Land: Combat & Identity in World War I* (Cambridge University Press, 1979), p. 201.

35. Quoted in Robert G. L. Waite, *Vanguard of Nazism* (New York: Norton, 1969), p. 42.

SUGGESTED READING

Albrecht-Carrie, René, *The Meaning of the First World War* (1965). How the war upset Europe's delicate equilibrium.

Bailey, Thomas, *Woodrow Wilson and the Lost Peace* (1963). A critical interpretation of the role of the United States at the peace conference.

Berghahn, V. R., *Germany and the Approach of War in 1914* (1975). Relates German foreign policy to domestic problems.

Essame, H., *The Battle for Europe, 1918* (1972). The last campaign.

Falls, Cyril, *The Great War* (1961). A good narrative of the war.

Fay, Sidney, *The Origins of the World War*, 2 vols. (1966). A comprehensive study of the underlying and immediate causes of the war; first published in 1928.

Fischer, Fritz, *Germany's Aims in the First World War* (1967). A controversial work, stressing Germany's responsibility for the war.

Fussell, Paul, *The Great War and Modern Memory* (1977). The influence of the Great War on British writers.

Gilbert, Martin, *The First World War* (1994). A recent survey; contains illuminating anecdotal material.

Geiss, Imanuel, ed., *July 1914* (1967). Selected documents.

Hale, Oron J., *The Great Illusion, 1900–1914* (1971). European thought, society, and politics just prior to World War I; a volume in the distinguished *Rise of Modern Europe* series.

Horne, Alistair, *The Price of Glory* (1967). Brilliantly recaptures the battle of Verdun.

Joll, James, *The Origins of the First World War* (1984). Excellent work of synthesis.

Koch, H. W., ed., *The Origins of the First World War* (1972). Useful essays, particularly those dealing with the glorification of war before 1914.

Lafore, Laurence, *The Long Fuse* (1971). A beautifully written study of the causes of the conflict.

Langer, W. L., *European Alliances and Alignments* (1964). Originally published in 1931, this now classic work treats the major international issues between 1871 and 1890.

Laqueur, Walter, and George Mosse, eds., *1914* (1966). A valuable collection of essays on the coming of war.

Leed, Eric J., *No Man's Land: Combat and Identity in World War I* (1979). The impact of the war on the men who participated in it.

Marshall, S. L. A., *The American Heritage History of World War I* (1966). Probably the best account available.

Panichas, George A., ed., *Promise of Greatness* (1968). Recollections of the war by people of prominence.

Remak, Joachim, *The Origins of World War I* (1967). A fine introduction.

Remarque, Erich Maria, *All Quiet on the Western Front* (1969). First published in 1929, this novel has become a classic.

Schmitt, Bernadotte, E., *The World in the Crucible, 1914–1919* (1984). The war and its aftermath. A volume in the distinguished *Rise of Modern Europe* series.

Straubing, Harold Elk, ed., *The Last Magnificent*

War (1988). Accounts of the war drawn from newspapers, magazines, and speeches.

Stromberg, Roland N., *Redemption by War: The Intellectuals and 1914* (1982). A superb analysis of the reasons that so many intellectuals welcomed the war.

Terraine, John, *To Win a War: 1918, the Year of Victory* (1981). The final compaign; contains numerous passages from primary sources.

Thomson, G. M., *The Twelve Days* (1964). An account of the twelve days preceding the outbreak of war.

Tuchman, Barbara, *The Guns of August* (1962). A beautifully written account of the opening weeks of World War I.

Watt, Richard M., *Dare Call It Treason* (1963). A brilliant study of the French army mutinies of 1917.

Williams, John, *The Other Battleground* (1972). A comparison of the home fronts in Britain, France, and Germany.

REVIEW QUESTIONS

1. How did the nationality problems in Austria-Hungary contribute to the outbreak of World War I?

2. What were the principal purposes of Bismarck's system of alliances?

3. What condition led to the formation of the Triple Entente? How did Germany respond to it?

4. After the assassination of Archduke Francis Ferdinand, what policies were pursued by Austria-Hungary, Germany, Russia?

5. Was World War I inevitable?

6. In assessing responsibility for the war, what arguments have been advanced by historians for each of the major countries involved?

7. Why did many Europeans welcome the war?

8. What battle plans did Germany and France implement in 1914? What prevented Germany from reaching Paris in 1914?

9. Identify and explain the historical significance of the battles of Verdun and the Somme.

10. Why did the United States enter the war?

11. What was Wilson's peace program? What obstacles did he face?

12. What happened to Austria-Hungary as a result of the war and the peace settlement?

13. How did World War I transform the consciousness of Europeans?

CHAPTER *30*

The Soviet Union:
Modernization
and Totalitarianism

ЛЮБИМЫЙ СТАЛИН-СЧАСТЬЕ НАРО

A fateful consequence of World War I, even before its final battles were fought, was the Russian Revolution of 1917. The Revolution occurred in two stages. In February, the tsarist regime was overthrown. The February (by the Julian calendar) revolution ushered in a period of liberal government and freedom, which soon led to a complete breakdown of law and order. Taking advantage of the chaos, hardened Marxist revolutionaries, called Bolsheviks, staged a second revolution in October and established a communist dictatorship.

The overthrow of the tsar showed that a government without mass support could not survive. The collapse of Russian liberalism in the first stage of the Revolution demonstrated the difficulty of establishing Western liberal-democratic forms of government in countries lacking a sense of unity, a strong middle class, and a tradition of responsible participation in public affairs. After World War I, liberal governments in central, eastern, and southern Europe suffered similar fates and were replaced by authoritarian regimes. European—and later, non-Western—dictators copied the Russian communists, who pioneered the first experiment of trying to match the accomplishments of the liberal democracies, including their power, with the culturally unprepared human resources inherited from tsarist times.

TSARIST AUTOCRACY

In the early nineteenth century, the Russian empire differed fundamentally from western Europe. Stretching through the Eurasian landmass from Germany to China and Japan, it covered one-sixth of the world's land surface. Yet it also suffered from incurable weaknesses. Unprotected by natural boundaries in its vast open spaces, it had been created by conquest. Its rulers lived in permanent

Soviet propaganda poster depicting Stalin, 1949. (*Sovfoto*)

CHRONOLOGY 30.1 From Russian Empire to Soviet Union

1825–1855	Reign of Nicholas I
1855	Reign of Alexander II begins
1861	Emancipation of the serfs
1870s	Rise of revolutionary movements
1881	Alexander II assassinated
1881–1894	Reign of Alexander III
1891	Trans-Siberian Railroad constructed
1892	Sergei Witte appointed minister of finance
1894	Reign of Nicholas II begins
1903–1905	Russo-Japanese War
1905	Revolution of 1905
1906	Imperial Duma established
1914	World War I breaks out
March 1917	Tsarist regime is overthrown
November 1917	Bolsheviks, led by Lenin, take command
1918–1920	Civil war and foreign intervention

dread of foreign invasion and internal breakup. Large distances, an adverse climate, and poor communications, as well as extensive ethnic, religious, and cultural diversity held together by force, made Russia a backward country compared with its western neighbors. The great movements that had shaped the outlook of the modern West—the Renaissance, the Reformation, the Scientific Revolution, the Enlightenment, and the Industrial Revolution—had barely penetrated the lands to the east.

Russia's fortunes in the nineteenth century depended on its political order, which centered more than in western Europe on the commands of the rulers. Although the tsarist government had reorganized its main institutions along the lines of Western models in the wake of the French Revolution, it took a conservative turn after Napoleon's defeat. It did so for good reason. Many returning Russian officers, asking why

Russia could not share the civilized life that they had seen in western Europe, turned revolutionary. Fear of revolution determined the character of the reign of Nicholas I (1825–1855) and of tsarist governments thereafter.

Aware of the subversive influence of foreign ideas and conditions, Nicholas I decreed an ideology of Russian superiority, called *official nationality*. The Russian people were taught to believe that the Orthodox creed of the Russian church, the autocratic rule of the tsar, and Russia's Slavic culture made the Russian Empire superior to the West. To enforce this contrived invincibility, Nicholas I created the Third Section, a secret agency of police spies, and controlled access to his country from Europe, drawing toward the end of his reign a virtual iron curtain to keep out dangerous influences. His ideal was a monolithic country, run, like an army, by a vigorous admin-

March 1918	Treaty of Brest-Litovsk
July 1918	Nicholas II and his family are murdered
March 1919	Communist International is formed
April 1920	Poland invades Russia, annexes Russian territory
November 1920	Remnants of the White Army are evacuated from the Crimean peninsula
1921–1928	New Economic Policy
1922	Stalin becomes general secretary of the Communist party
January 1924	Lenin dies
1924	Constitution of the Union of Soviet Socialist Republics takes effect
1928	First Five-Year Plan starts rapid industrialization
1929	Stalin in sole command; collectivization of agriculture begins
1936	Stalin constitution: socialism achieved
1936–38	Stalin's terror purges
June 1941	Hitler invades the Soviet Union

istration centered on the monarch; all Russians were to obey his wise and fatherly commands. But Nicholas's ambition to make Russia victorious in all comparisons with western Europe was thwarted in the Crimean War (1854–56), fought on Russian soil. English and French expeditionary forces defeated the Russian army and frustrated Russian efforts to gain political influence in the eastern Mediterranean area. Nicholas died before the war ended. A new regime began under Alexander II (1855–1881) in a mood of profound and widespread crisis. Alexander II was determined to preserve autocratic rule in Russia. However, he wanted Russia to achieve what had made western Europe strong: the energetic support and free enterprise of all its citizens. Whether stimulating popular initiative was possible without undermining autocracy was the key puzzle for him and for his successors to the end of the tsarist regime.

Alexander's boldest reforms included the emancipation of the serfs in 1861. They were liberated from bondage to the nobility and given land of their own, but not individual freedom. They remained tied to their village and to their households, which owned the land collectively. Emancipation did not transform the peasants into enterprising and loyal citizens. For the non-peasant minority, a package of other reforms brought new opportunities: limited self-government for selected rural areas and urban settlements, an independent judiciary, and the rule of law. Trial by jury was introduced, as well as a profession novel to Russians: the practice of law.

Meanwhile, Alexander reopened the borders, allowing closer ties with Europe and westernizing Russian society. The rising class of businesspeople and professional experts looked west and conformed to Western middle-class standards. There was some relaxation in the repression of non-Russian minorities. Railroads were constructed, which facilitated agricultural exports and permitted the importing of Western goods and capital. For some years, the economy boomed.

More significant in the long run was the flowering of Russian thought and literature among the intelligentsia. These were educated Russians whose minds were shaped by Western schooling and travel, yet who still were prompted by the "Russian soul" and an intensity of inward feeling unknown in Western society. They quarreled with fierce sincerity over whether Russia should pursue superiority by imitating the West or by cultivating its own Slavic genius, possibly through a Pan-Slavic movement. Pan-Slavism, which glorified the solidarity of Russians with other Slavic peoples of eastern Europe, was a popular cause. Even more than the tsars, the intelligentsia hoped for a glorious Russia that would outshine the West.

Yet tsarist autocracy undercut their hopes. The tsar would not permit open discussion likely to provoke rebellion. Liberals advocating gradual change were thwarted by censorship and the police. The 1860s saw the rise of self-righteous fanatics ready to match the chicanery of the police and foment social revolution. By the late 1870s, they organized themselves into a secret terrorist organization, and in 1881, they assassinated Alexander II. The era of reforms ended, but the revolutionary underground continued, soon led by Marxist intellectuals.

The next tsar, Alexander III (1881–1894), a firm if unimaginative ruler, returned to the principles of Nicholas I. In defense against the revolutionaries, he perfected the police state, even enlisting anti-Semitism in its cause. He updated autocracy and stifled dissent, but he also promoted economic development. Russia had relied too heavily on foreign loans and goods; it had to build up its own resources. It also needed more railroads to bind its huge empire together. So in 1891 the tsar ordered the construction of the Trans-Siberian Railroad. Soon afterward, Minister of Finance Sergei Witte used railroad expansion to boost heavy industry and industrialization generally.

In 1900, Witte addressed a farsighted memorandum to the young Nicholas II (1894–1917), who was hopelessly unprepared and out of tune with the times when he succeeded his father:

> *Russia more than any other country needs a proper economic foundation for its national policy and culture. . . . International competi-*
> *tion does not wait. If we do not take energetic and decisive measures so that in the course of the next decade our industry will be able to satisfy the needs of Russia and of the Asiatic countries which are—or should be—under our influence, then the rapidly growing foreign industries will . . . establish themselves in our fatherland and the Asiatic countries mentioned above. . . . Our economic backwardness may lead to political and cultural backwardness as well.*[1]

Forced industrialization, however, also brought perils. It propelled the country into alien and often hated ways of life, created a discontented new class of workers, and impoverished agriculture. In addition, it promoted mobility, literacy, and contact with western Europe. Thus, it helped to increase political agitation among the professional classes, intelligentsia, workers, peasants, and subject nationalities. Indispensable for national self-assertion and survival, industrialization strained the country's fragile unity.

The first jolt, the revolution of 1905, resulted from the Russo-Japanese War, in which Russia was subsequently defeated. Fortunately for the tsar, his soldiers stayed loyal. The autocracy survived, although now saddled with a parliament called the Imperial Duma, a concession to the revolution. The new regime, privately resisted by Nicholas II, started auspiciously. Russian art and literature flourished and the economy progressed. Agrarian reforms introduced the incentives of private property and individual enterprise in the villages. Nevertheless, on a deeper level, popular resentment against government-sponsored modernization festered, waiting for opportunities to explode.

The rulers of Russia between 1825 and 1914 had labored under enormous difficulties in their efforts to match the power and prestige of the great states of Europe. Two of them met a violent end: Alexander II was assassinated, and Nicholas II was murdered. The other two died in weariness and failure. Although the fear that the tsars inspired was real, their splendor was hollow. Their tragedy was that their high hopes for Russia's prominence in the world were incompatible with the reality of limited human resources, both their own and those of their peoples. This tragedy was understood neither by the liberal West nor by the tsars' critics among the intelligentsia, with whom they shared

The Tsar in Exile. Nicholas II and his children, now living in reduced circumstances, take the sun on a roof in Tobolsk, Siberia. The imperial family was later transferred to Ekaterinburg and then murdered in 1918. (*Hulton Deutsch Collection*)

the vision of a superior Russia. Their country's agony intensified as the competition for political power among nations escalated in World War I.

1917: THE YEAR OF REVOLUTIONS

The Collapse of Autocracy

Fears of revolution had long troubled foresighted Russians. In the opening years of the twentieth century, they sat, as some of them put it, on a volcano ready to erupt.

After the outbreak of war in 1914, the volcano came to life. On the German front, the Russian armies—ill equipped, poorly led, and suffering huge losses—soon began a long retreat to the east. The German government prepared plans for dismembering the Russian Empire. By 1916, the home front began to fall apart. Shops were empty, money valueless, and hunger and cold stalked the

poor quarters of cities and towns. But Tsar Nicholas II, determined to preserve autocracy, resisted any suggestion that he liberalize the regime for the sake of the war effort.

The people of Russia had initially responded to the war with a show of patriotic fervor. They Russianized the German name of their capital, Saint Petersburg, renaming it Petrograd. But by January 1917, virtually all Russians, and most of all the soldiers, were war-weary as defeat followed defeat. They had lost trust in their autocratic government: it had failed to protect the country from the enemy, and economic conditions had greatly deteriorated. Autocracy was ready to collapse at the slightest blow. In early March (February 23 by the calendar then in use*), a strike, riots in the food lines, and street demonstrations in Petrograd flared into an unpremeditated revolution. The soldiers, who in

*Until March 1918, events in Russia were dated by the Julian calendar, thirteen days behind the Gregorian calendar used in the West.

WOMEN DEMONSTRATE IN PETROGRAD, 1917. The collapse of the tsarist regime was followed by a period of political fermentation, meetings, and concern about food shortages. Women demonstrated for increased bread supplies. The poster reads, "Comrades, workers, and soldiers, support our demands!" (*VA/Sovfoto*)

1905 had stood by the tsar, now rushed to support the striking workers. The Romanov dynasty, after three hundred years of rule (1613–1917), came to an inglorious end a month before the United States entered the war "to make the world safe for democracy."

Even before the tsar had abdicated, two rival centers of government sprang up in Petrograd: first a council of soldiers and workers called the Petrograd *Soviet* (council), representing those who had fought in the streets and risked their lives; and soon afterward, a committee of various liberals afraid of revolution and the soviet. This committee claimed office as the Provisional Government—provisional until a representative Constituent Assembly (to be elected as soon as possible) could establish a permanent regime.

Thus, at the height of a disastrous war, mounting shocks mobilized the unresolved social and political tensions of many centuries, and the long-dreaded volcano erupted. Liberty came, hot and furious, to an utterly unprepared Russia, and soon reduced it to hopeless anarchy. Liberal democrats in Western countries had never suffered conditions like those that emerged in Russia.

The Problems of the Provisional Government

The collapse of autocracy was followed by what supporters in Russia and the West hoped would be a liberal-democratic regime, pledged to give Russia a constitution. In reality, however, the course of events from March to November 1917 resembled a free-for-all, a no-holds-barred fight for the succession to autocracy, with only the fittest surviving. Events also demonstrated, under conditions of exceptional popular agitation and mobility, the desperate state of the Russian Empire. Both Germany and national minorities in Russia took advantage of the anarchy to dismember the country.

Among the potential successors to the tsars,

the liberals of various shades seemed at first to enjoy the best chances. They represented the educated and forward-looking elements in Russian society that had arisen after the reforms of the 1860s: lawyers, doctors, professional people of all kinds, intellectuals, businesspeople and industrialists, many landowners, and even some bureaucrats. Their ideal was a constitutional monarchy, its leadership entrusted to the educated and propertied elite familiar with the essentials of statecraft. For them, freedom meant rule by the educated minority.

Unfortunately, the liberals acted as if conditions were normal and Russia still had a chance of winning the war. In fact, not enough steel was produced to supply both the railroads with rails and the army with artillery shells. Almost 2 million soldiers had deserted, "voting for peace with their feet," as Lenin, leader of the Bolsheviks, said; more were to be demobilized for lack of food.

The Provisional Government, representing the liberal classes, swept away the oppressive restrictions of tsarism, including discrimination on grounds of religion (notably against Jews) or nationality, and ended the death penalty. Now Russians could speak and act freely. Yet the new freedoms intensified the accumulated tensions in Russian life. As the Old Order crumbled, the Provisional Government could not create an administrative network capable of taking the place of the tsarist bureaucracy. More soviets of workers and soldiers sprang up; some villages even declared themselves independent. In the rising chaos, many liberals gave up all hope of a free Russia. As one of them said in early May, "on the day of the revolution Russia received more liberty than she could take, and the revolution has destroyed Russia. Those who made it will be cursed."[2] By July 1917, it had become clear that only brute force could uphold law and order.

In this setting, the Bolsheviks, under Lenin, were ready to try out their solution for Russia's supreme crisis: a dictatorship of the left exclusively based on the soviets, with mass support from the peasants in uniform, the peasants at the factory, and to some extent, even the peasants in the villages. Thus, the Bolsheviks, a small band of unknown but surprisingly well-prepared political soldiers, gained political power. Soon they called themselves communists.

Lenin and the Rise of Bolshevism

By the fall of 1917, revolutionary Bolshevism had a long history. Rooted in the Russian revolutionary tradition, it dated back to the early nineteenth century, when educated Russians began to compare their country with western Europe. In order to make their country modern, they, too, wanted constitutional liberty and the right to free speech and political agitation. Forbidden to speak out in public, the critics went underground, giving up their original liberalism as too pacifist and tame. Revolutionary socialism, with its idealistic vision and compassion for the masses, was a better ideology in the harsh struggle with the police. By the 1870s, many socialists had evolved into austere and self-denying professional revolutionaries, who, in the service of the cause, had no moral scruples, just as the police had no scruples in the defense of the tsars. Bank robbery, murder, assassination, treachery, and terror were not immoral if they served the revolutionary cause.

At first, the revolutionaries had staked their hopes on the Russian peasants as a progressive force capable of transforming peasant communal life into a superior socialist society. Yet already in the 1880s and 1890s, the more alert revolutionaries had learned industrial economics and sociology from Marx; from Marxism they had also acquired a vision of a universal and inevitable progression toward socialism and communism, which satisfied their semi-religious craving for salvation in this world, not the next. Marxism allied them with socialist movements in other lands, giving them an internationalist outlook. History, they believed, was on their side, as it was on the side of all the proletarians and oppressed peoples in the world. There also throbbed among all Russian revolutionaries a deep patriotic urge to end their country's inferiority. They dreamed of enabling their country to surpass the strongest Western nations in the highest ideals of human perfection drawn from Western civilization and enshrined in their socialist (or communist) vision.

By 1900, a number of able young Russians had rallied to revolutionary Marxism, almost all of them educated, and some from privileged families. The most promising was Vladimir Ilyich

V. I. LENIN. Red Army soldiers leaving for battle are addressed by Lenin in Moscow in May, 1920. Trotsky stands at the right, facing the camera. After his exile, Trotsky's image was deleted in other photographs of this scene. (*Sovfoto*)

Ulyanov, known as Lenin (1870–1924), the son of a teacher and school administrator who had attained the rank of a nobleman. Lenin had studied law, but he practiced revolution instead. His first contribution lay in adapting Marxism to Russian conditions, taking considerable liberties with the master's teaching. His second followed from the first: outlining the organization of an underground party capable of surviving against the tsarist police. It was to be a tightly knit conspiratorial elite of professional revolutionaries; its headquarters would be safely located abroad, and it would have close ties to the masses, that is,

to the workers and other potentially revolutionary elements.

To protect against police infiltration, Lenin rejected the democratic practice of Western Marxist parties. In 1902, he stated the guidelines for his revolutionary designs: "What is to a great extent automatic in a politically free country must in Russia be done deliberately and systematically by our organizations."[3] Put differently, the wealth and power achieved by voluntary civic cooperation in the Western democracies had to be achieved in the Soviet Union by compulsion under the command of the Communist party, an elite centralized dictatorial organization.

Two prominent Marxists were Leon Trotsky (1879–1940) and Joseph Stalin (1879–1953). Trotsky, whose original name was Lev Bronstein, was the son of a prosperous Jewish farmer from southern Russia and was soon known for his brilliant pen. Less prominent until after the Revolution, Stalin (the man of steel) was originally named Iosif Dzhugashvili; he was from Georgia, beyond the Caucasus Mountains. Bright enough to be sent to the best religious school in the area, he dropped out of the seminary after threatening another student with a knife and took up a revolutionary career. While they were still young, Lenin, Trotsky, and Stalin were all hardened by arrest, lengthy imprisonments, and exile to Siberia. Lenin and Trotsky later lived abroad, while Stalin, following a harsher course, stayed in Russia; for four years before 1917, he was banished to bleakest northern Siberia, and conditioned to ruthlessness for life.

In 1903, the Russian Marxists had split into two factions, the moderate Mensheviks, so named after finding themselves in a minority (*menshinstvo*) at a rather unrepresentative vote at the Second Party Congress, and the extremist Bolsheviks, who at that moment were in the majority (*bolshinstvo*). They might more accurately have been called the "softs" and the "hards." The "softs" (Mensheviks) preserved basic moral scruples; they would not stoop to crime or undemocratic methods for the sake of political success. For that the "hards" (Bolsheviks) ridiculed them, noting that a dead, imprisoned, or unsuccessful revolutionary was of little use. The "hards" were militant, radical revolutionaries who did not shrink from terrorist tactics.

Meanwhile, Lenin perfected Bolshevik revolutionary theory. He violated Marxist tradition by paying close attention to the revolutionary potential of peasants (thereby anticipating Mao Zedong). Lenin also looked closely at the numerous peoples in Asia who had recently fallen under Western imperialist domination. These peoples, he sensed, constituted a potential revolutionary force. In alliance with the Western—and Russian—proletariat, they might overthrow the worldwide capitalist order. Imperialism, he said, was caused by the giant monopolies of the Great Powers. Driven by their rivalry for profits, they had pushed their countries into colonial expansion and now into suicidal war. Lenin anticipated the anti-Western groundswell that arose from the great outpouring of European power and culture in the decades before the war; he envisioned that tide rising to a mighty world revolution. The Bolsheviks, the most militant of all revolutionary socialists, were ready to assist in that gigantic struggle.

The Bolshevik Revolution

On April 16, 1917, Lenin, with German help, arrived in Petrograd from exile in Switzerland. He asserted that the Provisional Government could not possibly preserve Russia from disintegration. Most of the soldiers, workers, and peasants would repudiate the Provisional Government's cautious liberalism in favor of a regime expressing their demand for peace and land. Nothing would stop them from avenging themselves for centuries of oppression. Lenin also felt that only complete state control of the economy could rescue the country from disaster. The sole way out, he insisted, was the "dictatorship of the proletariat," backed by the soviets of soldiers, workers, and peasants, particularly the poorer peasants.

Conditions favored Lenin, as he had predicted. The Bolsheviks obtained majorities in the soviets everywhere. The peasants were in active revolt, seizing the land themselves. The Provisional Government lost all control over the course of events.

The planning and execution of the Bolshevik coup was entrusted to Trotsky, who gloried in his role as a revolutionary leader. As a Marxist theorist, he made the overthrow of the Provisional Government into a universal model for proletarian revolutions. The coup's details were subsequently dramatized in Soviet literature and art as the grand opening of a new era. Thus dressed up, it has also impressed people in many lands. At the time, however, the Bolshevik coup was a minor event. On November 6 and 7 (October 24 and 25 by the old calendar), the Bolsheviks hardly "seized" power; rather, it fell into their laps.

The Bolsheviks quickly organized a government proclaiming "soviet democracy" but determined to establish a dictatorship. Only a dictatorship of the left, they said, had a chance of restoring government authority. The rest of the world, preoccupied with war, paid little attention. The *New York Times* on November 10 called the Bolsheviks "political children, without the slightest understanding of the vast forces they are playing with." Thus began a novel political experiment destined to change the world. Its ultimate aims were nothing less than to end class exploitation and to raise the poor and helpless peoples of backward lands to the power and wealth of Western countries.

Its immediate necessity, however, was merely to survive. The Bolshevik ascent to power in Petrograd was another step toward civil war—the real test of power for all forces eager to take the place of the tsars. The credit for Bolshevik survival belongs to Lenin.

THE BOLSHEVIKS SURVIVE

Lenin as Leader

Lenin's image was imprinted on the minds of Soviet citizens for more than half a century through eye-catching posters framed with slogans addressed to the masses. The posters depict Lenin in a dark business suit and sport cap, addressing a spellbound audience of workers and soldiers. His sweeping gestures, right arm outstretched as if to drive home his point, show him not commanding like Peter the Great, but pleading, persuading, cajoling, and sometimes threatening—a symbol to idolize. Lenin looked like a source of inexhaustible energy and confidence: he alone had grasped the opportunity for a socialist revolution; he had sustained a wavering, uncertain party and had led the advance into a totally unknown and risky future. Popular tradition endowed him with a religious aura.

Lenin pleaded that he was guiding the Russian proletariat and all humanity toward a higher social order, symbolizing—in Russia and much of the world—the rebellion of the disadvantaged against Western (or "capitalist") superiority. That is why, in 1918, he changed the name of his party from Bolshevik to Communist. For Lenin, as for Marx, a world without exploitation was humanity's noblest ideal. He matched his mission against that of Woodrow Wilson, who wanted to make the world safe for democracy. There were now two ideals of democracy: soviet style and American style. If individuals can be taken as symbols of historic turning points, Lenin counts among the most influential men of the twentieth century.

Dismemberment, Civil War, and Foreign Intervention

Staggering adversity confronted Lenin after his seizure of power. In the prevailing anarchy, Russia lay open to the German armies. Invoking the plea for national self-determination, the German government was quick to demand for its own benefit the liberation of territories held by Russia. Under the Treaty of Brest-Litovsk, signed in March 1918, the lowest point in Russian history in more than two hundred years, Russia lost Finland, Poland, and the Baltic provinces—all regions inhabited largely by non-Russians—plus the rebellious Ukraine, its chief industrial base and bread-basket. Yet Lenin had no choice but to accept the humiliating terms.

After the Treaty of Brest-Litovsk was signed, the civil war, which had been brewing since the summer of 1917, broke out in full. The anticommunist groups, generally called Whites in contrast to the communist Reds, were led by members of the old tsarist elite intent on defending their privileges. All received support from foreign governments, which freely intervened. The Germans, until their own revolution in November 1918, occupied much of southwestern Russia. England, France, and the United States sent troops to points in northern and southern Russia; England, Japan, and the United States also chan-

neled troops to Siberia. At first, they wanted to offset German expansion, but later they hoped to overthrow the Communist regime. In May and June 1918, the civil war rose to fever pitch.

In July 1918, Nicholas II and his entire family were murdered by communists. In August, a noncommunist socialist nearly assassinated Lenin, while the White forces in the south moved to cut off central Russia from its food supply. The communists, meanwhile, built up their own Red Army. Recruited from the remnants of the tsarist army and its officer corps, the Red Army was reinforced by compulsory military service and strict discipline; Trotsky reintroduced the death penalty, which had been outlawed by the Provisional Government. He also appointed political commissars to be responsible for the political reliability and morale of the troops. But the Red Army, like the armies of the Whites, lacked discipline; soldiers butchered their own comrades, as well as civilians. Their leaders, too, spared no lives to maintain control. Only the most ruthless commanders, including Trotsky and Stalin, prevailed.

The Allied victory in November 1918 and the American contribution to it ended the German menace, which would have wiped out the Russian state. Yet foreign intervention stepped up in response to the formation of the Communist International (Comintern), an organization founded in 1919 by Lenin to guide the international revolutionary movement, which he expected to issue from the world war. Lenin sought revolutionary support from abroad for strengthening his hand at home. His enemies reached into Russia to defeat at its source the revolution that they feared in their own countries.

Hard-pressed as Lenin's party was, by the autumn of 1920 it had prevailed over its enemies. The Whites were divided among themselves and discredited by their association with the tsarist regime. The Bolsheviks had greater popular support, the advantage of interior communications, and superior political skills. The last White forces, entrenched on the Crimean peninsula, were evacuated with British help in November 1920. At the same time, foreign interventionists called off their efforts.

Before winning the civil war, the communists faced a sudden invasion from Poland. After initial victories, the Red Army was routed and Lenin was forced to accept a new Polish-Russian boundary running deep inside Russian territory. By 1921, Soviet Russia had been virtually ejected from eastern Europe.

War Communism and the New Economic Policy

Despite all obstacles Lenin's party had prevailed. But the communist victory in the civil war had exacted a staggering price. Reds and Whites alike had carried the tsarist tradition of political violence to a new pitch of horror (some of it described in famous novels by Boris Pasternak and Mikhail Sholokhov). The entire population, including the Communist party and its leaders, suffered in the war. In 1921–22, a famine followed, taking still more millions of lives.

Adding to the extreme misery caused by the world war and civil war to the Russian people was the policy known as war communism. It was introduced in 1918 to deal with plummeting agricultural and economic production, rampant inflation, and desperate hunger in the cities. Under war communism the state took over the means of production and greatly limited the sphere of private ownership; it conscripted labor and, in effect, confiscated grain from the peasants. After the end of the civil war, people began to protest the harsh emergency measures. In March 1921, an uprising of sailors at the Kronstadt naval base and of workers in nearby Petrograd indicated the need for a change of course. The people who in 1917 had been ready to give their lives for the Revolution now rose against the repression that had been introduced during the civil war; they called for a restoration of soviet democracy. Trotsky ruthlessly suppressed that uprising, but the lesson was clear: the Communist regime had to retreat and restore a measure of stability to the country.

In 1921, the Communist party adopted the New Economic Policy, generally called NEP, which lasted until 1928. Under a system that Lenin characterized as "state socialism," the government retained control of finance, industry, and transportation—"the commanding heights" of the economy—but allowed the rest of the economy to return to private enterprise. The peasants, after giving part of their crops to the government, were free to sell the rest in the open market; traders could buy and sell as they pleased. With the resumption of small-scale capitalism, an air of normal life and cultural creativity returned. Key institutions of the new regime, meanwhile, established their routines.

The Communist Dictatorship

While the communists were waging a fierce struggle against the Whites, they instituted a dictatorship run by their party. Numbering about 500,000 members in 1921, the Communist party was controlled by a small, tight core of professional political leaders, often divided among themselves. This new elite's organizational skills allowed it to preserve its revolutionary drive in the face of failure, success, and internal disagreement. Those who did not pull their weight were purged.

Despite the lack of discipline in its ranks, the Communist party was more adaptable, energetic, and effective than the tsarist bureaucracy. Shaped by war, revolution, and civil war, it was also more ruthless. The savagery of the times and the backwardness of the people undermined or even destroyed the human values that Marx had channeled from the Enlightenment into his vision of the socialist society. These values, however, remained part of the faithful Communist's dream of human happiness in the new society.

For most Russians, being a good Communist was not easy. They had to be political activists, well versed in Marxism-Leninism, and they were continually admonished to observe strict party discipline, to toe the party line, and to set a model of communist dedication in every job they held. But reality was somewhat different. Especially in the lower ranks, sloppiness, corruption, and abuse of authority spoiled the high ideals.

The top leaders, however, were superior to tsarist officials. They combined a long experience of working with the masses and a fierce patriotic ambition to rescue their country from defeat and backwardness. They were inexperienced in statecraft, but they were ready to learn and explosively energetic.

Under its constitution, the "Russian Communist Party (Bolshevik)" was a democratic body. However, under the pressure of the civil war, power soon shifted to a smaller and more intimate group, the *politburo* (political bureau). There the leaders, Lenin, Trotsky, Stalin, and a few others, determined policy, assigned tasks, and appointed key officials. In the face of continuing crises, however, individual leaders like Lenin, or later Stalin, dominated their associates. And as the party grew, so did the need for centralization and bureaucratic organization; the higher echelons controlled the lower.

The party, in turn, dominated all public agencies; its key leaders held the chief positions in government. No other political parties were tolerated, and trade unions became agents of the regime. Never before had the people of Russia been so dominated by government. In attempting to transform their Soviet Russia into a modern industrialized state that would serve as a model for the world, the Bolsheviks imposed a new autocracy even more authoritarian than the old. They decided that Russia must be rebuilt on an uncongenial design adapted from the West and that this would be accomplished against the people's will, if necessary. In the view of the party leaders, the masses always needed firm guidance.

It was with the help of the Communist party, then, that Lenin from the start imposed his communist dictatorship, not shrinking from the use of terror. Already in November 1917, the Communists had set up an Extraordinary Commission (called the *Cheka*) to ferret out all counter-revolutionary activity. Staffed by hardened revolutionaries, it engaged in extreme terror not only against enemies of the regime, but also against the population at large. The Cheka founded the forced-labor camps that became notorious under Stalin's regime.

As former victims of tsarist repression, the Communists felt no moral objection to the use of stark terror. As Lenin admonished his followers, "cleanse the land of Russia of all sorts of harmful insects, of crook-fleas, and bedbugs," by which he meant "the rich, the rogues, and the idlers." He even suggested that "one out of every ten idlers be shot on the spot."[4] Those not shot found themselves, with Lenin's blessings, in the Cheka's forced-labor camps.

The Communists also made sure of continued popular support. Out of respect for the ideal of self-determination, the Communists held out hope for cultural and administrative autonomy among non-Russian minorities. At the same time, they pleased Russian nationalists by forcibly incorporating most of those non-Russian national groups that had tried to escape from the empire. By warding off foreign intervention, the Communists also claimed credit for defending Mother Russia.

The Communists abolished the power of the Orthodox church, the traditional ally of tsarism and the enemy of innovation. They were militant atheists, believing with Marx that religion was the "opium of the people"; God had no place in their vision for a better society. Yet the Orthodox church and other religions survived, much reduced in influence and closely watched, an enduring target for atheist propaganda.

The Communists also simplified the alphabet, changed the calendar to the Gregorian system prevailing in the capitalist West, and brought theater and all arts, hitherto reserved for the elite, to the masses. Above all, they wiped out—by expropriation, discrimination, expulsion, and execution—the educated upper class of bureaucrats, landowners, professional people, and industrialists. Their Russia was more than ever a country of backward peasants.

Shaping Soviet Society

The Russia of the Communists was "Soviet" Russia. It was the first regime in Russian history to base its legitimacy on the toiling masses. It spoke their rough language and expressed their crude sense of social justice, with some innovations dear to Western radicals.

The Communists' constituency, significantly, comprised both men and women. The party promised "to liberate woman from all the burdens of antiquated methods of housekeeping, by replacing them by house-communes, public kitchens, central laundries, nurseries, etc."[5] But traditional values, particularly in the Asian parts of the Soviet Union, hardly favored equality between the sexes, especially in political work. The practical necessity of combining work with family responsibility, moreover, tended to keep women out of managerial positions in the party and the organizations of the state, but the ideal remained alive.

The Bolsheviks derived much acclaim from their emphasis on redistributing housing, food,

FORGING SOCIALISM. Men and women work equally in this socialist realist propaganda poster from 1921. The caption reads, "By our weapons we routed the enemy. By our efforts we obtain bread. Let's get to work, comrades!" (*From* Art of the October Revolution, *Mikail Guerman (Aurora Publishers, Leningrad). Reproduced by permission of V/O Vneshtorgizdat.*)

and clothing and making education available to the masses. They were not opposed to some private property; they allowed items for personal use, provided they were in keeping with the standards of the common people. But they outlawed income-producing private property that enabled capitalists to employ (or exploit, as the Communists said) others for their own profit. With the disappearance of private enterprise, the state gradually became the sole employer, thereby forcibly integrating the individual into the reconstruction of the country. Socialism promised a far more intense mobilization of the country than a system based on private property. The Bolsheviks never ceased to stress that they worked strenuously for the welfare of the vast majority of the population. But they were also pledged to reeducate the masses to a higher standard of individual conduct and eco-

nomic productivity, which would be superior to capitalism. In the spring of 1918, Lenin argued that the Russian workers had not yet matched capitalist performance: "The Russian worker is a bad worker compared with the workers of the advanced, i.e., western countries." To overcome this fatal handicap, he urged competition—socialist competition—and relentlessly hammered home the need for "iron discipline at work" and "unquestioning obedience" to a single will, that of the Communist party. There was no alternative: "Large-scale machinery calls for absolute and strict unity of will, which directs the joint labors of hundreds and thousands and tens of thousands of people. A thousand wills are subordinated to one will."[6] In these words lay the essence of subsequent Soviet state-imposed industrialization.

The minds of the people, therefore, came under unprecedented government control. In education from the kindergarten through the university, in press and radio, and in literature and the arts, the Communist party tried to fashion people's thoughts to create the proper "consciousness." The party made Marxism-Leninism the sole source of inspiration, eliminating as best it could all rival creeds, whether religious, political, or philosophical. Minds were to be as reliably uniform as machine processes and totally committed to the party, as well as to the new Soviet Union.

Soviet patriotism was always a prime concern of ideological indoctrination. The Communists were determined to strengthen the unity of the Russian multinational empire, which the Revolution had endangered. They propagated Marxism-Leninism as a universal creed. All proletarians, they argued, shared a common class bond transcending ethnic and national differences. Proceeding from this assumption, the party promulgated in 1924 the first Soviet constitution, creating the Union of Soviet Socialist Republics (U.S.S.R.). Rallying patriotic pride, party leaders boasted that by its new constitution the country demonstrated its advanced level of social existence; it would attract other soviet socialist states, until eventually it would provide peace to the entire world through "the pacific co-existence and fraternal collaboration of peoples."[7] To prevent Soviet citizens from doubting their new superiority, the party prohibited all uncontrolled comparison with capitalist countries.

An Ideology for World Revolution

In foreign policy, Lenin was far bolder than any tsar: he turned Russian state ambition into an international revolutionary force.

The Russian Revolution deeply touched hitherto suppressed nationalistic ambitions for political self-determination and cultural self-assertion among a growing number of peoples around the world, especially in Asia. It appealed particularly to intellectuals who were educated in the West (or in westernized schools), yet who identified themselves with their downtrodden compatriots. Taught to worship the ideals of the French Revolution—liberty, equality, and fraternity—they noted that the Europeans (or white people everywhere) did not apply these ideals to people of different cultures and colors (if indeed they applied them among themselves). These intellectuals were determined to turn these ideals to their own advantage, if necessary by revolution. Like Lenin, they were of a divided mind: they favored self-determination for their own people, yet they also were eager to make their countries and cultures modern, that is, to reshape them after the Western model. These patriots included moderates like Gandhi and Nehru in India, who soon repudiated Lenin, and radicals like Ho Chi Minh in Vietnam, and Zhou Enlai and Mao Zedong in China, who became his disciples. Lenin made himself the spokesman for the rising anti-Western tide, soliciting support for the common aim of unhinging the capitalist world order based on Western superiority.

As a political tool for this purpose, Lenin created the Communist—or Third—International (Comintern). The most radical successor to earlier socialist international associations, it helped raise small Communist parties in western Europe which, in time, became dependable, although rather powerless, agents of Soviet Russia. In Asia, where no proletariat existed, Lenin tried to work closely with incipient nationalist movements and even envisaged setting up peasant soviets. He also held out the possibility that backward countries might skip the hated capitalist phase altogether, provided they allied themselves with the "leading socialist country," namely the Soviet Union. It was soon clear that the anti-Western agitation of the twentieth century would not follow the path of world revolution predicted by Lenin. Yet Lenin and the Bolshevik Revolution inspired admiration and instinctive loyalty among the colonial and semicolonial peoples in what would come to be called the Third World. The Communist experiment retained its global appeal until it collapsed in 1991.

Lenin contributed to a novel division in the world. In the uncertain times following World War I, the specter of world revolution created extravagant hopes and fears. Some people believed in the communist vision; others were thrown into a panic by it. The spread of communism was more than matched in western and central Europe, and in the Americas as well, by a vigorous anticommunism, which, in turn, contributed to the rise of right-wing, or fascist, movements. Propertied and patriotic men and women had good reason to be scared; world revolution threatened their sense of security, their religion, their very sanity. World opinion became polarized: fear of communism became an obsession in the West, as did the fear of capitalism in Russia and many poor countries around the world.

World revolution, however, was never a realistic prospect. The tide of Western ascendancy was running strong. Moreover, the Comintern was never a truly international force; it remained a tool of the Russian Communist party. But the fear it aroused served Lenin well: it made Soviet Russia appear strong when in fact the country was exhausted. At very little cost, the Comintern put prestige-conscious Russia back on the map of world politics. Having captured the attention of the world, Soviet Russia now stood out as the communist alternative to the capitalist West, rejecting the West and yet following it. Like the Western countries, the U.S.S.R. believed in industrial progress. Like them, it wanted to feel superior, above all in its vision of the future: a vision embedded in an unprecedented, risky experiment in social engineering, which inspired much imitation in countries trying to escape Western domination.

THE STALIN REVOLUTION

Stalin's Rise to Power

Lenin died in January 1924 and was subsequently idolized as the sacred icon of Soviet ideals. The task of achieving the goals that Lenin had set was taken up by Stalin. The "man of steel" was crude and vulgar, toughened by the revolutionary underground and tsarist prisons and by the roughest aspects of Russian life. Nobody in 1917 foresaw that this high-ranking Bolshevik would succeed the university-trained, cosmopolitan Lenin. Relentlessly energetic, but relatively inconspicuous among the more temperamental and intellectual key Bolsheviks, Stalin was given, in 1922, the unwanted and seemingly routine task of general secretary of the party. It became his responsibility, in the chaotic aftermath of the Revolution and the civil war, to give reality to the Leninist vision of the monolithic party as the ultimate guaranty of effective government in this vast multinational state.

Stalin did so to his own advantage, building up a reliable party cadre—apparatus men, or *apparatchiki,* as they came to be called—and dominating the party as not even Lenin had done. When in the protracted struggles for the succession to Lenin, he was challenged, particularly by Trotsky and his associates, it was too late to unseat him. None of Stalin's rivals could rally the necessary majorities at the party congresses. Although equally ruthless, none could match Stalin's drive and skill in party infighting or in making rough and anarchic people into docile members of the Communist party apparatus.

Like Lenin, Stalin was best known from his poster image. Soviet citizens saw him as an energetic man clad in a simple military tunic, devoid of show or pomp, a fatherly figure, a conciliatory chairman inspiring a sense of bureaucratic control suitable to the industrial era. Yet the image was a facade. Behind it lay a coarse, vindictive, impatient temperament, shaped in preindustrial Russia and surcharged with the furies of a lost war, a victorious revolution, and a protracted civil war. He represented a brutalized raw society rebelling against authority and wanting to rise to prosperity and glory. The real Stalin was an appalling mixture of contradictory qualities, raised to superhuman proportions by his dictatorial powers over a vast backward country, which had barely survived World War I.

Modernizing Soviet Russia

To Stalin, Russia's most pressing need was not world revolution but the fastest possible buildup of Soviet power through industrialization. The country could not afford to risk near-annihilation again, as it had done in the war and then in the civil war. Bolshevik pride dictated that the country be made strong as much as possible by Russian efforts. Stalin's slogan was "socialism in one country," which signified that Soviet Russia by itself possessed all the necessary resources for "surpassing and overtaking" capitalism in the shortest time possible. It was a staggering job.

Stalin decided on all-out industrialization at the expense of the toiling masses. Peasants and workers, already poor, would be required to make tremendous sacrifices of body and spirit to overcome the nation's weaknesses. The Bolshevik Revolution had cleared the way for decisive action. Dependent on and controlled by their government as never before, the Russian people could offer little resistance.

Stalin disbanded the NEP and decreed a series of Five-Year Plans, the first and most experimental one commencing in 1928. The industrialization drive was heralded as a vast economic and social revolution, undertaken by the state on a rational plan. The emphasis lay on heavy industry, the construction of railroads, power plants, steel mills, and military hardware like tanks and warplanes. Production of consumer goods was cut down to the minimum. All small-scale private trading, revived under the NEP, came to an end; the state shops and cooperatives were bare, and the service in them poor. Having just come within sight of their pre-1914 standard of living, Russians now found their expectations dashed for decades.

Thus, a new grim age began, with drastic material hardships and profound mental anguish. Few Soviet citizens understood the necessity of rigid central planning, but in the early years, young people particularly were fired to heroic exertions. They were proud to sacrifice themselves for the building of a superior society. When the Great Depression in the capitalist countries put millions out of work, no Soviet citizen suffered from unemployment; gloom pervaded the West, but confidence and hope, artificially fostered by the party, buoyed up Soviet Russia. Because of flaws stemming from lack of experience, the first Five-Year Plan had to be scrapped before running its course. Subsequent Five-Year Plans, however, gradually improved the quality of planning, as well as of production. At no time, though, did

LEON TROTSKY

Born in 1879, Lev Davidovich Bronstein was the son of a prosperous Jewish farmer in the Ukraine, drawn into the Russian revolutionary movement when still in his teens. From jail and Siberian banishment, he escaped, under the name of Leon Trotsky, to London. There, with Lenin's help, he turned into a gifted journalist and Marxist theorist, mapping the future as a worldwide permanent revolution.

After long years of exile in western Europe, his hour of glory struck when he returned to Russia after the collapse of the tsarist regime in World War I. In the fall of 1917 his intuitive sense of the public mood and his rhetorical brilliance made him the architect of the Bolshevik seizure of power in

the planning produce Western-style industrial efficiency.

Forced Collectivization

The revolution in Soviet agriculture was far more brutal, for the peasants had to be forcibly integrated into the planned economy through collectivization. Agriculture—the peasants, their animals, and their fields—had to submit to the same controls as industry. Collectivization meant the pooling of farmlands, animals, and equipment for the sake of more efficient large-scale production. The Bolshevik solution for the backwardness of Russian agriculture had long been that the peasants should become like workers. But knowing the peasants' distaste for the factory, their attachment to their own land, and their stubbornness, the party had hesitated to carry out its ambitious plans. In 1929, however, Stalin believed that, for the sake of industrialization, he had no choice. If the Five-Year Plan were to suc-

ceed, the government had to receive planned crops of planned size and quality at planned times. With collectivization, the ascendancy of the party over the people of Russia became almost complete.

The peasants paid a frightful price. Stalin declared war on the Russian countryside. The *kulaks* (the most enterprising and well-to-do peasants) were sent to forced-labor camps or killed outright. Their poorer and less efficient neighbors were herded onto collective farms at the point of a bayonet. The peasants struck back, sometimes in pitched battles. The horror of forced collectivization broke the spirit even of hardened officials. "I am an old Bolshevik," sobbed a secret police colonel to a fellow passenger on a train; "I worked in the underground against the Tsar and then I fought in the civil war. Did I do all that in order that I should now surround villages with machineguns and order my men to fire indiscriminately into crowds of peasants? Oh, no, no!"[8]

Defeated but unwilling to surrender their livestock, the peasants slaughtered their animals,

Petrograd. In the subsequent civil war he created the Red Army, prodding it to victory by his fierce rhetoric and ruthless brutality.

Beaten by Stalin in the struggle for power following Lenin's death in 1924, Trotsky was dropped from the politburo in 1926, expelled from the Communist party in 1927, and banished from the Soviet Union in 1929. A feared Marxist revolutionary, he was driven from Turkey to France, Norway, and finally Mexico, all the while writing books and articles on the Russian Revolution and the rise of fascism. A bitter foe of Stalin's totalitarianism, he was assassinated on Stalin's orders in 1940. For many Marxists, Trotsky died a widely admired martyr for a utopian vision.

gorging themselves in drunken orgies against the days of inevitable famine. The country's cattle herds declined to one-half, inflicting irreparable secondary losses as well. The number of horses, crucial for rural transport and farm work, fell by one-third. Crops were not planted or not harvested, the Five-Year Plan was disrupted, and in the period from 1931 to 1933 millions starved to death.

The suffering was most cruel in the Ukraine, where famine killed approximately 7 million people, many after extreme abuse and persecution.[9] For the sake of buying industrial equipment abroad so that industrialization could proceed on target, the Soviet Union had to export food, as much of it as possible and for prices disastrously lowered by the Great Depression. Let the peasants in the Ukrainian breadbasket perish so that the country could grow strong! Moreover, Stalin relished the opportunity to punish the Ukrainians for their disloyalty during the civil war and their resistance to collectivization. Typically, the local officials and activists who stripped the peasants

of their possessions and searched for hidden grain viewed themselves as idealists building a new society; they infused their own ruthlessness into the official orders. Their dedication to the triumph of communism overcame all doubts caused by the sight of starving people and the sounds of wailing women and children.

By 1935, practically all farming in Russia was collectivized. In theory, the collective farms were run democratically, under an elected chairman; in practice, the peasants followed, as best they could, the directives handed down from the nearest party office. People grumbled about the rise of a new serfdom; agricultural development had been stifled. Nevertheless, Stalin had reason to rejoice as he counted the results of collectivization: the kulaks had been wiped out as a class, and the peasants, ever rebellious under the tsars, had been cowed into permanent submission.

Total Control

To quash resistance and mold a new type of citizen, who would be motivated and disciplined, Stalin unleashed a third revolution, the revolution of totalitarianism. He followed Lenin's advice: the wealth and power achieved by voluntary civic cooperation in the Western democracies had to be achieved in the Soviet Union by systematic compulsion under the command of the Communist party. The aim was a total reconstruction of state and society, down to the innermost recesses of human consciousness. Stalin called for "a new man" suited to the needs of Soviet industrialism. Society was reshaped for the utmost productivity. In the process, the hallowed revolutionary ideal of equality was abandoned.

Soviet citizens had to work as hard as they could, with the rewards going to those who made special contributions toward plan fulfillment, to engineers, scientists, managers, and certain heroes of labor, like the famous miner Stakhanov, who set artificially inflated records of output. Workers were paid piece wages; the trade unions henceforth became tools of the state, enforcing work discipline. A new elite of party-trained industrial managers came into being. In addition, family discipline and sexual mores, which had become lax after the Revolution, were tightened by decree into a new work-oriented ethic.

In 1935, Stalin, summing up these changes, officially declared that socialism had been achieved in

BUILDING INDUSTRY IN RUSSIA. Foundations were dug by hand for the huge industrial complex at Magnitogorsk in 1934. This was part of Stalin's plan to transform Russia into an advanced, industrialized country. The *kulaks*, well-to-do peasant men and women who had been condemned to hard labor, bore the brunt of the work. (*TASS/Sovfoto*)

the Soviet Union. Extending the number of union republics to eleven, the Soviet Constitution of 1936 set forth major institutions and principles guiding the new society, often in terms reminiscent of Western constitutions. But the wording left no doubt about what was expected of Soviet citizens. They must "abide by the Constitution, observe the laws, maintain labor discipline, honestly perform public duties, respect the rules of socialist intercourse, and safeguard and strengthen public property" (theft of state property was a widespread practice). All offenders were called "enemies of the people" and threatened with dire punishment. The list of duties ended with the words "treason is the most heinous of crimes. The defense of the Fatherland is the most sacred duty of every citizen"—ominous words indeed.

The revolution of totalitarianism extended even further. All media of communications—literature, the arts, music, the stage—were forced into subservience to the Five-Year Plan and So-

viet ideology. In literature, as in all art, an official style was promulgated, called *socialist realism*. It aimed at describing the world as the party hoped to shape it.

Novels in the socialist realist manner told how the romances of tractor drivers and milkmaids, or of lathe operators and office secretaries, led to new victories of production under the Five-Year Plan. Composers found their music examined for remnants of bourgeois spirit; they were to write simple tunes suitable for heroic times. Everywhere, huge, high-color posters showed men and women hard at work, with radiant faces, calling others to join them; often Stalin, the wise father and leader, was shown taking the salute among them. In this manner, artistic creativity was locked into a utilitarian straitjacket of official cheerfulness; creativity was allowed only to boost industrial productivity. Behind the scenes, all artists were disciplined to conform to the will of the party or be crushed.

Education, from nursery school to university, was likewise harnessed to train dutiful and loyal citizens. Said one text on Soviet pedagogy:

> *We must cultivate in our children the realization that the Union of Soviet Socialist Republics is a land where a socialist society is being constructed for the first time in history. We must develop in them a feeling of pride in the most revolutionary class, the working class, and in its vanguard, the Communist Party. This party, the party of Lenin and Stalin, was able to organize the toiling masses for the construction of a new communist society. Through the victories of the Stalin five-year plans, our land was transformed into a mighty industrial country, the most advanced and most cultured. We must make every school child aware of the grandeur of our struggle and our victories; we must show him the cost of these great successes in labor and blood; we must tell him how the great people of our epoch—Lenin, Stalin, and their companions in arms—organized the workers in the struggle for a new and happy life.*[10]

Endeavoring to rally all Soviet people for that heroic struggle, Stalin gave communist political education a personal twist. He mobilized popular habits of hero worship, creating an image of himself as "The Greatest Genius of All Times and Peoples." Personal allegiance to a great man still counted as a political force among common folk; under Stalin, who in private remained rather modest, it became a tool of social engineering, part of his revolution of modernization. Projecting a superior leader as a symbol of unity and common purpose helped to overcome deep-seated doubts and divisions among the people. Never before had the glorification of a political figure (denounced by Stalin's successors as "the cult of personality") been carried to such extremes.

Stalin's Terror

Indoctrination alone could not overcome the resistance of the Russian masses to large scale and rigidly enforced regimentation required for rapid industrialization. Against that ingrained resistance, fostered by tradition, Stalin unleashed raw terror to break stubborn wills and compel conformity. Terror had been used as a tool of government ever since the Revolution (the tsars had also used it, moderately and intermittently). After the start of the first Five-Year Plan, show trials were staged, denouncing as saboteurs the engineers who found Stalin's too rapid tempo a hindrance to efficiency. The terror used to herd the peasants onto collective farms was of a larger scale. Stalin also used terror to crush opposition and to instill an abject fear not only in the ranks of the party, but also in Russian society at large. Through terror, society had to be purged of all resistance to Stalin's policies and all threats to his power.

Purges had long been used to rid the party of weaklings. After 1934, however, the purges became an instrument of Stalin's drive for unchallenged personal power. A party congress in that year had expressed doubts about Stalin's brutality in dealing with the peasants; it advanced a potential rival, Sergei Kirov. Soon afterward, Kirov was murdered at Stalin's request. In 1936, Stalin's vindictive terror broke into the open. The first batch of victims, including many founders of the Communist party, was accused of conspiring with the exiled Trotsky to set up a "terrorist center" and of scheming to terrorize the party; they were blamed for the murder of Kirov. The world watched the great show trials with amazement and horror as Stalin intimidated his people. After being sentenced to death, the first group was immediately executed. In 1937, the next group, including prominent communists of Lenin's day, was charged with cooperating with foreign intelligence agencies and wrecking "socialist reconstruction," the term for Stalin's revolution; they, too, were executed. Shortly afterward, a secret purge wiped out the military high command, leaving the Soviet army without leadership for years.

In 1938, the last and biggest show trial advanced the most monstrous accusation of all: sabotage, espionage, and attempting to dismember the Soviet Union and kill all its leaders (including Lenin in 1918). In the public hearings, some defendants refuted the public prosecutor, but in the end, all confessed before being executed.

The great trials, however, involved only a small minority of Stalin's victims; many more perished in silence. The terror first hit members of the party, especially the Old Bolsheviks, who had joined before the Revolution; they were the

MAP 30.1 The Union Republics of the U.S.S.R.

most independent-minded members and therefore the most dangerous to Stalin. But Stalin also diminished the cultural elite that had survived the Lenin revolution. Thousands of engineers, scientists, industrial managers, scholars, and artists disappeared; they were shot or sent to forced-labor camps, where most of them perished. No one was safe. To frighten the common people in all walks of life, men, women, and even children were dragged into the net of Stalin's secret police, leaving the survivors with a soul-killing reminder: submit or else.

The Human Price

The toll of the purges is reckoned in millions; it included Trotsky, who in 1940 was murdered in Mexico. The bloodletting was ghastly, as Stalin's purge officials themselves followed each other into death and ignominy.

The human price that Soviet Russia paid for Stalin's effort to wipe out his country's inferiority has been documented by the great Russian writer Aleksandr Solzhenitsyn in his work *The Gulag Archipelago.* Yet by Solzhenitsyn's own testimony, the responsibility for the atrocities was not Stalin's alone; the "wolfishness" of the terror flowed from Russian life itself. Speaking of the torturers, the "Blue Caps" who interrogated and often killed innocent victims of the terror, Solzhenitsyn asks: "Where did this wolf-tribe appear from among our people? Does it really stem from our own roots? Our own blood?" Devastatingly, he answers: "It is our own."[11]

Stalin, who had passed through the hands of the tsarist police and had participated in the carnage of the civil war, was untroubled by the waste of life. He believed that without the total obedience of the Russian people, the Soviet economy could not be effectively and quickly mobilized and that terror was necessary to compel compliance. By showing party officials and the Russian masses how vulnerable they were, how dependent on his will, Stalin intended to frighten them into servility. No doubt, the terror was also an expression of Stalin's sickly suspicious and vengeful nature. He saw enemies everywhere, took pleasure in selecting victims, and reveled in the show of his omnipotence. But because of inefficiency and disagreements within the government, his power was never as complete as it was advertised.

In foreign, even more than in internal, affairs, Stalin's policy was marked by fear; the danger of war was always uppermost in his mind. It was to Soviet advantage to make a show of strength, but underneath this facade Stalin pursued a conservative policy, husbanding Russia's resources for internal reconstruction and hoping that the capitalist states would fall out among themselves, allowing him to play the happy bystander and enter the fray for the kill after they had totally weakened each other. Stalin did not follow up Lenin's teaching about world revolution. He realized that the key to the future of Soviet communism lay in the power of the Soviet Union and that its power was never sufficient amid the dangers it confronted in the world. His personal sense of insecurity reflected the persistent insecurity of his country. By the end of the 1930s, after the Stalin revolution, yet another era of profound and cruel perils began for his country: World War II and the battle with Nazi Germany. If Hitler had won that war, the human devastation in Russian lands would have been infinitely worse than the suffering caused by Stalin's brutish efforts to prevent such a catastrophe.

STALINISM IN PERSPECTIVE

The Stalinist experiment profoundly excited opinion everywhere. Some Marxists saw their ideals realized; others felt that Stalin had betrayed the cause of socialism. But most westerners were appalled by Soviet totalitarianism, although, for profit or political expediency, some came to terms with the regime. For instance, in the face of the Great Depression and Japanese expansion, the United States officially recognized the Soviet Union in 1933. The purges disenchanted many early communist sympathizers. George Orwell in revulsion wrote *Animal Farm* and *1984,* and Arthur Koestler described prison experience in *Darkness at Noon.* In the countries of Asia, on the other hand, the progress of the Five-Year Plans was watched with envy and admiration: if Russia could raise itself by its bootstraps, could not others follow its example?

Stalin left no doubt about the ultimate justification for his policy. In 1931, bluntly disregarding Marxist-Leninist jargon and forgetting about Russian expansion into Asia, he said:

> *Those who fall behind get beaten. But we do not want to be beaten. No, we refuse to be beaten. One feature of the history of old Russia was the continual beatings she suffered for falling behind, for her backwardness. All beat her—for her backwardness, for military backwardness, cultural backwardness, political backwardness, for industrial backwardness, for agricultural backwardness. She was beaten because to do so was profitable and could be done with impunity. . . . You are backward, you are weak—therefore you are wrong, hence you can be beaten and enslaved. You are mighty, therefore you are right, hence we must be wary of you. Such is the law of the exploiters. . . . That is why we must no longer lag behind.[12]*

He set forth the stark reckoning of Russian history: the cost of foreign enslavement against the costs of a terror-driven mobilization; the dream of a Russia liberated from inferiority against the human price of totalitarianism.

Modernizing the peoples in the vast lands of Russia was bound to be an unprecedented and extremely cruel experiment of social engineering. After the humiliating collapse of the Russian empire in 1917, Lenin and Stalin were determined, with the help of Marxism, to rebuild the country as quickly as possible according to the Western model. Soviet industrialization took its lead from Western urban-industrial society. Stalin's constitution imitated Western constitutional language. Communist totalitarianism tried to copy the Western skills of spontaneous social cooperation. And most significantly, Soviet global ambition was designed to challenge Western domination of the world.

But catching up to the West was to be accomplished by utterly un-Western methods of regimentation, compulsion, and terror. The bitterness of the revolutionary movement, the battles of World War I, the excitements of the Revolution, and the passions of the civil war had not only shaped Stalin's ruthlessness, but also intensified the anarchic backwardness of the masses he tried to transform. The Communist party had to modernize the peoples of the Soviet Union against their deepest instincts, following a political tradition that had never respected human rights and always called for dictatorial power. These factors produced the totalitarian state and the gulags, or forced-labor prison camps.

Yet there were also positive aspects. Material welfare, literacy, and education improved; personal conduct became more socially aware. Above all, Stalin laid the foundations for the rise of the Soviet Union as a superpower, more secure and respected in the world than any previous Russian regime. The threat of being "beaten and enslaved" because of backwardness had been overcome—but at a stupendous human price. Yet in the wide-open Eurasian landmass, the collective security of the state, Stalin believed, necessarily took precedence over individual rights.

◆ ◆ ◆

Notes

1. Theodore H. Von Laue, *Sergei Witte and the Industrialization of Russia* (New York: Columbia University Press, 1963), p. 3.

2. V. A. Maklakov, quoted in *The Russian Provisional Government 1917*, vol. 3, documents selected and edited by Robert Paul Browder and Aleksandr F. Kerensky (Stanford, Calif.: Stanford University Press, 1961), p. 1276.

3. V. I. Lenin, "What Is to Be Done," in *The Lenin Anthology,* ed. Robert C. Tucker (New York: Norton, 1975), p. 83.

4. V. I. Lenin, "On Revolutionary Violence and Terror," in *Lenin Anthology,* p. 432.

5. "All-Russian Communist Party (Bolsheviks), 1919," in *Soviet Communism: Programs and Rules. Official Texts of 1919, 1952, (1956), 1961,* ed. Jan F. Triska (San Francisco: Chandler, 1962), p. 23.

6. V. I. Lenin, "The Immediate Tasks of the Soviet Government," in *Lenin Anthology,* pp. 448ff.

7. "Constitution of the Union of Soviet Socialist Republics, Part I: Declaration," in *A Documentary History of Communism,* ed. Robert V. Daniels (New York: Random House, 1960), 1:249.

8. Quoted in Isaac Deutscher, *Stalin: A Political Biography* (New York: Oxford University Press, 1966), p. 325.

9. Robert Conquest, *The Harvest of Sorrow: Soviet Collectivization and the Terror-Famine* (New York: Oxford University Press, 1986), p. 304.

10. "I Want to Be Like Stalin," from the *Russian Text on Pedagogy* by B. P. Yesipov and N. K. Goncharov, trans. George S. Counts and Nucia P. Lodge, with an introduction by George S. Counts (New York: John Day, 1947), pp. 36–37.

11. Aleksandr I. Solzhenitsyn, *The Gulag Archipelago,* vol. 1 (New York: Harper & Row, 1974), p. 160.

12. J. V. Stalin, "Speech to Business Executives" (1931), in *Documentary History of Communism,* 2:22.

Suggested Reading

Cohen, Stephen, *Bukharin and the Bolshevik Revolution* (1980). Argues that there existed more moderate alternatives to Stalin's policies.

Conquest, Robert, *The Harvest of Sorrow: Soviet Collectivization and the Terror-Famine* (1986). The human consequences of collectivization.

Deutscher, Isaac, *Trotsky: 1879–1940,* 3 vols., *The Prophet Armed* (1954), *The Prophet Unarmed* (1959), *The Prophet Outcast* (1963). The classic work on Trotsky.

Fitzpatrick, Sheila, *The Russian Revolution, 1917–1932* (1982). A good account of the political and social contexts of the Revolution.

Ginzburg, Eugenia, *Journey into the Whirlwind* (1967). A woman's experiences under the terror.

Laqueur, Walter, *Stalin: the Glasnost Revelations* (1990). Effects of the truth about Stalin on the Soviet people.

Mandelstam, Nadezhda, *Hope Against Hope: A Memoir* (1976). A searing account of life during the purges by the widow of one of the victims.

Medvedev, Roy, *Let History Judge: The Origins and Consequences of Stalinism,* rev. ed. (1990). Includes newly available material on Stalin's crimes of the 1930s.

Pasternak, Boris, *Doctor Zhivago* (1958). The tragedies of Russian life from Nicholas II to Stalin as seen through the eyes of a superbly sensitive and observant poet.

Scott, John, *Behind the Urals: An American Worker in Russia's City of Steel* (1942, repr. 1973). A firsthand account of life under the first Five-Year Plan.

Sholokhov, Mikhail, *And Quiet Flows the Don; The Don Flows Home to the Sea,* 2 vols. (1934, 1940). A Nobel Prize–winning novel about the brutalizing effects of war, revolution, and civil war.

Solzhenitsyn, Aleksandr I., *The Gulag Archipelago,* 3 vols. (1973–1975). The classic account of Stalin's terror.

Trotsky, Leon, *The Russian Revolution: The Overthrow of Tsarism and the Triumph of the Soviets* (1932). A classic account of the Bolshevik Revolution by its chief organizer; the chapters "Five Days" and "The Seizure of the Winter Palace" are especially valuable.

Tucker, Robert C., *Stalin as a Revolutionary* (1973). A psychological study of the young Stalin.

——, *Stalin in Power: The Revolution from Above, 1928–1941* (1990).

——, ed., *The Lenin Anthology* (1975). For those who want a taste of Lenin's writings.

——, ed., *Stalinism: Essays in Historical Interpretation* (1977). Essays on Stalin by prominent scholars.

Ulam, Adam B., *The Bolsheviks: The Intellectual and Political History of the Triumph of Communism in Russia* (1965). A full account built around Lenin.

Volkogonov, Dmitri, *Stalin: Triumph and Tragedy* (1991). The first Soviet biography based on hitherto unavailable archive material.

Von Laue, Theodore H., *Why Lenin? Why Stalin? Why Gorbachev?* 3rd ed. (1993). A brief survey of the rise and fall of the Soviet Union.

REVIEW QUESTIONS

1. How did the Soviet leaders view the position of Russia in the world? What were their aims and ambitions? How did their goals compare with those of other states?

2. How do you explain the fact that the Communist regime was far more ruthless in its methods of government than the tsarist regime? Which regime made Russia more powerful?

3. What do you think of the Leninist view (see page 757) that what was accomplished by voluntary cooperation in the West had to be achieved by compulsion in Russia? How do you account for the high degree of voluntary cooperation in American society? Why was it lacking in Russia?

4. In the light of the analysis offered in this chapter, how do you react to the outrage over Stalin's inhumanities? Was Stalin alone responsible? Was he aided by the Russian people? To what extent was the threat to the national security of a backward society responsible for his actions?

5. How would you define the differences between the conditions shaping American history and the conditions shaping Russian history in the years covered by this chapter? To what extent can American ways of thinking be applied to the conditions prevailing in Russia in the years treated in this chapter—or in general?

The Rise of Fascism:
The Attack on Democracy

*L*iberals viewed the Great War as a conflict between freedom and autocracy and expected an Allied victory to accelerate the spread of democracy throughout Europe. Right after the war, it seemed that liberalism would continue to advance as it had in the nineteenth century. The collapse of the autocratic German and Austrian Empires had led to the formation of parliamentary governments throughout eastern and central Europe. Yet within two decades, in an extraordinary turn of events, democracy seemed in its death throes. In Spain, Portugal, Italy, and Germany, and in all the newly created states of central and eastern Europe except Czechoslovakia, democracy collapsed, and various forms of authoritarian government emerged. The defeat of democracy and the surge of authoritarianism was best exemplified by the triumph of totalitarian fascist movements in Italy and Germany.

The emergence of fascist movements in more than twenty European lands after World War I was a sign that liberal society was in a state of disorientation and dissolution. The cultural pessimism, disdain for reason, and contempt for liberal values voiced by many intellectuals and nationalists before the war found expression after the war in the antidemocratic and irrational fascist ideologies, which altered European political life. Fascism marked the culmination of the dangerous trends inherent in the extreme nationalism and radical conservatism of the late nineteenth century.

As a Europe-wide phenomenon, fascism was a response to a postwar society afflicted with spiritual disintegration, economic dislocation, political instability, and thwarted nationalist hopes. It

A Nazi Rally. (*Wide World Photos*)

was an expression of fear that the Bolshevik Revolution would spread westward. It was also an expression of hostility to democratic values and a reaction to the failure of liberal institutions to solve the problems of modern industrial society. Regarding liberalism as bankrupt and parliamentary government as futile, many people yearned for a military dictatorship. To fascists and their sympathizers, democracy seemed an enfeebled old order ready to be overthrown.

In their struggle to bring down the liberal state, fascist leaders aroused primitive impulses and tribal loyalties; they made use of myths and rituals to mobilize and manipulate the masses. Organizing their propaganda campaigns with the rigor of a military operation, fascists stirred and dominated the masses and confused and undermined their democratic opposition, breaking its will to resist. Fascists were most successful in countries with weak democratic traditions. When parliamentary government faltered, it had few staunch defenders, and many people were drawn to charismatic demagogues who promised direct action.

The proliferation of fascist movements demonstrated that the habits of democracy are not quickly learned or easily retained. Particularly during times of crisis, people lose patience with parliamentary discussion and constitutional procedures, sink into nonrational modes of thought and behavior, and are easily manipulated by unscrupulous politicians. For the sake of economic or emotional security and national grandeur, they will often willingly sacrifice political freedom. Fascism starkly manifested the immense power of the irrational; it humbled liberals, making them permanently aware of the limitations of reason and the fragility of freedom.

The fascist goal of maximum centralization of power was furthered by developments during World War I: the expansion of bureaucracy, the concentration of industry into giant monopolies, and the close cooperation between industry and the state. The instruments of modern technology—radio, motion pictures, public address systems, telephone, and teletype—made it possible for the state to indoctrinate, manipulate, and dominate its subjects.

THE NATURE OF FASCISM

Fascist movements were marked by an extreme nationalism and a determination to eradicate liberalism and Marxism—to undo the legacy of the French Revolution of 1789 and the Bolshevik Revolution of 1917. Fascists believed that theirs was a spiritual revolution, that they were initiating a new era in history and building a new civilization on the ruins of liberal democracy. "We stand for a new principle in the world," said Mussolini. "We stand for the sheer, categorical, definitive antithesis to the world of democracy . . . to the world which still abides by the fundamental principles laid down in 1789."[1] The chief principle of Nazism, said Hitler, "is to abolish the liberal concept of the individual and the Marxist concept of humanity, and to substitute for them the Volk community, rooted in the soil and united by the bond of its common blood."[2]

Fascists accused liberal society of despiritualizing human beings and transforming them into materialistic creatures whose highest ideal was moneymaking. Idealistic youth and intellectuals rejoiced in fascist activism. They saw fascism as a revolt against the mediocrity of mass society and a reaffirmation of the noblest human qualities: heroism and dedication to one's people.

Fascists regarded Marxism as another enemy, for class conflict divided and weakened the state. To fascists, the Marxist call for workers of the world to unite meant the death of the national community. Fascism, in contrast, would reintegrate the proletariat into the nation and end class hostilities by making people at all levels feel that they were a needed part of the nation. Fascism thus offered a solution to the problem of insecurity and isolation in modern industrial society.

In contrast to liberalism and Marxism, fascism attacked the rational tradition of the Enlightenment and exalted will, blood, feeling, and instinct. Intellectual discussion and critical analysis, said fascists, cause national divisiveness; reason promotes doubt, enfeebles the will, and hinders instinctive, aggressive action. Fascism made a continual appeal to the emotions as a means of integrating the national community. This flow of emotion fueled irrational and dangerous desires and beliefs, which blocked critical judgment and responsible action. Glorifying action for its own sake, fascists aroused and manipulated brutal and primitive impulses and carried into politics the combative spirit of the trenches. They formed private armies, which attracted veterans—many of them rootless, brutal, and maladjusted men who sought to preserve the loyalty, camaraderie, and violence of the front.

Fascism exalted the leader—who, according to the fascist view, would intuitively grasp what was best for the nation—and called for rule by an elite of dedicated party members. The leader and the party would relieve the individual of the need to make decisions. Convinced that the liberal stress on individual freedom promoted competition and conflict, fascists pressed for monolithic unity: one leader, one party, and one national will.

Fascism drew its mass support from the lower middle class: small merchants, artisans, white-collar workers, civil servants, and peasants of moderate means, all of whom were frightened both by big capitalism and by Marxism. They hoped that fascism would protect them from the competition of big business and prevent the hated working class from establishing a Marxist state, which would threaten their property. The lower middle class saw in fascism a noncommunist way of overcoming economic crises and restoring traditional respect for family, native soil, and nation. Furthermore, many of these people saw fascism as a way of attacking the existing social order, which denied them opportunities for economic advancement and social prestige. Having no patience for parliamentary procedures or sympathy for democratic principles, they were drawn to demagogues who exuded confidence and promised direct action.

Although a radicalized middle class gave fascist movements their mass support, the fascists could not have captured the state without the aid of existing ruling elites: landed aristocrats, industrialists, and army leaders. In Russia, the Bolsheviks had to fight their way to power; in Italy and Germany, the old ruling order virtually handed power to the fascists. In both countries, fascist leaders succeeded in reassuring the conservative elite that they would not institute widepread social reforms or interfere with private property and would protect the nation from communism. Even though the old elite often abhorred fascist violence and demagoguery, it entered into an alliance with the fascists to protect its interests.

THE RISE OF FASCISM IN ITALY

Postwar Unrest

Although Italy had been on the winning side in World War I, it resembled a defeated nation. Food shortages, rising prices, massive unemployment, violent strikes, workers occupying factories, and peasants squatting on the uncultivated periphery of large estates created a climate of crisis. These dismal conditions contrasted sharply with the vision of a postwar world painted by politicians during the war. Italy required effective leadership and a reform program, but party disputes paralyzed the liberal government. With several competing parties, the liberals could not organize a solid majority that could cope with the domestic crisis.

The middle class was severely stressed. To meet accelerating expenses, the government had increased taxes, but the burden fell unevenly on small landowners, small business owners, civil service workers, and professionals. Moreover, the value of war bonds, purchased primarily by the middle class, had declined considerably because of inflation. Instead of being able to retrieve the good old days and their former status once the war ended, these solid citizens found that their economic position continued to deteriorate.

Large landowners and industrialists feared that their nation was on the verge of a Bolshevik-style revolution. They took seriously the proclamations of the socialists: "The proletariat must be incited to the violent seizure of political and economic power and this must be handed over entirely and exclusively to the Workers' and Peasants' Councils."[3] In truth, Italian socialists had no master plan to seize power. Peasant squatters and urban strikers were responding to the distress in their own regions and did not significantly coordinate their efforts with those in other localities. Besides, when workers realized that they could not keep factories operating, their revolutionary zeal waned and they started to abandon the plants. The workers' and peasants' poorly led and futile struggles did not portend a Red revolution. Nevertheless, the industrialists and landlords, with the Bolshevik Revolution still vivid in their minds, were taking no chances.

Adding to the unrest was national outrage at the terms of the peace settlement. Italians felt that despite their sacrifices—500,000 dead and 1 million wounded—they had been robbed of the fruits of their victory. Although Italy had received the Brenner Pass and Trieste, it had been denied the Dalmatian coast, the Adriatic port of Fiume, and territory in Africa and the Middle East. Nationalists blamed the liberal government for what they called a "mutilated victory." In 1919, a force of war veterans, led by the poet and adventurer Gabriele D'Annunzio (1863–1938), seized Fiume, to the delirious joy of Italian nationalists and the embarrassment of the government. D'Annunzio's occupation of the port lasted more than a year, adding fuel to the flames of Italian nationalism and demonstrating the weakness of the liberal regime in imposing its authority on rightist opponents.

Mussolini's Seizure of Power

Benito Mussolini (1883–1945) was born in a small village in east central Italy. Proud, quarrelsome, violent, and resentful of the humiliation he suffered for being poor, the young Mussolini was a troublemaker and was often brought before school authorities. But he was also intelligent, ranking first on final examinations in four subjects. After graduation, Mussolini taught in an elementary school, but this did not suit his passionate temperament. From 1902 to 1904, he lived in Switzerland, where he broadened his reading, lectured, and wrote. He also came under the influence of anarchists and socialist revolutionaries.

Returning to Italy, Mussolini was labeled a dangerous revolutionary by the police. As a reward for his zeal and political agitation, which led to five months in prison for inciting riots, in 1912 he was made editor of *Avanti,* the principal socialist newspaper. During the early days of World War I, he was expelled from the Socialist party for advocating Italian intervention in the war. After Italy entered the war, Mussolini served at the front and, during firing practice, suffered a serious wound, for which he was hospitalized.

In 1919, Mussolini organized the Fascist party to realize his immense will to power. The quest for power, more than a set of coherent doctrines, characterized the young movement. A supreme opportunist rather than an ideologist, Mussolini

MUSSOLINI WITH HIS TROOPS. The Italian dictator deliberately tried to sustain an image of a virile warrior. Although Mussolini established a one-party state, he was less successful than Hitler or Stalin in creating a totalitarian regime. (*Wide World Photos*)

exploited the unrest in postwar Italy in order to capture control of the state. He attracted converts from among the discontented, the disillusioned, and the uprooted. Many Italians, particularly the educated bourgeoisie who had been inspired by the unification movement of the nineteenth century, viewed Mussolini as the leader who would gain Fiume, Dalmatia, and colonies and win Italy's rightful place of honor in international affairs.

Hardened war veterans joined the Fascist movement to escape the boredom and idleness of civilian life. They welcomed an opportunity to wear the uniforms of the Fascist militia (Black Shirts), parade in the streets, and fight socialist and labor union opponents. Squads of Fascist Black Shirts (*squadristi*) raided socialist and trade union offices, destroying property and beating the occupants. As socialist Red Shirts responded in kind, it soon appeared that Italy was drifting toward civil war.

Hoping that Mussolini would rescue Italy from Bolshevism, industrialists and landowners contributed large sums to the Fascist party. The lower middle class, fearful that the growing power of labor unions and the Socialist party threatened their property and social prestige, viewed Mussolini as a protector. Middle-class university students, searching for adventure and an ideal, and army officers, dreaming of an Italian empire and hostile to parliamentary government, were also attracted to Mussolini's party. Intellectuals disenchanted with liberal politics and parliamentary democracy were intrigued by his philosophy of action. Mussolini's nationalism, activism, and anticommunism gradually seduced elements of the power structure: capitalists, aristocrats, army officers, the royal family, and the church.

In 1922, Mussolini made his bid for power. Speaking at a giant rally of his followers in late October, he declared: "Either they will give us the government or we shall take it by descending on Rome. It is now a matter of days, perhaps hours." A few days later, thousands of Fascists began the March on Rome. Some members of parliament demanded that the army defend the government against a Fascist coup. It would have been a relatively simple matter to crush the twenty thousand Fascist marchers, armed with little more than pistols and rifles, but King Victor Emmanuel III (1869–1947) refused to act. The king's advisers, some of them sympathetic to Mussolini, exaggerated the strength of the Fascists. Believing that he was rescuing Italy from terrible violence, the king appointed Mussolini prime minister.

Mussolini had bluffed his way to power. Fascism had triumphed not because of its own strength—the Fascists had only 35 of the 535 seats in parliament—but because the liberal government, irresolute and indecisive, did not counter force with force. In the past, the liberal state had not challenged Fascist acts of terror; now it feebly surrendered to Fascist blustering and threats. No doubt, liberals hoped that, once in power, the Fascists would forsake terror, pursue moderate aims, and act within the constitution. But the liberals were wrong; they had completely misjudged the antidemocratic character of fascism.

THE FASCIST STATE IN ITALY

Consolidation of Power

In October 1922, when Italy's liberal government capitulated, the Fascists by no means held total power. Anti-Fascists still sat in parliament and only four of the fourteen ministers in Mussolini's cabinet were Fascists. Cautious and shrewd, Mussolini resisted the extremists in his party, who demanded a second revolution: the immediate and preferably violent destruction of the Old Order. In this early stage of Fascist rule, when his position was still tenuous, Mussolini sought to maintain an image of respectability and moderation. He tried to convince the power structure that he intended to operate within the constitution, and he did not seek dictatorial power. At the same time, he gradually secured his position and turned Italy into a one-party state. In 1923, the Acerbo electoral law, approved by both chambers of the parliament, decreed that the party with the most votes in a national election (provided that the figure was not less than 25 percent of the total votes cast) would be granted two-thirds of the seats in the Chamber of Deputies. In the elections of 1924, which were marred by Fascist terrorism, Mussolini's supporters received 65 percent of the vote. Even without the implementation of the new electoral law, the opponents of fascism had been enfeebled. Mussolini had consolidated his power.

When socialist leader Giacomo Matteotti protested Fascist terror tactics, Fascist thugs killed him (in 1924). Although Mussolini had not ordered Matteotti's murder, his vicious attacks against his socialist opponent inspired the assassins. Repelled by the murder, some sincere democrats withdrew from the Chamber of Deputies in protest and some influential Italians called for Mussolini's dismissal. But the majority of liberals, including the leadership, continued to support Mussolini. And the king, the papacy, the army, large landowners, and industrialists, still regarding Mussolini as the best defense against internal disorder and Marxism, did not lend their support to an anti-Fascist movement.

Pressed by the radicals within the Fascist party, Mussolini moved to establish a dictatorship. In 1925–26, he eliminated non-Fascists from his cabinet and dissolved opposition parties. He also smashed the independent trade unions, suppressed opposition newspapers, replaced local mayors with Fascist officials, and organized a secret police to round up troublemakers. Many anti-Fascists fled the country or were deported.

Mussolini then turned on the extremist Fascists, the local chieftains (*ras*) who had led squadristi in the early days of the movement. Lauding violence, daring deeds, and the dangerous life, the ras were indispensable during the party's formative stage. But Mussolini feared that their radical adventurism posed a threat to his personal rule. And their desire to replace the traditional power structure with people drawn from their own ranks could block his efforts to cooperate with the established elite: industrialists, aristocratic landowners, and army leaders. Consequently, Mussolini expelled some squadristi leaders from the party and gave others positions in the bureaucracy to tame them.

Mussolini was less successful than Hitler and Stalin in fashioning a totalitarian state. The industrialists, the large landowners, the church, and to some extent even the army, never fell under the complete domination of the party. Nor did the regime possess the mind of its subjects with the same thoroughness as the Nazis did in Germany. Life in Italy was less regimented and the individual less fearful than in Nazi Germany or Communist Russia. The Italian people might cheer Mussolini, but few were willing to die for him.

Control of the Masses

Like Communist Russia and Nazi Germany, Fascist Italy used mass organizations and mass media to control minds and regulate behavior. As in the Soviet Union and the Third Reich, the Fascist regime created a cult of the leader. "Mussolini goes forward with confidence, in a halo of myth, almost chosen by God, indefatigable and infallible, the instrument employed by Providence for the creation of a new civilization," wrote the philosopher Giovanni Gentile.[4] To convey the image of a virile leader, Mussolini had himself photographed bare-chested or in a uniform with a steel helmet. Other photographs showed him riding horses, driving fast cars, flying planes, and playing with lion cubs. Mussolini frequently addressed huge throngs of admirers from his balcony. His tenor voice, grandiloquent phrases, and posturing—jaw thrust out, hands on hips—captivated audiences. Idolatry from the masses, in turn, intensified Mussolini's feelings of grandeur. Elementary school textbooks depicted Mussolini as the savior of the nation, a modern-day Julius Caesar.

Fascist propaganda inculcated habits of discipline and obedience: "Mussolini is always right." "Believe! Obey! Fight!" Propaganda also glorified war: "A minute on the battlefield is worth a lifetime of peace." The press, radio, and cinema idealized life under fascism, implying that fascism had eradicated crime, poverty, and social tensions. Schoolteachers and university professors were compelled to swear allegiance to the Fascist government and to propagate Fascist ideals, while students were urged to criticize instructors who harbored liberal attitudes. Millions of youths belonged to Fascist organizations, in which they participated in patriotic ceremonies and social functions, sang Fascist hymns, and wore Fascist uniforms. They submerged their own identities in the group.

Economic Policies

Fascists denounced economic liberalism for promoting individual self-interest, and socialism for instigating conflicts between workers and capitalists, which divided and weakened the nation. The Fascist way of resolving tensions between workers and employers was to abolish independent labor unions, prohibit strikes, and establish associations or corporations, which included both workers and employers from a given industry. In theory, representatives of labor and capital would cooperatively solve labor problems in a particular industry. In practice, the representatives of labor turned out to be Fascists who protected the interests of the industrialists. Although the Fascists lauded the corporative system as a creative approach to modern economic problems, in reality it played a minor role in Italian economic life. Big business continued to make its own decisions, paying scant attention to the corporations.

Nor did the Fascist government solve Italy's long-standing economic problems. To curtail the export of capital and reduce the nation's dependence on imports in case of war, Mussolini sought to make Italy self-sufficient. To win the "battle of grain," the Fascist regime brought marginal lands under cultivation and urged farmers to concentrate on wheat rather than other crops. Although wheat production thus increased substantially, total agricultural output declined because wheat was planted on land more suited to animal husbandry and fruit cultivation. To make Italy industrially self-sufficient, the regime limited imports of foreign goods, with the result that Italian consumers paid higher prices for Italian-manufactured goods. Mussolini posed as the protector of the little people, but under his regime the power and profits of big business grew and the standard of living of small farmers and urban workers declined. Government attempts to grapple with the depression were half-hearted. Aside from providing family allowances—an increase in income with the birth of each child—the Fascist regime did little in the way of social welfare.

The Church and the Fascist Regime

Although anticlerical since his youth, Mussolini practiced expediency. He recognized that coming to terms with the church would improve his image with Catholic public opinion. The Vatican regarded Mussolini's regime as a barrier against communism and as less hostile to church interests and more amenable to church direction than a liberal government. Pope Pius XI (1922–1939) was an ultraconservative whose hatred of liberalism and secularism led him to believe that the Fascists would increase the influence of the church in the nation.

In 1929, the Lateran Accords recognized the independence of Vatican City, repealed many of the anticlerical laws passed under the liberal government, and made religious instruction compulsory in all secondary schools. The papal state, Vatican City, became a small enclave within Rome over which the Italian government had no authority. Relations between the Vatican and the

Fascist government remained fairly good throughout the decade of the 1930s. One crisis arose in 1931 when Mussolini, pushed by militant anticlericals within his party, dissolved certain Catholic youth groups as rivals to Fascist youth associations; but a compromise that permitted the Catholic organizations to function within certain limits eased tensions. When Mussolini invaded Ethiopia and intervened in the Spanish Civil War, the church supported him. Although the papacy criticized Mussolini for drawing closer to Hitler and introducing anti-Jewish legislation, it never broke with the Fascist regime.

THE NEW GERMAN REPUBLIC

In the last days of World War I, a revolution brought down the German imperial government and led to the creation of a democratic republic. In October 1918, the German admirals had ordered the German navy to engage the British in the English Channel, but the sailors, anticipating peace and resentful of their officers (who commonly resorted to cruel discipline), refused to obey. Joined by sympathetic soldiers, the mutineers raised the red flag of revolution. The revolt soon spread, as military men and workers demonstrated for peace and reform and in some regions seized authority. Reluctant to fire on their comrades and also fed up with the war, German troops did not move to crush the revolutionaries.

On November 9, 1918, the leaders of the government announced the end of the monarchy, and Kaiser William II fled to Holland. Two days later, the new German republic, headed by Friedrich Ebert (1871–1925), a Social Democrat, signed an armistice agreement ending the war. Many Germans blamed the new democratic republic for the defeat—a baseless accusation, for the German generals, knowing that the war was lost, had sought an armistice.

In February 1919, the recently elected National Assembly met at Weimar and proceeded to draw up a constitution for the new state. The Weimar Republic—born in revolution, which most Germans detested, and military defeat, which many attributed to the new government—faced an uncertain future.

ROSA LUXEMBURG SPEAKING IN STUTTGART. A prominent member of the Social Democrats, Luxemburg rejected the argument of revisionists that capitalism could be reformed and revolution avoided. She was sentenced to prison for opposing Germany's entry into the war. Immediately after the war she emerged as one of the leaders of the newly established German Communist party, or Spartacists. The attempted uprising of the Spartacists in 1919 was crushed and Luxemburg was murdered by the Free Corps. (© *Topham, The Image Works*)

Threats from Left and Right

Dominated by moderate socialists, the infant republic faced internal threats from both the radical left and the radical right. In January 1919, the newly established German Communist party, or Spartacists, disregarding the advice of their leaders Rosa Luxemburg and Karl Liebknecht, took to the streets of Berlin and declared Ebert's government deposed. To crush the revolution, Ebert turned to the Free Corps: volunteer brigades of ex-soldiers and adventurers, led by officers loyal to the emperor, who had been fighting to protect the eastern borders from encroachments by the new states of Poland, Estonia, and Latvia. The men of the Free Corps relished action and despised Bolshevism. They suppressed the revolution and murdered Luxemburg and Liebknecht on January 15. In May 1919, the Free Corps also marched into Munich to overthrow the soviet republic set up there by communists a few weeks earlier.

The Spartacist revolt and the short-lived soviet republic in Munich (and others in Baden and Brunswick) had a profound effect on the German psyche. The communists had been easily subdued, but fear of a communist insurrection remained deeply embedded in the middle and upper classes—a fear that drove many into the ranks of the Weimar Republic's right-wing opponents.

In March 1920, the republic was threatened by the radical right. Refusing to disband as the government ordered, detachments of the right-wing Free Corps marched into Berlin and declared a new government, headed by Wolfgang Kapp, a staunch German nationalist. President Ebert and most members of the cabinet and National Assembly fled to Stuttgart. Insisting that it could not fire on fellow soldiers, the German army, the *Reichswehr,* made no move to defend the republic. A general strike called by the labor unions prevented Kapp from governing, and the coup collapsed. However, the Kapp Putsch

PAPERING A WALL WITH GERMAN MARKS. The inflation of 1923 made money virtually worthless, as this man demonstrates. (*UPI/Bettmann Newsphotos*)

demonstrated that the loyalty of the army to the republic was doubtful.

Economic Crisis

In addition to uprisings by the left and right, the republic was burdened by an economic crisis. During the war, Germany had financed its military expenditures not by increasing taxation, but through short-term loans, accumulating a huge debt that now had to be paid. A trade deficit and enormous reparation payments worsened the nation's economic plight. Unable to meet the deficit in the national budget, the government simply printed more money, causing the value of the German mark to decline precipitously. In 1914, the mark stood at 4.2 to the dollar; in 1919, at 8.9 to the dollar; and in early 1923, at 18,000 to the dollar. In August 1923, a dollar could be exchanged for 4.6 million marks, and in November, for 4 billion marks. Bank savings, war bonds, and pensions, representing years of toil and thrift, became worthless. Blaming the government for this disaster, the ruined middle class be-

came more receptive to rightist movements that aimed to bring down the republic.

With the economy in a shambles, the republic defaulted on reparation payments. Premier Raymond Poincaré (1860–1934) of France took a hard line. In January 1923, he ordered French troops into the Ruhr, the nerve center of German industry. Responding to the republic's call for passive resistance, factory workers, miners, and railroad workers in the Ruhr refused to work for the French. To provide strike benefits for the Ruhr workers, the government printed yet more money, making inflation even worse.

In August 1923, Gustav Stresemann became chancellor. The new government lasted only until November 1923, but during those one hundred days, Stresemann skillfully placed the republic on the path to recovery. Warned by German industrialists that the economy was at the breaking point, Stresemann abandoned the policy of passive resistance in the Ruhr and declared Germany's willingness to make reparation payments. Stresemann issued a new currency backed by a mortgage on German real estate. To reduce public expenditures, which contributed to inflation, the government fired some civil service workers and lowered salaries; to get additional funds, it raised taxes; to protect the value of the new currency, it did not print another issue. Inflation receded, and confidence was restored.

A new arrangement regarding reparations also contributed to the economic recovery. Recognizing that in its present economic straits Germany could not meet its obligations to the Allies or secure the investment of foreign capitalists, Britain and the United States pressured France to allow a reparation commission to make new proposals. In 1924, the parties accepted the Dawes Plan, which reduced reparations and based them on Germany's economic capacity. During the negotiations, France agreed to withdraw its troops from the Ruhr—another step toward easing tensions for the republic.

From 1924 to 1929, economic conditions improved. Foreign capitalists, particularly Americans, were attracted by high interest rates and the low cost of labor. Their investments in German businesses stimulated the economy. By 1929, iron, steel, coal, and chemical production exceeded prewar levels. The value of German exports also surpassed that of 1913. This spectacular boom was partly due to more effective methods of production and management and the concentration of related industries in giant trusts. Real wages were higher than before the war, and improved unemployment benefits made life better for the workers. It appeared that Germany had also achieved political stability, as threats from the extremist parties of the left and the right subsided. Given time and economic stability, democracy might have taken firmer root in Germany. But then came the Great Depression. The global economic crisis that began in October 1929 revealed how weak was the Weimar Republic.

Fundamental Weaknesses of the Weimar Republic

German political experience provided poor soil for transplanting an Anglo-Saxon democratic parliamentary system. Before World War I, Germany had been a semiautocratic state, ruled by an emperor who commanded the armed forces, controlled foreign policy, appointed the chancel-

lor, and called and dismissed parliament. This authoritarian system blocked the German people from acquiring democratic habits and attitudes. Still accustomed to rule from above, still adoring the power state, many Germans sought the destruction of the Weimar Republic.

Traditional conservatives—the upper echelons of the civil service, judges, industrialists, large landowners, and army leaders—were contemptuous of democracy and were avowed enemies of the republic. They wanted to restore a pre-1914 Prussian-type government, which would fight liberal ideals and protect the fatherland from Bolshevism. Nor did the middle class feel a commitment to the liberal-democratic principles on which the republic rested. The traditionally nationalistic middle class identified the republic with defeat in war and the humiliation of the Versailles treaty. Rabidly antisocialist, this class saw the leaders of the republic as Marxists who would impose on Germany a working-class state.

Right-wing intellectuals often attacked democracy as a barrier to the true unity of the German nation. In the tradition of nineteenth-century Volkish thinkers, they had contempt for reason and political freedom and glorified instincts, race, and action. In doing so, they turned many Germans against the republic, eroding the popular support on which democracy depends. German historian Kurt Sontheimer concludes:

The submission of a large part of German intellectual society to the National Socialist Weltanschauung . . . would have been inconceivable without the anti-democratic intellectual movement that preceded it and that, in its contempt for everything liberal, had blunted people's sensibilities to the inviolable rights of the individual and the preservation of human dignity. . . . Nothing is more dangerous in political life than the abandonment of reason. . . . The intellect must remain the controlling, regulating force in human affairs. The anti-democratic intellectuals of the Weimar period. . . . despised reason and found more truth in myth or in the blood surging in their veins. . . . Had they a little more reason and enlightenment, these intellectuals might have seen better where their zeal was leading them and their country.[5]

The Weimar Republic also showed the weaknesses of the multiparty system. With the vote spread over a number of parties, no one party held a majority of seats in the parliament (Reichstag), and so the republic was governed by a coalition of several parties. But because of ideological differences, the coalition was always unstable and in danger of failing to function. This is precisely what happened during the Great Depression. When effective leadership was imperative, the government could not act. Political deadlock caused Germans to lose what little confidence they had in the democratic system. Support for the parties that wanted to preserve democracy dwindled, and extremist parties that aimed to topple the republic gained strength.

Supporting the republic were Social Democrats, Catholic Centrists, and German Democrats; a coalition of these parties governed the republic during the 1920s.* Seeking to bring down the republic were the Communists, on the left, and two rightist parties, the Nationalists and the National Socialist German Workers' party, led by Adolf Hitler.

THE RISE OF HITLER

The Early Years

Adolf Hitler (1889–1945) was born in the town of Braunau am Inn, Austria, on April 20, 1889, the fourth child of a minor civil servant. Much of his youth was spent in Linz, a major city in Upper Austria. A poor student at secondary school, although by no means unintelligent, Hitler left high school and lived idly for more than two years. In 1907, the Vienna Academy of

---

*The Social Democrats hoped one day to transform Germany into a Marxist society, but they had abandoned revolutionary means and pursued a policy of moderate social reform. The largest party until the closing months of the Weimar Republic, the Social Democrats were committed to democratic principles and parliamentary government. The Catholic Center party opposed socialism and protected Catholic interests, but, like the Social Democrats, supported the republic. The German Democratic party consisted of middle-class liberals who also opposed socialism and supported the republic. Although the right-wing German People's party was more monarchist than republican, on occasion it joined the coalition of parties that sought to preserve the republic.

Arts rejected his application for admission. After the death of his mother in December 1907 (his father had died in 1903), Hitler drifted around Vienna, viewing himself as an art student. Contrary to his later description of these years, Hitler did not suffer great poverty, for he received an orphan's allowance from the state and an inheritance from his mother and an aunt. When the Vienna Academy again refused to admit him in 1908, he did not seek to learn a trade or to work steadily but earned some money by painting picture postcards.

Hitler was a loner, often given to brooding and self-pity. He found some solace by regularly attending Wagnerian operas (much admired by German nationalists for their glorification of German folk traditions), by fantasizing about great architectural projects that he would someday initiate, and by reading. He read a lot, especially in art, history, and military affairs. He also read the racial, nationalist, anti-Semitic, and Pan-German literature that abounded in multinational Vienna. This literature introduced Hitler to a bizarre racial mythology: a heroic race of blond, blue-eyed Aryans battling for survival against inferior races. The racist treatises preached the danger posed by mixing races, called for the liquidation of racial inferiors, and marked the Jew as the embodiment of evil and the source of all misfortune.

In Vienna, Hitler came into contact with Georg von Schönerer's Pan-German movement. For Schönerer, the Jews were evil not because of their religion, not because they rejected Christ, but because they possessed evil racial qualities. Schönerer's followers wore watch chains with pictures of hanged Jews attached. Hitler was particularly impressed with Karl Lueger, the mayor of Vienna, a clever demagogue who skillfully manipulated the anti-Semitic feelings of the Viennese for his own political advantage. In Vienna, Hitler also acquired a hatred for Marxism and democracy and the conviction that the struggle for existence and the survival of the fittest are the essential facts of the social world. His years in Vienna emptied Hitler of all compassion and scruples and filled him with a fierce resentment of the social order, which, he felt, had ignored him, cheated him, and condemned him to a wretched existence.

When World War I began, Hitler was in

Munich. He welcomed the war as a relief from his daily life, which lacked purpose and excitement. Volunteering for the German army, Hitler found battle exhilarating, and he fought bravely, twice receiving the Iron Cross.

The experience of battle taught Hitler to prize discipline, regimentation, leadership, authority, struggle, and ruthlessness. The shock of Germany's defeat and of revolution intensified his commitment to racial nationalism. To lead Germany to total victory over its racial enemies became his obsession. Like many returning soldiers, he required vindicating explanations for lost victories. His own explanation was simple and demagogic: Germany's shame was due to the creators of the republic, the "November criminals"; and behind them was a Jewish-Bolshevik world conspiracy.

The Nazi Party

In 1919, Hitler joined the German Workers' Party, a small right-wing group and one of the more than seventy extremist military-political-Volkish organizations that sprang up in postwar Germany. Displaying fantastic energy and extraordinary ability as a demagogic orator, propagandist, and organizer, Hitler quickly became the leader of the party, whose name was changed to National Socialist German Workers' party (commonly called Nazi). As leader, Hitler insisted on absolute authority and total allegiance—a demand that coincided with the postwar longing for a strong leader who would set right a shattered nation. Without Hitler, the National Socialist German Workers' party would have remained an insignificant group of discontents and outcasts. Demonstrating a Machiavellian cunning in politics, Hitler tightened the party organization and perfected the techniques of mass propaganda.

Like Mussolini, Hitler incorporated military attitudes and techniques into politics. Uniforms, salutes, emblems, flags, and other symbols imbued party members with a sense of solidarity and camaraderie. At mass meetings, Hitler was a spellbinder who gave stunning performances. His pounding fists, throbbing body, wild gesticulations, hypnotic eyes, rage-swollen face, and repeated, frenzied denunciations of the Versailles

THE SPELLBINDER. Hitler was a superb orator who knew how to reach the hearts of his listeners. The masses, he said, are aroused by the spoken, not the written, word. (*Roger-Viollet*)

treaty, Marxism, the republic, and Jews inflamed and mesmerized the audience. Many listeners—and his speeches generally attracted people already hostile to the Weimar Republic—were swayed by Hitler's earnestness, conviction, and self-confidence. They believed that Hitler and his movement could restore Germany's strength and pride. Hitler instinctively grasped the innermost feelings of his audience: its resentments and its longings. "The intense will of the man, the passion of his sincerity seemed to flow from him into me. I experienced an exaltation that could be likened only to religious conversion," said one early admirer.[6]

In November 1923, Hitler attempted to seize

power in Munich, in the state of Bavaria, as a prelude to toppling the republic. The attempt, which came to be known as the Beer Hall Putsch, failed, and the Nazis made a poor showing; they quickly scattered when the Bavarian police opened fire. Ironically, however, Hitler's prestige increased, for when he was put on trial, he used it as an opportunity to denounce the republic and the Versailles treaty and to proclaim his philosophy of racial nationalism. His impassioned speeches, publicized by the press, earned Hitler a nationwide reputation and a light sentence: five years' imprisonment, with the promise of quick parole. While in prison, Hitler dictated *Mein Kampf,* a rambling and turgid work, which contained the essence of his world-view.

The unsuccessful Munich putsch taught Hitler a valuable lesson: armed insurrection against superior might fails. He would gain power not by force, but by exploiting the instruments of democracy: elections and party politics. He would use apparently legal means to destroy the Weimar Republic and impose a dictatorship. As Nazi propaganda expert Joseph Goebbels would later express it, "We have openly declared that we use democratic methods only to gain power and that once we had it we would ruthlessly deny our opponents all those chances we had been granted when we were in the opposition."[7]

Hitler's World-View

Some historians view Hitler as an unprincipled opportunist and a brilliant tactician, who believed in nothing but cleverly manufactured and manipulated ideas that were politically useful in his drive for power. To be sure, Hitler was not concerned with the objective truth of an idea but with its potential political usefulness. He was not a systematic thinker like Marx. Whereas communism claimed the certainty of science and held that it would reform the world in accordance with rational principles, Hitler proclaimed the higher validity of blood, instinct, and will and regarded the intellect as an enemy of the soul. Hitler nevertheless possessed a remarkably consistent ideology. As Hajo Holborn explains:

Hitler was a great opportunist and tactician, but it would be quite wrong to think that ideology was for him a mere instrumentality for gaining power. On the contrary, Hitler was a doctrinaire of the first order. Throughout his political career he was guided by an ideology . . . which from 1926 onward [did] not show any change whatsoever.[8]

Hitler's thought comprised a patchwork of nineteenth-century anti-Semitic, Volkish (see page 618), Social Darwinist (see page 585), antidemocratic, and anti-Marxist ideas. From these ideas, many of which enjoyed wide popularity, Hitler constructed a world-view rooted in myth and ritual. Given to excessive daydreaming and never managing to "overcome his youth with its dreams, injuries, and resentments,"[9] Hitler sought to make the world accord with his fantasies—struggles to the death between races, a vast empire ruled by a master race, and a thousand-year Reich.

Racial Nationalism Nazism rejected both the Judeo-Christian and the Enlightenment traditions and sought to found a new world order based on racial nationalism. For Hitler, race was the key to understanding world history. He believed that Western civilization was at a critical juncture. Liberalism was dying, and Marxism, that "Jewish invention," as he called it, would inherit the future unless it was opposed by an even more powerful world-view. "With the conception of race National Socialism will carry its revolution and recast the world," said Hitler.[10] As the German barbarians had overwhelmed a disintegrating Roman Empire, a reawakened, racially united Germany, led by men of iron will, would carve out a vast European empire and deal a decadent liberal civilization its deathblow. It would conquer Russia, eradicate communism, and reduce to serfdom the subhuman Slavs, "a mass of born slaves who feel the need of a master."[11]

In the tradition of crude Volkish nationalists and Social Darwinists, Hitler divided the world into superior and inferior races and pitted them against each other in a struggle for survival. For him, this fight for life was a law of nature and of history. The Germans, descendants of ancient Aryans, possessed superior racial characteristics; a nation degenerates and perishes if it allows its blood to be contaminated by intermingling with lower races. Conflict between races was desirable, for it strengthened and hardened racial superiors; it made them ruthless—a necessary quality in this Darwinian world. As a higher race, the Germans were entitled to conquer and subjugate other races. Germany must acquire *Lebensraum* (living space) by expanding eastward at the expense of the racially inferior Slavs.

The Jew as Devil An obsessive and virulent anti-Semitism dominated Hitler's mental outlook. (See pages 620–625.) In waging war against the Jews, Hitler believed that he was defending Germany from its worst enemy. In Hitler's mythical interpretation of the world, the Aryan was the originator and carrier of civilization. As descendants of the Aryans, the Germans embodied creativity, bravery, and loyalty. As a counterpart, the Jew personified the vilest qualities. "Two worlds face one another," said Hitler in a statement that clearly reveals the mythical character of his thought, "the men of God and the men of Satan! The Jew is the anti-man, the creature of another god. He must have come from another root of the human race. I set the Aryan and the Jew over and against each other."[12] Everything Hitler despised—liberalism, intellectualism, pacifism, parliamentarianism, internationalism, communism, modern art, and individualism—he attributed to Jews.

For Hitler, the Jew was the mortal enemy of racial nationalism. The moral outlook of the ancient Hebrew prophets, which affirmed individual worth and made individuals morally responsible for their actions, was totally at odds with Hitler's morality, which subordinated the individual to the national community. Hitler once called conscience a Jewish invention. The prophetic vision of the unity of humanity under God and the belief in equality, justice, and peace were also contrary to Hitler's creed that all history is a pitiless struggle between races and that only the strongest and most ruthless deserve to survive.

Hitler's anti-Semitism served a functional purpose as well. By concentrating all evil in one enemy, "the conspirator and demonic" Jew, Hitler provided true believers with a simple, all-embracing, and emotionally satisfying explanation for their misery. By defining themselves as the racial and spiritual opposites of Jews, true believers of all classes felt joined together in a Volkish union. By seeing themselves engaged in a

heroic battle against a single enemy that embodied evil, they strengthened their will. Even failures and misfits gained self-respect. Anti-Semitism provided insecure and hostile people with powerless but recognizable targets on whom to focus their antisocial feelings.

The surrender to myth served to disorient the intellect and unify the nation. When the mind accepts an image such as Hitler's image of Jews as vermin, germs, and satanic conspirators, it has lost all sense of balance and objectivity. Such a disoriented mind is ready to believe and to obey, to be manipulated and to be led, to brutalize and to tolerate brutality; it is ready to be absorbed into the collective will of the community. That many people, including intellectuals and members of the elite, accepted these racial ideas shows the enduring power of mythical thinking and the vulnerability of reason. In 1933, the year Hitler took power, Felix Goldmann, a German-Jewish writer, commented astutely on the irrational character of Nazi anti-Semitism: "The present-day politicized racial anti-Semitism is the embodiment of myth, . . . nothing is discussed . . . only felt, . . . nothing is pondered critically, logically or reasonably, . . . only inwardly perceived, surmised. . . . We are apparently the last [heirs] of the Enlightenment."[13]

The Importance of Propaganda Hitler understood that in an age of political parties, universal suffrage, and a popular press—the legacies of the French and Industrial Revolutions—the successful leader must win the support of the masses. To do so, Hitler consciously applied and perfected elements of circus showmanship, church pageantry, American advertising, and the techniques of propaganda that the Allies had used to stir their civilian populations during the war. To be effective, said Hitler, propaganda must be aimed principally at the emotions. The masses are not moved by scientific ideas or by objective and abstract knowledge, but by primitive feelings, terror, force, and discipline. Propaganda must reduce everything to simple slogans incessantly repeated and must concentrate on one enemy. The masses are aroused by the spoken, not the written, word—by a storm of hot passion erupting from the speaker, "which like hammer blows can open the gates to the heart of the people."[14]

The most effective means of stirring the masses and strengthening them for the struggle ahead, Hitler had written in *Mein Kampf,* is the mass meeting. Surrounded by tens of thousands of people, individuals lose their sense of individuality and no longer see themselves as isolated. They become members of a community bound together by an esprit de corps reminiscent of the trenches during the Great War. Bombarded by the cheers of thousands of voices, by marching units, by banners, by explosive oratory, individuals become convinced of the truth of the party's message and the irresistibility of the movement. Their intellects overwhelmed, their resistance lowered, they lose their previous beliefs and are carried along on a wave of enthusiasm. "The man who enters such a meeting doubting and wavering leaves it inwardly reinforced; he has become a link to the community."[15]

Hitler Gains Power

When Hitler left prison in December 1924, after serving nine months, he proceeded to tighten his hold on the Nazi party. He relentlessly used his genius for propaganda and organization to strengthen the loyalty of his cadres and to instill in them a sense of mission. In 1925, the Nazi party counted about 27,000 members; in 1929, it had grown to 178,000, with units throughout Germany. But its prospects seemed dim, for since 1925, economic conditions had improved and the republic seemed politically stable. In 1928, the National Socialists (NSDAP) received only 2.6 percent of the vote. Nevertheless, Hitler never lost faith in his own capacities or his destiny. He continued to build his party and waited for a crisis that would rock the republic and make his movement a force in national politics.

The Great Depression, which began in the United States at the end of 1929, provided that crisis. As Germany's economic plight worsened, the German people became more amenable to Hitler's radicalism. The Nazis tirelessly expanded their efforts. Everywhere, they staged mass rallies, plastered walls with posters, distributed leaflets, and engaged in street battles with their opponents of the left. Hitler promised all things to all groups, avoided debates, provided simple explanations for Germany's misfortunes, and in-

sisted that only the Nazis could rescue Germany. Nazi propaganda attacked the communists, the "November criminals," the democratic system, the Versailles treaty, reparations, and the Jews. It depicted Hitler as a savior. Hitler would rescue Germany from chaos; he understood the real needs of the Volk; he was sent by destiny to lead Germany in its hour of greatest need. These propaganda techniques worked. The Nazi party went from 810,000 votes in 1928 to 6.4 million in 1930, and its representation in the Reichstag soared from 12 to 107.

The Social Democrats (SPD), the principal defenders of democracy, could draw support only from the working class; to the middle class, they were hated Marxists. Moreover, in the eyes of many Germans, the SPD was identified with the status quo, that is, with economic misery and national humiliation. The SPD simply had no program that could attract the middle class or give it hope for a better future.

To the lower middle class, the Nazis promised effective leadership and a solution to the economic crisis. For this segment of society, the Great Depression was the last straw, the final evidence that the republic had failed and should be supplanted by a different kind of regime. Germans of the lower middle class craved order, authority, and leadership and abhorred disputes of the political parties that provided neither. They wanted Hitler to protect Germany from the communists and organized labor. The traumatic experience of the Great Depression caused many bourgeois—until then apathetic about voting—to cast ballots. The depression was also severe in England and the United States, but the liberal foundations of these countries were strong. In Germany they were not, because the middle class had not committed itself to democracy, nor indeed did it have any liking for it. Democracy endured in Britain and the United States; in Germany, it collapsed.

But Nazism was more than a class movement. It appealed to the discontented and disillusioned from all segments of the population: embittered veterans, romantic nationalists, idealistic intellectuals, industrialists and large landowners frightened by communism and social democracy, rootless and resentful people who felt that they had no place in the existing society, the unemployed, lovers of violence, and newly enfranchised youth yearning for a cause. The Social Democrats spoke the rational language of European democracy. The Communists addressed themselves to only a part of the nation, the proletariat, and were linked to a foreign country, the Soviet Union. The Nazis reached a wider spectrum of the population and touched deeper feelings.

And always there was the immense attraction of Hitler. Many Germans were won over by his fanatical sincerity, his iron will, and his conviction that he was chosen by fate to rescue Germany. What a new party member wrote after hearing Hitler speak expressed the mood of many Germans: "There was only one thing for me, either to win with Adolf Hitler or to die for him. The personality of the Fuehrer had me totally in its spell."[16] Many others, no doubt, voted for Hitler not because they approved of him or his ideas, but because he was a strong opponent of the Weimar Republic, which they viewed as weak and contemptible. What these people wanted, above all, was the end of the republic they hated.

Meanwhile, the parliamentary regime failed to function effectively. According to Article 48 of the constitution, during times of emergency the president was empowered to govern by decree, that is, without parliament. When President Paul von Hindenburg (1847–1934), the aging field marshal, exercised this emergency power, the responsibility for governing Germany was in effect transferred from the political parties and parliament to the president and chancellor. Rule by the president, instead of by parliament, meant, for one thing, that Germany had already taken a giant step away from parliamentary government in the direction of authoritarianism.

In the election of July 31, 1932, the Nazis received 37.3 percent of the vote and won 230 seats, far more than any other party but still not a majority. Determined to become chancellor, Hitler refused to take a subordinate position in a coalition government. Franz von Papen, who had resigned from the chancellorship, persuaded Hindenburg, whose judgment was distorted by old age, to appoint Hitler chancellor. In this decision, Papen had the support of German industrialists, aristocratic landowners, and the Nationalist party.

As in Italy, the members of the ruling elite were frightened by internal violence, unrest, and the specter of communism. They thought Hitler a vulgar man and abhorred his demagogic incitement of the masses. But they regarded him as a useful instrument to fight communism, block social reform, break the back of organized labor, and rebuild the armament industry. Hitler had cleverly reassured these traditional conservatives that the Nazis would protect private property and business and go slow with social reform.

Like the Italian upper class, which had assisted Mussolini in his rise to power, the old conservative ruling elite intrigued to put Hitler in power. Ironically, this decision was made when Nazi strength at the polls was beginning to ebb. Expecting to control Hitler, conservatives calculated badly, for Hitler could not be tamed. They had underestimated his skill as a politician, his ruthlessness, and his obsession with racial nationalism. Hitler had not sought power to restore the Old Order, but to fashion a new one. The new leadership would be drawn not from the traditional ruling segments, but from the most dedicated Nazis, regardless of their social background.

Never intending to rule within the spirit of the constitution, Hitler, who took office on January 30, 1933, quickly moved to assume dictatorial powers. In February 1933, a Dutch drifter with communist leanings set a fire in the Reichstag. Hitler persuaded Hindenburg to sign an emergency decree suspending civil rights on the pretext that the state was threatened by internal subversion. The chancellor then used these emergency powers to arrest, without due process, Communist and Social Democratic deputies.

In the elections of March 1933, Nazi thugs broke up Communist party meetings, and Hitler called for a Nazi victory at the polls to save Europe from Bolshevism. Intimidated by street violence and captivated by Nazi mass demonstrations and relentless propaganda, the German people elected 288 Nazi deputies in a Reichstag of 647 seats. With the support of 52 deputies of the Nationalist party and in the absence of Communist deputies, who were under arrest, the Nazis now had a secure majority. Hitler then bullied the Reichstag into passing the Enabling Act (in March 1933), which permitted the chancellor to enact legislation independently of the Reichstag. With astonishing passivity, the political parties had allowed the Nazis to dismantle the government and make Hitler a dictator with unlimited power. Hitler had used the instruments of democracy to destroy the republic and create a dictatorship. And he did it far more thoroughly and quickly than Mussolini.

NAZI GERMANY

Mussolini's fascism exhibited much bluster and bragging, but Fascist Italy did not have the industrial and military strength or the total commitment of the people necessary to threaten the peace of Europe. Nazism, on the other hand, demonstrated a demonic quality, which nearly destroyed Western civilization.

Hitler's sinister, fanatical, and obsessive personality had a far greater impact on the German movement than Mussolini's character had on Italian fascism. Also contributing to the demonic radicalism of Nazism were certain deeply rooted German traditions, which were absent in Italy: Prussian militarism, adoration of the power state, and belief in the special destiny of the German Volk. These traditions made the German people's attachment to Hitler and Nazi ideology much stronger than the Italian people's devotion to Mussolini and his party.

The Leader-State

Totalitarian leaders want more than power for its own sake. In the last analysis, they seek to transform the world according to an ideology, an all-embracing vision, which constitutes a higher and exclusive truth. Like a religion, the totalitarian ideology provides its adherents with beliefs that make society and history intelligible and explain existence in an emotionally gratifying way. The ideology satisfies a human yearning for absolutes and creates true believers, who feel that they are participating in a great cause. Also like a religion, the totalitarian party gives isolated and alienated individuals a sense of belonging, a feeling of camaraderie; it enables a person to lose himself or herself in the comforting and exhilarating embrace of a mass movement. The radical Russian anarchist Bakunin had sensed the seductive power of the community when he stated: "I do not want to be I, I want to be *We*."[17]

The Nazis moved to subjugate all political and economic institutions and all culture to the will of the party. There could be no separation between private life and politics: ideology must pervade every phase of daily life and all organizations must come under party control. There could be no rights of the individual that the state must respect. The party became the state, and its teachings the soul of the German nation.

In contrast to earlier autocratic regimes, the totalitarian dictatorship is not satisfied with its subjects' outward obedience. Demanding unconditional loyalty and enthusiastic support from the masses, it strives to control the inner person: to shape thoughts, feelings, and attitudes according to the party ideology, which becomes an official creed. The aim is to create a "new man," one who dedicates himself body and soul to the party and its doctrines, a true believer stirred by a mission. Goebbels summed up this totalitarian goal as follows: "It is not enough to reconcile people more or less to our regime, to move them towards a position of neutrality towards us, we want rather to work on people until they are addicted to us."[18] An anonymous Nazi poet expressed the totalitarian credo in these words:

> We have captured all the positions
> And on the heights we have planted
> The banners of our revolution.
> You had imagined that that was all that we
>   wanted
> We want more
> We want all
> Your hearts are our goal,
> It is your souls we want.[19]

The Third Reich was organized as a leader-state, in which Hitler, the *fuehrer* (leader), embodied and expressed the real will of the German people, commanded the supreme loyalty of the nation, and held omnipotent power. As a Nazi political theorist stated, "The authority of the Fuehrer is total and all-embracing . . . it embraces all members of the German community. . . . The Fuehrer's authority is subject to no checks or controls; it is circumscribed by no . . . individual rights; it is . . . overriding and unfettered."[20] The German people owed complete loyalty to the fuehrer. In practice, however, the Nazi state was not a coherent and monolithic political system held together by commands issuing from one source. Rather, the nation was composed of organizations and individuals competing with one another for influence, power, and plunder.

To strengthen the power of the central government and coordinate the nation under Nazism, the regime abolished legislatures in the various German states and appointed governors who would make certain that Nazi directives were carried out throughout the country. The Nazis took over the civil service and used its machinery to enforce Nazi decrees. In this process of *Gleichschaltung* (coordination), the Nazis encountered little opposition. The political parties and the trade unions collapsed without a struggle.

In June 1933, the Social Democratic party was outlawed, and within a few weeks, the other political parties simply disbanded on their own. In May, the Nazis had seized the property of the trade unions, arrested the leaders, and ended collective bargaining and strikes. The newly established German Labor Front, an instrument of the party, became the official organization of the working class. Although there is evidence that the working class in 1933 would have resisted the Nazis, the leadership never mobilized proletarian organizations. With surprising ease, the Nazis had imposed their will on the nation.

Hitler made strategic but temporary concessions to the traditional ruling elite. On June 30, 1934, Nazi executioners swiftly murdered the leaders of the SA (the storm troopers who had battled political opponents) to eliminate any potential opposition to Hitler from within the party. With this move, Hitler also relieved the anxieties of industrialists and landowners, who feared that Ernst Röhm, the head of the SA, would persuade Hitler to remove them from positions of power and to implement a program of radical social reform, threatening their property.

The execution of the SA leaders (including Röhm) was also approved by the generals, for they regarded the SA as a rival to the army. In August, all German soldiers swore an oath of unconditional allegiance to the fuehrer, cementing the alliance between the army and National Socialism. The army tied itself to the Nazi regime because it valued the resurgence of militaristic values and applauded the death of the Weimar Republic. As German historian Karl Dietrich Bracher concludes, "Without the assistance of the Army, at first through its toleration and later

through its active cooperation, the country's rapid and final restructuring into the total leader state could not have come about."[21]

Economic Life

Hitler had not sought power to improve the living standards of the masses but to convert Germany into a powerful war machine. Economic problems held little interest for this dreamer, in whose mind danced images of a vast German empire. For him, the "socialism" in National Socialism meant not a comprehensive program of social welfare, but the elimination of the class antagonisms that divided and weakened the fatherland. Radicals within the party wanted to deprive the industrialists and landowners of power and social prestige and to expropriate their property. The more pragmatic Hitler wanted only to deprive them of freedom of action; they were to serve, not control, the state. Germany remained capitalist, but the state had unlimited power to intervene in the economy. Unlike the Bolsheviks, the Nazis did not destroy the upper classes of the Old Regime. Hitler made no war against the industrialists. He wanted from them loyalty, obedience, and a war machine. German businessmen prospered but exercised no influence on political decisions. The profits of industry rose, but the real wages of German workers did not improve. Nevertheless, workers lauded the regime for ending the unemployment crisis.

Nazism and the Churches

Nazism conflicted with the core values of Christianity. "The heaviest blow that ever struck humanity was the coming of Christianity," said Hitler to intimates during World War II.[22] Had Germany won the war, the Nazis would no doubt have tried to root Christianity out of German life. In 1937, the bishop of Berlin defined the essential conflict between Christianity and Nazism:

> *The question at stake is whether there is an authority that stands above all earthly power, the authority of God, Whose commandments are valid independent of space and time, country and race. The question at stake is whether*

individual man possesses personal rights that no community and no state may take from him; whether the free exercise of his conscience may be prevented and forbidden by the state.[23]

Nazism could tolerate no other faith alongside itself. Recognizing that Christianity was a rival claimant for the German soul, the Nazis moved to repress the Protestant and Catholic churches. In the public schools, religious instruction was cut back and the syllabus changed to omit the Jewish origins of Christianity. Christ was depicted not as a Jew, heir to the prophetic tradition of Hebrew monotheism, but as an Aryan hero. The Gestapo (secret state police) censored church newspapers, scrutinized sermons and church activities, forbade some clergymen to preach, dismissed the opponents of Nazism from theological schools, and arrested some clerical critics of the regime.

The clergy were well represented among the Germans who resisted Nazism; some were sent to concentration camps or executed. But these courageous clergy were not representatives of the German churches, which, as organized institutions, capitulated to and cooperated with the Nazi regime. Both the German Evangelical and German Catholic churches demanded that their faithful give Hitler their loyalty; both turned a blind eye to Nazi persecution of Jews; both condemned resistance and found much to admire in the Third Reich; and both supported Hitler's war. When Germany attacked Poland, starting World War II, the Catholic bishops declared: "In this decisive hour we encourage and admonish our Catholic soldiers, in obedience to the Fuehrer, to do their duty and to be ready to sacrifice their whole existence."[24] Both churches urged their faithful to fight for fatherland and fuehrer, pressured conscientious objectors to serve, and celebrated Nazi victories.

The German churches, which preached Christ's message of humanity, failed to take a stand against Nazi inhumanity for a variety of reasons. Many German church leaders feared that resistance would lead to even more severe measures against their churches. Traditionally, the German churches had bowed to state authority and detested revolution. Church leaders also found some Nazi ideas appealing. Intensely na-

tionalistic, antiliberal, antirepublican, and anti-Semitic, many members of the clergy were filled with hope when Hitler came to power. The prominent Lutheran theologian who "welcomed that change that came to Germany in 1933 as a divine gift and miracle"[25] voiced the sentiments of many members of the clergy. Such feelings encouraged prolonged moral nearsightedness, not a revolt of Christian conscience. When the war ended, the German Evangelical church leaders lamented:

[W]e know ourselves to be one with our people in a great company of suffering and in a great solidarity of guilt. With great pain do we say: Through us endless suffering has been brought to many people and countries. . . . We accuse ourselves for not witnessing more courageously, for not praying more faithfully, for not loving more ardently.[26]

Shaping the "New Man"

Propaganda had helped the Nazis come to power. Now it would be used to consolidate their hold on the German nation and shape a "new man," committed to Hitler, race, and Volk. Hitler was a radical revolutionary who desired not only the outward form of power, but also control over the inner person, over the individual's thoughts and feelings. The purpose of Nazi propaganda was to condition the mind to revere the fuehrer and to obey the new regime. Its intent was to deprive individuals of their capacity for independent thought. By concentrating on myths of the race and the infallibility of the fuehrer, Nazi propaganda sought to disorient the rational mind and give the individual new standards to believe in and obey. Propaganda aimed to mold the entire nation to think and respond as the leader-state directed. Even science had to conform to Nazi racial ideology. Thus, Johannes Stark, a Nobel Prize winner, declared that scientific thought is a function of race:

[N]atural science is overwhelmingly a creation of the Nordic-Germanic blood component of the Aryan peoples. . . . The Jewish spirit is wholly different in its orientation. . . . True, Heinrich Hertz made the great discovery of

electromagnetic waves, but he was not a full-blooded Jew. He had a German mother, from whose side his spiritual endowment may well have been conditioned.[27]

The Ministry of Popular Enlightenment, headed by Joseph Goebbels (1897–1945), controlled the press, book publishing, the radio, the theater, and the cinema. Goebbels, holder of a doctoral degree in the humanities, was intelligent and a master in the art of propaganda; he was also vain, cynical, and contemptuous of the very masses he manipulated. But the German people were not merely passive victims of clever and ruthless leaders. "The effective spread of propaganda and the rapid regimentation of cultural life," says Bracher, "would not have been possible without the invaluable help eagerly tendered by writers and artists, professors and churchmen." And the manipulation of the minds of the German people "would not have been effective had it not been for profound historically conditioned relations based . . . on a pseudo-religious exaggerated nationalism and on the idea of the German mission."[28] Although some intellectuals showed their abhorrence of the Nazi regime by emigrating, the great majority gave their support, often with overt enthusiasm. Some individuals rejected Nazi propaganda, but the masses of German people came to regard Nazism as the fulfillment of their nationalist longings.

The Nazis tried to keep the emotions in a state of permanent mobilization, for Hitler understood that the emotionally aroused are most amenable to manipulation. Goose-stepping SA and SS (elite military and police) battalions paraded in the streets; martial music quickened the pulse; Nazi flags decorated public buildings; loudspeakers installed in offices and factories blared the Nazi message, and all work stopped for important broadcasts. Citizens were ordered to greet each other with "Heil Hitler," a potent sign of reverence and submission.

The regime made a special effort to reach young people. All youths between the ages of ten and eighteen were urged and then required to join the Hitler Youth, and all other youth organizations were dissolved. At camps and rallies, young people paraded, sang, saluted, and chanted: "We were slaves; we were outsiders in our own country. So were we before Hitler

united us. Now we would fight against Hell itself for our leader."[29]

Nazification of Education The schools, long breeding grounds of nationalism, militarism, antiliberalism, and anti-Semitism, now indoctrinated the young in Nazi ideology. The Nazis instructed teachers how certain subjects were to be taught; and to ensure obedience, members of the Hitler Youth were asked to report suspicious teachers. Portraits of Hitler, along with Nazi banners, were displayed in classrooms. War stories, adventures of the Hitler Youth, and ancient Nordic legends replaced fairy tales and animal stories in reading material for the young. The curriculum upgraded physical training and sports, curtailed religious instruction, and introduced many courses in "racial science." Decidedly anti-intellectual, the Nazis stressed character building over book learning. They intended to train young people to serve the leader and the racial community—to imbue them with a sense of fellowship for their Volkish kin, that sense of camaraderie found on the battlefield. Expressions of individualism and independence were suppressed.

The universities quickly abandoned freedom of the mind, scientific objectivity, and humanist values. "We repudiate international science, we repudiate the international community of scholars, we repudiate research for the sake of research. Sieg Heil!" declared one historian.[30] Even before the Nazi takeover, many university students and professors had embraced Volkish nationalism and right-wing radicalism. Two years before Hitler came to power, for example, 60 percent of all undergraduates supported the Nazi student organization, and anti-Semitic riots broke out at several universities. Horst von Maltitz observes:

For seventy years or more, the professors had preached aggressive nationalism, the German destiny of power, hero worship, irrational political Romanticism, and so forth, and had increasingly deemphasized, if not eliminated, the teachings of ethical and humanist principles. . . . Essentially neither [professors nor students] wanted to have anything to do with democracy. In the Weimar Republic . . . both groups, on the whole, seemed equally deter-

*mined to tear down that Republic. The profes-
sors did their part by fiery lectures, speeches,
and writings; the students did theirs in noisy
demonstrations, torch-light parades, vandalism, and physical violence. . . . When Hitler
came to power, both professors and students
fell all over themselves to demonstrate their
allegiance.*[31]

In May 1933, professors and students proudly
burned books considered a threat to Nazi ideology. Many academics praised Hitler and the new
regime. Some 10 percent of the university faculty,
principally Jews, Social Democrats, and liberals,
were dismissed, and their colleagues often approved. "From now on it will not be your job to
determine whether something is true but whether
it is in the spirit of the National Socialist revolution," the new minister of culture told university
professors.[32] Numerous courses on Nazi ideology were introduced into the curriculum.

Giant Rallies Symbolic of the Nazi regime
were the monster rallies staged at Nuremberg.
Scores of thousands roared, marched, and worshiped at their leader's feet. These true believers,
the end product of Nazi indoctrination, celebrated Hitler's achievements and demonstrated
their loyalty to their savior. Everything was brilliantly orchestrated to impress Germans and the
world with the irresistible power, determination,
and unity of the Nazi movement and the greatness of the fuehrer. Armies of youths waving
flags, storm troopers bearing weapons, and
workers shouldering long-handled spades paraded past Hitler, who stood at attention, his
arm extended in the Nazi salute. The endless
columns of marchers, the stirring martial music
played by huge bands, the forest of flags, the
chanting and cheering of spectators, and the
burning torches and beaming spotlights united
the participants into a racial community. "Wherever Hitler leads we follow," thundered thousands of Germans in a giant chorus. The Nuremberg rallies were among the greatest theatrical
performances of the twentieth century.

Terror Terror was another means of ensuring
compliance and obedience. The instrument of terror was the SS, which was organized in 1925 to
protect Hitler and other party leaders and to
stand guard at party meetings. Under the leadership of Heinrich Himmler (1900–1945), a fanatical believer in Hitler's racial theories, the SS was
molded into an elite force of disciplined, dedicated, and utterly ruthless men. Myopic, narrow-
chested, and sexually prudish, Himmler contrived a cult of manliness. He envisioned the SS,
who were specially selected for their racial purity
and physical fitness, as a new breed of knights:
Nietzschean supermen who would lead the new
Germany.

The SS staffed the concentration camps established to deal with political prisoners. Through
systematic terror and torture, the SS sought to
deprive the inmates of their human dignity and to
harden themselves for the struggles that lay
ahead. Knowledge that these camps existed and
that some prisoners were never heard from again
was a strong inducement for Germans to remain
obedient.

Anti-Semitic Legislation

The Nazis deprived Jews of their German citizenship and instituted many anti-Jewish measures
designed to make them outcasts. Thousands of
Jewish doctors, lawyers, musicians, artists, and
professors were barred from practicing their professions, and Jewish members of the civil service
were dismissed. A series of laws tightened the
screws of humiliation and persecution. Marriage
or sexual encounters between Germans and Jews
were forbidden. Universities, schools, restaurants,
pharmacies, hospitals, theaters, museums, and
athletic fields were gradually closed to Jews.

In November 1938, using the assassination of a
German official in Paris by a seventeen-year-old
Jewish youth, whose family had been mistreated
by the Nazis, as a pretext, the Nazis organized an
extensive pogrom. Nazi gangs murdered scores of
Jews and burned and looted thousands of Jewish
businesses, homes, and synagogues all over Germany—an event that became known as Night of
the Broken Glass (*Kristallnacht*). Twenty thousand Jews were thrown into concentration camps.
The Reich then imposed on the Jewish community
a fine of 1 billion marks. These measures were a
mere prelude, however. During World War II,
genocidal murder of European Jewry became a
cardinal Nazi objective (see Chapter 33).

YOUNG NAZIS BURNING BOOKS IN SALZBURG, AUSTRIA, 1938. Heinrich Heine, the great nineteenth-century German-Jewish poet, once said that people who burn books end up burning people. (© *Topham/The Image Works*)

Mass Support

The Nazi regime became a police state, symbolized by mass arrests, the persecution of Jews, and concentration camps that institutionalized terror. Yet fewer heads rolled than people expected, and in many ways life seemed normal. The Nazis established the totalitarian state without upsetting the daily life of the majority of the population. Moreover, Hitler, like Mussolini, was careful to maintain the appearance of legality. By not abolishing parliament or repealing the constitution, he could claim that his was a legitimate government. By consolidating power in stages and retaining the institutions of the republic, the Nazis lulled both Germans and people in other countries into believing that legitimate statesmen governed Germany.

To people concerned with little but family,

job, and friends—and this includes most people in any country—life in the first few years of the Third Reich seemed quite satisfying. People believed that the new government was trying to solve Germany's problems in a vigorous and sensible manner, in contrast to the ineffective Weimar leadership. By 1936, the reinvigoration of the economy, stimulated in part by rearmament, had virtually eliminated unemployment, which had stood at 6 million jobless when Hitler took power. An equally astounding achievement in German eyes was the rebuilding of the war machine and the restoration of power in international affairs. It seemed to most Germans that Hitler had awakened a sense of self-sacrifice and national dedication among a people dispirited by defeat and depression. He had united a country torn by class antagonisms and social distinctions and given people a sense of pride. Workers had jobs, businessmen profits, and generals troops— what could be wrong?

Many intellectuals, viewing Hitlerism as the victory of idealism over materialism and of community over selfish individualism, lent their talents to the regime and endorsed the burning of books and the suppression of freedom. To them, Hitler was a visionary who had shown Germany and the world a new way of life—a new creed.

Thus, having regained confidence in themselves and their nation, many Germans rejoiced in Hitler's leadership, did not regret the loss of political freedom, and remained indifferent to the plight of the persecuted, particularly Jews. Moreover, Hitler's popularity and mass support rested on something far stronger than propaganda and terror, for he had won the hearts of a sizable proportion of the German people. To many Germans, Hitler was exactly as Nazi propaganda had depicted him: "He stands like a statue grown beyond the measure of earthly man."[33]

There was some opposition and resistance to the Hitler regime. Social Democrats and communists organized small cells. Some conservatives, who considered Hitler to be a threat to traditional German values, and some clergy, who saw Nazism as a pagan religion in conflict with Christian morality, also formed small opposition groups. But only resistance from the army could have toppled Hitler. Some generals, even before World War II, urged such resistance, but the overwhelming majority of German officers preferred the new regime or considered it dishonorable to break their oath of loyalty to Hitler. These officers would remain loyal until the bitter end. Very few Germans realized that their country was passing through a long night of barbarism, and still fewer considered resistance.

LIBERALISM AND AUTHORITARIANISM IN OTHER LANDS

The Spread of Authoritarianism

After World War I, in country after country, parliamentary democracy collapsed and authoritarian leaders came to power. In most of these countries, liberal ideals had not penetrated deeply; liberalism met resistance from conservative elites.

Spain and Portugal   In both Spain and Portugal, parliamentary regimes faced strong opposition from the church, the army, and large landowners. In 1926, army officers overthrew the Portuguese republic that had been created in 1910, and gradually, Antonio de Oliveira Salazar (1889–1970), a professor of economics, emerged as dictator. In Spain, after antimonarchist forces won the election of 1931, King Alfonso XIII (1902–1931) left the country, and Spain was proclaimed a republic. But the new government, led by socialists and liberals, faced the determined opposition of the ruling elite. The reforms introduced by the republic—expropriation of large estates, reduction of the number of army officers, dissolution of the Jesuit order, and closing of church schools—only intensified the Old Order's hatred.

The difficulties of the new Spanish republic mounted: workers, near starvation, rioted and engaged in violent strikes; the military attempted a coup; and Catalonia, with its long tradition of separatism, tried to establish its autonomy. Imitating the example of France (see page 794), the parties of the left, including the Communists, united in the Popular Front, which came to power in February 1936. In July 1936, General Francisco Franco (1892–1975), stationed in Spanish Morocco, led a revolt against the republic. He was supported by army leaders, the church, monarchists, landlords, industrialists, and the Falange, a newly formed fascist party. Spain was torn by a bloody civil war. Aided by Fascist Italy and Nazi Germany (see page 830), Franco won in 1939 and established a dictatorship.

Eastern and Central Europe   Parliamentary government in eastern Europe rested on weak foundations. Predominantly rural, these countries lacked the sizable professional and commercial classes that had promoted liberalism in western Europe. Only Czechoslovakia had a substantial native middle class with a strong liberal tradition. The rural masses of eastern Europe, traditionally subjected to monarchical and aristocratic authority, were not used to political thinking or civic responsibility. Students and intellectuals, often gripped by a romantic nationalism, were drawn to antidemocratic movements.

Right-wing leaders also played on the fear of communism. When parliamentary government failed to solve internal problems, the opponents of the liberal state seized the helm. Fascist movements, however, had little success in eastern Europe. Rather, authoritarian regimes headed by traditional ruling elites—army leaders or kings—extinguished democracy there.

With the dissolution of the Hapsburg Empire at the end of World War I, Austria became a democratic republic. From the start, it suffered from severe economic problems. The Hapsburg Empire had been a huge free-trade area, permitting food and raw materials to circulate unimpeded throughout the empire. The new Austria lacked sufficient food to feed the population of Vienna and needed raw materials for its industries. Worsening its plight was the erection of tariff barriers by each of the states that had formerly been part of the Hapsburg Empire. Between 1922 and 1926, the League of Nations had to rescue Austria from bankruptcy. The Great Depression aggravated Austria's economic position. Many Austrians believed that only an Anschluss (union) with Germany could solve Austria's problems.

Austria was also burdened by a conflict between the industrial region, including Vienna, and the agricultural provinces. Factory workers were generally socialist and anticlerical; the peasants were strongly Catholic and antisocialist. The Social Democrats controlled Vienna, but the rural population gave its support to the Christian Socialist party. Each party had its own private army: the workers had the *Schutzbund,* and the provincials the *Heimwehr.* During the Great Depression, Chancellor Engelbert Dollfuss (1892–1934) sought to turn the country into a one-party state. In February 1934, police and Heimwehr contingents raided Social Democratic headquarters. When the Social Democrats called a general strike, Dollfuss bombarded a workers' housing project, killing 193 civilians, and suppressed the Social Democratic party. Austria had joined the ranks of authoritarian states.

When Hitler came to power in Germany, Austrian Nazis pressed for Anschluss. In July 1934, a band of them assassinated Dollfuss, but a Nazi plot to capture the government failed. Four years later, however, Hitler would march into Austria, bringing about the Anschluss desired by many Austrians.

The new Hungary that emerged at the end of World War I faced an uprising by communists inspired by the success of the Bolsheviks in Russia. Béla Kun (1885–1937), supported by Russian money, established a soviet regime in Budapest in March 1919. But Kun could not win the support of the peasants and was opposed by the Allies, who helped Romania crush the revolutionary government. In 1920, power passed to Admiral Miklós Horthy (1868–1957), who instituted a brief white terror, which exceeded the red terror of the Kun regime. During the Great Depression, the Horthy government, which favored the large landholders, was challenged by the radical right, which preached extreme nationalism, anti-Semitism, and anticapitalism and tried to win mass support through land reform. Its leader, Gyula Gömbös (1886–1936), who served as prime minister from 1932 to 1936, sought to align Hungary with Nazi Germany. Wishing to regain territories lost as a result of World War I and aware of Hitler's growing might, Hungary drew closer to Germany in the late 1930s.

Poland, Greece, Bulgaria, and Romania became either royal or military dictatorships. In September 1940, a year after World War II had started, the fascist Iron Guard seized power in Romania and engaged in the mass murder of Jews. In January 1941, the Iron Guard was crushed by the military. The new state of Czechoslovakia, guided by President Tomáš Masaryk (1850–1937) and Foreign Minister Eduard Beneš (1884–1948), who were both committed to the liberal-humanist tradition of the West, preserved parliamentary democracy. Its most serious problem came from the 3.25 million Germans living within its borders, primarily in the Sudetenland (see page 831). The German minority founded the Sudetenland German party, which modeled itself after Hitler's Nazi party. Hitler later exploited the issue of the Sudetenland Germans to dismember Czechoslovakia.

The Western Democracies

While liberal governments were failing in much of Europe, the great Western democracies—the

United States, Britain, and France—continued to preserve democratic institutions. In Britain and the United States, fascist movements were merely a nuisance. In France, fascism was more of a threat because it exploited a deeply ingrained hostility in some quarters to the liberal ideals of the French Revolution.

The United States The central problem faced by the Western democracies was the Great Depression, which started in the United States. In the 1920s, hundreds of thousands of Americans had bought stock on credit; this buying spree sent stock prices soaring well beyond what the stocks were actually worth. In late October 1929, the stock market was hit by a wave of panic selling; prices plummeted. Within a few weeks, the value of stocks listed on the New York Stock Exchange fell by some $26 billion. A terrible chain reaction followed over the next few years. Businesses cut production and unemployment soared; farmers unable to meet mortgage payments lost their land; banks that had made poor investments closed down. American investors withdrew the capital they had invested in Europe, causing European banks and businesses to fail. Throughout the world, trade declined and unemployment rose.

When President Franklin Delano Roosevelt (1882–1945) took office in 1933, more than 13 million Americans—one-quarter of the labor force—were out of work. Hunger and despair showed on the faces of the American people. Moving away from laissez faire, Roosevelt instituted a comprehensive program of national planning, economic experimentation, and reform, known as the New Deal. Although the U.S. political and economic system faced a severe test, few Americans turned to fascism or communism. The government engaged in national planning but did not break with democratic values and procedures.

Britain Even before the Great Depression, Britain faced severe economic problems. Loss of markets to foreign competitors hurt British manufacturing, mining, and shipbuilding; rapid development of water and oil power reduced the demand for British coal, and outdated mining equipment put Britain in a poor competitive position. To decrease costs, mine owners in 1926 called for salary cuts; the coal miners countered with a strike and were joined by workers in other industries. To many Britons, the workers were leftist radicals trying to overthrow the government. Many wanted the state to break the strike. After nine days, industrial workers called off their strike, but the miners held out for another six months, only to return to work with longer hours and lower pay. Although the general strike had failed, it did improve relations between the classes, for the workers had not called for revolution and they had refrained from violence. The fear that British workers would follow the Bolshevik path abated.

The Great Depression cast a pall over Britain. The Conservative party leadership tried to stimulate exports by devaluing the pound and to encourage industry by providing loans at lower interest rates, but in the main, it left the task of recovery to industry itself. Not until Britain began to rearm did unemployment decline significantly. Despite the economic slump of the 1920s and the Great Depression, Britain remained politically stable, a testament to the strength of its parliamentary tradition. Neither the communists nor the newly formed British Fascist party gained mass support.

France In the early 1920s, France was concerned with postwar rebuilding. From 1926 to 1929, France was relatively prosperous. Industrial and agricultural production expanded, tourism increased, and the currency was stable. Although France did not feel the Great Depression as painfully as did the United States and Germany, the nation was hurt by the decline in trade and production and the rise in unemployment.

The political instability that had beset the Third Republic virtually since its inception continued, and hostility to the Republic mounted. As the leading parties failed to solve the nation's problems, a number of fascistic groups gained strength. On February 6, 1934, right-wing gangs threatened to invade the Chamber of Deputies. What brought on the crisis was the exposure of the shady dealings of Alexander Stavisky, a financial manipulator with high government connections. The resulting violence left hundreds wounded and several dead. The whole affair was too poorly organized to constitute a serious

Roger-Viollet

CHARLES MAURRAS

Some historians view *Action Française,* an ultra-nationalist, antidemocratic, and anti-Semitic, organization founded in 1898–99 by Charles Maurras (1868–1952), as a forerunner of the fascist movements that emerged in the aftermath of World War I. In the tradition of early nineteenth-century French conservatives, Maurras held that the collective takes precedence over the individual: "The primary reality, more real than the individual and more real also than the world," he declared, "is *la patrie,* the Country."* He regarded the religious individualism of the Reformation, the political individualism of the French Revolution, and the cultural individualism of romanticism as forces of national division and discord. The principle of equality, he said, permitted rule by the mediocre and the incompetent.

To save France from class war, political factions, capitalist exploitation and spiritual disintegration—all consequences of unbridled individualism in his eyes—Maurras championed integral nationalism. It sought the integration of the nation around Catholicism, France's ancestral religion; monarchy, a deeply rooted French tradition; and hierarchy, leadership based on birth and talent. Maurras valued France of the Old Regime, for it was monarchical, hierarchical, and community minded. Hostile and foreign influences—he meant specifically Masons, Protestants, Jews, alien residents, and recently naturalized citizens—must be

threat to the government. But to the parties of the left—socialists, communists, and radicals—the events of February 6–7 constituted a rightist attempt to establish a fascist regime.

Fear of growing fascist strength at home and in Italy and Germany led the parties of the left to form the Popular Front. In 1936, Léon Blum (1872–1950), a socialist and a Jew, became premier. Blum's Popular Front government instituted more reforms than any other ministry in the history of the Third Republic. To end a wave of strikes that tied up production, Blum gave workers a forty-hour week and holidays with pay and guaranteed them the right to collective bargaining. He took steps to nationalize the armaments and aircraft industries. To reduce the influence of the wealthiest families, he put the Bank of France under government control. By raising

deprived of political rights and influence. Such people, he argued, had no deep roots in the French nation; they could never be truly French. Maurras hoped that army leaders, inspired by Action Française's philosophy, would overthrow the Republic and reestablish monarchical rule.

Maurras was strongly anti-Semitic, holding that "Jewish capitalism" and "Jewish democracy" were corrupting the French soul. He attributed a destructive individualism to Judaism, for it had conceived the idea of one God who had endowed everyone with a conscience: "it is in the Law and the Prophets . . . that are to be found the first expressions in antiquity of the individualism, egalitarianism, humanitarianism, and social and political idealism that were to mark 1789."[†] He saw the Jews as agents of revolution and alien conspirators. The Action Française waged a fierce campaign against a pardon for Dreyfus, the Jewish army officer who was falsely convicted of treason. At times, it engaged in organized vandalism and violence against his supporters.

Student members of the Action Française joined with young royalists to form the *Camelots du Roi* (hawkers of the king), which sold the Action Française's newspaper in the street, acted as guards at the organization's meetings, and participated in anti-Republic and nationalist demonstrations. The organized violence of the Camelots du Roi presaged the fascist terror tactics after World War I. In this sense, the Camelots could be viewed as the first storm troopers.

Support for Action Française came principally from the army, the nobility, the clergy, and middle-class professionals. Between 1910 and 1926, the Action's membership ranged from thirty thousand to forty thousand. As such it was no threat to the state. But its cult of the fatherland, condemnation of democracy, celebration of war, virulent anti-Semitism, employment of organized violence, and call for a leader to resurrect the nation anticipated and coincided with fascism.

After France's defeat in World War II, Maurras supported the authoritarian Vichy regime and denounced the resistance movement. He applauded Vichy's laws that made Jews second-class citizens and was indifferent to the deportation of French Jews to German concentration camps. After the liberation of France, Maurras was sentenced to life imprisonment but was released in 1951 for medical reasons.

---

*Quoted in Michael Sutton, *Nationalism, Positivism and Catholicism: The Politics of Charles Maurras and French Catholics, 1890–1914* (Cambridge: Cambridge University Press, 1982), p. 26.
†Ibid., p. 8.

prices and buying wheat, he aided farmers. Conservatives and fascists denounced Blum as a Jewish socialist who was converting the fatherland into a communist state. "Better Hitler than Blum," grumbled French rightists.

Despite significant reforms, the Popular Front could not revitalize the economy. In 1937, the Blum ministry was overthrown and the Popular Front, always a tenuous alliance, fell apart.

Through democratic means the Blum government had tried to give France its own New Deal, but the social reforms passed by the Popular Front only intensified hatred between the working classes and the rest of the nation. France had preserved democracy against the onslaught of domestic fascists, but it was a demoralized and divided nation that confronted a united and dynamic Nazi Germany.

◆ ◆ ◆

NOTES

1. Quoted in Zeev Sternhill, "Fascist Ideology," in *Fascism: A Reader's Guide,* ed. Walter Laqueur (Berkeley: University of California Press, 1976), p. 338.

2. Quoted in John Weiss, *The Fascist Tradition* (New York: Harper & Row, 1967), p. 9.

3. Quoted in F. L. Carsten, *The Rise of Fascism* (Berkeley: University of California Press, 1969), p. 53.

4. Quoted in Max Gallo, *Mussolini's Italy* (New York: Macmillan, 1973), p. 218.

5. Kurt Sontheimer, "Anti-Democratic Thought in the Weimar Republic," in *The Path to Dictatorship, 1918–1933,* trans. John Conway, intro. Fritz Stern (Garden City, N.Y.: Doubleday Anchor Books, 1966), pp. 47–49.

6. Quoted in Joachim C. Fest, *Hitler,* trans. Richard and Clara Winston (New York: Harcourt Brace Jovanovich, 1974), p. 162.

7. Quoted in Karl J. Newman, *European Democracy between the Wars* (Notre Dame, Ind.: University of Notre Dame Press, 1971), p. 276.

8. Hajo Holborn, *Germany and Europe* (Garden City, N.Y.: Doubleday Anchor Books, 1971), p. 215.

9. Fest, *Hitler,* p. 548.

10. Quoted in Alan Bullock, *Hitler: A Study in Tyranny* (New York: Harper Torchbooks, 1964), p. 400.

11. *Hitler's Secret Conversations, 1941–1944,* with an introductory essay by H. R. Trevor Roper (New York: Farrar, Straus & Young, 1953), p. 28.

12. Quoted in Lucy S. Dawidowicz, *The War Against the Jews, 1933–1945* (New York: Holt, Rinehart & Winston, 1975), p. 21.

13. Quoted in Uri Tal, "Consecration of Politics in the Nazi Era," in *Judaism and Christianity Under the Impact of National Socialism,* eds. Otto Dov Kulka and Paul R. Mendes Flohr (Jerusalem: Historical Society of Israel, 1987), p. 70.

14. Adolf Hitler, *Mein Kampf,* trans. Ralph Mannheim (Boston: Houghton Mifflin, 1962), p. 107.

15. Ibid., p. 479.

16. Cited in Ian Kershaw, "Hitler and the Germans," in *Life in the Third Reich,* ed. Richard Bessel (New York: Oxford University Press, 1987), pp. 43–44.

17. Quoted in Hannah Arendt, *The Origins of Totalitarianism* (New York: Meridian Books, World Publishing, 1958), p. 330.

18. Quoted in David Welch, ed., *Nazi Propaganda* (Totowa, N.J.: Barnes & Noble, 1983), p. 5.

19. Quoted in J. S. Conway, *The Nazi Persecution of the Churches* (New York: Basic Books, 1968), p. 202.

20. Quoted in Helmut Krausnick, Hans Buchheim, Martin Broszart, and Hans-Adolf Jacobsen, *Anatomy of the SS State* (London: Collins, 1968), p. 128.

21. Karl Dietrich Bracher, *The German Dictatorship,* trans. Jean Steinberg (New York: Praeger, 1970), p. 243.

22. *Hitler's Secret Conversations,* p. 6.

23. Quoted in Hans Rothfels, "Resistance Begins," in *Path to Dictatorship,* pp. 160–161.

24. Quoted in Guenter Lewy, *The Catholic Church and Nazi Germany* (New York: McGraw-Hill, 1965), p. 226.

25. Quoted in Hermann Graml et al., *The German Resistance to Hitler* (Berkeley: University of California Press, 1970), p. 206.

26. Quoted in Conway, *Nazi Persecution,* p. 332.

27. Excerpted in George L. Mosse, ed., *Nazi Culture* (New York: Grosset & Dunlap, 1966), pp. 206–207.

28. Bracher, *German Dictatorship,* pp. 248, 251.

29. Quoted in T. L. Jarman, *The Rise and Fall of Nazi Germany* (New York: New York University Press, 1956), p. 182.

30. Quoted in Horst von Maltitz, *The Evolution of Hitler's Germany* (New York: McGraw-Hill, 1973), pp. 433–434.

31. Ibid., pp. 438–439.

32. Quoted in Bracher, *German Dictatorship*, p. 268.

33. Quoted in Fest, *Hitler*, p. 532.

SUGGESTED READING

Allen, William Sheridan, *The Nazi Seizure of Power* (1965). An illuminating study of how the people of a small German town reacted to Nazism during the years 1930–1935.

Bissel, Richard, ed., *Life in the Third Reich* (1987). Essays dealing with various aspects of life in Hitler's Germany; good overviews.

Bracher, Karl Dietrich, *The German Dictatorship* (1970). A highly regarded analysis of all phases of the Nazi state.

Broszat, Martin, *The Hitler State* (1981). A detailed anatomy of the internal structure of the Third Reich.

Bucheim, Heim, *Totalitarian Rule* (1968). The nature and characteristics of totalitarianism, by a German scholar.

Bullock, Alan, *Hitler: A Study in Tyranny* (1964). An excellent biography.

Burleigh, Michael, and Wolfgang Wippermann, *The Racial State: Germany 1933–1945* (1991). Persecution of Jews, Gypsies, mentally handicapped, and homosexuals; analysis of racially motivated social policies of the Nazi regime.

Cassels, Alan, *Fascist Italy* (1968). A clearly written introduction.

Conway, J. S., *The Nazi Persecution of the Churches* (1968). Nazi persecution of the churches and the capitulation of the clergy.

Fest, Joachim C., *Hitler* (1974). An excellent biography.

Haffner, Sebastian, *The Meaning of Hitler* (1979). A German journalist's inquiry into Hitler's successes and failures.

Jackel, Eberhard, *Hitler's Weltanschauung* (1972). An analysis of Hitler's world-view.

Kirkpatrick, Ivone, *Mussolini: A Study in Power* (1964). A solid biography.

Laqueur, Walter, ed., *Fascism: A Reader's Guide* (1976). A superb collection of essays.

Mack Smith, Denis, *Mussolini* (1982). By a leading historian of modern Italy.

Maltitz, Horst von, *The Evolution of Hitler's Germany* (1973). In trying to explain how it was possible, the author discusses the German roots of Nazism.

Mayer, Milton, *They Thought They Were Free* (1955). The lives of ordinary citizens who became Nazis.

Mosse, George L., *Nazi Culture* (1966). A representative collection of Nazi writings with a fine introduction.

Noakes, J., and G. Pridham, eds., *Nazism 1919–1945* (1983). A useful collection of primary sources in two volumes.

Paxton, Robert O., *Europe in the Twentieth Century* (1975). A first-rate text with an excellent bibliography.

Peukert, Detlev J. K., *Inside Nazi Germany* (1982). How ordinary citizens responded to Nazi rule.

Rogger, Hans, and Eugen Weber, eds., *The European Right* (1966). A valuable collection of essays on right-wing movements in various European countries.

Spielvogel, Jackson J., *Hitler and Nazi Germany* (1988). Clearly written, up-to-date survey.

Turner, Henry A., ed., *Reappraisals of Fascism* (1975). A collection of useful essays.

REVIEW QUESTIONS

1. How did fascist principles "stand for the sheer, categorical, definitive antithesis to the world of democracy . . . to the world which still abides by the fundamental principles laid down in 1789"?

2. Why did some Italians support Mussolini?

3. How did Mussolini bluff his way to power?

4. How did Mussolini try to extend his control over Italy?

5. What were Mussolini's policies toward the church? The economy?

6. In what ways was Mussolini less effective than Hitler in establishing a totalitarian state?

7. How was Hitler's outlook shaped by his experiences in Vienna?

8. What was the significance of the Munich putsch of 1923?

9. What were Hitler's attitudes toward democracy, the masses, war, the Jews, and propaganda?

10. What made Hitler's views attractive to Germans?

11. How was Hitler able to gain power?

12. How did the Nazis extend their control over Germany?

13. In what ways did Nazism conflict with the core values of Christianity? What was the general policy of the Nazis toward the churches? Why did the German churches generally fail to take a stand against the Nazi regime?

14. What was the purpose of the giant rallies?

15. By 1939, most Germans were enthusiastic about the Nazi regime. Explain this statement.

16. What lessons might democratic societies draw from the experience of fascist totalitarianism?

17. After World War I, in country after country, parliamentary democracy collapsed and authoritarian leaders came to power. Explain.

18. How did the United States, Britain, and France try to cope with the Great Depression?

CHAPTER 32

Thought and Culture in an Era of World Wars and Totalitarianism

*T*he presuppositions of the Enlightenment, already eroding in the decades before World War I, seemed near collapse after 1918—another casualty of trench warfare. Economic distress, particularly during the depression, also profoundly disoriented the European mind. Westerners no longer possessed a frame of reference, a common outlook for understanding themselves, their times, or the past. The core values of Western civilization—the self-sufficiency of reason and the inviolability of the individual—no longer seemed inspiring or binding.

The crisis of consciousness evoked a variety of responses. Some intellectuals, having lost faith in the purpose of Western civilization, turned their backs on it or found escape in their art. Others sought a new hope in the Soviet experiment or in fascism; still others reaffirmed the rational-humanist tradition of the Enlightenment. Christian thinkers, repelled by the secularism, materialism, and rootlessness of the modern age, urged westerners to find renewed meaning and purpose in their ancestral religion. A philosophical movement, called existentialism, which rose to prominence after World War II, aspired to make life authentic in a world stripped of universal values.

INTELLECTUALS AND ARTISTS IN TROUBLED TIMES

Postwar Pessimism

After World War I, Europeans looked at themselves and their civilization differently. It seemed that in science and technology they had unleashed powers that they could not control, and belief in the stability and security of European civilization

Guernica (detail) by Pablo Picasso. A Passionate Protest against Fascism and the Horrors of War. (*Giraudon/Art Resource, Copyright 1991 ARS, N.Y./SPADEM*)

appeared to be an illusion. Also illusory was the expectation that reason would banish surviving signs of darkness, ignorance, and injustice and usher in an age of continual progress. European intellectuals felt that they were living in a "broken world." In a time of heightened brutality and mobilized irrationality, the values of old Europe seemed beyond recovery. "All the great words," wrote D. H. Lawrence, "were cancelled out for that generation."[1] The fissures discernible in European civilization before 1914 had grown wider and deeper. To be sure, Europe also had its optimists—those who found reason for hope in the League of Nations and in the easing of international tensions and improved economic conditions in the mid 1920s. However, the Great Depression and the triumph of totalitarianism intensified feelings of doubt and disillusionment.

The somber mood that gripped European intellectuals in the immediate postwar period had been anticipated by Freud in a series of papers published in 1915 under the title "Thoughts for the Times on War and Death." The war, said Freud, stripped westerners of those cultural superimpositions that had served to contain a murderous primeval aggressiveness and it threatened to inflict irreparable damage on European civilization.

> We cannot but feel that no event has ever destroyed so much that is precious in the common possessions of humanity, confused so many of the clearest intelligences or so thoroughly debased what is highest. . . . [T]he war in which we had refused to believe broke out, and it brought —disillusionment. . . . It tramples in blind fury on all that comes in its way, as though there were to be no future and no peace among men after it is over. It cuts all the common bonds between the contending peoples, and threatens to leave a legacy of embitterment that will make any renewal of these bonds impossible for a long time to come.[2]

A pessimistic outlook also pervaded Freud's *Civilization and Its Discontents* (1930), in which he held that civilized life was forever threatened by the antisocial and irrational elements of human nature.

Other expressions of pessimism abounded. In 1919, Paul Valéry stated: "We modern civiliza-

tions have learned to recognize that we are mortal like the others. We feel that a civilization is as fragile as life."[3] "We are living today under the sign of the collapse of civilization,"[4] declared humanitarian Albert Schweitzer in 1923. In the midst of the depression, Arnold Toynbee wrote: "The year 1931 was distinguished from previous years . . . by one outstanding feature. In 1931 men and women all over the world were seriously contemplating and frankly discussing the possibility that the Western system of Society might break down and cease to work."[5] German philosopher Karl Jaspers noted in 1932 that "there is a growing awareness of imminent ruin tantamount to a dread of the approaching end of all that makes life worthwhile."[6]

Disillusionment and gloom also permeated works of fiction and poetry. The novels of Aldous Huxley rejected belief in progress and expressed a disenchantment with the modern world. Ernest Hemingway's *The Sun Also Rises* (1926) described a lost postwar generation. In *All Quiet on the Western Front* (1929), Erich Maria Remarque dealt with the horrors of the war and their impact. A German soldier in the novel ponders the war's effect on youth:

> I am twenty years old; yet I know nothing of life but despair, death, fear, and fatuous superficiality cast over an abyss of sorrow. I see how peoples are set against one another, and in silence, unknowingly, foolishly, obediently, innocently slay one another. I see that the keenest brains of the world invent weapons and words to make it yet more refined and enduring. . . . all my generation is experiencing these things with me. . . . What do they expect of us if a time ever comes when the war is over? Through the years our business has been killing. . . . Our knowledge of life is limited to death. What will happen afterwards?[7]

In the poem "The Second Coming" (1919), William Butler Yeats conveys his sense of the dark times:

> Mere anarchy is loosed upon the world,
> The blood-dimmed tide is loosed, and everywhere
> The Ceremony of innocence is drowned;
> The best lack all conviction, while the worst

Are full of passionate intensity.
Surely some revelation is at hand
Surely the Second Coming is at hand.[8]

T. S. Eliot's "The Waste Land" (1922) also expresses a feeling of foreboding. In his image of a collapsing European civilization, Eliot creates a macabre scenario. Hooded hordes, modern-day barbarians, swarm over plains and lay waste cities. Jerusalem, Athens, Alexandria, Vienna, and London—each once a great spiritual or cultural center—are now collapsing.[9]

Other writers and thinkers also focused on the crises facing the Western world. Carl Gustav Jung, a Swiss psychologist who broke with Freud, stated in *Modern Man in Search of a Soul* (1933):

I believe I am not exaggerating when I say that modern man has suffered an almost fatal shock, psychologically speaking, and as a result has fallen into profound uncertainty. . . . The revolution in our conscious outlook, brought about by the catastrophic results of the World War, shows itself in our inner life by the shattering of our faith in ourselves and our own worth. . . . I realize only too well that I am losing my faith in the possibility of a rational organization of the world, the old dream of the millennium, in which peace and harmony should rule, has grown pale.[10]

In 1936, Dutch historian Johan Huizinga wrote in a chapter entitled "Apprehension of Doom":

We are living in a demented world. And we know it. . . . Everywhere there are doubts as to the solidity of our social structure, vague fears of the imminent future, a feeling that our civilization is on the way to ruin. . . . almost all things which once seemed sacred and immutable have now become unsettled, truth and humanity, justice and reason. . . . The sense of living in the midst of a violent crisis of civilization, threatening complete collapse, has spread far and wide.[11]

The most influential expression of pessimism was Oswald Spengler's *The Decline of the West*. The first volume was published in July 1918, as the war was drawing to a close, and the second

volume in 1922. The work achieved instant notoriety, particularly in Spengler's native Germany, which was shattered by defeat. Spengler viewed history as an assemblage of many different cultures that, like living organisms, experience birth, youth, maturity, and death. What contemporaries pondered most was Spengler's insistence that Western civilization had entered its final stage and that its death could not be averted.

Spengler defined a culture as a spiritual orientation that pervades a people's literature, art, religion, philosophy, politics, and economics; each culture has a distinctive style, which distinguishes it from other cultures. The ancient Greeks, wrote Spengler, viewed themselves as living in a clearly defined and finite world. Hence, classical sculpture was characterized by the life-size nude statue; architecture, by the temple with small columns; and political life, by the small city-state rather than by a kingdom or an empire. Modern westerners have a different cultural orientation, said Spengler; they exhibit a Faustian urge to expand, to reach out. Thus, Europeans developed perspectival art, which permits distance to be depicted on a canvas; they sailed the oceans and conquered vast regions of the globe; and they invented the telephone and telegraph, making possible quick communication over great distances.

According to Spengler, cultures had to pass through three necessary stages: a heroic youth, a creative maturity, and a decadent old age. In its youth, during the Renaissance, said Spengler, Western culture experienced the triumphs of Michelangelo, Shakespeare, and Galileo; in its maturity, during the eighteenth century, Western culture reached its creative height in the music of Mozart, the poetry of Goethe, and the philosophy of Kant. But now, Faustian culture, entering old age, was showing signs of decay: a growing materialism and skepticism; a disenchanted proletariat; rampant warfare and competition for empire; and decadent art forms. "Of great painting or great music there can no longer be, for Western people, any question," Spengler concluded.[12]

To an already troubled Western world, Spengler offered no solace. The West, like other cultures and like any living organism, was destined to die. Its decline was irreversible and its death inevitable; the symptoms of its degeneration were already evident. Spengler's gloomy prognostication buttressed the fascists, who claimed that they were creating a new civilization on the ruins of the dying European civilization.

Literature and Art: Innovation, Disillusionment, and Social Commentary

Postwar pessimism did not prevent writers and artists from continuing the cultural innovations begun before the war. In the works of D. H. Lawrence, Marcel Proust, André Gide, James Joyce, Franz Kafka, T. S. Eliot, and Thomas Mann, the modernist movement achieved a brilliant flowering. Often these writers gave expression to the troubles and uncertainties of the postwar period.

Franz Kafka (1883–1924), whose major novels, *The Trial* and *The Castle,* were published after his death, did not receive recognition until after World War II. Yet perhaps better than any other novelist of his generation, Kafka grasped the dilemma of the modern age. There is no apparent order or stability in Kafka's world. Human beings strive to make sense out of life, but everywhere ordinary occurrences thwart them. They are caught in a bureaucratic web, which they cannot control; they live in a nightmare society dominated by oppressive, cruel, and corrupt officials and amoral torturers. In Kafka's world, cruelty and injustice are accepted facts of existence, power is exercised without limits, and victims cooperate in their own destruction. Traditional values and ordinary logic do not operate. Our world, thought to be secure, stable, and purposeful, easily falls apart.

In *The Trial,* for example, Josef K., an ordinary man who has no consciousness of wrongdoing, is arrested. "K. lived in a country with a legal constitution, there was universal peace, all the laws were in force; who dared seize him in his own dwelling?"[13] Josef K. is never told the reason for his arrest, and he is eventually executed, a victim of institutional evil that breaks and destroys him "like a dog." In these observations, Kafka anticipated the emerging totalitarian state. (Kafka's three sisters perished in the Holocaust.)

Kafka, a German-speaking Jew in the alien Slav environment of Czechoslovakia, was intimi-

Franz Kafka (1883–1924). The troubled Czech-Jewish writer expressed the feelings of alienation and aloneness that burden people in the modern age. (*The Bettmann Archive*)

dated by a tyrannical father. He died of tuberculosis at an early age. In voicing his own deep anxieties, Kafka expressed the feelings of alienation and isolation that characterize the modern individual. He explored life's dreads and absurdities, offering no solutions or consolation. In Kafka's works, people are defeated and unable to comprehend the irrational forces that contribute to their destruction. Although the mind yearns for coherence, Kafka tells us that uncertainty, if not chaos, governs human relationships. We can be sure neither of our own identities nor of the world we encounter, for human beings are the playthings of unfathomable forces, too irrational to master.

A brooding pessimism about the human condition pervades Kafka's work. One reason for the intensified interest in Kafka after World War II, observes Angel Flores, "is that the European world of the late 30's and 40's with its betrayals and concentration camps, its resulting cruelties and indignities, bore a remarkable resemblance to the world depicted by Kafka in the opening decades of the century. History seems to have imitated the nightmarish background evoked by the dreamer of Prague."[14]

Before World War I, the German writer Thomas Mann (1875–1955) had earned a reputation for his short stories and novels, particularly *Buddenbrooks* (1901), which portrayed the decline of a prosperous bourgeois family. At the outbreak of the war, Mann was a staunch conservative who disliked democracy. After the war, he drew closer to liberalism, supporting the Weimar Republic and attacking the Nazi cult of irrationalism.

In *Mario and the Magician* (1930), Mann explicitly attacked Italian fascism, and implied that it would require armed resistance. In 1931, two years before Hitler took power, Mann, in the article entitled "An Appeal to Reason," described National Socialism and the extreme nationalism it espoused as a rejection of the Western rational tradition and a regression to primitive and barbaric modes of behavior. Nazism, he said, "is distinguished by . . . its absolute unrestraint, its orgiastic, radically anti-humane, frenziedly dynamic character. . . . Everything is possible, everything is permitted as a weapon against human decency. . . . Fanaticism turns into a means of salvation . . . politics becomes an opiate for the masses . . . and reason veils her face."[15]

After Hitler's seizure of power, Mann went to Switzerland and eventually to the United States, where he remained a resolute foe of totalitarianism. In 1938, he described the crisis of reason that afflicted his generation: "The twentieth century has in its first third taken up a position of reaction against classic rationalism and intellectualism. It has surrendered to admiration of the unconscious, to a glorification of instinct. And the bad instincts have accordingly been enjoying a heyday."[16]

In *The Magic Mountain*, begun in 1912 and completed in 1924, Mann had reflected on the decomposition of bourgeois European civilization. The novel is set in a Swiss sanitarium, just prior to World War I. The patients, drawn from several European lands, suffer from tuberculosis and are diseased in spirit, as well as body. The sanitarium symbolizes Europe. It is the European psyche that is sick and rushing headlong into a catastrophe.

One patient, the Italian Ludovico Settembrini, stands for the humanist ideals of the Enlightenment: reason, individual liberty, and progress. While Mann is sympathetic to these ideals, he also indicts Settembrini for his naive faith in progress, his shallow view of human nature, which gives little significance to the will, and his lofty rhetoric. Overestimating the power of the rational, Settembrini foolishly believes that people will mend their ways once they are enlightened by reason. Thus, he even claims that he cured a sick person merely by looking at him "rationally." Settembrini represents a decaying liberalism.

Pitted against Settembrini is Leo Naphta, a Spanish-trained Jesuit of Jewish-Polish descent, who represents the revolt against reason in Mann's generation. Naphta completely rejects the Italian's liberal-humanist values. An authoritarian, he insists that people do not need freedom, but only authority and discipline imposed by state or church. He is a fanatic, accepting torture and terror as a way to impose authority. Convinced that the dictatorship of the proletariat is the means of salvation demanded by the age, Naphta embraces Marxism. Borrowing from medieval mysticism, Nietzschean irrationalism, and Marxist militancy, he attacks every facet of the existing liberal order.

Another character, a wealthy Dutch planter from Java, named Mynheer Peeperkorn, is nonintellectual, illogical, and inarticulate, but he radiates pure vitality and emotional intensity. This charismatic personality dwarfs the humanist Settembrini and the authoritarian Naphta and dominates the patients, who find him irresistible.

The Magic Mountain, which ends with the advent of World War I, raised, but did not resolve, crucial questions. Was the epoch of rational-humanist culture drawing to a close? Did bourgeois Europe welcome its spiritual degeneration in the same way that some of the patients in the sanitarium had a will to illness? How could Europe rescue itself from decadence?

D. H. Lawrence (1885–1930), the son of an illiterate British coal miner, was saddened and angered by the consequences of industrial society: the deterioration of nature, tedious work divorced from personal satisfaction, and a life-denying quest for wealth and possessions. He looked back longingly on preindustrial England

and wanted people to reorient their thinking away from moneymaking and suppression of the instincts. In *Lady Chatterley's Lover* (1928) and other works, he dealt with the clash between industrial civilization and the needs of human nature, between regimentation and passion.

Like nineteenth-century romantics, Lawrence found a higher truth in deep-seated passion than in reason; this led him to rail against Christianity for stifling human sexuality. Like Nietzsche, he believed that excessive intellectualizing destroyed the life-affirming, instinctual part of human nature. In 1913, he wrote:

> *My great religion is a belief in the blood, the flesh, as being wiser than the intellect. We can go wrong in our minds. But what our blood feels and believes and says is always true. The intellect is only a bit and a bridle. What do I care about knowledge. All I want is to answer to my blood without fribbling intervention of mind, or moral, or what not. . . . We have got so ridiculously mindful, that we never know that we ourselves are anything.*[17]

Shattered by World War I, disgusted by fascism's growing strength, and moved by the suffering of the depression, many writers became committed to social and political causes. Remarque's *All Quiet on the Western Front* was one of many antiwar novels. In *The Grapes of Wrath* (1939), John Steinbeck captured the suffering of American farmers losing their land when it became the Dust Bowl or driven from it by foreclosure during the depression. George Orwell's *The Road to Wigan Pier* (1937) recorded the bleak lives of English coal miners. Few issues stirred the conscience of intellectuals as did the Spanish Civil War, and many of them volunteered to fight with the Spanish republicans against the fascists. Ernest Hemingway's *For Whom the Bell Tolls* (1940) expressed the sentiments of these thinkers.

The new directions taken in art before World War I—abstractionism and expressionism—continued in the postwar decades. Picasso, Mondrian, Kandinsky, Matisse, Rouault, Braque, Modigliani, and other masters continued to refine their styles. In addition, new art trends emerged, mirroring the trauma of a generation that had experienced the war and lost its faith in Europe's moral and intellectual values.

In 1915 in Zurich, artists and writers founded a movement, called Dada, to express their revulsion against the war and the civilization that spawned it. From neutral Switzerland, the movement spread to Germany and Paris. Dadaists viewed artistic and literary standards with contempt and rejected both God and reason. They celebrated nihilism for its own sake. "Through reason man becomes a tragic and ugly figure," said one Dadaist; "beauty is dead," said another. Dada shared in the postwar mood of disorientation and despair. Dadaists regarded life as essentially absurd (*Dada* is a nonsense term) and cultivated indifference. "The acts of life have no beginning or end. Everything happens in a completely idiotic way," declared the poet Tristan Tzara, one of Dada's founders and its chief spokesman. Tzara elevated spontaneity above reason:

> *What good did the theories of the philosophers do us? Did they help us to take a single step forward or backward? . . . We have had enough of the intelligent movements that have stretched beyond measure our credulity in the benefits of science. What we want now is spontaneity because everything that issues freely from ourselves, without the intervention of speculative ideas . . . represents us.*[18]

For Dadaists, the world was nonsensical, and reality disordered; hence, they offered no solutions to anything. "Like everything in life, Dada is useless," said Tzara.[19]

Dadaists showed their contempt for art (one art historian calls Dada "the first anti-art movement on record"[20]) by deliberately producing works that seemed devoid of artistic value. Marcel Duchamp's *Bicycle Wheel* is an example, as is his *Mona Lisa* with a mustache. Despite the Dadaists' nihilistic aims and "calculated irrationality," says art historian H. W. Janson, "there was also liberation, a voyage into unknown provinces of the creative mind." Thus, Duchamp's painting with the nonsense title *Tu m'* was "dazzlingly inventive [and] far ahead of its time."[21]

Dada ended as a formal movement in 1924 and was succeeded by surrealism. Surrealists inherited from Dada a contempt for reason. They stressed fantasy and made use of Freudian

HARLEQUIN'S CARNIVAL, 1924 BY JOAN MIRÓ (1893–1983). In one of the first surrealist paintings, Miró makes visible an inner world of fantasy and humor populated by an array of imaginary creatures. (*Albright-Knox Art Gallery, Buffalo, New York, Room of Contemporary Art Fund, 1940. Copyright 1991 ARS, N.Y., ADAGP*)

insights and symbols in their art to reproduce the raw state of the unconscious and to arrive at truths beyond reason's grasp. To penetrate the interior of the mind, said André Breton, a French surrealist poet, the writer should "write quickly without any previously chosen subject, quickly enough not to dwell on and not to be tempted to read over what you have written."[22] Writing should not be dictated by the intellect but should flow automatically from the unconscious. Surrealists tried to portray the world of fantasy and hallucination, the marvelous and the spontaneous. Breton urged artists to live their dreams, even if it meant seeing "a horse galloping on a tomato." In the effort to break through the constraints of rationality so that they might reach a higher reality—that is, a "surreality"—leading

surrealists such as Max Ernst (1891–1976), Salvador Dali (1904–1989), and Joan Miró (1893–1983) produced works of undeniable artistic merit.

Artists, like writers, expressed a social conscience. George Grosz combined a Dadaist sense of life's meaninglessness with a new realism to depict the moral degeneration of middle-class German society. In *After the Questioning* (1935), Grosz, then living in the United States, dramatized Nazi brutality; in *The End of the World* (1936), he expressed his fear of another impending world war. Käthe Kollwitz, also a German artist, showed a deep compassion for the sufferer: the unemployed, the hungry, the ill, and the politically oppressed (see page 739).

In a series of paintings, *The Passion of Sacco*

ANGEL OF HEARTH AND HOME BY MAX ERNST (1891–1976). Ernst formed part of the transition from Dada to surrealism. His paintings, like the *Fireside Angel* (1937), expressed a profound anxiety. André Breton called him "the most magnificently haunted mind in Europe." (© *1995 Artists Rights Society (ARS), New York/SPADEM/ADAGP, Paris*)

and Vanzetti (1931–32), American artist Ben Shahn showed his outrage at the execution of two radicals. William Gropper's *Migration* (1932) dramatized the suffering of the same dispossessed farmers described in Steinbeck's novel *The Grapes of Wrath*. Philip Evergood, in *Don't Cry Mother* (1938–1944), portrayed the apathy of starving children and their mother's terrible helplessness.

In his etchings of maimed, dying, and dead soldiers, German artist Otto Dix produced a powerful visual indictment of the Great War's cruelty and suffering. Max Beckmann's service in the German army during World War I made him acutely aware of violence and brutality, which he expressed in *The Night* (1918–19) and other paintings. Designated a "degenerate artist" by the Nazis, Beckmann went into exile. In *Guernica* (1937), Picasso memorialized the Spanish village decimated by Nazi saturation bombing during the Spanish Civil War (see page 830). *White Crucifixion* (1938) by Marc Chagall, a

Russian-born Jew who had settled in Paris, depicted the terror and flight of Jews in Nazi Germany.

Communism: "The God That Failed"

The economic misery of the depression and the rise of fascist barbarism led many intellectuals to find a new hope, even a secular faith, in communism. They praised the Soviet Union for supplanting capitalist greed with socialist cooperation; replacing a haphazard economic system marred by repeated depressions with one based on planned production; and providing employment for everyone when joblessness was endemic in capitalist lands. American literary critic Edmund Wilson said that in the Soviet Union one felt at the "moral top of the world where the light never really goes out."[23] British political theorists Sidney and Beatrice Webb declared that there was no other country "in which there is

Culver Pictures

CHARLIE CHAPLIN

Charles Spencer (Charlie) Chaplin was born in London in 1889 to music hall entertainers. His mother, Hannah Chaplin, taught young Charles the art of pantomine. Touring the United States with an English company, he was hired by Mack Sennet to act in the popular Keystone Comedies. Insightful, intelligent, musical, and artistic, Chaplin transformed silent film comedy, which was largely slapstick, into an art form.

In *The Tramp* (1915), Chaplin played a gentleman tramp, the character with which he would always be identified. The "little tramp" wore baggy pants, a derby, fingerless gloves, and a shabby dress coat, handled a bamboo cane with great dexterity, and shuffled as he walked. Critics applauded Chaplin's skill as both actor and director in *The*

---

actually so much widespread public criticism and such incessant reevaluation of its shortcomings as in the USSR."[24] To these intellectuals, it seemed that in the Soviet Union a vigorous and healthy civilization was emerging and that only communism could stem the tide of fascism. For many, however, the attraction was short-lived. Sickened by Stalin's purges and terror, the denial of individual freedom, and the suppression of truth, they came to view the Soviet Union as another totalitarian state and communism as another "god that failed."

One such intellectual was Arthur Koestler. Born in Budapest of Jewish ancestry and educated in Vienna, Koestler worked as a correspondent for a leading Berlin newspaper chain. He joined the Communist party at the very end of 1931 because he "lived in a disintegrating society thirsting for faith," was moved by the suffering caused by the depression, and saw communism as the "only force capable of resisting the onrush of the primitive [Nazi] horde."[25] Koestler visited the Soviet Union in 1933, experiencing firsthand

both the starvation brought on by forced collectivization and the propaganda that grotesquely misrepresented life in Western lands. Although his faith was shaken, he did not break with the party until 1938, in response to Stalin's liquidations.

In *Darkness at Noon* (1941), Koestler explored the attitudes of the Old Bolsheviks who were imprisoned, tortured, and executed by Stalin. These dedicated Communists had served the party faithfully, but Stalin, fearful of opposition, hating intellectuals, and driven by megalomania, denounced them as enemies of the people. In *Darkness at Noon,* the leading character, the imprisoned Rubashov, is a composite of the Old Bolsheviks. Although he is innocent, Rubashov, without being physically tortured, publicly confesses to political crimes that he never committed.

Rubashov is aware of the suffering that the party has brought to the Russian people:

[I]n the interests of a just distribution of land we deliberately let die of starvation about five

Kid (1921), which also starred the six-year-old Jackie Coogan. The interaction between the little tramp and the young boy, who had been abandoned, brought tears and smiles to audiences. It also revealed Chaplin's social conscience. Abandoned by his alcoholic father, he knew poverty as a youth.

Chaplin's skill as a social commentator was demonstrated in two classic works: *Modern Times* (1936) and *The Great Dictator* (1940). In *Modern Times*, Chaplin satirized labor in the modern mechanized factory. In one memorable scene, Charlie is tightening nuts on a conveyer belt when the boss orders a speedup. Desperately trying to increase his pace, Charlie moves hyperactively and spasmodically. His mind is also affected. When he sees a secretary wearing a dress with ornaments resembling the nuts that he had been turning, Charlie chases her, determined to apply his wrench to the nut-like ornaments. In the *Great Dictator*, Chaplin mocked Mussolini and Hitler and expressed outrage at German anti-Semitism. He made the film, he said, for "the return of decency and kindness."

After World War II, Chaplin continued to act and direct, but his later works—*Monsieur Verdoux* (1947), *Limelight* (1952), and *A King in New York* (1957)—were not well received. Identified with leftist causes, Chaplin was refused reentry into the United States in 1952. Twenty years later, he returned to the United States and received on honorary Academy Award. In 1975, he was knighted by Queen Elizabeth II. He died at the end of 1977.

million farmers and their families in one year. . . . [to liberate] human beings from the shackles of industrial exploitation . . . we sent about ten million people to do forced labour in the Arctic regions and the jungles of the East, under conditions similar to those of antique galley slaves. . . . to settle a difference of opinion, we know only one argument: death. . . . Our poets settle discussions on questions of style by denunciations to the secret police. . . . The people's standard of life is lower than it was before the Revolution, the labour conditions are harder, the discipline is more inhuman. . . . Our Press and our schools cultivate Chauvinism, militarism, dogmatism, conformism and ignorance. The arbitrary power of the Government is unlimited, and unexampled in history. Freedom of the Press, of opinion and of movement are as thoroughly exterminated as though the proclamation of the Rights of Man had never been. We have built up the most gigantic police apparatus, with informers made a national institution, and with the most refined scientific system of physical and mental torture. We whip the groaning masses of the country towards a theoretical future happiness, which only we can see.[26]

Pained by his own complicity in the party's crimes, including the betrayal of friends, Rubashov questions the party's philosophy that the individual should be subordinated, and, if necessary, sacrificed to the regime. Nevertheless, Rubashov remains the party's faithful servant. True believers do not easily break with their faith. By confessing to treason, Rubashov performs his last service for the Revolution. For the true believer, everything—truth, justice, and the sanctity of the individual—is properly sacrificed to the party.

Reaffirming the Christian World-View

By calling into question core liberal beliefs—the essential goodness of human nature, the primacy of reason, the efficacy of science, and the

THE NIGHT, BY MAX BECKMANN (1884–1950). Max Beckmann's paintings gave expression to the disillusionment and spiritual unease that afflicted post-war Germany. When the Nazis included his works in the Degenerate Art Exhibition (1937), he left the country. In *The Night* (1918–19), Beckmann, himself a veteran of the front, depicts brutal men engaging in terrible violence. (*Kunstsammlung Nordrhein-Westfalen, Dusseldorf, © Estate of Max Beckmann/VAGA, New York, 1991*)

inevitability of progress—World War I led thinkers to find in Christianity an alternative view of the human experience and the crisis of the twentieth century. Christian thinkers, including Karl Barth, Paul Tillich, Reinhold Niebuhr, Christopher Dawson, Jacques Maritain, and T. S. Eliot, asserted the reality of evil in human nature. They assailed liberals and Marxists for holding too optimistic a view of human nature and human reason; postulating a purely rational and secular philosophy of history; and anticipating an ideal society within the realm of historical time. For these thinkers, the Christian conception of history as a clash between human will and God's commands provided an intelligible explanation of the tragedies of the twentieth century. Karl Barth (1886–1968), the Swiss-German Protestant the-

ologian, called for a reaffirmation of the Christ who inspires faith, the uniqueness of Christianity, and the spiritual power of divine revelation. The true meaning of history, he said, is not to be found in the liberals' view of the progress of reason and freedom or in the Marxist conception of economic determinism. Rather, it derives from the fact that history is the arena in which the individual's faith is tested.

Jacques Maritain (1882–1973), a leading Catholic thinker, denounced core elements of the modern outlook: the autonomy of the individual, the autonomy of the mind, and a nonreligious humanism. He urged that the Christian philosophy of Thomas Aquinas be revived, for he believed that it successfully harmonized faith and reason. A strong advocate of political freedom,

Maritain stressed the link between modern democracy and the Christian Gospels, which proclaimed "the natural equality of all men, children of the same God and redeemed by the same Christ . . . [and] the inalienable dignity of every soul fashioned in the image of God."[27] He insisted that "the democratic state of mind and . . . the democratic philosophy of life requires the energies of the Gospel to penetrate secular existence, taming the irrational to reason."[28] These energies would control the human propensity for self-centeredness, wickedness, and hatred of others. To survive, secular democracy must be infused with Christian love and compassion.

The English Catholic thinker Christopher Dawson (1889–1970) stresssed the historic ties between Christianity and Western civilization. He wrote in 1933: "If our civilization is to recover its vitality, or even to survive, it must . . . realize that religion is . . . the very heart of social life and the root of every living culture."[29]

In 1934, the British historian Arnold Toynbee (1889–1975) published the first three volumes of his monumental work, *A Study of History,* in which he tried to account for the rise, growth, breakdown, and disintegration of civilization. Underlying Toynbee's philosophy of history was a religious orientation, for he saw religious prophets as humanity's greatest figures and the world's major religions as humanity's greatest achievement. Toynbee attributed the problems of Western civilization to its breaking away from Christianity and embracing "false idols," particularly the national state, which, he said, had become the object of westerners' highest reverence.

Toynbee regarded nationalism as a primitive religion, inducing people to revere the national community rather than God. This deification of the parochial—tribal or local—community intensified the brutal side of human nature and provoked wars among people sharing a common civilization. To Toynbee, Nazism was the culmination of the worst elements in modern European nationalism, "the consummation . . . of a politico-religious movement, the pagan deification and worship of parochial human communities which had been gradually gaining ground for more than four centuries in the Western world at large."[30] The moral catastrophe of Nazism, he said, demonstrates the inadequacy of liberal humanism, for the Enlightenment tradition proved a feeble barrier to the rise and spread of Nazism. The secular values of the Enlightenment, divorced from Christianity, cannot restrain human nature's basest impulses. For the West to save itself, said Toynbee, it must abide by the spiritual values of its religious prophets.

Reaffirming the Ideals of Reason and Freedom

Several thinkers tried to reaffirm the ideals of rationality and freedom that totalitarian movements had trampled. In *The Treason of the Intellectuals* (1927), Julien Benda (1867–1956), a French cultural critic of Jewish background, castigated intellectuals for intensifying hatred between nations, classes, and political factions. "Our age is indeed the age of the *intellectual organization of political hatreds,*"[31] he wrote. Intellectuals, who stir up hatred between nations, said Benda, do not pursue justice or truth but proclaim that "even if our country is wrong, we must think of it in the right."[32] They scorn outsiders, extol harshness and action, and proclaim the superiority of instinct and will to intelligence; or they "assert that the intelligence to be venerated is that which limits its activities within the bounds of national interest."[33] The logical end of this xenophobia, said Benda, "is the organized slaughter of nations and classes."[34]

José Ortega y Gasset (1883–1955), descendant of a Spanish noble family and a professor of philosophy, gained international recognition with the publication of *The Revolt of the Masses* (1930). According to Ortega, European civilization, the product of a creative elite, was degenerating into barbarism because of the growing power of the masses, for the masses lacked the mental discipline and the commitment to reason that might preserve Europe's intellectual and cultural traditions. Ortega did not equate the masses with the working class and the elite with the nobility; it was an attitude of mind, not a class affiliation, that distinguished the "mass-man" from the elite.

The mass-man, said Ortega, has a commonplace mind and does not set high standards for himself. He is inert until driven by an external compulsion. He does not enter into rational dialogue with others, defend his opinions logically, or accept objective standards. Faced with a problem, he "is satisfied with thinking the first thing he finds in his head" and "crushes . . . everything that is different, everything that is excellent, individual, qualified, and select. Anybody who is not like everybody, who does not think like everybody, runs the risk of being eliminated."[35] Such intellectually vulgar people, declared Ortega, cannot understand or preserve the processes of civilization. The fascists exemplify this revolt of the masses, for "under fascism there appears for the first time in Europe a type of man who . . . simply shows himself resolved to impose his opinions. This is the new thing: the right not to be reasonable, the 'reason of unreason.'" The danger lay in "the masses . . . having decided to rule society without the capacity for doing so."[36] Rejecting reason, the mass-man glorifies violence: the ultimate expression of barbarism. If European civilization is to be rescued from fascism and communism, said Ortega, the elite must sustain civilized values and provide leadership.

A staunch defender of the Enlightenment tradition, Ernst Cassirer (1874–1945), a German philosopher of Jewish lineage, emigrated after Hitler came to power, eventually settling in the United States. Just prior to Hitler's triumph, in 1932, Cassirer wrote about the need to uphold and reenergize that tradition: "The age which venerated reason and science as man's highest faculty cannot and must not be lost even for us. We must find a way not only to see that age in its own shape but to release again those original forces which brought forth and molded this shape."[37]

In his posthumous work, *The Myth of the State* (1946), Cassirer described Nazism as the triumph of mythical thinking over reason. The Nazis, said Cassirer, cleverly manufactured myths—of the race, the leader, the party, the state—that disoriented the intellect. Germans who embraced these myths surrendered their capacity for independent judgment, leaving themselves vulnerable to manipulation by the Nazi leadership. Cassirer warned:

In politics we are always living on volcanic soil. We must be prepared for convulsions and eruptions. In all critical moments of man's social life, the rational forces that resist the rise of old mythical conceptions are no longer sure of themselves. In these moments the time of myth has come again. For myth has not been really vanquished and subjugated. It is always there, lurking in the dark and waiting for its

hour and opportunity. This hour comes as soon as the other binding forces of man's social life . . . lose their strength and are no longer able to combat the demonic mythical powers.[38]

To contain the destructive powers of political myths, Cassirer urged strengthening the rational-humanist tradition and called for the critical study of political myths, for "in order to fight an enemy you must know him. . . . We should carefully study the origin, the structure, the methods, and the technique of the political myths. We should see the adversary face to face in order to know how to combat him."[39]

Like Cassirer and many other German-Jewish intellectuals, Erich Fromm (1900–1980), a social theorist and psychoanalyst, settled in the United States after the Nazi seizure of power. In *Escape from Freedom* (1941), Fromm sought to explain the triumph of Nazism within the larger context of European history. When the Middle Ages ended, he said, the individual grew increasingly independent of external authority and experienced new possibilities for personal development. The individual's role in the social order was no longer rigorously determined by birth. Increasingly, the world was explained in natural terms, freeing people from magic, mystery, and authority; and the possibility for the full development of human potential here on earth was proclaimed. In the political sphere, this new orientation culminated in the democratic state. However, as westerners grew more "independent, self-reliant, and critical," they became "more isolated, alone, and afraid."[40]

During the Middle Ages, said Fromm, the individual derived a sense of security from a structured social system, which clearly defined the role of clergy, lords, serfs, and guildsmen, and from a Christian world-view, which made life and death purposeful. Modern westerners have lost this sense of security. Dwelling in vast cities, threatened by economic crises, no longer comforted by the medieval conception of life's purpose, they are often tormented by doubts and overwhelmed by feelings of aloneness and insignificance. People try to overcome this "burden of freedom" by surrendering themselves to a person or power that they view "as being overwhelmingly strong"; they trade freedom for security by entering into "a symbiotic relationship that overcomes . . . aloneness."[41]

Because modern industrial society has made the individual feel powerless and insignificant, concluded Fromm, fascism is a constant threat. Fromm would meet the challenge of fascism by creating social conditions that lead the individual to be free and yet not alone, to be critical and yet not filled with doubts, to be independent and yet feel an integral part of humankind.

George Orwell (1903–1950), a British novelist and political journalist, wrote two powerful indictments of totalitarianism: *Animal Farm* (1945) and *1984* (1949). In *Animal Farm,* based in part on his experiences with communists during the Spanish Civil War, Orwell satirized the totalitarian regime built by Lenin and Stalin in Russia. In *1984,* Orwell, who was deeply committed to human dignity and freedom, warned that these great principles are now permanently menaced by the concentration and abuse of political power. "If you want a picture of the future, imagine a boot stamping on a human face forever," says a member of the ruling elite as he tortures a victim in the dungeons of the Thought Police.[42]

The society of *1984* is ruled by the Inner Party, which constitutes some 2 percent of the population. Heading the Party is Big Brother—most likely a mythical figure created by the ruling elite to satisfy people's yearning for a leader. The Party indoctrinates people to love Big Brother whose picture is everywhere. Party members are conditioned to accept unquestioningly the Party's orthodoxy, with all its contradictions, twists, and reversals. Doublethink, the prescribed way of thinking, brainwashes people into holding two contradictory beliefs simultaneously. The Party's philosophy of government is revealed in three slogans: "WAR IS PEACE," "FREEDOM IS SLAVERY," "IGNORANCE IS STRENGTH." The Ministry of Truth resorts to thought control to dominate and manipulate the masses and to keep Party members loyal and subservient. Independent thinking is destroyed. Objective truth no longer exists. Truth is whatever the Party decrees at the moment. If the Party were to proclaim that two plus two equals five, it would have to be believed.

Anyone thinking prohibited thoughts is designated a Thoughtcriminal, a crime punishable by death. The Thought Police's agents are ubiquitous. Using hidden microphones and telescreens, they check on Party members for any signs of deviance from Party rules and ideology. Posters displaying Big Brother's picture carry the words "BIG BROTHER IS WATCHING YOU." Convinced that "who controls the past controls the future," the Ministry of Truth alters old newspapers to make the past accord with the Party's current doctrine. In this totalitarian society of the future, all human rights are abolished, people are arrested merely for their thoughts, and children spy on their parents. The society is brutalized by processions of chained prisoners of war, by public mass executions, and by the Two Minutes Hate ritual, which rouses the participants to a frenzy against Party enemies. A steady supply of cheap gin and pornographic literature keeps the masses (proles) dull-witted and out of political mischief.

Orwell's anti-utopian novel focuses on Winston Smith, who works for the Ministry of Truth and is arrested by the Thought Police for harboring anti-Party sentiments. Smith rebels against the Party in order to reclaim his individuality—to think and feel in his own way rather than in accordance with the Party's dictates. Tortured brutally, humiliated, and brainwashed, Smith confesses to crimes that both he and the Party know he did not commit.

The Inner Party seeks to capture the inner mind, to transform people into mindless robots. O'Brien of the Thought Police tells Smith: "You will be hollow. We shall squeeze you empty, and then we shall fill you with ourselves."[43] Thus, the Party does not kill Smith but "reshapes" him, by breaking his will and transforming him into a true believer in Big Brother. Smith comes to believe that "the struggle was finished. He had won the victory over himself. He loved Big Brother."[44]

EXISTENTIALISM

Intellectual Background

The philosophical movement that best exemplified the anxiety and uncertainty of Europe in an era of world wars was existentialism. Like writers and artists, existentialist philosophers were responding to a European civilization that seemed to be in the throes of dissolution. Although existentialism was most popular after World War II, expressing the anxiety and despair of many intellectuals who had lost confidence in reason and progress, several of its key works were written prior to or during the war.

What route should people take in a world where old values and certainties had dissolved, where universal truth was rejected and God's existence denied? How could people cope in a society where they were menaced by technology, manipulated by impersonal bureaucracies, and overwhelmed by feelings of anxiety? If the universe is devoid of any overarching meaning, what meaning could one give to one's own life? These questions were at the crux of existentialist philosophy.

Basic Principles

Existentialism does not lend itself to a single definition, for its principal theorists did not adhere to a common body of doctrines. For example, some existentialists were atheists, like Jean Paul Sartre, or omitted God from their thought, like Martin Heidegger; others, like Karl Jaspers, believed in God but not in Christian doctrines; still others, like Gabriel Marcel and Nikolai Berdyaev, were Christians; and Martin Buber was a believing Jew. Perhaps the essence of existentialism appears in the following principles, although not all existentialists would subscribe to each point or agree with the way it is expressed.

1. Reality defies ultimate comprehension; there are no timeless truths that exist independently of and prior to the individual human being. Our existence precedes and takes precedence over any presumed absolute values. The moral and spiritual values that society tries to impose cannot define the individual person's existence.

2. Reason alone is an inadequate guide to living, for people are more than thinking subjects who approach the world through critical analysis. They are also feeling and willing beings, who must participate fully in life and experience existence directly, actively, and passionately. Only in this way does one live wholly and authentically.

3. Thought must not merely be abstract speculation but must have a bearing on life; it must be translated into deeds.

4. Human nature is problematic and paradoxical, not fixed or constant; each person is like no other. Self-realization comes when one affirms one's own uniqueness. One becomes less than human when one permits one's life to be determined by a mental outlook—a set of rules and values—imposed by others.

5. We are alone. The universe is indifferent to our expectations and needs, and death is ever stalking us. Awareness of this elementary fact of existence evokes a sense of overwhelming anxiety and depression.

6. Existence is essentially absurd. There is no purpose to our presence in the universe. We simply find ourselves here; we do not know and will never find out why. Compared with the eternity of time that preceded our birth and will follow our death, the short duration of our existence seems trivial and inexplicable. And death, which irrevocably terminates our existence, testifies to the ultimate absurdity of life.

7. We are free. We must face squarely the fact that existence is purposeless and absurd. In doing so, we can give our life meaning. It is in the act of choosing freely from among different possibilities that the individual shapes an authentic existence. There is a dynamic quality to human existence; the individual has the potential to become more than he or she is.

Nineteenth-Century Forerunners

Three nineteenth-century thinkers—Søren Kierkegaard (1813–1855), Fyodor Dostoevski (see Chapter 28) and Friedrich Nietzsche (see Chapter 28)—were the principal forerunners of existentialism. Their views of reason, will, truth, and existence greatly influenced twentieth-century existentialists.

Kierkegaard A Danish religious philosopher and Lutheran pastor, Kierkegaard held that self-realization as a human being comes when the individual takes full responsibility for his or her life. The individual does so by choosing one way of life over another. In making choices, said Kierkegaard, the individual overcomes the agonizing feeling that life in its deepest sense is nothingness.

For Kierkegaard, the highest truth is that human beings are God's creatures. However, God's existence cannot be demonstrated by reason; the crucial questions of human existence can never be resolved in a logical and systematic way. In Kierkegaard's view, the individual knows God through a leap of faith, not through systematic reasoning. In contrast to the Christian apologists who sought to demonstrate that Christian teachings did not conflict with reason, Kierkegaard denied that Christian doctrines were objectively valid. For him, Christian beliefs were absurd and irrational and could not be harmonized with reason. True Christians, said Kierkegaard, confidently embrace beliefs that are incomprehensible, if not absurd.

Twentieth-century existentialists took from Kierkegaard the idea that an all-consuming dread is the price of existence. "I stick my finger into existence," said Kierkegaard—it smells of nothing. Where am I? What is this thing called the world? Who is it who has lured me into the thing, and now leaves me here? Who am I? How did I come into the world? Why was I not consulted?"[45] The sense that we live in a meaningless world drives us to the edge of the abyss. This overwhelming dread can cause us to flee from life and to find comfort in delusions. But it can also spark courage, since it is an opportunity to make a commitment. For both Kierkegaard and twentieth-century existentialists, the true philosophical quest is a subjective experience: the isolated individual, alone and without help, choosing a way of life, to which he or she is deeply committed. Only in this way does the individual become a whole person. Kierkegaard's dictum that "it is impossible to exist without passion"—that our actions matter to us—is at the heart of existentialism.

Dostoevski   Although existentialist themes pervade several of Dostoevski's works, it is in *Notes from Underground* (1864) that he treats explicitly the individual's quest for personal freedom, identity, and meaning and the individual's revolt against established norms—themes that are crucial to the outlook of twentieth-century existentialists.

Nietzsche   Friedrich Nietzsche was an important forerunner of existentialism for several reasons. He stated that philosophical systems are merely expressions of an individual's own being and do not constitute an objective representation of reality; there is no realm of being that is the source of values. Nor does religion provide truth, for God is dead. And, asked Nietzsche, is not this godless world absurd? Nietzsche held that modern westerners had lost all their traditional supports.

To overcome nothingness, said Nietzsche, individuals must define life for themselves and celebrate it fully, instinctively, and heroically. Nietzsche's insistence that individuals confront existence squarely, without hypocrisy, and give meaning to it—their own meaning—was vital to the shaping of existentialism.

Twentieth-Century Existentialists

Heidegger   The German philosopher Martin Heidegger (1889–1976), generally regarded as the central figure in the development of twentieth-century existentialist thought, presents a problem to students of philosophy. First, Heidegger rejected being classified as an existentialist. Second, he wrote in a nearly incomprehensible style, which obscured his intent. Third, in 1933, Heidegger, recently elected rector of the University of Freiburg joined the National Socialist party and publicly praised Hitler and the Nazi regime. The following year, he resigned as rector and gave no further support to the Third Reich, although he did continue to sympathize with some Nazi ideals. Heidegger's dalliance with Nazism caused some thinkers either to dismiss him or to minimize his importance as a valid philosopher.

Heidegger's principal book, *Being and Time* (1927), is a pathbreaking work in twentieth-century philosophy. In it, Heidegger asked: what does it mean *to be,* to say I am? Most people shun this question, said Heidegger; consequently, they live inauthentically, merely accepting a way of life set by others. Such people, he said, have "fallen from being"; they do not reflect on their existence or recognize the various possibilities and choices that life offers. Rather, they flee from their own selves and accept society's values without reflection. Neither their actions nor their goals are their own; they have forfeited a human being's most distinctive qualities: freedom and creativity.

To live authentically, declared Heidegger, the individual has to face explicitly the problem of Being; that is, one has to determine one's own existence, create one's own possibilities, and make choices and commitments. Choosing, said Heidegger, is not just a matter of disengaged thought, for the human creature is more than a conscious knower. The authentic life encompasses the feelings, as well as the intellect; it is a genuine expression of a person's whole being.

Coming to grips with death, said Heidegger, provides us with the opportunity for an authentic life. The trauma of our mortality and finiteness, the image of the endless void in which Being passes into non-Being, overwhelms us with dread; we come face to face with the insignificance of human existence, with directionless lives. To escape this dread, said Heidegger, some people immerse themselves in life's petty details or adopt others' prescribed values. But dread of death is also an opportunity. It can put us in touch with our uniqueness, our own Being, letting us take hold of our own existence to make life truly our own.

The authentic life requires, said Heidegger, that we see ourselves within the context of historical time, for we cannot escape the fact that our lives are bound by conditions and outlooks inherited from the past. Human beings are thrown into a world that is not of their own making. They dwell in a particular society, which carries with it the weight of the past and the tensions and conflicts of the present. Without knowledge of these conditions, Heidegger declared, events and things will always impose themselves on us, and we will not have the courage to reject conventions that we had no part in shaping.

Jaspers   Karl Jaspers (1883–1969), a German psychiatrist turned philosopher, was a leading figure in the existentialist movement. Jaspers fell into disfavor with the Nazi regime (he advocated liberal-humanist values and his wife was Jewish) and lost his position as professor of philosophy at Heidelberg University. Like Kierkegaard, Jaspers held that philosophy and science cannot provide certainty. Also like Kierkegaard, he sought to discover the genuine self through an encounter with life. Like Heidegger, he held that while death makes us aware of our finitude, thereby promoting anxiety, it also goads us to

focus on what is truly important and to do so immediately. Jaspers insisted that the individual has the power to choose. To be aware of this freedom and to use it is the essence of being human. He declared in 1930:

> *Man is always something more than what he knows of himself. He is not what he is simply once for all, but is a process; he is . . . endowed with possibilities through the freedom he possesses to make of himself what he will by the activities on which he decides.*[46]

Feelings of guilt and anxiety inevitably accompany free will, said Jaspers. Nevertheless, we must have the courage to make a choice, for it is in the act of choosing that the individual shapes his or her true self.

Although Jaspers rejected revealed religion, dogma, and the authority of churches, he did postulate what he called "philosophical faith." He thought of human existence as an encounter with Transcendence: "the eternal, indestructible, the immutable, the source [that] . . . can be neither visualized nor grasped in thought."[47] Jaspers did not equate Transcendence with God in the conventional sense, but the concept is laden with theistic qualities. Although not a traditional Christian, Jaspers was no atheist.

Sartre   The outlook of several French existentialists—Jean Paul Sartre (1905–1980), Maurice Merleau-Ponty (1908–1961), Albert Camus (1913–1960), and Simone de Beauvoir (1908–1987)—was shaped by their involvement in the resistance to Nazi occupation during World War II. Sartre, the leading French existentialist, said that their confrontation with terror and torture taught them "to take evil seriously." Evil is not the effect of ignorance that might be remedied by knowledge or of passions that might be controlled, said Sartre; rather, it is a central fact of human existence and is unredeemable. Facing capture and death, the members of the Resistance understood what it is to be a solitary individual in a hostile universe. Living on the cutting edge of life, they rediscovered the essence of human freedom: they could make authentic choices. By saying no to the Nazis and resisting them, they confronted existence squarely. They faced the central problem that concerned Sartre: what does it mean to be a human being?

JEAN PAUL SARTRE AND SIMONE DE BEAUVOIR. Existentialism is a major philosophical movement of the twentieth century. Sartre and de Beauvoir were two of its principal exponents. (*B/W Sygma-G. Pierre*)

Sartre served in the French army at the outbreak of World War II and was captured by the Germans. Released after the French surrender, he taught philosophy while serving in the Resistance. His principal philosophical work was *Being and Nothingness* (1943). In addition to his philosophical writings, Sartre, after World War II, gained international acclaim for his novels and plays, many of them, particularly *Nausea* (1938) and *No Exit* (1944), written from an existentialist point of view.

In contrast to Kierkegaard and Jaspers, Sartre defined himself as an atheist and saw existentialism as a means of facing the consequences of a godless universe. Atheistic existentialism, he said, begins with the person and not with God, a preestablished ethic, or a uniform conception of human nature.

For Sartre, existence precedes essence: that is, there are no values that precede the individual

metaphysically or chronologically to which he or she must conform. There exists no higher realm of Being and no immutable truths that serve as ultimate standards of virtue. It is unauthentic to submit passively to established values, which one did not participate in making. The individual has nothing to cling to; he or she is thrown into the world "with no support and no aid."[48]

It is the first principle of existentialism, said Sartre, that we must each choose our own ethics, define ourselves, and give our own meaning to our life. Through our actions, we decide how we shall create ourselves. According to Sartre, we are what we do; each individual is "nothing else than the ensemble of his acts, nothing else than his life. . . . man's destiny is within himself."[49] As free conscious beings, we are totally responsible for defining our lives and for giving them meaning and value. "Not only is man what he conceives himself to be, but he is also what he wills himself to be," Sartre said, and "existentialism's first move is to make every man aware of what he is and to make full responsibility of his existence rest on him."[50]

In Sartre's view, a true philosophy does not engage in barren discourses on abstract themes; it makes commitments and incurs risks. We are not objectified instruments, determined and shaped by material forces, as Marxism teaches. Nor do unconscious drives determine our actions, as Freud contended. Rather, we alone are responsible for who we are and for the feelings that torment, trap, and immobilize us. True, the conditions in which we find ourselves impinge on our existence, but it is up to us to decide what to do about them. Thus, said Sartre, a French man or woman had to choose between being a patriot or a traitor during the German occupation. Similarly, an alcoholic made poor choices and continues to make them.

We have the capacity to plunge decisively, audaciously into life and constantly to recreate ourselves. We have no control over the fact that we exist; existence is simply given to us. But each individual does decide his or her own peculiar essence. We do so by the particular way we choose to live. The realization that we have the freedom to decide for ourselves what meaning we give to our lives can be liberating and exhilarating. But it can also fill us with a dread that immobilizes or that leads us to seek refuge in a role selected for us by others. When we abdicate the responsibility of choosing a meaning for our lives, said Sartre, we live in "bad faith."

Camus Reared and educated in French-ruled Algeria, Albert Camus gained an instant reputation in 1942 with the publication of *The Stranger,* a short novel, and *The Myth of Sisyphus,* a philosophical essay. During World War II, he served in the French Resistance. His most important books in the decade after the war were two works of fiction, *The Plague* (1947) and *The Fall* (1956), as well as *The Rebel* (1951), a collection of interpretive essays on historical, philosophical, and esthetic topics.

Camus dealt with the existential theme of the individual struck by the awareness of God's nonexistence and of an impending rendezvous with an eternity of nothingness. Does this mean that my life is without meaning? That my actions do not matter? Camus rejected both suicide and

nihilism as responses to this absurdity of existence. Even though existence has no higher meaning and the universe is indifferent to us, we must still accept "the desperate encounter between human inquiry and the silence of the universe."[51] Ultimately, Camus saw a moralistic humanism that promoted human fraternity and human dignity as a worthwhile response to the absurdity of the human condition. Human beings should aspire to serve "those few values without which a world . . . isn't worth living in, without which a man . . . is not worthy of respect."[52]

In *The Stranger,* Meursault, an insignificant French shipping clerk, kills an Algerian Arab for no particular reason. It was as if shooting him or not shooting him came to the same thing. Convicted and sentenced to death, Meursault examines his own life, which he has lived without awareness, imagination, passion, or commitment, as revealed in the novel's opening lines: "Maman died today. Or yesterday, maybe, I don't know."[53] Meursault displays a shocking indifference to his mother's death not because of any hate for her, but simply because that is the way he lives. Neither her death nor his own life is very important to him. Committed to nothing, moved by nothing, and not given to introspection or reflection, he merely lives passively from day to day, a stranger to himself and to life. It is just such an attitude that human beings must strive to overcome, suggests Camus. Facing death, Meursault grasps an existential truth: even in a meaningless universe that is indifferent to his fate, he must strive to give meaning to his life.

For Camus, neither religion nor philosophy provides a basis for human values or can tell us with certainty what is right or wrong. No final authority can be found in a transcendental heaven or in reason's dictates. Thus, when a priest tries to make Meursault aware of his guilt and his spiritual needs, the condemned man responds: "He seemed so certain about everything, didn't he. And yet none of his certainties was worth one hair of a woman's head."[54] Values may not be absolute or eternal, maintained Camus, but he did urge living by values that advanced human dignity and warm human relations.

Religious Existentialism Several thinkers are classified as religious existentialists, among them Nikolai Berdyaev (1874–1948), an exile from

Communist Russia; Martin Buber (1878–1965), a Jew who fled Nazi Germany; and Gabriel Marcel (1889–1973), a French Catholic. During World War I, Marcel served with the French Red Cross, accounting for soldiers missing in battle. This shattering experience brought the sensitive thinker face to face with the tragedy of human existence. A growing concern with the spiritual life led him to convert to Catholicism in 1929.

The modern individual, said Marcel in 1933, "tends to appear to himself and to others as an agglomeration of functions." A person is viewed as an entrepreneur, a laborer, a consumer, a citizen. The hospital serves as a repair shop, and death "becomes, objectively and functionally, the scrapping of what has ceased to be of use and must be written off as a total loss."[55] In such a functional world, maintained Marcel, people are valued for what they produce and possess. If they do not succeed as merchants, bookkeepers, or ticket-takers, people judge them and they judge themselves as personal failures. Such an outlook suffocates spirituality and deprives the individual of the joy of existence. It produces an "intolerable unease" in the individual, "who is reduced to living as though he were in fact submerged by his function. . . . Life in a world centered on function is liable to despair because in reality this world is *empty*, it rings hollow."[56]

Marcel wanted people to surpass a functional and mechanical view of life and explore the mystery of existence—to penetrate to a higher level of reality. Marcel held that one penetrates ultimate reality when one overcomes egocentricity and exists for others, when one loves and is loved by others. When we exist through and for others, when we treat another person not as an object performing a function, but as a "thou" who matters to us, we soar to a higher level of existence. When we are actively engaged with others in concrete human situations, we fulfill ourselves as human beings; when we actively express love and fidelity toward others, life attains a higher meaning. Such involvement with others, said Marcel, provides us with a glimpse of a transcendent reality and is a testimony to God's existence. Marcel maintained that faith in God overcomes anxiety and despair, which characterize the modern predicament. It also improves the quality of human relationships, for if we believe that all people matter to God, they are more likely to matter to us.

THE MODERN PREDICAMENT

The process of fragmentation, which had begun in European thought and the arts at the end of the nineteenth century, accelerated after World War I. Increasingly, philosophers, writers, and artists expressed their disillusionment with the rational-humanist tradition of the Enlightenment. They no longer shared the Enlightenment confidence in either reason's capabilities or human goodness, and they viewed perpetual progress as an illusion.

For some thinkers, the crucial problem was the great change in the European understanding of truth. Since the rise of philosophy in ancient Greece, Western thinkers had believed in the existence of objective, universal truths: truths that were inherent in nature and applied to all peoples at all times. (Christianity, of course, also taught the reality of truth as revealed by God.)

It was held that such truths—the natural rights of the individual, for example—could be apprehended by the intellect and could serve as a standard for individual aspirations and social life. The recognition of these universal principles, it was believed, compelled people to measure the world of the here-and-now in the light of rational and universal norms and to institute appropriate reforms. Philosophy had the task of reconciling human existence with the objective order.

During the nineteenth century, the existence of universal truth came into doubt. A growing historical consciousness led some thinkers to maintain that what people considered truth was merely a reflection of their culture at a given stage in history—their perception of things at a specific point in the evolution of human consciousness. These thinkers, called historicists, held that universal truths were not woven into the fabric of nature. There are no natural rights of life, liberty, and property that constitute the individual's birthright; there are no standards of justice or equality that are inherent in nature and ascertainable by reason. It was people, said historicists, who elevated the beliefs and values of an age to the status of objective truth. The normative principles—the self-evident truths proclaimed by Jefferson—which for the philosophes constituted a standard for political and social reform and a guarantee of human rights, were no longer linked to the natural order, to an objective reality that could be confirmed by reason. As Hannah Arendt noted, "We certainly no longer believe, as the men of the French Revolution did, in a universal cosmos of which man was a part and whose natural laws he had to imitate and conform to."[57]

This radical break with the traditional attitude toward truth contributed substantially to the crisis of European consciousness that marked the first half of the twentieth century. Traditional values and beliefs, either those inherited from the Enlightenment or those taught by Christianity, no longer gave Europeans a sense of certainty and security. People were left without a normative order to serve as a guide to living.

Such an outlook fosters nihilism. For if nothing is fundamentally true—if there are no principles of morality and justice that emanate from God or can be deduced by reason—then it can be concluded, as Nietzsche understood, that everything is permitted. Some interpreters view Nazism as the culminating manifestation of a nihilistic attitude grown ever more brutal.

By the early twentieth century, the attitude of westerners toward reason had also undergone a radical transformation. Some thinkers, who had placed their hopes in the rational tradition of the Enlightenment, were distressed by reason's inability to resolve the tensions and conflicts of modern industrial society. Moreover, the growing recognition of the nonrational—of human actions determined by hidden impulses—led to doubts that reason plays the dominant role in human behavior. The intellect did not seem autonomous and self-regulating, but instead subject to the rebellious demands of unconscious drives and impulses. Men's and women's propensity for goodness, their capacity to improve society, and their potential for happiness seemed severely limited by an inherent irrationality. Indeed, civilization itself seemed threatened by people's instinctual needs, as Freud had proclaimed.

Other thinkers viewed the problem of reason differently. They attacked reason for fashioning a technological and bureaucratic society that devalued and crushed human emotions and stifled individuality; these thinkers insisted that human beings cannot fulfill their potential, cannot live wholly, if their feelings are denied. They agreed with D. H. Lawrence's critique of rationalism:

"The attribution of rationality to human nature, instead of enriching it, now seems to me to have impoverished it. It ignored certain powerful and valuable springs of feeling. Some of the spontaneous, irrational outbursts of human nature can have a sort of value from which our schematism was cut off."[58]

These thinkers pointed out that reason was a double-edged sword: it could demean, as well as ennoble, the individual. They attacked all theories that subordinated the individual to a rigid system. They denounced positivism for reducing human personality to psychological laws, and Marxism for making social class a higher reality than the individual. Rebelling against political collectivization, which regulated individual existence according to the needs of the corporate state, they assailed modern technology and bureaucracy. These creations of the rational mind, they claimed, had fashioned a social order that devalued and depersonalized the individual, denying people an opportunity for independent growth and a richer existence. According to these thinkers, modern industrial society, in its drive for efficiency and uniformity, deprived people of their uniqueness and reduced human beings to cogs in a mechanical system.

Responding to the critics of reason, other philosophers maintained that it was necessary to reaffirm respect for the rational tradition, first proclaimed by the ancient Greeks and given its modern expression by the Enlightenment philosophes. Reason, said these thinkers, was indispensable to civilization. What they advocated was broadening the scope of reason to accommodate the insights into human nature offered by the romantics, Nietzsche, Freud, modernist writers and artists, and others who explored the world of feelings, will, and the subconscious. They also stressed the need to humanize reason so that it could never threaten to reduce a human being to a thing.

In the decades shaped by world wars and totalitarianism, intellectuals raised questions that went to the heart of the dilemma of modern life. How can civilized life be safeguarded against human irrationality, particularly when it is channeled into political ideologies that idolize the state, the leader, the party, or the race? How can individual human personality be rescued from a relentless rationalism that reduces human nature and society to mechanical systems and seeks to regulate and organize the individual as it would any material object? Do we, as human beings, have the moral and spiritual resolve to use properly the technological and scientific creations of modern civilization, or will they devour us? Do the values associated with the Enlightenment provide a sound basis on which to integrate society? Can the individual find meaning in what many came to regard as a meaningless universe? World War II gave these questions a special poignancy.

◆ ◆ ◆

NOTES

1. Quoted in Barbara Tuchman, *The Guns of August* (New York: Macmillan, 1962), p. 440.

2. Sigmund Freud, "Thought for the Times on War and Death," in the *Standard Edition of the Complete Psychological Works of Freud,* vol. 14, ed. James Strachey (London: Hogarth Press, 1957), pp. 275, 278.

3. Quoted in Hans Kohn, "The Crisis in European Thought and Culture," in *World War I: A Turning Point in Modern History,* ed. Jack J. Roth (New York: Alfred A. Knopf, 1967), p. 28.

4. Quoted in Franklin L. Baumer, "Twentieth-Century Version of the Apocalypse," *Cahiers d'Histoire Mondiale (Journal of World History),* 1 (January 1954): 624.

5. Quoted in William McNeill, *Arnold J. Toynbee: A Life* (New York: Oxford University Press, 1989), p. 152.

6. Baumer, "Apocalypse," p. 624.

7. Erich Maria Remarque, *All Quiet on the Western Front,* trans. A. W. Wheen (Boston: Little, Brown, 1929), p. 224.

8. W. B. Yeats, "The Second Coming," in *Collected Poems of W. B. Yeats* (New York: Macmillan, 1956), pp. 184–185.

9. T. S. Eliot, "The Waste Land," in *Collected Poems, 1909–1962* (New York: Harcourt, Brace, 1970), p. 67.

10. Carl Gustav Jung, *Modern Man in Search of a Soul,* trans. W. S. Dell and Cary F. Baynes (New York: Harcourt, Brace, 1933), pp. 231, 234–235.

11. Johan Huizinga, *In the Shadow of Tomorrow* (London: Heinemann, 1936), pp. 1–3.

12. Oswald Spengler, *The Decline of the West,* trans. Charles F. Atkinson (London: Allen & Unwin, 1926), p. 40.

13. Franz Kafka, *The Trial,* trans. Willa and Edwin Muir (New York: Alfred A. Knopf, 1957), p. 7.

14. Angel Flores, ed., *The Kafka Problem* (New York: Gordian Press, 1975), p. xxi.

15. Thomas Mann, "An Appeal to Reason," excerpted in *Sources of the Western Tradition,* ed. Marvin Perry et al., vol. 2, 2nd ed. (Boston: Houghton Mifflin, 1991), pp. 351–352.

16. Thomas Mann, "Schopenhauer," in *Essays of Three Decades,* trans. H. T. Lowe-Porter (New York: Alfred A. Knopf, 1968), p. 409.

17. Harry T. Moore, ed., *The Collected Letters of D. H. Lawrence* (New York: Viking, 1962), 1:180.

18. Tristan Tzara, "Lecture on Dada (1922)," trans. Ralph Mannheim, in *The Dada Painters and Poets,* ed. Robert Motherwell (New York: Witterborn, Schultz, 1951), pp. 250, 248.

19. Ibid., p. 251.

20. Edward Lucie-Smith, in Donald Carrol and Edward Lucie-Smith, *Movements in Modern Art* (New York: Horizon Press, 1973), p. 49.

21. H. W. Janson, *History of Art,* 2nd ed. (Englewood Cliffs, N.J.: Prentice-Hall, 1977), p. 661.

22. André Breton, *What Is Surrealism?* trans. David Gascoyne (London: Faber & Faber, 1936), p. 62.

23. Quoted in David Caute, *The Fellow Travellers* (New York: Macmillan, 1973), p. 64.

24. Ibid., p. 92.

25. Richard Crossman, ed., *The God That Failed* (New York: Bantam Books, 1951), pp. 15, 21.

26. Arthur Koestler, *Darkness at Noon* (New York: Macmillan, 1941), pp. 158–159.

27. Jacques Maritain, *Christianity and Democracy*

(New York: Charles Scribner's Sons, 1944), p. 44.

28. Ibid., p. 62.

29. Quoted in C. T. McIntire, ed., *God, History, and Historians* (New York: Oxford University Press, 1977), p. 9.

30. Arnold J. Toynbee, *Survey of International Affairs, 1933* (London: Oxford University Press, 1934), p. 111.

31. Julien Benda, *The Betrayal of the Intellectuals,* trans. Richard Aldington (Boston: Beacon Press, 1955), p. 21.

32. Ibid., p. 38.

33. Ibid., p. 122.

34. Ibid., p. 162.

35. José Ortega y Gasset, *The Revolt of the Masses* (New York: Norton, 1957), pp. 63, 18.

36. Ibid., p. 73.

37. Ernst Cassirer, *The Philosophy of the Enlightenment,* trans. Fritz C. A. Koelln and James P. Pettegrove (Boston: Beacon, 1955), pp. xi–xii.

38. Ernst Cassirer, *The Myth of the State* (New Haven, Conn.: Yale University Press, 1946), p. 280.

39. Ibid., p. 296.

40. Erich Fromm, *Escape from Freedom* (New York: Avon Books, 1965), p. 124.

41. Ibid., pp. 173, 246.

42. George Orwell, *1984* (New York: Harcourt, Brace, 1949; paperback, The New American Library, 1961), p. 220.

43. Ibid., p. 211.

44. Ibid., p. 245.

45. Quoted in T. Z. Lavine, *From Socrates to Sartre: The Philosophic Quest* (New York: Bantam Books, 1984), p. 322.

46. Karl Jaspers, *Man in the Modern Age,* trans. Eden and Cedar Paul (Garden City, N.Y.: Doubleday Anchor Books, 1951), p. 159.

47. Quoted in John Macquarrie, *Existentialism* (Baltimore: Penguin Books, 1973), p. 246.

48. Jean Paul Sartre, *Existentialism,* trans. Bernard Frechtman (New York: Philosophical Library, 1947), pp. 28.

49. Ibid., pp. 38, 42.

50. Ibid., pp. 18–19.

51. Albert Camus, *The Rebel,* trans. Anthony Bower (New York: Alfred A. Knopf, 1956), p. 6.

52. Quoted in Germaine Brée, *Camus* (New Brunswick, N.J.: Rutgers University Press, 1961), p. 9.

53. Albert Camus, *The Stranger,* trans. Matthew Ward (New York: Vintage Books, 1988), p. 3.

54. Ibid., p. 120.

55. Gabriel Marcel, "On the Ontological Mystery," in *The Philosophy of Existentialism,* trans. Manya Harari (Secaucus, N.J.: Citadel Press, 1980), p. 10.

56. Ibid., p. 12.

57. Cited in Harry S. Kariel, *In Search of Authority* (Glencoe, Ill.: The Free Press, 1964), p. 246.

58. Cited in Anthony Arblaster, *The Rise and Decline of Western Liberalism* (Oxford: Basil Blackwell, 1984), p. 81.

SUGGESTED READING

See also books suggested for reading at the end of Chapter 28.

Barrett, William, *Irrational Man* (1958). Especially good on the intellectual and cultural roots of existentialism.

Blackham, H. J., *Six Existentialist Thinkers* (1952). Useful analyses of Kierkegaard, Nietzsche, Jaspers, Marcel, Heidegger, and Sartre.

———, ed., *Reality, Man and Existence* (1965). Essential works of existentialism.

Cain, Seymour, *Gabriel Marcel* (1963). A brief, informative survey.

Cruickshank, John, ed., *Aspects of the Modern European Mind* (1969). A useful collection of sources in modern intellectual history.

Jaspers, Karl, *Man in the Modern Age* (1930). A discussion of modern problems, particularly the impact of technology as seen from a half-century ago.

Kaufmann, Walter, ed., *Existentialism from Dostoevsky to Sartre* (1956). The basic writings of existentialist thinkers.

McIntire, C. T., ed., *God, History, and Historians* (1977). Selections from Christian thinkers; many deal with the crises of the twentieth century.

McIntire, C. T., and Marvin Perry, eds., *Toynbee Reappraisals* (1989). A collection of essays on Toynbee's life and thoughts.

Macquarrie, John, *Existentialism* (1972). A lucid discussion of existentialism.

Pawel, Ernst, *The Nightmare of Reason* (1984). A recent biography of Kafka.

Wagar, W. Warren, ed., *European Thought Since 1914* (1968). A valuable collection of sources.

REVIEW QUESTIONS

1. What factors contributed to a mood of pessimism in the period after World War I?

2. What signs of decay did Spengler see in Western civilization?

3. Better than any other novelist of his time, Kafka grasped the dilemma of the modern age. Discuss this statement. Do his insights still apply today?

4. In *The Magic Mountain,* Mann reflected on the decomposition of bourgeois European civilization. Discuss this statement.

5. What was D. H. Lawrence's attitude toward industrial society? Do you agree with him?

6. In what ways were both Dada and surrealism an expression of the times?

7. How did art and literature express a social conscience during the 1920s and 1930s?

8. Why were many intellectuals attracted to communism in the 1930s?

9. What is the theme of *Darkness at Noon?*

10. How did Toynbee interpret nationalism and Nazism?

11. What did Ortega mean by the "mass-man"? What dangers were presented by the mass-man?

12. Why did Benda entitle his book *The Treason of the Intellectuals?*

13. What was Cassirer's attitude toward the Enlightenment? How did he interpret Nazism?

14. How did Fromm explain the rise of Nazism?

15. What were some of the conditions that gave rise to existentialism? What are the basic principles of existentialism?

16. Why are each of the following considered forerunners of existentialism: Dostoevski, Kierkegaard, and Nietzsche?

17. In what ways do each of the following thinkers' works express existentialist themes: Heidegger, Jaspers, Sartre, Camus, and Marcel?

18. What do you like, or dislike, about existentialism?

CHAPTER 33

World War II: Western Civilization in the Balance

F rom the early days of his political career, Hitler dreamed of forging a vast German empire in central and eastern Europe. He believed that only by waging a war of conquest against Russia could the German nation gain the living space and security it required and, as a superior race, deserved. War was an essential component of National Socialist ideology; it also accorded with Hitler's temperament. For the former corporal from the trenches, the Great War had never ended. Hitler aspired to political power because he wanted to mobilize the material and human resources of the German nation for war and conquest. Whereas historians may debate the question of responsibility for World War I, few would deny that World War II was Hitler's war:

> It appears to be an almost incontrovertible fact that the Second World War was brought on by the actions of the Hitler government, that these actions were the expression of a policy laid down well in advance in Mein Kampf, and that this war could have been averted up until the last moment if the German government had so wished.[1]

Western statesmen had sufficient warning that Hitler was a threat to peace and the essential values of Western civilization, but they failed to rally their people and take a stand until Germany had greatly increased its capacity to wage aggressive war.

THE AFTERMATH OF WORLD WAR I

World War I had shown that Germany was the strongest power on the Continent. In the east, the German army had triumphed over Russia; in

German Bombers over London, 1940. (*Courtesy of the Trustees of the Imperial War Museum*)

CHRONOLOGY 33.1 Road to World War II

1931	Japan invades Manchuria
March 1935	Hitler announces German rearmament
October 1935	Italy invades Ethiopia
1936–1939	Spanish Civil War
March 7, 1936	Germany remilitarizes the Rhineland
October 1936	Berlin-Rome Axis is formed
November 1936	German-Japanese anticommunist pact
July 1937	Japan invades China
March 13, 1938	Anschluss with Austria, which becomes a German province
September 1938	Munich Agreement: Britain and France approve Germany's annexation of Sudetenland
1939	Franco establishes a dictatorship in Spain
March 1939	Germany invades Czechoslovakia
April 1939	Italy invades Albania
May 22, 1939	Pact of Steel between Hitler and Mussolini
August 23, 1939	Nonaggression pact between Germany and Russia
September 1, 1939	Germany invades Poland
September 3, 1939	Britain and France declare war on Germany

the west, Britain and France could have hoped for no more than a deadlock without the aid of the United States. The Treaty of Versailles had weakened Germany but not permanently crippled it.

In the decade after the war, responsibility for preserving the peace settlement rested essentially with France. The United States had rejected the treaty and withdrawn from European affairs; Soviet Russia was consolidating its Revolution; and Britain, burdened with severe economic problems, disarmed, and traditionally hostile to Continental alliances, did not want to join with France in holding Germany down. France sought to contain Germany by forging alliances with the new states of eastern Europe, which the French hoped would serve as a substitute for alliance with a now untrustworthy Communist Russia. Thus, in the 1920s, France entered into alliances with Poland, Czechoslovakia, Romania, and Yugoslavia. But no combination of small eastern European states could replace Russia as a counterweight to Germany. Against Hitler's Germany, the French alliance system would prove useless.

In the area of international relations, a feeling of hope prevailed during the 1920s. The newly created League of Nations provided a supranational authority to which nations could submit their quarrels. At the Washington Naval Conference (1921–22), the leading naval powers—the United States, Britain, France, Italy, and Japan—agreed not to construct new battleships or heavy cruisers for a ten-year period and established a ratio for these large ships between them. It was hoped that avoiding a naval arms race would promote international peace.

In the Locarno Pact (1925), Germany, France, and Belgium agreed not to change their existing borders, which meant, in effect, that Germany had accepted both the loss of Alsace and Lorraine to France and the demilitarization of the Rhineland—two provisions of the Versailles treaty. The Locarno Pact held the promise of a détente between France and Germany. But it was only an illusion of peace, for Germany gave no such assurances for its eastern border with Czechoslovakia and Poland, France's allies.

Other gestures that promoted reconciliation followed. In 1926, Germany was admitted to the League of Nations, and in 1928, the Kellogg-Briand Pact renouncing war was signed by most nations. The signatories condemned war as a solution for international disputes and agreed to settle quarrels through peaceful means. Ordinary people welcomed the Kellogg-Briand Pact as the dawning of a new era of peace, but because the pact contained no clauses for its enforcement, this agreement, too, fostered only the illusion of peace.

Nevertheless, between 1925 and 1930, hopes for reconciliation and peace were high. Recovery from the war and increased prosperity coincided with the easing of international tensions. As evidence of the new spirit of conciliation, France and Britain withdrew their forces from the Rhineland in 1930, four years ahead of the time prescribed by the Versailles treaty.

THE ROAD TO WAR

Hitler's Foreign Policy Aims

After consolidating his power and mobilizing the nation's will, Hitler moved to implement his foreign policy objectives: the destruction of the Versailles treaty, the conquest and colonization of eastern Europe, and the domination and exploitation of racial inferiors. In some respects, Hitler's foreign policy aims accorded with the goals of Germany's traditional rulers. Like them, Hitler sought to make Germany the preeminent power in Europe. During World War I, German statesmen and generals had sought to conquer extensive regions of eastern Europe, and in the Treaty of Brest-Litovsk, Germany took Poland, the Ukraine, and the Baltic states from Russia. But Hitler's racial nationalism—the subjugation and annihilation of inferior races by a master German race—marked a break with the outlook of the old governing class. Germany's traditional conservative leaders had never restricted the civil rights of German Jews and had sought to Germanize, not enslave, the Poles living under the German flag.

In foreign affairs, Hitler demonstrated the same blend of opportunism and singleness of purpose that had brought him to power. He behaved like a man possessed, driven by a fanatical belief that his personal destiny was tied to Germany's future. Here, too, he made use of propaganda to undermine his opponents' will to resist. The Nazi propaganda machine, which had won the minds of the German people, became an instrument of foreign policy. Nazi propaganda tried to win the support of the 27 million Germans living in Europe and the Americas, outside the borders of the Reich proper. To promote social and political disorientation in other lands, the Nazis propagated anti-Semitism on a worldwide basis and tried to draw international support for Hitler as Europe's best defense against the Soviet Union and Bolshevism. The Nazi anti-communist campaign "convinced many Europeans that Hitler's dictatorship was more acceptable than Stalin's and that Germany—'the bulwark against Bolshevism'—should be allowed to grow from strength to strength."[2]

As Hitler had anticipated, the British and the French backed down when faced with his violations of the Versailles treaty and threats of war. Haunted by the memory of World War I, Britain and France went to great lengths to avoid another catastrophe—a policy that had the overwhelming support of public opinion. Moreover, Britain suffered from a bad conscience regarding the Versailles treaty. Woefully unprepared for war from 1933 to 1938 and believing that Germany had been treated too severely, Britain was amenable to making concessions to Hitler. Although France had the strongest army on the Continent, it was prepared to fight only a defensive war—the reverse of its World War I strategy. France built immense fortifications, called the

Maginot Line, to protect its borders from a German invasion, but it lacked a mobile striking force, which could punish an aggressive Germany. The United States, concerned with the problems of the Great Depression and standing aloof from Europe's troubles, did nothing to strengthen the resolve of France and Britain. Since both France and Britain feared and mistrusted the Soviet Union, the grand alliance of World War I was not renewed. There was an added factor: suffering from a failure of leadership and political and economic unrest that eroded national unity, France was experiencing a decline in morale and a loss of nerve. It consistently turned to Britain for direction.

British statesmen championed a policy of appeasement: giving in to Germany in the hope that a satisfied Hitler would not drag Europe through another world war. British policy rested on the disastrous illusion that Hitler, like his Weimar predecessors, sought peaceful revision of the Versailles treaty and that he could be contained through concessions. This perception was as misguided as the expectation of Weimar conservatives that the responsibility of power would compel Hitler to abandon his National Socialist radicalism. Some British appeasers, accepting the view that Nazi propaganda cleverly propagated and exploited, also regarded Hitler as a defender of European civilization and the capitalist economic order against Soviet communism.

In *Mein Kampf,* Hitler had explicitly laid out his philosophy of racial nationalism and *Lebensraum* (living space). As dictator, he had established a one-party state, confined political opponents to concentration camps, and persecuted Jews. But the proponents of appeasement did not properly assess these signs. They still believed that Hitler could be reasoned with. Appeasement, which in the end was capitulation to blackmail, failed. Germany grew stronger and the German people more devoted to the fuehrer. Hitler did not moderate his ambitions, and the appeasers did not avert war.

Breakdown of Peace

To realize his foreign policy aims, Hitler required a formidable military machine. Germany had to rearm. The Treaty of Versailles had limited the

size of the German army to a hundred thousand volunteers, restricted the navy's size, forbidden the production of military aircraft, heavy artillery, and tanks, and disbanded the general staff. Throughout the 1920s, Germany had evaded these provisions, even entering into a secret arrangement with the Soviet Union to establish training schools for German pilots and tank corpsmen on Russian soil.

In March 1935, Hitler declared that Germany was no longer bound by the Versailles treaty. Germany would restore conscription, build an air force (which it had been doing secretly), and strengthen its navy. The German people were ecstatic over Hitler's boldness. France protested but offered no resistance. Britain negotiated a naval agreement with Germany, thus tacitly accepting Hitler's rearmament.

A decisive event in the breakdown of peace was Italy's invasion of Ethiopia in October 1935. Mussolini sought colonial expansion and revenge for the defeat that the African kingdom had inflicted on Italian troops in 1896. The League of Nations called for economic sanctions against Italy, and most League members restricted trade with the aggressor. But Italy continued to receive oil, particularly from American suppliers. Believing that the conquest of Ethiopia did not affect their vital interests and hoping to keep the Italians friendly in the event of a clash with Germany, neither Britain nor France sought to restrain Italy, despite its act of aggression against another member of the League of Nations.

Mussolini's subjugation of Ethiopia discredited the League of Nations, which had already been weakened by its failure to deal effectively with Japan's invasion of the mineral-rich Chinese province of Manchuria in 1931. At that time, the League formed a commission of inquiry and urged nonrecognition of the puppet state of Manchukuo created by the Japanese, but the member states did not restrain Japan. The invasion of Ethiopia, like the invasion of Manchuria, showed the League's reluctance to use force to resist aggression.

On March 7, 1936, Hitler marched troops into the Rhineland, violating both the Versailles treaty and the Locarno Pact. German generals had cau-

MAP 33.1 German and Italian Aggressions, 1935–1939 ▶

ICELAND

Germany and Italy
Italian possessions in Africa before 1935
German aggressions, 1935–1939
Italian aggressions, 1935–1939

0   200   400 Km.
0   200   400 Mi.

NORWAY

SWEDEN

FINLAND

North
Sea

DENMARK

Baltic Sea

ESTONIA

LATVIA

Moscow •

IRELAND

GREAT
BRITAIN

London •

Memel • LITHUANIA

Danzig • EAST
PRUSSIA

SOVIET UNION

NETHERLANDS

ATLANTIC
OCEAN

Brussels •
BELGIUM

Berlin
•

GERMANY

POLISH
CORRIDOR

Warsaw
•

RHINELAND
1936

SUDENTENLAND
1938

POLAND

Paris •

Weimar
•

Prague •

LUXEMBOURG

Nuremberg
•

CZECHOSLOVAKIA
1939

FRANCE

Munich
•

Vienna
•

SWITZERLAND

AUSTRIA
1938

HUNGARY

ROMANIA

SPAIN
(Civil War, 1936–1939)

• Madrid

ITALY

YUGOSLAVIA

*Black
Sea*

PORTUGAL

Barcelona
•

• Rome

BULGARIA

ALBANIA
1939

GREECE

TURKEY

Mediterranean Sea

LIBYA

ERITREA

AFRICA

ETHIOPIA
1935–1936

IT. SOMALILAND

A F R I C A

tioned Hitler that such a move would provoke a French invasion of Germany and reoccupation of the Rhineland, which the German army, still in the first stages of rearmament, could not repulse. But Hitler gambled that France and Britain, lacking the will to fight, would take no action.

Hitler had assessed the Anglo-French mood correctly. Britain was not greatly alarmed by the remilitarization of the Rhineland. After all, Hitler was not expanding the borders of Germany but only sending soldiers to Germany's frontier. Such a move, reasoned British officials, did not warrant risking a war. France viewed the remilitarization of the Rhineland as a grave threat. It deprived France of the one tangible advantage that it had obtained from the Treaty of Versailles: a buffer area. Now German forces could concentrate in strength on the French frontier, either to invade France or to discourage a French assault if Germany attacked Czechoslovakia or Poland, France's eastern allies. France lost the advantage of being able to retaliate by invading a demilitarized zone.

Three factors explain why France did not try to expel the twenty-two thousand German troops that occupied the zone. First, France would not act alone, and Britain could not be persuaded to use force. Second, the French general staff overestimated German military strength and thought only of defending French soil from a German attack, not of initiating a strike against Germany. Third, French public opinion showed no enthusiasm for a confrontation with Hitler.

The Spanish Civil War of 1936–1939 was another victory for fascism. Nazi Germany and Fascist Italy aided Franco; the Soviet Union supplied the Spanish republic. The republic appealed to France for help, but the French government feared that the civil war would expand into a European war. With Britain's approval, France proposed the Nonintervention Agreement. Italy, Germany, and the Soviet Union signed the agreement but continued to supply the warring parties. By October 1937, some sixty thousand Italian "volunteers" were fighting in Spain. Hitler sent between five and six thousand men and hundreds of planes, which proved decisive. By comparison, the Soviet Union's aid was meager.

Without considerable help from France, the Spanish republic was doomed, but Prime Minister Léon Blum continued to support nonintervention. He feared that French intervention would cause

Germany and Italy to escalate their involvement, bringing Europe to the edge of a general war. Moreover, supplying the republic would have dangerous consequences at home because French rightists were sympathetic to Franco's conservative-clerical authoritarianism. In 1939, the republic fell, and Franco established a dictatorship.

The Spanish Civil War provided Germany with an opportunity to test weapons and pilots. It also demonstrated that France and Britain lacked the determination to fight fascism. In addition, the war widened the breach between Italy and Britain and France that had opened when Italy invaded Ethiopia, and it drew Mussolini and Hitler closer together. In October 1936, Mussolini sent his foreign minister to meet with Hitler in Berlin. The discussions bore fruit, and on November 1, Mussolini proclaimed that a Rome-Berlin "Axis" had been created.

One of Hitler's aims was the incorporation of Austria into the Third Reich. The Treaty of Versailles had expressly prohibited the union of the two countries. But in *Mein Kampf,* Hitler had insisted that an Anschluss was necessary for German Lebensraum. In February 1938, under intense pressure from Hitler, Austrian Chancellor Kurt von Schuschnigg promised to accept Austrian Nazis in his cabinet and agreed to closer relations with Germany. Austrian independence was slipping away, and increasingly, Austrian Nazis undermined Schuschnigg's authority. Seeking to gain his people's support, Schuschnigg made plans for a plebiscite on the issue of preserving Austrian independence. An enraged Hitler ordered his generals to draw up plans for an invasion of Austria. Hitler then demanded Schuschnigg's resignation and the formation of a new government headed by Arthur Seyss-Inquart, an Austrian Nazi.

Believing that Austria was not worth a war, Britain and France informed the embattled chancellor that they would not help in the event of a German invasion. Schuschnigg then resigned, and Austrian Nazis began to take control of the government. Under the pretext of preventing violence, Hitler ordered his troops to cross into Austria, and on March 13, 1938, Austrian leaders declared that Austria was a province of the German Reich. The Austrians celebrated by ringing church bells, waving swastika banners, and attacking and humiliating Jews.

Czechoslovakia: The Apex of Appeasement

Hitler had obtained Austria merely by threatening to use force. Another threat would give him the Sudetenland of Czechoslovakia. Ethnic Germans, numbering some 3.25 million, predominated in the Sudetenland. The region contained key industries and strong fortifications; since it bordered Germany, it was also vital to Czech security. Deprived of the Sudetenland, Czechoslovakia could not defend itself against a German attack. Encouraged and instructed by Germany, the Sudeten Germans, led by Konrad Henlein, shrilly denounced the Czech government for "persecuting" its German minority and depriving it of its right to self-determination. The Sudeten Germans agitated for local autonomy and the right to profess the National Socialist ideology. Behind this demand was the goal of German annexation of the Sudetenland.

While negotiations between the Sudeten Germans and the Czech government proceeded, Hitler's propaganda machine accused the Czechs of hideous crimes against the German minority and warned of retribution. Hitler also ordered his generals to prepare for an invasion of Czechoslovakia and to complete the fortifications of the French border. Fighting between Czechs and Sudeten Germans heightened the tensions. Seeking to preserve peace, Prime Minister Neville Chamberlain (1869–1940) of Britain offered to confer with Hitler, who then extended an invitation.

Britain and France held somewhat different positions toward Czechoslovakia, the only democracy in eastern Europe. In 1924, France and Czechoslovakia had concluded an agreement of mutual assistance in the event that either was attacked by Germany. Czechoslovakia had a similar agreement with Russia, but with the provision that Russian assistance depended on France's first fulfilling the terms of its agreement. Britain had no commitment to Czechoslovakia. Some of the British officials, swallowing Hitler's propaganda, believed that the Sudeten Germans were indeed a suppressed minority entitled to self-determination. They also thought that the Sudetenland, like Austria, was not worth a war that could destroy Western civilization. Hitler, they said, only wanted to incorporate Germans living outside of Germany; he was only carrying the principle of self-determination to its logical

conclusion. Once these Germans lived under the German flag, Hitler would be satisfied. In any case, Britain's failure to rearm adequately between 1933 and 1938 weakened its position. The British chiefs of staff believed that the nation was not prepared to fight and that it was necessary to sacrifice Czechoslovakia to buy time.

Czechoslovakia's fate was decided at the Munich Conference (September 1938), attended by Chamberlain, Hitler, Mussolini, and Prime Minister Édouard Daladier (1884–1970) of France. The Munich Agreement called for the immediate evacuation of Czech troops from the Sudetenland and its occupation by German forces. Britain and France then promised to guarantee the territorial integrity of the truncated Czechoslovakia. Both Chamberlain and Daladier were praised by the people of Britain and France for keeping the peace.

Critics of Chamberlain have insisted that the Munich Agreement was a tragic blunder. Chamberlain, they say, was a fool to believe that Hitler could be bought off with the Sudetenland. Hitler regarded concessions by Britain and France as signs of weakness; they only increased his appetite for more territory. Second, argue the critics, it would have been better to fight Hitler in 1938 than a year later, when war actually did break out. In the year following the Munich Agreement, Britain increased its military arsenal, but so did Germany, which built submarines and heavy tanks, strengthened western border defenses, and trained more pilots.

Had Britain and France resisted Hitler at Munich, it is likely that the fuehrer would have attacked Czechoslovakia. But the Czech border defenses, built on the model of the French Maginot Line, were formidable. The Czechs had a sizable number of good tanks, and the Czech people were willing to fight to preserve their nation's territorial integrity. By itself, the Czech army could not have defeated Germany. But while the main elements of the German army were battling the Czechs, the French, who could mobilize a hundred divisions, could have broken through the German West Wall, which was defended by only five regular and four reserve divisions; then they could have invaded the Rhineland and devastated German industrial centers in the Ruhr. (Such a scenario, of course, depended on the French overcoming their psychological reluctance to take the offensive.) And there was the possibility that the Soviet Union

THE MUNICH CONFERENCE. Hitler and England's Prime Minister Neville Chamberlain at a fateful moment in history. Chamberlain was lauded as a keeper of the peace immediately after the Munich conference. However, Hitler used the following months to undermine the territorial integrity of Czechoslovakia. With the end of Czech independence, Hitler's intent to dominate Europe became apparent. (*Hulton Deutsch Collection*)

would have fulfilled its agreement and come to Czechoslovakia's aid.

After the annexation of the Sudetenland, Hitler plotted to extinguish Czechoslovakia's existence. He encouraged the Slovak minority in Czechoslovakia, led by a fascist priest, Josef Tiso, to demand complete separation. On the pretext of protecting the Slovak people's right of self-determination, Hitler ordered his troops to enter Prague. In March 1939, Czech independence came to an end.

The destruction of Czechoslovakia was of a different character from the remilitarization of the Rhineland, the Anschluss with Austria, and the annexation of the Sudetenland. In all these previous cases, Hitler could claim the right of German self-determination, Woodrow Wilson's grand principle. The occupation of Prague and the end of Czech independence, though, showed that Hitler really sought European hegemony. Outraged statesmen now demanded that the fuehrer be deterred from further aggression.

CHRONOLOGY 33.2 World War II

September 27, 1939	Poland surrenders
November 1939	Russia invades Finland
April 1940	Germany attacks Denmark and Norway
May 10, 1940	Germany invades Belgium, Holland, and Luxembourg
May 27–June 4, 1940	British and French troops are evacuated from Dunkirk
June 22, 1940	France surrenders
August–September 1940	Battle of Britain
September 1940	Japan begins conquest of Southeast Asia
October 1940	Italian troops cross into Greece
April 6, 1941	Germany attacks Greece and Yugoslavia
June 22, 1941	Germany launches offensive against Russia
December 7, 1941	Japan attacks Pearl Harbor: United States enters the war against Japan and Germany
1942	Tide of battle turns in the Allies' favor: Midway (Pacific Ocean), Stalingrad (Soviet Union), and El Alamein (North Africa)
April–May 1943	Uprising of Jews in Warsaw ghetto
September 1943	Italy surrenders to Allies, following invasion
June 6, 1944	D-day—Allies land in Normandy
August 1944	Paris is liberated; Poles rise up against German occupiers
January 1945	Soviet troops invade Germany
March–April 1945	Allies penetrate Germany
May 7, 1945	Germany surrenders unconditionally
August 1945	United States drops atomic bombs on Hiroshima and Nagasaki; Soviet Union invades Manchuria; Japan surrenders

Poland: The Final Crisis

After Czechoslovakia, Hitler turned to Poland, demanding that the free city of Danzig be returned to Germany and that railways and roads, over which Germans would enjoy extraterritorial rights, be built across the Polish Corridor, linking East Prussia with the rest of Germany. Poland refused to restore the port of Danzig, which was vital to its economy. The Poles would allow a German highway through the Polish Corridor but would not permit German extraterritorial rights. France informed the German government that it would fulfill its treaty obligations to aid Poland. Chamberlain also warned that Britain would assist Poland.

On May 22, 1939, Hitler and Mussolini entered into the Pact of Steel, promising mutual aid in the event of war. The following day, Hitler told his officers that Germany's real goal was the destruction of Poland. "Danzig is not the objective. It is a matter of expanding our living space in the east, of making our food supplies secure. . . . There is therefore no question of sparing Poland, and the decision remains to attack Poland at the first suitable opportunity."[3] In the middle of June, the army presented Hitler with battle plans for an invasion of Poland.

Britain, France, and the Soviet Union had been engaged in negotiations since April. The Soviet Union wanted a mutual-assistance pact including joint military planning, and demanded bases in Poland and Romania in preparation for a German attack. Britain was reluctant to endorse these demands, fearing that a mutual-assistance pact with Russia might cause Hitler to embark on a mad adventure that would drag Britain into war. Moreover, Poland would not allow Russian troops on its soil, fearing Russian expansion.

At the same time, Russia was conducting secret talks with Nazi Germany. Unlike the Allies, Hitler could tempt Stalin with territory that would serve as a buffer between Germany and Russia. Moreover, a treaty with Germany would give Russia time to strengthen its armed forces. On August 23, 1939, the two totalitarian states signed a nonaggression pact, which stunned the world. A secret section of the pact called for the partition of Poland between the two parties and Russian control over Latvia and Estonia (later the agreement was amended to include Lithuania). By signing such an agreement with his enemy, Hitler had pulled off an extraordinary diplomatic coup: he blocked the Soviet Union, Britain, and France from duplicating their World War I alliance against Germany. The Nazi-Soviet Pact was the green light for an invasion of Poland, and at dawn on September 1, 1939, German troops crossed the frontier. Two days later, when Germany did not respond to their demand for a halt to the invasion, Britain and France declared war on Germany.

THE NAZI BLITZKRIEG

Germany struck at Poland with speed and power. The German air force, the *Luftwaffe,* destroyed Polish planes on the ground, attacked tanks, pounded defense networks, and bombed Warsaw, terrorizing the population. Tanks opened breaches in the Polish defenses, and mechanized columns overran the foot-marching Polish army, trapping large numbers of soldiers. The Polish high command could not cope with the incredible speed and coordination of German air and ground attacks. By September 8, the Germans had advanced to the outskirts of Warsaw. On September 17, Soviet troops invaded Poland from the east. On September 27, Poland surrendered. In less than a month, the Nazi *blitzkrieg* (lightning war) had vanquished Poland.

The Fall of France

For Hitler, the conquest of Poland was only the prelude to a German empire stretching from the Atlantic to the Urals. When weather conditions were right, he would unleash a great offensive in the west. Meanwhile, the six-month period following the defeat of Poland was nicknamed the "phony war," for the fighting on land consisted only of a few skirmishes on the French-German border. Then, in early April 1940, the Germans struck at Denmark and Norway. Hitler wanted to establish naval bases on the Norwegian coast from which to wage submarine warfare against Britain, and to ensure delivery of Swedish iron ore to Germany through Norwegian territorial waters.

Denmark surrendered within hours. A British-French force tried to assist the Norwegians, but the landings, badly coordinated and lacking in air support, failed. The Germans won the battle of Norway. But the Norwegian campaign produced two positive results for the Allies: Norwegian merchant ships escaped to Britain to be put into service; and Winston Churchill (1874–1965), who had opposed appeasement, replaced Chamberlain as British prime minister. (The German victory in Norway eroded Chamberlain's support in the House of Commons, and he was forced to

MAP 33.2 World War II: The European Theater ▶

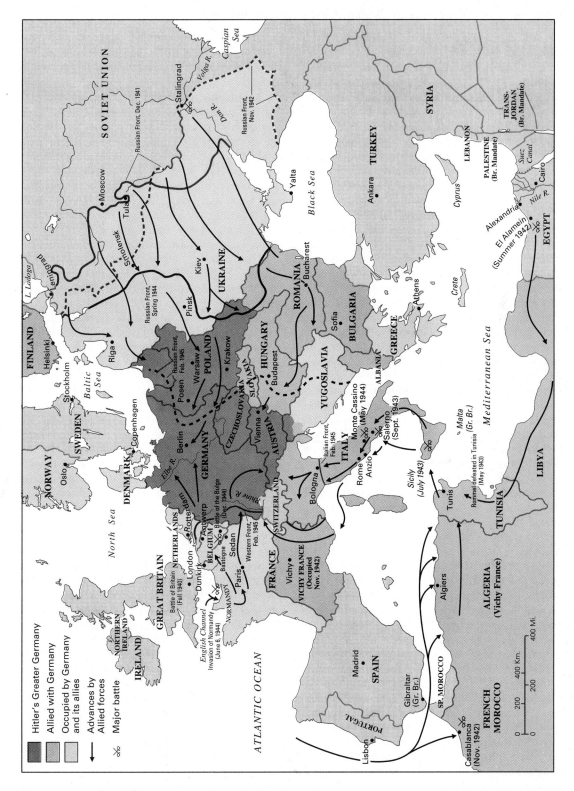

give up the helm.) Dynamic, courageous, and eloquent, Churchill had the capacity to stir and lead his people in the struggle against Nazism.

On May 10, 1940, Hitler launched his offensive in the west with an invasion of neutral Belgium, Holland, and Luxembourg. While armored forces penetrated Dutch frontier defenses, airborne units seized strategic airfields and bridges. On May 14, after the Luftwaffe had bombed Rotterdam, destroying the center of the city and killing many people, the Dutch surrendered.

A daring attack by glider-borne troops gave Germany possession of two crucial Belgian bridges, opening the plains of Belgium to German panzer (tank) divisions. Believing that this was the main German attack, French troops rushed to Belgium to prevent a German breakthrough, but the greater menace lay to the south, on the French frontier. Meeting almost no resistance, German panzer divisions had moved through the narrow mountain passes of Luxembourg and the dense Forest of Ardennes in southern Belgium. On May 12, German units were on French soil near Sedan. Thinking that the Forest of Ardennes could not be penetrated by a major German force, the French had only lightly fortified the western extension of the Maginot Line. The failure to counterattack swiftly was a second mistake. The best elements of the Anglo-French forces were in Belgium, but the Germans were racing across northern France to the sea, which they reached on May 20, cutting the Anglo-French forces in two.

The Germans now sought to surround and annihilate the Allied forces converging on the French seaport of Dunkirk, the last port of escape. But probably fearing that German tanks would lose mobility in the rivers and canals around Dunkirk, Hitler called them off just as the troops prepared to take the port. Instead, he ordered the Luftwaffe to finish off the Allied troops, but fog and rain prevented German planes from operating at full strength. The Allies took advantage of this breathing space to tighten their defenses and prepare for a massive evacuation. While the Luftwaffe bombed the beaches, some 338,000 British and French troops were ferried across the English Channel by destroyers, merchant ships, motorboats, fishing boats, tugboats, and private yachts. Abandoning their equipment on the beaches, the British saved their

armies to fight another day. Hitler's decision to hold back his tanks made the miracle of Dunkirk possible.

Meanwhile, the battle for France was turning into an even worse disaster for the French. Whole divisions were cut off or in retreat, and millions of refugees in cars and carts and on motorcycles and bicycles fled south to escape the advancing Germans. On June 10, Mussolini also declared war on France. With authority breaking down and resistance dying, the French cabinet appealed for an armistice, which was signed on June 22 in the same railway car in which Germany had agreed to the armistice ending World War I.

How can the collapse of France be explained? Neither French military leaders, who experienced the debacle, nor historians are in agreement as to the relative strength of the French and German air forces. It is likely that the Germans and the French (including the British planes based in France) had some three thousand planes each. But many French planes—in what still remains a mystery—stayed on the airfields. The planes were available, but the high command either did not use them or did not deploy them properly. Unlike the Germans, the French did not comprehend or appreciate the use of aviation in modern warfare. As for tanks, the French had as many as the Germans, and some were superior. Nor was German manpower overwhelming. France met disaster largely because its military leaders, unlike the Germans, had not mastered the psychology and technology of motorized warfare. "The French commanders, trained in the slow-motion methods of 1918, were mentally unfitted to cope with Panzer pace, and it produced a spreading paralysis among them," says British military expert Sir Basil Liddell Hart.[4] One also senses a loss of will among the French people: a consequence of internal political disputes dividing the nation, poor leadership, the years of appeasement and lost opportunities, and German propaganda, which depicted Nazism as irresistible and the fuehrer as a man of destiny. It was France's darkest hour.

According to the terms of the armistice, Germany occupied northern France and the coast. The French military was demobilized, and the French government, now located at Vichy, in the south, and headed by Marshal Pétain, the hero of World War I, would collaborate with the German authorities in occupied France. Refusing to recognize defeat, General Charles de Gaulle (1890–1970) escaped to London and organized the Free French forces. The Germans gloried in their revenge, and the French wept in their humiliation. The British gathered their courage, for they now stood alone.

The Battle of Britain

Hitler expected that, after his stunning victories in the west, Britain would make peace. The British, however, continued to reject Hitler's peace overtures, for they envisioned only a bleak future if Hitler dominated the Continent. "The Battle of Britain is about to begin," Churchill told his people. "Upon this battle depends the survival of Christian civilization. . . . if we fail, then . . . all we have known and cared for will sink into the abyss of a new Dark Age."[5]

With Britain unwilling to come to terms, Hitler proceeded in earnest with invasion plans. A successful crossing of the English Channel and the establishment of beachheads on the English coast depended on control of the skies. Marshal Hermann Goering assured Hitler that his Luftwaffe could destroy the British Royal Air Force (RAF), and in early August 1940, the Luftwaffe began massive attacks on British air and naval installations. Virtually every day during the "Battle of Britain," weather permitting, hundreds of planes fought in the sky above Britain. "Never in the field of human conflict was so much owed by so many to so few," said Churchill of the British pilots, who rose to the challenge. On September 15, the RAF shot down sixty aircraft, convincing Hitler that Goering could not fulfill his promise to destroy British air defenses, and on September 17 the fuehrer postponed the invasion of Britain "until further notice." The development of radar by British scientists, the skill and courage of British fighter pilots, and the inability of Germany to make up its losses in planes saved Britain in its struggle for survival. With the invasion of Britain called off, the Luftwaffe concentrated on bombing English cities, industrial centers, and ports. Every night for months, the inhabitants of London sought shelter in subways and cellars to escape German bombs, while British planes rose time after time to make the Luftwaffe pay the price. British morale never broke during the "Blitz."

Invasion of Russia

The obliteration of Bolshevism and the conquest, exploitation, and colonization of Russia were cardinal elements of Hitler's ideology. In Russia, the Nazi empire would take control of wheat, oil, manganese, and other raw materials, and the fertile Russian plains would be settled by the master race. German expansion in the east could not wait for the final defeat of Britain. In July 1940, Hitler instructed his generals to formulate plans for an invasion of Russia. On December 18, Hitler set May 15, 1941, for the beginning of Operation Barbarossa, the code name assigned for the blitzkrieg against the Soviet Union. Events in the Balkans, however, forced Hitler to postpone the date to the latter part of June.

Seeking to make Italy a Mediterranean power and to win glory for himself, Mussolini had ordered an invasion of Greece. In late October 1940, Italian troops stationed in Albania—which Italy had occupied in 1939—crossed into Greece. The poorly planned operation was an instant failure; within a week, the counterattacking Greeks advanced into Albania. Hitler feared that Britain, which was encouraging and aiding the Greeks, would use Greece to attack the oil fields of Romania, which were vital to the German war effort, and to interfere with the forthcoming invasion of Russia. Another problem emerged when a military coup overthrew the government of Prince Paul in Yugoslavia, which two days earlier had signed a pact with Germany and Italy. Hitler feared that the new Yugoslav government might gravitate toward Britain. To prevent any interference with Operation Barbarossa, the Balkan flank had to be secured. On April 6, 1941, the Germans struck at both Greece and Yugoslavia. Yugoslavia was quickly overrun, and Greece, although aided by fifty thousand British, New Zealand, and Australian troops, fell at the end of April.

For the war against Russia, Hitler assembled a massive force: some 4 million men, thirty-three hundred tanks, and five thousand planes. In the early hours of June 22, 1941, the Germans launched their offensive over a wide front. Raiding Russian airfields, the Luftwaffe destroyed twelve hundred aircraft on the first day. The Germans drove deeply into Russia, cutting up and surrounding the disorganized and unprepared

THE RUSSIAN FRONT. Some twenty-five million Russians perished in World War II, many of them the victims of German atrocities. (Soviet Life *from Sovfoto*)

Russian forces. The Russians suffered terrible losses. In a little more than three months, 2.5 million Russian soldiers were killed, wounded, or captured, and fourteen thousand tanks destroyed. Describing the war as a crusade to save Europe from "Jewish Bolshevism," German propaganda claimed that victory had been assured.

But there were also disquieting signs for the Nazi invaders. The Russians, who had a proven capacity to endure hardships, fought doggedly and courageously, and the government would not consider capitulation. Russian reserve strength was far greater than the Germans had estimated. The Wehrmacht (German army), far from its supply lines, was running short of fuel, and trucks and cars had to contend with primitive roads that turned into seas of mud when the autumn rains came. One German general described the ordeal: "The infantryman slithers in the mud, while many teams of horses are needed to drag each gun forward. All wheeled vehicles sink up to their axles in the slime. Even tractors can only move with great difficulty. A large portion of our

heavy artillery was soon stuck fast. . . . The strain that all this caused our already exhausted troops can perhaps be imagined."[6] Conditions no longer favored the blitzkrieg.

Early and bitter cold weather hampered the German attempt to capture Moscow. Without warm uniforms, tens of thousands of Germans suffered from frostbite; without antifreeze, guns did not fire. The Germans advanced to within twenty miles of Moscow, but on December 6, a Red Army counterattack forced them to postpone the assault on the Russian capital. The Germans were also denied Leningrad, which since September had been almost completely surrounded and under constant bombardment. During this epic siege, which lasted for two and a half years, the citizens of Leningrad displayed extraordinary courage in the face of famine, disease, and shelling that cost nearly 1 million lives.

By the end of 1941, Germany had conquered vast regions of Russia but had failed to bring the country to its knees. There would be no repetition of the collapse of France. The Russian campaign demonstrated that the Russian people would make incredible sacrifices for their land and that the Nazis were not invincible.

THE NEW ORDER

By 1942, Germany ruled virtually all of Europe, from the Atlantic to deep into Russia. Some conquered territory was annexed outright; other lands were administered by German officials; in still other countries, the Germans ruled through local officials sympathetic to Nazism or willing to collaborate with the Germans. On this vast empire, Hitler and his henchmen imposed a New Order.

Exploitation and Terror

"The real profiteers of this war are ourselves, and out of it we shall come bursting with fat," said Hitler. "We will give back nothing and will take everything we can make use of."[7] The Germans systematically looted the countries they conquered, taking gold, art treasures, machinery, and food supplies back to Germany and exploiting the industrial and agricultural potential of non-German lands to aid the German war economy. Some foreign businesses and factories were confiscated by the German Reich; others produced what the Germans demanded. Germany also requisitioned food from the conquered regions, significantly reducing the quantity available for local civilian consumption. German soldiers were fed with food harvested in occupied France and Russia; they fought with weapons produced in Czech factories. German tanks ran on oil delivered by Romania, Germany's satellite. The Nazis also made slave laborers of conquered peoples. Some 7 million people from all over Europe were wrested from their homes and transported to Germany. These forced laborers, particularly the Russians and Poles, whom Nazi ideology classified as a lower form of humanity, lived in wretched, unheated barracks and were poorly fed and overworked; many died of disease, hunger, and exhaustion.

The Nazis ruled by force and terror. The prison cell, the torture chamber, the firing squad, and the concentration camp symbolized the New Order. In the Polish province annexed to Germany, the Nazis jailed and executed intellectuals and priests, closed all schools and most churches, and forbade Poles from holding professional positions. In the region of Poland administered by German officials, most schools above the fourth grade were shut down. Himmler insisted that it was sufficient for Polish children to learn "simple arithmetic up to five hundred at the most; writing of one's name; a doctrine that it is a divine law to obey the Germans and to be honest, industrious, and good."[8] The Germans were particularly ruthless toward the Russians. Soviet political officials were immediately executed; many prisoners of war were herded into camps and deliberately starved to death. In all, the Germans took prisoner some 5.5 million Russians, of whom more than 3.5 million perished.

Extermination

Against the Jews of Europe, the Germans waged a war of extermination. The task of imposing the "Final Solution of the Jewish Problem" was given to Himmler's SS, and they fulfilled these grisly duties with fanaticism and bureaucratic efficiency. In exterminating the Jewish people, the Nazis were symbolically destroying essential values of the Western tradition—reason, freedom, equality, toleration, respect for human dignity, and individualism—which they despised and with which the Jews, because of their unique historical experience, were identified.

Regarding themselves as idealists who were writing a glorious chapter in the history of Germany, the SS tortured and murdered with immense dedication. The minds of the SS were dominated by the mythical world-view of Nazism, as the following tract issued by SS headquarters reveals:

Just as night rises up against the day, just as light and darkness are eternal enemies, so the greatest enemy of world-dominating man is man himself. The sub-man—that creature which looks as though biologically it were of absolutely the same kind, endowed by Nature with hands, feet and a sort of brain, with eyes and mouth—is nevertheless a totally different, a fearful creature, is only an attempt at a

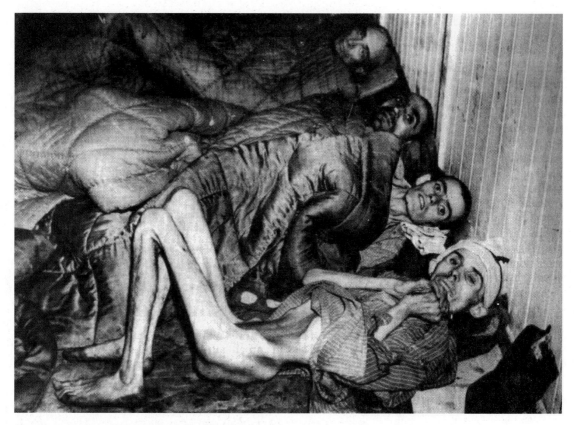

CONCENTRATION CAMP SURVIVORS. Thousands of emaciated and diseased inmates of German concentration camps died in the weeks after liberation by the Allies. These camps will forever remain a monument to the capacity of human beings for inhumanity. (© *Topham/The Image Works*)

human being, with a quasi-human face, yet in mind and spirit lower than any animal. Inside this being a cruel chaos of wild, unchecked passions: a nameless will to destruction, the most primitive lusts, the most undisguised vileness. A sub-man—nothing else! . . . Never has the sub-man granted peace, never has he permitted rest. . . . To preserve himself he needed mud, he needed hell, but not the sun. And this underworld of sub-men found its leader: the eternal Jew![9]

Special squads of SS—the *Einsatzgruppen,* trained for mass murder—followed on the heels of the German army into Russia. Entering captured villages and cities, they rounded up Jewish men, women, and children, herded them to execution grounds, and slaughtered them with machine-gun and rifle fire. Aided by Ukrainian, Lithuanian, and Latvian auxiliaries, along with contingents from the Romanian army, the Einsatzgruppen massacred some 2 million Jews. Units of the regular German army, the Wehrmacht, actively participated in the rounding up of Jews and sometimes in the actual shootings.

In Poland, where some 3.3 million Jews lived, the Germans established ghettos in the larger cities. Jews from all over the country were crammed into these ghettos, which were sealed off from the rest of the population. The German administration deliberately curtailed the food supply, and many Jews died of malnutrition, disease, and beatings. In the ghettos, the Polish Jews struggled to maintain community life and to preserve their spirit. They established schools (forbidden by the German authorities), prayed together (also forbidden), organized social services, and kept hidden archives so that future ages would have a historical record of their ordeal.

The mass killings, however, posed problems for the Germans. These murders were too public, whereas the Germans wanted to keep the Final Solution as secret as possible. Furthermore, the face-to-face killing of civilians, including women and children, could be too hard on the psyche of the personnel charged with carrying out such orders. To overcome these problems, the Germans transformed concentration camps, originally established for political prisoners, into killing centers, and they also built new ones for this purpose. Jews from all over Europe were rounded up—for "resettlement," they were told. The victims dismissed rumors that the Germans were engaged in genocide. They simply could not believe that any nation in the twentieth century was capable of such evil. "Why did we not fight back?"* a survivor asks, and answers: "I know why. Because we had faith in humanity. Because we did not really think that human beings were capable of committing such crimes."[10]

Jammed into sealed cattle cars, eighty or ninety to a car, the victims traveled sometimes for days, without food or water, choking from the stench of vomit and excrement and shattered by the crying of children. Disgorged at the concentration camps, they entered another planet.

> *Corpses were strewn all over the road; bodies were hanging from the barbed-wire fence; the sound of shots rang in the air continuously. Blazing flames shot into the sky; a giant smoke cloud ascended about them. Starving, emaciated human skeletons stumbled forward toward us, uttering incoherent sounds. They fell down right in front of our eyes gasping out their last breath.*
>
> *Here and there a hand tried to reach up, but when this happened an SS man came right away and stepped on it. Those who were merely exhausted were simply thrown on the dead pile. . . . Every night a truck came by, and all of them, dead or not, were thrown on it and taken to the crematory.*[11]

SS doctors quickly inspected the new arrivals, "the freight," as they referred to them. Rudolf

Hoess, the commandant of Auschwitz—the most notorious of the murder factories—described the procedure:

> *The "final solution" of the Jewish question meant the complete extermination of all Jews in Europe. I was ordered to establish extermination facilities at Auschwitz in June, 1941. . . . It took from three to fifteen minutes to kill people in the death chamber, depending upon climatic conditions. We knew when the people were dead because their screaming stopped. We usually waited about one-half hour before we opened the doors and removed the bodies. After the bodies were removed our special commandos took off the rings and extracted the gold from the teeth of the corpses. . . .*
>
> *The way we selected our victims was as follows. . . . Those who were fit to work were sent into the camp. Others were sent immediately to the extermination plants. Children of tender years were invariably exterminated since by reason of their youth they were unable to work. . . . We endeavored to fool the victims into thinking that they were to go through a delousing process. Of course, frequently they realized our true intentions, and we sometimes had riots and difficulties due to that fact. Very frequently women would hide their children under clothes, but of course when we found them we would send the children in to be exterminated.*[12]

The naked bodies, covered with blood and excrement and intertwined with each other, were piled high to the ceiling. To make way for the next group, a squad of Jewish prisoners emptied the gas chambers of the corpses and removed the gold teeth, which, along with the victims' hair, eyeglasses, and clothing, were carefully collected and catalogued for the war effort. Later, the bodies were burned in crematoriums specially constructed by I. A. Topf and Sons of Erfurt. The chimneys vomited black smoke, and the stench of burning flesh permeated the entire region. Jewish leaders in the United States and Britain, who got word of the killings, pleaded with the Allies to bomb the rail lines to Auschwitz and the gas chambers, but the Allies did nothing. The killing process went on relentlessly. (Between 1.1 million

---

*On Jewish resistance, see page 843.

and 1.5 million people died in Auschwitz; 90 percent of them Jews. Non–Jewish victims included political prisoners and Soviet prisoners of war.)

Auschwitz was more than a murder factory. It also provided the German industrial giant, I. G. Farben, which operated a factory adjoining the camp, with slave laborers, both Jews and non-Jews. The working pace at the factory and the ill treatment by guards was so brutal, reported a physician and inmate, that "while working many prisoners suddenly stretched out flat, turned blue, gasped for breath, and died like beasts."[13]

Auschwitz also allowed the SS, the elite of the master race, to shape and harden themselves according to the National Socialist creed. A survivor recalls seeing SS men and women amuse themselves with pregnant inmates. The unfortunate women were "beaten with clubs and whips, torn by dogs, dragged by the hair, and kicked in the stomach with heavy German boots. Then, when they collapsed, they were thrown into the crematory—alive."[14] By systematically overworking, starving, beating, terrorizing, and degrading the inmates, by making them live in filth and sleep sprawled all over each other in tiny cubicles, the SS deliberately sought to strip prisoners of all human dignity, to make them appear and behave as "subhuman," and even make them believe that they were "subman," as the National Socialist ideology asserted.

Many concentration camp inmates went mad or committed suicide; some struggled desperately, defiantly, and heroically to maintain their humanity. When prisoners, exhausted, starved, diseased, and beaten, became unfit for work, which generally happened within a few months, they were sent to the gas chambers. Perhaps the vilest assault on human dignity ever conceived, Nazi extermination camps were the true legacy of National Socialism, and the SS, the true end product of National Socialist indoctrination and idealism.

The SS were often ideologues committed to racist doctrines, which, they believed, were supported by the laws of biology. They were true believers driven by a utopian vision of a new world order founded on a Social Darwinist fantasy of racial hierarchy. To realize this vision of ultimate good, the Jews, whom Nazi ideology designated as the source of all evil, had to be destroyed. Other SS, and their army of collaborators, were simply ordinary people doing their duty as they had been trained to do, following orders the best way they knew how. They were morally indifferent bureaucrats, concerned with techniques and effectiveness, and careerists and functionaries seeking to impress superiors with their ability to get the job done. These people quickly adjusted to the routine of mass murder.

Thus, as Konnilyn G. Feig observes, the thousands of German railway workers "treated the Jewish cattle-car transports as a special business problem that they took pride in solving so well."[15] The German physicians who selected Jews for the gas chambers were concerned only with the technical problems, and those doctors who performed unspeakable medical experiments on Jews viewed their subjects as laboratory animals. The German industrialists who worked Jewish slave laborers to death considered only cost-effectiveness in their operations. So, too, did the firms that built the gas chambers and the furnaces, whose durability and performance they guaranteed.

An eyewitness reports that engineers from Topf and Sons experimented with different combinations of corpses, deciding that "the most economical and fuel-saving procedure would be to burn the bodies of a well-nourished man and an emaciated woman or vice versa together with that of a child, because, as the experiments had established, in this combination, once they had caught fire, the dead would continue to burn without any further coke being required."[16] Hoess, the commandant of Auschwitz, who exemplified the bureaucratic mentality, noted that his gas chambers were more efficient than those used at Treblinka because they could accommodate far more people. The Germans were so concerned with efficiency and cost that—to conserve ammunition or gas and not slow down the pace from the time victims were ordered to undress until they were hurried into the chambers—toddlers were taken from their mothers and thrown live into burning pits or mass graves.

When the war ended, the SS murderers and those who had assisted them returned to families and jobs, resuming a normal life, free of remorse and untroubled by guilt. "The human ability to normalize the abnormal is frightening indeed," observes sociologist Rainer C. Baum.[17] Mass murderers need not be psychopaths. It is a "disturbing psychological truth," notes Robert Jay Lifton, that "ordinary people can commit demonic acts."[18]

There have been many massacres during the

course of world history. And the Nazis murdered many non-Jews in concentration camps and in reprisal for acts of resistance. What is unique about the Holocaust—the systematic extermination of European Jewry—was the Nazis' determination to murder without exception every single Jew who came within their grasp, and the fanaticism, ingenuity, and cruelty with which they pursued this goal. Despite the protests of the army, the SS murdered Jews whose labor was needed for the war effort, and when Germany's military position was desperate, the SS still diverted military personnel and railway cars to deport Jews to the death camps.

The Holocaust was the fulfillment of Nazi racial theories. Believing that they were cleansing Europe of worthless life and a dangerous race that threatened Germany, Nazi executioners performed their evil work with dedication, assembly-line precision, and moral indifference—a gruesome testament to human irrationality and wickedness. Using the technology and bureaucracy of a modern state, the Germans killed approximately 6 million Jews—*two-thirds* of the Jewish population of Europe. Some 1.5 million of the murdered were children; almost 90 percent of Jewish children in German-occupied lands perished. Tens of thousands of entire families were wiped out without a trace. Centuries-old Jewish community life vanished, never to be restored. Burned into the soul of the Jewish people was a wound that could never entirely heal. Written into the history of Western civilization was an episode that would forever cast doubt on the Enlightenment conception of human goodness, rationality, and the progress of civilization.

Resistance

Each occupied country had its collaborators who welcomed the demise of democracy, saw Hitler as Europe's best defense against communism, and profited from the sale of war material. Each country also produced a resistance movement that grew stronger as Nazi barbarism became more visible and prospects of a German defeat more likely. The Nazis retaliated by torturing and executing captured resistance fighters and killing hostages—generally, fifty for every German killed.

In western Europe, the resistance rescued downed Allied airmen, radioed military intelligence to Britain, and sabotaged German installations. Norwegians blew up the German stock of heavy water needed for atomic research. The Danish underground sabotaged railways and smuggled into neutral Sweden almost all of Denmark's eight thousand Jews just before they were to be deported to the death camps. The Greek resistance blew up a vital viaduct, interrupting the movement of supplies to German troops in North Africa. After the Allies landed on the coast of France in June 1944, the French resistance delayed the movement of German reinforcements and liberated sections of the country. Belgian resistance fighters captured the vital port of Antwerp.

The Polish resistance, numbering some 300,000 at its height, reported on German troop movements and interfered with supplies destined for the eastern front. In August 1944, with Soviet forces approaching Warsaw, the Poles staged a full-scale revolt against the German occupiers. The Poles appealed to the Soviets, camped ten miles away, for help. Thinking about a future Russian-dominated Poland, the Soviets did not move. After sixty-three days of street fighting, remnants of the Polish underground surrendered, and the Germans destroyed what was left of Warsaw.

Russian partisans numbered several hundred thousand men and women. Operating behind the German lines, they sabotaged railways, destroyed trucks, and killed scores of thousands of German soldiers in hit-and-run attacks.

The mountains and forests of Yugoslavia provided excellent terrain for guerrilla warfare. The leading Yugoslav resistance army was headed by Josip Broz (1892–1980), better known as Tito. Moscow-trained, intelligent, and courageous, Tito organized the partisans into a disciplined fighting force, which tied down a huge German army and ultimately liberated the country from German rule.

Jews participated in the resistance movements in all countries and were particularly prominent in the French resistance. Specifically Jewish resistance organizations emerged in eastern Europe, but they suffered from shattering hardships. They had virtually no access to weapons. Poles, Ukrainians, Lithuanians, and other peoples of

AKG London

HANS AND SOPHIE SCHOLL

In February 1943, Hans Scholl, aged twenty-five, a medical student, and his twenty-two-year-old sister, Sophie Scholl, who was studying biology and philosophy, were executed by the Nazis for high treason. The Scholls belonged to the White Rose, a small group of idealistic students at the University of Munich that urged passive resistance to the National Socialist regime. The White Rose hoped that if more Germans were aware of the Nazi regime's inhumane character they would withdraw their loyalty.

The Scholls had once been enthusiastic members of the Hitler Youth, but over the years they grew increasingly disillusioned with Nazism. Their outlook was shaped by their anti-Nazi father, by a commitment to the German humanist tradition best represented by Schiller and Goethe, and by Kurt Huber, a professor of philosophy and psychology at their university, who spoke to trusted students of a duty "to enlighten those Germans who are still unaware of

eastern Europe with a long history of anti-Semitism gave little or no support to Jewish resisters—at times, even denounced them to the Nazis, or killed them. For centuries, European Jews had dealt with persecution by complying with their oppressors, and they had unlearned the habit of armed resistance that their ancestors had demonstrated against the Romans. The Germans responded to acts of resistance with savage reprisals against other Jews, creating a moral dilemma for any Jew who considered taking up arms. Nevertheless, revolts did take place in the ghettos and concentration camps. In the spring of 1943, the surviving Jews of the Warsaw ghetto, armed only with a few guns and homemade bombs, fought the Germans for several weeks.

Italy and Germany also had resistance movements. After the Allies landed in Italy in 1943, bands of Italian partisans helped to liberate Italy from fascism and the German occupation. In Germany, army officers plotted to assassinate the

fuehrer. On July 20, 1944, Colonel Claus von Stauffenberg planted a bomb at a staff conference attended by Hitler, but the fuehrer escaped serious injury. In retaliation, some five thousand suspected anti-Nazis were tortured and executed in exceptionally barbarous fashion.

THE TURN OF THE TIDE

The Japanese Offensive

While Germany was subduing Europe, its ally, Japan, was extending its dominion over areas of Asia. Seeking raw materials and secure markets for Japanese goods and driven by a xenophobic nationalism, Japan in 1931 had attacked Manchuria in northern China. Quickly overrunning the province, the Japanese established the puppet state of Manchukuo in 1932. After a period of truce, the war against China was renewed in July

the evil intentions of our government." Hans was also swayed by the persecution of Jews he had witnessed when he was in transport through Poland to the Russian front.

On walls in Munich, the Scholls painted signs: "Down with Hitler," and "Freedom." Stowing their anti-Nazi leaflets in luggage, the students traveled by railroad to several German cities to drop them off. The following excerpts come from three of the White Rose's four leaflets:

> *Who among us has any conception of the dimensions of shame that will befall us and our children when one day the . . . most horrible of crimes—crimes that infinitely outdistance every human measure—reach the light of day?" (First leaflet)*

> *Our present "state" is the dictatorship of evil. . . . it is your right—or rather, your moral duty—to eliminate this system. (Third leaflet)*

> *We are trying to achieve a renewal from within of the severely wounded German spirit.*

> *This rebirth must be preceded, however, by the clear recognition of all the guilt with which the German people have burdened themselves, and by an uncompromising battle against Hitler. (Fourth leaflet)**

On February 18, 1943, Hans and Sophie were spotted dropping leaflets in the univesity by the building superintendent, who reported them to the Gestapo. On February 23, Hans, Sophie, and Christoph Probst, also a medical student, were executed. Several days before she died, Sophie stated: "What does my death matter if through us thousands of people will be stirred to action and awakened?" Hans's last words, "Long live freedom," echoed through the prison. Kurt Huber and other members of the group were executed on July 13, 1943.

---

*Inge Scholl, Students Against Tyranny, trans. Arthur R. Schultz (Middletown, Conn.: Wesleyan University Press, 1970), pp. 36, 73, 81–82, 56.

1937. Japan captured leading cities, including China's principal seaports, and inflicted heavy casualties on the poorly organized Chinese forces, obliging the government of Jiang Jieshi (Chiang Kai-shek) to withdraw to Chungking in the interior.

In 1940, after the defeat of France and with Britain standing alone against Nazi Germany, Japan eyed Southeast Asia—French Indochina, British Burma and Malaya, and the Dutch East Indies. From these lands, Japan planned to obtain the oil, rubber, and tin vitally needed by Japanese industry and enough rice to feed the nation. Japan hoped that a quick strike against the American fleet in the Pacific would give it time to enlarge and consolidate its empire. On December 7, 1941, the Japanese struck with carrier-based planes at Pearl Harbor in Hawaii. Taken by surprise, the Americans suffered a total defeat: the attackers sank seventeen ships, including seven of eight battleships; destroyed 188 airplanes and

damaged 159 others; and killed 2,403 men. The Japanese lost only 29 planes. After the attack on Pearl Harbor, Germany declared war on the United States. Now the immense American industrial capacity could be put to work against the Axis powers—Germany, Italy, and Japan.

By the spring of 1942, the Axis powers held the upper hand. The Japanese empire included the coast of China, Indochina, Thailand, Burma, Malaya, the Dutch East Indies, the Philippines, and other islands in the Pacific. Germany controlled Europe almost to Moscow. When the year ended, however, the Allies seemed assured of victory. Three decisive battles—Midway, Stalingrad, and El Alamein—reversed the tide of war.

At Pearl Harbor, the Japanese had destroyed much of the American fleet. Assembling a mighty flotilla (eight aircraft carriers, eleven battleships, twenty-two cruisers, and sixty-five destroyers), Japan now sought to annihilate the rest of the United States Pacific fleet. In June 1942, the main

Japanese Empire, 1931
Japanese Empire, 1942
Extent of Japanese expansion
Allied advances

SOVIET UNION

ASIA

MONGOLIA

MANCHURIA

Peiping
(Peking) •

CHINA

KOREA

Hiroshima

Shanghai •

Nagasaki

JAPAN
Tokyo •

Taiwan

BURMA

THAILAND

FRENCH
INDOCHINA

Hong
Kong

MALAYA
Singapore •

Borneo

Sumatra

Java

Dutch East Indies

New
Guinea

INDIAN OCEAN

AUSTRALIA

Brisbane •

PACIFIC OCEAN

Attu

Kiska
1943

Aleutian Is.

Midway 1942

Hawaiian Is.
Pearl Harbor •

Iwo Jima
1945

Okinawa
1945

Mariana Is.

Saipan

Wake

Manila •

Philippine Is.

Leyte 1944

Guam
1944

Marshall
Is.

Caroline Is.

Tawara
1943

Gilbert Is.

Solomon Is.

Guadalcanal
1942

| 0 | 500 | 1000 Km. |
| 0 | 500 | 1000 Mi. |

body of the Japanese fleet headed for Midway, eleven hundred miles northwest of Pearl Harbor; another section sailed toward the Aleutian Islands, in an attempt to divide the American fleet. But the Americans had broken the Japanese naval code and were aware of the Japanese plan.

On June 4, 1942, the two navies fought a strange naval battle; it was waged entirely by carrier-based planes, for the two fleets were too far from each other to use their big guns. Demonstrating marked superiority over their opponents and extraordinary courage, American pilots destroyed 4 aircraft carriers and downed 322 Japanese planes. The battle of Midway cost Japan the initiative. With American industrial production accelerating, the opportunity for a Japanese victory had passed.

Defeat of the Axis Powers

After being stymied at the outskirts of Moscow in December 1941, the Germans renewed their offensive in the spring and summer of 1942. Hitler's goal was Stalingrad, the great industrial center located on the Volga River; control of Stalingrad would give Germany command of vital rail transportation. The battle of Stalingrad was an epic struggle in which Russian soldiers and civilians contested for every building and street of the city. So brutal was the fighting that at night half-crazed dogs sought to escape the city by swimming across the river.

A Russian counterattack in November caught the Germans in a trap. With his soldiers exhausted and short of food, medical supplies, weapons, and ammunition, Friedrich Paulus, commander of the Sixth Army, urged Hitler to order a withdrawal before the Russians closed the ring. The fuehrer refused. After suffering tens of thousands of additional casualties, their position hopeless, the remnants of the Sixth Army surrendered on February 2, 1943. Some 260,000 German soldiers had perished in the battle of Stalingrad, and another 110,000 were taken prisoner.

In January 1941, the British were routing the Italians in northern Africa. Hitler assigned General Erwin Rommel (1891–1944) to halt the British advance. Rommel drove the British out of Libya and, with strong reinforcements, might have taken Egypt and the Suez Canal. But Hitler's concern was with seizing Yugoslavia and Greece and preparing for the invasion of Russia. In the beginning of 1942, Rommel resumed his advance, intending to conquer Egypt. The British Eighth Army, commanded by General Bernard L. Montgomery, stopped him at the battle of El Alamein in October 1942. The victory of El Alamein was followed by an Anglo-American invasion of northwest Africa in November 1942. By May 1943, the Germans and Italians were defeated in North Africa.

After securing North Africa, the Allies, seeking complete control of the Mediterranean, invaded Sicily in July 1943 and quickly conquered the island. Mussolini's fellow Fascist leaders turned against him, and the king dismissed him as prime minister. In September, the new government surrendered to the Allies, and in the following month, Italy declared war on Germany.

Italian partisans, whose number would grow to 300,000, resisted the Germans, who were determined to hold on to central and northern Italy. At the same time, the Allies fought their way up the peninsula. The fighting in Italy would last until the very end of the war. Captured by partisans, Mussolini was executed (April 28, 1945) and his dead body, hanging upside down, was publicly displayed.

On June 6, 1944, D-day, the Allies landed on the beaches of Normandy in France. They had assembled a massive force for the invasion: 2 million men and 5,000 vessels. Although they suspected an imminent landing, the Germans did not think that it would occur in Normandy, and they dismissed June 6 as a possible date because weather conditions were unfavorable. The success of D-day depended on securing the beaches and marching inland, which the Allies did despite stubborn German resistance on some beaches. By the end of July, the Allies had built up their strength in France to a million and a half. In the middle of August, Paris rose up against the German occupiers and was soon liberated.

As winter approached, the situation looked hopeless for Germany. Brussels and Antwerp fell to the Allies; Allied bombers were striking German factories and mass-bombing German cities in

◀ MAP 33.3 World War II: The Pacific Theater

HIROSHIMA AFTER THE ATOMIC BOMB. The mass destruction of Hiroshima ushered in a new age. Nuclear weapons gave humanity the capacity to destroy civilization. (*The Bettmann Archive*)

terror raids that took a horrendous toll of life. Desperate, Hitler made one last gamble. In mid December 1944, he launched an offensive to split the Allied forces and regain the vital port of Antwerp. The Allies were taken by surprise in the battle of the Bulge, but a heroic defense by the Americans at Bastogne helped stop the German offensive.

While their allies were advancing in the west, the Russians were continuing their drive in the east, advancing into the Baltic states, Poland, and Hungary. By February 1945, they stood within one hundred miles of Berlin.

Also in February, the Allies in the west were battling the Germans in the Rhineland, and on March 7, 1945, American soldiers, seizing a bridge that the Germans had failed to destroy, crossed the Rhine into the interior of Germany. By April 1945, British, American, and Russian troops were penetrating into Germany from east and west. From his underground bunker near the chancellery in Berlin, a physically exhausted and emotionally unhinged Hitler engaged in wild fan-

tasies about new German victories. On April 30, 1945, with the Russians only blocks away, the fuehrer took his own life. In his last will and testament, Hitler again resorted to the vile lie: "It is not true that I or anybody else in Germany wanted war in 1939. It was wanted and provoked exclusively by those international statesmen who either were of Jewish origin or worked for Jewish interests."[19] On May 7, 1945, a demoralized and devastated Germany surrendered unconditionally.

After the victory at Midway in June 1942, American forces attacked strategic islands held by Japan. American troops had to battle their way up beaches and through jungles tenaciously defended by Japanese soldiers, who believed that death was preferable to the disgrace of surrender. In March 1945, twenty-one thousand Japanese perished on Iwo Jima; another hundred thousand died on Okinawa in April 1945 as they contested for every inch of the island. On August 6, 1945, the United States dropped an atomic bomb on

Hiroshima, killing more than seventy-eight thousand people and demolishing 60 percent of the city. President Harry S Truman said that he ordered the atomic attack to avoid an American invasion of the Japanese homeland, which would have cost tens of thousands of lives.

Truman's decision has aroused considerable debate. Some analysts say that dropping the bomb was unnecessary, that Japan, deprived of oil, rice, and other essentials by an American naval blockade and defenseless against unrelenting aerial bombardments, was close to surrender and had indicated as much. It has been suggested that with the Soviet Union about to enter the conflict against Japan, Truman wanted to end the war immediately, thus depriving the U.S.S.R. of an opportunity to extend its influence in East Asia. On August 8, Russia did enter the war against Japan, invading Manchuria. After a second atomic bomb was dropped on Nagasaki on August 9, the Japanese asked for peace.

THE LEGACY OF WORLD WAR II

World War II was the most destructive war in history. Estimates of the number of dead range as high as 50 million, including 25 million Russians, who sacrificed more than the other participants in both population and material resources. The war produced a vast migration of peoples unparalleled in modern European history. The Soviet Union annexed the Baltic lands of Latvia, Lithuania, and Estonia, forcibly deporting many of the native inhabitants into central Russia. The bulk of East Prussia was taken over by Poland, and Russia annexed the northeastern portion. Millions of Germans fled or were forced out of Prussia and regions of Czechoslovakia, Romania, Yugoslavia, and Hungary, places where their ancestors had lived for centuries. Material costs were staggering. Everywhere cities were in rubble; bridges, railway systems, waterways, and harbors destroyed; farmlands laid waste; livestock killed; coal mines wrecked. Homeless and hungry people wandered the streets and roads. Europe faced the gigantic task of rebuilding. Yet Europe did recover from this material blight, and with astonishing speed.

The war produced a shift in power arrangements. The United States and the Soviet Union emerged as the two most powerful states in the world. The traditional Great Powers—Britain, France, and Germany—were now dwarfed by these *superpowers*. The United States had the atomic bomb and immense industrial might; the Soviet Union had the largest army in the world and was extending its dominion over eastern Europe. With Germany defeated, the principal incentive for Soviet-American cooperation had evaporated.

After World War I, nationalist passions intensified. After World War II, western Europeans progressed toward unity. The Hitler years convinced many Europeans of the dangers inherent in extreme nationalism, and fear of the Soviet Union prodded them toward greater cooperation.

World War II accelerated the disintegration of Europe's overseas empires. The European states could hardly justify ruling over Africans and Asians after they had fought to liberate European lands from German imperialism. Nor could they ask their people, exhausted by the Hitler years and concentrating all their energies on reconstruction, to fight new wars against Africans and Asians pressing for independence. In the years just after the war, Great Britain surrendered India, France lost Lebanon and Syria, and the Dutch departed from Indonesia. In the 1950s and 1960s, virtually every colonial territory gained independence. In those instances where the colonial power resisted independence for the colony, the price was bloodshed.

The consciousness of Europe, already profoundly damaged by World War I, was again grievously wounded. Nazi racial theories showed that even in an age of sophisticated science the mind remains attracted to irrational beliefs and mythical imagery. Nazi atrocities proved that people will torture and kill with religious zeal and machinelike indifference. The Nazi assault on reason and freedom demonstrated anew the precariousness of Western civilization.

This assault would forever cast doubt on the Enlightenment conception of human goodness, secular rationality, and the progress of civilization through advances in science and technology. It bears out Walter Lippmann's contention that "men have been barbarians much longer than they have been civilized. They are only precariously civilized, and within us there is the propensity, persistent as the force of gravity, to revert under stress and strain, or under temptation, to our first natures."[20] Both the Christian and Enlightenment traditions had failed the West.

Some intellectuals, shocked by the irrationality and horrors of the Hitler era, drifted into despair. To these thinkers, life was absurd, without meaning; human beings could neither comprehend nor control it. In 1945, only the naive could have faith in continuous progress or believe in the essential goodness of the individual. The future envisioned by the philosophes seemed more distant than ever. Nevertheless, this profound disillusionment was tempered by hope. Democracy had, in fact, prevailed over Nazi totalitarianism and terror. Perhaps, then, democratic institutions and values would spread throughout the globe, and the newly established United Nations would promote world peace.

◆ ◆ ◆

Notes

1. Pierre Renouvin, *World War II and Its Origins* (New York: Harper & Row, 1969), p. 167.

2. Z. A. B. Zeman, *Nazi Propaganda* (New York: Oxford University Press, 1973), p. 109.

3. *Documents on German Foreign Policy, 1918–1945,* vol. 6 (London: Her Majesty's Stationery Office, 1956), series D, no. 433.

4. Basil H. Liddell Hart, *History of the Second World War* (New York: G. P. Putnam's Sons, 1970), pp. 73–74.

5. Winston S. Churchill, *The Second World War: Their Finest Hour* (Boston: Houghton Mifflin, 1949), 2:225–226.

6. Quoted in William L. Shirer, *The Rise and Fall of the Third Reich* (New York: Simon & Schuster, 1960), p. 860.

7. *Hitler's Secret Conversations, 1941–1944,* with an introductory essay by H. R. Trevor Roper (New York: Farrar, Straus & Young, 1953), p. 508.

8. Quoted in Gordon Wright, *The Ordeal of Total War* (New York: Harper Torchbooks, 1968), p. 124.

9. Quoted in Norman Cohn, *Warrant for Genocide* (New York: Harper Torchbooks, 1967), p. 188.

10. Gerda Weissman Klein, *All But My Life* (New York: Hill & Wang, 1957), p. 89.

11. Judith Sternberg Newman, *In the Hell of Auschwitz* (New York: Exposition, 1964), p. 18.

12. *Nazi Conspiracy and Aggression* (Washington, D.C.: United States Government Printing Office, 1946), 6:787–789.

13. Quoted in Joseph Borkin, *The Crime and Punishment of I. G. Farben* (New York: The Free Press, 1978), p. 143.

14. Gisella Perl, *I Was a Doctor in Auschwitz* (New York: International Universities Press, 1948), p. 80.

15. Konnilyn G. Feig, *Hitler's Death Camps* (New York: Holmes & Meier, 1979), p. 37

16. Quoted in Steven T. Katz, "Technology and Genocide: Technology as a 'Form of Life,'" in *Echoes from the Holocaust,* eds. Alan Rosenberg and Gerald E. Meyers (Philadelphia: Temple University Press, 1988), p. 281.

17. Rainer C. Baum, "Holocaust: Moral Indifference as the Form of Modern Evil," in *Echoes from the Holocaust,* eds. Rosenberg and Meyers, p. 83.

18. Robert Jay Lifton, *The Nazi Doctors* (New York: Basic Books, 1968), p. 5.

19. Excerpted in George H. Stein, ed., *Hitler* (Englewood Cliffs, N.J.: Prentice-Hall, 1968), p. 84.

20. Walter Lippmann, *The Public Philosophy,* (Boston: Little Brown, 1955), p. 86.

Suggested Reading

Adams, R.J.Q., *British Politics and Foreign Policy in the Age of Appeasement, 1935–1939* (1993). The nature, purpose, and meaning of appeasement.

Ambrose, Stephen E., *D-Day* (1994). Based on oral histories from people who were there.

Bartow, Omer, *Hitler's Army* (1992). Excellent material on the indoctrination of the German soldier.

Bauer, Yehuda, *A History of the Holocaust* (1982). An authoritative study.

Baumont, Maurice, *The Origins of the Second World War* (1978). A brief work by a distinguished French scholar.

Bell, P.M.H., *The Origins of the Second World War in Europe (1986)*. An intelligent survey.

Browning, Christopher R., *The Path to Genocide* (1992). Essays on launching the Final Solution; particularly good insights into the attitudes of lower- and middle-echelon bureaucrats who participated in mass murder.

Calvocoressi, Peter, and Guy Wint, *Total War* (1972). A good account of World War II.

Cohn, Norman, *Warrant for Genocide* (1967). An astute analysis of the mythical components of modern anti-Semitism.

Des Pres, Terrence, *The Survivors* (1976). A sensitive analysis of life in the death camp.

Eubank, Keith, *The Origins of World War II* (1969). A brief introduction; a good bibliographical essay.

Gilbert, Martin, and Martin Gott, *The Appeasers* (1963). A study of British weakness in the face of Hitler's threats.

Hilberg, Raul, *The Destruction of the European Jews* (1967). A monumental study of the Holocaust.

Hildebrand, Klaus, *The Foreign Policy of the Third Reich* (1973). An assessment of Nazi foreign policy.

Klee, Ernst, Willi Dressen, and Volker Riess, eds., *The Good Old Days* (1988). Documents show perpetrators and bystanders not only as indifferent to the suffering of Jews, but also deriving pleasure from it.

Marks, Sally, *The Illusion of Peace* (1976). The failure to establish peace in the period 1918–1933.

Marrus, Michael R., *The Holocaust in History* (1987). An excellent summary of key issues and problems.

Michel, Henri, *The Shadow War* (1972). An analysis of the European resistance movement, 1939–1945.

———, *The Second World War*, 2 vols. (1975). Translation of an important study by a prominent French historian.

Remak, Joachim, *The Origins of the Second World War* (1976). A useful essay, followed by documents.

Weinberg, Gerhard L., *A World at Arms* (1994). A recent study based on extraordinary knowledge of the sources.

Wiesel, Elie, *Night* (1960). A moving personal record of the Holocaust.

REVIEW QUESTIONS

1. What efforts promoted international reconciliation during the 1920s? How did these efforts foster only an illusion of peace?

2. What were Hitler's foreign policy aims?

3. Why did Britain and France practice a policy of appeasement?

4. Discuss the significance of each of the following: Italy's invasion of Ethiopia (1935), Germany's remilitarization of the Rhineland (1936), the Spanish Civil War (1936–1939), Germany's union with Austria (1938), the occupation of Prague (1939), and the Nazi-Soviet Pact (1939).

5. What factors made possible the quick fall of France?

6. What problems did the German army face in Russia?

7. Describe the New Order that the Nazis established in Europe.

8. In your opinion, what is the meaning of the Holocaust for Western civilization? For Jews? For Christians? For Germans?

9. Discuss the significance of each of the following battles: Midway (1942), Stalingrad (1942–43), El Alamein (1942), and D-day (1944).

10. What is the legacy of World War II?

PART SEVEN

The Contemporary World: The Global Age

since 1945

POLITICS AND SOCIETY	THOUGHT AND CULTURE
1940 Yalta agreement (1945) United Nations established (1945) Marshall Plan for recovery of Europe (1947) Cold war starts (1947) State of Israel established (1948) North Atlantic Treaty Organization (NATO) established (1949) Division of Germany (1949) Triumph of communism in China (1949)	Wiener, *Cybernetics* (1948) Orwell, *1984* (1949) de Beauvoir, *The Second Sex* (1949)

1950 Korean War (1950–1953)
European Economic Community (EEC) established (1957)
Sputnik launched; space age begins (1957)
	Camus, *The Rebel* (1951)
	Discovery of DNA by Crick and Watson
	   (1951–53)
	Djilas, *The New Class* (1957)
	Chomsky, *Syntactic Structures* (1957)
	Snow, *The Two Cultures and the Scientific
	   Revolution* (1959)

1960 Berlin Wall built (1961) Cuban missile crisis (1962) Vietnam War (1963–1973)	Pope John XXIII, *Pacem in Terris* (Peace on Earth) (1963) McLuhan, *Understanding Media* (1964) Levi-Strauss, *The Savage Mind* (1966)
1970 Détente in East-West relations (1970s)	Solzhenitsyn, *The Gulag Archipelago* (1974–1978)

1980 Gorbachev becomes leader of Soviet Union
   (1985)
Explosion at Chernobyl nuclear power plant
   (1986)
Peaceful overthrow of Communist governments in Eastern Europe (1989)
Berlin Wall demolished (1989)
	Gorbachev, *Perestroika* (1987)

1990 Reunification of Germany (1990)
Charter of Paris for a New Europe (1990)
Official end of cold war (1990)
Persian Gulf War (1991)
Yeltsin elected Russian president (1991)
Failed coup against Gorbachev ends rule of
   Soviet Communist party (1991)
Collapse of the Soviet Union (1991)
Czechoslovakia splits into Czech Republic
   and Slovakia (1993)
European Union ratifies the Maastricht
   Treaty (1993)
Yeltsin wins armed confrontation in Moscow
   (1993)
Elections for new Russian constitution and
   parliament (1993)	

CHAPTER 34

Europe After World War II: Recovery and Realignment, 1945–1985

At the end of World War II, Winston Churchill lamented: "What is Europe now? A rubble heap, a charnel house, a breeding ground for pestilence and hate."[1] Everywhere the survivors counted their dead. War casualties were relatively light in western Europe. Britain and the Commonwealth suffered 460,000 casualties; France, 570,000; and Italy, 450,000. War casualties were heavier in the east: 5 million people in Germany, 6 million in Poland (including 3 million Jews), 1 million in Yugoslavia, and more than 25 million in the Soviet Union. The material destruction had been unprecedentedly heavy in the battle zones of northwestern Europe, northern Italy, and Germany, growing worse farther east, where Hitler's and Stalin's armies had fought without mercy to people, animals, or the environment. Industry, transportation, and communication had come to a virtual standstill. Now members of families searched for each other; prisoners of war made their way home; Jews from extermination camps or from hiding places returned to open life; and displaced persons by the millions sought refuge.

Added to the human miseries was the historic fact that Europe had been dethroned from the central position in world affairs that it had occupied in recent centuries. It was politically cut in half; Soviet troops had overrun eastern Europe and penetrated into the heart of Germany. The Yalta agreement of February 1945, signed by Roosevelt, Churchill, and Stalin on Stalin's home ground in the Crimean peninsula, turned the prevailing military balance of power into a political settlement. The Soviet Union imposed its grim Eurasian tradition of dictatorship on the Western-oriented countries in the eastern and southeastern part of Europe.

Yet there was hope. In the spring of 1945, the United States rallied the victorious Allies, including the Soviet Union, to a farsighted political initiative, establishing the United Nations. In its charter,

Soviet May Day Parade, Moscow, 1964.
(*UPI/Bettmann*)

CHRONOLOGY 34.1 Europe, 1945–1985

1945	United Nations founded; Eastern Europe occupied by Red Army
1947	Cold war starts; Truman Doctrine; Marshall Plan inaugurated
1948	Stalinization of Eastern Europe
1949	NATO formed; first Soviet atomic bomb exploded
1953	Stalin dies
1956	Khrushchev's secret speech on Stalin's crimes; Polish October; Hungarian uprising is crushed
1957	European Economic Community established; sputnik launched—the space age begins
1961	Berlin Wall built, dividing the city of Berlin
1962	Cuban missile crisis
1963–1973	Vietnam War
1964	Khrushchev ousted; a new team of leaders, lead by Brezhnev, succeeds him
1968	Student uprising in France; Czechoslovakia's "socialism with a human face"
1969	American landing on the moon
1979	Soviet Union invades Afghanistan
1982	Brezhnev dies
1985	Gorbachev becomes U.S.S.R. leader

reflecting basic aspects of Western thinking, the new organization pledged

> To save succeeding generations from the scourge of war, which twice in our lifetime has brought untold sorrow to mankind, and to reaffirm faith in fundamental human rights, in the dignity and worth of the human person, in the equal rights of men and women and of nations large and small . . . to promote social progress and better standards of life in larger freedom.[2]

Three years later, the members of the United Nations underscored the charter's purpose in the Universal Declaration of Human Rights. The declaration announced that the "recognition of the inherent dignity and of the equal and inalienable rights of all members of the human family is the foundation of freedom, justice and peace in the world."[3] These ringing phrases, often restated in subsequent U.N. documents, extended to all humanity the ideals by which in recent times Western societies had professed to guide their political practice.

By promoting a global organization based on these ideals, the United States stepped forward as the heir and guardian of the Western tradition. A superpower, it was striving to shape the new world order of the global age that was emerging from the defeat of Germany and Japan. American political power was limited; however, the material wealth, of the United States, its industrial efficiency, and the ideals of democratic freedom embedded in its institutions helped rebuild democratic government and generate prosperity in western Europe. The United States also impressed people around the world, inspiring imitation even in hostile countries.

Thus, American influence speeded up the westernization of the world. Japan and Pacific Rim countries were drawn into the mainstream of Western business and culture. Decolonization created a multitude of new states in Asia and Africa; patterned, however painfully, after the Western model of statehood, they added immense complexity to the world's political landscape. For better or for worse, all the world's peoples were now becoming linked in rapidly increasing political and economic interdependence. Immigrants from poor countries streamed toward the rich.

These elemental changes took place over the next decades under the shadow of the cold war, the worldwide conflict between the two victors in World War II, the United States and the Soviet Union. Each offered its form of government and guiding ideals as a model for the entire world, in unequal competition. While proudly presenting their communist vision as the guide to the future, the Soviet leaders were also trying to help their vast country catch up to Western achievements.

THE COLD WAR

Origins

The cold war (the American financier Bernard Baruch coined the phrase in 1947) stemmed from the divergent historical experiences and the incompatible political ambitions of the United States and the Soviet Union. As the European continent lay in a shambles and even Great Britain had lost its preeminence, the proud outsiders to the west and east dominated the global scene. The challenge that started the cold war came from the east even before the end of World War II.

As the Red Army moved through eastern Europe, the fate of the peoples of that region hung in the balance. Would they have the right to self-determination and democratic freedom, favored elsewhere by the Western Allies? Or would Stalin treat them as a conquered people, knowing that left to their own devices they would return to their traditional anti-Russian orientation?

Attention first focused on Poland. The Western Allies, advancing from the Atlantic against Hitler's armies, were in no position to stop Stalin from doing as he wished. As the Red Army occupied Poland, Stalin installed a pro-Soviet regime. Other countries in eastern Europe suffered the same fate. Ever worried about the security of his country's western boundaries, Stalin incorporated the eastern European countries into a buffer zone for protection against Western attack. The local populations and their sympathizers in western Europe and the United States viewed the Soviet occupation of eastern Europe as a dire calamity. But short of starting another war, Western countries were powerless to intervene. For the next forty-five years or so, the two parts of the Continent would be known as Eastern Europe and Western Europe: two camps of opposing ideologies, communist and anticommunist.

Alarmed Americans viewed the Soviet occupation of eastern European countries as part of a communist expansion, which threatened to reach beyond Europe into the world. In March 1947, fearing Soviet penetration into the eastern Mediterranean and aware of British weakness in that area, President Truman proclaimed the Truman Doctrine: "It must be the policy of the United States to support free peoples who are resisting attempted subjugation by armed minorities or by outside pressures."[4] The Truman Doctrine was the centerpiece of the new policy of *containment,* of holding Soviet power within its then current boundaries. U.S. military and economic support soon went to Greece and Turkey. Thus, a sharp reversal took place in American foreign policy; with the special encouragement of the British government, prewar American isolation gave way to worldwide vigilance against any Soviet effort at expansion. Later that year, the United States took a further step toward

MAP 34.1 Western Europe After 1945

strengthening the West by establishing the Marshall Plan, aimed at helping Western Europe recover from the war (see page 863).

These measures were accompanied by a massive ideological mobilization of American opinion against the communist threat and a new apprehension about national security. As a result, the armed forces and the defense industries supporting them—the "military-industrial complex," in President Dwight D. Eisenhower's words—attained un-

precedented political power in U.S. politics. Never before in their history had Americans been so powerful as after World War II; and never before had they been so afraid of a challenge to their identity.

Like Western Europeans, Americans had reasons to fear Soviet expansionism. Although exhausted by the war and ever concerned about its security, the Soviet Union was tempted to restore Lenin's vision of world revolution. As he took over Eastern Europe, Stalin was held responsible—

wrongly, as it turned out—for starting a revolution in Greece in 1947. After Communists gained control in China in 1949, he was accused of authorizing Communist North Korea's invasion of South Korea in 1950, the cause of the Korean war. His successors supported their Vietnamese allies against Vietnam's French colonial masters and later against the Americans, who feared that a communist victory there would extend Soviet domination into the Pacific area. Soviet encouragement fueled anti-Western revolts in Asian and African countries rising to statehood. The U.S.S.R. also supported anti-American governments in Latin America—like Castro's Cuba, for one. Was Lenin's dream of world revolution to come true at last?

Worried about where Soviet ambition might lead, the United States redoubled its resolve to contain Soviet power by creating extensive alliances with other anticommunist states around the world. Of these alliances, the North Atlantic Treaty Organization (NATO) played the biggest role; it combined the armed forces of the major Western European states with the American forces stationed in Europe. Under President Eisenhower, the United States extended its military alliances into Asia. As Eisenhower stated, "These pacts stand as solemn warning that future military aggression and subversion against the free nations of Asia will meet united response."[5] Consequently, two more alliance systems were added to NATO (neither lasting very long): one united Turkey, Iran, Pakistan and Britain, and the other Pakistan, Thailand, the Philippines, Australia, and New Zealand. In the Western Hemisphere, the United States tried to make certain, by economic pressure, subversion, or military intervention, if necessary, that no pro-Soviet or even Marxist regime established itself. (It failed, however, in the case of Cuba.)

The Soviet Union, by contrast, could boast only one alliance system: the Warsaw Pact, formed in response to NATO. It consisted of the U.S.S.R.'s European satellites. In terms of military power, its global outreach was limited.

The Arms Race and the Space Race

Military alliances and forces were backed up by ever more powerful armaments. Sooner than expected, in 1949, the Soviet Union exploded its own atomic device. Thereafter, the arms race escalated to hydrogen bombs and intercontinental ballistic missiles (ICBMs). Threatened by Soviet ICBMs, the United States lost its territorial invulnerability, which its geography had assumed until then. The arms race proved a source of profound intellectual and moral alarm. Said Albert Einstein, "The unleashed power of the atom has changed everything save our modes of thinking, and thus we drift toward unparalleled catastrophes."[6] Catastrophe was barely avoided in 1962. When the Soviet Union, under Nikita Khrushchev, prepared to place nuclear missiles in Cuba, trying to offset U.S. missiles in Turkey, President John F. Kennedy demanded their removal. For a terrifying moment, as the world held its breath, the cold war threatened to turn into a hot nuclear exchange. Fortunately, Khrushchev was persuaded to back down. The Cuban missile crisis ended peacefully.

Meanwhile, the U.S.-Soviet rivalry had extended into outer space. In 1957, the Soviet government sent *sputnik* into orbit around the earth, shocking complacent Americans into a keen awareness of their vulnerability. For some years, the Soviet Union remained ahead in the prestigious field of space exploration, sending the first astronaut into orbit in 1961. The United States caught up in 1969, by landing a man on the moon. Eventually, other countries joined the American and Soviet ventures into space, for military or commercial gain. Thus, Western science and technology, spurred by the superpower rivalry, introduced human beings to the infinity of the cosmos.

All along science and technology had contributed to the escalation of the ominous arms race. Determined to gain the advantage in order to discourage an enemy attack, each side developed ever more sophisticated weapons and long-range delivery systems which, if used, could have destroyed all civilized life. In addition, other countries were acquiring nuclear arms: England, France, China, Israel, India, and Pakistan. The murderous weapons threatened to become a common tool of global politics. Fortunately, the increasing fear of nuclear war prompted efforts to scale down the arms race.

In 1968, one hundred members of the United Nations signed the Nuclear Non-Proliferation Treaty, promising to abstain from developing nuclear arms; other U.N. members soon joined them. In 1969, the super powers began the Strategic Arms Limitations Talks (SALT), agreeing in 1972 to a temporary limit on offensive strategic weapons. Further limitations

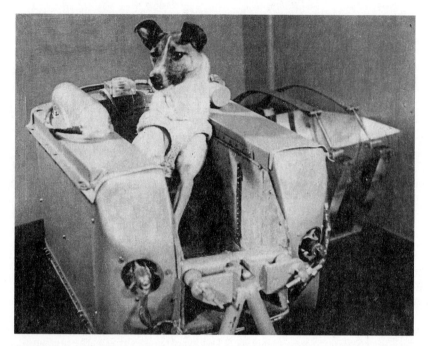

SPACE RACE. The world's first artificial satellite, Sputnik, was sent into orbit by the Soviet Union in 1957, beginning the space race between the superpowers. Shocked by the technological superiority of the Soviet Union, Americans called for increased funding for education in the sciences and expansion of the arms race. Here, the dog Laike sits ready for installation in Sputnik II. (*Sovfoto*)

negotiated under SALT II in 1979 were canceled to protest the Soviet invasion of Afghanistan. Subsequent efforts to negotiate a Strategic Arms Reduction Treaty failed until the early 1980's.

The arms race peaked in 1983 when President Reagan announced the Strategic Defense Initiative, popularly called "Star Wars." At enormous cost, it extended competition into outer space, seriously straining the economies of both countries.

From the start, the cold war had led humanity along the brink of nuclear apocalypse. It remained, however, a *cold* war, since the super powers abstained from armed confrontation as they tried to cope with new conditions in their countries and around the world.

The United States During the Cold War

At the end of World War II, the United States stood, as Winston Churchill observed, "at the pin-

nacle of world power."[7] Yet it had also reached a turning point in its history. Propelled from isolation into global leadership, it was immediately confronted with the Soviet expansion in Eastern Europe. To quote Churchill's famous words, "From Stettin in the Baltic to Triest in the Adriatic, an iron curtain has descended across the Continent."[8] Now the Western democracies had to close ranks against the communist menace. American leaders were profoundly alarmed: they now had the responsibility of rallying Western Europe, and possibly the world, against universal communism, a political force vaguely feared since the end of World War I and now backed up by the victorious Red Army.

This new wariness quickly raised to prominence a powerful national security establishment within the American government—an encroachment on traditional freedoms. The new Central Intelligence Agency (CIA) and the National Security Council were allied with the older Federal Bureau of Investigation (FBI), notorious for its anticom-

BOGGED DOWN IN VIETNAM. Americans defended South Vietnam against a threatened takeover by communist North Vietnam. Between 1964 and 1973, U.S. involvement in the unsuccessful Vietnam War cost tens of thousands of Vietnamese and American lives, ruined South Vietnam, and polarized U.S. public opinion over the morality of the war. (*Wide World Photo*)

munism. Thus fortified, the United States in 1950, with United Nations support, went to war for two years to defend South Korea against an invasion by Communist North Korea and its powerful Chinese ally. For a time thereafter, hysterical fear of communist infiltration into the government and among intellectuals gripped the American public. Most citizens, however, seemed content with the way American democracy continued to function. The postwar economic boom, which spread unprecedented material well-being, kept them satisfied and even fostered complacency.

In the 1960s, when trouble succeeded the good times long-hidden racial tensions surfaced, leading to the civil rights movement, urban riots by disaffected blacks, and some remedial legislation. In addition, a rebellious counterculture emerged among students, promoting disarmament, civil liberties, and racial equality, as well as defying traditional moral restraints.

The Vietnam War

The most divisive issue, however, was the war in Vietnam, where the Communist regime in the north threatened to take over South Vietnam as well. If the communists prevailed, apprehensive Americans argued, all the other countries in East and Southeast Asia would fall like dominoes to

SOVIET UNION
MONGOLIA
Ulaan Baatar
CHINA
Beijing
Vladivostok
NORTH KOREA
Pyongyang
SOUTH KOREA
Seoul
Pusan
JAPAN
Tokyo
Osaka
Shanghai
East China Sea
PACIFIC OCEAN
Taipei
TAIWAN
Guangzhou (Canton)
Hong Kong (Br.)
Macau (Port.)
PAKISTAN
Islamabad
Delhi
New Delhi
NEPAL
Kathmandu
BHUTAN
Thimbu
BANGLADESH
Dacca
Calcutta
INDIA
Bombay
MYANMAR (BURMA)
Rangoon
LAOS
Hanoi
Hainan
Vientiane
THAILAND
VIETNAM
Bangkok
South China Sea
Manila
PHILIPPINES
Bay of Bengal
CAMBODIA (KAMPUCHEA)
Phnom Penh
Ho Chi Minh City
Guam (U.S.)
Colombo
SRI LANKA
BRUNEI
Kuala Lumpur
MALAYSIA
Singapore
Borneo
Sumatra
Equator
0°
INDIAN OCEAN
INDONESIA
Jakarta
PAPUA NEW GUINEA
Port Moresby
AUSTRALIA
Perth
Sydney
Canberra
Melbourne
Tasmania
INDIAN OCEAN
0 500 1000 Km.
0 500 1000 Mi.
CHINA
Red R.
Dien Bien Phu
Hanoi
Haiphong
Gulf of Tonkin
Hainan
LAOS
Luang Prabang
NORTH VIETNAM
Mekong R.
Vientiane
Demarcation LIne, 1954
Hue
Da Nang
THAILAND
Ho Chi Minh Trail
Bangkok
CAMBODIA (KAMPUCHEA)
SOUTH VIETNAM
Gulf of Thailand
Phnom Penh
Saigon
South China Sea
0 100 200 Km.
0 100 200 Mi.

communist rule. Under President Lyndon B. Johnson, U.S. intervention in South Vietnam became the undeclared Vietnam War.

The U.S. government shipped to Vietnam nearly half a million soldiers, equipped with chemical weapons and advanced electronic gear. Yet victory eluded the American forces. The North Vietnamese government and its people withstood the cruelest punishment of bombs and chemical weapons ever inflicted on human beings. Nor was South Vietnam spared; virtually every South Vietnamese family saw relatives killed or maimed, and their farms and livelihoods ruined.

As domestic opposition to the war increased and North Vietnamese resistance could not be broken, President Richard M. Nixon, elected in 1968, realized that the war had to be ended by "peace with honor." While he initiated negotiations with North Vietnam, U.S. forces put pressure on the enemy by attacking communist bases and supply routes in neighboring Cambodia and Laos. Civilians were bombed more fiercely than had been the case in World War II. In 1973, by agreement with North Vietnam, the United States withdrew its forces from the area. In 1975, the North Vietnamese swept aside the inept South Vietnamese army and unified the country under a Communist dictatorship. Ho Chi Minh had triumphed against the mightiest nation in the world.

Yet defeat in Vietnam undermined neither America's domestic unity nor its position in the world. American political and economic preeminence peaked, to the electorate's satisfaction, during the presidency of Ronald Reagan. Admittedly economic progress slowed down, the gap between rich and poor widened, and social cohesion weakened. But the United States continued to stand out as a model of democracy, industrial productivity, and the good life, much admired around the globe.

BUILDING A NEW EUROPE

The United States made possible the rebuilding of Western Europe and its economic development in the years following World War II. American military presence and superiority in nuclear weapons

◄ MAP 34.2 Southeast Asia and the Vietnam War

protected Western Europe against the widely dreaded westward expansion of Soviet communism. To counter that threat, the United States and the countries of Western Europe established the North Atlantic Treaty Organization in 1949. NATO linked the armed forces of the United States, Canada, Portugal, Norway, Iceland, Denmark, Italy, Britain, France, and the Benelux countries (an acronym for Belgium, the Netherlands, and Luxembourg). Greece and Turkey soon joined; West Germany was included in 1956, and Spain in 1982. The American influence also provided the foundations for political stability under democratic constitutions, as well as for material prosperity based on free enterprise in a market economy.

Even before committing itself to a military presence, the United States had begun an extensive program of financial assistance for the economic recovery of Western Europe. In June 1947, Secretary of State George C. Marshall announced an impressive program of economic aid, formally called the European Recovery Program, but widely known as the Marshall Plan. By 1952, when the plan terminated, it had supplied Europe with a total of $13.15 billion in aid—a modest pump-priming for the subsequent record upswing in U.S., Western European, and even global prosperity. Western Europe recovered, and the United States gained economically strong allies and trading partners.

U.S. military and economic preeminence after the war also prepared the way for the spread of American culture and lifestyle abroad. The languages of Western Europe became permeated with American words and phrases. Young people especially favored American popular music, as well as American fashions. More generally, Western Europeans adopted the casual American way of life.

Most importantly, however, the United States set a model for economic and political cooperation. As Winston Churchill declared in 1946, "We must build a kind of United States of Europe."[9] Although sharing a common cultural heritage, Europeans have a diverse history and different national temperaments. After two ruinous world wars, people at last began to feel that the price of violent conflict had become excessive; war no longer served any national interest. Furthermore, the extension of Soviet power made

THE IRON LADY. The first British woman prime minister, Margaret Thatcher, aroused dormant patriotism in 1982 when British forces drove Argentinian invaders out of the Falkland Islands. Her government was committed to strong military and nuclear capability. (*Peter Jordan/Liaison*)

some form of Western European unity desirable. While procommunist sympathy lingered among workers and intellectuals, it hardly influenced the course of events.

Since the countries of Western Europe were not prepared to submerge their separate national traditions under a common government, they started with economic cooperation. Even that began rather modestly, with the creation of the European Coal and Steel Community (ECSC) in 1951. It drew together the chief Continental consumers and producers of coal and steel, the two materials essential for rebuilding Western Europe. The ECSC comprised France, West Germany, the three Benelux countries, and Italy.

Emboldened by the ECSC's success, the six countries in 1957 established the European Economic Community (EEC). Also known as the Common Market, it created a free market among the member states and sought to improve living conditions within them. In 1973, Great Britain, Ireland, and Denmark joined the original members in what now became the European Community (EC); in 1981, Greece, and in 1986, Spain and Portugal became members. The EC constituted the largest single trading bloc, conducting more than one-fifth of the world's commerce. In this framework of growing cooperation, the major countries of Western Europe experienced a political and economic revival, which contributed to Western superiority in the cold war.

Impoverished by the war and vulnerable in its dependence on imported food and raw material, Great Britain lost its leading role in world politics after World War II. It peacefully dismantled its colonial empire, while British seapower was replaced by the American navy and air force. The postwar Labour government, allied with powerful trade unions, provided Britons with a measure of economic security through social programs and extensive government control over important branches of the economy. Such controls, however, placed Britain at a disadvantage vis-à-vis its European competitors.

In 1979, at a low point in the economy, the voters elected a Conservative government, led by Margaret Thatcher, the "Iron Lady" and the first woman prime minister, who dominated English politics for the next decade. She fought inflation and rigorously encouraged individual initiative and free enterprise. During the Thatcher years, the British economy improved, and London regained its former luster as a financial center. Still, industries were declining, causing a rise in unemployment. Civic tensions—terrorism by the Irish Republican Army seeking to drive Britain from Northern Ireland, and resentment at the influx of Indians, Pakistanis, West Indians, and other people from former colonies—also took their toll. In addition, despite their EC membership, the English clung to their traditional insular detachment from their neighbors on the Continent.

Across the English Channel, France, liberated from German occupation, was reorganized democratically under the Fourth Republic and soon achieved respectable economic growth, despite frequent changes of government (twenty-six in twelve years). Defeat in Indochina and a civil war in Algeria between French settlers, backed by the French army, and Algerian nationalists produced a severe political crisis in 1958. It resulted in the presidency of General Charles de Gaulle, the leader of the Free French forces in World War II and president for a brief period after the war ended. De Gaulle established the Fifth Republic, with a strong executive authority, and sought to raise the country again to prominence by building its nuclear strength, making France independent of NATO, and renewing French influence in Africa. In 1962, he arranged a cease-fire in Algeria, allowing it to achieve independence. In 1968, the ever present domestic opposition erupted dramatically when students and workers, supported by the Communist party, staged demonstrations and street fights in Paris, demanding educational reform and social justice. Alarmed, de Gaulle quickly called a general election, in which a frightened electorate gave him a landslide victory. Unable to revise the constitution in his favor, however, he resigned in 1969.

The Fifth Republic continued with a government firmly based on a stable centrist majority, flanked by two radical parties. On the left, the Communist party gradually lost credibility because of its loyalty to Moscow. On the extreme right, the more dangerous *Front National* took hold, stirring up hatred against the increasing number of immigrants from North Africa. Under the pressure of the newcomers, the French, even more than the English, feared for their national identity.

Amid the economic and political uncertainties of the times, François Mitterrand, a moderate socialist and president since 1981, maintained the Gaullist tradition. His country was the third largest nuclear power and the fourth largest economy in the world, deriving 70 percent of its energy from nuclear power plants. All along, France was a leading architect of European unity without surrendering its French character.

Italy, half the size of France yet larger in population by a few million, became a democratic republic in 1946. Its government, however, has been weak and unstable. The average life span of an Italian cabinet to the present has been less than a year. A lengthy peninsula stretching out into the Mediterranean, the country offered a sharp contrast between north and south. The north was efficient and prosperous, whereas the south was backward and infiltrated by the Mafia. Centered in Sicily, the Mafia was a source of political corruption and even occasional terror against the government.

Division also characterized the political parties, from Communists to Christian Democrats. The Italian Communists, relatively free from corruption, well organized, and oriented toward Europe rather than Moscow, usually gained a quarter of the vote. On the other hand, the Christian Democrats—allied with the Vatican and constituting the majority party—were poorly disciplined, like the other noncommunist parties, and riven by corruption.

Yet the Italian economy proved to be a surprising success, despite the fact that the government was perennially in debt and unemployment ran high, especially in the south. Even more than France, Italy has been overrun by legal and illegal immigrants from Asia and Africa, straining the country's resources. It has been the most unruly of the major European countries, but no troublemaker for its neighbors.

In 1945, its cities in ruins, Germany had been

WILLY BRANDT

Willy Brandt (1913–1992) is one of the most remarkable political figures in recent European history. The child of a salesgirl in a German city on the Baltic Sea, he was reared by his maternal grandfather, a truckdriver. At the age of fourteen, he began writing articles for the local social-democratic newspaper. Escaping from the Nazis to Norway, he made a career as a journalist, spending World War II as an exile in Sweden. On his return to West Germany, he quickly rose to prominence in the Social Democratic party.

After his election in 1957 as mayor of West Berlin, the Western outpost in East Germany, he became a symbol of resistance to communism. By

defeated, occupied, and branded as a moral outcast. Divided among the four occupying powers—the United States, Britain, France, and the Soviet Union—the German nation was politically extinct. Extensive eastern lands were lost to Poland and the Soviet Union; some territory was returned to France. By 1949, two new and chastened Germanys had emerged. West Germany (the Federal Republic of Germany), formed from the three western zones of occupation, faced the hostile, Soviet-dominated East Germany (the German Democratic Republic). The former capital city of Berlin, inside East Germany, was similarly divided into western and eastern zones of occupation. The partition of Germany signified the destruction of Germany's traditional identity and ambition. The national trauma reached a climax in August 1961, when the East German government suddenly threw up a wall between East and West Berlin and tightly sealed off East from West Germany. West Germany thus became the crucial frontier of the cold war, radiating Western superiority into the Soviet bloc.

The cold war proved a boon to the West Germans; it contributed to their integration into the emerging new Europe and to the reduction of old hatreds. Located next door to the Red Army, the West Germans, along with the Western armed forces stationed on their soil, were in a strategic position for defending Western Europe. Moreover, German industrial expertise was indispensable for rebuilding the Western European economy. On this basis, West Germany (far larger than its Communist counterpart to the east and the most populous of all Western European countries) began to build a new political identity.

The architect of the new West Germany was Konrad Adenauer, its chancellor from 1949 to 1963. He sought to restore respect for Germany in cooperation with the leading states of Western Europe and the United States. As a patriot, he reestablished a cautious continuity with the German past; and shouldered responsibility for the crimes of the Nazi regime and assumed the payment of indemnifications and pensions to the Jewish victims and survivors of the Nazi era, as

1966, he was vice-chancellor and foreign minister of the Federal Republic of Germany. He was elected chancellor three years later. Calling the cold war a "sterile and dangerous confrontation," he took the initiative for peaceful accommodation, first with the Soviet Union and neighboring Poland and then between West and East Germany. This bold initiative earned him the Nobel Peace Prize in 1971.

While loyal to the European Community and NATO, he established economic and political cooperation with the Communist bloc, improving the international climate and cleansing the German image of its Nazi past. At the Warsaw ghetto memorial, he spontaneously fell to his knees in memory of the victims of the Holocaust; in 1973, he visited Israel. Revelations about a communist spy in his office forced his resignation from the chancellorship in 1974.

Brandt, however, remained active in German politics. From 1977 to 1979, he also chaired the Independent Commission on International Development Issues, whose members had been selected from leaders around the world. The commission issued a report, *North-South: A Program for Survival,* which indicated an alarming economic and political global future.

well as the payment of reparations to the state of Israel, which had been established in 1948. Under Adenauer's guidance, the West Germans also threw themselves into rebuilding their economy; the whole world soon admired the German "economic miracle." As a result, democracy put down roots among the West German people, strengthening their solidarity with their former European enemies. West Germany was admitted to NATO in 1957, and, together with East Germany, to the United Nations in 1972; it joined France in promoting the European Community.

After the Adenauer era, German voters shifted from center-right to center-left. Chancellor Willy Brandt (1969–1974) took the initiative for an "opening toward the East," contributing to a temporary relaxation of tensions between the superpowers. During these years, West German prosperity and a generous admission policy attracted ambitious immigrants, many from Turkey; the booming economy needed additional workers. Political extremists did not endanger political stability, except for one party, the Greens, which called attention to the destruction of the environment, industrial pollution, and the dangers of nuclear power. Loosely organized, the Greens expressed a romantic alienation from contemporary society and politics but achieved no lasting success. In 1982, the voters turned conservative, electing the leader of the Christian Democratic Union, Helmut Kohl, chancellor. Kohl continued Adenauer's policy of integrating West Germany, now the most prominent country in Western Europe, into the cold war alliance against Soviet communism.

THE SOVIET BLOC

For Soviet Russia, World War II was another cruel landmark in the succession of wars, revolutions, and crises afflicting the country since 1914. Nothing basically changed after its end. The vast country's weaknesses persisted, even though it had extended its boundaries far to the west. The liberation from terror and dictatorship, which many soldiers had hoped for as a reward for their heroism, never occurred. The epic struggle against the Nazi invaders had further hardened Stalin. Sixty-six years old in 1945, corrupted by unlimited power and unrestrained adulation, he displayed in his last years an unrelenting ruthlessness and a suspiciousness that turned into paranoia.

Stalin's assessment of Soviet Russia's condition at the end of the war was consistent with his previous thinking. He found no reason to relax control. Wherever he looked, he saw cause for concern. The government, the party, communist ideology, the economy—all were in disarray. The generals were riding high, threatening his own supremacy and that of the party. Ideological control had slackened during the war. The exhausted people were in danger of falling into a postwar slump, yearning for greater freedom in their personal lives. Tired and hungry as they were, how could they be goaded to work for the speedy reconstruction of their country, let alone the realization of the communist vision? Stalin's answer was more Five-Year Plans and more terror.

On this familiar note, the Soviet Union slid from war into the uneasy peace of the cold war, staggering through the hardships and hunger of the war's aftermath, mourning its dead soldiers, and desperately short of men. As before, the peasants were squeezed to the utmost to furnish the state with food without receiving more than the barest minimum in return. The urban-industrial population fared slightly better. Planning, much selfless hard work, manpower released from the army, and resources requisitioned from all occupied territories brought industrial production back to prewar levels within three years—no mean achievement.

With the return to Five-Year Plans came a deliberate tightening of ideological control. The target was any form of Western influence and personal withdrawal from the tasks set by the party. Thus, thousands of returning soldiers and prisoners of war, who had seen too much in the West, were sent to forced-labor camps; the Soviet intelligentsia was again terrorized into compliance with the party line.

A shrill, dogmatic superpatriotism became mandatory for all Soviet citizens. This patriotism extolled Russia's achievements, past and present, over those of the West. Even scientists had to submit, at a fearful cost to research (except in nuclear physics).

Soviet Russia's power was closely tied to the fate of the countries located to the west and southwest. When the Red Army poured into the lands of eastern and central Europe in 1944–45 on their way to Berlin, Stalin was faced with a historically unique opportunity: Soviet Russia controlled the entire area up to the Elbe River in the heart of Germany, a huge territorial buffer against future invasions. Stalin seized the opportunity. As the Red Army fought its way west, eastern European communists, trained in the Soviet Union, followed behind them. The Baltic states (Lithuania, Latvia, and Estonia)—part of the Russian Empire until 1918, then independent, and, after brief Soviet occupations, lost to Hitler in World War II—were reincorporated into the Soviet Union as "soviet socialist republics." Elsewhere, Stalin respected, outwardly at least, the national sovereignty of the occupied countries by ruling through returning native communists and whatever sympathizers he could find.

By the end of 1948, however, the countries of eastern and southeastern Europe, as well as eastern Germany, had emerged as "people's democracies." The Soviet Union continued to claim the right, based on conquest, of intervening at will in the internal affairs of its satellites. Thus, the pall of Stalinism hung over war-torn and impoverished Eastern Europe. The puppet regimes leveled the formerly privileged classes, curtailing or abolishing private enterprise. The economy was socialized and rigid, and hasty plans were implemented for industrialization and the collectivization of agriculture. Religion and the churches were repressed, and political liberty and free speech stamped out. Even the "proletarian masses" derived few benefits from the artificial revolution engineered from Moscow, because Stalin drained the countries under his control of their resources for the sake of rebuilding the Soviet Union. Contact with Western Europe or the United States was banned. Each satellite country existed in isolation, surrounded by borders fortified with barbed wire and watchtowers set along mined corridors cut through the landscape. Fear reached deep into every house and into individual

MAP 34.3 Eastern Europe After 1945 ▶

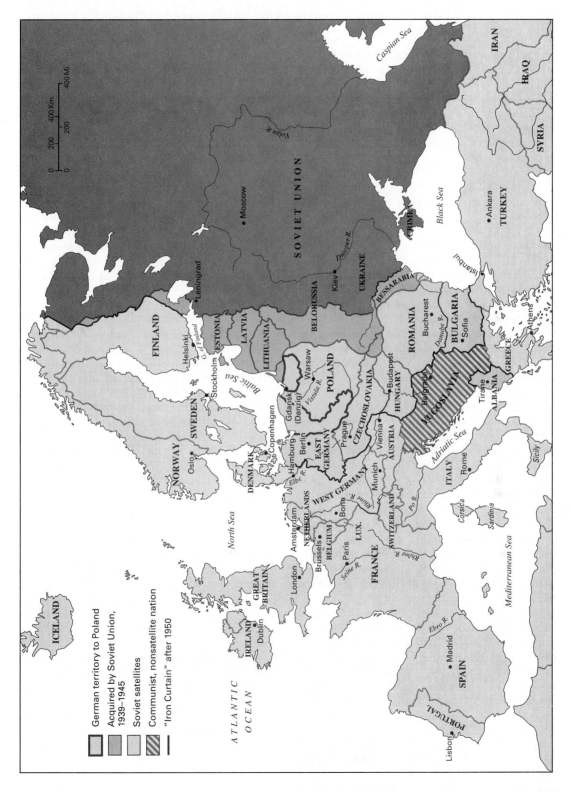

ICELAND

ATLANTIC OCEAN

IRELAND
Dublin

GREAT BRITAIN
London

NORWAY
Oslo

SWEDEN
Stockholm

DENMARK
Copenhagen

North Sea

NETHERLANDS
Amsterdam

BELGIUM
Brussels

LUX.

FRANCE
Paris
Seine R.

Rhône R.

SPAIN
Madrid

PORTUGAL
Lisbon

Ebro R.

Corsica

Sardinia

Mediterranean Sea

Sicily

ITALY
Rome
Po R.

SWITZERLAND

WEST GERMANY
Bonn
Rhine R.
Munich

Hamburg
Elbe R.

EAST GERMANY
Berlin

AUSTRIA
Vienna

Prague

CZECHOSLOVAKIA

POLAND
Warsaw
Vistula R.

Gdansk (Danzig)

FINLAND
Helsinki
G. of Finland

Baltic Sea

ESTONIA

LATVIA

LITHUANIA

Leningrad

Moscow

SOVIET UNION

Volga R.

Dnieper R.

BELORUSSIA

UKRAINE
Kiev

Caspian Sea

CRIMEA

Black Sea

BESSARABIA

ROMANIA
Bucharest

HUNGARY
Budapest

Danube R.

YUGOSLAVIA
Belgrade

BULGARIA
Sofia

ALBANIA
Tirane

Adriatic Sea

GREECE
Athens

Istanbul

TURKEY
Ankara

IRAN

IRAQ

SYRIA

Scale:
400 Mi.
400 Km.
200
200
0
0

Legend:
German territory to Poland
Acquired by Soviet Union, 1939–1945
Soviet satellites
Communist, nonsatellite nation
"Iron Curtain" after 1950

souls as little Stalins copied their mentor's style in East Berlin, Warsaw, Prague, Budapest, and Sofia.

All Communist parties (by whatever name) were guided by Moscow; Soviet troops remained strategically stationed in the area. The Warsaw Treaty Organization (the Warsaw Pact), which was a military instrument for preserving the ideological and political unity of the bloc and for counterbalancing NATO, coordinated the armies of the satellite countries with the Red Army.

Stalin's Last Years

In his last years, Stalin withdrew into virtual isolation, surrounded by a few fawning and fearful subordinates, and his sickly suspicion worsened. Before he died, he "recognized" a plot among the doctors who treated him and personally issued orders for their torture (which killed one of them). When on March 5, 1953, the failing dictator died of a stroke, his assistants sighed with relief, but many people wept. To them, Stalin was the godlike leader and savior of the nation.

One of the most remarkable people of the twentieth century, Stalin was a towering figure, in the Russian mold of Ivan the Terrible or Peter the Great. The human costs of his labor were immense, but of his achievements in raising Soviet power there can be no doubt. By 1949, sooner than expected, Soviet Russia possessed the atomic bomb. By 1953, at the same time as the United States, it had the hydrogen bomb as well. Nuclear weapons guaranteed the country's unprecedented external security. Never before had its territories been so well protected from foreign invasion.

Stalin also bequeathed to his successors a tamed and even cowed population, more malleable and submissive than any previous generation. But one traditional source of insecurity remained: the humiliating comparison with the superior West, carefully suppressed but ever present. Relaxing controls by opening the country to the outside world would not only slacken the rigid communist discipline, but also discredit the Marxist-Leninist ideology, which had helped to raise the Soviet Union to its superpower status. Stalin's successors faced an impossible task. How could they preserve its status while reducing the inhuman brutality of Stalinism, which had enforced the rapid mobilization of the country's resources and led to its postwar global preeminence?

Khrushchev: A New Course Stalled

After Stalin's death, a team, headed by Nikita Khrushchev (1954–1964), assumed leadership. Khrushchev was the driving force behind the "thaw" that emptied the forced-labor camps and allowed most of the nationalities forcibly resettled during the war to return to their native regions. Privileged Russians were allowed to catch a glimpse of the West. Khrushchev himself visited the United States, observing that "We must study the capitalist economy attentively . . . study the best that the capitalist countries' science and technology have to offer . . . in the interests of socialism."[10] In a secret speech (soon known around the world) at the Twentieth Party Congress in February 1956, Khrushchev even dared to attack Stalin himself. His audience gasped with horror as he recited the facts: "Of the 139 members and candidates of the party's Central Committee who were elected at the 17th Congress (1934), 98 persons, i.e., 70%, were arrested and shot."[11] In this vein, Khrushchev cited example after example of Stalin's terror. Without criticizing the Soviet system, Khrushchev acknowledged and rejected the excesses of Stalinism.

Khrushchev's revelations created a profound stir around the world and prompted defection from Communist ranks everywhere. Among the Soviet satellite countries, the first rumbles of protest were heard in June 1956, in Poland. The crisis came to a head in October: would Poland revolt, inviting invasion by the Red Army, or would Khrushchev ease Soviet control? The Soviet boss yielded in return for a Polish pledge of continued loyalty to the Soviet Union. Thereafter, Poland breathed more freely, clinging to its Catholic faith as a cornerstone of its national identity.

Although the "Polish October" ended peacefully, events moved to a brutal showdown in Hungary. The Stalinists had suppressed national pride in Hungary for too long. On October 20, 1956, an uprising in Budapest led to an anti-Soviet outburst. Feeling rose to fever pitch and forced Soviet troops to withdraw from the country. Next, a moderate Communist government, eager to capture popular sentiment, called for Western-style political democracy and Hungary's withdrawal from the Warsaw Pact. Thoroughly alarmed, and with the backing of Mao and even Tito, the Soviet leaders struck back. On November 4, 1956, Soviet troops re-entered Hungary and crushed all opposition.

Subsequently, Russian space exploits inspired new confidence in the Soviet system. The foundations of the space program had been laid by Stalin, and in 1957 the first space satellite, *sputnik,* was launched. In 1962, Yuri Gagarin circled the earth in a space capsule. Both triumphs were enviously watched by alarmed Americans. Khrushchev had boasted to them in 1959: "We will bury you." In 1962, he claimed that "Soviet society has become the most highly educated society in the world,"[12] predicting that by 1970 the Soviet Union would "surpass the strongest and richest capitalist country, the USA, in per capita production."[13] Not surprisingly, the cold war grew hotter in those years as Khrushchev made some provocative moves, threatening access to West Berlin and trying to place Soviet nuclear missiles in Cuba. In both cases, American pressure forced him to withdraw. Breaking relations with Communist China, he also reduced Soviet influence in the Far East. Khrushchev scored no victories in the cold war.

Eager to prod his people toward higher levels of dedication and productivity, Khrushchev presented a new party program. He impatiently pressed for industrial and technological progress, disregarding the heavy human and ecological damage that was to burden his country far into the future. His ceaseless reorganizations antagonized wide sections of state and party administration. In October 1964, while he was on vacation, his comrades in the politburo unceremoniously ousted him for "ill health" or, as they later added, his "hare-brained schemes." He was retired and allowed to live out his years in peace.

Brezhnev: Confidence and Stagnation

Like Stalin, Khrushchev was succeeded by a group of leaders acting in common. Among these men, Leonid Brezhnev (1964–1982) gradually rose to the fore. Under his leadership, the government of the U.S.S.R. turned from a personal dictatorship into an oligarchy: the collective rule of a privileged minority. Brezhnev's style stressed reasoned agreement rather than command. Soviet officials breathed more easily, and Soviet society in turn grew less authoritarian.

The post-Stalin permissiveness was never without risks, however, even under the milder regime of Brezhnev, as was shown in Czechoslovakia in 1968. A new group of Czech Communists, led by Alexander Dubček, sought to liberalize their regime. Their goal was a "humanist democratic socialism," or "socialism with a human face"—a Communist party supported by public goodwill rather than by the secret police.

On August 21, East German, Polish, Hungarian, and Soviet troops, under the provisions of the Warsaw Pact, carried out a swift and well-prepared occupation of Czechoslovakia but failed to break the rebellious will of its Communists. While Soviet tanks rumbled through Prague, an extraordinary Czechoslovak party congress secretly met in choked fury. Never had the Soviet leaders encountered such united resistance by a Communist party. Nonetheless, the revolt ended in failure. The party was purged; all reforms were canceled; and the country was reduced to abject hopelessness. But the Soviet Union paid a high price. A cry of moral outrage resounded around the world; protests were heard even in Moscow.

In the other satellite countries of Eastern Europe caution and moderation prevailed during the Brezhnev years. Soviet leaders could point to the positive results of their control over the eastern and southeastern parts of Europe. They had promoted industrialization in predominantly agrarian and comparatively backward countries; they had reduced the gap between rich and poor, substantially advancing education and cultural opportunity. They had also muted the instability and violence so evident in the region in the past.

In the 1970s, international relations entered a limited phase of peaceful cooperation, called *détente.* At the same time, the Soviet Union achieved a rough parity in nuclear weapons with the United States; henceforth it was protected by deterrence just like the United States. For a brief period, the country enjoyed some civic contentment; it inspired Brezhnev's boast that "capitalism is a society without a future."[14] His

SOVIET TANKS IN PRAGUE, CZECHOSLOVAKIA, AUGUST, 1968. The Warsaw Pact invasion, led by the Soviet Union, crushed Dubček's liberalization of communist rule. (*AP/Wide World Photos*)

confidence led in 1979 to the Soviet invasion of Afghanistan, in support of a faltering pro-Soviet regime.

The good Brezhnev years, whose memory was to endure for a long time, permitted a relaxation of the authoritarian discipline. The country could be opened, cautiously, to the outside world. Young people, for instance, were allowed access to Western styles of music and dress. More issues of state policy were opened to public debate and more latitude granted to artistic expression. Interest in religion revived.

Meanwhile prominent dissidents were punished, but less brutally than in the past. Andrei

Sakharov, the distinguished scientist who had helped develop the Soviet hydrogen bomb and subsequently became a vigorous advocate of human rights, was exiled from Moscow and placed under house arrest. Other outspoken critics, such as Alexander Solzhenitsyn and Andrei Amalrik, were expelled from the country (or allowed to emigrate). Less prominent dissidents were confined to mental hospitals, following a practice begun under the tsars. Jews who wanted to emigrate were refused permission. Yet the brief era of public satisfaction induced widespread complacency and corruption. Comparisons with the West also caused a loss of patriotic dedication. Brezhnev had reason to complain about moneygrubbing, hooliganism, capitalist tendencies, red tape, and indifference. Voices were heard on the street protesting that Marxism-Leninism "tastes like stale bread." Not surprisingly, economic productivity declined, and opposition stirred among the Soviet satellite states, most of all in Poland. The Soviet claim to superiority faded, arousing profound concern in the highest ranks of the Communist party: the Soviet Union was falling behind in the cold war.

In Eastern Europe, Moscow's efforts to integrate its satellites' economies into the even less advanced Soviet economy never succeeded. One by one, the satellite governments resumed ties with capitalist states, incurring considerable indebtedness in the process. How could the Soviet government retain control over its satellites while allowing them greater independence?

Brezhnev's successors were old men who survived in office for only a short time. In 1985, at last a younger, energetic Communist, Mikhail Sergeyevich Gorbachev, assumed control, admitting privately that "everything is rotten through and through." Maybe Brezhnev had been wrong: perhaps the Soviet system rather than capitalism had no future.

DECOLONIZATION

Meanwhile, the cold war between the two superpowers had spread into Asia and Africa—into the Third World, as it came to be known. Western imperialism had everywhere introduced Western institutions, goods, and ideals. World War II had stirred up the non-Western peoples living under Western colonial rule to liberate themselves. When World War II ended, the militancy of anticolonial movements increased. The political agitation of the war, in which many colonial soldiers had loyally fought for their masters, sparked the desire for political independence. After all, freedom and self-determination had been prominent Allied war slogans. Exhausted by the war, European colonial powers had little strength left for colonial rule.

In this setting, the mighty groundswell of decolonization, supported by the superpowers and the ideals of the United Nations, eventually abol-

JOMO KENYATTA (C. 1894–1978). Wearing a leopard skin over his western suit, Kenyatta brandishes a fly whisk, a symbol of authority. Imprisoned by the British for his opposition to colonial rule, he became the leader of independent Kenya in 1963. Under his slogan *Harambee* (pulling together), he built a strong stable government, and a capitalist-oriented economy. (*Anthony Howard/Camera Press/ Retna*)

ished all overseas empires and propelled their former subjects into independent statehood. Decolonization quickly became a major issue in the cold war as the two superpowers competed with each other for control over the emerging states of Africa and Asia. The Soviet Union, dedicated by its ideology to the liberation of all oppressed peoples, tried to steer the colonial independence movements into its orbit, supporting them with advisers and weapons. The Western powers, with their superior resources, tried to guide their former colonial subjects toward a pro-Western allegiance, likewise offering military, political, and financial assistance. Both sides, in their ignorance of local cultures, found themselves entangled in

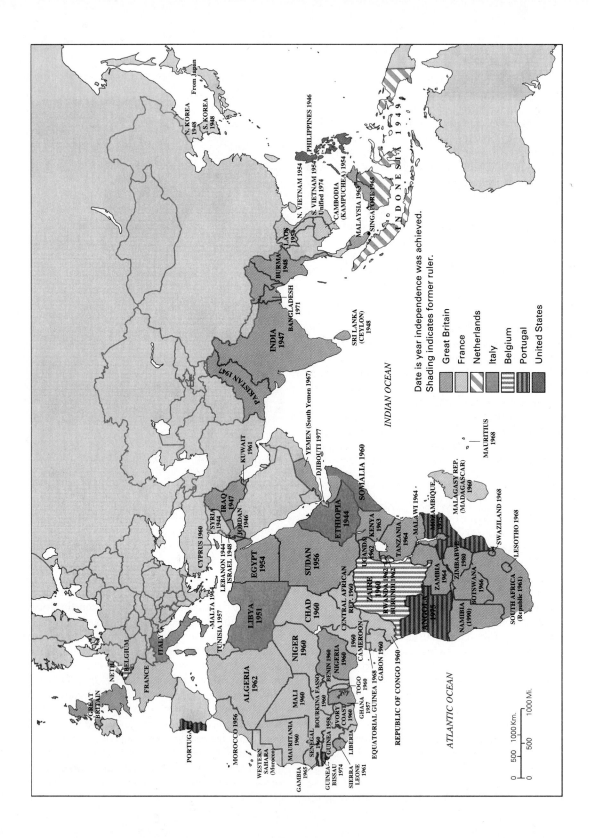

Date is year independence was achieved.
Shading indicates former ruler.

Great Britain
France
Netherlands
Italy
Belgium
Portugal
United States

INDIAN OCEAN

ATLANTIC OCEAN

N. KOREA 1948
S. KOREA 1948
From Japan

PHILIPPINES 1946
N. VIETNAM 1954
S. VIETNAM 1954
Unified 1974
CAMBODIA (KAMPUCHEA) 1954
MALAYSIA 1963
SINGAPORE 1963
INDONESIA 1949
LAOS 1954
BURMA 1948
BANGLADESH 1971
SRI LANKA (CEYLON) 1948
INDIA 1947
PAKISTAN 1947

YEMEN (South Yemen 1967)
DJIBOUTI 1977
KUWAIT 1961
IRAQ 1947
JORDAN 1946
SYRIA 1944
LEBANON 1944
ISRAEL 1948
CYPRUS 1960
MALTA 1964
TUNISIA 1957
EGYPT 1954
LIBYA 1951
SUDAN 1956
ETHIOPIA 1944
SOMALIA 1960
UGANDA 1962
KENYA 1963
MALAWI 1964
TANZANIA 1964
MOZAMBIQUE 1975
MALAGASY REP. (MADAGASCAR) 1960
MAURITIUS 1968
SWAZILAND 1968
LESOTHO 1968
CENTRAL AFRICAN REP. 1960
ZAIRE 1960
RWANDA 1962
BURUNDI 1962
ZAMBIA 1964
ZIMBABWE 1980
BOTSWANA 1966
ANGOLA 1975
NAMIBIA (1990)
SOUTH AFRICA (Republic 1961)
CHAD 1960
CAMEROON 1960
GABON 1960
EQUATORIAL GUINEA 1968
REPUBLIC OF CONGO 1960
NIGER 1960
NIGERIA 1960
BENIN 1960
TOGO 1960
GHANA 1957
IVORY COAST 1960
BURKINA FASO 1960
ALGERIA 1962
MALI 1960
MAURITANIA 1960
GAMBIA 1965
SENEGAL 1960
GUINEA 1958
GUINEA-BISSAU 1974
SIERRA LEONE 1961
LIBERIA 1847
MOROCCO 1956
WESTERN SAHARA (Morocco)

GREAT BRITAIN
FRANCE
BELGIUM
NETH.
PORTUGAL
ITALY

0   500   1000 Km.
0   500   1000 Mi.

the intricacies of local power struggles, especially in tropical Africa, which was frequently involved in protracted civil wars bordering on anarchy.

Decolonization began in 1946 in Asia, when the United States granted independence to the Philippines. In 1947, India and Pakistan attained sovereign statehood; in 1948, independent Burma and Ceylon (later renamed Sri Lanka) emerged. In 1949, Holland was forced to grant independence to Indonesia. More ominously in that year, China turned communist, encouraging anticolonialism in Asia and Africa. After granting independence to Laos in 1954, the French were driven from Cambodia and Vietnam the same year, leaving the Americans to defend South Vietnam against the communist revolutionaries of North Vietnam until 1975.

After the middle fifties, the European rulers started the process of decolonization in Africa, turning over power to indigenous leaders. In 1956, France freed its northern African colonies, Morocco and Tunisia, and four years later, Senegal, in West Africa. (Algeria, however, did not gain independence until 1962, after a cruel war.) In 1957, the British Gold Coast, renamed Ghana, achieved independence—the first sub-Saharan country to do so. Its leader, Kwame Nkrumah, had already indicated his guiding policy, which also inspired other African leaders: "Capitalism is too complicated a system for a newly independent nation. Hence the need for a socialistic society" and possibly for "Emergency measures of a totalitarian kind."[15] In 1961, Nkrumah toured the Soviet bloc.

Pushed by the trend of the times, the Belgians in 1960 pulled out of the Congo, precipitating a civil war in the unprepared country. The Congo's first leader, Patrice Lumumba, appealed for Soviet help, until he was ousted by Mobutu Sese Seko, who in 1971 renamed his country Zaire. He stayed in power indefinitely, supported by Western nations eager to exploit his country's valuable raw materials.

Decolonization swept through African lands ruled by Britain. In 1961, Tanganyika became independent, joining with Zanzibar to form Tanzania in 1964 under the leadership of Julius Nyerere. He presided until the 1980s over a socialist development program, assisted by communist China. In 1962, Uganda was decolonized; it was led by Milton Obote as a socialist one-party state, until he was overthrown in 1971 by Idi Amin, a barbarous dictator, who lasted in power until 1980. Nigeria, an ethnically divided state, attained independence in 1960 but was soon caught in a civil war costing a million lives. In that war, Britain, Italy, and the Soviet Union, in an unusual alignment, competitively assisted the Nigerian government, while France aided the separatists. In 1964, having gained independence the previous year, Kenya turned into a republic under Jomo Kenyatta, who ruled as an authoritarian president in a one-party state leaning toward the West. The following year, a white supremacist party defied Britain by declaring unilateral independence in the British colony of Rhodesia. It finally yielded to African rule in 1980, and Rhodesia became the new state of Zimbabwe.

The Portuguese held on to their African colonies as long as possible, quitting Angola in 1975 and leaving it embroiled in a civil war between the American-supported government and a liberation movement supported by the Soviet Union, with Cuban assistance. Only the Republic of South Africa, independent since 1910, remained under repressive white minority rule during this period.

Decolonization everywhere sparked protracted and often brutal struggles of building modern states among peoples who were utterly unprepared for this effort by their colonial rulers, and who were also divided by their past animosities, as well as by the competition between the superpowers. Given their lack of preparation, Western practices like capitalism and democracy proved too complex for achieving effective statehood. The Soviet model seemed more suitable; besides, it offered the new leaders the attraction of absolute power. Yet how long could that model hold its own against the capitalist rival, whose riches exerted an even stronger attraction? Decolonization inevitably expanded the influence of Western ways of life in the newly independent nations, even though one-party governments and dictatorships remain in power in many African countries.

◄ MAP 34.4 Former European Colonies

◆ ◆ ◆

NOTES

1. Quoted in Walter Laqueur, *Europe Since Hitler* (Baltimore: Penguin Books, 1970), p. 118.

2. "The Charter of the United Nations," *Yearbook of the United Nations* (Dordrecht, Netherlands: Martin Nijhoff, 1989), 39:1378.

3. "Universal Declaration of Human Rights," *Yearbook of the United Nations, 1948–49* (New York: Columbia University Press, 1950), p. 535.

4. "The Truman Doctrine," in *Major Problems in American Foreign Policy: Documents and Essays,* ed. Thomas G. Paterson (Lexington, Mass.: Heath, 1978), 2:290.

5. Dwight D. Eisenhower, "State of the Union Message by President Eisenhower January 6, 1955," in *The Eisenhower Administration: A Documentary History,* ed. Robert L. Branyan and Lawrence H. Laresen (New York: Random House, 1971), 1:448.

6. Ralph E. Lapp, "The Einstein Letter That Started It All," *New York Times Magazine,* August 2, 1964, p. 64.

7. Winston S. Churchill, "Sinews of Peace; Address, March 5, 1946," *Vital Speeches of the Day,* March 15, 1946, p. 329.

8. Churchill, "Sinews of Peace," p. 331.

9. Quoted in Roger Morgan, *West European Politics Since 1945* (London: Batsford, 1972), p. 91.

10. *Current Soviet Policies II. The Documentary Record of the 20th Party Congress and Its Aftermath* (New York: Praeger, 1957), p. 141.

11. Nikita S. Khrushchev in *The Crimes of the Stalin Era: Special Report to the 20th Congress of the Communist Party of the Soviet Union,* annotated by Boris I. Nicolaevsky (New York: The New Leader), 1956, p. 20.

12. *Current Soviet Policies IV. The Documentary Record of the 22nd Congress of the Communist Party of the Soviet Union* (New York: Columbia University Press, 1962), p. 64.

13. *Current Soviet Policies IV,* p. 15.

14. Leonid Brezhnev, *Following Lenin's Course* (Moscow: Progress Publishers, 1976), 5:480.

15. Kwame Nkrumah, *The Autobiography of Kwame Nkrumah* (Edinburgh: Thomas Nelson, 1957), p. x.

SUGGESTED READING

Childs, David, ed., *Honecker's Germany* (1985). East Germany's economy, culture, and foreign relations, written four years before reunification.

Craig, Gordon, *The Germans* (1982). Key aspects of post–World War II Germany in historical perspective.

Friend, Julius W., *Seven Years in France: François Mitterrand and the Unintended Revolution, 1981–1988* (1989). France in the Mitterrand years—communism's decline, the rise of the *Front National,* socialism's adaptability.

Gelb, Norman, *The Berlin Wall* (1987). An on-the-spot account of the building of the wall and its effect on Berlin, the former two Germanys, and East-West relations.

Kennedy, Paul, *The Rise and Fall of the Great Powers: Economic Change and Military Conflict from 1500 to 2000* (1987). An economic analysis of five hundred years of Western civilization and a projection into the future.

Kennedy, Robert F., *Thirteen Days: A Memoir of the Cuban Missile Crisis* (1969). An account of President Kennedy's handling of the crisis by his brother, a member of the White House inner circle.

LaPalombara, Joseph, *Democracy Italian Style* (1987). A guide to the modern Italian state and a portrayal of how the convoluted Italian political system works.

Marsh, David, *The Germans: Rich, Bothered and Divided* (1990). A good source of relevant information and perceptive analysis.

Medvedev, Roy, *Khrushchev: The Years in Power* (1976). A sympathetic biography by a prominent former dissident.

Riddell, Peter, *The Thatcher Decade: Britain in the 1980s* (1989). A *Financial Times* editor analyzes the Iron Lady's policies and leadership style against the background of a changing British society.

Schell, Jonathan, *The Fate of the Earth* (1982). On

the results of nuclear war; still relevant, despite the end of the cold war.

Solzhenitsyn, Alexander, *Cancer Ward* (1968). A novel using a cancer ward in a hospital as a metaphor for Stalin's Soviet Union. Based on the author's experiences.

———, *One Day in the Life of Ivan Denisovich* (1963). The first account of life in one of Stalin's forced-labor camps to reach the public.

PERIODICALS

Bulletin of the Atomic Scientists (Chicago). Founded by concerned scientists in 1945 to study the connections between global politics and nuclear weapons.

Current Digest of the Post-Soviet Press (Columbus, Ohio). Provides weekly translations of the most significant items in the Soviet press.

Current History (Philadelphia). Current analyses of European and Soviet affairs.

Foreign Affairs (New York). The foremost American periodical on foreign relations.

Foreign Policy (Washington, D.C.). A scholarly analysis of current world issues.

International Affairs (London). A British journal dealing with global politics.

New York Review of Books (New York). Carries excellent articles on world affairs.

REVIEW QUESTIONS

1. What were the origins of the cold war? Could it have been avoided?

2. Some people called the cold war "the third world war." Would you agree?

3. What do you consider the biggest changes that have taken place in Western Europe after 1945?

4. What was the postwar role of the United States in Western Europe? How did it contribute to the present strength of Western Europe?

5. How do you assess Stalin's accomplishments in rebuilding the Soviet Union after the end of World War II?

6. How did Khrushchev and Brezhnev change the Stalinist heritage? What effect did their policies have on the Soviet people?

7. How firm was the hold of the Soviet Union on its Eastern European satellites?

8. What benefits were expected from decolonization? What were the actual consequences?

CHAPTER *35*
The Troubled Present

*S*ince 1985, momentous events have utterly changed the world. The superpower polarization of world politics has ended, and a new, multicentered, unstable world order has emerged. Western civilization and its ideals have been transformed into a transcultural worldwide modernity. The global, interdependence, ever growing closer, is now loosely centered in three major geographic areas: North America, the Far East, and Europe. Underneath the global uniformity, however, the traditional cultural diversity still simmers, obstructing interdependence and occasionally breaking forth in fierce ethnic wars. The lands freed from Soviet domination have been under severe stress as they try to establish democratic governments and market economies.

The end of the cold war has introduced a new uncertainty into human affairs. On the one hand, global interdependence promotes peaceful cooperation; on the other, it foments cultural disorientation, causing contagious violence. Optimists and pessimists disagree about the prospects for the future. Thus, we move from the known past through the troubled present into the twenty-first century.

THE END OF THE COLD WAR

One of the most striking events in recent history has been the collapse of the Soviet Union, the largest state in the world. Because of Stalin's brutal efforts to overcome his country's backwardness, the Soviet Union had expanded into central Europe at the end of World War II, and then it acquired nuclear weapons. Thus, it emerged as "the other superpower," challenging Western, specifically American, ascendancy around the world. While moderating Stalin's ruthlessness, his

United Nations peacekeeping troops in Cambodia.
(*Jason Bleibtreu/Sygma*)

879

CHRONOLOGY 35.1 From the Cold War to Globalism

1985	Gorbachev becomes U.S.S.R. leader
1989	Year of liberation in Eastern Europe; Berlin Wall demolished
1990	Soviet republics call for independence; Soviet economy in crisis; reunification of Germany; Charter of Paris for a New Europe; official end of cold war
1991	Persian Gulf War; Yeltsin elected Russian president; collapse of Soviet Union; Yugoslav federation breaks up and war begins
1992	Bosnia declares independence
1993	Czechoslovakia splits into Czech Republic and Slovakia; elections for new Russian constitution and parliament; European Union ratifies Maastricht Treaty
1994	South Africa elects multiracial government

successors continued basic Soviet policies, trying to match Western wealth and power by imposing an artificial social discipline on their reluctant peoples. Yet, despite striking achievements in science and technology, and despite considerable improvements in education and social welfare, they could not reduce the gap in living standards and the quality of life between the Soviet system and Western capitalism. By comparison, the West was making impressive progress. This fact, increasingly recognized throughout the Soviet bloc, undermined its carefully enforced communist conformity.

Disloyalty grew throughout the multinational and multiethnic Soviet empire. By the 1980s, it had become common knowledge, admitted in the highest ranks of the Communist party, that the Soviet system had stifled rather than advanced creativity and efficiency. What then could be done? Loosening the centralized controls might endanger the unity of the country; upholding the regime by military force would discredit it still further. To everybody's surprise, events unfolded suddenly and without violence, but with unexpected consequences affecting the entire world.

Gorbachev's Challenge

It was the fate of Mikhail Gorbachev to preside over his country's collapse. He became the Soviet Union's leader in 1985, at the age of fifty-four.

Self-confident, energetic, and articulate, Gorbachev in his early years of power talked freely to people in all stations of life. Keenly aware of his country's problems and eager to confront them, he did not hesitate to state them bluntly. "The practical actions of Party and state agencies," he announced in February 1986, "lag behind the demands of the times and of life itself. Problems . . . grow faster than they are solved. Sluggishness, ossification in the forms and methods of management decrease the dynamism of work. . . . Stagnation begins to show up in the life of society."[1] A sobering demonstration in inefficiency and mismanagement occurred in late April 1986: because of staff misjudgment, a reactor at the nuclear power plant at Chernobyl exploded, spewing dangerous radiation high into the atmosphere. Poisonous fallout covered much of Europe. Wherever Gorbachev looked, he observed a profound crisis in his country's fortunes.

Resolving that crisis required a double effort. "For our internal progress," Gorbachev stressed in 1987, "we need normal international relations."[2] The Soviet Union had to try to catch up with the rapid advance of prosperity and high technology in Western Europe, North America, and the Pacific Rim countries. Its earlier claims to

MAP 35.1 Post-Cold-War Europe and the Former Soviet Union ▶

880

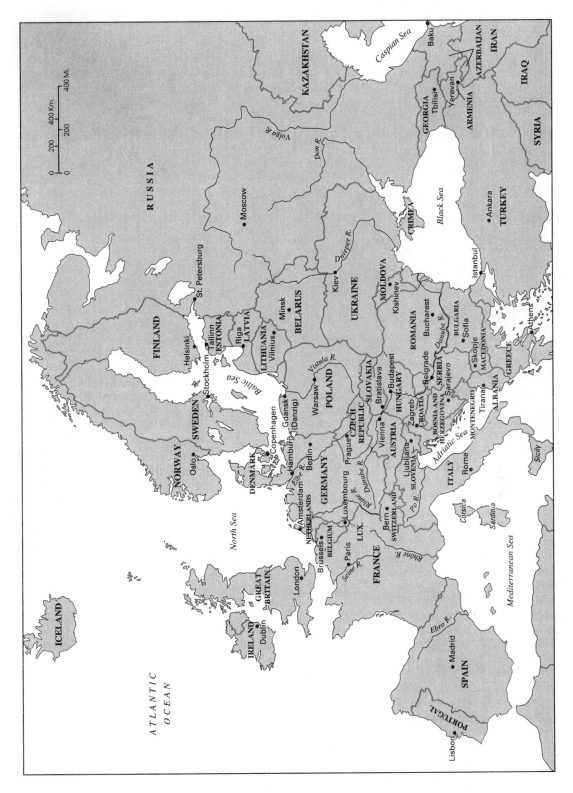

ATLANTIC OCEAN

ICELAND

IRELAND
Dublin

GREAT BRITAIN
London

NORWAY
Oslo

SWEDEN
Stockholm

FINLAND
Helsinki

RUSSIA
Moscow
St. Petersburg

KAZAKHSTAN

Volga R.

Don R.

Caspian Sea
Baku

AZERBAIJAN
ARMENIA
Yerevan

GEORGIA
Tbilisi

IRAN

IRAQ

SYRIA

TURKEY
Ankara

Black Sea

CRIMEA

Istanbul

Athens

GREECE

ESTONIA
Tallinn

LATVIA
Riga

LITHUANIA
Vilnius

BELARUS
Minsk

Kiev
Dnieper R.

UKRAINE

MOLDOVA
Kishinev

ROMANIA
Bucharest

Danube R.

BULGARIA
Sofia

Skopje
MACEDONIA

Tirana
ALBANIA

Baltic Sea

Stockholm

DENMARK
Copenhagen

Gdańsk (Danzig)

POLAND
Warsaw

Vistula R.

CZECH REPUBLIC
Prague

SLOVAKIA
Bratislava

HUNGARY
Budapest

SERBIA
Belgrade

BOSNIA AND HERZEGOVINA
Sarajevo

MONTENEGRO

CROATIA
Zagreb

Adriatic Sea

North Sea

NETHERLANDS
Amsterdam

GERMANY
Hamburg
Berlin

Elbe R.

BELGIUM
Brussels

LUXEMBOURG
LUX.

Rhine R.

Danube R.

AUSTRIA
Vienna

SLOVENIA
Ljubljana

Po R.

ITALY
Rome

SWITZERLAND
Bern

FRANCE
Paris

Seine R.

Rhône R.

Corsica

Sardinia

Sicily

Mediterranean Sea

Ebro R.

SPAIN
Madrid

PORTUGAL
Lisbon

400 Mi.
400 Km.
200
200
0
0

881

MIKHAIL GORBACHEV. Soviet leader Gorbachev and his wife visit Vilnius, the capital of Lithuania, following the declaration of independence by the Lithuanian Communist Party. Gorbachev warned demonstrators, "If we should separate, it is the end of perestroika." (*Alain Nogues/Sygma*)

superiority had clearly been presumptuous. Consequently, Gorbachev abandoned the Soviet anti-Western orientation. He strove to integrate his country into the main currents of modern life through a dramatic retreat from communist theory and practice.

Gorbachev's domestic reforms proceeded under the barrage of two slogans: *perestroika* (restructuring) and *glasnost* (openness). The reforms aimed at "a genuine revolutionary transformation" of Soviet life and institutions.[3] The goals that Lenin and Stalin had tried to reach through totalitarian controls were now to be achieved by the opposite method of voluntary civic cooperation. Perestroika promised to reorganize the state and society and to revive individual creativity, which rigid bureaucracy had deadened. Liberated

at last, Soviet citizens were to take the initiative in government at the grassroots level and participate in national affairs. Thus, with the help of the most advanced technology, they could satisfy their yearning for a higher standard of living. Glasnost, in turn, was to take the Stalinist lid off public opinion and permit at long last an uninhibited discussion of the country's problems. It would rid public thinking of the official propaganda lies and promote open debate. As Gorbachev observed in 1986, "Communists always need the truth."[4] Both perestroika and glasnost sought to transform the Soviet system into a true democracy. Meanwhile, contacts with the outside world increased. Western ideals, culture, and respect for human rights penetrated Soviet minds as never before, reinforcing Gorbachev's pleas for greater humaneness and for revitalizing spiritual life.

Summed up by Gorbachev as "the most thorough-going upheaval in our country's history,"[5] these changes entailed unforeseen perils. They led to the defection of the Soviet satellites in Eastern Europe.

1989: The Year of Liberation

Perestroika and glasnost spread among the peoples of Eastern Europe, resentful of Soviet domination and worried by widespread economic hardships. During 1989 and 1990, Eastern Europeans showed their distaste for Communist leadership and demanded freedom and self-determination. Poland took the lead.

Traditionally anti-Russian, the Poles had long stirred in protest against their country's economic decline. The slightest relaxation of Soviet control encouraged Polish nationalism, which had always found expression in the Roman Catholic church. When a Polish cardinal became Pope John Paul II in 1978, patriotism surged. In 1980, workers, led by an electrician, Lech Walesa, succeeded, with the blessing of the church, in forming an independent labor union, called Solidarity. Pressured by relentless strikes, the government briefly recognized the union, despite threats of Soviet intervention.

In December 1981, however, a military dictatorship, under General Wojciech Jaruzelski, imposed martial law. Solidarity persisted under-

THE WALL CAME TUMBLING DOWN. The Berlin Wall, symbol of the division of Germany, was breached in November 1989. Young people excitedly clambered onto the partially demolished wall, while East and West Berliners thronged the streets. (*Regis Bossu/Sygma*)

ground until 1988, when public pressure forced Jaruzelski to end his dictatorship and appoint a civilian government. Solidarity was legalized in January 1989; in April the Communist party gave up its monopoly of political power. In the first free election, Solidarity triumphed, leading to the formation of a noncommunist government. After ten years of struggle, Poland, the largest country in Eastern Europe, had achieved political independence by essentially peaceful means. In December 1990, Lech Walesa was elected president.

Encouraged by events in Poland, Hungary abolished its Communist bureaucracy in May 1989. Before the end of the year, a multiparty system, consisting of some fifty parties, was in place, with two noncommunist parties, the Democratic Forum and the Alliance of Free Democrats, competing for leadership. Inspired by revived nationalism, Hungary had embraced the ideals of democracy and free enterprise.

A more dramatic upheaval occurred in East Germany. While the Communist government

VÁCLAV HAVEL

The Czech playwright and president, Václav Havel, was born in 1936 to prosperous parents in Prague. After military service, he joined a theater group in Prague as a stagehand and discovered his vocation. His plays, written in the 1960s and 1970s, were satires and parables of life under totalitarianism. They were banned by the Communist government from performance or publication in Czechoslovakia but produced abroad to wide acclaim.

In 1977, Havel was among the founders of the dissident human rights movement, Charter 77, and became its spokesman. His activities exposed him to constant police harassment, and he was imprisoned for five years.

His career as a political leader began in 1989, when communism crumbled in eastern Europe. In celebrated the country's fortieth anniversary as a "socialist workers' paradise," with Gorbachev as an honored guest, a popular revolution was brewing. People left for West Germany through the recently opened border of Hungary and Czechoslovakia. The elderly Communist leader, Erich Honecker, was deposed by his own government, and on November 6, when almost a million antigovernment demonstrators crammed the streets of East Berlin, the Communist government resigned. On November 9, in an explosion of patriotic fervor, the Berlin Wall was breached (the day is now a public holiday in united Germany). Young people danced on top of the wall and tens of thousands of East Germans flocked into West Berlin, welcomed with flowers, champagne, and money for buying West German goods. East Germany was ready to be united with West Germany, with Gorbachev's approval.

The exhilaration over breaching the Berlin Wall reverberated in the countries still under Communist rule, like Bulgaria. There, Todor Zhivkov was the longest-serving dictator in the Soviet bloc. Bulgaria had been the most docile Soviet satellite, until Gorbachev pleaded for reform, to which Zhivkov was bitterly opposed. One day after the dramatic events in Berlin, he voluntarily resigned. By mid-December 1989, a multiparty system was installed. Bulgaria had joined the quest for democratic government and private enterprise.

The end of the year produced the final victories in the revolution of 1989. Romania's Nicolae Ceausescu, persisting in his own ruthless dictatorship, had paid no attention to the drift of the times. But on December 21, a mass demonstration, organized on his behalf in the capital city of Bucharest, was disrupted by students. The crowd followed their lead, and even the army turned against Ceausescu. On December 25, he and his wife were tried and executed. The most repulsive representative of Communist rule, defying to the last the trend toward democratic freedom, had ignominiously fallen.

On the day of Ceausescu's death, Czechoslovakia joined the triumphant finale of the crusade

the absence of democratic politicians, intellectuals in Prague established the Civic Forum to guide the country toward democracy. Havel, with his talent for promoting unity, became the chief negotiator. His skillful leadership contributed to Czechoslovakia's astonishingly swift and smooth transition to democracy. In recognition of his immense popularity, he was elected president in December 1989.

Although the era of intellectuals in politics was brief, Havel remained in office. He resigned in 1992, protesting the division of Czechoslovakia, but returned as president of the Czech Republic. He has used his moral authority in the service of government and his literary gifts in political writings, explaining the policies, problems, and achievable hopes of his country to Czechs and to readers worldwide.

against communism with the election of Václav Havel as president. The most daring and articulate dissident in his country, Havel had led a swift "velvet revolution" against the Czech Communist government. The election of this previously imprisoned dissident playwright, a profound thinker deeply committed to the Western humanist tradition, was a joyous landmark in a momentous year of liberation.

The message spread quickly into Yugoslavia, a fragile federation of six ethnically conscious member republics, among whom Serbia was dominant. Less rigidly controlled than other Eastern European countries, Yugoslavia enjoyed close relations with Western Europe. Yet in 1989, the government could not prevent public protest, encouraged by the news of the Communist downfall in other lands. On December 26, its Communist party caved in and suggested the formation of a multiparty system, which was duly adopted in January 1990. The new freedom soon broke up the unity of the Yugoslav federation— with bitter war to follow in Bosnia.

The Yugoslav Communists were the last to surrender in the revolution of 1989. Except for Albania, where the Communist party held on until free elections in February 1991, all of Eastern Europe had liberated itself from Soviet domination—a breathtaking change, accomplished unexpectedly within a single year and dealing a deadly blow to the Soviet Union itself.

THE COLLAPSE OF THE SOVIET UNION

The repudiation of communism in Eastern Europe intensified the disintegration of Soviet rule at the center. Gorbachev's glasnost released the bitterness accumulated under Stalinist repression; it revealed the widespread environmental damage caused by promoting industrial progress at any price; and it activated the immense diversity of attitudes and values among the people, which polarized opinions and spawned vicious infighting.

The cohesion of the Soviet Union weakened as well. Clamoring for independence, the Lithuanians, Latvians, and Estonians set off similar demands among Ukrainians, Byelorussians, Georgians, Armenians, and the peoples of central Asia. Interethnic violence escalated disastrously. The biggest blow to Soviet unity came in 1990, when the Russian republic, the largest member of the Soviet Union, declared its limited independence under the leadership of Boris Yeltsin. Gorbachev was willing to establish a new federal union of sovereign republics, balancing the understandable desire for local self-management with the need for unionwide cooperation. But how in the centrifugal rush toward self-determination could common interests gain sufficient recognition?

As political fragmentation increased, the economy, battered by natural disasters such as the Armenian earthquake of 1988, deteriorated. The inefficient system of producing and distributing food and consumer goods collapsed. The breakdown of effective government led to crime, corruption, and violence—evils always simmering under the surface of Soviet life and now encouraged by contact with the outside world. In late 1990, a Moscow newspaper described the public mood in grim terms:

Our society is in many ways inexorably drifting toward the danger point of ungovernability

YELTSIN'S FINEST HOUR. In August 1991, hardline communists staged a coup against Gorbachev. Tank units, sent to Moscow to intimidate Yeltsin and liberals in the government, were surrounded by thousands of protesters. Yeltsin courageously defied the hardliners, climbing on a tank to rally the protesters. The coup collapsed in three days, but the Communist party, Gorbachev's leadership, and the Soviet Union itself were doomed. (*Sovfoto*)

and decline. Economic collapse, paralysis of political authority, outbreaks of ethnic unrest, the illusory nature of social safeguards, rampant crime, and the visible impoverishment of a starving, tired people, which has spawned a general spiritual emptiness, apathy, bitterness and confusion—these are but a few signs . . . of mounting and potentially explosive public discontent. . . . As the store shelves grow emptier, narrow-minded, rudimentary sentiments have become increasingly prevalent: why the hell do we need this restructuring, all this openness, with pluralism to boot? We'd rather have sausage and order.[6]

Obviously, the spiritual rebirth and the revolution in people's minds that Gorbachev had hoped for had not occurred. In October 1990, he himself conceded in the face of failure that "unfortunately, our society is not ready for the procedures of a law-based state. We don't have that level of political culture, those traditions. All that will come in the future."[7]

The future, however, deepened the country's disunity. On August 19, hardline Communists, hostile to Gorbachev's reforms, staged a coup, imprisoning him in his Crimean vacation home and deposing him as president of the Soviet Union. Citing popular discontent, widespread lawlessness, and the decline of Soviet power in the world, they declared a state of emergency in preparation for a new Communist dictatorship.

Yet the conspirators, all of them high officials appointed by Gorbachev, grossly misjudged popular attitudes. Revulsion against the Communist party was even stronger than the yearning for sausage and order. The KGB's vanguard forces defected to Yeltsin, who led a fervent street protest at risk to his life. The emotional outburst in favor of freedom and democracy quickly spread from Moscow to Leningrad (recently renamed Saint Petersburg, as under the tsars) and other cities. The coup collapsed in less than three days, with utterly unexpected consequences. When Gorbachev returned to Moscow, he faced, as he said, "a different country." The chief victims of the coup, apart from its leaders, were the key sources of Soviet power: the Communist party, now repudiated by Gorbachev himself and swept aside by public disdain, and the Soviet Union's unity.

Within two weeks, twelve of the fifteen union republics—the Baltic republics of Latvia, Lithuania, and Estonia foremost among them—declared their independence. The remaining republics soon followed suit. On December 24, 1991, the Soviet Union was officially dissolved and Gorbachev dismissed from his office. The only trace left of the former unity was the ill-defined Commonwealth of Independent States (CIS), formed in November by Russia, the Ukraine, and White Russia (Belarus). The CIS held out a vague hope for future cooperation among the diverse peoples sharing the resources and perils of the vast open Eurasian space; it was eventually joined by all the former Soviet republics apart from the Baltic states.

The huge empire that for centuries had cast its shadow over Europe and the world had perished. Even more significantly, the Soviet system, which had challenged the Western ascendancy since the end of World War I, had collapsed, together with its ideological presumption of worldwide communist happiness. Freedom, democracy, and private enterprise—the ideals of the American superpower—had won the cold war, unchallenged in the 1990s by any rival vision. Hopes ran high for a more humane future in an era of universal peace and democracy. But were the world's peoples prepared to live up to the vision spread by the Western experience?

THE POST–COLD WAR WORLD

The end of the cold war marked a sharp break with the past. The competition between the two superpowers and their rival ideologies, which had polarized world politics, now gave way to a new affirmation of the world's political diversity, encouraged by the victorious ideals of democratic freedom and self-determination. Ethnic and religious minorities began to struggle for recognition and independence; political tensions within and between states, hitherto subdued by superpower rivalry, flared up. The collapse of the Communist dictatorships was followed by the agonies of liberation among the peoples of eastern and central Europe and the former Soviet Union. Suddenly, the world had become more unmanageable and complex. A new political constellation, however, offered an element of stability.

The Global Triangle

Global power is now shared by three geographical areas endowed with comparable economic and political strength, all in keen competition with each other, but compelled to maintain peaceful relations by their tight interdependence. They share the common vision of a westernized modernity, as well as the uncertainties of the new global openness.

The leading role belongs to the United States, the strongest and richest country. With its 260 million inhabitants, it ranks third in population, after China and India, and it is still a superpower thanks to its nuclear weapons and military bases in Europe and Asia. It proved its might during the Gulf War in 1991, when it defeated Saddam Hussein, with token help from allied countries. The aggressive Iraqi dictator had invaded Kuwait in order to dominate the oil-rich Middle East. Restrained subsequently from military operations by growing domestic problems, the United States expanded its commercial relations with neighboring Canada and Mexico through the North American Free Trade Agreement (NAFTA). It expects to extend this agreement throughout the Western Hemisphere. "The free trade area of the Americas will stretch from Alaska to Argentina . . . this hemisphere will be the world's largest market,"[8] said President Bill Clinton in December 1994. The United States also benefits from its innumerable economic ties around the world, which intensify its cultural outreach. Its ideals are the guide for the global future; its style of life, the envy of people around the world.

In East Asia, a more loosely related group of states with economic power and political influence has risen to prominence, headed by Japan. Although it has only limited political clout, lacks nuclear weapons or a seat on the U.N. Security Council, and is still resented by its wartime victims, Japan has gained impressive economic influence in Asia, America, and Europe, more than holding its own against its Chinese neighbor.

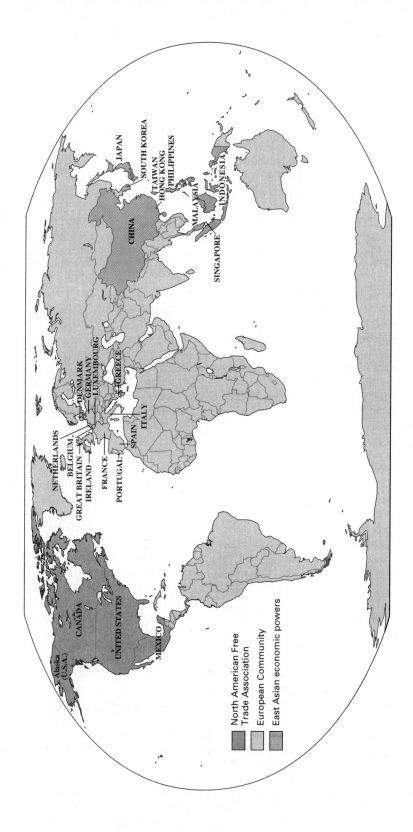

NETHERLANDS
BELGIUM
GREAT BRITAIN
IRELAND
FRANCE
PORTUGAL

DENMARK
GERMANY
LUXEMBOURG
GREECE

SPAIN
ITALY

JAPAN
SOUTH KOREA
TAIWAN
HONG KONG
PHILIPPINES
MALAYSIA
INDONESIA

CHINA

SINGAPORE

CANADA
UNITED STATES
Alaska (U.S.A.)
MEXICO

North American Free
Trade Association

European Community

East Asian economic powers

China, a nuclear power with a Security Council seat, is burdened by its huge population, 1.2 billion people. Its society, characterized in 1923 by its widely traveled statesman Sun Zongshan as "a sheet of loose sand," lacks the civic unity needed for effective democracy. Its government holds the country together by dictatorial force based on outdated communist ideology but grants sufficient freedom to private enterprise for booming economic development. Yet China's economic potential is limited by the persistent underdevelopment of its infrastructure.

Next to these two giants, the "little dragons" of the Pacific Rim—Taiwan, Hong Kong, Singapore, and South Korea—are economic powerhouses on their own, inspiring neighbors like Malaysia and Indonesia to follow their example. Inhabited by energetic and talented people energized by Western influence, East Asia is playing an increasingly prominent role in the world.

Western Europe occupies the third corner of the global triangle. The source of Western civilization and growing in economic and political unity, it constitutes a massive presence in world affairs. The largest single trading entity, in charge of one-fifth of the world's economy, it also contains two nuclear powers, France and England, both of them members of the U.N. Security Council. Linked militarily with the United States through NATO, western Europe is a center of both political and military might.

Western Europe's highly interactive historic diversity is still visible. Its member states, both large and small—all committed to democratic government in their various ways—struggle to retain their traditional identities as they cope with domestic difficulties. High unemployment, fear of refugees and immigrants, soaring government debt, social discontent, shifting parliamentary majorities, and the need to maintain their economic competitiveness pose major challenges. Fearful voters, absorbed in their domestic problems, have moved to the right, slowing down the trend toward European integration. Germany's reunification, which has imposed burdensome costs on the country, has also shifted the European balance of power in Germany's favor, caus-

ing concern among its neighbors. With its population of 80 million, Germany is by far the largest state in Europe. Will it continue to integrate itself submissively into the western European community of nations, or will it try to dominate it?

Meanwhile, ambitious plans transformed the European Community into the European Union. According to the Maastricht Treaty, drafted in 1991 in November 1993, the European Union is scheduled to have a common currency by the end of the century and will formulate a common foreign policy. Eventually, it will approach the coherence of a unified state. Given the persistence of national ambitions among member states, however, timely realization of these plans is unlikely. Additional obstacles are raised by the European Union's projected eastward expansion. Inclusion of the prosperous and democratic Scandinavian countries will be easy. But how can Poland, the Czech republic, Slovakia, and Hungary, under consideration for admission, meet the membership requirements of a stable democratic government and a market economy? Even more worrisome, how is the new Europe to relate to the post-Soviet turmoil in the countries beyond—in the Balkans, and above all in Russia and the other lands of Eurasia? Western Europeans and their American allies look eastward with justified concern.

Eastern Europe After 1989

At the start, events in eastern and central Europe took a surprisingly promising course. The evidence of progress under freedom and democracy in the West had penetrated deep into the eastern lands and had heightened popular expectations beyond anything the Communist regimes could offer. The revolutionary changes of 1989 were an overwhelming victory for Western forms of government and ways of life.

By 1990, however, the euphoria of the previous year began to vanish. New problems loomed ahead: how could democratic government and market economies be adapted to the tension-ridden traditions of that troubled area, now suspended between the remnants of Communist rule and the glittering promise of Western life? In 1991, Václav Havel summed up those strains of the transition as follows:

◀ MAP 35.2 Three Major Trading Blocs

We are witnesses to a bizarre state of affairs: society has freed itself, true, but in some ways it behaves worse than when it was in chains. Criminality has grown rapidly, and the familiar sewage that in times of historical reversal always wells up from the nether regions of the collective psyche has overflowed into the mass media, especially the gutter press. But there are . . . more serious and dangerous symptoms: hatred among nationalities, suspicion, racism, even signs of fascism; politicking, an unrestrained, unheeding struggle for purely particular interests, unadulterated ambition, fanaticism of every conceivable kind, new and unprecedented varieties of robbery, the rise of different mafias; and a prevailing lack of tolerance, understanding, taste, moderation, and reason.[9]

Under these conditions, politicians found it difficult to establish an effective democratic consensus. Political parties proliferated, forming unstable coalition governments eager to promote economic development. In January 1990, Poland began a quick transition from a Soviet-style economy to a market economy open to the world. A year later, Czechoslovakia started on a similar course. Hungary, the most enterprising of the communist countries, loosened its economy further. Yet everywhere the well-meant efforts produced disappointing results. The Soviet Union's collapse deprived eastern European states of their former markets and of cheap energy imports; the outdated eastern European industries could not compete on the world market. Despite help from western European countries, inflation and unemployment rose frighteningly. People were unprepared for an open market economy and suspicious of capitalism.

As a result of the economic and psychological insecurities, the pace of privatization slowed down, most prominently in Poland, where in 1993 a majority voted in favor of leadership under an ex-Communist. A similar trend surfaced in Hungary a year later, when the former Communist party, renamed the Hungarian Socialist Workers party, took office after a massive election victory. The Czechs, bound by tradition to western European culture, fared somewhat better; after January 1993, they were relieved of their association with backward Slovakia, which

asserted its right to independence. Ruled at the start by an ex-Communist nationalist, Slovakia soon lapsed into economic and political misery. Farther east and out of the political limelight, Bulgaria passed through a fairly peaceful adjustment, while Romania continued to suffer from its communist heritage, and Albania began to resemble a Third World country.

Conditions were worst in Yugoslavia. Cobbled together after World War I as an artificial state, composed of sharply different ethnic groups dominated by Serbia, Yugoslavia was torn apart by the nationalist ambitions set off by the collapse of the Soviet Union. In July 1991, Slovenia and Croatia voted for independence; in April 1992, Bosnia seceded, ending Serbian control. Now ethnic hatred exploded, centered on Bosnia, a splintered mountainous region. Its population—44 percent Muslim, 32 percent Catholic Croat, and 11 percent Orthodox Serb—was scattered in multiethnic communities, with few ethnically consolidated areas.

The three ethnic groups ruthlessly fought each other, the Bosnian Serbs attempting to join with Serbia in a "greater Serbia." They conquered 70 percent of Bosnia, conducting a brutal "ethnic cleansing" of Muslims, while submitting Sarajevo, Bosnia's capital, to bloody bombardment. All sides, but most of all the Serbs, committed heinous atrocities, provoking moral outrage but no foreign intervention. While the United Nations dispatched minor peacekeeping forces and imposed sanctions on Serbia, the European Community and the United States were unable to negotiate a peaceful settlement. Unless ethnic arrogance gives way to cooperation, there appears to be little hope for Bosnia—the most tragic country in the uneasy buffer zone between the prosperous countries to the west and the troubled vastness of Eurasia.

Post-Communist Russia

The Russian Federal Republic with its nearly 150 million people dispersed over eleven time zones, from eastern Europe to the Bering Strait, is beset by profound problems. Ethnic separatism runs strong. Assertive regionalism undercuts the authority of the government in Moscow, which is increasingly divided by bitter partisanship.

THE SIEGE OF MOSTAR. Fleeing Serbian attacks in Bosnia, Muslims crowded into the city of Mostar in Croatia. The Croatians, alarmed by their numbers, tried to drive them away by shelling their area of the city. The Muslims huddled in cellars without water, light, or sanitation. Here, an inhabitant, running to escape shellfire, brings water and provisions. The siege lasted nine months and destroyed the Muslim area of Mostar. (*Laurent van der Stock/Liaison*)

After the collapse of the Soviet Union, Boris Yeltsin emerged as the charismatic leader of the new Russia, committed, with Western support, to promoting democratic government and a market economy. Closer in temperament to the Russian mentality than Gorbachev, he enjoyed sufficient popularity to be confirmed as president by a plebiscite in April 1993. Yet in trying to create an effective government, he was frustrated by the sharp political divisions among the peoples of Russia.

Political partisanship was progressively embittered by the rapid deterioration in all aspects of life. The country was caught in cultural disorientation worse than under Gorbachev. The communist ideology was discredited, but Western culture, although enviously admired, did not fit into the Russian experience, shaped by tsars and communists. Where could Russians find guidance for their lives: in the Russian past, in the reign of the last tsar, or in a new anti-Western nationalism? The young generation proved to be especially vulnerable to their country's confusion.

Initially, Yeltsin and his Western-oriented advisers hoped for an accelerated conversion of the Russian economy to private enterprise through a policy called "shock therapy." But in unprepared Russia, the sudden imposition of Western business practices led toward economic chaos. While small-scale consumer-oriented enterprises responded reasonably well to privatization, it proved impossible to convert the heavy industries into competitive, privately managed enterprises. Burdened by outdated equipment, how could they survive in an open market economy? Yet closing them would be a major threat to public order; their huge labor force would be deprived of employment and of all the supporting social services provided by the state industries. To prevent such a crisis, the government kept printing ever more rubles for preserving useless industries. As a result, the annual rate of inflation rose to 1,000 percent in 1993–94, impoverishing the bulk of the population. The economy slid out of control. Under these circumstances, massive foreign aid, avidly solicited but only cautiously supplied, could be of little help.

The drastic decline in the standard of living was accompanied by the breakdown of civic order, health services, and moral standards. The collapse was more alarming than in eastern Europe. Corruption, crime, prostitution, and drunkenness escalated as people were forced ruthlessly to fend for themselves. The biggest threat came from the rise of armed gangs, commonly called mafias, which penetrated the new private enterprises, often with the help of the police or government agencies. The decline in cultural values and, perhaps worse, the collective humiliation caused by the collapse of Russian prestige abroad, aggravated the misery. The biological consequences were disturbing: life expectancy was reduced and the birthrate fell sharply.

In this political climate, Yeltsin's hard-line opponents in the Supreme Soviet staged their final confrontation. On October 3 and 4, 1993, a bloody shootout took place in front of the "White House" (the office building of the Supreme Soviet) between the hard-liners and army units supporting Yeltsin. Yeltsin's victory dispersed the Supreme Soviet; its leaders were jailed. Soon afterward, Yeltsin introduced a new constitution, strengthening the role of the president; he also called for a new election, for the first time under democratic rules. The outcome of that election of December 12, 1993, however, shocked Russia and the world. Not only did the conservatives hold their own, but they thrust into the limelight a flamboyant chauvinist, anti-Semite, and authoritarian, Vladimir Zhirinovsky, a man given to irresponsible yet vote-catching statements. He was going to take Alaska back from the United States, expand Russia to the Indian Ocean, and establish Russian rule around the world. Patriotic Russians wondered: how could democratic elections be trusted if they advanced a man like Zhirinovsky?

In response to the election, Yeltsin slowed down his policy of liberalizing the economy. The social costs were too high. Blamed for the deterioration of life in Russia and caught in the crossfire between supporters of a liberal-democratic future and those who urged a return to authoritarianism, Yeltsin gradually lost his charismatic appeal. Given the mounting adversities, however, it is doubtful if any individual could have revitalized Russia in line with the popular expectations of a better life after communism.

Yet despite the horrendous problems—the environmental degradation, outdated industrial equipment, rising public cynicism, loss of moral responsibility, and the attendant political disorder—public services continue, and no one starves. Because of the country's size and nuclear weapons, the government still considers itself a great power, entitled to worldwide respect, even though it is operating under drastically adverse conditions. It certainly seeks to exert a measure of control over the "near abroad"—the former Soviet republics—in order to advance the geopolitical unity of Eurasia for what it deems the common good.

Profound uncertainty prevails in the states that succeeded the former Soviet republics. Open elections notwithstanding, all of them are still ruled by ex-Communist governments. The Ukraine, with its 50 million inhabitants (including a large Russian minority), is troubled by a deep economic crisis; it is also quarreling with Russia over control of Crimea and the ex-Soviet navy stationed there. Georgia suffers from devastating ethnic strife and civil war. Impoverished Armenia is fighting neighboring Azerbaijan over Nagorno-Karabakh, an Armenian enclave in Azeri territory. The central Asian republics, highly dependent on the Russian economy, are sticking most closely to Russia within the framework of the Commonwealth of Independent States.

After centuries of compulsory unity, the diverse and divided peoples of Eurasia have to learn how to manage by themselves. Untrained in the skills of civic cooperation, which are the key to effective government and economic growth, they face harrowing trials for a long time to come. Their misery illustrates the hardships of peoples around the world who must try to bridge the gap between their past cultural conditioning and the pressures of modernization. It also increases the insecurity of the new global age.

GLOBAL PROSPECTS

The end of the cold war has produced an unprecedented new age for all humanity. Universal westernization has been transformed into a perilous, wide-open globalism. Never before have so many people—soon to reach 6 billion—been thrust together in such inescapable intense interaction. Television, videotapes, and computer networks recognize no boundaries; people move from country to country, uprooted and subject to conflicting pressures. All want to share the benefits of modernity. At the same time, the ideal of freedom stimulates them to assert their cultural or personal identity, regardless of the price. What then in this novel era are the prospects for the future?

Causes for Hope

The logic of global interdependence indicates a progressive advance from traditional local or national existence to the global framework. Achieving an adequate standard of living and human happiness for an ever larger part of humanity, not to mention human survival in the age of nuclear weapons, depends on peaceful worldwide cooperation. The global community extends now from states to regional associations, and moves vaguely, toward some form of global government however imperfect, like the United Nations.

The United Nations, a product of the high-flown wartime hopes expressed in its Charter and Universal Declaration of Human Rights, is an organization for maintaining worldwide peace and justice. From its imposing headquarters in New York City, it operates around the globe, its membership comprising virtually all governments in existence (184 in 1994). Russia has the most territory, and Saint Kitts and Nevis in the Caribbean the least. The People's Republic of China is the most populous (1.2 billion people in 1991). The richest are the Americans and the Japanese; the poorest are the peoples of Ethiopia and Mozambique.[10]

The core of the United Nations is the Security Council, composed of the five major founding members: the United States, Britain, France, Russia, and China. Each of them possesses the right to veto any action proposed by their peers or by any of the ten nonpermanent members serving a two-year term. The veto power severely limits U.N. action: on what issues can the divergent countries agree? The Security Council is associated with the General Assembly, which is dominated by the non-Western and ex-colonial members, all determined to shift attention to their needs. Thus, the United Nations has become more representative of the world's troublesome diversity but more cumbersome in its organization.

The range of U.N. responsibilities is impressive. It includes population control, health, women, children, human rights, food and agriculture, the environment, world trade, atomic energy, and weapons. Yet the major emphasis has been on development; the United Nations has declared each decade since 1960 a "development decade." Concern over development has become linked with anxiety over the global environment. In June 1992, the organization convened the Earth Summit in Rio de Janeiro, the largest gathering yet of world leaders. It established a program of sustainable development, balancing human needs against environmental degradation. Two years later, another U.N. conference, in Cairo, put the spotlight on population control in developing countries, with special emphasis on the rights of women.

Peacekeeping has been another problematic U.N. effort. The United Nations was not able to prevent the Korean and Vietnam Wars, nor over one hundred lesser wars in Asia and Africa, but it helped in the Gulf War to stop the aggression of Iraq's Saddam Hussein. U.N. peacekeeping forces have been sent to all the major trouble spots, including Bosnia, Somalia and other African countries. As their ineffectiveness in Bosnia and Somalia has shown, however, outsiders can hardly prevent violence if the insiders choose to fight. Besides, the costs of the peacekeeping forces overstrain the U.N. budget. Member countries (including the United States) have frequently been unwilling to pay their dues to the United Nations or commit themselves politically to its initiatives.

The United Nations is assisted by a variety of intergovernmental organizations, which try to

CHANGE IN SOUTH AFRICA. The former president of South Africa, F. W. de Klerk, talking with his successor, Nelson Mandela. The election in 1994 of a multiracial government headed by President Mandela, closed a bitter chapter of repressive white rule in South Africa. All African countries now have indigenous or multiracial governments. (*Reuters/Bettmann*)

cope with the complexities of promoting peace and economic development. One of them, the General Agreement on Tariffs and Trade (GATT), has a long record of advancing worldwide free trade; it will be succeeded by the even more powerful World Trade Organization. The more numerous nongovernmental organizations represent private efforts to advance worldwide cooperation in a broad range of concerns, including human rights as promoted by Amnesty International. In addition, academic, professional, and business people hold their own international conferences and meetings, and athletes from all over the world compete in the Olympic games. Obviously a global community is in the making.

Meanwhile, regional organizations are springing up around the world, enlarging local and national perspectives for cooperation. In Europe, for example, the powerful European Union is linked to the organization for security and cooperation in Europe (formerly the Conference on

Security and Cooperation in Europe), formed in 1975. The organization is concerned with eastern Europe and Russia, as well as western Europe. In 1990, it officially declared the end of the cold war and drew up the Charter of Paris for a New Europe, joining the countries liberated from Soviet rule to their western neighbors in a "common European home," as Gorbachev expressed it. By the logic of global interaction, human perspectives everywhere are being enlarged. People isolated until now are being exposed to new opportunities for personal development; mentally and physically, they have become mobile in their search to improve their lot.

Interdependence, assuring the rich of material security and offering help to the poor, calls for reducing the threat of a nuclear holocaust. In late 1994, Russia and the United States concluded the START negotiations, which had been broken off in the 1980s. The treaty provides for significant reduction in the number of American and Russian nuclear warheads and for safe disposal of the rest. In addition, diplomatic efforts continue to limit, under the U.N. Nuclear Non-Proliferation Treaty, the number of countries possessing nuclear weapons. In any case, world wars like those earlier in the twentieth century seem outdated, and no advantage can be gained from a war fought with nuclear weapons.

Additional hope arises from the increase in the number of democratic governments in the world. Popular participation in government guarantees peaceful civic cooperation. The most striking success acclaimed throughout the world was achieved in 1994 in South Africa, where a representative multiracial government under Nelson Mandela, chosen in a fair election, replaced repressive white rule.

Looking around the world, we are entitled to a mood of confidence. The advances in all fields of learning have been astounding. Science and technology, more closely linked than ever, have increased human control over nature beyond the wildest dreams of earlier ages. Physicists have explored the atom down to the smallest components of matter; biologists have laid bare the genetic structures of animate matter. Human beings have set foot on the moon. Rockets with sophisticated equipment have been sent to the distant reaches of the solar system. Advances in electronics have brought the whole world to remote villages in Asia and Africa through radio and television. Computers, indispensable to scientists and engineers, have penetrated everyday life in finance, business, and in ordinary households. In the arts and literature, the interaction of cultural influences from all parts of the world has been a creative stimulus.

In support of optimism, a Canadian observer cites encouraging statistical evidence. In the past thirty years, world per capita food production has increased by 20 percent; we live in a better-fed world, despite a 1.8 billion population increase. In developing countries, average life expectancy has increased from fifty-three to sixty-five years, while women have four rather than six children. World trade has increased by 6 percent. And in the nine years before 1993, the number of democratic countries has risen from 99 to 107. In short, "life for the majority of the world's citizens is getting steadily better in almost every category."[11]

Causes for Concern

At the same time, however, there are reasons for pessimism. Despite all progress, the bulk of humanity is still miserable; more people means more poverty. Inadequate supplies of food, clean water, and medical help diminish the opportunities of more than half the world's population. Underfed, diseased, and untrained people perpetuate or even increase the already widespread poverty. Under these conditions, stable governments have little chance to emerge, and without stable governments, effective economic development seems impossible.

Since World War II, all efforts to bridge the gap between rich and poor nations have failed; in fact, the gap has widened. Modern communications have raised the expectations of poor people around the globe, but their societies suffer from staggering burdens that impede development: soaring populations, widespread illiteracy, malnutrition, disease, and huge debts. Furthermore, global military expenditures exceed the combined gross national product of China, India, and sub-Saharan Africa. The military outlays of Third World countries grow even faster, as a percentage of their GNP, than those of the developed countries. More money is spent on trading weapons on the international market than on trading grains.

The Population Explosion A major source of worry is the rapid growth of the world's population. Western science, medicine, humanitarianism, and economic progress have produced an unprecedented population explosion, especially in Asia, Africa, and Latin America. For countless millennia the world's population had remained almost stationary, slowly beginning to grow in the eighteenth century. At the height of Western imperialism, in 1900, the world's population had reached 1.6 billion. Fifty years later, it had grown to 2.5 billion, and by 1994, skyrocketed to 5.5 billion. Despite immense losses of life in two world wars, totalitarian terror, local famines, and other calamities, the world's population has almost quadrupled within a century—the century of intensifying global interdependence.

Despite an expected overall decline in birthrates, the population continues to expand. Projections to the year 2025 indicate that the world's population will increase to somewhere between 7.6 billion and 9.4 billion. By the second half of the twenty-first century, according to the World Bank, total population may stabilize between 10 and 11 billion; other projections run as high as 14.5 billion.[12] This staggering population increase threatens the global environment's capacity to support human life. Individuals have to find their way among ever larger masses of people; the masses overwhelm their governments with ever larger problems at home and in international relations. The burden is especially great for non-Western nations, whose populations grow most rapidly. In poverty-stricken sub-Saharan Africa, for example, the annual population growth rate of 3.2 percent is the highest in the world. If the rate is unchecked, the current population of 600 million people in this area could more than double within thirty-five years, to 1.6 billion.[13]

The Threat to the Environment As the world's population increases—by an estimated 88 million people per year in the 1990s—the world's natural resources, already strained by the population explosion of the past century, become proportionally scarcer and the natural environment is damaged. Since 1950, it has been estimated, the world lost nearly one-fifth of its cropland topsoil because of erosion; and one-fifth of its tropical rain forests, a vital reserve of animal and plant species, has been cut down. In Africa, the overly rapid population increase has led to widespread land degradation. Traditionally self-sufficient in foods, its peoples now depend on imported grain. There, as in Latin America, people eat less. In Africa, as in India, grasslands are overgrazed and cattle starve. The Saharan desert is spreading southward at an alarming rate. Moreover, industrialization in developing countries has reduced the amount of land available for agriculture to feed the burgeoning populations, while increasing environmental pollution. In Africa, Latin America, and parts of Asia, the 1980s have been called an unmitigated disaster.[14]

Developed countries, too, suffer from environmental degradation. They are losing arable land, because of erosion, spreading urbanization and road construction, or urban waste disposal. Chemical waste pollutes the underground water supplies, lakes, rivers, and even oceans. The beaches

of the Mediterranean are notoriously dirty. Clean drinking water or water for irrigation is becoming scarcer. The radiation from nuclear waste from power plants and weapon factories poses special dangers. More visibly, exhaust from millions of cars and trucks dims the skies of most cities; air pollution is worse in the big cities of poor countries, worst perhaps in Mexico City. The fumes from coal-burning power plants produce acid rain, which destroys valuable forests in many parts of Europe and North America. The extent of environmental damage resulting from headlong industrialization in the former Soviet Union and eastern European countries has only recently come to light.

The fumes of burned fossil fuels—coal and oil—have an even more threatening effect. Emitting carbon dioxide into the air, they cause a progressive warming of the global atmosphere, a process aggravated by the destruction of tropical rain forests essential for organically absorbing atmospheric carbon dioxide. While scientists debate the issue, there is no question that global warming leads to adverse worldwide climatic changes and a rising water level of the oceans, endangering vital human settlements along the coasts. Another closely watched consequence of the use of modern conveniences is the depletion of the ozone layer in the higher atmosphere, caused by chlorofluorocarbons in aerosol sprays and refrigerators. The ozone layer reduces the penetration of the sun's ultraviolet light to the earth's surface; its depletion endangers all organic life.

The tradition of Western scientific alertness has promoted in recent years a growing public awareness of the adverse impact of modern life on the natural environment on which all life depends. International agreements testify to the new global sense of environmental responsibility. In 1989, an international conference meeting in The Hague declared that "the right to life is the right from which all other rights stem. Guaranteeing this right is the paramount duty of those in charge of all States throughout the world. Today, the very conditions of life on our planet are threatened by the severe attacks to which the earth's atmosphere is subjected."[15]

These good intentions are not easily carried out. Are Americans, Europeans, or Japanese willing to submit to the drastic changes in their lifestyles required for cutting down their use of gasoline for transportation? Are people willing to adjust their national priorities? In any case, the preservation of a life-sustaining natural environment is more than a national responsibility; it calls for incisive international agreements. The globalization of Western civilization has created a range of problems and challenges unprecedented in human experience. These problems and challenges demand a global awareness.

Cultural Disorientation   An even more serious reason for concern is the ever more widespread cultural disorientation. It undermines the collective cooperation that not only upholds existing societies, but is more urgently needed in the enlarged framework of global interdependence. In most parts of the world, tradition is subtly or grossly subverted by Western practices and lifestyles. Some people still feel close to their ancestors' values. The young generation, however, is generally carried away by the most superficial aspects of Western life, which hardly reflect the creative sources of Western civilization. The majority of non-Western peoples thus live in suspension between the familiar and often still cherished past and the admired modern present. While tradition is undermined, the essentials of Western civilization, particularly the commitment to democratic values, are misunderstood or are seen as dangerous alien ideas.

Cultural disorientation causes bitter disunity within states and governments. How is it possible to create a sufficient consensus for effective government among disoriented and divided peoples? The Soviet experiment of forcing unwilling people to work together under totalitarian compulsion has been discredited, except perhaps in China. It is being replaced by new experiments, inspired by the Western ideals of freedom, democracy, and a market economy. Yet in unprepared countries suffering from cultural disorientation, the twin ideals of personal freedom and democratic institutions tend to collide. Where neither a tradition of voluntary sociopolitical cooperation or sufficient ground for common convictions exists, the Western idea of freedom leads to anarchy rather than democracy. In addition, the highly visible contrast between local poverty and the wealth of the developed countries discredits even the best-intentioned governments; they, rather than their confused and divided peoples, are blamed for the continued miseries. As the daily news shows, governments in Asia, Africa,

Latin America, and now eastern Europe face endless difficulties. Authoritarianism, dictatorship, or civil war are widespread; or, as in India, government crises occur in quick succession.

Worldwide mobility has also given Western peoples a taste of the cultural disorientation that they have spread among nonwesterners. Non-Western lifestyles, values, and religions are spreading into Western society. The confluence of so many different peoples, languages, and ways of life is a challenge to Western traditions; minds are inundated by an unmanageable flood of discordant information and divisive tendencies. In the complexity of modern life, human energies are strained; the pressures of life increase. The affirmation of cultural pluralism threatens consensus, and discord causes social and political disruption, often combined with violence.

According to one observer of the social, political, and moral disintegration is at its worst along the West African coast.

> *West Africa is becoming* the *symbol of worldwide demographic, environmental, and societal stress, in which criminal anarchy emerges as the real "strategic" danger. Disease, overpopulation, unprovoked crime, scarcity of resources, refugee migrations, the increasing erosion of the nation-states and international borders, and the empowerment of private armies, security firms, and international drug cartels are now most tellingly demonstrated through a West African prism. West Africa provides an appropriate introduction to the issues . . . that will soon confront our civilization.*[16]

In short, "scarcity, crime, overpopulation, tribalism, and disease are rapidly destroying the fabric of our planet."[17] All promote the universal trend toward violence as the deadly tool of collective or even individual self-assertion.

National, Ethnic and Religious Conflicts   Suspended between disparate cultural influences, ordinary people crave the dignity of a secure national, ethnic, or religious identity. They feel nostalgic about the certainties that had prevailed within their own traditional communities. To defend these certainties, they often become intolerant, hostile, or violent toward outsiders. The search for identity runs counter to the need for

FUNERAL IN BOSNIA. A funeral of one of the tens of thousands of Muslim victims of the civil war in the former Yugoslavia, which has been raging since 1992. The principal aggressor has been Serbia, intent on seizing territory in Bosnia and Croatia in order to create a "greater Serbia." (*Anthony Suau/Liaison*)

extended global cooperation, but it is growing in all parts of the world.

When the ideological unity of communism broke down in the Soviet Union and eastern Europe, nationalism, previously suppressed by authoritarian governments, erupted. In the former Yugoslavia, Serbs carried out an ethnic cleansing campaign against Muslims and Croats in order to create a "greater Serbia." Less violent hostilities plague other multiethnic Balkan states. In eastern Europe, Czechoslovakia split into the Czech Republic and Slovakia. In the former Soviet Union, nationalism, combined with claims for ethnic autonomy or independence, has led to civil wars in the Caucasus area and central Asia. The unity of Russia itself is threatened by ethnic minorities agitating for territorial autonomy.

Divisive self-affirmation, whether through nationalism, ethnicity, or religion, also prevails within western Europe. Northern Ireland, where Catholics fight Protestants, presented, until recently, the worst case. Basques in Spain, Scots in Scotland, and Walloons in Belgium clamor for separatism. In the Middle East, North Africa, and reaching into Europe, Muslim fundamentalists terrorize Muslims adjusting to Western lifestyles, while Israelis and Palestinians clash in the Gaza Strip and on the West Bank of the Jordan River. In India, Hindus fight against Muslims and Sikhs. Africa explodes with tribal conflicts; the most atrocious one is in Rwanda between the Hutus and the Tutsis. Even in the United States, the call for cultural pluralism hardens religious and political attitudes; the tensions promote violence.

Rather than enlarging human fellowship, close contact among peoples living according to different customs encourages an angry defense of traditional creeds and ways of life. Burdened by the overload of information and stimuli conveyed by the media from around the world, people yearn for simple truths to guide them in their ever more complicated daily existence. Wherever we look, the new globalism presents a major challenge for the future.

Coping with the Future

Optimists and pessimists, as well as pro-Western and anti-Western voices, clash furiously as we approach the twenty-first century. All face the crucial question: how can peaceful competitive global interdependence be advanced in view of the growing violence? How can tiny individuals on our crowded planet gain a sense of control over their personal circumstances, as well as over the times in which they live?

How is it possible to gain the world-mindedness that would enable us to be cooperative citizens of our earthly habitat even under grave adversity? Can the present generation of Western peoples, above all Americans, understand the newly created global community? Can they help shape its development according to the highest ideals of Western civilization: reason, freedom, and respect for human dignity?

◆ ◆ ◆

NOTES

1. Mikhail Gorbachev, "Political Report to the 27th Party Congress," *Digest of the Soviet Press*, March 26, 1986, p. 4.

2. Mikhail Gorbachev, *Perestroika: New Thinking for Our Country and the World* (New York: Harper & Row, 1987), p. 11.

3. Mikhail Gorbachev, "Political Report to the 27th Party Congress," *Current Digest of the Soviet Press*, March 26, 1986, p. 12.

4. Ibid., p. 26.

5. Mikhail Gorbachev, "On the Path to a Market Economy; Speech . . . [to] the USSR Supreme Soviet," *Current Digest of the Soviet Press*, October 24, 1990, p. 3.

6. "Drifting Toward the Danger Point" [from *Izvestia*], *Current Digest of the Soviet Press*, November 21, 1990, p. 26.

7. Quoted in Anthony Lewis, "Et Tu Eduard," *New York Times*, December 21, 1990, sec. A, p. 39.

8. James Brooke, "U.S. and 33 Hemisphere Nations Agree to Create Free-Trade Zone," *New York Times*, December 11, 1994, sec. 1, p. 1.

9. Václav Havel, *Summer Meditations* (New York: Alfred A. Knopf, 1992), p. 2.

10. This information is taken from *The Statesman's Year-Book 1993–1994* (New York: St. Martin's Press, 1993).

11. Marcus Gee, "Surprise! The World Gets Better," *World Press Review*, 41 (July 1994): 18–20.

12. Paul Kennedy, *Preparing for the Twenty-First Century* (New York: Random House, 1993, p. 23.

13. John Darnton, "'Lost Decade' Drains Africa's Vitality," *New York Times*, June 19, 1994, sec. 1, p. 10.

14. *State of the World, 1990* (New York: Norton, 1990), p. 136.

15. Ibid., p. 13.

16. Robert D. Kaplan, "The Coming Anarchy," *Atlantic Monthly*, 273 (February 1994): 46.

17. Ibid., p. 44.

SUGGESTED READING*

Beschloss, Michael, and Strobe, Talbott, *At the Highest Levels* (1993). An insider's account of the tumultuous events of 1989–1993 and the end of the cold war.

Buchan, David, *Europe: the Strange Superpower*

*For periodicals, please refer to Chapter 34, page 877.

(1993). A critical survey of diplomacy and defense in the European Community.

Feshbach, Murray, and Alfred Friendly, *Ecocide in the USSR* (1992). Environmental deterioration and health problems in the Soviet Union.

Garton-Ash, Timothy, *The Magic Lantern: The Revolution of '89 Witnessed in Warsaw, Budapest, Berlin and Prague* (1990). A lively account of the death of communism in Eastern Europe, conveying the exhilaration of the time.

Gorbachev, Mikhail S., *Perestroika: New Thinking for Our Country and the World* (1987). The authoritative account by the Soviet leader, covering both domestic and foreign affairs.

Halberstam, David, *The Next Century* (1991). The possibilities and limitations of the United States at the end of the century.

Havel, Václav, *Summer Meditations* (1992). An excellent selection of essays by the president of Czechoslovakia.

Kennedy, Paul, *Preparing for the Twenty-First Century* (1993). An analysis of the demographic, technological, and ecological challenges in the coming decades.

Lewin, Moshe, *The Gorbachev Phenomenon*, expanded ed. (1991). Gorbachev's reforms in the perspective of fifty years of social and political change.

Pond, Elizabeth, *Beyond the Wall: Germany's Road to Unification* (1993). An account of the new Germany by a veteran journalist with an optimistic view of the future of Europe.

Remnick, David, *Lenin's Tomb* (1993). A superb, Pulitzer Prize–winning account of the last years of the Soviet Union.

Sachs, Jeffrey, *Poland's Jump to the Market Economy* (1993). An account of the dramatic economic restructuring in Poland since 1989. (The author has been an economic adviser in Poland and Russia.)

State of the World. A Worldwatch Institute Report on Progress Toward a Sustainable Society (1984 to date). Annual report on changes and adjustments in social, economic, and environmental relationships worldwide.

REVIEW QUESTIONS

1. Gorbachev has been praised by Europeans and Americans and condemned by his fellow Russians. How do you assess Gorbachev's role?

2. Why was the "revolution" of 1989 in eastern Europe a relatively peaceful one?

3. How stable, in your opinion, is the new world order that emerged after the cold war?

4. How do you react to Václav Havel's description of the consequences of the transition to democracy? Does it also apply to Russia?

5. How, in the light of Russian history, the conditions of the country, and the attitude of its peoples, do you react to a Russian patriot's opinion, expressed after the election of December 1993: "Universal suffrage, dumped on Russia like the other fruits of European liberties, does not work in Russia"?

6. What is the purpose of the United Nations? To what extent has its purpose been carried out in the years since 1945?

7. What is your attitude regarding the conflict between modernization and the preservation of traditional cultures? With which side of the conflict do you agree?

8. Do you consider yourself an optimist or a pessimist? What do you see as the major problems confronting your generation?

Index